PETER THOMSON AND SON

PETER THOMSON AND SON

Mid-Victorian Furniture Styles and Designs

PETER THOMSON AND SON

A combined publication of their
Victorian furniture design
and instruction books:

THE CABINET MAKER'S SKETCH BOOK 1851
BY PETER THOMSON
Originally published by William Mackenzie,
Glasgow, Edinburgh, London and New York

THE CABINET-MAKER'S ASSISTANT 1852-3
BY PETER THOMSON
Originally published by Blackie and Son,
Glasgow, Edinburgh, London and New York

THE PRACTICAL CABINETMAKER'S DESIGN BOOK C1870
BY HORATIO THOMSON
Originally published by J. Campbell, Glasgow

ANTIQUE COLLECTORS' CLUB

© 2011 Antique Collectors' Club
World Copyright Reserved

ISBN 978-1-85149-646-4

British Library Cataloguing-in-Publication Data
A CIP catalogue record for the book is available from the British Library.

Printed in China
Antique Collectors' Club Ltd., Woodbridge, Suffolk

The paper used in this publication
is from sustainable resources.

CONTENTS

Watercolour by
Horatio Thomson,
courtesy
The Hunterian,
Glasgow University.

Rabbs' Close, Saltmarket.

INTRODUCTION

Thomson is a common name in Scotland and quite a few Thomsons have become well known and famous: Alexander 'Greek', the architect, Peter, the golfer, James, the poet, William, (Lord Kelvin) the scientist are just a few who immediately come to mind, but there are many more.

By republishing these design books it is hoped that Peter Thomson, will, in time, join the ranks of 'Famous Scots', as the pre-eminent designer of British Mid-Victorian Furniture.

Whilst listed in the 1841 Census of Glasgow as a Cabinet-Maker, aged 27, it appears that this is the only record that indicates Peter had received some formal training, although no relevant entries have been found in any training institution. From 1846 to 1851 he is listed in the Glasgow Post Office Directories as an 'Ornamental designer in furniture and cabinet work'. In the General Directory, and also in the1849-50 Trade Directory, he is listed as a 'Pattern Drawer'.

From 1850-51 until 1863-64 no listings could be found in any directory, but he reappears in 1864-65 in the P.O. Directory as a 'Designer' in the General Directory section. This description also appears for the next two years with an addition in the Trade Directory as a 'Designer to Calico Printers'. For the next two years the General entry changes to 'Designer of Furniture, Ship's Cabins etc', whilst the Trade Directory remains the same.

His final three years, from 1869-70 to 1871-72, show listings in the General Directory only as a 'Cabinet Furniture Artist', a term which so far, we have been unable to unravel.

Both books were initially issued in parts, firstly the *Cabinet Maker's Sketch Book* through William Mackenzie and secondly the *Cabinet-Maker's Assistant* through Blackie and Sons. It is probable that the *Sketch Book* was never issued as a volume (no two copies we have examined are exactly the same) and those that are in existence are the bound copies of the parts. However, the Blackie archives at Glasgow University disclose that they printed the *Assistant* in parts in 1852 and then as a volume in 1853. Continuing demand required printing again in 1859 and also1862. Ontario Library claims to have two copies dated 1863 but there is no proof of later issues. By being issued in parts, little recognition is given to the author, but as each plate carries his name, P. Thomson, the originator (delineateur) cannot be disputed.

Most libraries and institutions believe that the *Assistant* was published before the *Sketch Book* because the title page of the *Sketch Book* states 'Author of the Cabinet-Maker's Assistant', but there are two known copies of the *Sketch Book* which have the following page bound in:

ADVERTISEMENT

The Publisher, desirous to do everything in his power to render the Sketch Book, if possible, still more worthy the extensive patronage already bestowed upon it, has induced Mr. Thomson to visit Paris, for the purpose of inspecting the various Manufactures and Collections of Furniture in that capital, so celebrated for its taste in the Decorative Art.

Mr. Thomson is now in London, where there is at present a rich field presented to the designer, in the collections of furniture from all parts of the world to be found in the Great Exhibition; amongst which we see every variety of taste in designing, combined with the utmost skill in execution. Subjoined is a letter received from Mr. T during his stay in Paris.

> Drakes Excelsior Hotel, Rue St.Honore
> Paris, 18th. September, 1851

Mr. Mackenzie,
    Dear Sir,

Since my arrival in Paris I have visited Versailles and most of the public places here, and have occupied my leisure moments in making rough outlines of some of the most striking articles I have seen. The Grandeur of the Palaces and Churches, especially the Magdalene far exceeds anything I had ever conceived; and I am certain that my visit to this place will be suggestive of many ideas that will be of benefit to my new work..

I intend to return to London in a few days, and shall remain there till the close of the Great Exhibition.

You therefore may expect me in Glasgow about the middle of October.

> I am, Dear Sir, yours truly,
> P.Thomson

It is evident that the reference to his 'new work' really meant the *Assistant* and that he, at that point, had agreed that Mackenzie could publish it, hence the title page reference; subsequently there must have been a dispute and Thomson switched to Blackie. The *Assistant* also has a page of bed designs in the French manner, undoubtedly inspired by his visit to Paris which also confirms that it was published after the *Sketch Book*.

As the Library of Congress indicates that the *Sketch Book* was issued in 20 parts, the probable sequence of events was that the first part was issued about May 1851 and allowing for two per month, it would have continued until February 1852, thus allowing Blackie to start issuing the 22 parts of the *Assistant* (Blackie Archives) some months later and the bound volume in 1853.

It is extremely unfortunate for Peter Thomson that two twentieth-century publications with worldwide markets failed to give him credit for his designs; when Dover Publications of America decided to republish the *Assistant* in 1970 they asked John Gloag to write an introduction, wherein he states that 'as such it could be found, well-thumbed and in constant use, on the benches of small, independent cabinet-makers and in the larger workshops of such manufacturing centres as High Wycombe'. The back cover continues with 'it was the most successful copybook of its time; its designs and embellishments were repeated on countless articles of furniture' But there is no discussion or mention of Peter Thomson. Though it was obvious that Edward Joy had done some research on the designer, unfortunately, in the introduction to the *Pictorial Dictionary of British 19th Century Furniture Design*, he attributes the many illustrated designs taken from the *Assistant* to 'Blackie' and in fact, Joy's description of the book is titled 'Blackie's Cabinet-Maker's Assistant'.

Last year we discovered that the Winterthur Library copy of the *Assistant* (1853 Blackie) contained the initial subscribers list, which they have kindly permitted us to reprint; it contains over 600 names including Charles Bielefeld, Druce and Co., Holland and Sons, Jackson and Graham, Smee and Son, Lamb of Manchester and so on; the Blackie archives indicate that their usual print run was either 5000 or 10000 (although Glasgow based, they already had branches in London, Edinburgh and New York) but no specific records relating to the *Assistant* could be found.

Both books came to, and were used in Australia – the dining room furniture in Government House, Sydney was made by a local cabinet-maker, Andrew Lenehan in 1857 using the *Assistant's* designs. Professors McIntyre and Webster in the Canadian Encyclopedia state 'all these styles and their variants could be found in such popular handbooks as A.J. Downing's *The Architecture of Country Houses* (1850) or Blackie and Sons *The Victorian Cabinet-maker's Assistant 1855.*'

By 1854 the *Assistant* had arrived in America and is listed in the Patent Office records of November of that year. The Smithsonian Institute's Restoration Course now lists it in the American section as recommended reading.

As Blackie Publications were widely distributed they would undoubtedly have been sent to many other countries seeking 'Modern' furniture designs and a description of the technical methodology used to make them.

Despite all our efforts, including two prolonged periods in Glasgow, we have found no clues regarding Peter Thomson's activities from the time his books were made public until the reappearance of his name in the Directories of 1864. One probable explanation for this disappearance is that he was 'head-hunted' by one of the major furniture manufacturers, but this can be only surmise and so far, we have been unable to discover any of his later designs in any of the fields into which he ventured.

Peter died during the bronchitis plague in Glasgow on 13 October 1871 and the funeral undertakers were none other than Wylie and Lockhead.

HORATIO THOMSON

Horatio was born in 1850 and graduated from the Glasgow School of Art with two prizes; he appears to have followed in his father's footsteps for some time, leading to the publication of the *Practical Cabinet Maker's Design Book* published by J. Campbell of Glasgow, probably around 1870, although no information regarding this printer can be found. Subsequently, Horatio had some success as an artist. A collection of his watercolours depicting Glasgow buildings (now demolished), is held in the Hunterian. In the 1881 Census he was described as a 'Decorative Furniture Artist', but by the 1891 Census, he had become a 'Boat Designer' and by 1901 a 'Draughtsman'.

MUMFORD'S GEGGIE, SALTMARKET.

Watercolour by
Horatio Thomson,
courtesy
The Hunterian,
Glasgow University.

SUBSCRIBERS

FOR THE

CABINET-MAKER'S ASSISTANT:

A SELECTION FROM THE GENERAL SUBSCRIPTION LIST, AND CONSISTING OF THE LEADING CABINET-MAKERS, UPHOLSTERERS, &c., THROUGHOUT THE KINGDOM.

LONDON.

R. Adams, Cumberland-st., Middlesex Hospital.
M. Alexander, Black Horse-yard, Rathbone-pl.
Henry Andrews, Waterloo-road.
J. Antrobus, Thomas-street, Bethnal Green.
E. J. Archer, New Oxford-street.
George Archer, Banner-street, St. Luke's.
J. Aspinwall, Lower Grosvenor-street.
R. Atkins, Argyle-place, Regent-street.
W. and J. Bailes, Charlotte-street, Fitzroy-sq.
W. Banting and Son, St. James's-st., Piccadilly.
James Barnes, Providence-row, Finsbury.
C. Barnett, Bacchus-walk, Hoxton.
Joseph Barr, Curtain-road.
William Barr, Cumberland-street, Curtain-road.
William Barralett, Holywell-row, Finsbury.
James Barrett, South-street, New North-road.
John Baits and Son, Hardwick-place, Commercial-road.
G. Bayley, Carver, York-street, Shoreditch.
W. Baylis, Waterloo-road.
S. and G. Bertin, Hoxton-square.
Charles Bielefeld, Papier-Maché Works, Wellington-street, Strand.
J. Binns, Ogle-mews, Foley-place.
William and Samuel Binns, High Holborn.
T. Bird, Ship-yard, Wardour-street.
Samuel Bird, Worship-street.
H. J. Blackburn, George-street, Portman-sq.
John Bolton, Bunhill-row.
William Bourne, Barnes-place, Mile-End-road.
Charles Bower, Vauxhall-bridge-road.
G. Brand and Son, Berner's-street, Oxford-st.
Broadwood and Winchester, Wardour-st., Soho.
E. Browne, Curtain-road.
J. Browne, Leadenhall-street.
Thomas Brown, Curtain-road.
Thomas Burgin, Great Winchester-street.
John Card, Cumberland-street, Curtain-road.
Edmund Carly, Bolingbroke-row, Walworth-rd.
C. Chapman, Sloane-street.
F. and W. Chapman, Davies-street, Oxford-st.
Thomas Chick, Liverpool-road, Islington.
G. A. Clare, Mount-street, Grosvenor-square.
J. B. Clarke, Dean-street, Soho.
James Cobbett, Deptford-bridge, Greenwich.
Edward Coote, Boot-street, Hoxton.

C. Cousins, Draughtsman, Oxford-street.
W. Crafer, John-row, Hoxton.
J. Craft, Strap-street, Kingsland-road.
John Cross, King-street, Golden-square.
Henry Crowther, Titchbourne-st., Edgeware-rd.
William Cutbill, Holywell-row, Finsbury.
G. Davis, Gloucester-place.
Henry Davis, Caroline-place, Goswell-street.
John Daw, Bath-street, City-road.
W. Dawe, Theberton-street, Islington.
B. Dawes, Soho-square.
H. Devon, Carver, Old-street-road.
Michael Dobinson, New Bond-street.
D. Donatti, Chapel-street, Curtain-road.
Downing and Wilson, High Holborn.
John Dowson, London-street, Greenwich.
William Draper, Newman-street, Oxford-street.
Druce and Co., Bazaar, Baker-street.
R. Dunball, Horse-shoe-alley, Moorfields.
O. J. Dunn, Philpot-street, Commercial-road.
Durley and Co., Oxford-street.
R. Durley, Mary-le-bone Passage, Oxford-street.
Charles Ellis, Bedford-street, Covent-garden.
Thomas Epps, Kennington Green.
R. Evans, Mansion-house-place, Camberwell.
Andrew Eve, Turner, Charlotte-st., Fitzroy-sq.
Robert Ewin, High-street, Islington.
T. Farnham, City-road.
T. Fenn, Carver, Chapel-street, Soho.
James Flood, jun., Charles-st., Middlesex Hosp.
Charles George, Old-street-road.
Thomas Gepp, Crown-row, Mile-End-road.
W. Gilbert and Co., Kingsland-row.
W. Gittens, High-street, Camden Town.
Edward Glancey, Bellchamber Passage, Red Cross-street.
Goulding and Son, Eldon-street, Finsbury.
John Gregory, Old-street.
Ebenezer Grieg, Farringdon-street.
E. Hacker, Nichold-street, Shoreditch.
R. W. Hackett, Jury-street, Aldgate.
Hampton and Russell, Leicester-square.
Harding and Son, Fore-street.
G. Harman, Admiral-terrace, Vauxhall.
R. Harris, High Holborn.
W. Haseldane, Eldon-street, Finsbury.
S. Hatchwell, Edward-street, Langham-place.
Thomas Hattersley, Portman-pl., Maida-hill.

George Helman, Carver, John-st., Curtain-rd.
J. Henderson, Windmill-street, Rathbone-pl.
Henessey and Pelley, King-street, Soho.
T. and A. Heweston, Wardour-street, Soho.
Holland and Sons, Mary-le-bone-st., Golden-sq.
R. Horsey, Carver, Tottenham-street, Tottenham-court-road.
Howard and Sons, Berners'-street, Oxford-st.
E. Howell, William-street, Lisson-grove.
Huddlestone and Son, Nassau-street, Middlesex Hospital.
W. I. R. and E. Hunter, Moorgate-street.
E. Hyrons and Co., John-street, Fitzroy-square.
J. Jackson, Fashion-court, Spitalfields.
Jackson and Graham, Oxford-street.
R. S. Jarmar, Lower Vale-place, Hammersmith.
Joseph Jay, Church-street, Hackney.
Jenks and Son, Broad-street, Cheapside.
Thomas Jenks, Dorset-street, Fleet-street.
W. Jounaux, Carver, Ogle-mews, Foley-place.
C. B. St. Julian, Carver, Windmill-st., City-road.
F. Kane, Berners'-mews, Middlesex Hosp.
William Kerr, Tottenham-court-road.
J. W. Kidwell, Peter-street, Sun-street.
Lambert and Son, Clapham-road.
T. Lambert, Carver, Upper Clifton-st., Finsbury.
John Lear, Carver, Steven-street, Tottenham-court-road.
J. Leith, Wardour-street, Soho.
John Lennon, Providence-row, Finsbury.
Hugh Leslie, South Molton-street, Oxford-st.
G. Levy, Carver, Cumberland-place, Newington.
J. Linningdine, Featherstone-street.
William Law, Devonshire-street, Queen-square.
R. Low, Hollen-street, Soho.
J. Lowrey, Carver, Cornwall-road, Lambeth.
Lucker and Co., Waterloo-street, St. Luke's.
G. Maddox, Welbeck-street, Cavendish-square.
W. Marchant, Curtain-road.
G. Martin, Addington-street, Lambeth.
James Martin, Hoxton-market.
William Maxey, Boot-street, Hoxton.
J. F. Meekin, Baker-street, Portman-square.
James Miller, St. James's-street, St. Luke's.
Thomas Miller, Old-street-road.
William Mills, Oxford-street.
Chas. Mitchellin, Carver, Ogle-mews, Foley-pl.
T. Mitchell, Wilson-street, Finsbury.

SUBSCRIBERS' NAMES.

R. More, Hart-street, Bloomsbury.
Henry Morehen, Cumberland-st., Curtain-road.
William Morgan, New-street, Hoxton.
C. Morris, Cumberland-street, Hackney-road.
James Morris, Hoxton Old Town.
E. Nash, Duke-street, Stamford-street.
Thomas Nash and Son, Leigh-st., Burton-cres.
George Newton, Cleveland-st., Middlesex Hosp.
John Owen, Carver, Old-street-road.
Henry Oxley, London-road.
J. Paulson, Deal-street, Mile-end, New Town.
M. Pepper, Carver, Castle-st., Oxford-market.
John Perry, London-wall.
John Pew, Stafferton-row, Walworth-row.
R. Phillips, Mary-le-bone-street, Golden-square.
T. Pike, Rushton-street, Hoxton.
Thomas Ponsonby, Regent-circus.
J. J. Pope, Titchfield-street.
H. T. A. Potter, High-street, Camden Town.
F. Presig, Trevor-terrace, Knightsbridge.
Charles Price, Great Leonard-street.
W. Priest, Walter-street, Farringdon-street.
Prosser and Hadley, Ornamental Saw-works,
    Clipstone-street.
W. Ratcliff, Weymouth-terrace, Hackney-road.
Richard Rayner, Little Britain.
William Rivet and Sons, Crown-st., Finsbury.
Robert Rough, Mansion-house-street.
Robert Ruffle, Great Queen-street.
William Russell, Curtain-road.
E. Samson, Old-street.
Thomas Samson, Hoxton-square.
J. Scarffe, Brompton.
Astley Searle, Camberwell-green.
J. L. Seaton, Frederick-place, Hampstead-road.
S. W. Silver and Co., Cornhill.
J. W. Simson, Bow-street, Covent-garden.
Smee and Son, Little Moorfields.
James Smith, Old-street-road.
James Smith, Hoxton Old Town.

William Smith and Co., Albion House, Pimlico.

W. S. Smith, Pantechnicon, Belgrave-square.
H. Sowden, Old Kent-road.
J. L. Stacey, Tabernacle-row, City-road.
John Stalon, Carver, Berwick-street, Soho.
C. and T. Styles, Paul-street, Finsbury.
James Tanner, Honduras House, Hoxton.
A. Tarrant, Hollen-street, Soho.
H. Taylor, Long Alley, Moorfields.
Taylor, Bros., Fret Cutters, Berners'-mews.
Taylor, Jordan, and Co., Machine Carving Works,
    Belvidere-road.
Joseph Taylor, Broad-street, Bloomsbury.
S. Taylor, Haydon-square, Minories.
N. Tindale, Portland-place, Commercial-road.
Samuel Varley, Great Leonard-street.
William Waine, High-street, Newington.
C. Waites, Lemon-street, Whitechapel.
John Ward, Upper York-row, Walworth-road.
Jeremiah Warren, Wilson-street, Finsbury.
J. Welsh, Booth-street, Hoxton.
J. Whitbourne, Park-street, Dorset-square.
Thomas White, Borough-road.
J. Willatts, Myrtle-street, Hoxton.
Henry Williams, Union-street, Borough.
M. Willson, Great Queen-street.
J. Wilson and Sons, Wigmore-st., Cavendish-sq.

Richard Woodward, Kirby-st., Hatton-garden.
L. and M. Worms, Whitechapel-road.
J. Wright, Cleveland-street, Fitzroy-square.
W. and J. Wright, Wardour-street, Oxford-st.

LIVERPOOL.

John Abbott, Islington.
Joseph Asbery, Newington.
Arbuthnot Blair, Bold-street.
Bradley Brothers, Bold-street.
Robert Chatham, Carver at Duke's, Renshaw-st.
Wm. Cosgreaves, Carver, Sir Thomas's-buildings.
Robert Crossley, Cases-street.
Samuel Cutter, Bold-street.
Henry Dickson, Park-road.
John Duke, Renshaw-street.
N. and T. Dutton, Great George-street.
R. Edmundson and Sons, Bold-street.
Charles Forrest, Foreman, Bradley Brothers,
    Lawton-place.
A. Grant, London-road.
John Griffith, Carver at Duke's, Renshaw-street.
G. Hall, Carver, Leigh-street.
Hand and Son, Bold-street.
Henry Harris, Chair-maker, Renshaw-street.
Holden and Co., Church-street.
Edward Holt and Son, Duke-street.
James Hughes, Bold-street.
J. Lolley, Foreman at Blair's, Atherton-street.
Charles M'Allister, Upholsterer, Seel-street.
John Pemberton, Duke-street.
James Priest, Carver, Stanley-street.
William Rainford, Renshaw-street.
Ray and Swann, Renshaw street.
H. B. Roberts, Perry-street.
Rossal and Gradwell, Bold-street.
Mr. Shirratt, Carver, Slater-street.
J. Smith, Carver at Blair's, Atherton-street.

William Taylor, Seel-street.

William Turner, Islington.
Urquhart and Adamson, Bold-street.
Alexander J. Wells, Carver, Bittern-street.
James Winstin, Foreman at Duke's, Renshaw-st.
Henry Wright, Renshaw-street.

MANCHESTER.

John Abraham, Oldham-street.
Robert Abraham, King-street.
James Acarnley, Hardman-street.
George Blackburn, Rusholme.
Thomas Brown, Medlock-street.
Thomas Deagle, Clarendon-street.
John Etheridge, Oldham-road.
George Fynney, Stretford-road.
John Gilchrist, Victoria Bridge, Salford.
William Gilbert, New Buckley.
John Hanibal, Bank Parade.
S. Harris, Great Jackson-street.
George Harrison, Chatworth-street.
T. Johnson, Lower Brook-street.
James Kendally, Oxford-road.
John Lamb, John Dalton-street.
John Lee, King Street.
John Mathly, Grosvenor-street.
T. Merridan, Lower Brook-street.

Thomas Morland, Charter-street.
Thomas Moss, Medlock-street.
William M'Donald, Oxford-road.
William Naylor, Rosamond-street.
Henry Ogden, John Dalton-street.
Newberry Ogden, John Dalton-street.
Charles M. Ogg, London-road.
Pember and Latham, Stretford-road.
Francis Price, Great Ducie-street.
James Price, Ward-street.
W. Stephenson, Garden-street, Medlock.
Edward Taylor, Great Ducie-street.
Joseph Wainwright, Great Jackson-street.
Henry Wilde, Stretford New-road.
Joseph Wilde, Grosvenor-street.
Henry Wilson, King-street.
James Wyatt, Oldham-road.
William Yeates, Princess-street.

PRESTON.

William Bowker, Bowker-street.
William Brumfit, Oxford-street.
Richard Butters, Mount-street.
John Couburn, Friargate.
Duckett and Westhead, Friargate.
William Evans, Elizabeth-street.
William Exton and Son, Lancaster-road.
John Gardner, jun., Frenchwood-street.
George Gillett, Fishergate.
George Healey, Derby-street.
James Huntington, Stoneygate.
Charles Innerdale, Meadow-street.
Lodge and Co., Lune Street.
Thomas W. Lyod, Library-street.
William Penny, Avenham-street.
James Rooney, Lord-street.
John N. Smith, North-road.
Henry Snape, Walton-le-Dale.

Henry Tunstall, Market-place.

LANCASTER.

William Bousfield, Upholsterer, Crown-stre
T. Redmaine, Penny-street.
Edward Simpson, Penny-street.
John Simpson, Penny-street.
John Warbrick, New-street.
W. J. Whitehead, New-street.

BURNLEY.

Stephen Ellison, Hammerton-street.
Robert Nichol, Lane-bridge.
William Pollard, Bethesda-street.
Richard Rawlinson, Parker-lane.
John Robinson, Pickup-croft.
William Robinson, Cheapside.
William Sutcliffe, St. James-street.
James Taylor, Cheapside.
Thomas Winkley, St. James-street.

COLNE.

Benjamin Brown, Colne.
James Hargreaves, Bacup.
John Hartley, Bacup.

SUBSCRIBERS' NAMES.

Holland and Whitehead, Barrowford.
Stephen Parkinson, Barrowford.
Henry Robinson, Haslingden.
William and Robert Smith, Haslingden.

MACCLESFIELD.

Joseph Dickson, Chestergate.
William Hollinhead, Carver, Mill-street.
Thomas Johnson, Mill-street.
Thomas Kimble, jun., Chestergate.
Joseph Mosely, Water-cotes.
John Plant, Mill-lane.
S. Plant, Mill-lane.

BLACKBURN.

Henry Austen, Over Darwen.
David Howarth, Old-square.
J. Quick, Northgate.
Lawrence Wolstenholme, Northgate.

WARRINGTON.

Richard Charles, Sankey-street.
Robert Garnett, Bridge-street.
James M'Intire, Church-street.

BOLTON.

William Downing, Bradshaw-gate.
Mr. Dunny, Bridge-street.
William Metcalfe, Church-street.
John Taylor, Halshaw Moor.

CARLISLE.

Joseph Hope.

BIRMINGHAM.

Frederick Appleton, Bull-street.
Mr. Ashford, Digbeth.
G. Bodenham, High-street.
J. Cole, Barr-street.
William Eades, Carver and Gilder, Mosely-street.
Stephen Ethell, Ann-street.
George Hall, Snow-hill.
John Hansen, Carver and Gilder, Pershore-street.
Mr. Hinsman, New-street.
James F. Hitchings, Constitution-hill.
Robert Humphrey, Carver, Little Charles-street.
William Malpas, Washington-street.
Mr. Moody, Pershore-street.
William Purser, Broad-street.
Jas. Reynolds, Foreman at Ashford and Jenkins', Digbeth.
J. Taylor, Brad-street.

WORCESTER.

Charles Blessett, New-street.
Henry Clackson, Carver at Foxin's.
Alfred Davies, Sidbury.
Charles Frame, Upholsterer, Mealcheapen-street.
William George, High-street.
Henry Insull, Bank-street.

Francis Jones, at Cook's, Broad-street.
William Pindar Wells, St. Swithin-street.

LEAMINGTON.

William Beatie, Carver, Warwick-street.
Edward Bentley, Oxford-street.
W. and J. Cook, Warwick-street.
William Fairfax, Spencer-street.
William Lawick, Warwick-street.
George Lock, Carver, Regent-street.

HEREFORD.

J. Bradley, Union-street.
Thomas Merrick, King-street.
John Millson, St. Martin-street.
Francis Morris, St. Owen-street.

KIDDERMINSTER.

Charles Allcock, Mill-street.
John Dewsbury, Hagley-Road, Old Swinford.
S. J. Harrison, Stourbridge-street.

NOTTINGHAM.

W. Brandreth, 13, Melton-street.
J. Hall and Son, Pilcher-gate.
S. Smith, Talbot-street.

DERBY.

Basford and Son, 60, London-road.

LEEDS.

Jos. Addy, Wormald's-yard.
W. Barker, Lady-lane.
J. H. Bland, North-street.
Messrs. Constantine and Co., South Parade.
F. Danby, Upperhead-row.
J. Drake, High-street.
G. W. England, Commercial-street.
H. Hardy, Lambert's-yard.
J. Hebblethwaite, West-street.
Messrs. Hodgson and Wild, Woodhouse-lane.
J. Holburn, Wade-lane.
Thomas Holy, Woodhouse-lane.
Messrs. I. Kendell and Co., West Bar.
John Mountain, Wellington-lane.
George Nelson, Albion-street.
J. W. Nicholson, Kirkgate.
George Padget, Meadow-lane.
Josiah Teale, Camden-court.
E. Tolson, Leighton-lane.

YORK.

John Brown, Monk Bar.
Joseph Hield, Gilleygate.

BRADFORD.

Edward Archer, Tyrrel-street.
Albert Bentley, Market-street.
Cowan and Son, Northgate.

Isaac Craven, Darley-street.
Duckworth and Watson, Well-street.
Dunn and Stoddart, Market-street.
S. Emmott, Northgate.
Charles Grayson, Kirkgate.
Joseph Harrison, Wool-pack-yard.
S. Hartley, Leeds-road.
J. Marshall, Manchester-road.
Thomas Mills, Market-street.
Joseph Poole, Silbridge-lane.
Pratt and Prince, North Parade.
J. Robinson and Son, Smith-st., Manchester-rd.
Richard Robinson, Victoria-street.
William Thompson, Northgate.
F. Wilkinson, Market-place.

SHEFFIELD.

William Abbot, Foreman, Carver-street.
Charles Burley, Fargate.
———— Davis, Carver-street.
Charles Davis, Foreman, New Church-street.
J. Didsbury, Foreman, Carver-street.
Thomas Eadon, New Church-street.
George Green, Cherry-tree-green.
Joseph Green, Carver-street.
Enoch Hacey, Foreman, New Church-street.
Arthur Haybell, Rockingham-street.
William Johnston, Fargate.
John Morris, Hollis-croft.
William Newbould, Foreman, Barker-pool.
Samuel Roebuck, Chaster-street.
J. W. Shore, Carver-street.
William Skelton, Angel-street.
Isaac Turnell, Piniston-street.
George Wilson, Carver-street.

HALIFAX.

William Crowther, Lord-street.
J. Hanson, Southgate.
Hibblethwaite and Knowles, Bull-close-lane.
John Hustler, Water-house-street.
John Jessop, Northgate.
William Nicholson, Albion-court.
John Scholfield, Carlton-place.
Joseph B. Spencer, Upper Brunswick-street.

BATH.

J. Barnes, Milk-street.
J. Bodey, Park-street.
G. Chidley, James'-street.
W. Craymer, Artist, Marlborough-hill.
W. Darke, Carver, Merchant-street.
J. Edwards, St. Augustine-place.
Henry Eyles, James'-street.
G. Gwillian, Park-street.
G. Hawkins, Old Bond-street.
Hulbert and Hancock.
J. Kirkham, Pulteney-street.
J. Thatcher, Old Market.
W. H. Turner, St. Michael's-hill.
J. Vincent, Berkeley-place.

PLYMOUTH.

Mr. Baker, Union-street.
William Brown, Batter-street.

Mr. Hopping, King-street.
George B. Eyre, 56, Exeter-street.
Lane Brothers, 7, James'-street.
Thomas Rendle, 46, Old Town-street.
W. Rendle, Buckwell-street.
Charles Roan, Union-street.

EXETER.

J. Gove, Milk-street.
Theodore James, Queen-street.
Kingdom and Son, Fore-street.
Robert Reynolds, 3, Paris-street.

DEVONPORT.

Samuel Marcombe, 56, Duke-street.
J. Richards, 27, Market-street.
F. C. Rickard, 25, St. Aubyn-street.

PENZANCE.

J. T. Brewer, Queen-street.
Thomas Carne, 17, Marine-terrace.
Mr. Fleming, Chapel-street.
J. Perkins and Co., Builders.
George D. Read.
George Tregarthen, Victoria-place.
Robert J. Wallace, Victoria-place.
White and Bennett.

GLASGOW.

Andrew Allan, 16 and 18, London-street.
T. G. Allan, 71, Cowcaddens.
M. and J. Allan, 10, Watt-street.
Alexander Allan, Piano - forte - Maker, 109, Eglinton-street.
Thomas Anderson, 221, Buchanan-street.
Charles Archer, 101, Holm-street.
John Ballardie, 342, Argyle-street.
Alexander Bissett, 100, Sauchiehall-street.
William Boyd and Son, 4, Hyde Park-street.
William Brown, 239, Argyle-street.
William Caldwell, 146, West Nile-street.
Robert Cameron, 285, Argyle-street.
Cochran and Provan, 44, Gordon-street.
Thomas Colquhoun, 103, St. Vincent-street.
Alexander Cree, 27, Gordon-street.
John Davidson and Co., 87, Argyle-street.
Duncanson and Forbes, 2, Maxwell-street.
J. Forrest and Son, 64, Sauchiehall-street.
A. Fotheringham, 86, Wellington-street.
Andrew Galloway, 105, Hope-street.
W. and J. Harvie, 75, North Wellington-street.
James Heggie, 230, Buchanan-street.
Archibald Hunter, 3 and 4, Terrace-street.
Thomas Knox, 44, Renfield-street.
George Lawson, 42, Argyle-street.
Bryce Martin, 38, St. George's-road.
James Miller, 130 and 131, Trongate.
Robert Miller and Son, 29, Stirling-street.
E. and A. Murphy, 53, Montrose-street.
J. and J. M'Culloch, 37, Renfield-street.

Daniel M'Ewan, 6, Union-street.
John Macintosh, 106, Hope-street.
James Mackenzie, 197, Argyle-street.
P. M'Kinnon, 77, Carrick-street.
William M'Murray, 15, St. Enoch-square.
John Napier, Shipbuilder, Vulcan Foundry.
Walter Newton, 226, Argyle-street.
William Nisbet, 19, Croy-place.
Charles Park, 162 and 164, West Regent-st.
James Reid, 26, Renfield-street.
George Scott at J. Richmond and Co's., 57, Buchanan-street.
William Scott, 59, Candleriggs.
John Simpson, 102 and 104, London-street.
Peter Smith, 53, West George-street.
W. G. Smith, 82, Trongate.
Robert Struthers, 89, Buchanan-street.
John Toshack, 5, Wellington-street.
James Walker, 5, Warwick-street.
Robert Whyte, 111, St. Vincent-street.
W. and J. Wotherspoon, 80, West Nile-street.
Wylie and Lochhead, 28, Argyle-street.

GREENOCK.

William Archibald, 73, West Blackhall-street.
Robert Blair, West Blackhall-street.
Hugh Cameron, Bank-street.
G. Cowan, 7, Sir Michael-street.
Fisher and Hall, 4, Church-place.
J. M'D. Rugvy, 14, West Blackhall-place.
William Shaw, 43, Hamilton-street.

PAISLEY.

William Bunten, 99, High-street.
Thomas Maitland, 15, Wellmeadow-street.
J. Pinkerton, 39, Wellmeadow-street,
J. Vallance, 33, Wellmeadow-street.

AYR.

William Afflesh and Son.
John Reid.
John Wilson and Co.

KILMARNOCK.

Alexander and Craig.
James Hood.

TROON.

Robert Alexander.

EDINBURGH.

Allardice and Sclanders, 12, George-street.
Anderson and Paterson.
John Boyd, 2, York-place.
Burke and Grant, 4, Dublin-street.
Cruikshanks and Veitch.
William Finlay, 14, St. Andrew-square.
Thomas Goldie, 12, Queensferry-street.

Harper and Henderson, Jamaica-street-lane.
William Hillhouse, 1, Rose-court.
William Hogg, 30, Dundas-street.
James Kay and Son, 1, Teviot-row.
Thomas Keddie, 13, Melville-place.
Charles Macfarlane, Carver and Gilder.
George Potts, Foreman to Mr. C. Trotter.
J. and T. Scott, 10, George-street.
James Sherriff, 5, Hope-street.
Robert Simpson, 29, Frederick-street.
John Trail.
H. Wharton, 2, North St. Andrew-street.

FALKIRK.

John Budge, Rainsford.
Alexander Johnston, High-street.
John Middlehurst,   ,,
James Miller,   ,,
Robert Nelson,   ,,
Alexander Reid,   ,,
James Smart,   ,,

BERWICK-ON-TWEED.

William Fair, Hyde-hill.
Thomas Paxton, Hyde-hill.
Thomas Smart, Tweedmouth.

DUNDEE.

James Alexander, Constitution-road.
David Anderson, Nethergate.
David Batchelor, Barrack-street.
Alexander Boyd, Nethergate.
James Fairweather, Meadow-entry.
John Fairweather, Reform-street.
Robert Herd, King-street.
George M'Donald, Union-street.
John M'Lean, Murraygate.
James Ramsay, Black's-croft.
William Ramsay, Overgate.
Peter Sanderson, Meadow-side.
Andrew Smith, Yeaman-shore.
Andrew W. Smith, Nethergate.
James Wallace, Scouring-burn.
Thomas Watson, Perth-road.
John Wynd, jun., Bucklemaker's-wynd.

ABERDEEN.

Thomas Baird, 171, Union-street.
John Barnett, 33, St. Nicholas'-street.
John Edmond, Chronicle-lane.
Nathaniel Ross, Chronicle-lane.
John Smith, 43½, Castle-street.
William Stephen, 157, Union-street.

BELFAST.

Dawson Bell, 10, Ann-street.
William Gray, 14, William-street South.
Samuel Latimore, 4, Church-street.
Archibald Sloan, 33, Castle-place.

A PICTURE ALBUM OF THOMSON STYLES

This album contains photographs of antique furniture which can be attributed to Thomson designs.

1. Cedar Telescope Table, Made by A. Lenehan. Government House, Sydney. Courtesy Historic Houses Trust
2. As above, Centre Pedestal Detail
3. As above, Leg Detail
4. Cedar Slab Sideboard, Government House, Sydney. Courtesy Historic Houses Trust, NSW
5. As above, Leg Detail
6. Rosewood Sideboard with Fretwork Doors. Courtesy National Trust for Scotland and Georgian Antiques
7. Mahogany Bookcase with Fretwork Doors to Base
8. As above, Door Detail
9. Cedar Bookcase. Courtesy Melbourne Club, Melbourne
10. Mahogany Drum Face Clock
11. Mahogany Drum Face Clock
12. Rosewood Chiffonier with Raised Fretwork Back and Doors Courtesy Tim Wilmot
13. Walnut Hall Seat with Fretted Back and Ends
14. Mahogany Hall Seat, Government House, Ottawa. Courtesy National Capital Commission, Ottawa
15. Mahogany Hall Table, Government House, Ottawa. Courtesy National Capital Commission, Ottawa
16. Cedar Slab Sideboard. Courtesy Melbourne Club, Melbourne
17. Mahogany Side Table with Fretwork End Supports. Courtesy Alan Hislop
18. Cedar Slab Sideboard
19. Mahogany Drawing Room Sofa
20. Half Tester Mahogany Bedstead
21. High Back Walnut Bedstead
22. Fretwork Fire Screen
23. Cedar Dining Chair, Courtesy Bonhams and Goodman.
24. Walnut Hall Seat
25. Mahogany Hall Chair, Government House, Ottawa. Courtesy National Capital Commission, Ottawa

1

2

3

5

4

6

7

8

15

16

17

18

19

20

21

22

23

24

25

CONTENTS AND LIST OF PLATES

This table of contents was missing from the original and has been added by Jim Martin and the publisher.

TO

Charles Trotter Esq.r

EDINBURGH

THIS WORK

Is by kind Permission

DEDICATED

AS A MARK OF RESPECT

By his Much Obliged & Humble Servant

The Author.

THE

CABINET-MAKERS' SKETCH BOOK.

LINEAR PERSPECTIVE.

CHAPTER I.

1. LINEAR PERSPECTIVE may be defined to be the drawing of objects in their exact proportions, with respect to height, length, and breadth, as they appear to the eye when placed in any position. This may be illustrated by placing a pane of glass, or other transparent substance, betwixt the eye and an object, and by keeping the eye steady, and tracing the different lines upon the object; if these lines be distinctly marked on the transparent plane, there would be a *linear perspective* view of the object.

2. It is necessary for the person commencing to learn perspective—if he has not got a previous knowledge of mechanical drawing—to understand the use of the instruments commonly used. We will here, in the first place, explain some of these, and show the manner of using them.

The *drawing-board* is generally made of deal, of a size according to the intended use. We would here recommend one for drawing perspective of about two feet nine inches, or three feet long, by two feet or two feet four inches broad, made of 1 inch or 1¼ inch stuff, neatly planed and clamped at the edges to keep it from warping. The paper might be fastened upon it, either by drawing-board pins, which is a very good and the most expeditious method, or by sealing wax, or by paste, which is done in the following manner:—Having cut the paper to the size required, wet the back of it with a sponge dipped in clean water, passing it over several times, and leaving it a short time till the water is absorbed, and the paper lies flat; run a rim of paste round the edge, about three quarters of an inch wide; then turn the wetted side of the paper downward on the drawing-board, and press the pasted rim close to the board with a paper knife, or some hard substance, pressing as much of the paste out as possible, that the paper may adhere firmly to the board. The face of the paper should be then wetted in the centre with a sponge, taking care not to pass it on the pasted rim: without this precaution, the centre would be dry before the edges, and the paste would not hold.

The best sort of drawing-boards are those made in a panel form: in these, there is an outside frame rebated on the inside, into which there is a moveable panel fitted, also rebated, to allow of the panel coming nearly flush with the upper surface of the frame. The paper is placed upon this panel, and then put into its place, where it is fastened by two pieces of wood in the back. This is undoubtedly the best sort of drawing-board, as it keeps the paper stretched, and answers well for drawings which have a deal of minute work about them, and also for colouring.

The next instrument is the T *square*, which is so well known that we would just recommend it to be made straight and strong, not to bend when drawing near its end; those made with a

A

screw, for drawing lines at any inclination, are most preferred. There are also small pieces of mahogany of a right-angled triangular form, called *set squares,* which by moving along the edge of the T square, lines can be drawn at angles for which the squares are made—those with 45° and 60° are very useful.

Compasses are very useful instruments in mechanical drawing. They should be fine pointed, and move freely at the joint, which should not, however, be too slack, for then a little compression might move them from their position. Those with fixed legs are called dividers. When the moveable leg is taken out, there is a leg which can be put into its place, having a piece of lead pencil fastened into it, for drawing circular lines in lead, and also another for circular ink lines.

Drawing-pens are very useful instruments for drawing lines in ink, after being marked out with lead. The handle is made mostly of brass or ivory, having two steel prongs on the one end, which can be brought close, or widened (betwixt which the ink is placed), by means of a screw, for drawing the lines fine or broad. There are also *bow-pens,* for drawing small circles in ink, which are very useful, and similar ones for drawing lead lines.

Parallel rulers are for drawing parallel lines: they are generally made of two pieces of wood, connected by two pieces of brass, fastened to them near the ends, allowing the wood to move freely: by holding on or pressing upon it, the other can be moved, and it is still held in its parallel position by the pieces of brass. Parallel rules moving on rollers are to be preferred.

These instruments, with scales, and a few others occasionally used, are those employed in mechanical drawing; those used in perspective will be described farther on. It may be remarked, that there are cases or boxes of instruments, containing compasses, drawing-pens, scales, &c., of different prices, from a few shillings to a number of guineas, to be got in almost every town of note in the three kingdoms—the student, by seeing them applied, will learn their use far better than by a written description.

3. It is presumed that the student is acquainted with practical geometry—raising perpendiculars, describing squares, triangles, circles, ellipses, pentagons, hexagons, &c.; if not, we would recommend him to learn that in Bonnycastle's Mensuration, or some other work, as there are many, and it would therefore be useless to enter upon the subject here.

4. There are five ways in which mechanical drawings are generally done:—1st, The *ichnographic* or *ground plan* of an object is the seat of the different parts, showing their correspondence, situation, and magnitude, without any reference to the height. 2d, The *orthography* or *elevation,* which is the appearance any object would present if an eye could view every part perpendicularly. 3d, *Sections*—these are cuts made through the object, showing its internal arrangements. If the section be parallel to the front, it is called a *longitudinal section,* and if from front to rear, a *transverse* or *lateral section;* any other is called an *oblique section.* 4th, The *scenographic*— that is, the representation of objects as they appear to the eye when in any position—or the *perspective view.* The scenographic is better applied to the perspectives of objects, as houses, for instance, when scenery is introduced. 5th, The *development*—this is the representation of any circular, elliptical, or polygonal figure, &c., when taken and spread out upon a plane, thereby giving the appearance of an orthographic projection or elevation. Having gone thus far, we will begin now and explain some of the fundamental parts of the science.

Fig. 1.

Fig. 2.

5. If a person stand at the middle of one end of a long road, which is supposed horizontal, straight, and of a uniform breadth, the sides will seem to approach nearer and nearer to each other as they are farther from his eye; and if the road be very long, the sides of it at the farthest end will seem to meet, and there an object that would cover the whole breadth of the road, and be of a height equal to that breadth, would appear to be a mere point.

If A B and C D, fig. 1, be two parallel sides of a road, and o the place of the observer—suppose the road to be divided into squares, A c *i e, e i·k f,* &c., the person standing at o will see these two sides as if they were gradually approaching towards one another, as in fig. 2 ; and the squares will seem to diminish in size as they are farther from the eye—so that the first square, A c *i e,* fig. 1, will appear as A c *i e,* fig. 2 ; the second square, *e i k f,* fig. 1, will appear as *e i k f,* fig. 2 ; and so on till the last square, which would vanish into a point, as s in fig. 2, where A s and c s meet.

6. The point, s, where the parallel sides of the road seem to meet, is called the *point of sight,* and is still opposite to the observer, and at the height of the eye. The place where the observer's eye is placed is called the *place of the observer,* or the *point of view.* The line, P s, passing through the point of sight, is called the *horizon.*

CHAPTER II.

1. In the annexed figure it is intended to show more particularly the principles upon which this kind of perspective depends. G I K L is called the *ground plane,* upon which there is a square, P R S Q, to be drawn in perspective; F A B C is the *plane of the picture,* upon which the representation is to be made; E is the *point of view,* sometimes called the *point of sight ;* it is the place of the observer's eye, and hereafter shall be called the *point of view,* and the *point of sight* shall be applied to the point opposite the eye in the horizon, to which lines and planes perpendicular to the plane of the picture converge. M N is the horizon of the picture, or the representation of the meeting of the sky and water, if an observer were looking at the ocean; and it may be remarked that the horizon, M N, is still on a level with the eye. If a sketch

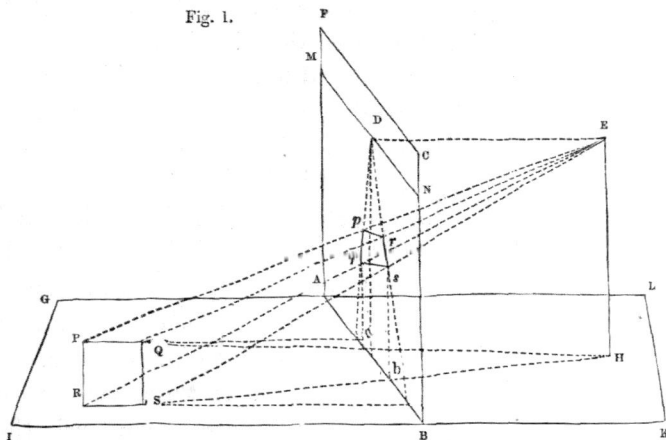

Fig. 1.

were made on the top of a mountain, the horizon would then be high up ; and if made from a valley or some low place, the horizon would then be low down : and in every linear perspective drawing, there must be a *horizon* or *horizontal line.* We might suppose M N was the representation of the line or visible connection of sky and land ; and this apparent meeting or line, though below the level of the eye, is still put at the eye's height, as the distance from the eye to the picture is so small, that there can be no sensible difference in taking the horizontal line, M N, at the height of the eye.

E D is perpendicular to the horizon, M N ; the point, D, is called the *point of sight ;* the line, A B, in which the plane of the picture and the ground plane intersect, is called the *section line :* now, if lines be drawn from P Q R S to E, the points, *p q r s,* where these lines intersect the plane of the picture, being joined, will form the perspective representation of the square. The operation just mentioned may be said to be of no very great use in drawing perspective, as a transparent plane cannot always be held before an object, for perspectives are made of houses, bridges, machinery, &c., before any of them are built or constructed ; indeed, if perspective consisted only in this, it were very contracted, and therefore of no great importance. We see, therefore, recourse must be had to other means. The point, H, in the ground plane, directly under the eye, is the point to which the lines are drawn from the object ; we have drawn two in the diagram, as more would only have caused confusion : and from the points, *a b,* where they meet the section line, we raise

7

perpendiculars until they meet lines drawn to the point of sight in *q s*, from the points where P Q and R S meet the section line produced. If two other lines had been drawn from P R to H, and perpendiculars raised as before, they would have marked out *p r;* if then, *p r, q s*, &c., be joined, there would be formed *p q r s*, the perspective representation. This will be better understood by the following, with respect to the square.

2. *To put a square in perspective.* Let A B C D be the square which is to be drawn, and E the point of view. We will suppose, in the first case, that the plane of the picture, or the section

Fig. 2.

Fig. 3.

Fig. 4.

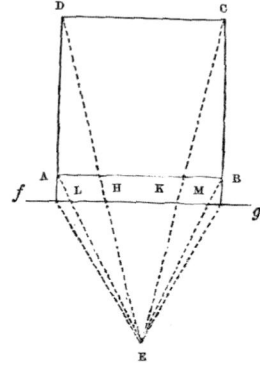

line, *f g*, coincides with the side, A B, of the square, and that the point of view is exactly opposite the side, A B, of the square, the visual rays, E D, E C, are drawn, making the side, D C,

Fig. 5.

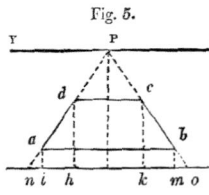

appear equal to H K. The side of the square is eight feet, and is laid down at the scale of an eighth of an inch to the foot. In fig. 3, *a b* is made equal to A B, fig. 2, because it touches the section line or plane of the picture, and therefore it is the real size. Draw the horizontal line, Y Z, at the height of the eye, about five feet four inches, and as the observer stands opposite the middle of the side, *a b*, the point of sight, P, will be also opposite the middle; join P *a*, P *b*, make *h k* equal to H K, and put half on each side of the central line, and draw the perpendicular *h d, k c*, and join *c d*—then *a b c d* will be the perspective representation.

Fig. 6.

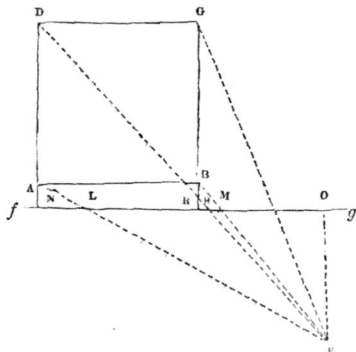

3. In the second case we, will suppose that the plane of the picture does not touch the side of the square, but the observer is still standing opposite the middle of the side, as in fig. 4.

Draw the visual rays, E A, E D, E C, E B; then the apparent sizes of D C and A B will be H K, L M; then, in fig. 5, draw the base line *n o*, and at the proper height the horizontal line Y Z; leave off *h k, l m, n o*, respectively equal to H K, L M, A B, one half on each side of the central line; join *n* P, *o* P, and draw the perpendiculars, *l a, h d, k c, m b*, and join *a b, c d*; then *a b c d* will be the square.

4. In the third case, we will suppose the observer stands to one side, and that the plane of the picture does not coincide with the side of the square, the plane of the picture being still parallel to the side of the square, as in fig. 6.

Fig. 7.

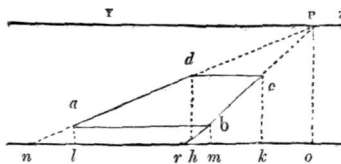

Let the visual rays be drawn as before, and let E *o* be the principal one, or the one directed to the point of sight. In fig. 7, let *n o* be the base, and Y Z the horizontal line, P the point of sight, *o* P the principal visual ray; leave off *o n, o l, o r*, &c., equal to O N, O L, O R, &c.; join *n* P, raise the perpendiculars, *l a, h d*, &c., and join *a b, c d*; then *a b c d* is the square. Now, the attentive reader will easily see the connection of this method with that mentioned in description of fig. 1. The point, E, in figs. 2, 4, and 6, is the same as H, fig. 1, which is the point perpendicularly under the eye on the ground plane. The lines, though drawn from the object to it, mark out on the section line the apparent length and breadth virtually the same as if they were drawn to the point of view. Again, in fig. 1, from the points where the visual rays cut the section line, perpendiculars were raised, meeting lines passing to the point of sight; the same is adopted in figs 3, 5, and 7, where the perpendiculars are also raised, meeting lines passing to the same point.

In the three examples which we have given with respect to the square, and in other subsequent examples, we might have done with one figure, but we would like to impress these first principles upon the mind of the reader in as easy a manner as possible; we have therefore adopted two figures, that it may be the better understood. It is evident, that if A B C D, in figs. 2, 4, and 6, had been a right-angled parallelogram or rectangle, its perspective could have been as easily made; and if A B, in fig. 6, had touched the section line, it would have been easier.

Fig. 8.

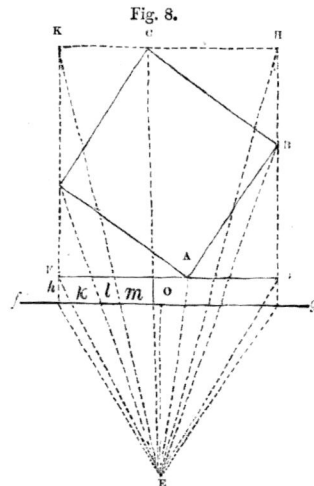

We might also mention, that if A B C D had been a pavement divided into squares, or of it were a square garden, or a rectangular one with straight walks and flower plots, it could be very easily drawn by going upon the same principle which we have adopted.

5. There is still another case with respect to the square, viz. :— when the section line is oblique to all of the sides, as in fig. 8.

Draw F G parallel to the section line, as also K H, and draw the perpendiculars, K F, H G; draw the visual rays, E F, E D, &c., and E O, the principal one.

Fig. 9.

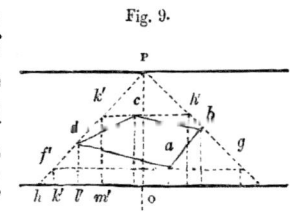

Now, let the base line and also the horizontal one be drawn, fig. 9, as before, and also *f' g' h' k'*, the perspective representation of F G H K, and let *o p* correspond with E O the principal visual ray; leave *o h'*, *o k'*, &c., equal to *o h*, *o k*, &c., and let the perpendiculars be raised till they meet the lines passing to the point of sight, &c., marking out the points, *f'*, *k'*, &c., corresponding with those in fig. 8, as also *a b c d*, which points being joined, mark out the perspective representation.

We have drawn all the lines necessary on the figures, so that the student will clearly see the method of proceeding.

CHAPTER III.

1. It will be seen, by reference to the preceding chapter, that in the three cases of the square which were taken into consideration, in which the plane of the picture was parallel to two of its sides, these sides were parallel to one another in the representation, and the other two sides converged to the point of sight; but (in 5) where the sides were oblique to the plane of the picture, it was seen, that in the representation, the two sides, which in the former cases were parallel, are no longer so, but converge to a point on the horizontal line, whilst the other two converge to another point also on the horizontal line. This will take place if they be accurately constructed; whereas, those lines which circumscribe the square, converge to the point of sight, or are parallel to one another, as the case may be. These points to which the lines converge are called *vanishing points*, and are in general on the horizon.

2. Linear perspective is of two kinds. The first is called *direct* or *parallel;* it is the same as described in Chap. II. This is the easier sort: it is so called, because, in the face of the object (which is parallel to the plane of the picture) in the representation, the horizontal lines are parallel,

B

whilst on the end or flank these lines converge to the point of sight. The second kind is called *indirect,* because those lines which, in the former case, were parallel to one another and to the horizon, in this are not, but converge to the vanishing point; and also those on the end or flank, which in the former case converged to the point of sight, in this they converge to a vanishing point.

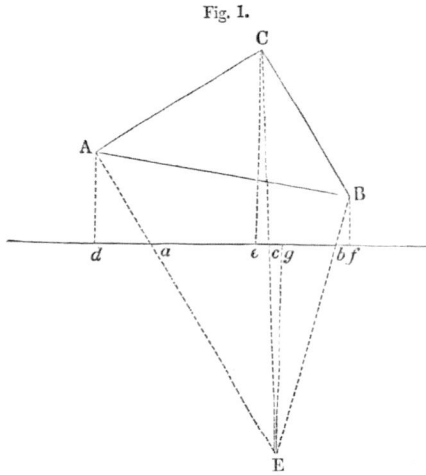

Fig. 1.

As the two kinds are differently managed, and the *direct* being the easier, we shall consider it first:—

3. By proceeding nearly in the same manner as that adopted (in 5), we could, by direct perspective, put the plan of any object into this sort of it when the figure is bounded by right lines; and, as will subsequently be seen, the plan of any figure, no matter by what sort of lines bounded. Now, that we may be perfectly understood in this, we will put first a triangle, and then any rectilineal figure, by this method into perspective.

4. To put a triangle into perspective by the direct method.

Let A B C, fig. 1, be the triangle, *d f* the section line, E the point of view. Draw the visual rays, E A, E C, E B, cutting the section line in *a c b;* draw also the perpendiculars, A *d,* B *f,* C *e,* and the principal visual ray, E *g.*

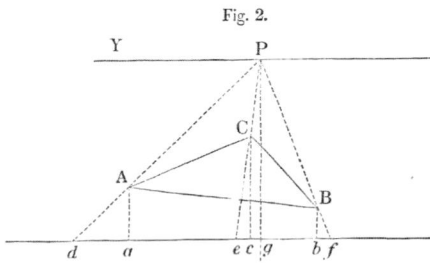

Fig. 2.

In fig. 2, draw the base line, *d f,* at the proper height, also the horizontal line, Y Z. Let *g* P represent the principal visual ray, proceeding to the point of sight, P; leave off *g d, g a,* &c., equal to *g d, g a,* &c. Draw lines to the point of sight, P, from *d, e, f,* and raise perpendiculars from *a, b, c,* to meet these lines respectively, and they will mark out the points, A, B, C, which being joined, give the required representation.

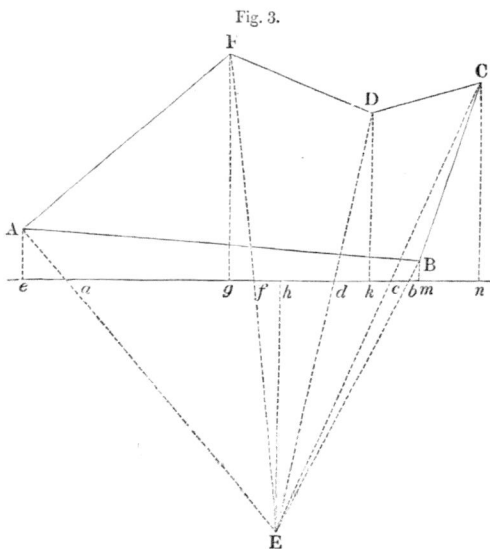

5. To put any rectilineal figure into perspective by the direct method.

Since any rectilineal figure is composed of triangles connected with one another, it follows that the figure can be easily put into perspective when the method of putting the triangle is known.

Let A B C D F, fig. 3, be the rectilineal figure, *e n* the section line, E the point of view; draw the visual rays, E A, E F, &c., and the perpendiculars, A *e,* F *g,* &c.

Fig. 3.

Then, in fig. 4, draw the base line, *e n,* the horizontal line, Y Z, and take the point of sight, P, and let P *h* be the principal visual ray. Leave off *h e, h a,* &c., respectively, equal to *h e, h a,* in fig. 3, and draw the lines *e* P, *g* P, *k* P, *m* P, *n* P, to the point of sight, and from the points *a, f,* &c., draw perpendiculars until they respectively meet the other lines in the points A, F, &c.; these points being joined will give the representation.

6. Having now shown the method of putting the plan of any object, when bounded by right lines, into this perspective, before proceeding to the consideration of objects with regard to height, we would recommend the reader who may read this, and who would wish to become acquainted with this useful branch of science, to make all the figures two or three times the size here shown, and afterwards progressively introduce others which the fancy may dictate—such as quadrila-

terals, pentagons, hexagons, &c.—as a short practice will sooner and more efficiently bring it home to the mind than any descriptions, no matter how well and how easily written.

We are well aware, from a very particular examination of the principles of direct perspective contained in various works, such as Ferguson's, Hayter's, and a voluminous work by a French Jesuit, translated by Chambers, &c., &c., that the way we treat it is different from theirs a little; yet ours is conducted in the same manner as that adopted in indirect perspective—with this difference, that in the latter there are vanishing points to which the lines converge, whereas it is to the point of sight they converge in the former, as described by writers on this branch; and it is our opinion, that it is founded upon rational principles, and deducible from mathematical precedents, and easy in its application.

7. With respect to the distance the observer should stand from the object, some lay it down as a rule to stand off the distance of the two visible sides taken together—as, if the object were a house, to stand off a distance equal to the length of the two sides which are seen; whilst others consider this too little, and we think it answers better to stand farther off than this—say about as much, and one-fourth or one-third as much more. It greatly depends on taste; but there are some positions which give better perspectives than others, as is very soon learned from practice. Others stand off such a distance as the angle comprehended between the extreme visual rays which proceed to the object, may be about 60° as the angle, A E B, in fig. 2 of Chapter II.

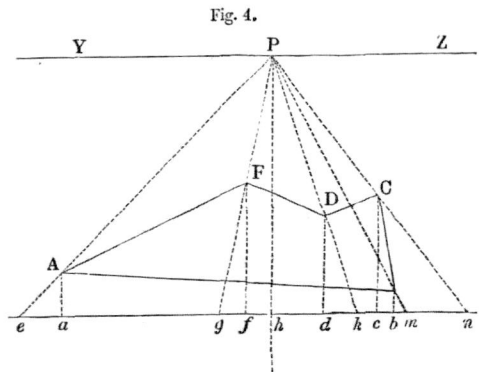
Fig. 4.

CHAPTER IV.

To put a cube, parallelopiped, or a box in perspective.—Let the dimensions of it be 7 feet long, 4 broad, and 3 high. Make the plan, A B C D, fig. 1; draw the section line, *e g;* take E, the point of view at a distance, equal to A B and B C together, from the object, and draw the visual rays, E A, E B, &c., and produce D A, C B, to *e* and *f*.

In fig. 2, draw the base line, and at the proper height, say about five feet four inches, the horizontal line, Y P; take the point of sight, P, leave off *g e, g a,* &c., equal to *g e, g a,* &c.; in fig. 1, draw *e* P, *f* P, to the point of sight, P, and raise the perpendiculars, A *a,* B *b,* C *c,* D *d;* join A B C D, then A B C D is the perspective representation of the rectangular base.

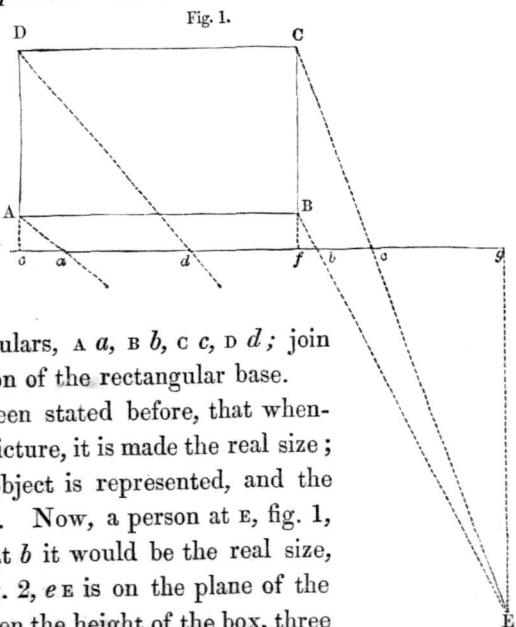
Fig. 1.

Here we would remark more fully what has been stated before, that whenever any part of an object touches the plane of the picture, it is made the real size; that is, with respect to the scale by which the object is represented, and the smaller, the greater the distance from the observer. Now, a person at E, fig. 1, would see an object at D, smaller than at B; but at *b* it would be the real size, because it touches the plane of the picture. In fig. 2, *e* E is on the plane of the picture, and perpendicular to the base line, *e g;* if then the height of the box, three feet, be left off on *e* E, and a line drawn to the point of sight, P, the point, F, where it cuts the perpendicular, A F, will give A F the perspective height required, the parallel, F G, and also the line, G P, intersecting the perpendicular from C in H, and then draw the parallel, H L; this then will give the required representation.

A perpendicular from f would have answered equally as well for the height line. If the

Fig. 2.

Fig. 3.

object were a cube, its perspective would be found in the same way; and if the object touched the section line, its perspective would be still more easily found.

2. *To put a pyramid in perspective.*—Let it be a triangular one, each side of which is six feet, and the perpendicular height seven.

Let A B C, fig. 3, be the plan of the pyramid, O the centre, take E the point of view, and let the section line be parallel to side, A B, and touch the angle, C; draw the visual rays, and the principal one, E g, and the perpendiculars, A e, O C, B f.

In fig. 4, let P be the point of sight, Y Z the horizontal line, and $e\ g$ the base line; leave off $g\ e$, $g\ a$, &c., equal to $g\ e$, $g\ a$, &c., in fig. 3; and because the lines, A e, O C, B f, are perpendicular to the section line in fig. 4, they will converge to the point of sight. Raise

Fig. 4

Fig. 5.

the perpendiculars, A a, O o, B b, and they will give the points, O, A, B, the latter two of which being joined with C, gives the perspective of the base. Draw the perpendicular, C G, and leave off the height on it, seven feet, and draw the line, G P, to the point of sight, P: the point H, where it cuts the perpendicular from the centre O, is the vertex of the pyramid, which being joined with A, B, and C, gives the required representation. Only one side of it is seen when the point of view is opposite the middle of that side.

If A B C, fig. 3, were the plane of the base of a frustrum of a pyramid, and the dotted lines $a'\ b'\ c'$ its top, its perspective would be found by putting the small triangle in perspective, as in fig. 4, and raising perpendiculars until they would meet the lines from A B and C to H, and then joining these points for the top, the base being previously formed as before.

It is evident from this, that any pyramid, whether triangular, rectangular, octagonal,

&c., or any frustrums of these, might in this manner be put in perspective, and also any prism.

3. *To put the block of a house in this perspective.*—In fig. 5, let the dotted lines indicate the outline of the walls, and the drawn lines the roof; the section line touches one side of the roof.

In fig. 6, P is the point of sight, Y z the horizontal line, *a c* the height line, which touches one corner of the roof, *a b* the base line. The roof being the most difficult part, is done in the following manner:—The height, *a g*, to the spouting, is left off on *a c*, and its depth (five or six inches), and then two lines are drawn horizontal to the other side, and then from its extreme projection, which is found by plan lines, two lines are drawn to the point of sight. Now the height to the under side of the projection of the roof must be perspec-

Fig. 6.

tively laid off, and it, together with the line of projection, and two short lines (one at *g* to the point of sight, the other at the remote corner horizontal), will show the *soffit* or under side of the projection of roof. For the height, leave off *a c* equal to the whole height, and run a line to the point of sight, cutting a perpendicular in *d*, which corresponds with D in fig. 5, and then a horizontal line, cutting the perpendiculars in *e* and *f*, which points again with E and F, fig. 5, and then draw lines to the extremities of the roof. The plinth may be easily put round the two sides, and the rest of it is easy.

CHAPTER V.

The drawing of curves in perspective, or curvilinear perspective, is more complex, and therefore more difficult, than that of right-lined or rectilinear perspective. The ellipse, hyperbola, parabola, &c., are seldom drawn in perspective; if so, the method of points, which are here pointed out for the circle, are equally applicable with respect to them. It is evident, that if the eye be directly over the centre of a circle, or in a line drawn perpendicular to its plane from the centre, its perspective representation will also be a circle; for, if the plane of the picture be put betwixt the eye and the original circle, and of course parallel to it, and lines drawn from the eye to the circumference of the original, these lines would evidently trace out a circle on the plane of the picture.

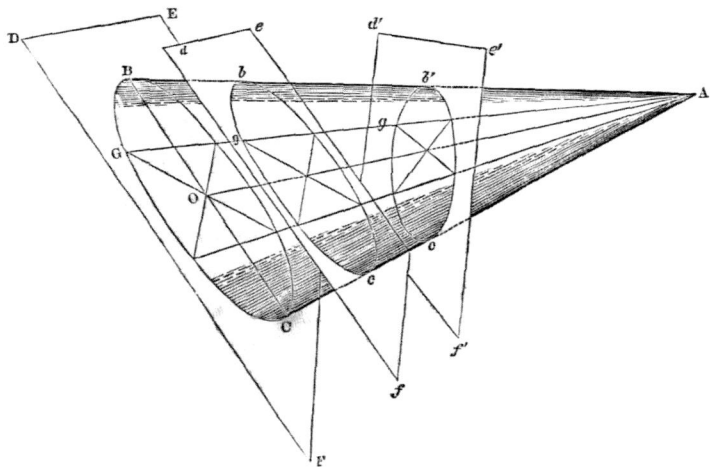

Fig. 1.

Let D E F be a plane on which there is the circle, B G C, and o its centre, and o A the principal visual ray, passing through the eye, A; now, if rays be supposed to pass from every point of the circumference to A, these rays will form a cone, and every plane, parallel to the original D E F,

C

13

will be cut by these rays in a circle. If the plane, *d e f,* be parallel to D E F, and which might represent the plane of the picture, it will be cut also in a circle, as *b g c;* it will be greater or less than the original, according as it is farther off, or nearer to the eye, than it. In mathematical language, the diameter of this circle is to the original in the ratio of their distances.

Fig. 2.

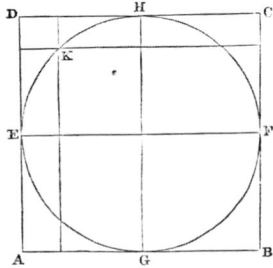

Now, suppose another plane, as *d' e' f'*, intersects the cone of rays, but is not parallel to the original, it can be proved mathematically that *b g c,* the perspective representation, will be an ellipse: it may be said the perspective of a circle is generally an ellipse.

If the eye of the observer be in the same plane with that of the circle, it will then appear as a straight line. A familiar example of this may be seen in a tea-cup, which, if a person hold in his hand, with the eye over the middle of it, will then appear as a circle; and if it be gradually turned round, it will assume the forms of ellipses, becoming more and more elongated, until finally it appears as a straight line, or it will assume appearances of ellipses of every possible eccentricity, from zero, or the circle, to one of the diameters, or the straight line.

2. *To put a circle in perspective.*—Let E F G H be a circle; draw two perpendicular diameters, E F, G H, and tangents at their extremities; then A B C D is a square.

If this square be put in perspective by the method previously pointed out, and the points, F, G, H, E, found, there would then be four points given, through which the circle must pass. This way will do where great accuracy is not required, but the number of points may be increased. The point, K, may be taken in the curve, and through it parallels to the sides; the perspective of K may then be found, and also in the same way any number of points as may be thought necessary, and then the circle traced out with the hand.

The following way finds eight points which perhaps might be accurate enough for general use.

Let A C B D be a circle, say four feet in diameter, and M the point from which it is viewed; draw the two diameters, A B, C D, perpendicular to one another, and such that C D is perpendicular to the section line, O E, Draw any two lines, E F, G H, parallel to C D, and cutting the circle; and draw lines from the various points to the point of view. In fig. 4, draw the line O E, and parallel to it Y Z, the horizontal line, and take into it P, the point of sight; leave off O E, O C, &c., O *e*, O *d*, &c., equal to O E, O C, &c., and O *e*, O *d*, &c., in fig. 3.

Because E F, C D, are perpendicular to the section line in fig. 3, in fig. 4 they will run to the point of sight, P, and then perpendiculars from *e d,* &c., will meet these lines in points *e', d',* &c., which mark out points in the circumference of the circle; and with a steady hand the perspective of the circle may be traced out after the rest of the points have been found in the same manner.

Fig.

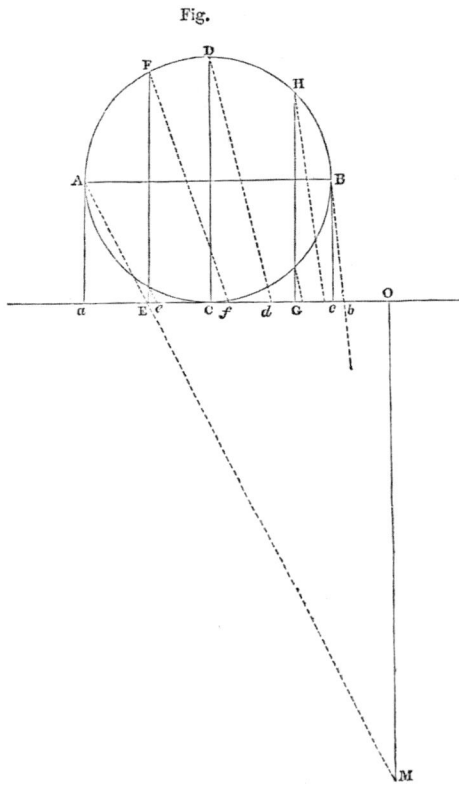

which in this case touches the circle.

Fig. 4.

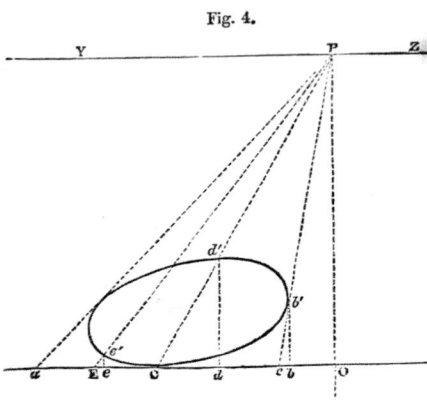

3. In a former chapter, the method of putting any rectilineal figure into perspective was shown, and by the method of points, as applied to the circle, any curvilineal figure may also be put into it; and as all figures on the same plane, no matter how irregular they may be, are bounded by straight lines or curves, (or the figure may be called *mixtilineal*,) it is evident that the methods for these two conjoined will be the mode of proceeding in general cases.

4. *To put a cone in perspective.*—Let A B C, fig. 5, be the plane of a cone three feet in diameter at base, and four feet high. Let F O be the section line, and E the point of view, eight feet from the cone; let D be the seat of the vertex; draw D F perpendicular, and draw the visual ray, E D.

Fig. 5.

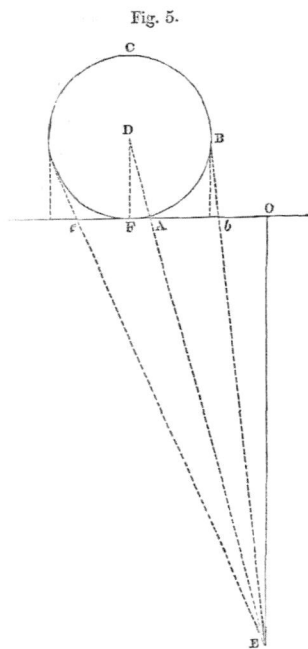

Fig. 6.

In fig. 6, let Y Z be the horizontal line, P the point of sight, and O F the base line; the base of the cone being a circle, it must therefore be first put into perspective. Make O F, O A, equal to O F, O A, in fig. 5, draw the perpendiculars F G, A D, and leave off the height of the cone on F G, four feet, and from this point draw a line to P; then where it cuts perpendicular from A in D, D will be the vertex; then draw tangents from D to the curve—they will form slant sides of the cone. Or if O e, O b, be made equal to O e, O b, in fig. 5, and perpendiculars drawn, they will touch the curve in two points, to which, if lines be drawn from D, they will form the slant sides of the cone. In fig. 5, e b is the representation of the apparent size of the diameter of the circle, found by drawing lines to represent visual rays to touch the circle.

5. *To put a cylinder in perspective.*—The top and bottom are equal circles; the bottom circle

Fig. 7.

Fig. 8.

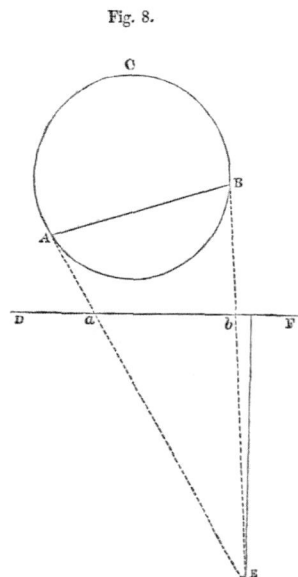

can first be put into perspective, and then the top one directly over it. The plane of the picture touches the cylinder; F G is the line on which the height is laid off; Y Z is the horizontal line, and P the point of sight, as before. The two lines, A B and C D, may be made to touch the circles in A B, and C D; or these points may be found by the method shown in the last example.

6. *To put a globe in perspective.*—If the plane of the picture be perpendicular to the visual ray, passing to the centre of the sphere, the representation will be a circle; but if it be not

perpendicular, the representation will be an ellipse. Let A B C be the plane of the sphere, E the point of view, and D F the section line. Now, if lines be drawn from E to touch the sphere in A and B, A B will be the apparent size of the diameter, and *a b* its representation. A section of the sphere through A B will be a small circle of the sphere, of which A B is the diameter; and all the visual rays from E to touch the sphere, will touch the circumference of this circle. The perspective of the globe will then be found by putting this circle into perspective by the method previously shown.

PRACTICAL GEOMETRY.

LET not the practical student be repelled from the study of this treatise, as if there were something unintelligible in the word GEOMETRY. A geometrical form is simply a regular form, or a form of which the development is founded on some definite rule—a geometrical rule or law. A piece of lump-sugar, casually broken from a larger mass of the same substance, or a clod of earth turned over by the plough, or the outline of the sea-coast, cannot be said to possess a geometrical form, in the ordinary sense of the phrase ; because we followed no law of form in giving a separate existence to the former objects, nor can we recognise any regularity in the form of any one of the three. In each case, the form is rather a compound of a multitude of other forms equally irregular, thrown together in an irregular manner. In a more comprehensive sense, indeed, it may be affirmed, without contradiction, that the form of the clod, such as it is, has resulted from the recognised laws of gravity and cohesion, and must of course possess some definite relation of parts ; but without being hypercritical, and raising any argument on this point, which is really beside the question, every intelligent artisan will understand the nature of the distinction, as regards form or outline, between *shapeless* masses of wood, iron, earth, or loaf-sugar, and the erect, square, and rounded mass of a steam cylinder, or the precise exactitude of a spur-wheel.

Again, to approach still nearer, by comparison, to the distinctive idea of geometrical forms, there are many forms which, while they are not geometrical, are nevertheless characterised by a simplicity, harmony, and grace, which set them at a wide distance from such rude forms as those we have been contemplating. We need only allude to the human form, as a pre-eminent example of the distinct class of forms now alluded to. The simplicity of the human form is greatly owing to its being composed solely of curve lines ; now, not only are straight lines excluded from the figure, but circular lines also, at least so far as that they never constitute any feature in the outline. In tracing the contour of the body in any given attitude, or from any given point of view, we no sooner arrive at an elevation or a depression which begins to assume a circular outline, than it sweeps into another curve, either rounder or flatter than the one which precedes it, or of which the convergency may be reversed, so as to form an undulation. If we may be permitted to apply the language of geometry at all, we would say that the radius of curvature perpetually varies, and is frequently reversed ; and that the utmost approximation to a geometrical analysis of the figure would be the remote generality, that it is composed of very short segments of circles, directly and reversely running into one another. That this definition is of no practical utility, however, is very evident from the fact, that no one ever yet could delineate the human form on geometrical principles, as we daresay no one ever attempted it. He who could seriously set himself to accomplish such an impossibility would be scouted, pitied, or laughed to scorn.

In the meantime, to cut short these preliminary remarks, we hope we have succeeded in assisting the student to understand what geometrical forms *are not*. It behoves us now to explain to him what geometry *is*, and to initiate him into such of the problems of geometry as are necessary for

D

17

his aid in the practical delineation of his compositions. In approaching this introductory exposition, we mean to state and illustrate only such propositions as are of directly practical use in the delineation of all ordinary matters of design, to the exclusion of such as may safely be left to remain within the pasteboard walls of Euclid. We utter this apparently irreverent sentence—irreverent towards the memory of the immortal Euclid—with the proviso, that we speak of what is wanted only for the immediate necessities of the draughtsman—of what he cannot do without. We know from experience that many an artisan will consent to devote his attention to the acquisition of a few plain methods of doing a few plain things, when he would be effectually scared from the regular study of a system embracing the development of the principles of geometry. We heartily recommend the study of Euclid's Elements of Geometry to such as are able and willing to bestow upon it the leisure and application necessary for its prosecution, as they will thereby not only acquire a complete conception of the nature of the science, but will also provide themselves with a fund of general ideas on the relations of figure, which will, in many cases, be of very great advantage to them.

Geometry, then, is the science which treats of the properties and relations of *magnitudes*; that is, of things which have length, or length and breadth, or length, breadth, and thickness. The word is derived from two Greek words, signifying *the earth* and *measure*, obviously embodying the idea of measuring the earth. Some more specific explanations, however, are required; and we shall now explain what are the *things* referred to in the definition.

A *solid* is that which extends in three directions; that is, which has length, breadth, and thickness. The application of these distinctive terms to the three dimensions of a body, is simply a matter of convenience. In applying the reasonings of geometry to a solid, it does not matter though the solid were turned upside down, or round about; whether its thickness or height should exchange its name for its length, or its length under one aspect should be called its breadth under another aspect.

A *surface* or *superficies* is that which has only length and breadth. It may be called the boundary of a solid, as it has no thickness.

A *line* has only length, without either breadth or thickness; and it may properly be distinguished as the boundary of a surface, the simple termination of it.

A *point* has neither length, breadth, nor thickness; it has simply position. For example, the intersection or crossing of two lines which pass through each other, is a point; it obviously has a position or locality, but cannot be said to have either length, breadth, or thickness. In like manner, the extremity of a line is a point; it terminates the line.

In attempting to represent lines and points on the surface of paper by means of drawing instruments, the representations can never more than approximate to the things intended to be shown. For the finest line that can be drawn will have *some* breadth; and, indeed, if it had no breadth, it could not be visible. In the same way, a point may be represented by a very minute dot or puncture on the surface; still, as it covers *some* surface, it is not a geometrical point; it is only an approximation, or something very near what is intended. Since, then, all material representations of objects on paper, by means of lines, are really only approximations in proportion to the fineness of the lines employed, those drawings will be the most correct in which the finest lines are employed, other circumstances being the same. It should be understood, then, that the foregoing definitions are not without their practical value, as they set before the student the standard of perfection to which, if not really attainable, he should strive to approach as nearly as possible.

In studying the following definitions, the reader is requested to refer, where necessary, to the accompanying Table of Geometrical Figures for illustrations of the objects of the definitions.

A *straight line* is the shortest way between the points constituting its extremities. Straightness is exemplified in the strings of a violin when screwed up into a state of tension. If a straight line were bent at particular points in its length, it would become a *series* of straight lines, termed in familiar language a *zig-zag*.

A *curve line* is one which continually changes its direction between its extremities. It is evidently not the shortest way between its extremities; neither is it a zig-zag, as this is composed of straight lines.

A *plane surface,* or *plane* simply, is a surface which contains the smallest extent of surface that can be enclosed by its boundaries. This is exemplified in the end of a drum, which, when screwed up or stretched into musical trim, is perfectly *flat,* as we would say in ordinary language. And it is clear that the shortest distance between any two points on the surface of the drum-end, must lie in that surface; that is, in general, if any two points be taken in a plane, the straight line which joins them will lie wholly in that plane. For illustration of this, if we apply a "straight edge" to the stretched surface of the drum, we shall find that it coincides with that surface, into whatever direction it may be turned.

A *curve surface* is one which is continually deflected, no part of it being a plane. The shell of an egg presents a curve surface, whether it be viewed externally or internally. The exterior surface of the superficies is denominated a *convex* surface, and the interior a *concave* surface.

Parallel lines are straight lines in the same plane, which are equally distant from each other at every part. They, consequently, never can meet, though produced or extended ever so far either way.

A *rectilineal angle* is the quantity of divergence of two straight lines, which either meet or cut each other at a point, without regard to the lengths of the lines. As there are numberless positions in which the lines meeting or intersecting may be placed in relation to each other, so there may be numberless angles at which they may stand. These may be arranged into three classes—right angles, obtuse angles, and acute angles.

Fig. 1.

A *right angle* is formed by one line standing on another, so that the adjacent angles may be equal, *each* of these angles being a right angle. Thus the line, D B (fig. 1), standing on the line, A B C, forms with it the two angles at B; and if these angles be equal, then each is a right angle. Further, the line, D B, is called a *perpendicular* to the line, A C, in virtue of its right angular position.

Here we may shortly explain, that, in designating an angle, we employ the letters used to denote its sides. Thus, the angle contained by the lines, A B and D B, is called the angle, A B D; and that contained by D B and B C is the angle, D B C.

An *obtuse angle* is one which is greater than a right angle. Thus, if the dot line, F I (fig. 2), be at right angles to the line, E F G, the line, F H, inclining to one side of the perpendicular, F I, will form the obtuse angle, E F H.

Fig. 2.

An *acute angle* is one which is less than a right angle. Thus, the line, F H (fig. 2), inclining toward F G, off the perpendicular, forms the acute angle, H F G.

A *plane triangle* is a surface bounded by three straight lines. When three sides are all equal, it is termed *equilateral;* when two of them are equal, it is called *isosceles;* all other plane triangles are classed as *scalene* triangles. Any side may be called the *base.* Triangles are denominated also according to the magnitudes of their angles. When the three angles are acute, a triangle is called *acute-angled;* when one angle is obtuse, it is *obtuse-angled;* when one is a right angle, the triangle is named a *right-angled* triangle.

In a right-angled triangle, the side opposite the right angle is called the *hypothenuse;* the other sides are called, indiscriminately, one of them the *base,* and the other the *perpendicular.*

A *quadrilateral* figure is that which is bounded by four straight lines. When the opposite sides are parallel, it is called a *parallelogram.* When a parallelogram has right angles, it is called a *rectangle;* when a rectangle has all its sides equal, it is termed a *square;* when a parallelogram has no right angles, it is termed a *rhomboid;* when the four sides of a rhomboid are equal, it is termed a *rhombus* or *lozenge.*

1. Let A B (fig. 8) be the line, and c the point without it. On c, as a centre, with a conveniently long radius, describe an arc, cutting the line, A B, at the points, D E.

2. On the points, D E, as centres, and with a longer radius (the longer the more accurate the work is likely to be), describe the arcs intersecting at F.

3. Set a straight edge to the points, c and F, and draw a straight line from c to the line, A B. This will be the perpendicular required.

If there be no room below the line, A B, the intersections, F, may be taken above, that is, between the point, c, and the line. This mode is not, however, so good as the one already described, because it is not likely to be so exact.

Second.—When the point is near the end of the line.

1. In the figure annexed to the second case of Prob. II. (fig. 6), let D be the given point, and A B the straight line. From D draw any straight line, D A, meeting A B at A.

2. Bisect A D at c, and on c, as a centre, with c A as a radius, describe an arc, cutting A B at B.

3. Draw D B for the perpendicular required.

PROBLEM IV. To describe a square on a given straight line.

Fig. 9.

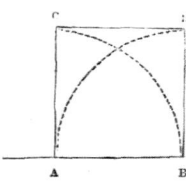

1. Let A B (fig. 9) be the straight line, or the base of the proposed square. Draw A c and B D perpendicular to the base, from its extremities, and make each of them equal to A B.

2. Draw the line, c D; this will complete the square, A B C D, on the line, A B.

A rectangle may be constructed in the same manner. Having determined one of the sides, perpendiculars are drawn from each end of it, of the proper equal lengths, and their extremities joined.

When the centre line of a rectangle is given, the figure may be very accurately described in the following manner :—

Fig. 10.

1. Let A B (fig. 10) be the centre line, and c the middle of the length of the figure. Draw the perpendicular, D E, through the point, c.

2. Set off c F and c G on each side, equal to half the length of the rectangle.

3. Set off c H and c I on the line, D E, each equal to half the breadth of the rectangle; with the same radius, and from the centres, F G, describe arcs, K, L, M, N.

4. From the intersections at H I, and with the half-length as radius, describe arcs, O, P, Q, R, cutting the others. The four lines joining the extreme points of intersection will constitute the rectangle.

PROBLEM V. To draw a line parallel to a given line.

First.—To draw the parallel at a given distance.

1. Let A B (fig. 11) be the given line. Open the legs of the compasses to the required dis-

Fig. 11.

Fig. 12.

tance, and from any two points, c and D, (the farther apart the better,) describe two circular arcs on the side towards which the parallel is to be drawn.

2. Apply a straight edge tangentially to the arcs at E and F, and draw the straight line, G H; this will be a parallel to the given line.

Second.—To draw the parallel through a given point.

1. Let c (fig. 12) be the point; from c draw any oblique line, c D to A B.

2. From c and d, as centres, describe arcs, D E and C F.

3. Make D E equal to C F, and through the points, C, E, draw the parallel, G H. This is the line required.

The methods of describing squares and rectangles, already given, are also available for drawing parallels, though they are not so generally ready of application as the foregoing.

PROBLEM VI. To divide a straight line into any number of equal parts.

1. Let A B (fig. 13) be the straight line, to be divided into, say, five equal parts. Through the points, A and B, draw two parallels, A C, B D, forming any convenient angle with A B.

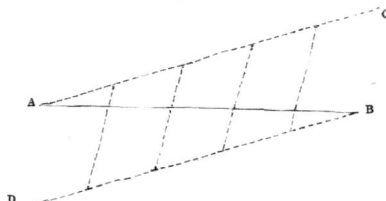

Fig. 13.

2. Take any convenient distance, and lay it off four times (one less than the number of parts required) along the lines, A C and B D, from the points, A and B respectively; and join the first on A C to the fourth on B D, the second on A C to the third on B D, and so on. The lines so drawn will divide A B into the required number of equal parts.

With the assistance of the straight edge and the triangle, or a couple of triangles, this process may be considerably expedited. Thus, having drawn an oblique line, A C, from the point, A, lay off five equal parts on it; set the edge of the triangle to the point, B, and the fifth graduation on A C (fig. 14), slide the triangle parallel to itself in the direction, B A, and draw parallels from the points of division on A C to the line A B; the latter will thus be divided into five equal parts.

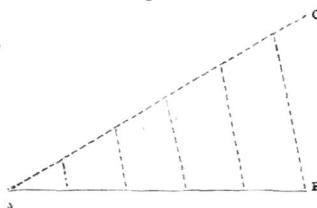

Fig. 14.

PROBLEM VII. To construct an equilateral triangle.

1. Let A B (fig. 15) be the length of the side of the triangle. On A and B, as centres, describe arcs, cutting each other at c.

2. Join A C and B C; the triangle, A B C, thus formed, is equilateral.

Fig. 15.

PROBLEM VIII. To construct a triangle, having its three sides of given lengths.

1. Let A B (fig. 16) equal the base of the triangle. On A, as a centre, with a radius equal to one of the sides, describe an arc.

2. On B, as a centre, with a radius equal to the third side, describe an arc, cutting the former at c.

3. Join A C and B C. The triangle is thus completed as required.

This problem is useful in enabling us to locate a point, the distance of which from two other

Fig. 16.

Fig. 17.

Fig. 18.

points is known. Thus, the position of the point, c, is readily ascertained by the foregoing process, when its distances from the points A and B are given.

PROBLEM IX. To draw a straight line so as to form any required angle with another straight line.

1. Let B A C (fig. 17) be the given angle, and D E the line upon which an equal angle is to be drawn at the point, D. From the points A and D, with any convenient radius, describe arcs F G and H I.

2. Set off the length of the arc F G, contained between the lines A B and A C, upon the arc H I; and draw D I. The angle, E D I, will be equal to the given angle, B A C.

PROBLEM X. To bisect a given angle.

1. Let B A C (fig. 18) be the given angle. On A, as a centre, describe an arc, cutting the sides of the angle at D and E.

2. On D and E, as centres, describe arcs, cutting each other at F. The line A F will bisect the angle, as required.

PROBLEM XI.—To find the centre of a circle, or of a segment of a circle.

First.—For the centre of a circle.

Fig. 19.

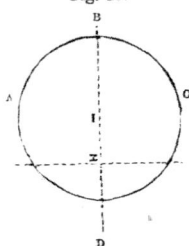

1. Let A B C D (fig. 19) be a circle, of which the centre is to be found. Draw and chord A C.

2. Bisect the chord at E, and draw B D perpendicular to it, bounded both ways by the circumference. Then B D is a diameter.

3. Bisect B D at F; this point will be the centre of the circle.

Or the following method may be adopted; and it is the more expeditious of the two.

1. From any point, B, in the circumference, with a radius not greater than that of the circle, describe a circular arc.

Fig. 20.

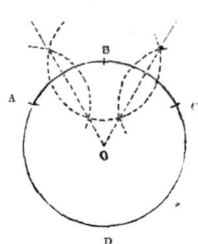

2. From two other points, A and C (fig. 20), beyond this arc, one on each side, describe other arcs with the same radius, each cutting the first arc in two points.

3. Through the two points of intersection thus found, draw straight lines meeting at the point o. This will be the centre of the circle.

Second.—For the centre of a circular segment or arc. The second process for finding the centre of a circle may also be applied to find the centre of a segment. In the diagram annexed to the description of that process, if the segment, A B C, be given, its extremities, A and C, and any intermediate point, B, may be taken for the centres on which the curves are described, and the centre, o, will be found, as already explained. If the curve be greater than a semicircle, as A D C, the same process is applicable; or if it be much greater, the first method may be resorted to. It is obviously of importance that the points, A, B, and C, be well apart, and about equally distant too, and also that the arcs employed be of as large a radius as convenient, as the process is then likely to be more accurate.

PROBLEM XII.—To draw a tangent to a circle through a given point.

There are several varieties of this problem, depending upon the position of the given point, and the accessibility of the centre.

Fig. 21.

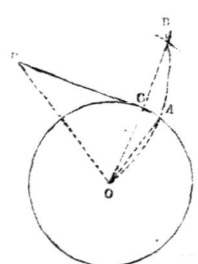

First.—When the point is outside the circumference, and the centre given.

1. Let P (fig. 21) be the point, and o the centre of the circle, A. With the radius, P o, on the centre, P, describe the arc, o A B.

2. With the diameter of the given circle, as radius, on the centre, o, cut the arc at B; join o B, and bisect it at C. The line, P C A, will be a tangent to the circle, touching it at A. Here it may be observed, that as the line, P C A, is perpendicular to o B, it is identical with the line employed in the process for bisecting the line, o B; thus there may be but one operation in performing this bisection, and drawing the line, P A.

The tangent may be drawn in the following manner also. Draw B o to the centre ; upon P o as a diameter describe a semicircle, cutting the circle in A ; the line P A is the tangent.

Second. When the given point is in the circumference, and the centre given.

1. Let A (fig. 22) be the given point. Draw o A D, making A D equal to o A ; and draw B A C perpendicular to it, and B A is the tangent required.

Third. When the centre is inaccessible, as the given point is in the circumference.

1. Let A B C (fig. 23) be the given arc, and A the given point. Set off from A two equal arcs, A B, B C, and draw the straight lines, A B and A C.

2. Make the angle B A D equal to the angle B A C. Then A D is the tangent.

This is a very simple operation, and it may be employed with advantage even though the centre be given.

Fig. 22. Fig. 23.

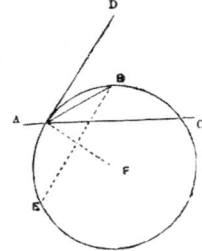

Another mode is to set off on each side of the point A, equal arcs A B and A E ; to join E B, and to draw a perpendicular, A F, to it, and finally to draw A B perpendicular to A F.

PROBLEM XIII.—To describe a circle that shall pass through three given points.

The second process for finding the centre of a circle (Prob. XI.) is exactly applicable for this purpose. Referring to the accompanying figure, suppose A, B, and C, to be the three given points ; the point o being found by the method there delineated, it is the centre of the circle required, and by taking the distance to any of the points A, B, C, as a radius, the circle may be described passing through all the three points.

Also this problem is obviously identical with that which requires to circumscribe a triangle, as in this case a circle is to be described passing through the three points terminating its angles ; the problem which proposes to describe an arc of a circle passing through the extremities of a straight line with a given *rise*, is but another form of the one now discussed. For example, in the figure accompanying the first process under Problem XI., if A B be the straight line, and E B the given rise, being a perpendicular to it at the middle point E, it is clearly a case of the 12th problem ; as we have the three points, A, B, C, and we wish to describe an arc passing through these three points. This problem will be useful for finding the diameter of any large object, when only a part of the circumference is accessible.

PROBLEM XIV. To draw a number of radial lines upon the circumference of a circle, the centre being inaccessible.

1. If the radii are at equal distances, divide the circumference, or a part of it, into the required number of equal parts, at the points A, B, C, &c.

2. On the points A, B, c, &c., as centres, with radii larger than a division, describe arcs cutting each other at *b, c,* &c. ; thus, from A and c, as centres, describe arcs intersecting at *b ;* and from B and D, as centres, describe arcs cutting *a, c ;* and so on. The lines, A B *b,* c *c,* &c., will be radial lines, as desired.

Fig. 24.

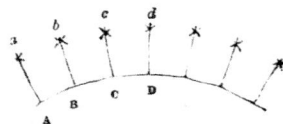

In presenting the foregoing methods of performing geometrical operations, no account is taken of the use that might be made of the common T square, and the triangles, or of the parallel ruler. These instruments will, however, where applicable, assist considerably on many occasions, in simplifying the solution of the problems, and with an accuracy generally quite sufficient for practical purposes. When, for example, a tangent is to be drawn to a circle through a given point in the circumference, one edge of the triangle might be set to the radius at that point, and the parallel ruler set to the perpendicular edge of the triangle, and then shifted to the circumference, where the tangent could be drawn, or, if the tangent be parallel to an edge of the board, the T square will suffice to draw it.

F

PROBLEM XV. On a given line to describe a regular pentagon.

Let A B (fig. 25) be the given line, bisect A B at C, and draw C F perpendicular to A B. Set off on this line, a length, C D, equal to A B, the given side of the required pentagon. Draw A D, and produce it indefinitely, make D E equal to half A B. From A, as a centre, with the length A E, as a radius, describe the arc E F, cutting C F in F.

Fig. 25.

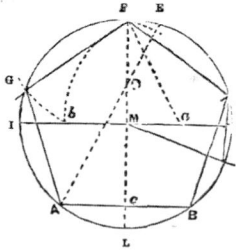

2. From A F and B as centres, with A B as a radius, describe arcs cutting each other in A and H.

3. Draw the lines A F and H B, when A G F H B will be the pentagon required.

PROBLEM XVI. To describe a pentagon in a given circle. Let A G F H B (fig. 25) be the given circle.

1. Draw the diameters, I K and L F, perpendicular to each other; bisect M K in *a*. Upon *a*, as a centre, with the distance *a* F, describe the arc F *b*. Upon F, as a centre, with the distance F *b*, describe the arc *b* G, cutting the circle at G. Join G A, and carry it round the circle five times, and it will produce the required pentagon. The arcs contained between the extremities of any side of the pentagon, as H K, being bisected as at H K, will give the side of a decagon, or ten-sided figure, inscribed in the same circle.

PROBLEM XVII. To construct a hexagon on a given line.

Fig. 26.

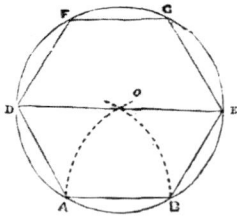

1. Let A B (fig. 26) be the given line. On the extremities of this line, with the extent of the line as a radius, describe arcs intersecting each other at C.

2. On C, as a centre, with the same radius, describe a circle. From the intersections at D and E, with the arcs before described, set off D F and E G on the circle.

3. Join A D, D F, F G, and E B, which will form the hexagon required.

When the circumscribing circle is given, the following method may be adopted.

Take the radius of the given circle in the compasses, and apply it to the circumference, which will divide it into six equal parts. Draw a chord to each arc, and the six chords will form the hexagon required.

PROBLEM XVIII. To inscribe a regular octagon in a given square.

Fig. 27.

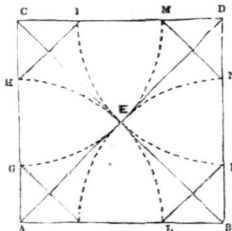

Let A B C D (fig. 27) be the given square. Draw the diagonals, A D and B C, intersecting at E.

Upon A B C D as centres, with a radius E C, describe the arcs, H F L, K E N, M E G, and F E I. Join K G, H I, M N, and F L, and the required octagon is produced.

If a circle is given, in which to inscribe a regular octagon, it may be done in the following simple manner.

1. Draw two diameters at right angles to each other.

2. Bisect the four arcs thus obtained, and draw chords to each; which chords shall form the octagon required.

PROBLEM XIX. To describe any regular polygon upon a given line.

Let A B (fig 28) be the given line. Produce A B any length in either direction, as A C. From A as a centre, with A D as a radius, describe a semicircle, divide it into as many equal parts as the polygon is to have sides; in the present instance we have chosen five, as *a* D *b c*, the number of points required to produce a pentagon.

2. Draw lines through all the divisions (minus one), as A D, A *b* F, A C F.

3. From D and B as centres, with A B as a radius, describe arcs, cutting A E in E, and A F in F. Draw the lines D E, E F, and F B; when A D E F B shall be the polygon required.

PROBLEM XX. To describe any regular polygon in a given circle.

1. Let A F B D (fig. 29) be the given circle. Draw the diameter, A B. From E, as a centre, erect the perpendicular, E F C, cutting the circle at F. Divide E F into four equal parts, and set off three similar divisions from F to C.

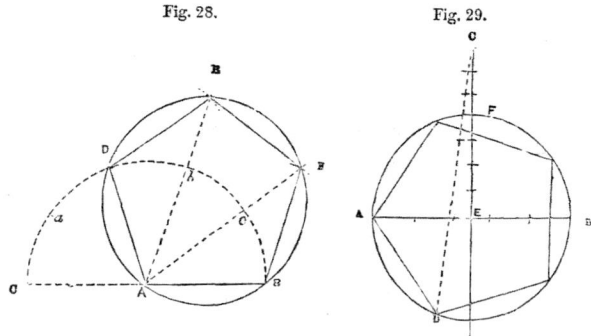

Fig. 28.   Fig. 29.

2. Divide the diameter, A B, into as many equal parts as the polygon is required to have sides.

3. From C, through the second division in the diameter, draw the line C D, and A D shall be the side of the polygon required.

In each of these examples we have shown a pentagon, on account of its simplicity, but the same rule is applicable to polygons of any number of sides.

THE ELLIPSE.

The fact of circular surfaces changing their appearance with the different positions of the observer's eye, is so well known as to render any observations on that head needless; but in order to delineate them under all circumstances, it is essentially requisite that the student should understand that the elliptical curve thus assumed by the circular one is strictly regular, and is to be produced by rules as fixed and certain, as that by which we describe the circle itself. With the assistance of the annexed figure (30), which we have selected as a familiar explanation of the principles of the ellipse, the student will have ro difficulty in understanding the plain definition of it. The line A B, passing through the length of the figure, is called its *transverse axis.*

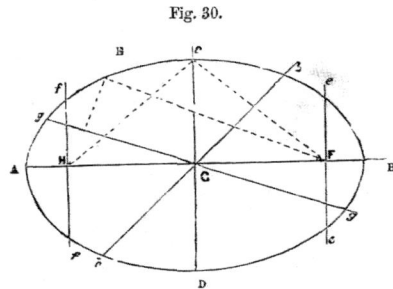

Fig. 30.

The point G, which bisects the transverse axis, is the *centre* of the ellipse. The line C D, crossing this centre at right angles to the transverse axis, is termed the *conjugate axis.*

The point F in the transverse axis, and corresponding point H at the same distance from the centre on the other side, are called the *foci* of the ellipse.

A right line *ff* or *e e* passing through a focus of the figure at right angles to the transverse axis, and terminated at either end by a curve, is called the *latus rectum,* or sometimes the *parameter.*

A straight line passing in any direction through the centre of the figure, and terminated at either end by the curve, as *g g* or *h h,* is called a *diameter.*

A line drawn through any diameter parallel to a tangent at the extremity of that diameter terminated by a curve, is called a *double ordinate.*

The ellipse is constructed by the motion of a point about the centre of the figure G, beginning its course at the extremity of a diameter, as at A, and taking such a path as that its distance from one of the foci, together with its distance from the other, shall be, in every point throughout its course, exactly equal to the whole length of the transverse axis, A B. A practical application of this principle is to be found in the following method, which is often resorted to in the workshop for producing an ellipse. In the preceding figure, if the transverse and conjugate axes are given, the *foci* are determined by taking half the tranverse axis, as A G, and with that extent in the compasses, and on the extremity c of the conjugate as a centre, describing an arc, which cuts A B in the points F and H, which are the *foci*.

If pins are fixed in these points, and a thread equal in length to the transverse axis is fastened to them by its extremities, a pencil so applied to the thread as to keep it continually stretched, or forming two straight lines, will, if progressively moved about the centre, describe the ellipse. Thus, in the figure before us, H C F may be supposed to be thread, which, if gradually moved round the centre, will, at different points of its travel, take the position of the inclined lines H and E F, describing by the entire revolution of the pencil the ellipse, A C B D.

PROBLEM XXI. The transverse and conjugate diameters of an ellipse being given, as A B and C D, to describe the curve itself through a number of points, to be determined at the extremities of any number of diameters at pleasure.

Fig. 31.

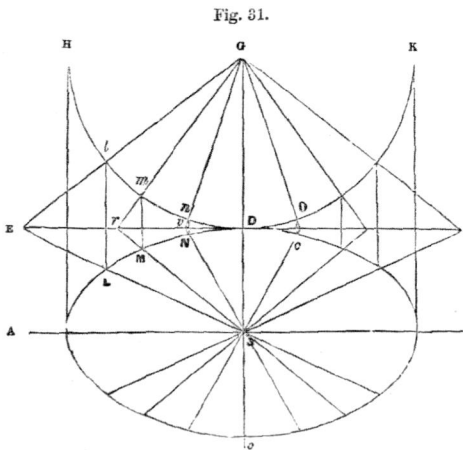

1. Through the extremity, D (fig. 31), of the conjugate axis, draw E F parallel to the transverse axis; extend the line C D to G, and make it equal to A S or S B, half the transverse axis.

2. Upon G, with the radius G D, describe the circle, H D K; through the centre, s, draw the lines, s, L, E, s, M, r, &c. at pleasure, respectively cutting the line E F at E r, &c. Join the points thus determined on the line E F with the centre G, and mark the points of intersection produced on the arc, H D K, at l, m, n, o, &c.; draw lines from H, l, m, &c., parallel to G D, until they respectively intersect the extremities of the diameter at A, L, M, N, &c.; these points will be in the periphery of the ellipse, and a curve traced through them will describe the figure.

A figure which is often substituted for the ellipse for practical purposes, but is decidedly inferior to it in point of regularity and beauty of contour, may be drawn by means of circles in the following manner :—

Fig. 32.

1. Let A B (fig. 32) be a given transverse diameter; divide A B into three equal parts, by the points o v. From o and v as centres, with o A or v B as a radius, describe equal circles, D V F and E G O, cutting each other in the points I and K.

2. Draw the lines K O D, I V G, I O F, and K V E, cutting the circles in the points D E F and G.

3. From I and K as centres, with K D or I G as a radius, describe the curvilineal tangents, D E and F G, when the figure, A D, E B, G F, will be the ellipse required.

There are various methods of describing ellipses *mechanically* at present in use, probably the best of which is that invented by Mr. Ridley. By this instrument every species of ellipse, from a circle down to a right line, may be correctly formed.

The instrument consists mainly of a beam, a, carrying three sliding sockets, b c d (fig. 33), which may be set at any distance from each other. On the sockets, b and d, small sheaves are fitted to revolve on pins, and the centre one, c, is fitted to receive a pencil or tracer.

To explain the action of this apparatus, we shall suppose A B to be the transverse, and C D the conjugate axis of the required ellipse, intersecting each other at E. The inner edge of a square, F, is now to be applied to the lines, c, E, B, at such a parallel distance therefrom as to allow the centres of the sheaves on the sliding bar to move exactly over the centre of the lines constituting the axes of the ellipse. To adjust the position of the sockets to produce the given ellipse, the distance between the pencil and the sheave, *b*, is made equal to half the length of the transverse axis, and *c d* equal to half the conjugate. If now the bar is moved along the edge of the square, as shown by the dotted lines, the tracing point will describe one quarter of the ellipse, each of the remaining portions being described in a similar manner.

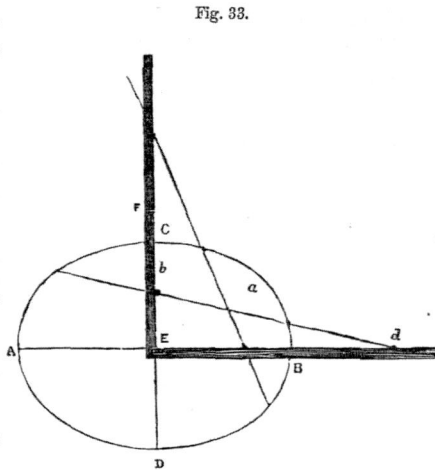

Fig. 33.

This simple apparatus has since been considerably improved; instead of the plain square of wood, two grooved pieces of metal crossing each other at right angles, so as to form four squares, are substituted. The pins in the pencil beam are fitted to slide in the grooves which are made along the upper side of the squares. In this manner, the whole of the ellipse may be described at once, with the exception of the slight portion which the thickness of the square covers; these are easily filled in by hand.

We now come to the consideration of the two curvilineal figures, the parabola and hyperbola, which, together with the ellipse, are generally treated under the head of Conic Sections, that is, as curves produced by the intersection of a flat surface with the curve surface of a cone.

Let A B C (fig. 34) represent a vertical section through the centre of a cone, the figure which is produced is a triangle.

If the entire cone is cut by a plane passing through it in the direction of D E, parallel to the base, the figure produced will be similar to the base, that is, a circle.

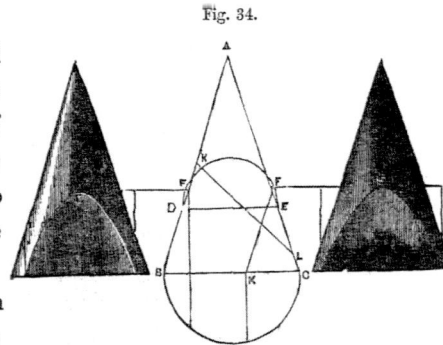

Fig. 34.

If the section is made in the direction F K, parallel with the opposite sloping side of the cone, as A B, the curve described on the surface will be a parabola. If the intersecting plane pass through the cone in the direction F I, perpendicular to the base and parallel to the axis, the curve produced on the surface of the cone by the section is an hyperbola.

If the intersecting plane pass through the cone in any oblique direction, as K L, the curve described on its surface will be an ellipse. As we have already explained the construction of the ellipse, we shall now proceed to examine that of the parabola.

THE PARABOLA.

In order to enter fully upon the geometrical construction of this figure, we shall, in the first place, exhibit its mechanical formation, so as to enable us to set before the student the most explicit rules for application in practice.

In the annexed figure (35), let A B C be a straight-edged ruler, and A B D a common joiner's square; and let a thread of a length equal to B D be fixed by one extremity to the end of the square D, and the other to any point E, between the two rulers. If now the side A B of the square be moved along the edge of the ruler, A B C, and a pencil is applied to the edge B D, so as always to keep the thread stretched, at the same time that it allows it to slip round its point F, the pencil will describe a curve, F L H I, which is a parabola.

G

The point E, about which the thread moves, is called the *directrix*.

A line H K, drawn through the focus E, and perpendicular to the directrix, is called the *axis* of the figure.

The point H, in which the axis cuts the curve, is called the *vertex* of the figure.

A line G N, passing through the focus E, at right angles to the axis, and terminated by the curve, is the *parameter*.

Any line which can be drawn within the limits of the curve, parallel to the axis, as J K, is called a *diameter*.

If a tangent were drawn to J K at J, the extremity of the diameter, a line L O, drawn parallel to it, is called a *double ordinate*.

That part of any diameter which is contained within any part of the curve itself and its ordinate, as J K, is termed an *abscissa*.

Fig. 35.

Fig. 36.

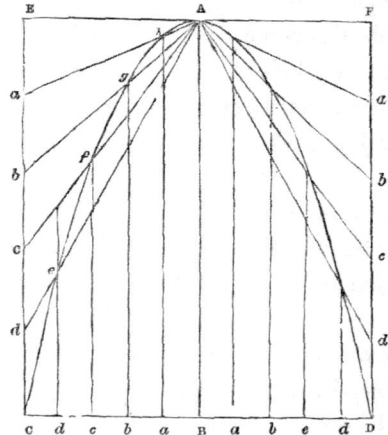

PROBLEM XXII. Let A B (fig. 36) be the given axis of a parabola, and C D a double ordinate. It is required to delineate the curve by a process which shall determine a number of points in its course.

1. Through A draw E F, parallel to the double ordinate, C D. Through C and D draw the perpendiculars, C E and E F, parallel to A B.

2. Divide B C and B D into any number of equal parts, as five. Likewise divide C E and D F in a similar manner.

3. Through the points *a b c* and *d* in C D, on each side of the point B, draw the perpendiculars *a e b f c g d h*, &c., and through the points *a b c* and *d*, in C E and D F, draw lines to the upper extremity A, of the transverse axis A B, respectively, cutting the perpendiculars drawn from the line C D, in the points *e f g h*, then will the points of intersection to the right and left of the transverse axis be situated in the curve of the required parabola, and which will be completed by tracing a line steadily through them.

THE HYPERBOLA.

In giving a familiar explanation of the properties of this curve, we shall again have recourse to the mechanical process of its formation, to the end that we may the more easily define its leading characteristics.

Referring to the accompanying woodcut (fig. 37), we shall suppose the points B and C to be determined, and a straight ruler, A B, to be made moveable on one of its extremities, about the point B, as a centre. To the end A of this ruler, one end of a thread is attached, the other being fixed at the determined point C. Now, let a pencil be applied to the thread, so as to press a portion of it against the edge of the ruler, as A D, and keep the other portion, D C, tightly stretched. The ruler being made to traverse on the given point B, at the same time that the pencil D moves along its edge, always preserving the tension of the threads; and the motion of the pencil or point D, will be in the curve D F G, which is that of an hyperbola.

If the extremity of the ruler, which now moves on the point B as a centre, was removed to C, and there made to traverse in a similar manner, the end of the thread now set at C, being now placed at B, the curve described would be an *opposite hyperbola*.

Fig. 37.

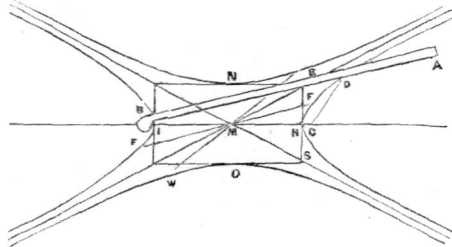

The points B and C, on which the ruler traverses, are called the *foci*.

A line terminated by the curves of the hyperbola and its opposite, and which, if continued at either extreme, would pass through either of the foci, as I H in the figure, is called the *transverse axis*. A line passing through the centre M of the figure to the right and left of it, and terminated by the intersection of the arc of a circle, which is described on the point H as a centre, with the distance C M as a radius, is called the *conjugate axis*. Any line, as V W, drawn through the centre M, is called a *diameter*. If a tangent, with either of the curves, be drawn to the extremity of V W, another line, as F F, drawn parallel to that tangent, and through the centre M, is called a *conjugate diameter* to that at the extremity of which the tangent was drawn. A line drawn through any diameter parallel to its conjugate diameter, and terminated by the curve, is called a *double ordinate*. If any diameter be continued within the curve, and is terminated by the curve and a double ordinate, the part within is termed an *abscissa*. A line drawn through the focus of the figure, and at right angles to the transverse axis, is called the *parameter*.

If through the extremity of the transverse axis, I H, a line, R S, is drawn parallel to the conjugate axis, N O, and equal to N O, having H R and H L respectively equal to M N and M O, their right lines drawn through the centre M, and the points R and S, as are the lines M X and M Y, are called *asymptotes*.

When the transverse and conjugate diameters are equal, the hyperbola is termed *equilateral* or *right-angled*.

The recapitulation of these dry and uninteresting terms may appear formidable to the student, but he must bear in mind that a complete knowledge of these is essentially necessary to enable him to comprehend and construct any hyperbolic curves with which he may meet in practice. For curves of a large size, the foregoing mechanical system of construction is very useful and accurate; but, as before adverted to, in order to attain a complete knowledge of the subject, as well as to be able to cope with the different forms which occur, it is necessary to understand correctly their geometrical construction.

Fig. 38.

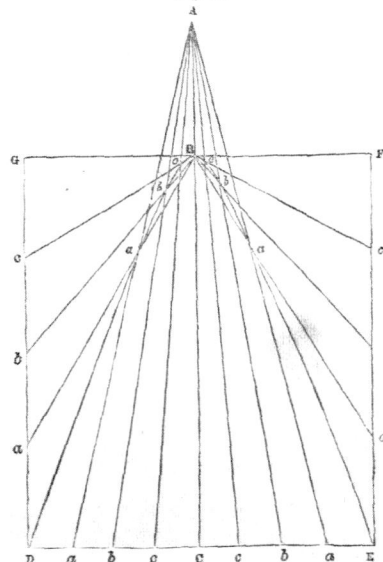

PROBLEM XXIII. The diameter of an hyperbola, A B (fig. 38), its abscissa, B C, and double ordinate, D E, being given, it is required to delineate the curve by determining a certain number of points which shall be in its course.

1. Through B draw G F parallel to D E, and from the extremities, D and E, of the ordinates, draw D G and E F parallel to the abscissa, B C, cutting G F in the points F and G.

2. Divide C D and C E, each into any number of equal parts, as four; and through the points of division, *a b c*, on each side of the point C, draw lines to A.

3. Divide D G and E F into the same number of equal parts, and from the points of division on D G and E F, draw lines to B. A curve drawn through the intersections at *a b c*, on each side the diameter, will be that of the hyperbola required.

PROBLEM XXIV. The transverse and conjugate diameters, A B and C D (fig. 39), being given, it is required to determine a certain number of points in the curve with a view to its delineation.

Through the extremity B, of the diameter A B, draw F G parallel to C D, the other diameter; and make B F and B G equal to the semi-diameters E C or E D. Through the points F and G thus determined, draw E H and E J, which will be the symptotes of the figure.

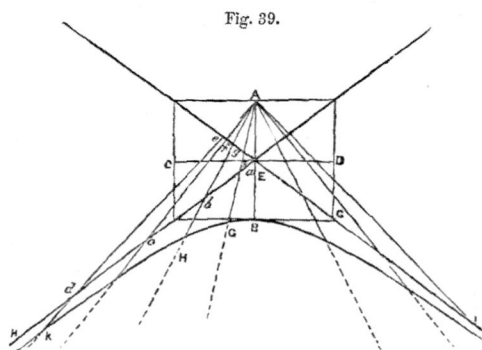

Fig. 39.

From A, as before, draw lines at pleasure towards the curve to be described, as A G, A H, A J, A K, cutting the asymptotes at the points *a b c d*, and *e f g*, and *h*, &c. Set off the distances A *h*, H *g*, A*f*, A *e*,respectively, from the points *a b c* and *d* on the lines from A; and the points G H, J K, will be in the curve required.

If the student has gone over this course of practice in the construction of geometrical curves, by performing the examples themselves on a large scale, he will be enabled, in his future operations, to make use of them in any drawings which come before him in his every-day practice. There are numerous other useful curve lines which admit of regular definitions, as the Cycloid, Epicycloid, &c. The first of these curves, the Cycloid (fig. 40), may be defined in a familiar manner, by supposing it to be the periphery of a cart-wheel rolling along a level road. Thus the circle A B, in the annexed woodcut, may be supposed to represent the cart-wheel rolling in the direction A B A, and A to be the given point in its periphery. Under these conditions, the track of the point A during one revolution will be indicated by the curve line, A C A, G A, which is termed the cycloidal curve. The properties of the cycloid may be briefly defined as follows :—If the generating circle is placed in the centre of the curve, its diameter coinciding with the axis, A B, and if from any point there be drawn a tangent, C E, the ordinate, C D E, perpendicular to the axis, and the chord of the circle, then

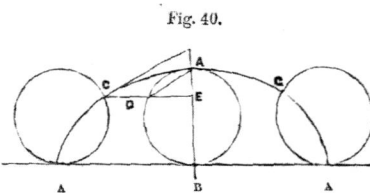

Fig. 40.

The right line, C D, = the circular arc, A D.

The cycloidal arc, A C, = double the chord, A D.

The semi-cycloid, A C A, = double the diameter, A B, and

The tangent, C F, is parallel to the chord, A D.

If the ball of a pendulum is caused to move in a cycloidal curve, its vibrations will be isochronous ; that is, they will all be performed in precisely the same amount of time.

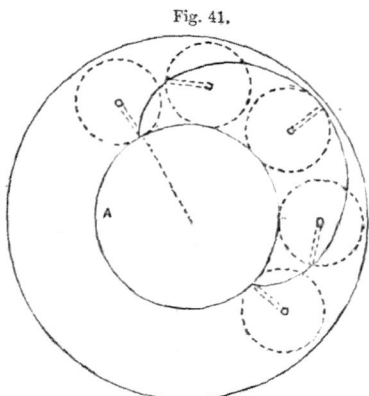

Fig. 41.

The epicycloid (fig. 41) differs from the cycloid in this, that it is generated by a point in one circle rolling upon the circumference of another, instead of a level surface. The cycloid may, however, be brought under the same definition, by regarding the straight line as the circumference of a circle whose diameter is infinitely great.

This definition of the curve will be understood by reference to the accompanying figure, in which A is the *generating* or rolling circle, and B the *fundamental* one, or that upon which it rolls in describing the exterior epicycloidal curve, C D. If the generating circle, instead of rolling on the outside, were to roll within he interior circle, a point in the former would describe an interior epicycloid, or, as it is more recently termed, the hypocycloid.

ORDERS OF ARCHITECTURE.

CHAPTER I.

THE moderns have applied the term "order" to those architectural forms with which the ancient Greeks and Romans composed the exteriors of their temples. There are generally understood to be five orders of Architecture, namely—the Tuscan, the Doric, the Ionic, the Corinthian, and the Composite. The Doric, the Ionic, and the Corinthian orders were originally designed by the Greeks, who knew nothing of the Tuscan and the Composite orders. The Romans borrowed the three Grecian orders, and modified them to suit their own purposes; and to these they added the Tuscan and Composite orders. The latter orders, however, have little claim to be separately classed, as they have much in common with the former three. The Tuscan order, by its title, enables us to assign its origin to Tuscany, which is indeed the more certain by the fact, that the Tuscans were originally a colony of Dorians. The Composite order, as the name implies, is compounded from the other orders, and may be called in truth a corrupted Corinthian. The characteristics of an order are determined not so much by the ornaments with which it is embellished, as by the essential proportions of its parts.

It appears then from this, that there are three Grecian and five Roman orders; and the Doric, Ionic, and Corinthian being common to both, they are distinguished as Grecian Doric, Roman Doric, and similarly for the Ionic and Corinthian.

The leading members of an order are—1. a platform; 2. perpendicular supports; and 3. a lintelling or covering connecting the tops of the supports, and covering the edifice. The proportioning of these parts to the edifice and to each other, with the addition of suitable decorations, constitutes an *order* or *rule*. The principal member is the upright support or column, the accompanying members being subservient to this leading feature; the bottom of the column rests either on a general platform, or upon a particular square plinth. The lower part of the column resting upon the square plinth is usually encompassed with a selection of mouldings, which, from their position, are, in conjunction with the plinth, termed the Base of the column. The upper end is likewise covered with a plinth, which, in conjunction with the accompanying mouldings on the upper end of the column, is termed the Capital of the column. The body of the column, or that part situated between the base and the capital, is called the Shaft. The lintelling or covering which lies upon the columns is denominated the Entablature, and is subdivided into three parts—the Architrave, Frieze, and Cornice. The architrave represents a mere lintel, embracing the tops of the columns; the frieze is intended to signify generally the ends of the cross-beams resting upon the lintels, having the spaces between them filled up, and having also a plain moulding to separate it from the architrave, and to conceal the horizontal joint formed by the two members; the upper member or cornice represents the projecting eaves of a Greek roof, showing the ends of the rafters. The whole is distinctly exemplified in the Grecian Doric order.

Mouldings.—Before going into the details of the orders, it will be necessary to give an account of the various mouldings employed in Greek and Roman architecture. And, in the first place,

H

33

mouldings may be defined to be prismatic or annular solids, formed by plane and curved surfaces, which are employed as ornaments, and are considered as forming constituent parts of an order. If we conceive a straight moulding to be cut through at right angles to its length, the section thus formed is termed its profile, and exhibits exactly its characteristic outline, from which its name is derived. Annular mouldings, again, or such as are formed upon a round surface, as the surface of a column, must be cut by a plane passing through the centre line or axis of the column, in order to exhibit their characteristic sections or profiles.*

A prevailing gracefulness of outline characterises the mouldings of the Grecian orders, which at once distinguishes them from the more unpretending and simpler mouldings of the Romans. Various modes are employed for describing the Roman, and more especially the Greek mouldings, so various are their applications and the modifications of form to which they are subject. The Roman mouldings, however, are usually composed of circular arcs. The Grecian mouldings exhibit every variety of conic section—elliptical, parabolical, and hyperbolical—the circle being seldom employed but in small cavettos and mouldings of contrary flexure.

The regular mouldings are eight in number, and are thus named:—The Fillet or Band, the Torus, the Astragal or Bead, the Ovolo, the Cavetto, the Cyma recta, the Cyma reversa or Talon, and the Scotia.

The *fillet, a,* fig. 1, is the smallest rectangular member in any composition of mouldings. When it stands upon a flat surface, its projection from the surface is generally made equal to its height. In general it is employed to separate other members.

In the following descriptions, the extreme points of the curves are always assumed to be given.

The *torus* and *astragal,* shaped like ropes, are intended to bind and strengthen the parts to which they are applied. In form the torus is a semicircle, which projects from a vertical diameter. Thus, in fig. 2, let *a b* be the vertical diameter, from which the torus projects; bisect, or divide in two equal parts, the line, *a b,* at the point, *c;* from *c* as a centre, describe the semicircle, *a d b;* this will be the profile of the torus, which, it will be noticed, is surmounted by a fillet, *b e.* The astragal is described in the same way as the torus, the only distinction between them being that, when employed in the same order, the astragal is smaller than the torus. The torus is generally employed in the bases of columns; the astragal, both in bases and capitals.

The *ovolo* is a member strong at the extremity, and obviously intended for support; it is usually employed above the eye, as a supporter to the essential members of the composition. The Roman ovolo consists of a quadrant or a less portion of a circle, and is described as in fig. 3, the height and projection being given. And first, let the height be equal to the projection. Draw *a b* equal to the height, and *b c* at right angles with, and equal to, *a b,* for the projection. The quadrant, *a c,* described from the centre, *b,* with a radius, *b a,* or *b c,* is the contour of the ovolo. But, when the projection is less than the height, as in fig. 4, draw *a b* and *b c,* as before, at right angles, *a b* being the height, and *b c* the projection. From the point, *a,* draw an arc of a circle, *b d,* with the radius, *a b,* and from the point, *c,* with the same radius, describe another arc, cutting the former arc at *d;* the point, *a,* is the centre from which the ovolo is to be described, with the radius, *d a,* or *d c;* this being done, the curve, *a c,* is the contour of the ovolo.

* It is by some considered preposterous to lay down rules for the construction of contours, which are said to be subjected to no law of form, except what is furnished by the individual's own taste. Seeing, however, that beautiful outlines may doubtless be traced by means of regular geometrical constructions, we think the insertion of the more common of these methods will be useful to those who cannot readily sketch for themselves.

The Greek ovolo, fig. 5, unlike the Roman ovolo, cannot be described by means of circular arcs; it must be described by finding a number of points in it. For this purpose draw the tangent, *a c*, from the lower extremity, *a*, indicating the inclination of the curve at that point; draw also the vertical line, *d b c*, through the extreme point, *b*, or projection of the curve. Draw *b e* parallel to *c a*, and *a c f* parallel to *c b*; make *e f* equal to *a e*; divide the lines *e b* and *b c* into the same convenient number of equal parts; draw straight lines from the point, *a*, to the points of division in *b c*, and similarly draw straight lines from the point, *f*, through the points of division in *b e*, meeting successively the lines drawn from *a* to *b c*; the points of intersection of the pairs of lines thus drawn will be as many points in the contour of the moulding, and a curve line traced so as to embrace these points will be the greater part of the contour. The remaining part, *b g*, if required to be determined in the same manner, may be found by drawing lines from *a* instead of *f*, through the points in *b e*, and from *f* to *b d*, instead of from *a* to *b c*. Of course this will give a good deal

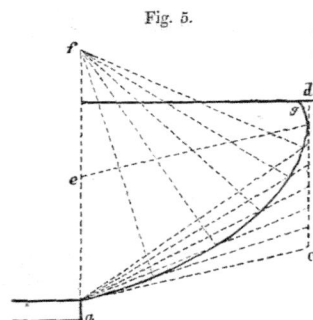

Fig. 5.

more of the curve than is necessary. The curve drawn in this manner is a portion of an ellipse, somewhat greater than a fourth of the whole circumference. The recess of the moulding, *b g d*, at its projecting point, is denominated a *quirck*. Fig. 5 is, from its great projection relatively to its height, adapted for capitals of Doric columns. With less projection, it would be suitable for entablature.

To describe the *hyperbolical ovolo*—fig. 6—as employed in Doric capitals; having given the projection, *b*, of the curve, and the lower extremity, *a*, draw the line, *a c*, in the direction of the lower end of the curve, and *b c* vertically through the point, *b*; draw *a g* vertically from *a*, and *b e* and *c d* perpendicular to *a g*; set off *e f* equal to *a d*, and *e g* equal to *a e*; join *b f*, and divide *b f* and *b c* into the same convenient number of equal parts; draw straight lines from *a* to the points of division in *b c*, and also straight lines from *g* through the points in *f b*; the successive intersections of these lines, as in the foregoing case, are the positions of as many points in the contour. This is the general form of the ovolos in the capitals of the Grecian Doric. It will be seen that the lower part towards *a* is nearly straight, and is succeeded by four fillets, shown in section on a large scale, and rounded away on the under sides into the fundamental line, *n o*.

The *cavetto*—figs. 7, 8, and 9—which is the reverse of the ovolo, both in regard to form and to the weakness of the extreme parts, is well adapted for purposes of shelter for the other members. It is always employed as a finishing, and is here applied where strength is required. It is never used in bases or capitals, but frequently in entablatures; thus in the Roman

Fig. 6.

Doric order, it forms the crowning member of the cornice, and is evidently employed to overhang and shield the under members. The cavetto is described in the same way as the Roman ovolo; by arcs of circles, which may be either full quadrants or of less extent. The Greek cavetto—fig. 9—is somewhat elliptical, and may be described by a combination of two circular arcs, thus : Let *a b* be the projection of the moulding, and *a c* the vertical line ; from the point, *a,* draw *b d* vertically from *b*, and make it equal to *b e*, which is two-thirds of *b a* ; from the centre, *d,* describe the arc, *b i* ; draw *i n* perpendicular to *e d*, make *n o* equal to *n i*, draw *o p* perpendicular to *a c*, and meeting *e d* produced in *p,* and from the centre, *p,* thus found, describe the arc, *i o*. The contour, *b i o c*, will represent the Greek cavetto.

The *conge* or *scape*—figs. 10 and 11—is a species of cavetto, and is not recognised as a distinct moulding. In section it is partly concave and partly straight, the latter part being vertical. It is employed in the columns of some of the orders, for joining the capitals and bases to the shafts. Let *a b* be the projection of the moulding from the vertical line, *a e*, which it is required to touch ; and first, if the projection, *a b*, is equal to the height of the curve, make *a c*—fig. 10—equal to *a b* ; and

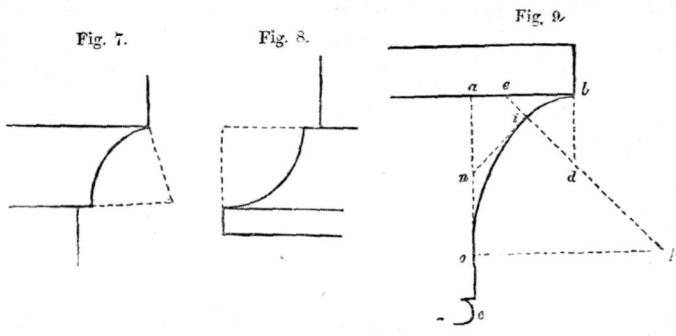

Fig. 7. Fig. 8. Fig. 9.

from the points, *b* and *c*, as centres, with *a b* or *a c* as a radius, describe the arcs intersecting at *d* ; from *d,* with the same radius, describe the arc, *b c* ; this completes the contour of the conge. The centre, *d,* may likewise be found by drawing *b d* vertically, and making it equal to *a b*.

If the conge contains less than a quarter of a circle, as in fig. 11, let *b e* be the tangent to the curve at the point, *b* ; on the vertical, *a f,* set off the distance, *c d*, equal to *c b* ; draw *b e* at right angles to *b c*, and *d e* at right angles to *c d* ; from the point, *e,* as a centre, describe the arc, *b d* ; this completes the contour of the moulding, *b d f*.

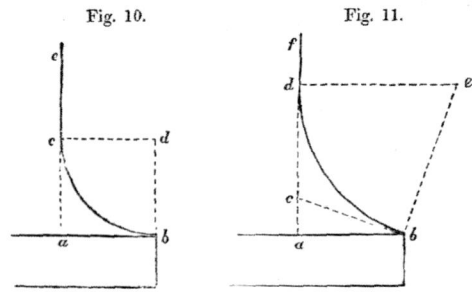

Fig. 10. Fig. 11.

These are the simple Roman forms of the conge. It is obvious that the curve may be varied into a combination of arcs of different radii, in the same way as the cavetto—fig. 9—which would render it more appropriate for Grecian profiles.

The *cymatium*, or *ogee*, is the term applied to a moulding of which the section is compounded of a concave and convex surface. There are two species of cymatium : the cyma recta, or simply, the cyma, and the cyma reversa or talon. The Roman cymatium is usually composed of circular arcs, which may either be equal to or less than a fourth of a circumference.

Thus, in the accompanying figures, 12 and 13, the former of which represents the cyma recta, and the latter the talon, let *a* and *b* be the extremities of the curve, join *a b* and bisect, or divide it equally at the point, *c* ; from the points *a* and *c* as centres, with the same radius, describe arcs cutting at the point, *e d* ; likewise, from the points, *b* and *c*, as centres, with the same radius, describe arcs cutting at the point, *e* ; from the points, *d* and *e*, thus found, as centres, describe

Fig. 12. Fig. 13.

the arcs, *a c* and *c b* ; then the curve of double flexure, *a c b*, fig. 12, is the cyma recta, and the curve, *a c b*, fig. 13, is the cyma reversa or talon. In the former, it will be observed, the concave portion of the surface is uppermost, whereas in the latter it is undermost. If the curve is required to be made quicker, a shorter radius than *a c* or *c b* must be used in describing the two parts of the contour. The projection of the upper end of the curve over the under, as *n b*, fig. 12, is generally equal to the height, *a n*, of the moulding.

The Greek cyma-recta differs little from the Roman, except in that its projection over the under fillet is less than that of the latter, and that its curvature is also less. It may be described similarly to the Roman cyma (fig. 12) by means of circular arcs, described with radii of greater length than $a\,c$ or $c\,b$. The nature of the Greek cyma-reversa, or talon, is represented in fig. 14; the curvature of the moulding is much more deeply marked than that of the Roman talon. The concave portion, $a\,e$, is deeply indented, and the convex portion, $b\,n\,e$, projects considerably, and is *quirked* or turned inwards at b. The following is a simple mode of constructing the moulding, first introduced by Mr. A. M. Nicholson:—Join the points, $a\,b$, the extremities of the curve; bisect $a\,b$ at the point c; upon $b\,c$, as a diameter, describe the semicircle $c\,d\,b$, and on $a\,e$ describe the semicircle $a\,e\,c$; draw perpendiculars, $d\,o$ and c, from any number of points in $b\,c$ and $c\,a$, meeting the circumferences of the semicircles; from the same points draw a series of horizontal lines, as represented in the figure, equal in length to the corresponding perpendiculars, $o\,n$ equal to $o\,d$, for example. The curve line, $b\,n\,e\,a$, traced through the extremities of the lines, will be the contour of the moulding.

Fig. 14.

The curve might be rendered flatter by using arcs of circles of a diameter greater than $a\,c$ or $c\,b$, as, of course, the height, $o\,d$, of the arcs would not be so great as it is in the figure; this will be exemplified in describing fig. 17, which follows; also, if the upper part, $b\,n\,c$, be required to be larger than the under part, $c\,a$, of the contour, this may be effected by shifting the point, c, nearer to a, before drawing the circular arcs.

The cyma, like the cavetto, is always used as a finishing, and never applied when strength is required, as it is weak in the extreme parts, though it is applicable as a means of shelter to crowning members. The talon, on the contrary, strong towards its extremity, is, like the ovolo, well adapted for supporting weight.

The *scotia*, fig. 15, like the fillet, is employed in bases to separate, contrast, and increase the effect of other mouldings, and conveys a graceful turn to the profile. To describe the scotia, the extremities, a and b, of the moulding being given:—Draw the perpendicular, $a\,c$, then $b\,c$ is the projection of the moulding; draw the perpendicular, $b\,e$; add one-half of $a\,c$ and two-thirds of $b\,c$ into one length, which set off from b to d; from the centre, d, with the radius, $b\,d$, describe the semicircle, $b\,f\,e$; join $e\,a$, and produce it to f; then join $d\,f$, cutting $a\,c$ in g; from g, as a centre, describe the arc $a\,f$; this arc, in conjunction with $b\,f$, completes the contour, $a\,f\,b$, of the scotia.

Fig. 15.

Another mode of describing the scotia is represented in fig. 16. Join the extremities, a and b, and bisect $a\,b$ in c; draw $e\,c\,d$ horizontally, and make $c\,d$ equal to the required recess of the curve, and $c\,e$ equal to $c\,d$; draw $f\,d\,g$ parallel to $a\,b$; divide $a\,f$ and $a\,c$ into the same convenient number of equal parts, and to the points of division in $a\,f$ draw straight lines from d; draw also straight lines from e, through the points in $a\,c$, till they meet successively the lines drawn to $a\,f$. Having performed the same operation on the upper side, the series of intersections thus found are points in the curve, and by tracing a line through them the contour will be completed.

Fig. 16.

Fig. 17.

In fig. 17, a method is given in some respects similar to the preceding. Having joined $a\,b$, describe upon it the semicircle, $a\,d\,b$; from the centre, c, draw a series of lines perpendicularly from $a\,b$, meeting the circumference, $a\,d\,b$; draw also a series of horizontal lines from the same points in $a\,b$, as shown in the figure, making these lines equal to the corresponding lines in the semicircle, $c\,e$ equal to $c\,d$, for

I

example; the extremities of these lines will be as many points in the curve. If the recess of the curve is required to be less than *e c*, as, for instance, *c n*, then set off *c o* equal to *c n*, and describe an arc, *a o b*, from the centre, *i*, which will be found after one or two trials; performing the same operation as in the other case, we find the contour, *a n b*.

In comparing these three modes of describing scotias, it is to be remarked that the second is the most generally applicable, whether the recess and the projection be great or small compared with the height. In the third mode, when the projection is small, the form of the curve approximates to that of the circular arc employed in describing it. Both of these modes of description are applicable to mouldings of any recess and projection. The mode first described, to produce graceful contours, should be confined to those of medium proportions, when, for example, the projection is two-fifths of the height, as in fig. 15.

The shaft of a column, like the mouldings which constitute the other portions of the column, may be described with various contours. The shaft is never cylindrical, that is, of equal diameter throughout; it is always tapered to a certain extent towards the upper end. The degree of taper is termed the diminution of the shaft; the diminution usually applied to columns ranges between one-fourth and one-sixth of the diameter at the bottom of the shaft. The following simple modes of diminishing the shaft of a column may be applied, when the diameter at the top and bottom are determined :—

Let the vertical line, A B, Plate A, fig. 1, be the altitude of the column, and B c the half diminution at the upper end of the shaft; divide A B into any number of equal parts, A *a*, *a b*, . . . and also B c into the same number of equal parts, B 1, 1 2, . . . draw the horizontal lines, *a f*, *b g*, . . . and draw other lines from the points 1, 2, . . . slanting towards A, to meet the horizontal lines respectively at the points *f*, *g*, *h*, . . . that is, the line drawn from 1 towards A, to meet the line *a f* at the point *f*, the line from 2, towards A, to meet *b g* at *g*, and so on; the points, *b*, *c*, *d*, *e*, and *f*, thus found, will be points in the contour of the shaft, and by joining them into one bent line, A *f g h i k* c, this line will be the contour, or entasis, as it has been termed, of the column.

But suppose that less swell or bulging is to be given to the shaft; then, in fig. 2, divide A B, as before, into a number of equal parts, and B c into two equal parts at D; divide D c into as many equal parts as A B; then proceed, exactly as in fig. 1, to find the points, *f*, *g*, *h*, *i*, *k*, in the contour. This will obviously bring the outline nearer to a straight line from A to B. In this figure, E F is supposed to be the axis or centre line of the column, E G and E A being the semi-diameters at the bottom, and F N, F c, the semi-diameters or radii at the top. To explain a third mode of determining the entasis of the shaft: On A G as a chord, describe the circular arc, A O G, proportionally less than a semicircle, as the swell is intended to be less; from the point N draw the vertical line, N P, parallel, of course, to E F; divide the arc, G P, into any number of equal parts, G 1, 1 2, 2 3, . . .; divide the altitude, E F, into the same number of equal parts; through the points of division draw the horizontal lines, *f l*, *s m*, *h n*, . . . and draw the vertical parallel lines, 1 *l*, 2 *m*, 3 *n*, . . . meeting the others respectively at the points *l*, *m*, *n*, *o*, *p*; the curve line drawn through these points will be the entasis of the column.

In many instances the shafts of columns are not finished with plain round surfaces; their surfaces are frequently *fluted*, that is, indented by longitudinal flutes or grooves, throughout the whole extent of the shaft. The flutes, when cut, are applied entirely round the shaft, and their profile, which is shown by the section of the column, taken horizontally, is generally an arc of a circle, equal to, or less, than the semi-circumference.

There are two varieties of fluting represented in profile in figs. 3 and 6, Plate A, and shown also in elevation by figs. 4, 5, and 7, 10. In figs. 6 and 7, it will be observed that the flutes are regularly separated by fillets; while in figs. 3 and 4, no such intervention exists, the flutes meet each other edge to edge, and form a sharp angle or arris at their junction; the intervention of the fillets, as they strengthen the projecting angles, permits of the flutes being cut much deeper than when they follow each other consecutively. The circumference of fluted columns are always measured, in the one case, over the exterior surfaces of the fillets, and, in the other, over the angles formed by the flutes.

To describe the flutes of a column without fillets: Let A B, fig. 3, be the diameter of the shaft at the lower end; bisect A B at G, and describe the semicircle A E F B; draw A D and B C perpendicular to A B, and D C parallel to A B, touching the circle; draw also D E G and C F G to the centre; divide the semi-circumference into half as many equal parts as there are flutes in the whole circumference; more particularly, let there be twenty flutes in the circumference, then ten of these are due to the semicircle, A E F B, and they ought to be so disposed as to have nine of them whole, and the tenth divided between the two extremities, A and B, in order that a flute may stand directly in front, as seen in the figure, where the line, D C, touches the circle. To this end, then, divide the arc, E F, into five equal parts, and continue the division towards A and B, making two whole divisions and a half, as F d and d c, and c B. These points of division determine the arrises of the flutes. To strike the form of the flute, describe arcs from the centres, c and d, with the radius, c d, intersecting at e; from e, with the same radius, describe the concave surface, c d; this forms the flute—the same process is applied to find the others. Having drawn the concentric semicircle, a b, for the diameter of the shaft at the upper end, if radial lines be drawn from the arrises of the flutes in the circle, A E F B, towards the centre, G, the points at which they meet the circle, a b, will be the arrises of the fluting at the upper end of the shaft, which is described similarly to that at the bottom. The figure, as now completed, becomes a half-plan of the shaft of the column. Fig. 4 is a bottom elevation of the column, derived from the plan, as indicated by the dot lines; and fig. 5 is a top elevation

To describe flutes with fillets in the shaft of a column: Let A B, fig. 6, Plate A, be the diameter of the column; bisect it at G, and describe a semicircle, as before, upon the diameter, A B; draw A D and B C perpendicular, and D C parallel to A B, touching the circle; join D G and C G. Let there be twenty-four flutes in the circumference; there will then be eleven whole and two half-flutes in the semi-circumference, and five wholes and two halves in the quarter circumference. If, therefore, this space be divided into six equal parts, the points of division will be the centres from which the flutes are described, and by running on the divisions to the points A and B, the centres for the whole semi-circumference will be ascertained, and will divide it into twelve equal arcs. Take any one of these arcs, F d, and divide it into five equal parts; then, with two of these parts as a radius, from each of the aforesaid centres, describe a semicircle; this will be the section of the flute; the flutes of the interior circle, representing the upper diameter of the shaft, are found by drawing radial lines, which appears sufficiently obvious from the figure. Figs. 7, 8, and 9, are elevations of the bottom of the column, as found from the plan by means of the dot lines; fig. 9 represents the most usual mode of finishing the flutes at the bottom of the shaft; fig. 10 is the corresponding elevation of the upper end.

In describing by relative dimensions the proportions of each particular order of architecture, it is desirable, for the sake of perspicuity and facility of reference, that in all the orders one common standard of measurement should be adopted, to which the proportional dimensions of all the parts of each order should be referred, being expressed in parts of that standard. For this purpose the diameter of the shaft of the column at the base, in each order, is taken as the standard of reference for all the parts or members of the particular order. The advantage of this is twofold; for, first, the proportions of an order are seen by a few glances; and, secondly, the relative proportions of corresponding parts in different orders are likewise readily ascertained. On this principle we shall proceed in defining the orders separately. The diameter at the base, in each order, is divided into 60 equal parts, denominated seconds, and constituting the scale of parts for the particular order; this affords a ready means of accurately noting the proportions, which are expressed in seconds and fractions of seconds, when these occur.

OF THE GRECIAN DORIC ORDER.

This order, illustrated by Plate A, is the most ancient of the orders, and, while employed by the Greeks, was without a base. The surface of the shaft is usually worked into twenty very flat flutes, meeting each other at an edge—this will be explained by the half-plan given in the plate. The edge is sometimes a little rounded; the upper member of the capital is a square abacus or thin plinth, under which there is a large and elegant ovolo of great projection; on the base or lower part of the ovolo there are three fillets, or annulets, which project from the surface of the ovolo, and have, of course, equally recessed spaces betwixt them; the flutings of the column terminate on the under sides of the lowest of these fillets, being finished by a cavetto or a conge. The general outline formed by the junction of the conge with the ovolo, constitutes a cyma-reversa, the effect of which is most graceful.

The architrave consists of one vertical face, with a continuous band or fillet at its upper edge; to the under side of this band are suspended a series of smaller fillets, with drops or guttæ; these fillets are of the same length as the breadth of the triglyphs in the frieze, and are placed exactly below them.

The frieze consists of rectangular projections and recesses, placed alternately. The projections or tablets are diversified on the face by two vertical channels, and two half ones cut on the right and left edges, constituting three whole channels, and hence called *triglyphs*. The square spaces alternating with the triglyphs are named *metopes*, and are frequently decorated with sculptures.

The cornice is distinguished by a conspicuous *corona*, a term applied to a vertical or inclined plane surface which considerably overhangs the members underneath. To the corona, immediately over the triglyphs, blocks named *mutules* are suspended, of which the soffit or under side is inclined downwards from the roof; the mutules are also furnished with guttæ or drops depending from their soffits.

The proportions of the different members of the Doric order, as practised by the Greeks, range within considerably wide limits. The following are the average proportions for the members of the order. Taking the diameter at the bottom of the shaft as the standard of measurement, the column is six diameters in height. The diameter at the upper end of the shaft is three-fourths of a diameter; that is, the shaft diminishes one-fourth of the diameter. The height of the capital is half a diameter; that of the ovolo, including the annulets, and that of the abacus, are each one-quarter of the upper diameter, the annulets together being one-fifth of one of the parts. The horizontal dimension of the abacus is six times its height.

The height of the entablature is one-third of that of the column, or two diameters. If it be divided into eight equal parts, these are distributed between the architrave, the frieze, and the cornice, in the proportion of 3, 3, 2: thus, the height of the architrave is equal to that of the frieze, and that of the cornice is two-thirds of either. The inner edge of the triglyph at the angle of the building is in a vertical line with the axis of the column; the breadth of the triglyph is three-fifths of its height, which is also that of the frieze, and the breadth being divided into nine equal parts, two are occupied by each glyph or channel, one by each semiglyph, and one by each of the three interglyphs, or flat surfaces between the glyphs.

All this is shown in the annexed figure, which is a horizontal section of a portion of the entablature, viewed from below, and taken through the frieze. It exhibits the section of the triglyphs, as well as the arrangement of the mutules in the cornice, with their drops. The metopes are square; the height of the capital of the triglyph is one-seventh of its whole height, and that of the metope one-ninth. The height of the cornice being divided into five equal parts, the lowest is given to the fillet, the mutule, and the drops; the next two to the corona, and the remaining two parts are subdivided and disposed of as shown in the detail figure, Plate A. The projection of the cornice over the capital of the triglyph is equal to its height; and being divided into four equal parts, three are given to the projection of the corona, and they are further subdivided as shown in the plate.

The number of annulets in the capital vary from three to five; and the number of horizontal grooves separating the shaft from the capital, vary from one to three.

In the scales which we have attached to the outline drawing of the order, three sets of dimensions are given, the nature of which are indicated by the initial letters at the bottom of the scales. The first scale contains the "particular heights" of all the members of the order, expressed in seconds, each figure standing opposite the member to which it refers. The second scale contains the "general heights" of the members, each division of the order being specified. The third scale contains the "projections" of all the particular members, beyond the centre line of the column, expressed in seconds.

OF THE GRECIAN IONIC ORDER.

The Ionic order, like the Doric, may be primarily divided into column and entablature; in its secondary divisions, however, a new element is introduced, as, besides the shaft, capital, architrave, frieze, and cornice, it is provided with a base to the column.

The origin of the Ionic order is problematical; its capital, which is its principal characteristic, has been compared to the curls in the head-dress of females, to the spiral horns of rams, the bark of some trees when dried in the sun, the form of various sea-shells, and so on. The order is a medium between the grave solidity of the Doric, and the elegance and delicacy of the Corinthian.

In the architrave and frieze, all appearances of triglyphs and guttæ are omitted; in the cornice, instead of the bold mutules of the Doric, the ends of several pieces of wood are substituted, which are by way of support to the covering tiles, and are represented by dentils or teeth. The other portions of the cornice are analogous to those in the Doric, and consist principally of a cyma, ovolo, and cornice. The great recess of the mouldings under the cornice gives it a striking prominence; this relieves its apparent heaviness, though both the dentil band and the cymatium of the frieze are introduced under it.

The base of the column consists of two tori, separated by a scotia, with fillets, and a square plinth, on which the column rests; though in some cases the plinth is dispensed with, and the column stands immediately upon the general platform which supports the whole.

In the volute of the capital, the lower edge of the channel which runs between the upper and under spirals, is formed into a curve bending downwards in the middle, and revolving about the spirals on both sides. The volute rests upon the ovolo, astragal, and fillet, which terminate the shaft. The ovolo is always cut into eggs, surrounded by borders, with tongues between them. The shaft is, in general, cut into twenty-four flutes, with fillets between them, and the flutes are sometimes made with an elliptical section, which makes them flatter than when they are circular. The taper of the shaft is also less than that of the Doric.

Besides the special dimensions, given in Plate B, of the Ionic order, the following may be noted as the general proportions of the order. The column is eight and a half diameters in height; the diameter of the upper end of the shaft is five-sixths of a diameter; the taper of the shaft is one-sixth. The height of the base, including the plinth, is half a diameter; the heights of the tori and the scotia are nearly equal; the upper fillet of the scotia projects as much as the

K

upper torus. The projection of the lower torus beyond the lower radius of the shaft, is one-fifth of a diameter. The height of the capital is half a diameter; the height of the volute is seven-twelfths of a diameter; dividing the height of the volute into three equal parts, the top of the lower one reaches to the bottom of the ovolo, and the second division to the top of the festoon, on the axis of the column. The curvature of the outer spiral springs immediately from the ovolo with which the volute is crowned.

Dividing the whole height of the order into twenty-one parts, four of these go to the entablature, which is, therefore, two diameters in height; the height is equally distributed between the architrave, the frieze, and the cornice. Dividing the height of the architrave into four parts, one part is due to the mouldings of the upper portion or capital; subdividing the capital into nine equal parts, give one to the upper fillet, three to the cavetto, four to the ovolo, and one to the bead. Divide the height of the frieze into six equal parts, and give the upper part to the talon, which forms the capital. Divide the cornice into three equal parts; subdivide the upper and lower thirds, each into six parts; in the upper third, give one part to the upper fillet, four to the cyma-recta, and one to the lower fillet, and turn one down into the middle third, for the ovolo under : dispose of the parts in the lower third as appears by the scale.

The projection of the cornice over the cymatium of the frieze is equal to its height; the projections of the subordinate members will be obvious at once from the scales attached.

The volutes of the Ionic capitals are composed of two or more spirals of the same kind, which, after making a number of revolutions, terminate at the centre upon a central point resembling a button, denominated the eye of the volute. The spirals, which project from the surface to give them relief, are termed the *hems* of the volute; the interspaces being called the *channels*.

These definitions will be understood on referring to the detail drawings of the Ionic order, in Plate B. There the front elevation of the capital is represented, showing the central eye, and the spirals terminating in it. The back elevation of the capital is the same as the front. The flanks, shown as side elevations in fig. 1, Plate B, have somewhat the appearance of a balustre. In the plan, fig. 2, this portion of the capital, supposed to be viewed from the under side, appears square in its general outline. Fig. 3 is a vertical section of the capital, exhibiting the profile in flank; fig. 4 is a vertical section, drawn to the same centre line, and in a plane at right angles to that of the preceding section, exhibiting the contour of the front and back elevations of the capital. From these figures it will be observed, that the volutes fit like a cap upon the circular tablet formed by the ovolo. There are no precise rules for the form of the capital in flank, except, perhaps, that the parallel beads which decorate the scroll should run directly into the interspaces of the carvings upon the ovolo; otherwise, the configuration of the parts is left to the taste of the designer. The shaft of the column has been represented fluted in these details, that the correspondence of the flutes with the carvings upon the ovolo may be shown.

To describe the Ionic volute: the number of revolutions or quarters of which the spirals are to consist being given, the vertical height, also, of the spiral, and the diameter of the eye :—Let A B, Plate B, fig. 5, be the height of the volute, and let the spiral make three revolutions, consisting, therefore, of twelve quarters; bisect A B at the point c, and from A B cut off A D, equal to the given radius of the eye; divide D C into as many given parts as there are quarter revolutions in the spiral to be drawn (which in this case are twelve in number), at the points 1, 2, 3, . . . 11, 12. To prevent confusion, we have indicated this division upon a parallel line, D' C'; draw C E at any angle with C D, and make it equal to two of these parts; join D E, and from the points 1, 2, 3 . . . draw straight lines, 1 F, 2 G, 3 H, . . . parallel to C E; taking c d equal to one part, draw df perpendicular to A B, and equal to 12 E; draw fg perpendicular to df, and equal to 11 Q; draw again gh perpendicular to fg, and equal to 10 P. Proceed in this manner until all the sides of this winding fretwork are drawn; then, the points $d, f, g, \ldots p, q, r$, so found, are the centres from which the quadrants which compose the spiral must be successively described. For this purpose, produce df to 1, fg to 2, gh to 3, and so on; the quadrants, as they are described, will be limited by these lines; from the centre, d, with the radius, d B, describe the quadrant, B 1; from the centre, f, with the radius, f, describe the quadrant, 1, 2; from g, with the radius, g 2, describe in like manner the quadrant, 2, 3; proceed in this way till the last arc, 11, 12, is described from the centre, q, with the radius, q 11; then, finally, describe the circle at the centre, from the point, r, and with the radius, r 12. If the operation be accurately performed, this radius, r 12, will be equal to A D, as required, and the spiral line will be completed.

But as the process, as it is now described, is very liable to inaccuracy, the method of finding the centres shown on a larger scale at fig. A, is at once more expeditious and more certain. Having drawn df perpendicular to the vertical line, bisect it at e; draw er perpendicular to df, equal to de or ef, and join dr and fr; divide er into three equal parts, es, st, tr, and draw isk and nto parallel to df; draw fg perpendicular to df, and equal to 11 Q; draw gh and ih respectively parallel and perpendicular to df, meeting at the point h; draw the diagonals gp and hq parallel to dr and fr, and draw the perpendiculars kl, op, rq, nm. In this way all the centres are determined, namely, $d, f, g, h, \ldots . o, p, q, r$.

To describe the second spiral line, which, with the first one, comprehends the thickness of the hem, a similar process is applicable. Set off B R for the thickness of the hem at that part, and, supposing the hem to diminish in thickness by equal amounts for each half revolution, divide B R into six equal parts; as the spiral describes six half revolutions, it will diminish in thickness one-sixth of B R for each half revolution; set off, therefore, A s equal to 5-6ths of B R, then R s is the height of the second spiral. Bisect R s at T, and set off s v equal to the radius of the eye; then, dividing T v into 12 equal parts, the method already described for finding the centres may be applied.

The method already described, though it is well adapted to the description of the single spiral, is not applicable where there are many spirals. In this case, the principle of the logarithmic spiral may be employed. The nature of this spiral is such, that being divided into equal angular segments, as quadrants or half quadrants, its distances from the centre, at the ends of the segments successively, decrease in a geometrical ratio.

To describe the Ionic volute, on the principle of the logarithmic spiral · the centre, the vertical height, and the distance between the first and second revolutions of the outer spiral being given.

Definition.—The vertical line o A, fig. 6, drawn from the centre o of the spiral, and expressing also the height of it above the centre, is termed the *cathetus*.

If then o A be the cathetus, o the centre, and A I the distance between the first and second revolutions, produce A o to E, and draw G o c at right angles to A E; bisect the angles at the centre by the straight lines B o F and D o H; find a mean geometrical proportional between o A and o I, and make o E equal to it; find also a mean proportional between o A and o E, and make o c equal to this mean. Having thus found the consecutive points A, B, and c, the distances of which from the centre are in geometrical progression, the others in succession will be found by the aid of proportional compasses. Having set the compasses, so that the ratio of the lengths of the legs on the opposite sides of the centre pin may be that of o A to o B, it is obvious that if the distance A o, be taken between the longer ends, the shorter ends will measure the distance B o; and, in like manner, that if the longer ends be set to B o, the shorter ends will measure c o. Farther, by taking c o in the one end, we have D o in the other; and proceeding in this way, we may find successively the distances E o, F o, G o, &c., which furnish as many points in the spiral; and, by tracing a curve line through the points thus found, the spiral will be completed. The divisions marked off upon the line A G indicate the commencements of the other spirals, of which the volute consists, which, it will be observed, are disposed in three sets.

Another method of setting off the spiral by means of proportional compasses, without pricking the paper, is to construct a scale of parts A B o, fig. 7. This method also expedites the process considerably. Having found o A and o B, as before, and set the compasses in the manner already described, make o A, fig. 7, equal to o A, fig. 6, by the longer ends of the compasses, and mark off o b. the distance between the shorter ends. Take again o b, between the longer ends, and mark o c, between the short ends; similarly, from o c find o d, and so on, till the distance o i, is found. And here the accuracy of the process may be tested, as o i, fig. 7, should be equal to o I, fig. 6. Join the points of division in A i to the point B; draw the horizontal line i E, and from E draw the vertical E F, cutting i B at the point G; draw again the horizontal and vertical lines G H and H K I. Then the three scales A O, E F and H I, will afford eight points in each of the three revolutions of the first spiral A C E G I: o b is equal to o B, o c equal to o C, o d equal to o D, and so on; and lastly, o i or F E is equal to o I. Following the same process, the eight divisions on the scale F E give eight points in the second revolution I K L, and the scale I H gives eight points to the third revolution L M N.

The points thus determined for the spiral may be transferred to the edge of a slip of paper, and thence marked by a pencil point upon the drawing, fig. 6.

The same scale, fig. 7, may be employed for the other spiral lines in the volute, the commencements of which are marked on the line A I, fig. 6, for, by dividing the parallel line A i, which is equal to A I, in the same manner as A I, and drawing horizontal lines from these several points of division, as indicated in the figure by dot lines, the perpendiculars drawn from the points at which these lines meet A B, furnish scales for the first revolutions respectively. For example, if we draw a horizontal line L M from the point L, meeting A B at the point M, the perpendicular M O N becomes a scale of parts for setting off the first revolution of the spiral which starts at the same point L, fig. 6. The scales P R Q and S U T, formed in the same manner as before, serve to define the second and third revolutions of the same spiral. In this way, then, it is clear we can readily construct a set of scales for each individual spiral. Another mode of finding a series of points in a spiral is represented by the scale, fig. 8.

Referring for convenience to fig. 6, divide the whole height A E into 16 equal parts, making the portion A O above the centre equal to 9 parts, and leaving of course 7 for the portion O E. In fig. 8, make O E equal to O E, fig. 6, and draw a perpendicular O A equal to O A, fig. 6; join A E, and on E as a centre describe the arc A P; divide that arc into 28 equal parts, and join the points of division to the centre E. The straight line A O intersected by these radii at the points, b, c, d, &c., forms the scale for the first spiral: thus o A is the distance o A, fig. 6; o b gives the distance o B, o c gives the distance o C; o d gives the distance o D, and so on; till lastly o n gives the radius o N of the eye, which is described by a circle on the centre o. Having thus marked off a series of points in the curve, it may be completed either by describing arcs of circles connecting the points which have been set off, or by tracing by hand a curve line through them. The other spiral lines of the volute may be described in like manner by making a new scale for each.

In this example, the radius of the eye has been made equal to the first four divisions of the line A, the remaining 24 divisions being distributed along the spiral. We may, of course, secure any number of divisions for the radius of the eye; if we are to secure 8 divisions, for example, then as 24 are due to the spiral, the arc must be divided into 24 + 8 or 32 parts.

OF THE GRECIAN CORINTHIAN ORDER.

The Corinthian is the third and last of the Grecian orders. Upon this order the ancients lavished the utmost efforts of their creative genius; it is the most magnificent and elegant of the orders.

The great distinguishing feature of this order is its capital. The capital consists of a solid body or nucleus in the shape of a bell, and hence commonly called the bell of the capital; the bell is surrounded with two tiers of foliage, consisting of acanthus leaves, of which there are 8 in each tier; the upper end of the shaft finishes with an astragal, which appears to bind together the leaves at the roots; surmounting these are 8 caulicoli, or twisted and fluted stalks, springing from between the leaves of the upper tier, and spreading each into two open volutes, which sup-

port the abacus: the abacus consists of a square tablet, concave on the four sides or edges, and having the acute angles thus formed cut away; the edge of the abacus is wrought into an ovolo and a cavetto, separated by a fillet—one of the upper tier of leaves fronts each side of the abacus; the space beneath the abacus, unoccupied by the leaves, is taken up with slender caulicoli or stalks, which spring from between every two leaves, and proceed to the corners, and to the centres of the sides of the abacus, where they are formed into delicate volutes. The centre of each side of the abacus is adorned with a rosette, or small flower.

The base of the column, as represented in Plate E, is the same as the Ionic base, consisting of two tori, separated by a scotia, the whole resting on a square plinth. The shaft of the column should be fluted when the entablature is enriched.

In the cornice of the entablature the dentil band is preserved, as in the Ionic order, and is overhung by a fascia, from which enriched medallions project. The entablature bears a close resemblance to that of the Ionic order.

The following are the general proportions of the Corinthian order:—In its general arrangement, it is similar to the Ionic: the column is ten diameters in height; the diameter at the upper end is five-sixths of that at the under end, the taper being therefore one-sixth. The height of the base is half a diameter; the projection of its upper torus is equal to that of the upper fillet of the scotia. The height of the capital is $1\frac{1}{6}$ diameters, of which one diameter is occupied by the leaves and volutes, the remaining sixth being given to the depth of the abacus; the height occupied by the leaves and

Fig. 1.

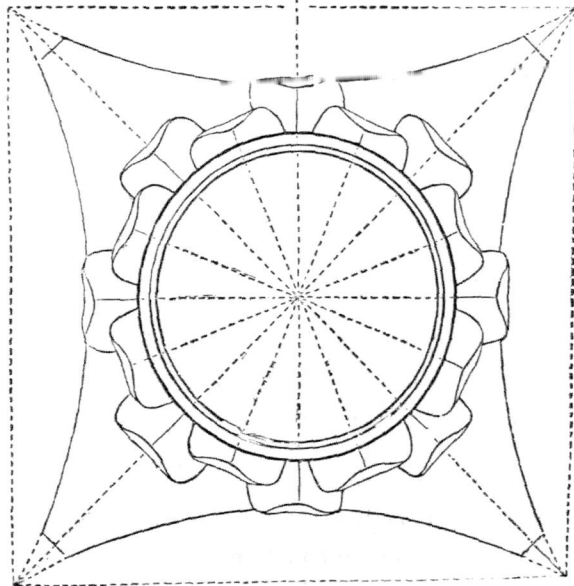

Fig. 2.

volutes being divided into three equal parts, the lower part is due to the lower tier of leaves, the second part to the second tier, and the third part to the caulicoli and volutes. The height of the principal volutes is three-fourths of one of these parts. The droop or descent of the tips of the leaves is one-third of the height assigned to them; their form is seen more explicitly in the engravings, which give the general form of the foliage before it is cut, in which fig. 1 is the elevation, and fig. 2 the semi-plan of the capital. It will be seen that the circumference of the bell is divided between eight leaves in each tier. The abacus, which is seen in both these figures,

L

is supposed to be cut from a square plinth, shown in dot lines in the plan, the diagonals of which measure two diameters of the column; the curvature of each side is an arc of a circle, of which the centre is formed by constructing an equilateral triangle upon the side of the square, the vertex of the triangle being the centre. Figs. 3 and 4 show the general form and manner of raffling the leaves.

Fig. 3

Fig. 4.

Dividing the whole height of the order into five parts, one of these is due to the entablature, which is therefore one-fourth of the height of the column, or two and a half diameters high. The architrave is three-fourths of a diameter high, the frieze is two-thirds, and the cornice one and a twelfth. Dividing the height of the architrave into five parts, one of these is due to the fillet, the quirked cyma-reversa, and the bead; the other four parts are divided equally among the three fascia which compose the remainder of the architrave. The frieze is commonly ornamented, though frequently left quite flat and plain. The height of the cornice being divided into three parts, they are disposed among the members in the manner exhibited by Plate C. The projection of the cornice over the frieze is equal to its height; the projections of the members of which it is composed are given on the plate. The modillions which overhang the dentil band are represented in fig. 5.

Fig. 5.

OF THE ROMAN DORIC ORDER.

In the progress of their conquests, the Romans extended their dominions over the colonies of Greece, over Greece itself, and over some parts of Asia. It was not till they had acquired the mastery of these, their more polished neighbours, that they possessed any opportunity of becoming acquainted with the architecture of Greece, as well as with its sculptures and paintings. The columnar architecture of the Romans, imitating that of the Grecians, is evidently of the same family, though greatly inferior in simplicity and harmony. The Doric order of the Romans, which we are now to describe, affords an illustration of this remark; it strikingly contrasts with the simple and energetic Doric of the Grecians, and is by no means an improvement on this beautiful order of architecture.

The column of the Roman Doric had originally no base, but the addition of a base is certainly an improvement, and renders the parts of the order consistent with one another. The capital has a greater number of members than that of the Grecian, and are of a light and round character, while those of the other are broad and flat. The shaft is more slender than the other, and is very seldom fluted; when it is fluted, the flutes are separated by fillets, as in fig. 6, Plate A, and are twenty in number; the shaft is finished at the upper end with an astragal and a fillet, which support the capital, instead of one or more channels, as in the Grecian. In the capital, three fillets, with a quarter-round and a semi-torus, are intended to represent the ovolo and annulets of the Greek capital; and the height of the abacus, instead of being plain, is divided into a projecting fillet, a cyma, and a fascia.

The architrave is, like the other, furnished with a band along its upper edge, from which the fillets and guttæ depend. The guttæ, also, are six in number, but are coniform instead of cylindrical, and project from the surface of the architrave fully more than half their diameter. The face of the architrave is vertical, and stands in a line with the superior diameter of the column, though it is sometimes set a trifle within the point. In the frieze, the triglyphs project from, instead of being coincident with, the architrave; and those next the angle of the building are, as represented in Plate C, placed directly over the centre of the column, instead of being on the angle; the glyphs, of which there are two wholes and two halves, are finished square at the upper edge, and the tops slope downwards towards the back at the same angle with the sides.

In the cornice, the members are all lighter than those of the Grecian (there is, in fact, a greater subdivision), with the exception of the mutules, which are boldly developed, and have no guttæ.

Besides the special dimensions which we have given in Plate C, we may state the following general proportions of the order:—Dividing the whole height of the order into five equal parts, one of these is given to the entablature, the height of which is therefore one-fourth of that of the column. The column tapers one-sixth throughout the shaft, and is eight diameters high, of which one diameter is distributed equally between the capital and the base. The plinth in the base is one-third of the height. The height of the capital is nearly equally divided between the abacus with its mouldings, the ovolo with its fillets, and the neck.

The entablature is two diameters in height, and being divided into eight equal parts, these are distributed among the cornice, the frieze, and the architrave, in the proportions of 3, 3, and 2. This distribution contrasts strongly with that of the entablature of the Doric. The height of the architrave, which is half a diameter, being divided into three, one of the parts is due to the band, fillet, and guttæ, of which the height of the band is equal to that of the fillet and guttæ together. The frieze is three-fourths of a diameter in height: it is divided horizontally into triglyphs and metopes, of which the former are each half a diameter in breadth, and on the whole depth of the frieze—dividing the breadth of the triglyph into twelve parts, the extreme twelfths are due to the semiglyphs, and the remaining ten parts are distributed equally between the two whole glyphs and the three vertical plane surfaces, or *shanks*, which separate them, two parts being given to each member. The plat-band or fascia, which crowns the triglyph, is one-eighteenth of its height. The cornice is three-fourths of a diameter high. The breadth of the dentils is the same as that of the triglyphs, and their projection is equal to their breadth.

THE ROMAN IONIC ORDER.

The Roman Ionic is the modification of the original Grecian, practised by the Romans after their conquest over the Greeks. The general proportions of the Roman and Grecian Ionics are nearly alike; the minutiæ and detail, however, are considerably different. This will be perceived at once on referring to the plates of these orders—Plates B and D.

In the column of the Roman Ionic, the attic base is always employed. The capital is considerably distinguished from that of the Grecian by the straightness of the under edge of the channel of the volutes over the quarter round, and the absence of the hem which bordered the under side of this channel in the Grecian. The shaft may be either plain or fluted, with twenty or twenty-four flutes, in plan a trifle more than semicircular. The fillets between the flutes should have between one-third and one-fourth of their width. The egg and dart ornament of the quarter round in the capital should correspond with the flutes of the column, there being an egg exactly over each flute, and a dart, of course, over each fillet. The volutes may be described according to the methods already given for those of the Grecian order.

Dividing the whole height of the order into five parts, one of these pertains to the entablature, the others to the column: the height of the entablature is, therefore, one-fourth of that of the column. The shaft of the column tapers one-sixth; the whole height of the column is nine diameters, half a diameter is given to the base, and seven-twentieths, or twenty-one minutes, to the capital.

The entablature is two and a quarter diameters high. Dividing its height into five equal parts of twenty-seven minutes, two of these parts go to the depth of the cornice, and the remaining three are divided equally between the architrave and the frieze. The faces of the frieze, and the lowest member of the architrave, are directly on the outline of the upper end of the shaft; this gives them a less heavy aspect than the corresponding members of the Grecian, which project considerably. The projection of the cornice from the face of the frieze is equal to its height.

The Ionic entablature is occasionally reduced to two-ninths of the height of the column; this may readily be accomplished without altering its internal proportions, by making its module or scale of parts less, by one-ninth, than the diameter of the column, and setting off its parts from this scale in the proportions exhibited in the plate. In the decoration of the interior of apartments, when much delicacy is required, the height of the entablature may, according to Nicholson, be reduced to even one-fifth of the column, by observing the same method, and making the module only four-fifths of the diameter.

OF THE ROMAN CORINTHIAN ORDER.

This order, Plate D, is the only one in which the Romans have truthfully represented the original from which it is derived. In detail, this order is but slightly different from its prototype.

Dividing the whole height of the order into five parts, one part is due to the entablature, which is therefore one-fourth of the column, as in the Grecian. The height of the column is ten diameters, and the entablature, consequently, two and a half diameters. The cornice is one diameter, or two-fifths of the entablature, high; the remaining three-fifths are divided equally between the frieze and the architrave, three-fourths of a diameter to each. These general proportions, it will be observed, are the same as those of the Roman Ionic order. The entablature of the latter is frequently substituted in the Corinthian order.

THE COMPOSITE ORDER.

The Composite order is derived from the three original orders, or, more strictly perhaps, from the Roman Ionic and Corinthian, being a compound of the two orders. There are a great variety of designs recognised as the Composite order; we have given the design in Plate D from Chambers, who, in composing it, endeavoured to avoid the faults and unite the perfections of those with which he was acquainted. The entablature has one-fourth of the height of the column; the column is ten diameters high, consequently the entablature is two and a half diameters, of which the cornice has one diameter, and the frieze and the architrave each three-fourths of a diameter. The base is precisely the same as in the other orders: the shaft is fluted similarly to the Ionic; the capital retains the two tiers of acanthus leaves in the Corinthian, and also the abacus in the same order; the Ionic scroll, however, is introduced between these members. The cornice differs from the Corinthian only in having the medallion square, and composed of two fascias.

The entablature of the Composite order may be reduced to two-ninths of the column, which, to avoid fractions, may be called two modules and a half, taking the module at nine-tenths of a diameter. If it be reduced to one-fifth, the module will be four-fifths of the diameter ; where such a diminution is desirable, it will be preferable to adopt the Ionic cornice, which, consisting of fewer parts, will retain its due importance without affecting the mass.

THE TUSCAN ORDER.

This order is the fifth and last of the Roman orders. It derives its name from the ancient Etruscans, who were employed by the Romans in building, and are said to have been its inventors. Without any great stretch of comparison, the order appears to be a simplification of the Roman Doric, having little else to distinguish it from this order, besides its massiveness and plain appearance.

The total height of the order, Plate D., being divided into five equal parts, four of them are given to the column, and the other parts to the entablature. The column is seven diameters high; it is thus shorter in proportion to its diameter than any other of the orders. The capital is a semi-diameter high; the base, with the lower cincture of the shaft, is also half a diameter. The entablature, one-fourth of the column, is one-and-three-quarters diameters high; it is divided in the same proportion as the other Roman orders, two-fifths of its height being given to the cornice, and the other three-fifths divided equally between the architrave and frieze. The projection of the cornice over the vertical faces of the inferior members is equal to its height.

A

Fig. 5.

Fig. 3.

Fig. 4.

Fig. M.

Fig. 6.

Fig. 7.

Fig. 8.

Fig. 9.

Fig. 2.

Fig. 1.

A

ORDERS OF ARCHITECTURE

GRECIAN DORIC ORDER.

Triglyph

Square Metope

B

ORDERS of ARCHITECTURE.
ROMAN IONIC ORDER.

Profile of the Capital.

Side of the Capital.

Plan of 1-4th of Capital.

Cornice 54

Frieze 40½

Architrave 40½

Capital 21

Shaft 6 diams. 9 minutes.

Base 16

B

ORDERS of ARCHITECTURE.
GRECIAN IONIC ORDER.

Cornice 40

Frieze 40

Architrave 40.

Capital 30

Shaft 1¾ diams.

Base 30.

51

ORDERS of ARCHITECTURE

ROMAN DORIC ORDER.

Cornice 45

Frieze 45

Architrave 30

Capital 30

Shaft 7 diams.

Base 30

ORDERS of ARCHITECTURE

GRECIAN CORINTHIAN ORDER.

Cornice 65

Frieze 40

Architrave 45

Capital 70

Shaft 8⅓ diams

Base 30

B

Fig. 1.

56 Minutes

Fig. 2.

Fig. 3.

Fig. 4.

Fig. 5.

Fig. 6.

Fig. 7.

Fig. 8.

Fig. A

53

Plan of the Capital

Angular View of the Capital

TABLE OF GEOMETRICAL FIGURES FOR PURPOSES OF GENERAL REFERENCE,

TO ILLUSTRATE THE TREATISE ON PRACTICAL GEOMETRY.

LINES.

STRAIGHT LINE. Shortest distance between two points.

CURVE LINE. Neither straight nor zig-zag; its direction continually varying.

MIXED LINE. Composed of straight lines and curves.

ZIG-ZAG LINE. A series of straight lines.

HORIZONTAL LINE. A level line; parallel to the horizon.

VERTICAL LINE. Perpendicular to the horizon.

PERPENDICULAR LINE. Forming with another line two right angles. It is not necessarily vertical, and if not so, the line which it meets is oblique.

PARALLEL LINES. In the same plane and equally distant from each other at every part.

ANGLES.

ANGLES. The quantity of divergence of two lines which meet. The lines are the arms of the angle; the point of meeting is the corner of the angle.

CURVILINEAL ANGLE. The angle formed by two curve lines meeting.

MIXTILINEAL ANGLE. Formed by a straight line and a curve line.

RIGHT ANGLE. The angle formed by two straight lines, perpendicular the one to the other.

ACUTE ANGLE. Less than a right angle.

OBTUSE ANGLE. Greater than a right angle.

TRIANGLES.

EQUILATERAL TRIANGLE. The three sides of which are equal.

ISOSCELES TRIANGLE. Two sides of which are equal.

RIGHT-ANGLED TRIANGLE. Having one right angle.

SCALENE TRIANGLE. All the sides are unequal.

ACUTE-ANGLED TRIANGLE. Having the three angles acute.

OBTUSE-ANGLED TRIANGLE. Having one obtuse angle.

A line which is not perpendicular to another is oblique.

QUADRILATERALS.

ISOSCELES TRAPEZOID. Having two opposite sides equal.

SQUARE. Having four right angles, and four equal sides.

RECTANGLE. Having four right angles, and only two equal sides.

RHOMBUS, OR LOZENGE. Having its sides equal, and only its opposite angles equal.

RHOMBOID. Having its sides parallel, and only its opposite sides equal.

TRAPEZIUM. Having neither pair of its sides parallel.

TRAPEZOID. Having two sides parallel.

RIGHT-ANGLED TRAPEZOID. Having two right angles.

DIAGONAL. Line joining the summits of two angles of a figure, not adjacent.

REGULAR POLYGONS.—HAVING EQUAL SIDES AND EQUAL ANGLES.

PENTAGON. Five sides and five angles equal.

HEXAGON. Six sides.

HEPTAGON. Seven sides.

OCTAGON. Eight sides.

NONAGON. Nine sides.

DECAGON. Ten sides.

UNDECAGON. Eleven sides.

DUODECAGON. Twelve sides.

CIRCLES.

ARC. A part of a circumference.

CHORD. A line joining two points of a circle, or the extremities of an arc.

SEGMENT. Part of a circle cut off by a chord.

SECTOR. Space cut off by two radii.

INSCRIBED LINE. A line terminated both ways by the circumference.

INSCRIBED ANGLE. The summit at the circumference, and the sides consisting of two chords.

INSCRIBED TRIANGLE. The summits of the three angles at the circumference.

CIRCUMFERENCE. A curve line, of which the points are equally distant from a point or common centre. The curve is the area bounded by the circumference.

DIAMETER. A line passing through the centre, and terminated both ways by the circumference.

RADIUS. A line drawn from the centre to the circumference; equal to half a diameter; all the radii are equal.

SPIRAL. Starting from a centre, and removing from it gradually.

HELIX. Turning on a cylinder, and uniformly advancing lengthwise.

TANGENT CIRCLES.

CIRCUMSCRIBED POLYGON.

ELLIPSE.

TANGENT. Touching the circle without cutting it.

SECANT. Cutting the circle at two points.

CONCENTRIC LINES. Having a common centre and parallel.

ECCENTRIC LINES. Having different centres.

GENERATE. Joining a radius to the circumference.

SOLIDS.

QUADRANGULAR PYRAMID. Having a square for the base.

TRIANGULAR PYRAMID. Having three sides in the base, and terminating in a point.

HEXAGONAL PYRAMID. Having a hexagon for the base.

CONE. Having a circle for its base, and terminated by a point.

CYLINDER. Generated by the motion of a circle parallel to itself, and at right angles to its own plane.

INCLINED PYRAMID.

INCLINED CYLINDER.

QUADRANGULAR PRISM. Having four sides in the base.

TRUNCATED PRISM. Having the plane of one end oblique to the sides.

HEXAGONAL PRISM. Having six equal sides in the base.

TETRAHEDRON. Having the faces composed of four equilateral triangles.

HEXAEDRON. Having six faces, equal squares.

OCTAEDRON. Having eight faces, equilateral triangles.

DODECAEDRON. Having twelve faces, equal pentagons.

ICOSAEDRON. Having twenty faces, isosceles triangles.

TRIANGULAR PRISM. Having three sides in the base.

SPHERE. The curve surface of which is at all points equally distant from the centre.

SPHEROID. A flat sphere; like an ellipse in side revolution.

PUBLISHED BY JAMES AINSWORTH 47 & 58 PICCADILLY, MANCHESTER.

PLATE XIX

Inches 12   9   6   3   0   1   2   3   Feet

WILLIAM MACKENZIE _ GLASGOW & EDINBURGH

56

Fig 1

J   H   G   F

Fig 2

Glass
6   7   8   9

Fig 1
J   H   P

Fig 2
6 7 8
9

Back of
Clock

Fig 1

Back of
Clock

Fig 2

Fig 3

Glass
C   Brass   A
D
E   B

Fig 3
E C C B A

1 2 3   4   5

Fig 4

Gilt
Fig 4   Glass
1
Brass
2   3
4
5

P. Thomson

J. Scott.

Inches 12   9   6   3   0   1   2 Feet

WILLIAM MACKENZIE _ GLASGOW, EDINBURGH & LONDON.

BRACKETS & GLASS FRAMES OVER

WILLIAM MA‑KENZIE, GLASGOW, EDINBURGH & LONDON

W.D.Dawson.

Inches 12 9 6 3 0 1 2 3 4 5 6 7 8 9 10 11 Feet

59

PLATE XI

HALL CHAIRS

WILLIAM MACKENZIE _ GLASGOW & EDINBURGH

J.Scott

60

PLATE XXIX.

BACK OF HALL CHAIR

WILLIAM MACKENZIE, GLASGOW & EDINBURGH

61

PLATE II

DETAILS FOR HALL TABLES

WILLIAM MACKENZIE GLASGOW & EDINBURGH

WILLIAM MACKENZIE — GLASGOW & EDINBURGH

63

WILLIAM MACKENZIE, GLASGOW EDINBURGH & LONDON

Inches
Feet.

WILLIAM MACKENZIE . GLASGOW & EDINBURGH

Inches 12   9   6   3   0   1   2   3 Feet

TRUSSES

WILLIAM MACKENZIE — GLASGOW, EDINBURGH & LONDON

WILLIAM MACKENZIE, GLASGOW, EDINBURGH, LONDON
AND NEW YORK

SIDEBOARDS

WILLIAM MACKENZIE, GLASGOW, EDINBURGH & LONDON.

SIDEBOARD DOORS

For very Rich Wood

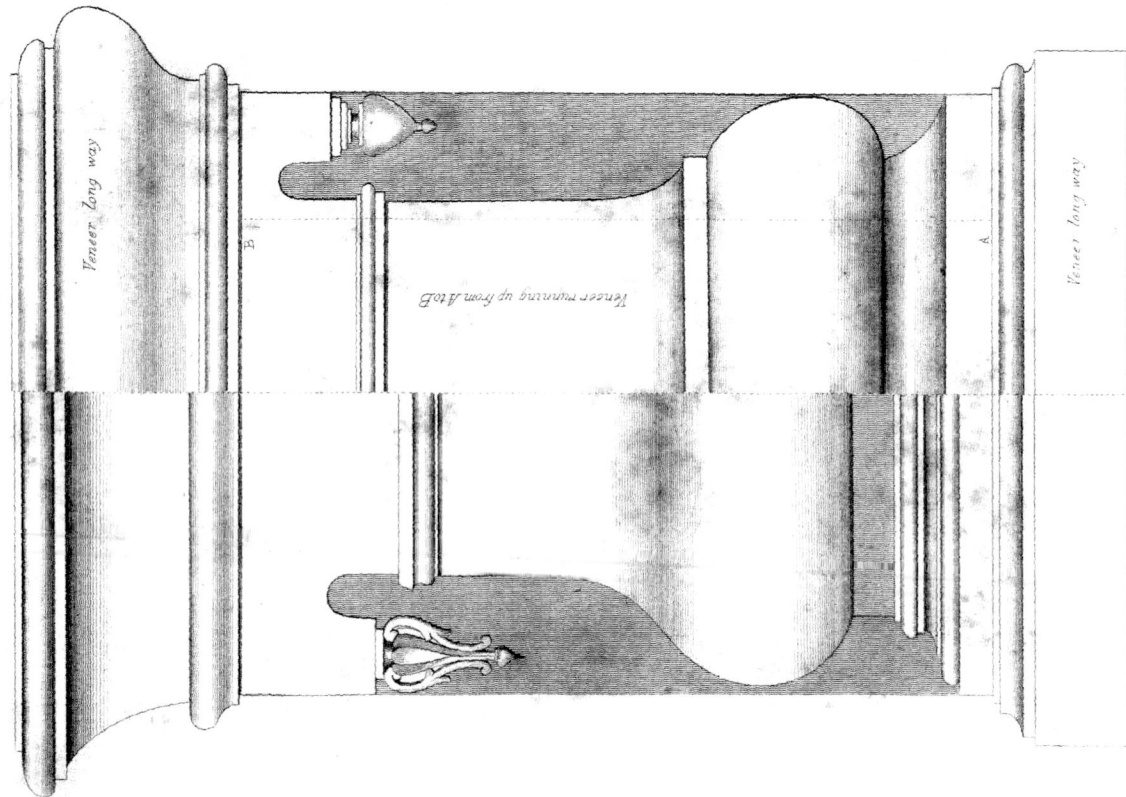

Veneer long way

Veneer running up from A to B

Veneer long way

For Good Wood

WILLIAM MACKENZIE GLASGOW & EDINBURGH

J Ramage

PLATE XVII

BRACKETS FOR CHIFFONNIÈRES HALF SIZE

J Scott

WILLIAM MACKENZIE — GLASGOW & EDINBURGH

73

WINE COOLERS

WILLIAM MACKENZIE GLASGOW EDINBURGH & LONDON

WILLIAM MACKENZIE, GLASGOW, EDINBURGH & LONDON

Inches   12   9   6   3   0   1   2 Feet

WILLIAM MACKENZIE GLASGOW EDINBURGH & LONDON

Pierced

Pierced

Pierced

Pierced

Pierced

Pierced

Pierced

Pierced

WILLIAM MACKENZIE GLASGOW EDINBURGH · LONDON
AND NEW YORK

WILLIAM MACKENZIE _ GLASGOW, EDINBURGH & LONDON

SOFAS

WILLIAM MACKENZIE, GLASGOW, EDINBURGH & LONDON

WILLIAM MACKENZIE. GLASGOW EDINBURGH & LONDON

EASY CHAIRS

WILLIAM MACKENZIE, GLASGOW, EDINBURGH, & LONDON.

83

TABLE CLAWS

WILLIAM MACKENZIE — GLASGOW & EDINBURGH.

FIRE SCREEN & TABLE LEGS

One Foot

Scale to Centre Figure

Inches 12 · · 3 · 6 · 9

Scale to Table Legs

0 · 3 · 6 · 9 · One Foot

Inches 12

WILLIAM MACKENZIE - GLASGOW & EDINBURGH

W. Warwick

87

TABLE PILLARS

SOFA LEGS

One Foot

Inches 12   9   6   3   0

WILLIAM MACKENZIE, GLASGOW & EDINBURGH.

WILLIAM MACKENZIE, GLASGOW, EDINBURGH & LONDON

WILLIAM MACKENZIE, GLASGOW, EDINBURGH & LONDON

PIER TABLE

93

DRAWING ROOM TABLE RIMS

FULL SIZE FOR WORK & CARD TABLES AND HALF SIZE FOR LOO TABLES.

R Dawson

WILLIAM MACKENZIE, GLASGOW, EDINBURGH & LONDON.

94

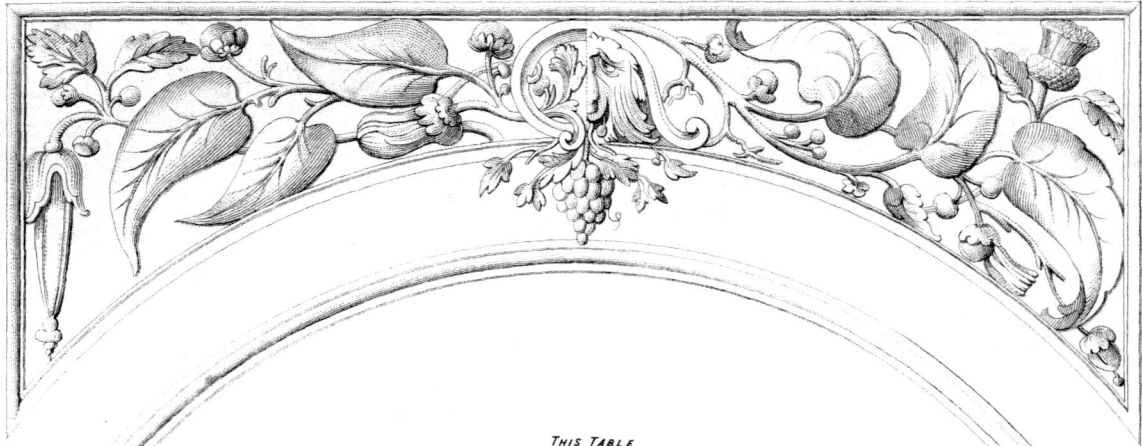

THIS TABLE

must be drawn from the wall when required for

a Large Party. The centre circular back folds down when out,

Two supporters are hinged on the back of the part which folds down when

the back is flat, There might be a double back one half to fold to the front upon

the top and the other to fold to the back which would form a Round Table: The Use

of this Table is to hold the Dishes which may be required on the Centre or Dinner Table.

There ought to be two of these Tables in a Dining Room, one placed on each side of the Sideboard.

Inches 12 9 6 3 0   1   2   3   4   5

WILLIAM MACKENZIE GLASGOW EDINBURGH & LONDON

CABINETS

WILLIAM MACKENZIE, GLASGOW, EDINBURGH & LONDON.

96

WILLIAM MACKENZIE, GLASGOW, EDINBURGH & LONDON.

2

1

B

B

D

P. Thomson

D

A

3   4   5 Feet

PLATE XXXIII.

Inches 12 9 6 3 0   2   3 Feet

J. Scott.

WILLIAM MACKENZIE — GLASGOW EDINBURGH & LONDON.

P. Thomson

WILLIAM MACKENZIE, GLASGOW & EDINBURGH

W. Warwick

PLATE XXX

P. Shamham

T. Watt.

P. Chamran

WILLIAM MACKENZIE, GLASGOW, EDINBURGH & LONDON.

PLATE XV

DETAILS FOR BEDS

Fig. 3

Fig. 2

Fig. 5

Fig. 7

Fig. 1

Fig. 4

WILLIAM MACKENZIE GLASGOW & LONDON

WILLIAM MACKENZIE, GLASGOW, EDINBURGH & LONDON.

WARDROBES

WILLIAM MACKENZIE GLASGOW EDINBURGH & LONDON

WILLIAM MACKENZIE, GLASGOW, EDINBURGH & LONDON

108

WILLIAM MACKENZIE — GLASGOW, EDINBURGH & LONDON.

WILLIAM MACKENZIE. GLASGOW EDINBURGH & LONDON.

(FULL SIZE)

WILLIAM MACKENZIE — GLASGOW & EDINBURGH

PLATE III

WARDROBE DETAILS

WILLIAM MACKENZIE, LONDON, GLASGOW & EDINBURGH

Inches   Feet

Thomson

WILLIAM MACKENZIE, GLASGOW, EDINBURGH & LONDON

115

WILLIAM MACKENZIE _GLASGOW. EDINBURGH & LONDON.

WILLIAM MACKENZIE _ GLASGOW EDINBURGH & LONDON

PLATE XXV

FIRE SCREENS

CABINET FOR STUDIO

WILLIAM MACKENZIE, GLASGOW, EDINBURGH & LONDON

122

BOOKCASE

WILLIAM M.CKENZIE _GLASGOW EDINBURGH & LONDON.

123

WILLIAM MACKENZIE, GLASGOW EDINBURGH & LONDON

WILLIAM MACKENZIE, GLASGOW, EDINBURGH & LONDON.

WILLIAM MACKENZIE, GLASGOW & EDINBURGH

TABLE FEET FOR CARD, FULL, AND LOO, HALF SIZE.

MILLAR JA MENZIE GLASGOW EDINBURGH LONDON AND NEW YORK

WILLIAM MACKENZIE _ GLASGOW EDINBURGH & LONDON

Inches

Feet

WILLIAM MACKENZIE _GLASGOW, EDINBURGH & LONDON.

PLATE II

RAILINGS

WILLIAM MACKENZIE, GLASGOW & EDINBURGH

J. Scott

Inches 12 9 6 3 0   1   2   3   4   5   6 Feet

131

One Foot   0   3   6   9   12 Inches

WILLIAM MACKENZIE, GLASGOW, EDINBURGH, LONDON
AND NEW YORK

WILLIAM MACKENZIE,— GLASGOW. EDINBURGH & LONDON

133

WILLIAM MACKENZIE, GLASGOW EDINBURGH & LONDON

PLATE XXXII

WILLIAM MACKENZIE GLASGOW EDINBURGH & LONDON.

DESCRIPTION OF PLATE,

HINTS FOR YOUNG TRADESMEN, No. I.

Fig. 1, on this Plate, represents a sideboard front, with a diagram explanatory of the method of delineating it. For the benefit of apprentices, we may here explain the system of working out the figure with the compasses, the practice of which will initiate the young artist into several processes of a like character.

The oval may be drawn in a variety of ways, but the diagram before us will show both the method of delineation and the rule for finding it. The circle, 1 to 7, is divided into equal parts, as the regulator of the figure. By placing the 1 higher and the 7 lower, or the reverse, the oval will be made long or flat at pleasure. The point of the compasses is first placed at 1 on the circle, the leg being extended to 1 on the large sweep, thus drawing a portion of a circle to the first dotted line on the right. Then sweep from 2, and extend the compasses as before, up to 7. The upper portion is done in the same way—extending from the lower 4 to the upper 4 all round to 1, where the circle intersects the dotted line. The dotted line from 4, up through the sweep, gives the list on the top.

Mouldings of this character are termed Roman, although, strictly speaking, a Roman moulding is produced by parts of circles, whilst Greek mouldings are formed of ovals. Now this figure is formed of parts of ovals, and, owing to its roundness, has been claimed by the Romans as altered by them from the Greek; like the Composite order of architecture, which is a compound of Corinthian and Ionic.

The small ogee below is divided into four equal parts, with the points on one line.

Fig. 2 is a perspective elevation of a portion of a chair. In delineating this, it is to be remembered that 18 inches is the ordinary height of a chair seat from the floor. First we must determine the size of the front, which is usually equal to the height. The front is then to be divided into four equal parts—that is, one part blank, one part the front of the chair, and the other two the side. At the upper corner, to the left, the dotted line, running three parts, cuts the depth of the back leg; the dotted line coming from the right to the centre, on the ground line, cuts the leg a second time. Generally, the point of sight is put 5 feet 6 inches high by the scale beneath the figure; but if this were done, it would appear to be suspended. In the figure before us, this point is only 2 feet 6 inches from the floor to the eye.

Fig. 3 is drawn on the same principle, adapted for cubes, such as wardrobes, sideboards, and cheffoniers. In the case of a wardrobe, the point of sight may be about five feet from the floor. To lay it down, first draw the four fronts; then, from the right corner on the upper line, draw the dotted lines. This done, the line from C to B is to be drawn, cutting the square of the blocks. Then raise the perpendicular, and, with the T-square, draw the horizontal line, showing the top. Afterwards draw a line from corner to corner on the shaded side, giving the centre of the blocks, and, raising the square, draw the top line.

HINTS FOR YOUNG TRADESMEN

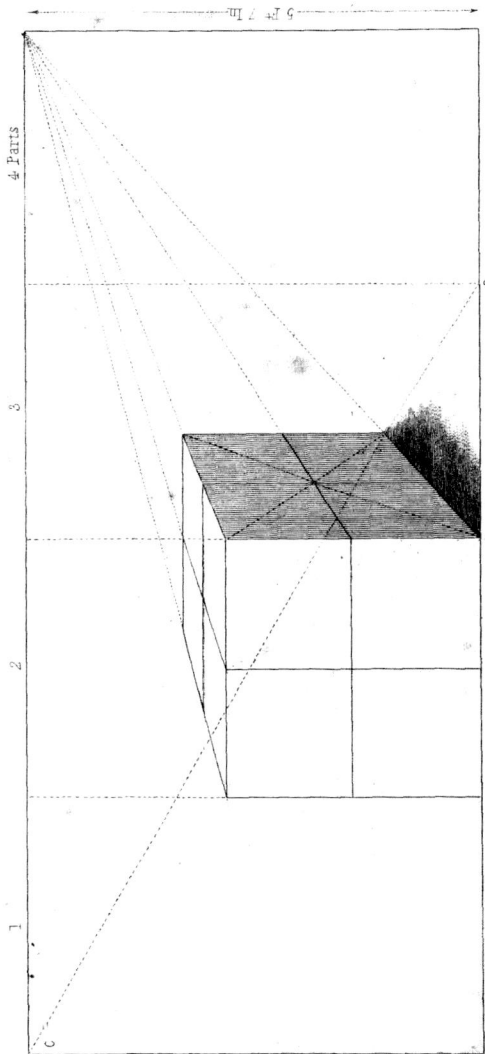

To Represent 8 Square Blocks.

139

DESCRIPTION OF PLATE.—CORNICES.

Fig. 1, on Plate, is well adapted for a bookcase of large dimensions. On a smaller scale it will answer well for a large wardrobe. It is, however, more suitable for the former; and as in a large library the cornices usually go up to the ceiling, it would, on this account, show to fine effect. The extent between G and the dotted line near the centre of the screw-nail, represents a piece of fir—the upper part being held on by the screw. On this is planted the top moulding of solid mahogany or oak. Beneath, the double line represents the portion which is veneered, down to the bead. Round, under this again, is another veneer, continued through the under curve as far as B, which is solid. The oval moulding is solid, and is planted on the fir, as also is the short length between the large moulding and bead. The bead itself is solid, and the succeeding longer, or frieze portion again is veneered. The under bead and portion at G is solid, to allow of working out the under hollow. The upper piece of fir, where the top moulding is planted on, is glued on before it is veneered.—See the dotted line cutting the veneer.

To delineate this, place the compass leg at A, and extend to A, sweeping round, to give the requisite size of wood for a blocking, which, as it is not seen, may be square. Next place the compass point at c, and extend it to c, and perform the same operation, and afterwards the like from B to B. Then, for the large mouldings, place the compasses at D, and extend to D, then from E to E, on the sweep. We are thus explicit, in order that the young apprentice may see his way perfectly clear.

In commencing to delineate this cornice, the perpendicular and horizontal pieces of fir must first be framed; then plant on B first, afterwards the large moulding, then the two beads and c below. The top moulding and three beads may be gilt.

Fig. 2 exhibits the groundwork of an S, and forms the plan of an oval. After laying down the perpendicular and horizontal lines, describe the three circles. The intersecting lines cut the outer circle, for the start of the oval. The compass point is to be placed at the top of the circle, on the perpendicular line—extending the leg to the top of the small circle, sweeping round for the start of the oval.

To form the oval, the compass point is to be placed at the upper edge of the top of the small circle, extending to the under edge of the under small circle; the point is then to be placed on the cross line, sweeping round on the horizontal line, which gives the extent of the flat sides of the oval, and the same on the side.

Fig. 3 very nearly resembles fig. 1, and requires little description.   The compass point is to be placed at A, and extended to A, outside, for the sweep.   The same must be done from B to B, and C to D.   This cornice will answer well for a rich bed in mahogany.   Either of the two, reversed, will give the base for a fire-screen, stand, or other article of a similar class.

Fig. 4 is a diagram to give the height above a cornice in a room, whether for a wardrobe or bed.   It affords its own explanation.

DESCRIPTION OF PLATE.—SIDEBOARD DETAILS.

In fig. 1 are shown the dotted lines for working the compasses round the sweeps of the large moulding. A, Is the top above the drawer. B, Is first worked to fit the moulding, and is afterwards shaped as shown, and glued on the moulding. This detail is ¼ inch thick when finished.

Fig. 2 is treated in a similar manner. The ogee moulding is veneered lengthways, and the drop is planted on after the veneer is polished. The two vertical dotted lines in the outline, or profile, show the drawer front, and the cross line from A to the lower part of D is the drawer front.

Fig. 3 very closely resembles fig. 1. The three points are clearly shown by the dotted lines; so also is the drawer front.

In fig. 4, the only difference is the carved ornaments on the front at B, which is first fitted on the large moulding, and then carved. The outline, B C, is the section.

Fig. 5 is a truss in the same style, intended to suit fig. 3. It may either be pierced or sunk, but is shown sunk. Of course, in this view, only a single pendant is shown, but there are four in reality, turned from beneath the first bead and list. The flowers may be planted on, and about half the breadth of the front of the truss at the top, and a quarter of the breadth at the under side, yet as free and graceful as possible.

PLATE XIX

SIDEBOARD DETAILS, STAGES, HALF SIZE

WILLIAM MACKENZIE GLASGOW & EDINBURGH

DESCRIPTION OF PLATE.—BED AND DETAILS.

The end of this bed is the only important feature. The cornice is not so high at the sides and the end next the wall. The curtain at the end is higher than at the sides, as shown. The part of the curtain at the edge of the post is fixed, the other portion, working out on rings, going into the hollow on a straight rod, which is concealed under the cornice. For the covering of the cornice below, there is a piece of flat wood which carries the hollow right through. On the sides, the curtain works on a rod to the centre, or even to the head of the bed. The pillar is veneered, and goes up through the cornice by means of a round tenon. The mouldings are all sunk in after the pillar is cleaned off, and then the ornaments are fitted on. Bay wood is the best for the pillar, veneered with very rich Boa Constrictor mahogany, or myrtle. The moulding and ornaments to be of the same colour of wood, but plain, as they are well opened up. The footboard demands our attention only in details. Its section is exhibited at G, H, J, K, and L. The cornice again is shown on a large scale at A, B, C, D, and E.

A

B

C

A

B

C

D

E

G

H

J

K

L

G

H

F

F

K

L

Scale to Details

1? Inches   1 Foot

Inches   12   9   6   3   0   1   2   3   4   Feet

WILLIAM MACKENZIE GLASGOW & EDINBURGH

WILLIAM MACKENZIE, GLASGOW & EDINBURGH

150

WILLIAM MACKENZIE - GLASGOW EDINBURGH & LONDON

151

STATE BEDSTEAD.

THE

CABINET-MAKER'S

ASSISTANT:

A SERIES OF

ORIGINAL DESIGNS FOR MODERN FURNITURE,

WITH DESCRIPTIONS AND DETAILS OF CONSTRUCTION.

PRECEDED BY PRACTICAL OBSERVATIONS

ON THE MATERIALS AND MANUFACTURE OF CABINET-WORK,

AND

INSTRUCTIONS IN DRAWING ADAPTED TO THE TRADE.

BLACKIE AND SON:
GLASGOW, EDINBURGH, LONDON, AND NEW YORK.
MDCCCLIII.

contact; they are then to be passed along the stone in a perpendicular position, until both the tips appear to agree exactly. The pen is then to be held steadily in the left hand, while, with the right, the oil-stone is rubbed against the backs of the blades at the point, until both are brought to an edge of equal fineness. The inner side of the blades should not be touched, further than to remove the barbs that may have arisen, and should be kept quite flat. The instrument must next be examined, and the points retouched, if they require it, until they are perfect. Cabinet-makers, from being accustomed to the setting of edge tools, will find little difficulty in keeping their pens in good order; they must, at the same time, recollect that too great care cannot be bestowed on them. When laid aside, the ink ought always to be cleaned out, and on no account should it be allowed to dry in the pens, as it is not only cleaned with greater difficulty, but the points will become corroded and destroyed.

Dotting Pen.—It is frequently convenient in drawing, to employ an interrupted or dotted line. The drawing of such a line by hand, occupies a good deal of time, but when well executed is the best method; an instrument may, however, be used which effects a considerable saving of labour. It consists of two steel blades precisely similar to the drawing pen in form, but between the points is placed a small notched wheel or roller, as seen at E in the figure. The ink is inserted between the blades, as in the pen, when the wheel, being drawn along any surface, will leave a line composed of equidistant points or short lines. There is a little uncertainty in using this kind of roller, as it will not always begin to mark when required, or always mark regularly. The best way is to get it to work upon a separate piece of paper, and then to apply it to the drawing where desired. If the line produced should fail in regularity, it is not possible to go over it again with the roller without producing blots. There are generally several sets of wheels for producing lines of different characters; these may be changed in the instrument by relaxing the screw, which allows the pivots to escape from the holes at the extremities of the blades.

The size of compasses varies with their use; they are to be had from three or four inches in length upwards; a convenient size is from five to six inches, which, with its arm, will describe a tolerably large circle in a drawing; they are made as much as twelve inches in length in metal, and above that they are of wood, with metal points and crayon holders.

Bow Compasses.—Small circles are generally described by compasses of a suitable size, called *bow compasses*, these are very convenient from the facility with which they may be used, being provided with a short handle, by means of which they may be turned round between the finger and thumb. The instrument consists of a small pair of compasses, as represented in the engraving, the legs of which open about a centre A; one of the legs is fitted permanently with a pen, which is furnished with a joint at C, in order that it may be set as nearly perpendicular as possible to the surface on which the circle is described. The stiffness of this joint can be regulated by the screw at C, and the strength of the line by the screw F, as already described. In these small compasses, it is found very convenient to have them provided with what is called a needle point; this consists of an arrangement at the extremity of the leg, by which a fine needle may be secured by a small clamping screw E, so that when the point loses its efficiency another may be substituted.

The pencil bow compasses is represented in the annexed engraving. It is similar in construction to the last described, having a joint at C, in the leg which forms the pencil holder; this may either be an arrangement of tubes fitting into one another, as previously described, or it may be as in the figure, where the pencil is clipped in a socket which is tightened by a screw F. This instrument is also provided with a needle point. Excellent bow compasses are made with the ordinary points, and without the joint at C; the advantage of the joint is, that by its means the pen point *may be brought* more nearly perpendicular in describing circles with it, which is of some importance, the line drawn being much clearer than when the pen slopes.

It is frequently necessary to describe smaller circles than even the bow compasses can well be made to do; for this purpose, a pair of very fine spring compasses is employed. They are made both with pen and pencil points; that in the engraving is provided with the latter. In these, as in the already described spring dividers, there is no joint, the instrument being made of a single piece of steel, the part D forming the spring. The opening between the points is regulated by the screw and nut B, the former, passing through an opening in one leg, is secured to the other at A. By means of such instruments, very minute circles may be described with great accuracy. The figure represents the compasses of the full size, but they are frequently made smaller.

Rulers.—Having described the different kinds of compasses by which the circle is described, it remains to notice the *plane scale*, or *straight edge*, by means of which straight lines are drawn. These rulers are made of various materials, most of the hard woods being employed, as well as ivory, and different metals; they are of any length, according to the wants of the draughtsman. Those generally used in drawing are composed of wood or ivory, but more frequently the former; these materials being preferable, on account of their lightness; a metal ruler, when of any length, being inconveniently heavy in using it; the latter, however, has the very important advantage of retaining its form more truly, while wood is very apt to warp, a defect which, when it does occur, renders the ruler in a great measure useless. An excellent kind of ruler, when well made, is one with a thin slip of brass let into the edge, and against which the marking point glides; these are generally made of pear-tree, a wood that seems to answer the purpose admirably. From their liability to suffer from time and use, rulers must be frequently verified. This may be done by drawing a line carefully along the edge, and then reversing the ruler, so that it may be presented on the other side of the line as exactly as possible, and drawing a second line over the first; on examination, it will be seen whether both coincide or not; if they do not, the rule is false, and ought not to be used until the defect is remedied. Great care is necessary in drawing these proof lines, for although it may appear an easy matter to draw a line along the edge of a ruler, it requires some little practice to do so truly, that is, to copy its edge with exactitude; the hand must be held so that the pen or pencil may not deviate in the least, during its progress, from its inclination to the surface when first applied, more especially sideways. It may be remarked, that it is a much easier thing to describe a circle truly, than to draw a perfectly straight line. This is well exemplified in the ease with which the turner produces a true circle in his work, and the difficulty that the joiner experiences in making his edges accurately straight.

In selecting or proving rulers, they may be compared with one another; by placing the edges of two close together and holding them against the light, any irregularities will shew themselves by a greater or less breadth of light being allowed to pass between them. If they are quite close, the two rulers may either be curved so as to fit one another, or they may be perfectly straight; if a third is now found to agree with both, in comparing them together by this method, then they are all three correct and to be depended on. By the application of this principle, perfectly straight metal edges are easily produced. Three thin flat bars are prepared as far as possible with the file; they are perfected by grinding their edges alternately together, interposing a little fine emery and oil; by changing the bars successively and repeatedly, and at proper intervals, the straight edge is sure to be produced at last. The bars may be an eighth of an inch thick, two inches wide, and must not very much exceed two feet six inches in length. Pressure on any particular part must be avoided as much as possible in the grinding.

Pencils.—For general purposes, the pencils used for drawing lines and circles ought to be rather of a hard quality; these produce a much clearer line than the softer kinds, and, when good, the marks or lines may be easily removed by the India rubber without trouble. Pencils are to be had which are made expressly to fit into compasses; but it will be found better to use a piece of a good lead pencil, and pare it away nicely until it is of a proper size; the side of the wood in which the lead does not lie, ought to be slipped off altogether.

A convenient mode of cutting the pencil for drawing straight lines, is to bring the lead to a fine edge, taking care to keep one side of the wood as flat as possible, and parallel with the edge. By applying the flat side of the pencil to the ruler, the point is brought close to it, and is prevented by its form from turning during its progress; the line may thus be much more accurately and easily drawn than with a round point; this particular form of the lead enables it not only to draw a clearer line, but to retain its sharpness much longer than any other. The same method may be applied in cutting the points of pencils for the compasses.

China Ink.—The other material that is employed in drawing with the compasses is generally China ink. This ought to be of the best quality; the common kinds of it are all more or less filled with gritty or sandy particles, which interfere with the flowing of the ink from the pen, besides being of a dull brown colour. The quality of the ink may be easily ascertained by applying the end of the cake to the tongue, when, if there are any coarse particles or sand in its texture, they will be felt immediately. In using it, the ink ought to be rubbed down with a little clean water upon a plate or saucer, until the fluid is brought to any depth of colour required, but not so thick that it will not flow freely from the pen; a little experience will soon show how far this may be carried. In rubbing down the cake, it ought to be turned occasionally, so that the edges may be rounded off, this prevents it from splintering off in little bits which are troublesome. Common ink may also be employed, but it is not so good as the China ink, being more apt to run and blot when lines are drawn close to each other with it, or where many lines are drawn from the same point; also, if a drawing is required to be subsequently tinted, the ink runs when wetted, producing a very disagreeable effect.

In drawing a straight line, its position is usually indicated by two points; when these are marked, they ought to be made as small and distinct as possible, so as to leave no room for uncertainty in placing the ruler. It is then applied exactly to the points, leaving as much space as the thickness of the marking point requires; this is easily found by trial, if necessary, by placing the point precisely over each mark, and arranging the ruler accordingly; but practice will enable any one to judge very closely of the proper distance without this trouble. Care ought to be taken to place the marks through which a line is to be drawn, at as great a distance from one another as convenient; by this, any slight inaccuracy in placing the ruler is diminished. Serious inconvenience arises sometimes from neglect of this, as a deviation from its true direction, that may be inappreciable or immaterial in a short line, may become again very apparent when others are combined with it, or are dependent on it. The points which direct a line are most frequently indicated or found by the intersection of two lines, or two arcs of circles; certain precautions are necessary sometimes, in order that the exact place of the intersection may be clearly seen—for this purpose the lines must not be made to cross each other at a very small angle, if it can be avoided, because the less this is, the greater uncertainty is there of the exact place of the intersection; also, when the lines are not made very fine and clear, the difficulty of ascertaining it is much increased, particularly with a very small angle. The lines ought to cross each other well, so that the point of intersection may be clearly and distinctly evident. It must always be recollected that the nearer the points are to each other which give the direction of a long line, the more care must be taken to have no uncertainty, for any error that may be committed is increased in proportion to the length of the line drawn.

We have now described the nature of the few instruments that are essentially necessary for the production of circles and straight lines in drawing, and have endeavoured to point out the most convenient modes of using them for this end. Circles and straight lines, in themselves, are of small service, unless directed by intelligence to the attainment of a specific object; it is the province of practical geometry to show how they may be combined among themselves and together, for the production of results which may either add to our knowledge, or be applicable to some practical and useful purpose. In this way geometry becomes connected with all the mechanical arts, and among the rest not the least important one, with that of the cabinet-maker. This is evident if drawing alone were considered, which is indispensable in his calling: but in his work and operations he frequently carries into effect the problems of geometry. The kind of drawing, also, which he employs, is essentially geometric, and dependent on geometric principles; it is of the utmost importance to him, therefore, that he should become familiar with the principles, as well as with the different processes of drawing.

The business of the cabinet-maker is either to execute any piece of work that he may undertake in an accurate and efficient manner, in accordance with a given design, or to produce the design himself. His power of execution either way, depends on his knowledge of drawing; in the one case, it will enable him to comprehend more clearly, and with greater facility, the intentions of another, and so to work with greater certainty and precision in carrying out the design; and in the other, it will enable him to express his own ideas in an intelligible form. Nothing can more conduce to this end, and to the attainment of skill in the workman, than the acquirement of strict geometric principles. In the comparison of work, that is always the best which approaches more nearly to geometric precision in the lines and surfaces; nor is this merely conducive to external beauty, for the strength and durability of any structure, independent of the material, depends on such precision, and any inaccuracy not only frequently impairs outward beauty, but produces, in a corresponding degree, a real want of firmness and stability.

The limits of this work preclude the possibility of entering fully on the theoretical part of the sciences connected with drawing; but in the subsequent parts, we shall endeavour to impart such practical explanations of the principles of its different departments, as may enable the cabinet maker with ease to execute such drawings as he may require, or to give form to subjects of his own invention. This art, as applied to mechanical purposes, is so based upon geometric principles, that it becomes essentially necessary for the student to make himself familiar with the construction of plane geometric figures; a series of these, the most applicable to the purposes of the cabinet-maker, are offered in the following pages, and it is strongly recommended to the beginner to commence by drawing these carefully and accurately. It would be of great service to him were he to endeavour to become acquainted with so much of the elementary principles of geometry, that he may be able to prove, by demonstration, the truth or fallacy of the processes which are employed, and not merely to rest satisfied that they are correct; this would not only fix the problems more firmly in his memory, and be highly conducive to advancement in his daily pursuits, but also afford him a source of great enjoyment and rational recreation in his leisure hours.

It must not be imagined that there is any mystery attached to the acquirement of this kind of knowledge; the elementary parts of geometry, so far as will be found necessary, are exceedingly easy, and of evident application in the various constructions. All that is required, is a little attention in following out a connected train of reasoning from the simplest principles, which are in themselves self-evident. It must be borne in mind, that if they are understood with so much readiness, they are apt to escape from the recollection with equal facility, if not impressed by unwearied practice, and by being repeated and reflected upon in all their details, until they may become so familiar as to present themselves when occasion requires.

The young draughtsman, then, ought to make himself thoroughly acquainted with the terms used and with the constructions in practical geometry; these he should be able to draw with readiness, not only from a copy, but from recollection. No other instruments ought to be employed but the ruler and compasses, avoiding the use of squares and other aids that may be ordinarily useful or convenient in drawing; by this means, he will more readily attain to the mastery of his instruments. He ought to bestow all the pains he can upon the figures, endeavouring to produce them as clear and neat as he can. This attained, will be one important step in his progress as a draughtsman. He may probably experience some difficulty at first, and be apt to condemn his own awkwardness in the use of the compasses; this he must expect, and not be discouraged by it. A very little practice and experience will soon give dexterity; nothing of the kind can be acquired without some trouble at first; and it must be recollected, that the more care and attention that is bestowed at the outset, the greater will be the subsequent progress, as there will thus be less to overcome, or perhaps, to correct at an after period.

PRACTICAL GEOMETRY.

Geometry is that science which treats of the magnitude and forms of the objects by which we are surrounded, as relates to the three dimensions of *length*, *breadth*, and *thickness*, and also of portions of space considered as possessing these dimensions.

Theoretical geometry demonstrates the absolute truths of the science by abstract reasoning.

Practical geometry, by rules deduced from the demonstrations of theoretic geometry, teaches the truthful construction of figures upon given conditions.

The whole system of geometry is founded upon simple and self-evident truths, which cannot receive, and do not require, any proof or demonstration. In practical geometry it is unnecessary to enumerate these, but the definition and application of some of the terms used in the science is requisite for the right understanding of the intention of the problems and their solutions.

Definitions.—A *point* is that which has position, but no magnitude nor dimensions, neither length, breadth, nor thickness.

A *line* is length, without breadth or thickness. The extremities of lines are points, and when two lines cross each other, their intersection is a point. In practice, it is usual to consider as points and lines the smallest marks that can be formed by mechanical means; these are strictly and truly solid bodies, possessing the three dimensions of length, breadth, and thickness; but in practical geometry they are understood as occupying no space.

A *surface, or superficies,* is an extension, or a figure of two dimensions, length and breadth, but without thickness. A shadow gives a very good notion of a superficies; its length and breadth can be measured, but it has no depth or thickness. The quantity of space contained in any surface is called the *Area.*

A *body, or solid,* is a figure of three dimensions, namely, length, breadth, and depth or thickness. The term may be applied to any visible object, but in geometry it is understood to signify the space contained within the different surfaces.

Lines may be drawn in any direction, and are called accordingly either right, or curved, or mixed of these two.

A right, or straight line, lies all in the same direction between its extremities, and is the shortest distance between two points. In description, it is generally indicated by a letter placed at each end, as the line A B.

Every line which is not a straight line is a *curved line.* It continually changes its direction between its extreme points. The variety of curves is unlimited. Plane geometry includes only one, the circle; the rest are divided into different sections according to their properties.

A mixed line is composed of straight and curved lines connected in any form.

Parallel lines are always at the same perpendicular distance from one another, and they never meet though ever so far produced. Curved lines may also be parallel, when the perpendicular distance between them remains always the same.

Oblique, or converging, straight lines change their distance, and would meet or intersect each other, if produced, on the side of the least distance.

A rectilineal angle is formed at the common point of origin, or intersection of two straight lines. Thus, the straight lines B A and B C, diverging from the point B, form an angle of which B is called the *Vertex.* The lines containing an angle are called the *Sides.* In description, a letter is generally placed at the vertex, as B, and also one somewhere on each of the sides, as A and C, and the angle is called "the angle A B C," placing the letter which indicates the vertex between the other two. The angle may sometimes be called "the angle B," or, "at B," when there is no risk of mistake. The magnitude of an angle does not depend on the length of the sides, but on the greater or less divergence of the lines which contain it.

Angles are either *right* or *oblique,* and the latter either acute or obtuse, according as they are greater or less than a right angle.

A right-angle is formed when one line meeting another, or standing upon it, makes the angles on both sides of it equal to each other; and the straight line which stands on the other is said to be *perpendicular to it.*

An *acute angle* is any angle that is less than a right-angle, as *b.*

An *obtuse angle* is any angle that is greater than a right-angle, as *c.*

An angle is measured by the portion of the circumference of a circle intercepted between the sides containing it, and which is described from the vertex as a centre. All circles being similar figures, and bearing the same proportion to their diameters, similar sectors of different circles are to one another as the whole circles, and the arcs of the similar sectors are to one another as the circumferences; hence, it is not the actual length of the arc that determines the quantity of the angle, but the proportion that it bears to the whole circumference, of which it is a part. The arc of a circle being thus the measure of angular magnitude, for its expression by number, the whole circumference is divided into 360 equal parts, called *degrees;* and for those angles that do not contain whole numbers of these parts, each degree is divided into sixty equal parts, called *minutes;* and these again are subdivided into sixty *seconds,* and so on. Degrees, minutes, and seconds, are indicated by the signs °, ′, ″, placed over the numbers which represent them; thus, 51°, 25′, 52·85″, is read fifty-one degrees, twenty-five minutes, fifty-two seconds, and eighty-five hundredth part, and represent an angle which is measured by the seventh part of the circumference of a circle. It is evident that the right-angle is measured by the fourth part of a circumference, as in the diagram, where A B C is a right-angle, and the interceped arc is a quadrant or quarter of a circle. This is divided into 90°, or one-fourth part of 360. By drawing lines from the centre B, through each point of division, the angle is divided into equal angles, in the present case, into nine equal parts, each containing 10°; and the angle which each of these lines makes with B C, the horizontal line is called an angle of 10° or 20°, &c. The right-angle thus containing 90°, the acute angle contains a less, and the obtuse angle any greater number of degrees.

The division of the circle into 360°, is called the

sexagesimal division; among other advantages, it possesses the important property, that 360 may be divided by a great many whole numbers, without a remainder. It is proper to mention, that in some French works the circle will be found divided into 400°, for the measurement of angles, and these are subdivided by 10, &c. The quadrant, or right angle, is thus made to consist of 100°. This is called the centesimal division.

Any angle which is more than two right angles, is called a *reverse angle*.

When any angle is less than two right angles, the deficiency is called the *supplement of the angle*.

When any angle is less than a right angle, the deficiency is called the *complement of the angle*.

Superficies are either *plane* or *curved*.

A *plane*, or *plane superficies*, is that with which a straight line may every way coincide; or, if the line touch the plane in two points, it will touch it in every point. This affords one of the most accurate and ready tests by which the truth of a plane surface is determined, the workman applying a straight edge, or one as nearly straight as can be, to his work in various directions; if the edge is found to touch the surface in all its points, and in every way that it is applied, he concludes that his object has been attained.

A *curved superficies* is such as will not coincide with a straight line in every direction. There are certain curved surfaces to which the straight line may be applied; but when this is the case, it is only in one sense that it can be so, as will readily be understood; for instance, a straight line may be applied to the surface of a cylinder, as a garden roller, in the direction of its length, but in no other, leaving the ends out of the question.

Plane figures are bounded either by right lines or curves.

Plane figures bounded by right lines have names, according to the number of their sides or of their angles, for they have as many sides as angles.

Three is the least number of straight lines by which space can be circumscribed. These lines incline to each other, and meeting, form three angles. The figure is hence called a *triangle*. The straight lines which form it are called the *sides of the triangle*.

These figures receive different denominations from the relation of their sides and angles.

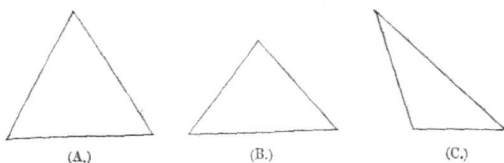

(A.)   (B.)   (C.)

The *equilateral triangle* is that which has all its sides equal. (A.)

The *isosceles triangle* is that which has two of its angles equal. (B.)

A triangle all of whose sides are unequal, is called a *scalene triangle*. (C.)

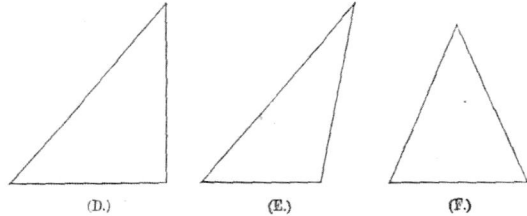

(D.)   (E.)   (F.)

A *right angled triangle* is that which has one of its angles a right angle. (D.)

An *obtuse angled triangle* is that which has an obtuse angle. (E.)

An *acute angled triangle* is that which has all its angles acute angles. (F.)

For the convenience of reference, different letters are marked at each of the angles of the triangle, and it is described by means of those letters; as the triangle A B C.

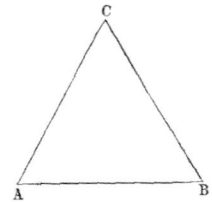

Any side of a triangle may be called its *base*, and the opposite angular point its *vertex*; thus, A B, one of the sides of the triangle A B C, may be called the base, and the angle at C the vertical angle of the triangle.

The *altitude of a triangle* is a line which is drawn from the angle opposite to the base line, perpendicular to it, or the base produced when necessary; thus, C D is the altitude of the triangle A B C, the base A B being produced so as to meet it. In the same way, C D is the altitude of the right angled triangle A D C.

The side of a right angled triangle which is opposite to the right angle, is called the *hypotenuse* of the triangle; thus, A C is the hypotenuse of the right angled triangle A D C.

The triangle is the simplest of all the rectilineal figures, and the most important in geometry, as by its means the properties of all other figures bounded by straight lines, and which may be resolved into component triangles, are investigated and determined.

Figures of four sides and angles are called *quadrilaterals*, or *quadrangles*, and receive different denominations according to the relations of those sides and angles.

b

A *parallelogram* is a quadrilateral which has both its pairs of opposite sides parallel, and it takes the following particular names:—namely, rectangle, square, rhombus, and rhomboid.

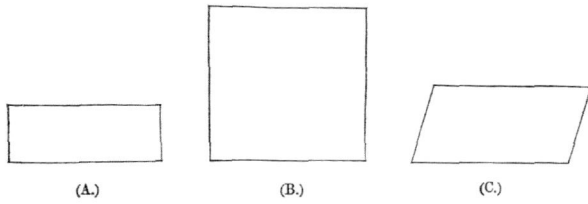

(A.)　　　　　　(B.)　　　　　　(C.)

A *rectangle* is a parallelogram having all its angles right angles, the term being generally applied to those figures in which the opposite pairs of sides are of unequal lengths. (A.)

A *square* is an equilateral rectangle having all its sides equal, and all its angles right angles. (B.)

When the angles of a parallelogram are oblique, and the opposite pairs of sides are unequal in length, the figure is called a *rhomboid.* (C.)

A *rhombus* is an equilateral rhomboid, having all its sides equal, but its angles oblique. The figure is also called a *lozenge.*

(D.)　　　　　　(E.)　　　　　　(F.)

A *trapezoid* has only one pair of opposite sides parallel. (D.)

A *trapezium* is a quadrilateral which has not its pairs of opposite sides parallel. (E.)

Those angles of a quadrilateral which are at each extremity of one of the sides, are called *adjacent angles*, as B A D and A D C, while those which are not so, as A B C and A D C, are called *opposite angles.* A straight line, as A C, which joins the opposite angles, is called a *diagonal.* (F.)

A quadrilateral is generally described by means of letters which are placed at each of the angles of the figure, as the quadrangle A B C D, or sometimes the letters indicating the opposite angles are alone employed, as the parallelogram A C.

Plane figures having more than four sides, are in general called *polygons*, and they receive other particular names according to the number of their sides or angles.

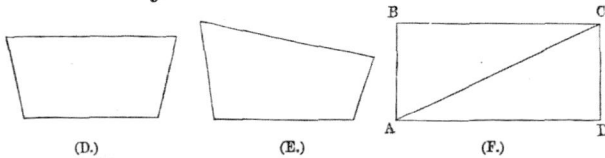

(G.)　　　(H.)　　　(I.)　　　(K.)

A *pentagon* is a polygon of five sides. (G.)

A *hexagon* is a polygon of six sides. (H.)

A *heptagon* is a polygon of seven sides. (I.)

An *octagon* is a polygon of eight sides. (K.)

A *nonagon* has nine, a *decagon* ten, an *undecagon* eleven, and a *dodecagon* twelve sides. Polygons that have more than twelve sides (except that of fifteen, which is called a *quindecagon*) are generally designated by the number of their sides.

A polygon is *regular* when it has all its sides equal, and all its angles equal, as in the above figure of the pentagon, hexagon, &c. It may be remarked that the equilateral triangle and the square, are both of them regular polygons of three and four sides respectively, and are sometimes called, the former a *trigon*, and the latter a *tetragon.*

An *irregular polygon* has its sides or angles unequal, or both, as in the figure which is called an *irregular pentagon.*

The *angle* of any regular polygon is that formed by the meeting of two of its sides.

The *centre* of a regular polygon is that point within it which is equidistant from similar points in each of the sides.

The *angle at the centre* is that which is formed by the meeting of two lines at the central point, which are drawn from the ends of one of the sides.

A *circle* is a plane figure bounded by one curved line, which is everywhere equally distant from a point within it called the *centre*. The space contained is the circle, the containing line is called the *circumference*; *b c d* is the circumference of the circle, and *a* the centre. It may not be improper to remark that the terms circle and circumference are frequently confused; thus we say, "Describe a circle from a given point," instead of saying, "Describe the circumference of a circle from a given point;" the circumference being the curved line thus described, everywhere equally distant from the centre; whereas the circle is, strictly speaking, the superficial space included within the circumference.

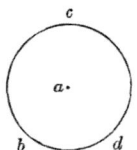

The *radius* of a circle is a straight line drawn from the centre to the circumference, as *b a* or *b c.* All the radii of a circle are equal.

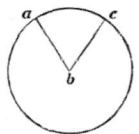

The *diameter* of a circle is a right line drawn through the centre, and terminated both ways by the circumference, as *a b.* The diameter of a circle is equal to twice the length of the radius.

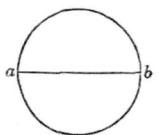

An *arc* of a circle is any part of the circumference, as *c e d* or *c f d*.

A *chord* is a straight line joining the extremities of any arc, as *c d*, which, it is to be observed, is equally that of the arc *c e d* or *c f d*, and the chord is said to subtend them. The diameter is the greatest chord of a circle, and it divides it into two equal parts called *semicircles*.

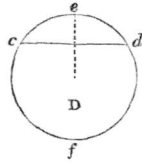

A *segment* is any part of a circle bounded by an arc and its chord, as *c e d* or *c f d*; each of these are segments into which the circle is divided by the chord *c d*.

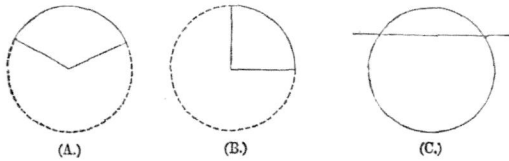

(A.)   (B.)   (C.)

A *sector* is any part of a circle bounded by an arc, and two radii drawn to its extremities. (A.)

A *quadrant*, or quarter of a circle, is a sector having a fourth part of the circumference for its arc, and its two radii are perpendicular to each other. (B.)

A *secant* is a straight line that cuts a circle, being drawn from a point without the circumference. (C.)

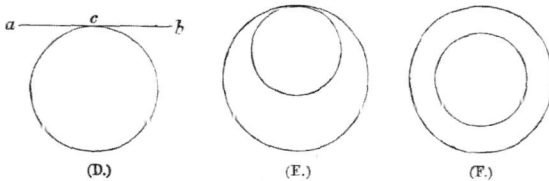

(D.)   (E.)   (F.)

A straight line which touches a circle without cutting it, is called a *tangent*, as *a b*, which touches the circle in *c*; and this point *c* is called the *point of contact*. (D.)

Circles may also be tangential, that is, when they have a single point of contact; and they may either touch each other externally or internally, as (E.)

Concentric circles are such as are described from the same centre. (F.)

Circles which are not described from the same centre, are said to be *eccentric* to one another.

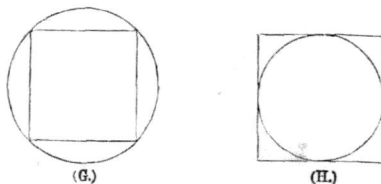

(G.)   (H.)

A right lined figure is *inscribed in a circle*, or the circle *circumscribes* it, when all the angular points of the figure are in the circumference of the circle. (G.)

A right lined figure circumscribes a circle, or the circle is inscribed in it, when all the sides of the figure touch the circumference of the circle. (H.)

" *Identical* figures, are such as have all the sides and all the angles of the one, respectively equal to all the sides and all the angles of the other, each to each ; so that if the one figure were applied to, or laid upon the other, all the sides of the one would exactly fall upon and cover all the sides of the other; the two becoming as it were but one and the same figure."

Similar figures have all the angles of the one equal to all the angles of the other, each to each ; and the sides about the equal angles, proportional.

PROBLEM 1.—At a given point in a straight line, to make an angle equal to a given angle.

Let E be a point in a straight line E F, at which it is required to make an angle equal to a given angle A B C. From the vertex B, with any radius B *g*, describe an arc of a circle meeting the sides B A and B C in points *g* and *h*. From the point E, with the same radius, describe an arc meeting E F in *k*, and of indefinite length towards *l*. From *k*, with a radius equal to the distance between the points *g* and *h*, describe an arc intersecting *k l* in *l*. The arc *k l* is thus made equal to *g h*. From E, draw a straight line through *l* towards D, then will the angle D E F be equal to the given angle A B C. In the solution of this problem, when the angle is very obtuse, it will be found advantageous to divide the arc which measures it into two parts, and to measure each of them successively upon the arc of construction ; by this means, the true point of intersection required, will be more distinctly seen than when the arcs cut each other at a very small angle. It must be remarked of the solution of the problem here given, that the character of the given angle has not been specified in the enunciation ; that is, it is not said whether it is to be considered as an acute or a reverse angle, or whether the greater or the lesser portion of the circumference of the circle that may be described from the vertex, and intercepted by the sides, is to be taken as its measure ; but the construction need not differ, since the distance *d e* of the extremities of the lesser and greater arcs is the same. This is the principle of an instrument made use of by all artizans, called a *bevel*, which is very convenient for the drawing and transference of angles. In its absence, the workman may verify his operations by

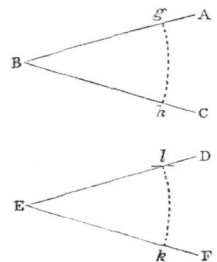

means of the above problem ; as, for instance, in the production of a many sided figure, say of six sides, all the angles being equal. Having drawn the figure on paper, or otherwise, and measured equal distances from an angle upon the sides containing it ; the same distances are measured, and marked upon the work, from the angle to be proved. The distance, then, between the two points on the drawing, may be taken by a pair of callipers, compasses, or other means at hand ; and if the corresponding distance on the work is the same, the angle is correct. If the reverse angle is greater, the marked points will be within the ends of the callipers ; and if less, beyond them.

PROBLEM 2.—At a given point in a straight line, to erect a perpendicular to it.

Let C be a given point in a straight line AB, at which it is required to erect a perpendicular to it. From C, measure upon A B equal distances, Cd and Ce, on each side of it. From d and e as centres, with any radius greater than Cd or Ce, describe arcs intersecting each other, as at f. From C draw a straight line through f. This is the perpendicular required.

PROBLEM 3.—From a given point, to let fall a perpendicular upon a given straight line.

Let C be a given point, from which it is required to let fall a perpendicular upon a straight line AB. From C as a centre, with any radius, describe an arc of a circle which will cut AB in two points, d and e. From d and e as centres, with any radius greater than the half of d e, describe intersecting arcs, as at f, on the other side of AB. A line drawn through the two points C and f, will be the perpendicular required. It is evident that the second point f, might be marked between C and the line, or beyond it, if necessary ; but it is generally best to find it on the side of AB, on which the given point is not placed, for the more distant the points are from one another, the less risk there is of making a considerable error in the angle, when the line is drawn.

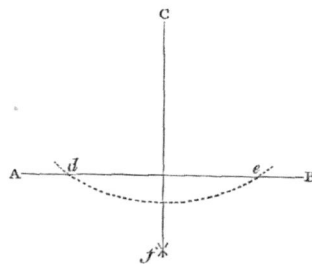

It may here be observed, that the perpendicular drawn to any line from any point, is the shortest distance between them.

PROBLEM 4.—From a given point, at, or nearly opposite to the extremity of a straight line, to let fall a perpendicular on it.

Let C be a given point, opposite to the extremity of a straight line A B, from which it is required to let fall a perpendicular on it. From any point e, in A B, as a centre, with a radius equal to the distance e C, describe an arc of a circle, extending it on both sides of A B. From f, any other point in A B, by preference between e and B, with a radius equal to f C, describe arcs, intersecting the first at points C and D. A straight line C D, drawn through C and D, will be the perpendicular required.

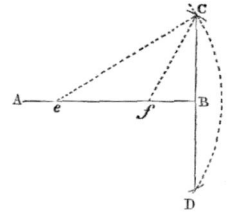

PROBLEM 5.—From the extremity of a straight line, to erect a perpendicular to it.

Let it be required to erect a perpendicular to a given straight line A B, from its extremity B. From any convenient point c, describe an arc of a circle greater than a semicircle, and cutting A B in d. Through d and c draw a straight line to meet the arc in a point e. Join e B by a straight line. This is the perpendicular required. Or,

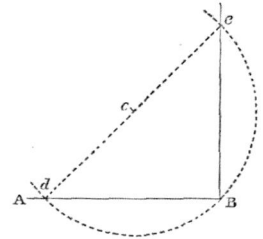

Let A B be the straight line, and A the point at which it is required to erect a perpendicular to it. From A, with any radius A E, describe an arc of a circle ; and from E, with the same radius, a second, intersecting the first in C. Through E and C draw a straight line of indefinite length ; and from C, with the radius A E, describe an arc intersecting it at the point D. Draw D A, which is the perpendicular required. Both these solutions are modifications of the same principle, namely, that the angle in a semicircle is a right angle ; that is, all the angles formed by lines drawn from the extremities of the diameter to meet in points in the circumference, are right angles. The draughtsman will do well to bear this principle in mind, as it is of such easy application in the drawing of lines perpendicular to one another. It is plain that the construction is applicable to any point in the line, whether situated at the extremity or not. The following is also a convenient method :—

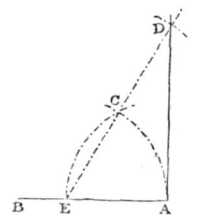

Let A B be the given line, and B the extremity at which it is required to erect a perpendicular to it. From B, with any radius B c, describe a large arc of a circle. From c, with the same radius, describe an arc intersecting it at d, and from d a second intersecting it at e; from e and d, with any radius, describe arcs intersecting each other at f, and draw f B, which is the perpendicular required.

PROBLEM 6.—To erect a perpendicular to a straight line by means of a scale of equal parts.

Let D be a scale of five equal parts, and let B be the extremity of a straight line A B, at which it is required to erect a perpendicular to it. From B, upon B A, make B e equal to three of the parts upon the scale. From B, with a radius equal to four of them, describe an arc of a circle towards C, and from e, with the whole five parts, describe an arc intersecting the first at a point C. A straight line drawn through C and B, is perpendicular to A B as required.

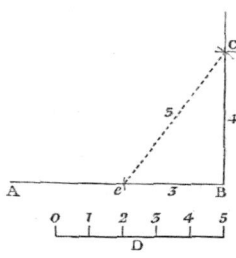

This method of drawing or proving perpendiculars will be found exceedingly convenient, either on a large scale or in the absence of the usual means; for it is plain that a temporary square may be readily constructed by the aid of the principle, and with great exactitude when the scale is good. The following is also a method of drawing perpendiculars that may be adopted with advantage, particularly on a large scale.

PROBLEM 7.—From a given point in a straight line, to erect a perpendicular to it by rectilineal construction, that is, by employment of the ruler alone.

Let A B be the given straight line, and C, a point in it, from which it is required by straight lines only to erect a perpendicular to it. In A B take any point D, and from it draw a line D E forming any angle with A B, and equal in length to the distance D C. Through E and C draw a straight line, and produce it beyond A B to G, until C G is equal to C D;

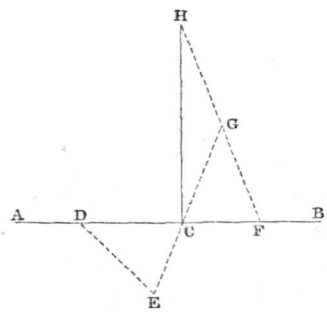

make C F equal to C E. Through F and G draw a line, and produce it beyond G to H, until G H is equal to F G or C D. A straight line drawn from C through H, will be perpendicular to A B as required.

It is generally by means of an instrument called a *square*, that lines are drawn perpendicularly, or at right angles with one another. Two of the edges or sides of this should meet each other, and make an angle of 90°. There are several forms of the instrument in use, according with the different purposes to which it is applied. In these it very often happens that, either from faulty construction or the effects of air and usage, the angle is not perfectly true. They ought therefore to be verified before employing them, where great exactitude is required, as without this, any error that exists is sure to become a source of serious inconvenience, frequently involving a very great amount of needless labour. In order to see whether a square is true, it is only necessary to draw a line, as A B, with a good rule or straight edge, upon a plane surface; the square is then adjusted as for drawing a perpendicular, and a line C D drawn, forming an angle A C D. The square being now turned, and placed in the angle B C D, if both the angles are found to be equal, the instrument is true; but if they are unequal, it is false; and it is easily seen whether its angle is greater or less than it ought to be, and also how much.

PROBLEM 8.—Through a given point, to draw a line parallel to a given line.

Let C be a point through which it is required to draw a line parallel to a given line A B. From C, draw a line meeting A B in a point d. From d, with the radius d C, describe an arc C e, meeting A B in e. From C as a centre, with the same radius, describe an arc d f, and make it equal to the arc C e. Through C and f draw a straight line. This line is parallel to A B as required. This solution of the problem depends on a property of parallel lines, that they make equal alternate angles with a line which intersects them; that is, if C d is a line intersecting the parallel lines A B and f C, the angles f C d and C d B, are equal. Hence, if the point C were at such a distance from A B as to render it inconvenient to employ the line C d as a radius for the arcs of construction, it would be sufficient to make the alternate angles equal by the employment of a shorter radius. Otherwise—

Let A B be the given line, and C the given point through which a line parallel to it is required to be drawn. From C, describe an arc touching A B in e, from any point d in A B; with the same radius C e, describe an arc as at f, and through C draw a straight line touching this arc at f, which will be the parallel line required. Otherwise—

This problem may be solved by rectilineal construction, that is, by means of the ruler alone.

Let it be required to draw a line through a given point C, parallel to a line A B. From C draw a straight line to intersect A B in any point D, and produce it until D E is equal to D C. From E draw another line to intersect A B at any point F, and produce the line to G, until F G is equal to F E. Through C and G draw a straight line. This line is parallel to A B. This is an exceedingly convenient method of drawing parallel lines, especially on a large scale.

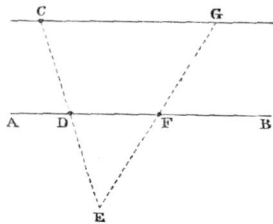

PROBLEM 9.—To draw a straight line parallel to a given line at a given distance from it.

Let it be required to draw a straight line parallel to a given straight line A B, at a distance from it equal to m n. In the given line A B, take any two points e and f as centres, and from them, with a radius equal to m n, describe the arcs g and h; a line C D drawn to touch these arcs without cutting them, will be parallel to A B as required.

The principle here employed, is one of constant recurrence in the different methods adopted for the production of parallel lines; namely, that the perpendicular distance between parallel lines remains constantly the same. A workman will draw, with great precision upon his work, a line parallel to one of its edges at a given distance, by means of a rule held firmly in one hand, while a pencil is kept by the other at the free end, and both are moved along and guided by the edge. From the above principle, it will be seen that every thing during the drawing of the line must occupy the same relative position, otherwise the perpendicular distance will vary, and the lines would not be parallel. This is also the principle of the carpenter's gauge, by which a much surer result is obtained, from the comparative immovability of the parts. The various kinds of planes

by which different mouldings are produced, are also examples of the production of parallel lines dependent on the same principle.

PROBLEM 10.—To find a point that shall be at two given distances from two given straight lines.

Let A B and C D be the two given lines, and let it be required to find the point that shall be at a distance from A B, equal to m n, and from C D, equal to o p. Parallel with A B, and at a distance from it equal to m n, draw a line e f (Prob. 9), and also a line g h parallel to C D, at a distance from it equal to o p. The point E, where these lines intersect each other, is that sought, being evidently at the given distances from the lines.

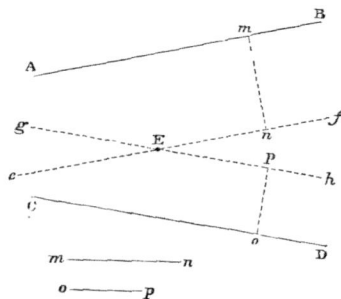

PROBLEM 11.—Through a given point to draw a line, to form an angle with a given line, which shall be equal to a given angle.

Let C be a point through which it is required to draw a line, to form an angle with a given line A B, which shall be equal to a given angle D e B. Join C and e by a straight line from e, with any convenient radius e f, describe an arc f g, between the lines e D and e C. From C, with the same radius, describe an arc F G, equal to f g, and on the other side of C e. Through C and G draw a line to meet A B in a point E; then is the angle C E B equal to the given angle D e B, and the side E C is drawn through the point C, as required. Here D e and C E have been made parallel, they are consequently intersected by A B, so that D e B and C E B are corresponding angles, and therefore equal.

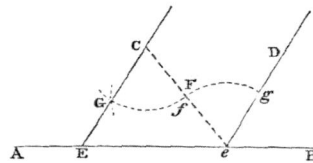

PROBLEM 12.—To find the middle point of a given straight line, or to divide it into two equal parts.

Let A B be the given straight line. From A and B, the extremities of the given line, as centres, with any convenient radius which is evidently greater than the half of it, describe arcs of circles intersecting each other at points C and D, on opposite sides of A B. Through C and D draw

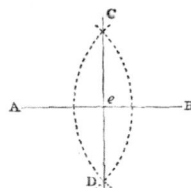

a straight line ; this will intersect A B at a point *e,* which is its middle point, or the parts A *e* and B *e,* into which it is divided, are equal. The two points C and D might also be determined on the same side of A B, if convenient ; but the method given is the shorter, when practicable. When A B is of a length to render the construction inconvenient, equal parts may be marked off from each end of the line, and the portion remaining between them bisected ; the middle of this part is the middle of the whole line.—Many workmen are in the habit of resolving this Problem by trials with the compass, until a distance is found which may nearly be the half of the line ; but this process is certainly longer than the geometric construction, and the result never so exact, since, after a few attempts to save time, he generally rests satisfied with an approach to the true measure.

PROBLEM 13.—To bisect a given angle, that is, to divide it into two equal parts.

Let it be required to divide a given angle A B C, into two equal parts.
From the vertex B, with any radius B *d,* describe an arc *d e,* meeting the sides B A and B C in points *d* and *e,* respectively.
From *d* and *e* as centres, with any radius, describe arcs intersecting each other as at *f.* A straight line B D drawn through B and *f,* will divide the given angle into two equal angles A B D and C B D, as required. It is evident that by repeating the process of bisection, the angle may be divided into 4, 8, 16, &c., parts, or into any number which is the product of two, multiplied repeatedly into itself. Otherwise—

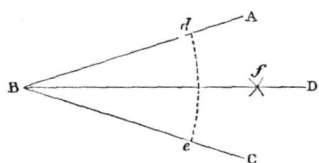

The Problem may be solved by rectilineal construction, or by the ruler alone :—

Let B A C be the given angle which it is required to divide into two equal angles. Upon A B, one of the sides, mark any two points D and E. Upon A C, make A F equal to A D, and A G to A E. Join D G and F E by straight lines ; these will intersect each other at a point H. A straight line drawn through A and H, will divide the angle B A C into two equal angles, B A H and C A H.

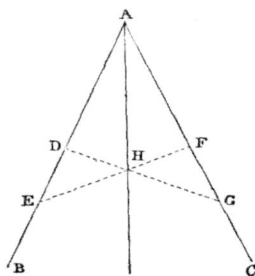

This latter method of dividing an angle will be found useful occasionally, when it is necessary to operate on a large scale ; two cords, of any kind, being substituted for the intersecting lines.

PROBLEM 14.—To trisect a right angle, or to divide it into three equal parts.

Let A B C be a right angle. From the vertex B, with any radius B *d,* describe an arc or quadrant, meeting the sides B A and B C in points *d* and *g.* From the point *d,* with the same radius, describe an arc intersecting *d g* in a point *f* ; and from *g,* with the same radius, an arc intersecting it at a point *e.* Straight lines drawn from B, through the points *e* and *f,* will divide the right angle A B C into three equal parts, as required.

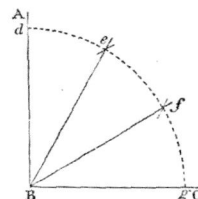

It is evident, that, as a right angle contains 90°, and the radius of a circle is the chord of the sixth part of the circumference, equal to 60°, the difference, or 30°, is the third part of the quadrant by which a right angle is measured.

It must be observed that the solution of the general problem to divide any given angle into three equal parts, cannot be effected by a geometric construction produced by the ruler and compass alone. Instruments have, however, been invented by which this may be effected, but the workman will probably find it a more convenient method to employ careful trials with the compass for this purpose, taking care to measure the third part of the arc which measures the angle, and *not* of the chord of that arc, as is very commonly done.

PROBLEM 15.—Upon a given straight line, to construct an equilateral triangle.

Let A B be a given straight line, on which it is required to construct an equilateral triangle. From the extremities A and B of A B as centres, with a radius equal to A B, describe arcs of circles intersecting each other at a point C. Draw straight lines C A and C B. Then A B C is an equilateral triangle.

PROBLEM 16.—Upon a given base line to make an isosceles triangle, each of whose other two sides shall be equal to a given line.

Let it be required to construct an isosceles triangle upon a given base line A B, and each of the other sides to be equal to a given line *m n.* From A and B as centres, with a radius equal to *m n,* describe intersecting arcs at C. Draw straight lines C A and C B. Then is A C B the isosceles triangle required.

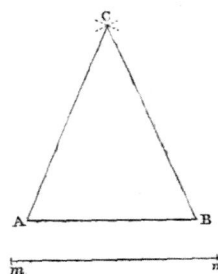

PROBLEM 17.—To construct a triangle, of which the sides shall be equal to three given straight lines, any two of which are greater than the third.

Let it be required to construct a triangle whose sides shall be equal to three given straight lines, *ab, ac,* and *c b.* Draw a straight line A B, and make it equal to *a b.* From A as a centre, with a radius equal to *ac,* describe an arc of a circle towards C; and from B, with a radius equal to *bc,* describe an arc intersecting the first at a point C. Draw straight lines C A and C B. Then is A B C the triangle required.

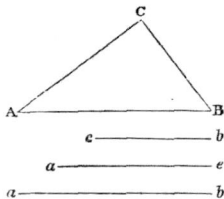

It may here be noticed with respect to triangles, that they are permanent in their figures, that is, the sides which determine it will form one figure only; and in practice, no force applied to a constructed triangle, if loosely attached at the angles, will change its form, unless one that destroys some part of the material of which it is composed.

PROBLEM 18.—To construct a triangle of which one angle and the two containing sides are given.

Let it be required to construct a triangle of which two of the sides are given equal to *ab* and *bc,* and the angle *a'b'c'* which is contained by them. Draw a straight line B C, and make it equal to *bc,* one of the given lines. At the point B in it, make an angle *a'* B C, equal to the given angle *a'b'c'* (Prob. 1), and produce the side B *a'* to A until it is equal to *b a.* Join A C by a straight line, which is the third side of the figure, and the required triangle is constructed.

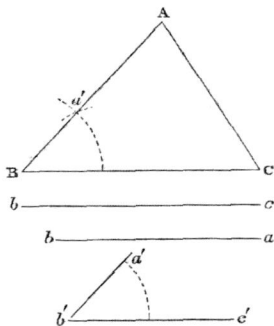

PROBLEM 19.—To construct a triangle of which one side is given, and the two adjacent angles.

Let *a b* be the given side, and *cab* and *cba* the two adjacent angles given; it is required to construct the triangle. Draw a straight line A B, equal to *a b.* At A make an angle *c'* A B, equal to *c a b* (Prob. 1), and at B make an angle *c''* B A on the same side of A B, and equal to *c b a.* Produce the sides A *c'* and B *c''* of these angles until they meet in a point C. Then is A B C the triangle required.

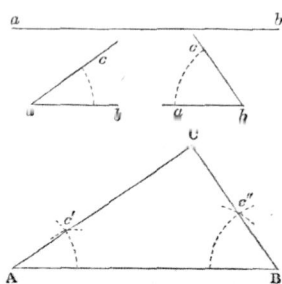

PROBLEM 20.—To construct a triangle of which a side is given, and two angles, one of which is opposite to the given side.

Let it be required to construct a triangle of which *a b* is a given side, *c a b* and *a c b* two angles, of which *a c b* is to be placed opposite to the given side *a b* in the triangle. Draw a straight line A B, equal to *a b,* and at the extremity A make an angle *c'* A B, equal to *c a b* (Prob. 1). Produce the side A *c'* indefinitely towards D, and at *e,* any point in A D, and on the side of it towards A B, make an angle A *ef,* equal to *a c b* (Prob. 1). Lastly, through B draw a straight line parallel to the side *e f* (Prob. 8), meeting A D in a point C. Then is A B C the triangle required.

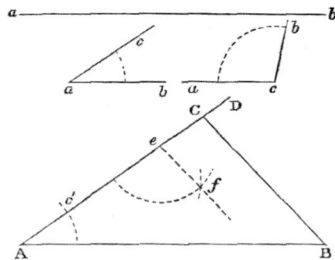

PROBLEM 21.— To construct a triangle of which two of the sides are given, and an angle opposite to one of them.

Let it be required to construct a triangle of which the two given sides are *a b* and *b c,* of which *b c* is greater than *a b,* and let *a b c* be the given angle which is to be placed opposite to one or other of the given sides. This problem evidently divides itself into two cases, according as the angle is to be placed opposite to the greater or the lesser line. First, let the angle be opposite to the greater line *b c.* Draw a straight line A B, equal to *a b* the shorter line. At A, one of its extremities, make an angle *c'* A B, equal to the given angle *a b c* (Prob. 1). Produce the side A *c'* indefinitely towards D, and from B as a centre, with a radius equal to *b c,* describe an arc intersecting A D in a point C. Join C B by a straight line. Then is A B C the triangle required.

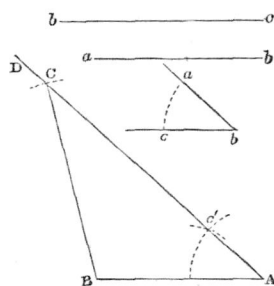

Next, let the angle be placed opposite to the lesser line *a b.* In this case, the construction affords two solutions. Draw a straight line B C, equal to *b c,* and at one extremity C, make an angle *a'* C B, equal to the given angle *a b c* (Prob. 1). Produce the side C *a'* towards D indefinitely. From B as a centre, with the radius equal to *a b*, describe an arc of a circle, which will intersect C D in points A and A'. Join B A and B A' by straight lines. Then each of the triangles A B C and A' B C, have two of their sides, A B, B C of the one, and A' B, B C of the other, respectively equal to the given lines *a b* and *b c*, and the angle at C made equal to *a b c*, opposite to a side B A or B A', equal to the lesser line *a b*.

In the latter part of this problem, it is assumed that a triangle may be constructed with the given quantities. Sides and angles may be proposed with which no triangle could be formed on the conditions given; when this is the case, the construction will always show it.

PROBLEM 22.—The hypothenuse, and one side of a right angled triangle being given, to find the other side.

Let A B be the hypothenuse, and C D the side. Bisect the hypothenuse, A B, in *e* (Prob. 12); from *e* as a centre, with a radius equal to *e* A, or *e* B, describe the arc C B. From A as a centre, with a radius equal to the length of the given line C D, describe another arc, intersecting the former at C. Join C A, and C B; then C B will be the required side of the right angled triangle A B C.

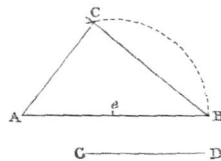

The last eight Problems contain all the methods of constructing triangles that are of any importance to the cabinet maker, they may be variously applied, and some of them will be found very useful in the construction of plans, &c., particularly when any of the sides are interrupted, so as to prevent a direct measure being taken. It may have been observed, that in the Problems, certain of the parts being given, the rest were derived from them; this proceeds from the constant dependence of the parts of triangles upon one another. Of these relations, the most remarkable and important is a property of the angular magnitudes, that their sum is always equal to two right angles, or 180°, neither more nor less. This is common to all triangles, however they may vary in form. A triangle consists of six parts, namely, three sides and three angles; but as one of the angles is always the result of the other two, the number of variable parts is only five; any three of these being ascertained, the triangle may be completely described, as seen in the Problems.

PROBLEM 23.—To make a triangle similar to a given triangle upon a given line, which is to correspond to one of the sides indicated.

Let A B C be the given triangle, and H K the given line which is to correspond to the side A B in the triangle. From the angular points A and B of the given triangle, with any radius, describe the arcs *d e* and *f g*. From the extremity H of H K, with the same radius, describe an arc *m n*, and make it equal to *d e*. From K, with the same radius, describe an arc *o p*, and make it equal to *f g*. From H, through the point *n*, draw a straight line; and from K, through the point *p*, draw also a straight line; these, being produced, will meet in a point L; then the triangle H L K will be similar to the triangle A B C, with the side H K corresponding to the side A B, as required. It is evident, that if the given line H K were equal to A B, the two triangles would be identical, and the construction would then be much simpler, being that of Problem 17, in which the triangle is constructed, the three sides being given. The following, also, is a very useful method:—

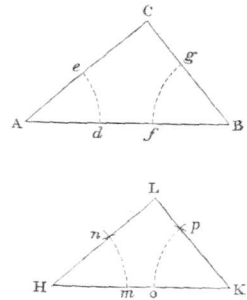

Let A B C be the given triangle, and C D the given line which is to correspond with B C in the triangle. From C draw C E parallel to B A, and from D draw D E, parallel to C A (Prob. 8), producing both the lines until they meet in the point E. Then is C D E a triangle similar to the given triangle A B C, and C D in it corresponds to the side B C, as required. Here C D has been made a continuation of the side B C of the triangle; but not necessarily so, for it may be placed anywhere in the same plane, provided it is parallel with B C, and the construction completed as in the Problem; this will be found of great convenience in practice. A remarkable property of the right angled triangle may here be pointed out, which is, that if a line be drawn from the right angle perpendicularly upon the hypothenuse, the triangle will be divided into two triangles, which are similar to one another, and to the whole triangle.

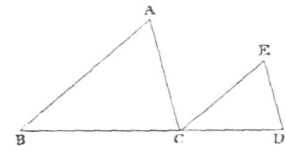

Upon the construction of similar triangles depends, in general, the solution of those Problems in which proportions are found.

PROBLEM 24.—To divide a given line into any number of equal parts.

Let B C be the given line, and let it be required to divide it into five equal parts. From one extremity B, draw a line B A, forming any angle with B C, but, by preference, acute. Upon B A, measure five equal parts from B to A; join draw a line; also through b' and B; these lines, produced, will meet in a point F. Draw lines e' F, d' F, and c' F; these will intersect A B at points C, D, and E, and divide it into parts that are correspondingly proportional to those of ab; that is, A B : ab :: A C : ac :: C D : cd, &c., as required; the corresponding parts bearing the same proportion among themselves that the whole lines have.

PROBLEM 29.—To divide a given line in any given ratio.

Let it be required to divide a given line A B into parts that shall have the ratio to one another that ac has to bc. From one extremity A of A B, and at any angle, draw a line A c'' equal to ac. On the other side of A B, from B draw a line B c' parallel to A c'' (Prob. 8), and equal to bc. Join c' c'' by a straight line; this will intersect A B at a point D, and divide it into parts A D and D B, which have the ratio to each other that ac has to bc, or A D : D B :: ac : bc.

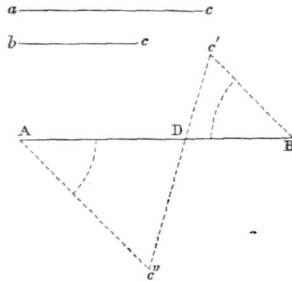

The ratio may be given in number. Let $ac : bc$ be as 4 : 3. The parallel lines being drawn as before, but of indefinite length, four equal parts must be measured upon A c'', and three of the same parts upon B c'; the construction is then completed by joining the extremities of the measured parts.

Should it be required to solve the problem by number, the proportion stands: As the sum of the terms of the given ratio is to the whole line in number, so is one of the terms of the ratio to the corresponding part of the divided line. Let the ratio be as 4 to 2, and let the given line or number be 9; then, as the sum of 4 and 2, or 6, is to 9, so is 4 to 6, or 2 to 3; consequently, 6 and 3 are the numbers sought. The workman will do well to exercise himself in these arithmetical solutions of the problems of proportion, as well as in their geometrical construction, for they are of great importance in the course of his operations, as no work can be correctly enlarged or diminished without their aid.

PROBLEM 30.—To find the centre of a given circle.

Let A C B D be the given circle, the centre of which it is required to find. Draw any chord A B, and at its middle point raise a perpendicular to it (Prob. 12), producing it both ways to meet the circumference of the circle in points C and D. This straight line C D is the diameter of the circle; and its middle point

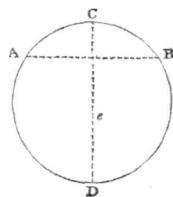

is the centre. Bisect C D therefore in e (Prob. 12), which is the centre sought.

PROBLEM 31.—To describe a circle, the circumference of which shall pass through three given points that are not in the same straight line.

Let it be required to describe a circle that shall pass through three given points, A, B, and C, which are not in the same straight line. Connect the points by two lines in any way, as A B and B C. Raise perpendiculars to the middle of each (Prob. 12), and produce these until they meet in a point D. This point is the centre of the circle, which is to be described with a radius equal to the distance between it and any one of the points, as D A, D B, or D C.

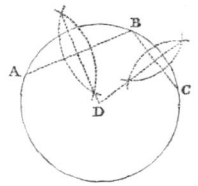

PROBLEM 32.—The arc of a circle being given, to complete the circle.

Let it be required to complete the circle of which A B C is the arc given. Mark any point B in the arc, and join B A and B C by straight lines. Raise perpendiculars to the middle of each of these lines (Prob. 12), which, being produced, will intersect each other in a point D. From D, with the radius D A, D B, or D C, describe the remaining portion of the circle. This is evidently another form of the preceding problem.

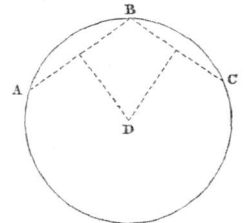

PROBLEM 33.—To divide a given arc of a circle into two equal parts, or to bisect it.

Let it be required to divide a given arc A B C into two equal parts. Draw the chord A C, and raise a perpendicular to its middle point D (Prob. 12). This, being produced, will cut the arc at a point B, and divide it into two equal parts, B A and B C.

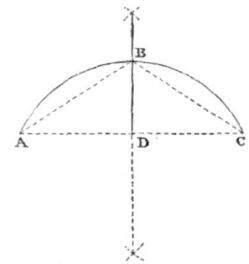

PROBLEM 34.—The arc of a circle being given, to draw perpendiculars to it from any points in it without finding the centre.

Let A B be the given arc; and first let e be a point in it, remote from the extremities, from which it is required to raise a perpendicular to the arc. On each side of e, measure equal

and C G, from C to L, M, and N, respectively. Join K L, L M, M N, and N K by straight lines; then is K L M N a square constructed about the point C, with a side equal to A B, as required.

PROBLEM 38.—To construct a rectangle whose sides shall be equal to two given straight lines.

Let A B and C D be the given straight lines. Draw a line E F equal to A B, and at each of its extremities, E and F, raise E H and F G perpendicular to it (Prob. 5), and equal to C D. Join G H by a straight line. Then is E F G H the rectangle required.

PROBLEM 39.—To construct a rhomboid with two given straight lines, and with an angle equal to a given angle.

Let A and B be the given sides, and H C I the given angle. Draw a straight line D E equal to A, and at one extremity D, make an angle L D E equal to the given angle H C I (Prob. 1). Produce the side D L indefinitely; and from D, with a radius equal to B, describe an arc intersecting it at F. From F as a centre, with the radius A or D E, describe an arc towards G; and from E, with the radius B or D F, another arc intersecting it at a point G. Join F G and G E by straight lines. Then is D E G F the rhomboid required, whose sides are respectively equal to A and B, and with an angle equal to the given angle.

PROBLEM 40.—To construct a rhombus or lozenge, of which the diagonals are given.

Let a b and c d be the given diagonals. Draw a straight line A B equal to a b, and a straight line F G, intersecting A B at right angles at its middle point E (Prob. 12). From A draw a line A H, parallel to E F (Prob. 8) and equal to c d. Join H B by a straight line; this will intersect F G at a point C. Upon E G, make E D equal to E C. Join A C, B D, and A D; then is A C B D the rhombus required.

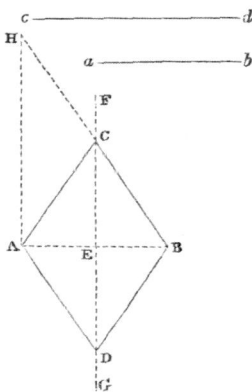

PROBLEM 41.—To construct a trapezium, the four sides being given, and one angle.

Let a b, a c, c d, and b d be the given sides, and c a b the given angle. Draw a straight line A B equal to a b, and at one extremity A, make an angle c' A B equal to c a b (Prob. 1). Produce the side A c' to C, until A C is equal to a c. From C, with a radius equal to c d, describe an arc towards D, and from B, with a radius equal to b d, describe another intersecting it at a point D. Join C D and B D; then is A C D B the trapezium required. It is plain, that any pair of the sides may be made to contain the angle, and any order assumed for the succession of the sides. It may be observed, that it is a necessary condition for the possibility of constructing the figure, that any three of the sides shall be greater than the fourth.

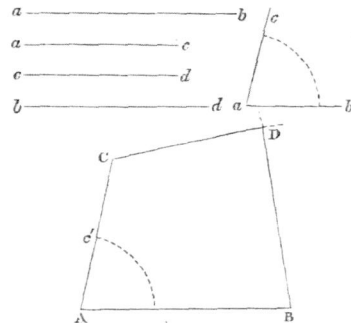

PROBLEM 42.—To construct a trapezoid, the four sides being given.

Let a b, c d, a c, and b d be the given sides, of which let a b and c d be parallel in the figure. Draw A B equal to a b, and upon it, from B, measure c d from B to F. From A, with a radius equal to a c, describe an arc of a circle towards C; and from F, with a radius equal to b d, describe a second arc intersecting the first at a point C, and join C A; this line is equal to c a. From B draw a line parallel to C F (Prob. 8), and equal to b d. Join C D, which is thus parallel to A B and equal to c d; then is A C D B the trapezoid required. In the solution of this problem with the lines given, any two of the sides may be made parallel; but this cannot be done with all the quantities that might be proposed, the necessary condition being that, of the given lines, the difference of those that can be made parallel shall be greater than the difference between the other two sides.*

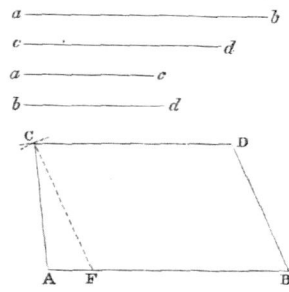

* It will easily be seen, by trial, that, as these differences approach to equality, the distance between the lines that are parallel diminishes; until, upon becoming equal, the possibility of construction ceases. It is also obvious, as in the last Problem, that any three of the lines shall be greater than the fourth.

PROBLEM 43.—An isosceles triangle being given, to draw a line parallel to the base line, so that it shall be equal to each of the equal parts of the other two sides intercepted between it and the base line.

Let A B C be the given triangle. From any point D, in A C, draw a line D E parallel to A B, and equal to D A (Prob. 8). Through A and E draw a line, and produce it to meet C B in a point F. From F draw a line F G parallel to A B. This line is equal to each of the parts G A and F B, of C A and C B, respectively, which are intercepted between it and the base. It is manifest, that a line may be drawn parallel to the base line, that shall have any given ratio to the parts intercepted between it and the base. For this purpose, the line of construction D E must be made in the given ratio to D A, and the construction completed as in the Problem.

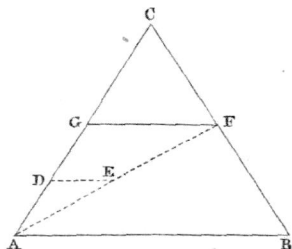

PROBLEM 44.—Upon a given line, to construct a trapezoid, the other three sides of which shall each be equal to a given line, which is greater than the third part of that given.

Let A B be the given straight line, and c d the given side. Bisect A B in E, and c d in e (Prob. 12). From E, on A B, make E C and E D on each side of it equal to the half of c d. From C and D raise perpendiculars to A B (Prob. 2), of indefinite length. From A and B, with a radius equal to c d, describe arcs intersecting the perpendiculars in points F and G, respectively. Draw A F, F G, and B G; then is A B G F the trapezoid required.

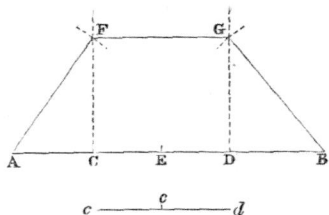

All the quadrilaterals possess the remarkable property that, if the sides are bisected, and the successive middle points connected by straight lines, a parallelogram of some sort is produced. That is, let A B C D be a trapezium, each of whose sides is bisected in points E, F, G and H, respectively; these points being joined by straight lines, a parallelogram E F G H is produced. It may be observed, that the area of this parallelogram is the half of that of the trapezium.

The application of the diagonal in quadrilaterals is of great importance in most structures, since it confers stability. If any figure is constructed of four pieces of wood, or other material, connected at the angles by means of joints, it is plain that its character may be changed, the parts being movable; but if a diagonal piece is added, the figure is immediately converted into two triangles, each of which being, as before observed (Prob. 17), permanent in its form, their combination is also permanent. This is a method of rendering work firm that is familiar to every workman. The change that takes place in the form of a parallelogram by the parts being made movable, is applied in the construction of a kind of parallel rule much made use of in drawing.

The diagonal lines afford a valuable means of verifying work. In the square and the rectangle, it must be recollected that the diagonals are equal. In the parallelograms that are oblique angled, the diagonals are unequal; the greater being opposite to the greater angles. The two diagonals of any parallelogram mutually bisect each other; and in those that are equilateral, as the square and the lozenge, the diagonals intersect each other at right angles.

PROBLEM 45.—Two straight lines convergent to an inaccessible point being given, and a point between, or beyond them, to draw a line through the given point that shall, if produced, meet them at their point of convergence.

Let A B and C D be the converging lines, and E a point between them, through which it is required to draw a line to converge with them. Through E draw a straight line M E F, to meet A B and C D in points M and F. Parallel to M F (Prob. 8), at any convenient distance, draw a line M'G, meeting A B and C D at points M' and G. Find a fourth proportional to M' G in the ratio of M F to M E, that is, make M F : M E : : M' G : M' H (Prob. 25). Through H and E draw a straight line; this line will converge with A B and C D towards their point of meeting. When the given point E' is beyond the lines, the construction is similar; or the proportion is M' F : M G : : M E : M H. Otherwise—

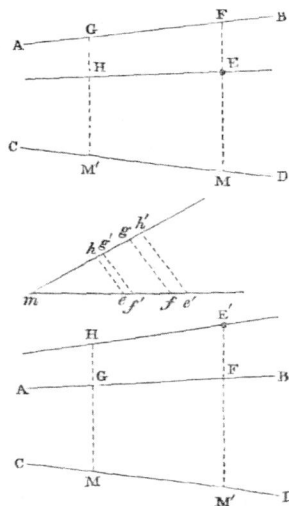

Let A B and C D be the convergent lines, and E a point through which it is required to draw a line that shall converge with them. In A B, take any convenient points A and G, and F any point in C D. Join A F and F G by straight lines. Join also A E and E G. From K, or any point in A B, at a convenient distance from G, draw K H, parallel to A F (Prob. 8), meeting C D in H. From H draw H L parallel to F G, meeting A B in L. From L draw a line L M parallel to G E, and from K a line parallel to A E, meeting L M in a point N. Through E and N draw a straight line; this line converges with A B and C D toward their inaccessible point of meeting. The construction is similar when the given point is beyond the lines.

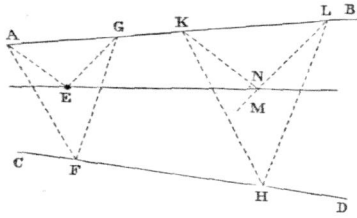

PROBLEM 46.—Two convergent lines being given, which would meet, if produced, in an inaccessible point, to find a point in each that shall be equidistant from that point.

Let A B and C D be the two convergent lines. From E, any point in A B raise E F perpendicular to it (Prob. 2), and meeting C D in F. From F raise F G perpendicular to C D, meeting A B in G. Bisect the angle E F G (Prob. 13) by the straight line F H, meeting A B in H. Then are F and H points equidistant from the point in which A B and C D would meet, if produced, to their inaccessible point of meeting.

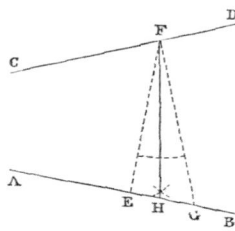

PROBLEM 47.—Two convergent lines being given, which would meet, if produced, in an inaccessible point, to draw a line between them that would bisect the angle formed by them at the point of meeting.

Let A B and C D be the convergent lines. Let E F be drawn joining the points E and F, which are equidistant from the point of meeting of the given lines (Prob. 46), and draw a line H I perpendicular to its middle point G (Prob. 12). This line, if produced with the convergent lines, would bisect the angle formed by them at their point of meeting, as required.

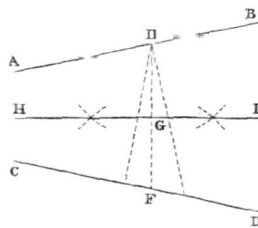

The Problem may also be solved by the following method :—

Let C H and C B be the convergent lines. From H, any point in C H, raise H G perpendicular to it (Prob. 2), and of any convenient length. From E, any point in C B, raise E F a perpendicular to it, making it equal to H G. Through G draw a line parallel to C H (Prob. 8), and through F a line parallel to C B; these lines, being produced, will intersect each other in a point S. From S with any sufficient radius, describe an arc A B, meeting the given lines in points A and B. Bisect this arc (Prob. 33), that is, from A and B, with any radius, describe intersecting arcs at D. Through D and S draw a straight line. This line, if produced, would bisect the angle formed by the given lines at their point of meeting.

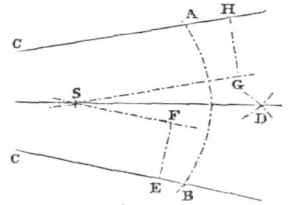

There are many other methods by which lines may be drawn to inaccessible points; those given are the simplest, and will be found sufficient. The cabinet-maker will find them available in perspective drawing, in which they are of great importance.

PROBLEM 48.—Three points, not in a straight line, being given, to find the altitude of the arc of a circle that will pass through them, the position of the chord being determined, but without having the centre.

Let it be required to find the altitude of an arc of a circle that will pass through three given points A, B, and C, the line joining A and C being the chord. Draw straight lines B A and B C between the points, and bisect the angle A B C thus formed, by the straight line B D (Prob. 13). Raise E F perpendicular to the middle point E, of A C (Prob. 12). At g, any point in E F, make an angle E g m, equal to A B D, the half of the angle A B C (Prob. 1). Through A, draw a line parallel to g m (Prob. 8), which will meet E F at a point F. Then E F is the required altitude of the arc. It is obviously necessary to determine the position of the chord, since any of the lines forming the triangle A B C may be assumed as such, and thus affect the altitude. This Problem, as well as the two following, depends on a property of segments of circles, that they contain one angle and no other; that is, if lines are drawn from the extremities of an arc to meet in any points in that arc, all the angles formed by them will be equal. In the case of the angle contained by a semicircle, this has already been pointed out, and that it contains a right angle; any segment which is less than a semicircle, contains an obtuse

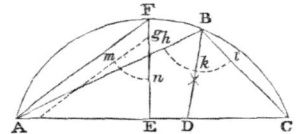

angle; and in any segment which is greater than a semicircle, the angle contained is acute.

PROBLEM 49.—Three points not in a straight line being given, to find a number of other points in the arc of the circle that will pass through them, without employment of the centre.

Let A, B, and C, be the three given points, and let A C be the chord line. Join A B and B C by straight lines. From A and C, with the same radius, describe arcs *d e* and *f g*, making *d h* equal to *k g*, and *k f* equal to *h e*. Divide *h e* and *k f* each into the same number of equal parts; divide also *d h* and *k g* into the same number of equal parts. From A draw a straight line through the first point of section from *d*, upon the arc *d h*; and from C draw a line through the first part of section from *g*, in the arc *g k*: these lines will intersect each other in a point *l*, which is one of the points required. Proceed in the same manner with the other points of section on the arcs, taking them successively from *d* towards *e*, in the arc *d e*, and from *g* towards *f*, in the arc *g f*; other points in the arc will thus be found, as *m*, *n*, and *o*, and means may be taken for drawing the curve. The most expeditious and accurate method is probably by means of a thin slip of wood. The points having been found, nails may be placed in them, and the slip of wood bent round these; the curve may then be traced on the side of it next to the nails. It may be observed that, if the whole arcs *d e* and *f g* are divided into equal parts, the points of the arc so found will be equidistant.

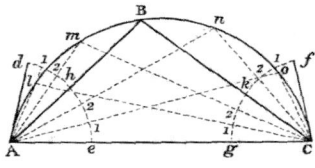

PROBLEM 50.—An arc of a circle being given, to find a number of points in the supplementary part of the circle, without having the centre.

Let A B C be the given arc. Draw the chord A C, and from A and C draw lines to meet in any point B, of the arc. At the extremities A and C of A C, make angles C A *k* and A C *m*, each equal to A B C; that is, make the arcs *h k* and *l m* each equal to *f g*. Divide the arcs *h k* and *l m*, each into the same number of equal parts. Lines drawn from A, through the points of section in the arc *h k*, in succession, from *k* to *h*; and lines drawn from C through the points of section in the arc *l m*, in succession,

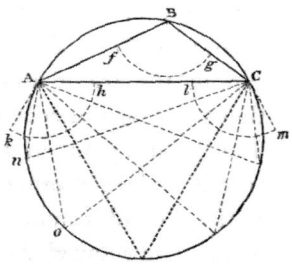

from *l* to *m*, will intersect each other at points *n*, *o*, &c., which are points in the circumference of the circle of which A B C is an arc.

PROBLEM 51.—From a given circle, to cut off a segment that shall contain an angle equal to a given angle.

Let A B D be the given circle, and *a b c* the given angle. At any point B in the circle, draw B C, a tangent to it; and at B make an angle C B *e*, equal to *a b c* (Prob. 1); produce the side B *e* to meet the circumference in a point A; then is A D B a segment of a circle that will contain an angle equal to that given. The reason of this is, that the angles formed by a tangent, and a chord drawn to the same point in a circle, are equal to those in the alternate segments, into which the circle is divided by the chord; that is, the angles A B C and A D B are equal; and if the tangent C B were produced from B, the angle which it would make with the chord B A would be equal to that which is contained by the segment A B of the circle. This principle has been applied in the last Problem.

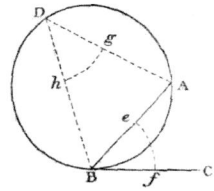

PROBLEM 52.—To describe the arc of a circle, of which the chord and the height or versed sine are given.

Let *a b* be the given chord, and *c d* the given height of the arc. Draw A B equal to *a b*, and D C perpendicular to its middle point D, and equal to *d c* (Prob 2). Produce the line also from D indefinitely towards E. Join A C by a straight line, and bisect it (Prob. 12) by a line drawn perpendicular to it, producing it to meet D E in a point F. Then is F C or F A the radius of the circle, of which the required arc is a part; and it may be described from F as a centre. Otherwise—

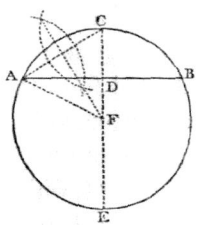

Let *a c* be the given chord, and *d b* the given height of the arc. Draw A C equal to *a c*, and bisect it by a line drawn perpendicular to it, making D B equal to *d b*, and the part D E of indefinite length. Join A and B by a straight line. At the extremity A of A B, make an angle B A *k*, equal to the angle A B E (Prob. 1),

d

187

intervening space, then the middle point of the line which joins them is the centre sought. When that distance is greater or less than the half of the distance of the points from each other, the centre will be either between the line which joins the points and the given line, or beyond them.

PROBLEM 63.—To describe two circles, with given radii, that shall touch each other, and also a given straight line.

Let it be required to describe circles with radii respectively equal to C D and E F, which shall touch each other, and also a given line A B. From any point g in AB, raise g k a perpendicular to it (Prob. 2), and equal to C D, the greater of the two given radii. Upon g h measure E F from g to k, and through k draw k m parallel to A B (Prob. 8). From h, with a radius equal to the sum of C D and E F, describe an arc of a circle intersecting k m in a point m. From h, with a radius equal to C D, describe a circle; and from m, with the radius E F, also describe a circle. These two circles will touch each other, and also the given line A B, as required.

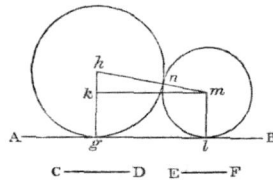

PROBLEM 64.—Two circles being given, one of which is not contained by the other, to draw straight lines that shall be tangents to both.

Let the given circles be described about centres A and B, of which that about A is the greater. Draw any radius A H of the greater circle, and

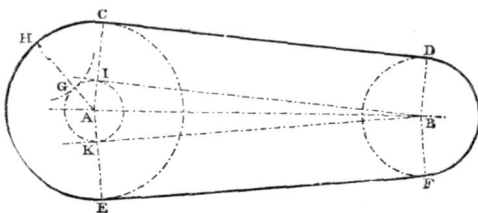

upon it from H, make H G equal to B D, the radius of the lesser. From centre A, with the radius A G, describe a circle. From B, draw tangents B I and B K to this circle (Prob. 55), and from A, draw radii through the points I and K, to meet the greater circle in points C and E. Through C and E draw lines parallel to I B and K B, respectively (Prob. 8). These lines will touch the circle about B, in points D and F, and they will be tangents to both the circles as required. Otherwise—

Let the given circles be described about centres A and B, of which that about A is the greater. Through A and B draw a straight line, producing it indefinitely beyond the lesser circle. From the

centre A, draw any radius A D, and from B, draw a radius B E, parallel to A D (Prob. 8), and on the same side of the line A B. Through D and E

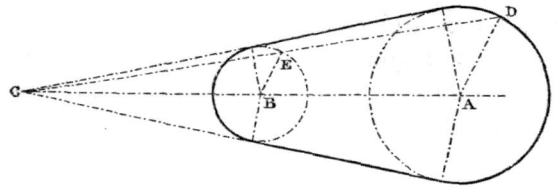

draw a line extending it to meet the production of A B in a point C. From C draw tangents to the circle about B (Prob. 55), which, being extended, will also be tangents to that about A, as required.

PROBLEM 65.—Two diverging lines being given, to describe a circle that shall touch them both, and one of them at a given point.

Let B E and B F be two given lines divergent from a point B, and let A be a given point in one of them, B E. Upon B F make B C equal to B A. From A, raise a perpendicular to B E (Prob. 2), and from C a perpendicular to B F; these, being produced, will intersect each other at a point D. From D as a centre, with the radius D A or D C, describe a circle. This will touch each of the lines and B E at the given point A. When the point B is not accessible, points of equal distance from it may be determined by Prob. 46, and the construction completed as above; or the line which bisects the angle drawn, and the point where it intersects the perpendicular is the centre sought.

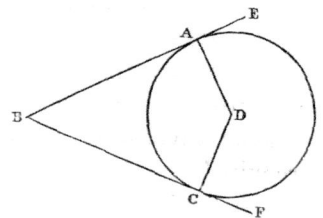

PROBLEM 66.—To describe a circle with a given radius that shall touch two given straight lines which are not parallel.

Let m n be a given radius, with which it is required to describe a circle that shall touch two given lines A B and C D which are not parallel. At any point E in C D, raise E F perpendicular to it (Prob. 2), and equal to m n; through F draw G H parallel to C D (Prob. 8). At any point I in A B raise I K perpendicular to it, and also equal to m n; and through K draw L M parallel to A B. The two lines G H and L M will intersect each other in

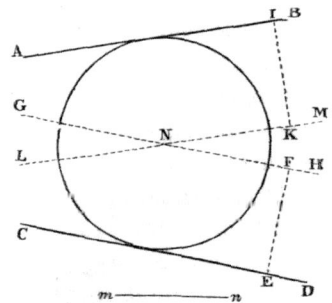

a point N. From this point, with the radius mn, describe a circle; this will touch the given lines, as required.

PROBLEM 67.—To describe a circle that shall touch three given straight lines, one of which is not parallel with the other two.

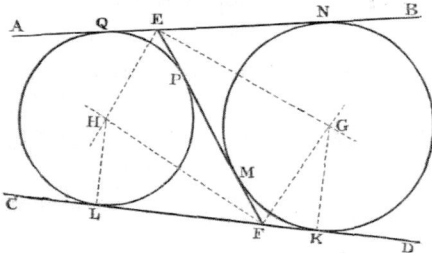

Let AB, CD, and EF, be the three given lines. Bisect each of the angles D F E and B E F by straight lines (Prob. 13), which, being produced, will intersect each other in a point G. From G let fall a perpendicular G K upon C D (Prob. 3), and from G, with the radius G K, describe a circle; this will touch each of the given lines at points K, M, and N, respectively. A second circle may be described which also fulfils the given conditions. Bisect each of the angles C F E and A E F (Prob. 13), by lines which, produced, will intersect each other at a point H; let fall H L perpendicular to C D (Prob. 3), and from H, with the radius H L, describe a circle; this will also touch each of the lines at points L, P, and Q, respectively.

PROBLEM 68.—To describe a circle, with a given radius, that shall touch a given circle at a given point.

Let ab be the given radius, and, first, let it be required to touch a given circle, described about a centre C internally, at a point A. Draw the radius C A, and from A make A B equal to ab. From B, with the radius ab, describe a circle; this will touch that about C internally at the point A as required. Next, let it be required to touch a given circle described about a centre C externally, at a point B. Draw the radius C B, and produce it beyond the circle, until B A is equal to ab. From A, with the radius A B, describe a circle; this will touch that about C externally, at the point B, as required. Should it be required to find the point of contact of two circles that touch each other, it must be recollected that the straight line which passes through their centres will also pass through the point of contact, or will do so when produced, if necessary.

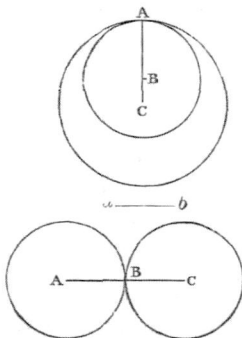

PROBLEM 69.—To describe a circle with a given radius, to be touched externally by two given circles.

Let ab be the given radius, and let the given circles be described about centres C and D, with radii C E and D F, respectively. Produce ab from b, until bf is equal to D F. From D as a centre, with a radius equal to af, describe an arc of a circle towards G. From b, upon bf, make bc equal to C E; and from C, with a radius equal to ac, describe an arc intersecting the first at a point G. From G as a centre, with the radius ab, describe a circle; this will be touched externally by the given circles, as required.

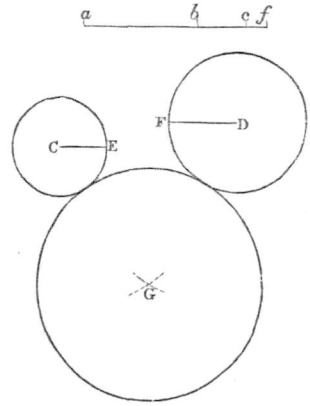

If it is required that the circle to be described should be touched internally by the circles, the difference between each of the radii of the given circles and the radius given, must be employed for finding the centre. By combining these means, the circle may be described so as to be touched externally by one, and internally by the other, given circle. The construction will show when the Problem becomes impossible, that is, when the conditions cannot be fulfilled with the things given.

PROBLEM 70.—To describe a circle about a given triangle.

Let A B C be the given triangle. Draw straight lines E G and F H perpendicular to the middle points E and F of any two of the sides, as A B and A C of the triangle (Prob. 12). These, being produced, will intersect each other at a point K. From K as a centre, with a radius K A, K B, or K C, equal to the distance between it and any of the angles of the triangle, describe a circle. This will circumscribe the triangle, as required. This problem evidently reduces itself into describing a circle through three points which are not in a straight line. It must be observed, that the centre will be either within or without the figure, according as the triangle is acute, or obtuse angled. When it is right angled, the centre is the middle point of the hypothenuse, or that side which is opposite to the right angle.

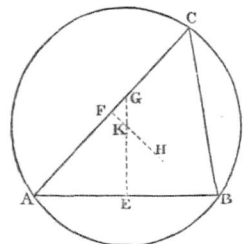

PROBLEM 71.—To inscribe a circle in a given triangle.

Let A B C be the given triangle. Bisect any two of the angles, as B A C, and B C A, by straight lines (Prob. 13), which, being produced, will intersect each other in a point D. From D let fall a perpendicular (Prob. 3), upon any one of the sides, as A C, meeting it in a point E. From D as a centre, with the radius D E, describe a circle. This will touch each of the sides of the triangle, and they will be tangents to it.

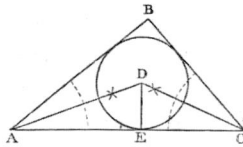

PROBLEM 72.—To describe a circle within three given lines, which would form a triangle, if produced to inaccessible points.

Let A B, D C, and E F, be the given lines, and let the vertical angle of the triangle which they would form, be contained by C D and F E. Draw the straight line m n, which would bisect the angle formed by the production of D C and B A (Prob. 47); also r n, to bisect that formed by A B and E F. These will intersect each other at a point n. From n let fall a perpendicular n s on one of the sides, as A B (Prob. 3), and from n, with the radius n s, describe a circle. This will touch each of the given lines, and be inscribed within them, as required.

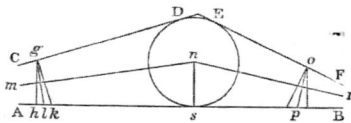

PROBLEM 73.—To divide the circumference of a circle into five and ten equal parts, and to inscribe a regular pentagon or decagon.

Let the given circle be described about a centre o. Draw the diameters A C and B D at right angles to one another (Prob. 2). Bisect the radius A o in E (Prob. 12), and from E, with the radius E B, describe an arc, to meet A C in F. The distance B F is the chord of the fifth part of the circumference. It is to be measured, therefore, from B to G, and H, &c., and the points of section being connected successively by straight lines, the inscribed pentagon will be produced. Bisect the arc H B in k (Prob. 33), then is B k, or H k, the tenth part of the circumference, and it may be measured upon it for the production of the inscribed decagon, if required. The distance o F, is also the chord of the tenth part of the circumference, and may be employed in the construction.

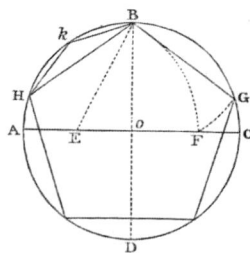

PROBLEM 74.—Upon a given straight line, to construct a regular decagon.

Let A B be the given line. Bisect it in C (Prob. 12), and from B raise B D perpendicular to it (Prob. 5), and equal to A B. Produce A B from B, until C E is equal to C D. From A and B as centres, with the radius A E, describe intersecting arcs at F; and from F, with the same radius, describe a circle. This circle will circumscribe a regular decagon, of which the side is equal to A B. Upon its circumference, therefore, measure A B from B to G, G to H, &c.; connect the successive points of section by straight lines, and the figure required will be produced.

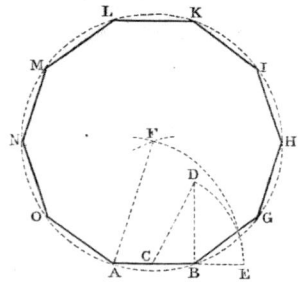

PROBLEM 75.—Upon a given straight line, to construct a regular pentagon.

Let A B be the given line. From B, one of its extremities, raise B c perpendicular to it (Prob. 5), and equal to the half of A B. Through A and c draw a straight line, and produce it beyond c, until c d is equal to c B. From A and B as centres, with a radius equal to the distance B d, describe arcs intersecting each other at e. From e, with the radius e A or e B, describe a circle. This will circumscribe a pentagon whose side is equal to A B. Upon its circumference measure A B, from B to F, F to G, G to H. Connect the successive points of section by straight lines, and the figure A B F G H will be the pentagon required.

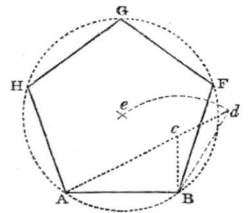

PROBLEM 76.—To divide the circumference of a given circle into six and twelve equal parts, and to inscribe an equilateral triangle, a regular hexagon or six-sided figure, and a dodecagon or regular twelve-sided figure.

Let the given circle be described about a centre B. Draw any radius B A, and from A, with the same radius, describe an arc, meeting the circumference in points C and D. Join C D by a straight line; and from C, with the radius C D, describe an arc intersecting the circumference in E; join C E and D E by

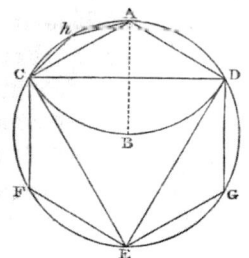

ight lines; then is C D E the inscribed equi-
ral triangle required. From C and D, with a
ius equal to A B, describe arcs intersecting the
umference in points F and G; it will thus be
ided into six equal parts at the points A, D, G, E,
and C. Straight lines drawn between these
nts will form the inscribed hexagon. Bisect
h of the arcs as A C in h, and join the points
, h C, &c.; each of these is the twelfth part of
circumference, and may be measured upon it
the completion of the dodecagon if required.

PROBLEM 77.—To divide the circumference of a
en circle into twelve equal parts, and to inscribe
hin it a regular dodecagon or twelve-sided
re.

Let the given circle be described about a centre C.
w two diameters,
B and C D, at right
les to one another
ob. 2). From A,
h the radius A C of
circle, describe arcs
rsecting the cir-
ference in points F
G; from D, at I
H; from B, at K
L; and from E, at
and N. These, with the points A, B, E, and D,
ide the circumference into twelve equal parts.
form the inscribed dodecagon, join the successive
nts of section, as D K, K I, I B, &c., by straight
s, and it will be produced, as required.

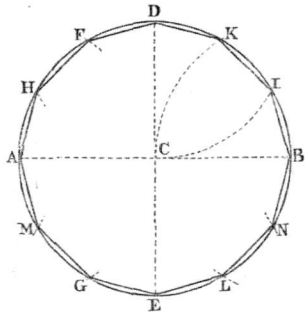

n Problem 14, the same process was employed
the bisection of a right angle, and the principle
then explained. It is plain, that as the cir-
aference of a circle measures four right angles,
ll the angles about any point, if each of these is
ided into three equal parts, the whole circum-
nce will be divided into twelve parts, all of
ch are equal.

PROBLEM 78.—Upon a given straight line to
struct a regular hexagon.

Let A B be the given line. From A and B as
tres, with the radius A B,
cribe arcs intersecting
h other in C. From C,
h the radius C A, describe
ircle. This is the circle
t may be circumscribed
ut a hexagon, whose side
equal to A B. Upon its
cumference measure A B from B to D, D to E,
to F, F to G, and G to A. Join the successive
nts of section thus found by straight lines.
en is A B D E F G the hexagon required.

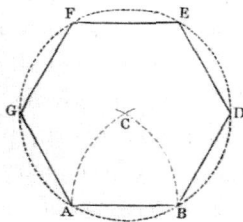

PROBLEM 79.—Upon a given line to construct a
regular dodecagon.

Let A B be the given line. Raise C D perpendicular to the middle
point C of A B, and
of indefinite length
(Prob. 12). From B,
with the radius B A,
describe an arc inter-
secting C D in a point
E. From E, upon E D,
make E F equal to E A
or E B or A B. From
F, with the radius F B
or F A, describe a circle. This circle will circumscribe a dodecagon, whose side is equal to A B.
Upon its circumference measure A B from B to G,
G to H, H to I, &c. The successive points of
section being joined by straight lines, the required
dodecagon is completed.

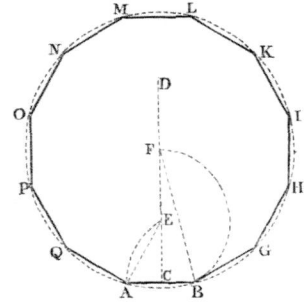

PROBLEM 80.—Within a given square, to inscribe
the greatest possible regular octagon.

Let A B C D be the given square. Draw the
diagonals A C and B D, intersecting each other at the point
e. From each of the angles
A, B, C, and D, with a radius
equal to e D, the half of one
of the diagonals, describe arcs
of circles, meeting each of the
sides of the square in points
g n, f k, h m, l o. Join the points f o, g h, k l, m n
by straight lines, and the required octagon will be
produced.

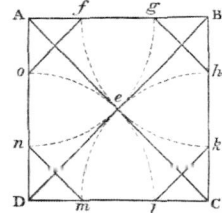

PROBLEM 81.—Upon a given straight line, to
construct a regular octagon.

Let A B be the given straight line. Produce
A B both ways, towards
k and l. From the ex-
tremities A and B of the
given line, raise A E
and B F perpendicular
to it (Prob. 5), and of
indefinite length. Bisect
each of the angles E A k
and F B l (Prob. 13)
by straight lines, A H and B C, which are to be
produced until each of them is equal to A B. From
H and C draw lines H G and C D, parallel to A F
and B E (Prob. 8), and equal to A B. From G
and D, with a radius equal to A B, describe arcs
intersecting A E and B F in points E and F,
respectively. Join G E, E F, and F D, by straight
lines; then is A B C D E F G H a regular octagon
constructed upon A B, as required.

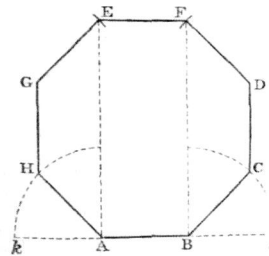

PROBLEM 82.—To divide the circumference of a circle into four and eight equal parts, and to inscribe within it a square, and regular octagon.

Let the given circle be described about the centre M. Draw any diameter A C, and perpendicular to it draw the diameter B D (Prob. 2); the circumference is thus divided into four equal parts, at the points A, B, C, and D. Join A B, B C, C D, and D A by straight lines; Then is A B C D a square inscribed within the circle. Bisect each of the quadrants A B, B C, &c., in points e, f, g, and h, respectively (Prob. 33); these points, with the former, will divide the circumference into eight equal parts. Join A e, e B, B f, &c., by straight lines; then A e B f C g D h is a regular octagon, and it is inscribed within the circle, as required.

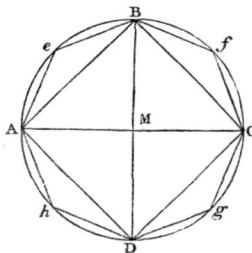

PROBLEM 83.—About a given circle, to describe a square, and a regular octagon.

Let A C B D be the given circle. Draw two diameters, A B and C D, at right angles to one another (Prob. 2). At the points A, B, C, and D, draw tangents to the circle (Prob. 54), and produce them both ways to meet two and two in points E, F, G, and H. Then E F G H is a square circumscribing the circle. Draw the diagonals E G and F H, and, at the points where these intersect the circumference of the circle, draw tangents to it, as h k, &c. (Prob. 54), to meet the sides of the square. These, with the intercepted portions of the sides of the square, will form a regular octagon circumscribing the circle, as required.

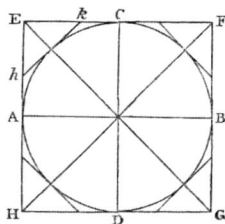

PROBLEM 84.—About any given regular polygon, to circumscribe a circle.

Let A B C D E be the given regular polygon. Bisect any two of the angles, as E A B and C B A, by straight lines (Prob. 13); these, if produced, will intersect each other at a point F. From F, with the radius F A, or the distance to any of the angular points, describe a circle. This will circumscribe the figure, as required. When the number of the sides of the polygon is even, the line

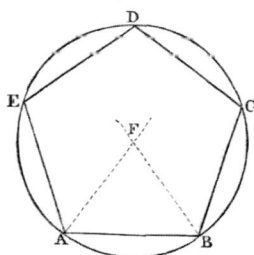

which joins two opposite angles is the diameter of the circle which will circumscribe it, and its middle point will be the centre required.

PROBLEM 85.—Within a given regular polygon, to inscribe a circle.

Let e f g h k be a given regular pentagon, within which it is required to inscribe a circle. Draw straight lines perpendicular (Prob. 12) to the middle points C and D of two of the sides, as k h and k e, respectively. These, being produced, will intersect each other at a point B. From B as a centre, with a radius B C or B D, describe a circle; this will be inscribed within the figure, or will touch each of its sides, as required.

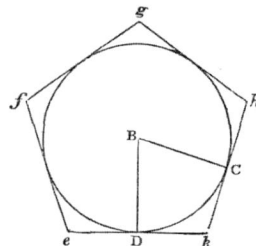

In this Problem, when the number of sides of the polygon is even, the line which joins the middle points of two parallel sides is the diameter of the circle, which may be inscribed in the figure; and its middle point is the centre sought.

The construction of the regular polygons is generally effected by the division of the circumference of the circle into equal parts, and connecting the successive points of section by straight lines. The division of the circle into *all* numbers of equal parts, however, is not possible by geometric methods; but certain numbers are derived from its primary geometric divisions, which are two, five, or ten, and six equal parts: and from these others are derived.

From the foregoing geometric divisions of the circumference of the circle, may be derived its partition into greater numbers of parts by the continued bisection of the arcs so found, and their differences, and so to construct the inscribed polygon. Hence, from the hexagon, by continued bisection, will arise regular polygons of 12, 24, 48, 96, &c. sides; from the square, those of 8, 16, 32, 64, &c. sides; from the pentagon and decagon, those of 20, 40, 80, 160, &c. sides. The differences of these systems also afford arcs which divide the circumference equally—that between the hexagon and decagon giving rise to its division into 15 parts; and hence, polygons of 30, 60, 120, &c. sides, may be constructed, and so on.

The division of the circumference of the circle into seven, nine, eleven, and other parts, cannot be effected geometrically, and the corresponding figures inscribed; approximations must, therefore, be had recourse to, and some of these afford results which do not differ much from the truth.

PROBLEM 86.—To divide the circumference of a circle approximately into seven equal parts, and to inscribe within it a heptagon.

Let the given circle be described about a centre A, with a radius A B. Draw the chord B C equal to A B, the radius of the circle.   From A let fall A K perpendicular to B C, meeting it in K (Prob. 3).   This line, A K, is nearly equal to the chord of the seventh part of the circumference of the circle.   Measure it, therefore, upon the circumference from any point B to D, D to E, &c. Join the successive points of section by straight lines.   Then is B D E F G H I a heptagon inscribed within the circle.

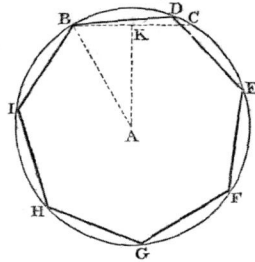

PROBLEM 87.—To divide the circumference of a given circle approximately into nine equal parts, and to inscribe within it a nonagon.

Let the given circle be described about a centre A.   Draw a diameter B C, and from A a radius A D, perpendicular to it (Prob. 2).   Bisect A D in E (Prob. 12). From any convenient point F in the diameter, and on the same side with A D, raise F G perpendicular to it, of indefinite length (Prob. 2).   Upon F G measure five equal parts F 1, 2, 3, &c.   Divide their sum F 5, into three equal parts (Prob. 24) F a, a b, b 5. Next, bisect the space b 3 in H (Prob. 12).   Draw a straight line through 5, and the point E in A D, to meet the diameter B C, or its production, if necessary, in a point K ; and between K and H draw a straight line.   This will intersect A D at a point L.   Then is D L very nearly the chord of the ninth part of the circumference of the circle.   Measure D L, therefore, upon it from any point D to M, M to N, &c.; connect the successive points of section by straight lines, and D M N O P Q R S T will be a nonagon inscribed in the given circle. This is a very close approximation.

PROBLEM 88.—To divide the circumference of a given circle approximately into eleven equal parts, and to inscribe within it an undecagon.

Let the given circle be described about a centre A.   Draw a radius A B of the circle.   Bisect it in C (Prob. 12); bisect C B in D, C D in E, and

C E in F.   Then is A F the chord of the eleventh part of the circumference of the circle very nearly.   From any point B in it, measure A F, from B to G, G to H, &c., connect the successive points of section by straight lines, and B G H I K L M N O P Q will be the inscribed undecagon.

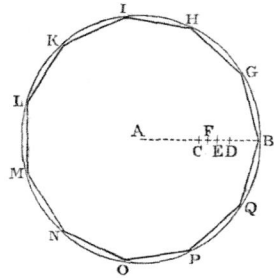

PROBLEM 89.—A regular polygon being given, to construct another having the same perimeter, but double the number of sides.

Let the given polygon be a regular pentagon, of which the side is A B.   Bisect two of the adjacent angles of the figure, as those at A and B (Prob. 13), by straight lines, which, being produced, will meet in a point C, and form a triangle A B C. Upon a line D E, equal in length to the half of A B, construct (Prob. 23) a triangle D F E, similar to the triangle A B C.   Erect a perpendicular from the middle of D E, and produce it beyond F to G, until F G is equal to F D or F E.   From G, with a radius G D or G E, describe a circle. This is the circle which will circumscribe a decagon whose side is equal to D E.   Upon its circumference measure D E as often as it will contain it, and construct the decagon, which will be that required.

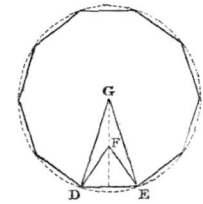

PROBLEM 90.—A regular polygon being given, to construct another having the same perimeter, but any different number of sides.

Let the given polygon be a regular hexagon whose side is A B, and let it be required to construct a regular octagon having an equal perimeter. Divide A B into eight equal parts (Prob. 24).   Draw a line D E equal to A C, which contains six of these parts, and upon it construct (Prob. 81) an octagon, which will be that required.   In this case the polygon required has a greater number of sides than that given.   Let it be reversed, or let the octagon be given whose side is D E. Divide D E into six equal

e

195

parts, and produce it from E to F, until E F is equal to two of them. Draw A B equal to D F, and upon it construct a hexagon (Prob. 78), which will be that required. In the same manner, whatever difference there may be in the number of sides, always divide the side of the given polygon into the same number of equal parts as there are sides required in the new figure, adding to, or deducting from it, according to the difference.

PROBLEM 91.—On a given straight line, to construct a polygon of any number of sides.

Let A B be the given line, and let it be required to construct a regular heptagon upon it. Produce A B from B indefinitely, and from B as a centre, with any radius as B A, describe a semicircle. Divide the semicircle into seven equal parts (Prob. 86), and draw B D through the second division from C, making it equal to B A. B A and B D are two sides of the required figure. Bisect each of them respectively in e and f, and raise perpendiculars at these points, which, being produced, will meet in a point G. From G, with the radius G A, describe a circle, upon the circumference of which measure AB from D to H, &c.; join the points of section by straight lines, and the required heptagon will be produced. In this manner, a polygon of any number of sides may be produced, always dividing the semicircle into the required number of sides, and drawing a line to the second division, in order to find the position of a second side. Otherwise—

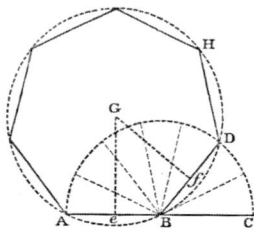

Let A B be a given line, on which it is required to construct a pentagon. Produce A B indefinitely from B, and from B as a centre, with any radius as B A, describe a semicircle upon A C. Divide the semicircle into five equal parts (Prob. 73). From B draw a straight line B D, through the second of these divisions from C, which will be equal to BA. Through the remaining points of section draw lines B H and B K of indefinite length; and from D and A, with the radius A B, describe arcs intersecting them at points H and K. Join D H, H K, and K A, by straight lines, and the required pentagon will be produced.

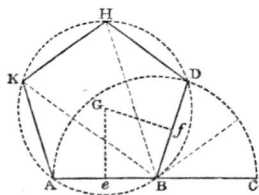

The principle of the construction is, that the exterior angle, as D B C of the polygon, is equal to the angle at the centre. The methods are very convenient occasionally, as the exterior angle may be marked by any of the instruments usually employed in the measurement of angles; and the particular angle for each polygon is easily ascertained by calculation, being four right angles, or 360° divided by the number of sides. For convenience, the following table exhibits the angles of the first ten polygons :—

No. of Sides.	Name of Polygon.	Angle at Centre.	Angle of Polygon.	Angle at base of elem. triangle.
3	Trigon or triangle ...	120°	60°	30°
4	Tetragon or square ...	90	90	45
5	Pentagon................	72	108	54
6	Hexagon	60	120	60
7	Heptagon................	$51\frac{3}{7}$	$128\frac{4}{7}$	$64\frac{2}{7}$
8	Octagon	45	135	$67\frac{1}{2}$
9	Nonagon	40	140	70
10	Decagon	36	144	72
11	Undecagon	$32\frac{8}{11}$	$147\frac{3}{11}$	$73\frac{7}{11}$
12	Dodecagon	30	150	75

The angle of the polygon, or that formed by the meeting of two of its sides, is equal to the difference between 180° and the angle at the centre; for example, the angle at the centre of the regular octagon is 45°, which, subtracted from 180°, leaves 135° for the angle of the polygon.

The triangle B C D, in the following problem, is called the elementary triangle of the polygon; that is, any regular polygon may be decomposed into as many identical elementary triangles as the figure has sides. The angle at B is that at the centre of the polygon; those at the base are equal each to the half of the angle of the polygon; for example, in the octagon, the angles at the base of the elementary triangle corresponding with C and D, are each of them the half of 135° or $67\frac{1}{2}°$. It is plain that polygons may be constructed by means of their elementary triangles, a method that will be very serviceable to the cabinet-maker.

The following Problem shows a convenient method of employing the above table :—

PROBLEM 92.—To inscribe any regular polygon in a given circle, by means of the angle at the centre.

Let A be a given circle, within which let it be required to inscribe a regular hexagon. At B, the centre of the circle, by means of any instrument employed in the measurement of angles, mark an angle of 60°, which is that of the hexagon. Produce the sides containing it, until they meet the circumference of the circle in points C and D. The chord of the arc C D is that of the sixth part of the circumference of the circle, and may be measured upon it for the construction of the polygon.

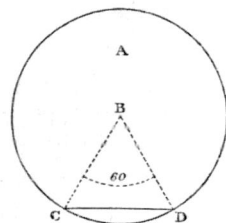

PROBLEM 93.—Within a given circle, to inscribe a regular polygon of any number of sides.

Let A D B F be the given circle, within which let it be required to inscribe a regular pentagon. Draw the diameter A B, and divide it into five equal parts (Prob. 24). From the middle point e of A B, raise a perpendicular (Prob. 2), and produce it beyond the circumference of the circle, until F C is equal to three-fourths of the radius e F. Draw a straight line C D through the second division from the extremity A, and meeting the circle in D. The chord of the arc A D will be nearly the length of the side of the inscribed pentagon, and may be employed accordingly. Otherwise—

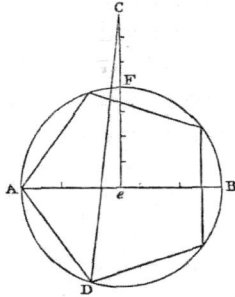

Let A E F B g be the given circle, within which it is required to inscribe a hexagon. Draw the diameter A B. From the middle point C of A B, raise a perpendicular to it (Prob. 2), producing it beyond the circle, until g D is equal to three-fourths of the radius C g of the circle. Divide the radius C A, into six equal parts (Prob. 24), and from D draw a line D E, through the second division from C, producing it to meet the circumference in a point E. Draw E F parallel to the diameter A B, meeting the circle in F. E F is the length of one of the sides, and being applied successively to the circumference of the circle, the required polygon will be produced.

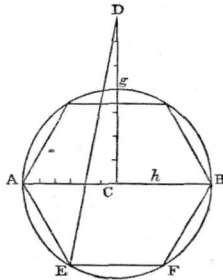

In a like manner, polygons of any numbers of sides may be inscribed within given circles, always dividing the diameter or the radius into a number of equal parts, corresponding with the number of sides of the required polygon. It must be recollected that these methods are only approximations.

The solution of this general problem for the inscription of polygons has given rise to many very beautiful and ingenious constructions, but these are all liable to the same objection, namely, that they are not strictly correct, or are not so in all cases, although they may approach sufficiently near the truth to be very useful general rules. Those given will be found to be very available in practice, and have the advantage of being exceedingly simple; but, where possible, it is always better to employ the true geometrical construction, as given in the previous problems, for each of the polygons up to twelve sides.

The following table exhibits the relations of the side of any of the first ten polygons, with the radius of the circumscribing circle, each in its turn being taken as unity:—

No. of Sides.	Length of Radius when the Side is 1.	Length of the Side when the Radius is 1.
3	·57735	1·73205
4	·70710	1·41421
5	·85065	1·17557
6	1·00000	1·00000
7	1·15237	·86777
8	1·30657	·76536
9	1·46190	·68404
10	1·61804	·61803
11	1·77470	·56347
12	1·93188	·51763

By the above table, it is easy to find either the length of the radius of the circumscribing circle, the side of the polygon being given, or, the side of the polygon, the radius of the circumscribing circle being given; the question being simply one of finding a fourth proportional to three given terms. In the first case, let the given side of a pentagon be 3, then 1 : ·85065 :: 3 : 2·55195 the length of the radius required. In the second case, let the given radius of a circle circumscribing a pentagon be 2·55195, then 1 : 1·17557 :: 2·55195 : 3, the side of the pentagon required.

Three of the polygons, only, are so constituted, that by the adaptation of their sides and angles to each other, the repetition of the same figure about a point in a plain surface will completely fill the space about it. These are the equilateral triangle, the square, and the hexagon. The interior triangle of an equilateral triangle is one-third of two right angles; consequently, six such triangles have their vertices in the same point. The angle of a square is a right angle, and four squares may be arranged about a point; and that of the hexagon being two-thirds of two right angles, three hexagons will thus meet in the same point. But although these are the only three regular polygons that will alone fill up the space about a point, they may be combined among themselves, and with others, so as to do so; the necessary condition being, that the sum of the angles of the different figures so meeting shall be equal to four right angles. The following is a list of all the various combinations that fulfil this condition:—

1. When three polygons are combined, there are ten arrangements, and the number of sides must be 3,7,42; 3,8,24; 3,9,18; 3,10,15; 3,12,12; 4,5,20; 4,6,12; 4,8,8; 5,5,10; and 6,6,6.

2. When four polygons are combined, there are four arrangements, and the number of sides must be 3,3,4,12; 3,3,6,6; 3,4,4,6; and 4,4,4,4.

3. When five polygons are combined, there are two arrangements, and the number of sides must be 3,3,3,4,4; and 3,3,3,3,6.

4. And when six polygons are combined, there is only one arrangement, and they must be all equilateral triangles. All these may be placed without regard to order, but their regular combination gives rise to many beautiful arrangements, which are of great importance in ornamentation.

PROBLEM 94.—To cover a surface with equilateral triangles.

Construct an equilateral triangle A B C (Prob. 15), in order to have two lines A C and B C divergent at an angle of 60°.

Upon these lines measure equal parts A a, a b, &c., upon A B; and A a′, a′ b′ &c., upon A C; each equal to the side of the equilateral triangle that is to be employed. From the points a, b, &c., upon A B, draw lines parallel to A C (Prob. 8), and from the points a′, b′, &c., in A C, draw lines parallel to A B. Join a′ a, b′ b, &c., by straight lines, and the surface will be divided into a number of equilateral triangles, as A a a′, &c., which completely cover it.

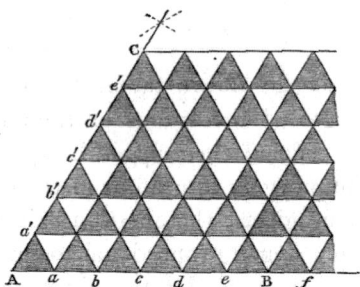

PROBLEM 95.—To cover a surface with regular hexagons.

Draw two straight lines, A B and A C, divergent from A, and making an angle C A B, with one another, equal to 60° (Prob. 15). Upon each of these, measure the side of the hexagon from A to a, a to b, &c., upon A B, and from A to a′, a′ to b′, &c., upon A C; divide the surface into equilateral triangles as in the last problem. It will easily be seen, that about each point, as m, there are six equilateral triangles, which together form a hexagon, as a b k h b′ a′, of which the diagonals a h, b b′, and a′ k, may be obliterated. By proceeding in the same manner with the several groups of triangles, the surface will be left covered with regular hexagons, as required.

PROBLEM 96.—To cover a surface with regular hexagons and equilateral triangles.

Let the lines of construction be drawn as in Prob. 15, and the surface divided into equilateral triangles, whose sides are equal to the sides of the required figures. Three groups of the triangles which form hexagons, connected two and two, as at d, e, and f, are to be employed for the hexagonal figures, and the remaining triangle will fill up the intervening space. In this case, the space about a point is filled up by two hexagons and two equilateral triangles.

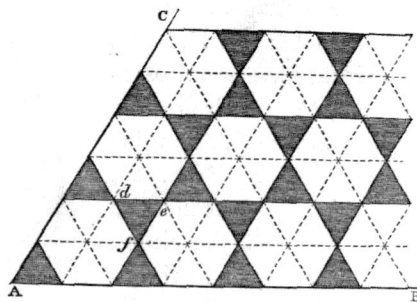

PROBLEM 97.—To cover a space with lozenges, arranged in groups of three.

Draw two straight lines A B and A C, forming an angle C A B, equal to 60°. divide the space, as in Prob. 94, into equilateral triangles, and arrange them into hexagonal groups, divide each hexagon, as a b c d e f, into lozenges, by means of the radii g b, g d, and g f, drawing the radii in each polygon parallel with those in the others. The surface will thus be divided as required.

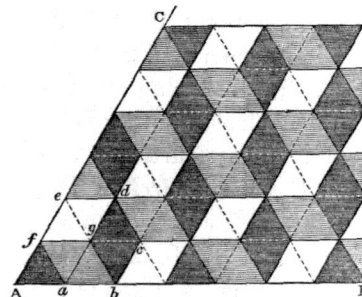

A kind of polygon that is much used in ornament, is a figure in which the angles are alternately salient, and re-entrant; this produces a very beautiful star-formed figure. The character of such polygons varies with the number of the angles; they are generally derived from the regular polygons, and are constructed by the same means, that is, by the division of the circumference of a circle. For this purpose, instead of connecting the successive points of section on the circumference, the alternate points are joined, or lines are drawn between those that are at any equal interval; always passing over two, or three, or more points, according to the number in the polygon, and the character of the star that it is desired to produce.

PROBLEM 98.—To cover a surface with regular octagons and squares.

Draw two straight lines A B and A C at right angles to one another (Prob. 5). Upon each, measure the breadth of the octagon to be employed, from A to d, d to e, &c., upon A B; and from A to *d'*, *d'* to *e*, &c., upon A C. From *d'*, *e'*, and *f'* draw lines parallel to A B (Prob. 8), and from *d, e, f*, and *g*, draw lines parallel to A C. The surface is thus divided into squares. Draw A F diagonally through the squares. Take A*h*, the half of the diagonal of one of the squares, and from *d, e, f*, and *g* upon A B, and *d', e'*, and *f'* upon A C, measure the distance on each side of them, upon the respective lines A B and A C, the points, 1.1', 2.2', 3.3', &c., will thus be found; from each of these points draw lines parallel to A F (Prob. 8) the diagonal of a series of the squares; these will intersect the lines forming the squares, and indicate the angles of the octagonal figures, which must be connected by straight lines where necessary, and it will be found, that the surface is covered with squares and octagons, as required.

PROBLEM 99.—To construct regular star-formed polygons.

Let it be required to construct all the regular star-formed polygons of nine points. Let the circumference of a circle be divided into nine equal parts, at points 1, 2, 3, &c. (Prob. 87.) First, join the alternate points of section, as 1 3, 3 5, &c., until all the points are connected, and the line has returned again to the first point. This will produce the figure whose points contain the greatest angle.

Next, in joining the points, draw lines between the first and fourth points, thus passing over two, 4 and 7, 7 and 1. In this way an equilateral triangle is produced. By commencing again with 2, and afterwards with 3, and proceeding in the same manner, two other triangles will result, which combined, will produce the figure.

Lastly, join the first and the fifth points; the

fifth and the ninth, the ninth and the fourth, and so on, passing three points; when the line has returned again to the first point, the figure will be completed. There are thus three star-formed polygons derived from the nonagon, and these are all that it is possible to construct from it.

The number of these figures that can be constructed from any regular polygon, is the half of the number of its sides diminished by three, when the number is odd; and when the number is even, it is half of the number of sides diminished by four. In the above case, the nonagon was used. If nine is diminished by three, there remains six, the half of which is three, the number produced. It is to be observed that it is not necessary that the star should be inscribed within the circle, or the polygon of construction; the same forms will be produced by drawing the lines beyond the points, until they meet, the only difference being, that the figures which result will be much larger than in the former case. These star-formed polygons are of great service in the construction of inlaid work of all kinds, as floors, &c., affording appropriate forms for the purpose. In the general application of the principle to ornament, it may also be observed, that the connection of the points may be effected by curved lines, as circles, or by regularly and systematically mixed lines; by this means an infinite variety of forms may be produced, which are well adapted for frets, and so forth. Many of the beautiful, and apparently complicated figures, so frequently employed in Moorish ornament, are constructed upon this simple principle, which affords unlimited scope for ingenuity in the designer, and the display of his art in the tasteful division and filling up of spaces that may be appropriately occupied by such ornament.

The construction of similar figures is probably one of the most familiar forms under which geometry presents itself, being the principle upon which all objects are repeated or imitated, as in models, drawings, plans, &c.; or where any object is represented, these being merely similar figures constructed upon a certain scale or proportion.

In the case of similar triangles (Prob. 23), it has been explained, that certain of the parts being equal, the whole figures were similar, whether they were equal or not. It is plain that, as any polygonal figure may be divided into a number of triangles, according to the number of its sides, and each of these may be repeated, with their corresponding sides proportionally greater or less, that by dividing such a figure into its component triangles, and reconstructing these, commencing with a side either equal or proportional, and placing them in the same relation with one another, the group of triangles will present a form which is either equal to, or greater or less than the original figure, according as the corresponding sides have been made equal or proportional. To this principle of similar triangles is reducible the system of construction, adopted in making one figure similar to another.

PROBLEM 100.—To make a figure identical with a given rectilineal figure.

Let *a b c d e f* be the given rectilineal figure. Divide the figure into its component triangles, that is, draw the diagonals *d f*, *c f*, and *a c*. Draw a straight line A F equal to *a f* for the corresponding side, and upon it construct a triangle A C F, equal to *a c f* (Prob. 23). Upon A C construct a triangle A B C, equal to *a b c*; upon C F a triangle C D F, equal to *c d f*; and upon D F a triangle D E F, equal to *d e f*. Then is the whole figure A B C D E F identical with *a b c d e f*, as required. This is evident; for each of the triangles successively constructed being identical with those of the given figure, and with corresponding sides and angles, the whole, collectively, must be so also.

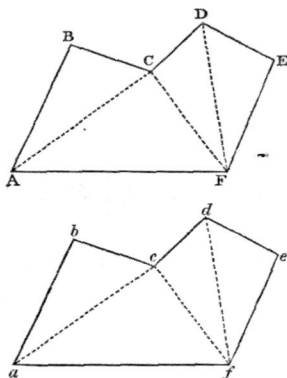

PROBLEM 101.—To make a figure similar to a given rectilineal figure, upon a straight line which is to correspond to a side indicated.

Let *a b c d e* be the given figure, and let A E be the given line which is to correspond to *a e* in the figure. Divide the given figure into its component triangles, by drawing the diagonals *b e* and *b d*. Upon A E construct a triangle A E B, similar to *a e b* (Prob. 23); upon E B a triangle E D B, similar to *e d b*; and upon B D a triangle B C D, similar to *b c d*. Then is the whole figure A B C D E similar to the given figure *a b c d e*.

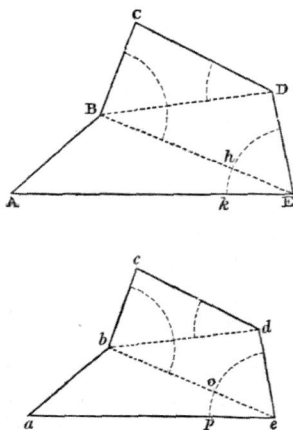

PROBLEM 102.—To make a figure similar to a given rectilineal figure, upon a given line which is parallel to one of the sides, and is to correspond with that side in the figure.

Let *a b c d e f* be the given figure, and let A B be the given line which is parallel to, and is to correspond with, the side *a b* in the figure. Through the extremities A and *a* draw a line, extending it within the figure, and through B and *b* draw a line to meet it in a point *g*.

From this point *g* draw lines through each of the other angles, *c*, *d*, *e*, and *f*, of the figure, extending them beyond it indefinitely. From B draw a line B C parallel to *b c* (Prob. 8), meeting the production of *g c* in a point C. From C draw a line C D parallel to *c d*, meeting the production of *g d* in D. In the same manner draw D E parallel to *d e*, E F to *e f*, and join F A, which is parallel to *f a*. Then is A B C D E F similar to the given figure *a b c d e f*.

PROBLEM 103.—To make a figure similar to a given rectilineal figure, by means of projections from a diagonal.

Let *b c d e a f g* be the given figure. Draw within the figure the greatest diagonal possible, *a b*; and from each of the other angles let fall perpendiculars upon it (Prob. 3), as *c h*, *d k*, *e l*, *f m*, and *g n*. Draw A B a straight line equal to *a b*. Upon it, from A, measure A *m'* equal to *a m*, *m' l'* equal to *m l*, &c., until A B is similarly divided with *a b*. At the points *h'*, *k'*, *l'*, raise perpendiculars *h'* C, *k'* D, *l'* E (Prob. 2), equal respectively to *h c*, *k d*, and *l e*. From *m'* and *n'* on the other side of A B, raise perpendiculars *m'* F, *n'* G, each equal respectively to *m f* and *n g*. Join the points B C, C D, &c., by straight lines; then is B C D E A F G a figure identical with that given. If the figure is required to be constructed with a side, either greater or less, the line of construction A B must be drawn in the given proportion, and divided similarly with *a b* (Prob. 28); the perpendiculars must also be made proportional, each to each.

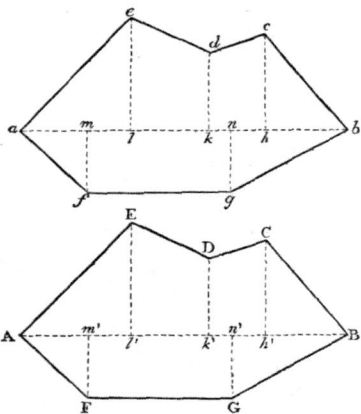

It is to be observed, that it is not necessary that the line to which the perpendiculars are drawn should be within the figure; it may be placed anywhere, either within or beyond it; the lengths of the perpendiculars indicating the position of the angles, or other points that may be determined for the construction of the new figure. In this way curved lines of all kinds are very accurately repeated. The following problem depends on the above principle, and the line of construction becomes the axis of symmetry.

PROBLEM 104.—A rectilineal figure being given, to construct another equal and similar figure, but reversed.

Let A B C D E be the given rectilineal figure.
From each of the angles of the figure draw lines parallel to one another (Prob. 8), in the direction towards which the new figure is to be produced, and intersect them by a straight line F G perpendicular to them (Prob. 2). Make F A′ equal to F A, H B′ to H B, I E′ to I E, K C′ to K C, and G D′ to G D. Draw straight lines between A′ and B′, B′ and C′, &c., then A′ B′ C′ D′ E′ will be a figure, equal and similar to that given, but reversed, or the two figures will be symmetrically placed with respect to the axis F G.

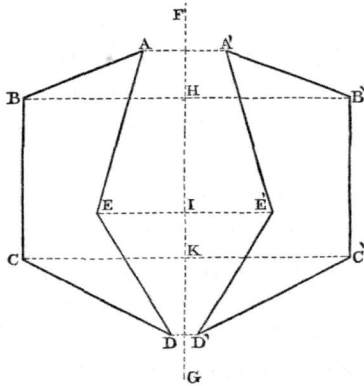

PROBLEM 105.—A rectilineal figure being given, to construct another equal and similar to it, by means of parallel lines.

Let a b c d e f be the given figure. From each of the angles of the figure draw parallel lines of indefinite length (Prob. 8). Upon each of these measure equal distances from the angular points, as a A, b B, &c.; connect the points as they correspond in the figure, as A B, B C, &c., by straight lines; then A B C D E F will be the figure required. This is a very expeditious method, and has great advantages in practice.

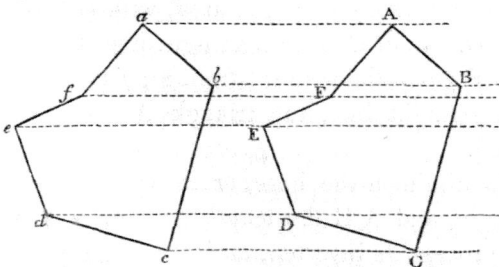

PROBLEM 106.—To construct a rectangle of an area equal to a given rhomboid, upon the same or an equal base.

Let A B D C be the given rhomboid, of which A B is the base. Produce the side D C from C towards E indefinitely. From A and B raise perpendiculars to A B (Prob. 5), producing them to meet D E in points E and F. Then is A B F E a rectangle of an area equal to the rhomboid A B C D. The area of a rhomboid is equal to its base multiplied into its altitude. Let A B = 4, and the altitude B F = 2; then the area = 4, multiplied by 2, = 8, the area.

It is plain that the converse of this problem may also be effected in a similar manner; or a rhomboid may be constructed of an area equal to a given rectangle. Let A B F E be the given rectangle. At A, one extremity of the base line, make an angle C A B equal to any given angle; and from B draw B D parallel to A C (Prob. 8), to meet the production of E F in D; then A B D C is the rhomboid required. The principle of these constructions is, that parallelograms, on the same or equal bases, and between the same parallel lines, are equal; that is, if E D were extended to any length, all the parallelograms that could be constructed upon A B as a base, and between the parallel lines A D and E D, would be equal to one another. This principle is of the utmost importance, since by its means the conversion of all kinds of figures is effected, and their measure obtained.

The conversion of a rhomboid into a rectangle may be effected by means of a species of dissection, which may sometimes be very advantageously applied in practice.

Let a b c d be a rhomboid upon a base a b. Draw b e perpendicular to a b. Make b f equal to a e, and also f g. Draw lines f h and g k parallel to b e. The parts into which the rhomboid is now divided may be placed so as to form the rectangle A B C D, by arranging them so that b f is connected in a parallel manner with a e, f g with e h, and g c with h d.

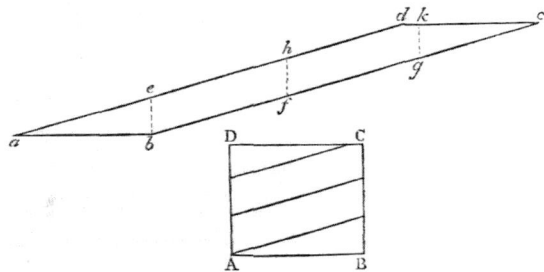

PROBLEM 107.—To construct a right-angled triangle of an area equal to a given triangle, upon one of its sides as a base line.

Let A B C be the given triangle, and A B the base. Through C draw a line C D, parallel to A B (Prob. 8). From B, one of the extremities of A B, raise B E perpendicular to it (Prob. 5), and produce it to meet D C in a point E. Join E A by a straight line. Then is A B E a triangle right-angled at B, which is equal to the given triangle A B C.

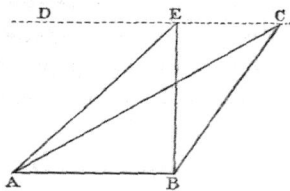

The area of a triangle is found by taking half the product of the base multiplied into the altitude. B E is the altitude of the two triangles A B C and A B E. Let A B=3 ft., and B E=4 ft., then $\frac{3\times4}{2}$=6 ft., the area of both the triangles.

PROBLEM 108.—To make a rectangle equal in area to a given triangle, the base line being determined.

Let A B C be the given triangle, of which B C is the base line. From A let fall the perpendicular A D (Prob. 3) upon the base B C; this is the altitude of the triangle. Bisect A D in E (Prob. 12). Through E draw a line parallel to B C (Prob. 8), and from B and C raise perpendiculars to meet the parallel to B C in points F and G (Prob. 5). Then is B C G F a rectangle of an area equal to the given triangle A B C. It is evident that the area of the rectangle is the base multiplied into half the altitude.

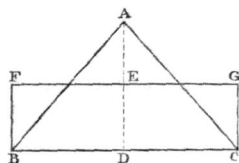

PROBLEM 109.—To make a square of an area equal to a given triangle.

Let A B C be the given triangle, and B C the base line. Draw A D the altitude, and bisect it in E (Prob. 12). Produce the base B C from C until C F is equal to D E, half the altitude. Bisect B F in G (Prob. 12); and from G, with the radius G F or G B, describe a semicircle. From C raise a perpendicular to B C (Prob. 2), and produce it to meet the semicircle in a point H. Upon C H construct a square C H I K (Prob. 36). This

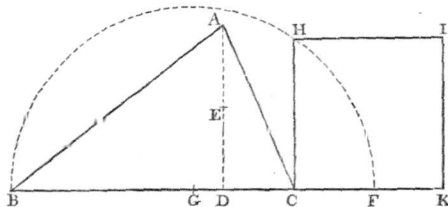

square is of an area equal to the given triangle A B C. The side of a square which is equivalent to any triangle, is thus a mean proportional between the base line and half the altitude of the triangle. Let B C=6 ft., and A D=4 ft., or D E, the half of A D=2 ft., the square root of 6×2= 3·464, &c., or about 3 ft. 5½ inches, the side of the square sought.

The side of the square may also be found, when the length of the sides forming the triangle are known. Thus, from half the sum of the sides deduct each side successively; then multiply the half sum by the three remainders continually. The square root of the product is the area of the triangle; and the square root of the area is the side required.

PROBLEM 110.—A triangle being given, to change it into one equal to it, but having an altitude or base greater or less in a given proportion.

First, let the altitude be changed. Let A B C be a given triangle, of which A B is the base; and let it be required to construct another of an equal area, but with an altitude equal to ef. Produce the base A B from B, towards D indefinitely. Join f B by a straight line; and from C draw a straight line parallel to f B (Prob. 8), extending it to meet the produced base line in a point D. Join f D by a straight line. Then is A f D the required triangle, equal in area to that given.

In order to increase the altitude of the triangle, or if A f D were the triangle given, and that it were required to make the altitude greater, the above process is simply inverted; or C D is first drawn, and then f B parallel with it; C and B are then joined, and the triangle is produced.

Next, let the base be changed. Let A B C be the given triangle; and let it be required to construct a triangle of equal area, with a base equal to A D. Join C D by a straight line, and from B draw B f parallel with it (Prob. 8); f D being joined by a straight line, the triangle A f D is that required.

To diminish the base, or if A f D is the given triangle, and A B the length of the new base line, the process is inverted, as in the first part of the problem.

Under Problem 106 it was observed, that parallelograms, placed upon the same or equal bases, and between the same parallel lines, were equal to one another. The same applies to triangles which are themselves the halves of parallelograms of some sort. Hence, if a line parallel to A D were drawn through *f*, all the triangles that could be constructed upon A D as a base, and having their vertices in that line, would be equal to one another. The same applies to the triangles that could be drawn upon A B, with the vertices in a line parallel with it, drawn through C.

PROBLEM 111.—To make a triangle equal to one, and similar to another given triangle.

Let it be required to construct a triangle that shall be equal to a given triangle, D E F, and similar to another, A B C. Make a triangle, D G H, equal to D E F (Prob. 110), with an altitude equal to that of A B C. Find a mean proportional between A B and D H; that is,

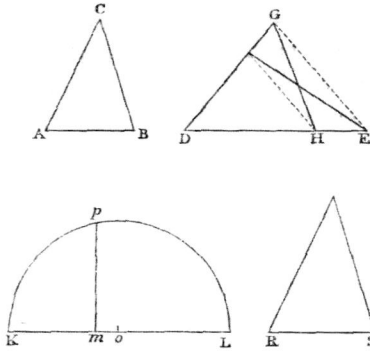

draw L K, and make K *m* equal to A B, and *m* L to D H. Bisect K L in *o*, and describe a semicircle in it. From *m* raise a perpendicular to meet the semi-circumference in a point *p*, then *m p* is the base of the triangle required. Draw R S equal to *m p*, and upon it construct a triangle (Prob. 23) similar to A B C, which will be that required.

PROBLEM 112.—To make a rectangle of an area equal to a given trapezoid.

Let ABCD be the given trapezoid. Produce the shorter of the two parallel sides both ways towards E and F. Upon A B measure D C from A to G. Bisect the difference G B in H (Prob. 12), and from A and

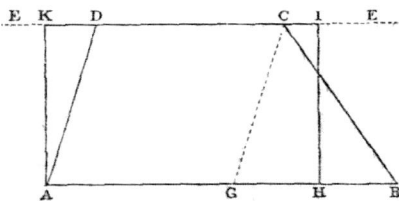

H raise perpendiculars (Prob. 5) to meet E F in points I and K respectively; then is A H I K a rectangle of an area equal to the given trapezoid. The area of a trapezoid is equal to the rectangle contained by its altitude, and half the sum of the parallel sides. This is manifest; for C G B is a triangle, and its area is equal to a rectangle under its base, and half the altitude (Prob. 108); or which is the same thing, to that under half the base, and the whole altitude. Hence A H I K is equal to the area of A G C D, together with the rectangle under G H and H I. Let A B=6 ft., D C=4 ft., and the altitude H I=2 ft., then $\frac{6+4}{2}=5$, and $5 \times 2=10$ ft., equal the area of the trapezoid.

PROB. 113.—To make a triangle of an area equal to a given trapezium.

Let A B C D be the given trapezium, and A B the base. Draw a diagonal, D A, and from C draw a line parallel to D A (Prob. 8), to meet the production of the base, in a point E. Join E D by a straight line. Then is E D B a triangle of an area equal to the trapezium A B C D.

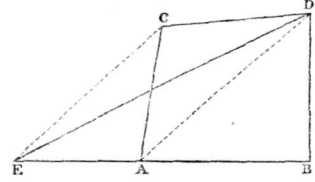

PROBLEM 114.—To make a triangle of an area equal to a given pentagon.

Let A B C D E be the given pentagon. Produce one side, as A B, both ways indefinitely. Draw the diagonals D A and D B. From E draw a line parallel to D A (Prob. 8), meeting the produced base in a point F, and join F and D by a straight line. From C draw a line parallel to D B, to meet the base produced in G, and draw D G. Then is F D G a triangle equal in area to the given pentagon.

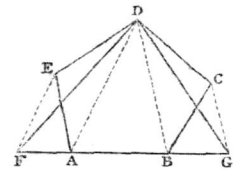

PROBLEM 115.—To make a triangle of an area equal to a given irregular hexagon.

Let A B C D E F be the given irregular hexagon. Join C E by a straight line, and from D draw a line parallel to it (Prob. 8), to meet the production of B C in a point G, and join E G by a straight line; the hexagon is thus reduced to a pentagon, A B G E F, of equal area. Next, join E A by a straight line, and from F draw a line parallel to it, to meet the production of A B in a point H; and join H E, which will produce the trapezium H B G E.

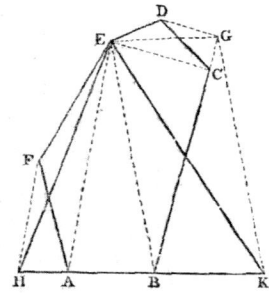

Now, join E B by a straight line, and from G draw a line parallel to it, to meet the production of A B in K, and join K E; the trapezium is thus reduced to an equal triangle, H E K, which is equal to the given hexagon. Here it is seen, that by the construction of equal triangles between parallels, the figure has been reduced one side successively at each step, and an equivalent figure formed, until at last the triangle is produced. It is evident that a triangle, by this means, may be made equal to any rectilineal figure. The area of any figure may be easily ascertained by this construction; for if it is accurately drawn by a scale, and the process of

f

conversion conducted with care, the resulting triangle may be measured by the same scale, and the area found as indicated in Problems 107 and 109, either multiplying the altitude into half the base, or by employment of the second method, which is that generally used in ascertaining the areas of triangles.

PROBLEM 116.—To make a triangle of an area equal to any given regular polygon.

Let it be required to make a triangle equal to a given hexagon. From the centre, C, let fall a perpendicular upon one of the sides, A B, of the figure (Prob. 3); this is the altitude of the elementary triangle, A B C, of the hexagon. Draw a straight line, D E, making it equal to the perimeter of the given polygon; upon it construct a triangle whose altitude shall be equal to that of the elementary triangle A B C. This triangle will be equal in area to the given hexagon.

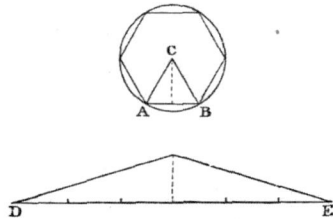

PROBLEM 117.—A regular polygon being given, to construct another, having an equal area, but a different number of sides.

Let it be required to construct a regular nonagon, whose area shall be equal to a given pentagon. Divide a side, as A B, of the figure into nine equal parts (Prob. 24). Upon a straight line D E, equal to five of these parts, construct a triangle D E H, with an altitude equal to that of A C B, the elementary triangle of the pentagon. Construct a triangle, F G L, having its vertical angle, F L G, equal to the angle at the centre of a nonagon which is 40°, and make its altitude equal, also, to that of the elementary triangle of the pentagon. Find the base of a triangle that shall be equal to D E H, and similar to F L G (Prob. 111), that is, find a mean proportional, l n, between D E and F G; this is the side of the required nonagon. Draw N O equal to l n, and upon it construct a nonagon (Prob. 91) which will be equal in area to the given pentagon, as required.

PROBLEM 118.—To make a rectangle equal in area to a given trapezium.

Let A B C D be the given trapezium. Draw B D, a diagonal of the figure, and from each of the angles, A and C, let fall perpendiculars upon B D, meeting it at points f and g (Prob. 3). Bisect B D in e (Prob. 12). Draw a straight line H K equal to B e, the half of the diagonal; and from its extremities raise perpendiculars H M and K L to it (Prob. 5), making each of them equal to the sum of the perpendiculars A f and C g. Join M L by a straight line; then H K L M is a rectangle equal in area to the given trapezium. The area of a trapezium is found by number, by multiplying the sum of the perpendiculars C g and A f by the diagonal, and taking half the product. Let the diagonal of a trapezium = 8 ft., and the perpendiculars let fall upon it from the other angles be respectively 2 ft. and 3 ft., then 2×3=5, and 5×8=40, the half of which is 20 ft., the area of the figure.

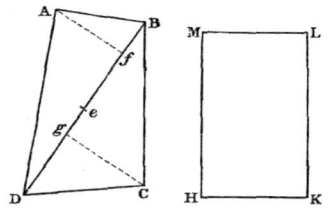

PROBLEM 119.—To make a rectangle of an area equal to a given regular polygon.

Let A B C D E be a given regular pentagon, of which the centre is F. Draw a straight line H I, and make it equal to half the sum of the sides of the pentagon. Upon it make a rectangle, with an altitude H K (Prob. 38), equal to F G, the perpendicular distance between the centre F and a side of the given figure. Then is H I L K a rectangle, equal in area to the given pentagon.

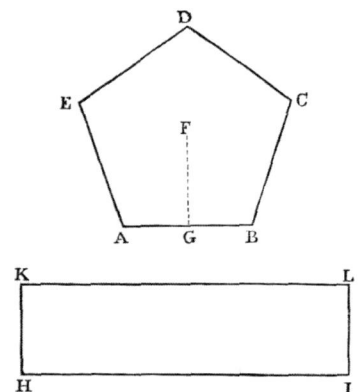

The arithmetical rule for finding the area of the regular polygons is to multiply half the perimeter, or of the sum of the sides of the figure, by the perpendicular, let fall from the centre upon one of the sides. The areas of the first ten regular polygons may be found by multiplying the square of the side, by the corresponding number in the following table:—

No. of sides.	Name of polygon.	Multipliers, or area when the side is 1.	No. of sides.	Name of polygon.	Multipliers, or area when the side is 1.
3	Equilateral triangle	·4330127	8	Octagon	4·8284271
4	Square	1·0000000	9	Nonagon	6·1818242
5	Pentagon	1·7204774	10	Decagon	7·6942088
6	Hexagon	2·5980762	11	Undecagon	9·3656399
7	Heptagon	3·6339124	12	Dodecagon	11·1961524

These numbers represent the areas of the polygons with the side 1, and similar figures are to one another as the squares of their sides; hence the rule—Let the side of a pentagon=3 ft., then 3×3 =9, and 9×1·72=15·48 ft., or nearly 15 ft. 6 in., the area of the pentagon.

PROBLEM 120.—To make a rectangle equal in area to a given rectangle, and with a side equal to a given line.

Let A B C D be the given rectangle, and E F the given line, on which it is required to construct a rectangle of equal area. Find a line having the same proportion to the shorter side A D of the given rectangle, that E F has to

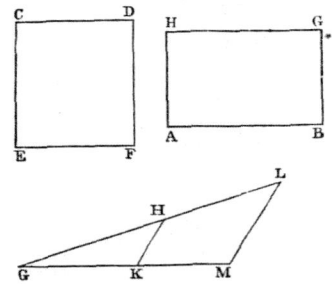

A B; that is, from any point I, draw two divergent lines. Upon one of them make I N equal to A B, and I M equal to E F; upon the other make I L equal to A D. Join L M by a straight line, and from N draw M K parallel with it. Then is I K the side sought. From E and F raise perpendiculars to E F, making them equal to I K, and join G H; then is E F G H a rectangle equal in area to that given. This very useful problem is easily solved by arithmetic. Let A B=6 ft., and A D= 2 ft., and let the given line E F be equal to 4 ft., the fourth side is found by simply dividing the product of 6 multiplied by 2, which is the area of the given rectangle, by 4; the result is 3 ft., which is the quantity sought. Otherwise—

Let C D E F be the given rectangle, and A B the given line. Produce the sides C D and E F indefinitely; produce also the sides C E and D F to G and H, making E G and F H each equal to A B. Draw G F, extending it from F to meet C D, produced in a point L. From L draw L K parallel to D H (Prob. 8), and also equal to it, and join G K by a straight line; then is F M K H the rectangle required, equal in area to that given.

In a similar manner rhomboids may be drawn, equal to given rectangles. The solution of the problem depends on an important property of parallelograms, that if, through any point in a diagonal, lines are drawn parallel to the sides, the figure is divided into four lesser parallelograms. Two of these, through which the diagonal passes, are similar

to one another, and also to the whole figure; these are said to be about the diagonal. The remaining two, through which the diagonal does not pass, are called their complements, and are equal in area, although not always similar figures. This indicates an easy method of making a rectangle similar to a given rectangle, and with a given side. F or G L being the diagonal of G K L C, if G H, any given side, be measured upon G C, and H F and E F drawn, then G H F C is the required rectangle.

PROBLEM 121.—To make a square equal in area to a given rectangle.

Let A B C D be the given rectangle. Produce one side A B from B to E, until B E is equal to B C. Bisect A E in K (Prob. 12), and from K, with the radius K A or K E, describe a semicircle upon it. From B raise B H perpendicular to A E (Prob. 2), meeting the semicircle in H. Upon B H describe a square (Prob. 36) B F G H; this is of an area equal to the given rectangle. The side of a square, which is equivalent to any rectangle, is a mean proportional between its containing sides. If A B=8, and B C=2, then B H is the square root of 8×2, which is 4, and the proportion is 2 : 4 :: 4 : 8, and each area is 16.

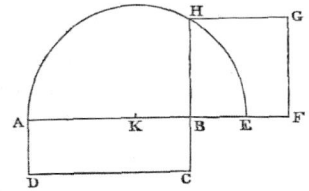

PROBLEM 122.—On a given line, to make a rectangle equal to a given square.

Let C D E F be the given square, and A B the given line. Find a third proportional to A B, and a side of the square (Prob. 26); that is, from any point G, draw two divergent lines. Upon one of them measure E F, a side of the square, from G to K; and upon the other measure A B from G to H, and from H to L. Join H K by a straight line, and from L draw a line L M parallel with it (Prob. 8), to meet the new line in a point M; then is M K the third proportional sought. Upon A B make a rectangle A B G H, whose altitude A H is equal to K M (Prob. 38). This rectangle is equal in area to the given square. If A B=9 ft., and E F, the side of the square=6 ft., then A H=$\frac{6\times6}{9}$=4, and the proportion is 9 : 6 :: 6 : 4, the area of each being 36. Otherwise—

Let A B C D be the given square, and E F the given line. Produce one side of the square, as D C to G, until D G is equal to E F. Join A G by a straight line, and parallel with it draw a line from D (Prob. 8) to meet the production of B C in H. Through H draw a line parallel to D G (Prob. 8), and to meet perpendiculars drawn from D and G (Prob. 5), in points I and K. Then is D G K I a rectangle equal to the given square; and its side D G is equal to the given line E F. When the given side is less than the side of the given square, the construction must be somewhat modified; that is, let D I be the given side. I K must be drawn parallel to D C, and B C produced to meet I K in H. D H is then drawn, and A G parallel with it, to meet D C produced in G, when K G being drawn, the rectangle is complete.

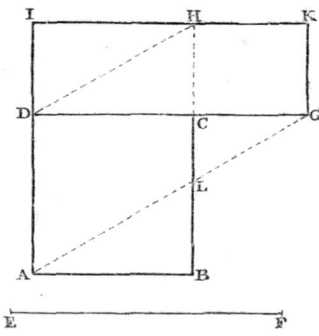

PROBLEM 123.—To divide a given straight line, so that the rectangle contained by its segment shall be equal to a given rectangle.

Let A B be the given line, and C D E F the given rectangle. Find D G the side of the square, which is equivalent to the given rectangle (Prob. 121). Upon A B describe a semicircle, and from B, one extremity, raise B G′ perpendicular to it (Prob. 5), and equal to D G. From G′, draw a line G′ H parallel to A B (Prob. 8), and meeting the semicircle in H. From H, let fall a perpendicular H I upon A B (Prob. 3), meeting it in I. Then is AB divided at this point into two parts, A I and I B, which will contain a rectangle equal in area to that given; that is, AIKL is equal to CDEF. The principle of this construction is plainly reversing the process for finding a mean proportional between two lines. The arithmetical computation is, from the square of half the line, to deduct the area of the given rectangle, the

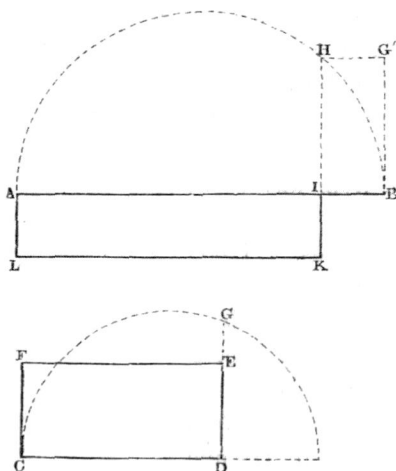

square root of the remainder, added to and deducted from half the line, will give the value of the respective parts. Let the area of the given rectangle = 36, and the given line = 15, then $\frac{15}{2} = 7.5$, the square of which is 56.25; and $56.25 - 36 = 20.25$, the square root of which is 4.5; this added to and deducted from 7.5, will be $7.5 - 4.5 = 3$, and $7.5 + 4.5 = 12$, then $12 + 3 = 15$, equal to the given line; and $12 \times 3 = 36$, which is the area required.

PROBLEM 124.—To produce a line, so that the rectangle contained by the whole line produced, and the produced part, shall be equal to a given rectangle.

Let A B be the given line, and C D E F the given rectangle. Find D G, the side of the square that is equal to the given rectangle (Prob. 121). Bisect A B in H (Prob. 12), and from one extremity B, raise B G′ perpendicular to it (Prob. 5), and equal to D G. Produce A B from B, until H K is equal to the distance H G′.

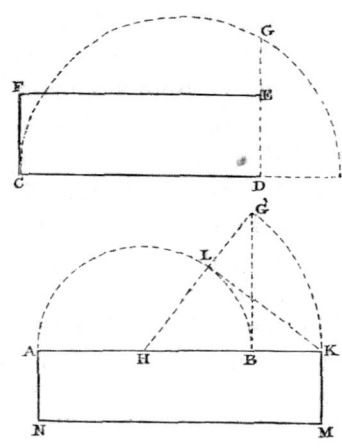

Then is A B produced to K, so that the rectangle contained by the whole line A K, and the part K B, or A K M N, is equal in area to the given rectangle.

The construction of figures that are equal in area to the sum of others is mainly effected by a property of the right-angled triangle, which is one of the most remarkable and beautiful in geometry. This is, that the squares described upon its sides have constant relations to one another; that upon the hypothenuse being always equal to the sum of the other two; and necessarily, that the difference between that upon the hypothenuse and one of the others, is equal to the remaining square; and as the areas of similar figures are to one another as the squares of their corresponding sides, it follows that similar figures of any kind, described upon a right-angled triangle, will have the same relations to one another that squares have, or that the figure upon the hypothenuse will be equal in area to the sum of the other two.

PROBLEM 125.—To make a square equal in area to the sum of two given squares.

Let A and B be the given squares. Construct a right-angled triangle D C E, right-angled at C, and having the sides about it equal each to a side of one of the given squares. The square D E F G, constructed upon the hypothenuse, is equal in area to the sum of those given. By arithmetic, the side of the square that is equal to two others is readily found, being the square root of the sum of the areas; for example, it will be recollected that, in Prob. 6, a method of drawing perpendiculars was given by means of a scale of equal parts, and that the numbers 3, 4, and 5, were employed. Let the side of A equal 3 ft., and that of B, 4 ft.; the areas of the squares will be, respectively, 9 and 16, which, added together, make 25; the square root of which is 5, or the side D C of the equivalent square is 5 ft.

PROBLEM 126.—To make a square equal in area to the difference of two given squares.

Let A and B be the given squares. Construct a right-angled triangle C D E, of which the side C D is equal to a side of the lesser square A; and C E, the hypothenuse, equal to the side of the greater square B (Prob. 22). The square D E F G, constructed upon the side D E of this triangle, is equal to the difference between the given squares. By number, let the side of A = 3, its area will be 9; let the side of B = 5, the area will be 25. The difference between these areas, or 25—9 = 16, is the area of the square upon D E; and the square root of 16, which is 4, is the side D E of the square.

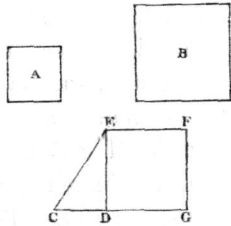

PROBLEM 127.—To make a square equal in area to the sum of any number of given squares.

Let it be required to make a square that shall have an area equal to three given squares A, B, and C. Construct a right-angled triangle F D E, making the sides D F and D E, containing the right angle, each equal to a side of one of the squares, as of B and C respectively. Upon F E construct a right-angled triangle G F E, making F G equal to the side of the third square A. The square E G H K con-

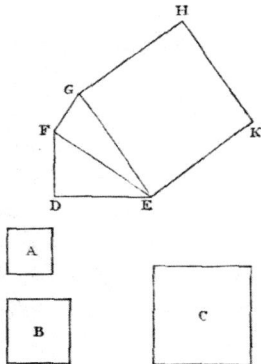

structed upon the hypothenuse G E of this triangle, is equal in area to the three given squares. It is evident that, by proceeding in this method, a square may be constructed, equal in area to any number of given squares; that is, by always adding one to the sum of those already found. By number, the side of the equivalent square is found by simply extracting the square root of the sum of all the areas added together. The same is applicable to any kind of figure, by employing a corresponding side of each, and constructing a similar figure upon the last found hypothenuse.

PROBLEM 128.—To make a square, whose area shall be equal to a given square, any required number of times.

Let A B C D be the given square, and let it be required to make a square of three times the area. Produce two of the sides, as A B and A D, indefinitely towards m and n. Draw the diagonal B D of the square, and make A E upon A n equal to it. Draw E B, and make A F upon A n equal to it. Then the square A F G H, which is constructed upon A F, has an area equal to three times that of A B C D. By proceeding in the same manner, always measuring upon A n, the distance between B and that last found, any number of equal squares may be added together. It is to be observed, that the diagonal of a square is always equal to the side of the square which has double the area.

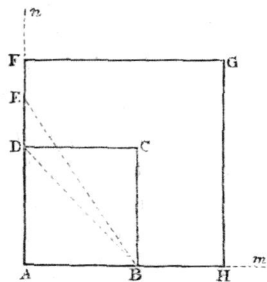

PROBLEM 129.—To make a figure similar and equal to two given similar figures.

Let it be required to make a figure similar and equal to two given similar figures, a b c d and e f g h. Construct a right-angled triangle, A B C, having the sides containing the right angle equal to a b and e f, two corresponding sides of the given figures. Upon A C, the hypothenuse, construct a figure A C D E, similar to one of the given figures (Prob. 101); this is equal in area to the two that were given.

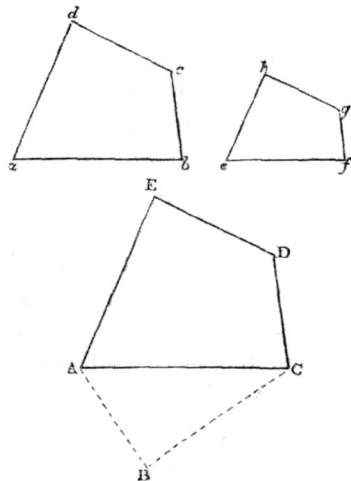

PROBLEM 130.—Upon a given line, to make a parallelogram equivalent to two given parallelograms.

Let A B be a given line, on which it is required to construct a rectangle, equal in area to two given rectangles, A C D E, and B C F G. Having constructed (Prob. 17) a triangle, A B C, with the given line A B, and one side of each of the rectangles, produce the sides E D and G F of the rectangles, until they meet in a point L. Through L and C, draw a straight line, extending it beyond the triangle until M N is equal to C L. Through N, draw a line parallel (Prob. 8) to A B, and from A and B draw perpendiculars to A B (Prob. 5), to meet the parallel drawn through N, in points H and K; then is A B H K the rectangle required, which is equal in area to those given. It must be observed, that it is not necessary that the parallelograms should be rectangular; they may be oblique-angled, and also dissimilar, the only condition being, that the given line which is to form a side of the new figure, must not be greater than the sum, nor less than the difference of the two sides of the parallelograms employed in the construction. This will show itself by the impossibility of constructing the triangle with the lines.

PROBLEM 131.—To make a square that shall be equal in area to any required part of a given square.

Let it be required to construct a square, equal in area to one-third of a given square A. Find a mean proportional between a side of the square and its third part, that is, draw B C equal to a side of the square, and produce it to D, making C D equal to a third part of it (Prob. 24). Upon B D describe a semicircle, and from C raise a perpendicular to it, producing it to meet the semicircle in E. Upon C E construct a square (Prob. 36); this will be equal in area to the third part of that given, as was required.

PROBLEM 132.—A rectilineal figure being given, to make a similar figure that shall be equal to any determined part of it.

Let a b c d be the given figure, and let it be re-

quired to make a similar figure that shall have two-thirds of its area. Draw a straight line, a' b', equal to a b, and produce it to e, until a'e is equal to two-thirds of a b (Prob. 24). Find a mean proportional a' a'' between a' b' and a' e (Prob. 27), and upon this line, or on A B, which is equal to it, construct a figure A B C D, similar to that given (Prob. 101), making A B correspond to a b in the figure, and the area will be two-thirds of the given figure a b c d. The areas of figures are as the squares of their corresponding sides; let a b = 6, then a' a'', the mean proportional between a b and a' e, which is two-thirds of it, or 4, will be 4·9; the squares of these numbers are in the required ratio, or as 24 to 36. By an extension of the problem the side of a similar figure in any ratio may be found, as a' e may be made any multiple of a b, and the mean proportional will be the side of a figure of a proportionally increased area.

PROBLEM 133.—To make a rectilineal figure that shall be similar to one, and equal to another given rectilineal figure.

Let it be required to construct a figure similar to A B C, an equilateral triangle, and equal to

D E F G, a given rectangle. Upon A B, the base of the triangle, make a rectangle A B H I of equal area (Prob. 108), and upon the side B H make a rectangle B H K L, equal to D E F G (Prob. 120). Find a mean proportional, H M, between I H and H K (Prob. 27), and upon this line, or H′M′, which is equal to it, construct an equilateral triangle H′ M′ M (Prob. 15); this is similar to A B C, and equal to the rectangle given.

PROBLEM 134.—To divide a given square into any number of proportional spaces, by means of concentric squares, whose sides shall be parallel to those of the given square.

Let A B C D be the given square, and let it be required to divide it into three equal spaces, by means of concentric squares. Draw the diagonals A C and B D, intersecting each other in E. Divide E A, one-half of the diagonal, into the required number of proportionate parts, which in the present case is three equal parts, E F, F G, and G A (Prob. 24). Upon E A describe a semicircle, and from F and G raise perpendiculars to E A (Prob. 2), meeting the semicircle in points H and K respectively. Make E L, upon E A, equal to the distance E H, and E M equal to the distance E K. From L and M draw lines L N and M O, parallel to A B (Prob. 8), and meeting the diagonal B D. Upon these lines make squares L N P Q, and M O R S (Prob. 36). These concentric squares divide that given into three equal spaces as required.

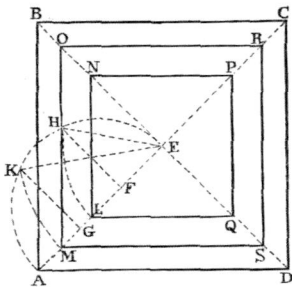

PROBLEM 135.—A rectangle being given, to divide it so that its parts may form a polygonal band of the same area.

Let A B C D be the given rectangle, and let it be required to divide it into parts that will form a

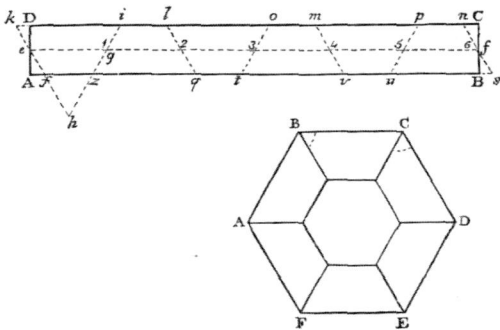

hexagonal band. Bisect A D in e (Prob. 12), and draw e f parallel to A B or D C, and divide it into six equal parts, 1, 2, 3, &c. (Prob. 24.) Upon

e g make an equilateral triangle e g h (Prob. 15), and produce the sides h g and h e to meet D C, and D C produced, in i and k. Make k l, l m, and m n, each equal to twice e g. Make also i o, o p, f q, q v, v s, z t, and t u, each equal to twice e g. Draw l q, m v, and n s, which will be parallel to k f; draw also o t and p u, which will be parallel to i z. The rectangle is thus divided into parts that may be arranged as A B C D E F, into a regular hexagonal band. The rectangle may be divided so as to form any polygonal band, by making the angles i z B, and k f A, equal to the external angle of the polygon, or i z A equal to the internal angle, and then drawing lines alternately parallel through the points of equal division, upon the middle line e f, as in the problem.

PROBLEM 136.—Within a given triangle to construct the greatest possible rectangle.

Let A B C be the given triangle. Bisect two of the sides, as C A and C B, in points D and E, respectively (Prob. 12). Join D E by a straight line; this line is parallel to A B. From D and E let fall perpendiculars upon A B (Prob. 3), meeting it in points F and G, respectively. Then is D E G F the greatest rectangle that the triangle will contain. The area of the rectangle is always equal to half that of the triangle; it is consequently found by multiplying half the altitude into half the base. It is to be observed, that the character of the rectangle will vary with the side that is assumed as the base, but the area always remains the same.

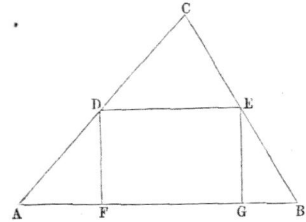

PROBLEM 137.—In a given triangle to inscribe the greatest possible square.

Let A B C be the given triangle. From any point D, in A C, let fall a perpendicular upon A B (Prob. 3), meeting it in E. Draw D F at right angles to D E, and equal to it (Prob. 5). Through A and F draw a line, and produce it to meet C B in a point G. From G draw a line G H, parallel to A B (Prob. 8), and meeting A C in H. From G and H let fall perpendiculars upon A B, meeting it at points K and L. Then is K L G H a square, and the greatest that can be constructed in the given triangle. It is plain, that by the same means a rectangle may be constructed within the triangle, whose sides shall have a given ratio; for this purpose D E and D F must be made to have

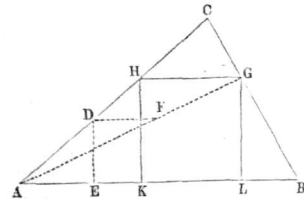

the required ratio, and the construction completed as before.

PROBLEM 138.—To draw a straight line equal to the circumference of a given circle.

Let A B be the given circle. Draw the diameter A B, and divide it into seven equal parts (Prob. 24) 1, 2, 3, &c. Draw a straight line C D, and upon it measure the diameter three times, C 1, 1·2, 2·3, and make 3 D equal to one seventh part of A B; then is the whole line C D nearly equal to the circumference of the given circle.

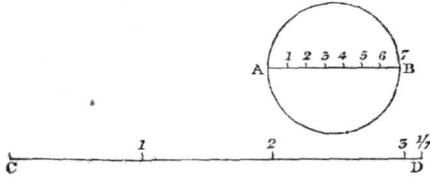

The absolute measurement of the circumference of the circle has not been effected by geometry; but there are various methods of obtaining an approximate expression of the relation of the circumference with the diameter, and from this the area and other measures are deduced; and any difference that there may be between the results obtained, and the unknown true expression, may be reduced beyond any conceivable quantity, so that, in practice, this want of exactness is of less moment.

In the mensuration of the circle, it is considered as a regular polygon, with sides that are, or may be made infinitely small; by a very simple computation it has thus been found, that the ratio of the diameter to the circumference of a circle, when expressed to ten decimal places, is greater than 1 to 3·1415926535, and less than 1 to 3·1415926536. In practice, there are several modes of more or less accuracy employed for expressing this measure of the circle. For many purposes, the ratio of the diameter to the circumference being taken, as in the construction in the problem, at 1 to 3¼, or, which is the same thing, as 7 to 22, is sufficient; the ratio of 1 to 3·1416 is employed when greater accuracy is required. It has been found that the ratio of 113 to 355 also expresses the relation with great exactness, being true to six places of decimals. The practical application is very evident, as it becomes a simple question of proportion when the diameter is given in number; thus, as 7 is to 22, so is the given diameter to a fourth proportional, which is the circumference; or, if the given diameter is 12 ft., then 7 : 22 : : 12 : 37·714 ft., which is the circumference nearly, in terms of the unit of the diameter, or any of the other ratios may be employed instead of 7 to 22. The diameter is derived from a given circumference, by inverting the terms of the ratio, or, as 22 is to 7, so is the given circumference to a fourth proportional, which is the

diameter sought. If the circumference is 12 ft., then 22 : 7 : : 12 : 3·81 ft., the diameter. There are also other methods by construction which afford remarkable approximations.

PROBLEM 139.—To draw, by construction, a straight line nearly equal to the given semi-circumference of a circle.

Let A B C be the given semicircle, described on the diameter A C, from the centre D. Raise A E perpendicular to A C (Prob. 5), and equal to three times the radius A D. Draw the radius D B perpendicular to A C (Prob. 5), and from B describe an arc intersecting the semicircle in G. Draw C F perpendicular to A C, to meet the radius D G produced in a point F, and join E F by a straight line; this line is very nearly equal to the semi-circumference given; that is, making the radius D A, 1 the semi-circumference is made equal to 3·14162, instead of 3·14159, &c.

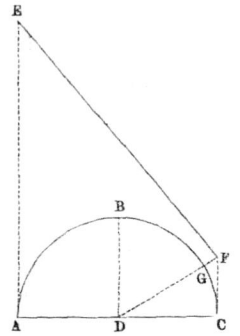

PROBLEM 140.—An arc of a circle being given, to make a straight line equal to it, the rest of the circle not being described.

Let A B be the given arc. Draw the chord A B, and produce it from one extremity B indefinitely. Bisect the arc in C (Prob. 33), and measure A C, the chord of half the arc, upon A B, produced from A to F and from F to D. Divide B D into three equal parts, and make D E equal to one of them. The whole line A E is nearly equal in length to the given arc. This method is very exact for small arcs, but the proportion between the chord of the arc and its height, should not be less than 8 to 1. The arithmetical rule is, from eight times the chord of half the arc, to deduct the chord of the arc, the third part of the difference is the quantity required. By using the above proportion of 8 to 1, the chord of half the arc = 4·1229, which multiplied by 8 = 32·9832, then $\dfrac{32\cdot9832 - 8}{3} = 8\cdot3277$, which is the length of the arc.

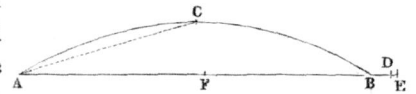

PROBLEM 141.—An arc of a circle being given of which the centre is known, to make a straight line equal to it.

Let A B be the given arc. From one extremity B draw a straight line through the centre d of the circle, and extending beyond it until e C is equal to three-fourths of the radius. From B draw also a line at right angles to B C, of indefinite length.

From C, through A, draw a straight line, producing it to meet the perpendicular to B C, in a point F; then is B F a line nearly equal in length to the arc A B. A modification of this method has been employed, for the solution of the general problem, for the division of the circumference of the circle into any number of equal parts, and inscribing the polygon.

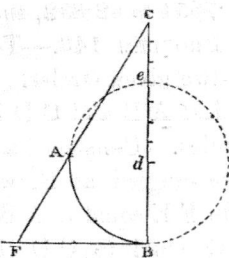

The length of an arc of a circle may sometimes be conveniently found by bending a thin slip of wood round the curve; the length of this, when extended in a straight line, will be very near the length required. Another method is similar to that adopted (Prob. 138), for finding the circumference of a circle, and consists in considering the arc as a portion of a polygon; a small part of it may be taken between the points of a pair of compasses, and this measured upon the curve accurately, as often as it will contain it, either with or without a remainder. The distance may then be repeated the same number of times on a straight line, and the length of the remainder, if any, added; the whole line will then be nearly the length of the arc. It is evident, that the smaller the distance taken by the compasses, the more nearly ought the result to be to the truth.

PROBLEM 142.—To make a triangle equal in area to a given circle.

Let the given circle be described about a centre B, with the radius B A. Let a straight line C D, be drawn equal to the circumference of the circle (Prob. 138), and from any point E in it, raise E F perpendicular to it (Prob. 2); join F C and F D by straight lines; then is the triangle C F D equal in area to the given circle. If the altitude of the triangle is made as g h, equal to the diameter of the circle, then the base C E must be made equal to the semi-circumference. And in the same manner the base and altitude of the equivalent triangle may be altered; for, if the altitude is increased, the base must be diminished in the same proportion, and the area of the figure will still remain the same.

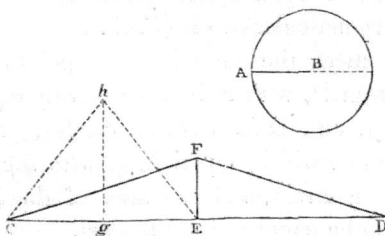

PROBLEM 143.—To make a rectangle equal in area to a given circle.

Let the given circle be described about a centre B. Draw a radius B A of the circle. Draw also a straight line C D, equal in length to the semi-circumference (Prob.139), and upon it make a rectangle C D E F, whose altitude, D E, is equal to the radius B A of the circle (Prob. 38). This rectangle is equal in area to the circle. The circumference of a circle being only approximately commensurate with the diameter, or the half diameter or radius, its area can only be determined with a degree of accuracy corresponding with that of the expression for the circumference. In the problem, the area is made by number to be the radius multiplied into the semi-circumference; or, if the radius is 4 feet, the whole circumference, by Prob. 138, is 25·143 feet, the half of which, or 12·571, is the semi-circumference; and this, multiplied by 4, will give 50·284 feet, which is very nearly the area of the circle.

PROBLEM 144.—To make a square equal in area to a given circle.

Let the given circle be described about a centre B, with a radius B A. Find a mean proportional between the semi-circumference and the radius of the circle, that is, draw a straight line C D, and produce it from D to E, until D E is equal to the radius A B. Upon C E, describe a semicircle, and at D raise a perpendicular to it, to meet the semicircle in a point F; then F D is the line sought. Draw G H equal to it, and upon it construct a square (Prob. 36). This square is equal in area to the given circle. By number, the value of the side of the square is easily ascertained. Let the radius be 4 feet, as in the last Problem. The area was found to be 50·284; the square root of this number, or 7·091 feet, is the side of the equivalent square.

The following very useful rules are derived from the foregoing, and some other Problems:—

1. To find the area of a circle, multiply half the circumference by the radius.

Or, multiply the square of the diameter by ·7854.

Or, multiply the square of the circumference by ·07958.

2. To find the side of a square of an area equal to that of a circle, multiply the diameter by ·8862.

9

Or, multiply the circumference by ·2821.

3. To find the diameter of a circle which shall contain a given area, divide the area by ·7854, and the square root of the quotient will be the diameter.

Or, multiply the area by 1·27324, and the square root of the product is the diameter.

4. To find the diameter of a circle of an area equal to a given square, multiply the side of the square by 1·1284.

5. To find the circumference of a circle which shall contain a given area, divide the area by ·07958, the square root of the quotient will be the circumference.

Or, multiply the area by 12·56637, and the square root of the product will be the circumference.

6. To find the circumference of a circle of an area equal to a given square, multiply the side of the square by 3·545.

7. To find the side of a square inscribed in a circle, multiply the diameter by ·7071.

Or, multiply the circumference by ·2251.

8. To find the area of an inscribed square, multiply the area of the circle by ·6366.

9. To find the diameter of a circle to circumscribe a square, multiply the side of the square by 1·4142.

PROBLEM 145.—To make a circle equal in area to the ring included between the circumferences of two concentric circles.

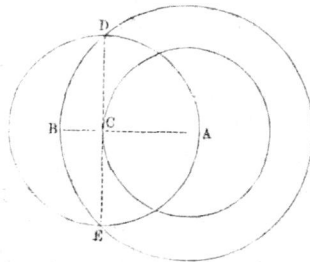

Let it be required to describe a circle whose area shall be equal to the circular ring included between the circumferences of two circles, described from a centre A, and whose breadth is B C. From A draw a radius A B of the greater circle, cutting the inner circle in C. Through C draw a line at right angles to A B (Prob. 2), meeting the circumference of the greater circle in D and E. From C as a centre, with the radius C D or C E, describe a circle. This will be equal in area to the given circular ring. The area of the ring is evidently the difference between the areas of the two circles; and the radius of the equivalent circle is a mean proportional between half the sum and half the difference of the diameters. Let the greater diameter = 12, the lesser = 8, then $\frac{8+12}{2} = 10$, and $\frac{12-8}{2} = 2$, the mean proportional between 10 and 2 is 4·4721, which is the radius sought, and 8·9442 is the diameter. The area may be found by Prob. 144 to be 8·9442 × 8·9442 × ·7854 = 62·832, &c. A more direct method is to multiply the sum of the diameters by their difference, and the product by ·7854; that is, 12 + 8 = 20, and 12 — 8 = 4, then 20 × 4 × ·7854 = 62·832, the area, as before.

PROBLEM 146.—To make a circle equal in area to two given circles.

Let A B and C D be the given diameters of two circles. Construct a right-angled triangle E F G, right-angled at F, with a side F E equal to A B, and F G equal to C D (Prob. 18). Bisect the hypothenuse E G in H (Prob. 12); and from H as a centre, with the radius H E or H G, describe a circle. This will be equal in area to both the circles of which the diameters were given. The difference of two circles may also be found in a similar manner, proceeding in the same way as for finding the differences of squares, as in Prob 126.

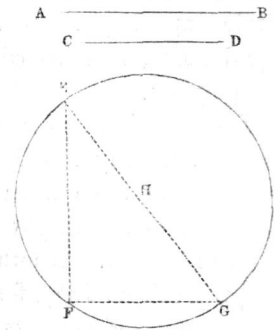

PROBLEM 147.—To divide a given circle into any number of equal or proportional parts by means of concentric circles.

Let the given circle be described about a centre D, with the radius D A, and let it be required to divide it into five equal parts by means of concentric circles. Divide the radius D A into five equal parts (Prob. 24), and upon it describe a semicircle. From each of the points of division upon the radius raise perpendiculars to it (Prob. 2), to meet the semicircle in points e, f, g, and h. From D, with radii respectively equal to D e, D f, D g, and D h, describe circles, each of the rings formed will be equal in area to the fifth part of the given circle, and the area of the inner circle will also be equal to its fifth part.

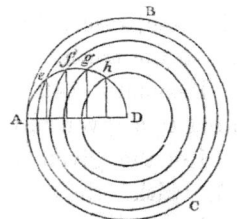

PROBLEM 148.—To divide a given circle into parts that shall be in any given proportion to one another, by means of concentric circles.

Let the given circle be described about a centre D, with a radius D A, and let it be required to divide the circle into parts that shall be in the proportions of one, two, and three. Divide the radius A D into six equal parts, or the sum of the terms. Upon A D describe a semicircle; and from the first and third points of division on it, from the centre, raise perpendiculars to it, to meet the semicircle in points *f* and *e* respectively. From D, with a radius equal to D *f*, describe a circle, and also from D, with the radius D *e*, describe a circle. The whole circle A B C will thus be divided as required; or the outer circular ring will be three times the inmost circle, and the intermediate will have twice its area.

PROBLEM 149.—To divide a given circle into any number of parts, which shall be equal to each other both in area and perimeter.

Let A B C D be the given circle, and let it be required to divide it into five parts that shall be equal to each other both in area and perimeter. Draw the diameter A C of the circle, and divide it into five equal parts (Prob. 24), at points *e, f, g,* and *h*. On A *e* describe a semicircle; and, on the same side of the diameter, describe semicircles upon A *f*, A *g*, and A *h*. Next, on the other side of the diameter, describe a semicircle upon C *h*; and, on the same side of it, semicircles upon C *g*, C *f*, and C *e*. The given circle will thus be divided into four parts that are equal both in area and perimeter.

ON THE CONSTRUCTION OF ELLIPSES AND SOME OTHER CURVED LINES.

Those curved lines, formed by the intersection of a cone by planes in different directions, are of the greatest importance in all the arts and sciences, on account of the great beauty of their forms, and the facility of their adaptation. These are extensively employed by the cabinet-maker in many ways, and their introduction into mouldings and other members, confers a graceful variety to the outline, which might not be otherwise attainable. Of these lines the ellipse is probably the most frequently used; it is that figure which is formed by the intersection of a cone by a plane which cuts *both* the slanting sides in any direction not parallel to the base; for it is evident that if the plane were parallel to the base, the section would be a circle. The other conic sections are the *parabola* and the *hyperbola;* the parabola is formed by the intersection of the cone by a plane in a direction parallel to one of the sides, and the hyperbola by any other section that does not cut both the sides.

Different names are given to lines drawn within the ellipse, and to certain points in it, which it is necessary to explain, as they are employed in their construction.

The two most distant opposite points, C and D, in the circumference of an ellipse, are called the *vertices*. And a straight line C D, drawn between the vertical points is called the *transverse axis*.

The middle point A, of the transverse axis, is called the *centre* of the ellipse, and any lines, K L, G H, &c., drawn through the centre to meet the circumference both ways, are called *diameters*. The diameters of an ellipse are not equal, as in the circle, but differ in length; the transverse axis C D being the longest, while the shortest, E F, is that which is perpendicular to it, and receives a particular denomination, being called the *conjugate* axis. The transverse and conjugate diameters, from their being the greatest and least diameters, are also called the *axis major* and *axis minor*. Two diameters of an ellipse are conjugate to one another, when one of them is parallel to a tangent to the curve drawn through the extremity of the other; thus, K L is conjugate to G H, being parallel to M E, a tangent to the ellipse at G, the extremity of G H; and conversely G H is conjugate to K L.

An *ordinate* to any diameter, is a line drawn parallel to its conjugate or to the tangent at its extremity, and terminated by the diameter and the curve; thus, *a* T being parallel to K L or M E, is an ordinate to the diameter G H; and when it is produced to meet the curve in the other direction, as at U, it is called a *double ordinate*. Every double ordinate is bisected by the diameter to which it belongs.

An *absciss* is a part of any diameter contained between its vertex and an ordinate to it, as C *b* or D *b*, also G *a* or H *a*.

There are two points *b* and *b* in the transverse axis C D, which are called the *foci* of the ellipse, and are so situated, that if two lines are drawn to them, from each point in the circumference of the figure, the sum of the two lines will always be the same, or equal to the greater diameter; that is, the sum of E *b* and E *b* is equal to C D. This affords an easy means of determining the points when both the axes of the figure are known; thus, from E, one extremity of the conjugate diameter, with a radius equal to A C or A D, describe an arc of a circle, cutting the transverse axis C D, in points *b* and *b*, which are the points required. The determination of these is of great importance in constructing the figure.

The double ordinate cd, which passes through the focus, is called the *parameter* of the diameter c D, and it is a third proportional to C D and E F, the conjugate diameter.

PROBLEM 150. — To describe an ellipse, the transverse and conjugate axes being given.

First Method.—Let ab be the given transverse axis, and cd the conjugate. Draw A B equal to ab, and from its middle point E raise E C perpendicular to it, and equal to ec, the half of cd. From C, with the radius E A,

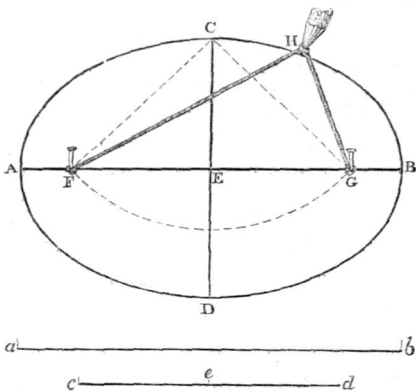

describe an arc intersecting A B in points F and G, which are the foci of the ellipse. In these points let pins of any kind be placed, and to them let the ends of an inelastic cord of suitable thickness be fastened, making its whole length equal to A B. If a pencil or other marking point be now looped in the cord, stretching it at the same time to its full extent, so that it forms two sides of a triangle, as F H G, and the pencil is moved round steadily until it returns to its first position, taking care always to keep the cord fully extended, a curved line will be traced, which is an ellipse, and it will have the given diameters.

Second Method.—Instruments are also constructed by which the ellipse is described by a continuous motion; of these, that most commonly employed is called a trammel. It consists of a fixed and a movable part. The fixed part is generally made of two rectangular bars E G and F H fastened together, so as to have a uniform thickness; on one side of this cross are two grooves, at right angles to one another. The movable part

is a rod or bar of wood or metal $k\,m$, upon which are three sliders, so constructed that they may be fastened securely at any point upon the bar, either by

screws or wedges; two of these, k and l, are, on the under side, provided with cylindrical pins, which fit exactly into the grooves, so that they may move freely, but without shaking, and the third slider m is contrived for holding a pencil or other marking point.

In order to use the instrument, let A C be the given transverse axis, and B D the semi-conjugate axis. Having drawn B D at right angles to the middle point D of A C, let the trammel be placed upon the line, so that the middle of one of the grooves, as E G, may be exactly over the transverse diameter A C, and the other D F over D B in the same manner; the intersection of the grooves will thus be over the centre of the ellipse. The sliders upon the bar must next be arranged. Let the tracing point m be fastened at a distance from l, one of the cylindrical pins, so that $l\,m$ may be equal to D B, the semi-conjugate diameter; and let the second slider k be fastened upon the bar, so that $l\,k$ is equal to the difference between A D, the semi-transverse diameter, and D B, the semi-conjugate, that is, the whole distance $m\,k$ is equal to A D. The pin l being now placed in the groove E G, and k in F H, by moving the bar round, and keeping the pins in the grooves, the pencil will trace an ellipse. By both these methods the true ellipse is described, but as it is not always convenient to employ them, different means are adopted by which any number of true points of the figure may be obtained, and these connected by a uniform curve, or when less exactness is required, figures approaching to the elliptical form may be produced by arcs of circles.

PROBLEM 151.—To describe an elliptical figure, by finding any number of true points in the curve, the transverse and conjugate axis being given.

First Method.—Let A B be the transverse, and D E the conjugate axis given, and let them be

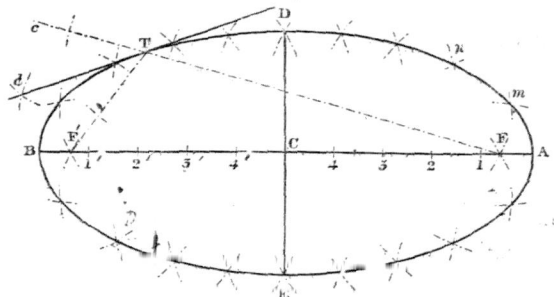

drawn so as to intersect each other at right angles at the middle point C. Find the foci F and F' of the ellipse, by describing an arc from D or E, with the radius C B, the half of A C. Assume any number of points, 1, 2, 3, &c., in the transverse axis A C, or it may be divided into any number of equal parts. Then from each of the foci as centres, with radii, the sum of which shall be equal to A B, describe intersecting arcs, that is, from F; with the radius A 1 describe an arc, and intersect it at *m* by a second, described from F' with a radius B 1. From F, with the radius A 2, describe an arc, and intersect it at *n* by a second described from F' with a radius B 2, and so on for all the points; these points of intersection will all be in the curve, and a line drawn through them will be the ellipse required. A convenient method of drawing the curve where practicable, is to place pins in all the points, and to bend a flexible and elastic slip of wood or metal round them on the convex side, and when it is nicely adjusted so as to touch all the pins, the curve may be drawn on the concave side, repeating the process when the curve is of a length to render that necessary.

The method of drawing a tangent to an ellipse is also shown in the diagram. Let T be a given point, at which it is required to draw a tangent to the curve. From F draw a line through T, producing it beyond the curve towards *c*. From F' draw F' T. Bisect the angle *c* T F' by the straight line *d* T; this line, produced both ways, is a tangent to the ellipse at T, as required.

Second Method.—Let A B and C D be the given axis, mutually bisecting each other at right angles

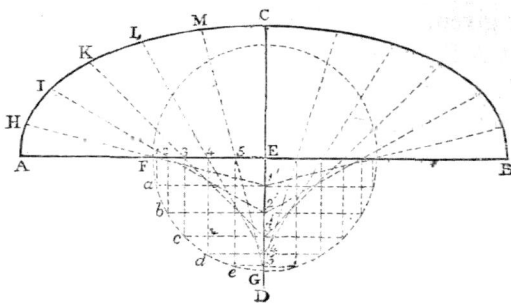

at E. From A upon A B, make A F equal to C E, the semi-conjugate axis; and from E, with the radius E F, describe a circle. Divide the quadrant F G into any number of parts, as into six equal parts at *a*, *b*, *c*, &c. From these points of section draw lines parallel to E G, meeting E F in points 1, 2, 3, &c., marking them from F to E; draw also lines parallel to E F, meeting E G in points 1', 2', &c., and mark them from E to G. Through 1 and 1' draw a line, and produce it to H, until 1 H is equal to A F or E C. Through 2 and 2' draw a line, and produce it to I, until I 2 is equal to A F. Proceed in the same manner with the other points marked with the same numbers, and the extremities A H I K L M C will be so many points in the elliptical curve, which may be drawn as in the last method; or small arcs of circles may be described through each three of the points. This is an exceedingly useful mode of constructing the ellipse, as the points in the curve may be found

by means of any kind of ruler, or even a piece of stiff paper; for if a distance is marked upon its edge equal to A E, the semi-transverse axis, and A F equal to the semi-conjugate axis, if the points E and F are applied to the diameters A B and C D, drawn at right angles to one another, the third point A is in the elliptical curve, and its position may be marked; the method will be readily understood by reference to the diagram.

Third Method.—Let A C be the transverse axis, and B E the conjugate, mutually bisecting each other at right angles. Draw B F parallel to A D, and F A parallel to B D. Divide F A into three equal parts, and join B 1 and B 2 by straight lines. Divide A D also into three equal

parts, and through the points E and 1 in A D, draw a line to meet B 1 in *k*, and through E and 2 draw a line to meet B 2 in *m*, the points *k* and *m* are each of them points in the ellipse. Bisect B *k* at *h* by a line perpendicular to it, and extended to meet the production of B E in G, and join *k* G. Bisect K *m* in *l* by a perpendicular line, producing it to meet *k* G in *n*, and join *m n*, intersecting A D in *o*. From G, with the radius G B, describe an arc of a circle passing through *k* and B, and extending it to P, until B P is equal to *k* B. From *n*, with the radius *n k*, describe an arc *m k*, and from *r* in P G, with the same radius, describe P *s*. From *o*, with the radius *o m*, describe the arc *m* A, and from *i*, the arc *s* C; a semi-ellipse will thus be produced, and the whole figure may be completed by repeating the same construction on the other side of A C.

Fourth Method.—When the transverse axis only is given, a figure approaching to the true ellipse may be constructed by dividing the given diameter, A B, into three equal parts at points *f* and *g*; from these points as centres, with the radius *f* A, describe circles which will intersect each other at C and F. Draw the diameters C D, C E, F G, and F H.

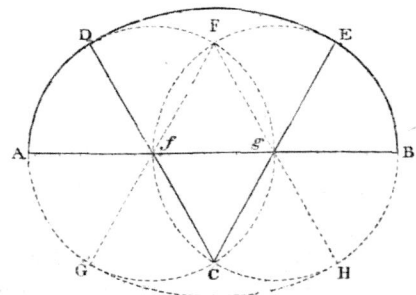

From C, with the radius C D, describe an arc D E; and from F, with the same radius, describe the arc G H. These arcs, with the intercepted arcs D A G and E B H, will complete the elliptical figure. It is not necessary that the line A B should be equally divided, for A *f* and B *g* being made equal, an equilateral triangle may then be constructed upon the remaining space, *f g*, the sides of which are to be produced to meet the circles described from *f* and *g*, and the vertex of the triangle is the centre from which the intermediate arc, D E, may be described. By this construction, the figure produced becomes very irregular, when the points *f* and *g* are placed too near to the extremities, A and B of the diameter.

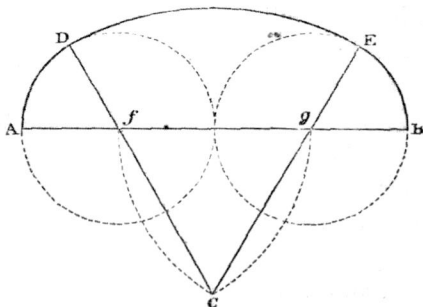

PROBLEM 152.—Two conjugate diameters of an ellipse being given, to describe the curve.

First Method—By means of ordinates.—Let M R and V H be the given diameters, intersecting each other at the centre C, of the ellipse; and let V H be the greater. From C, with the radius C V, describe a circle. Divide C H, the semi-transverse diameter, into any number of equal parts, at the points D, E, F, and G; and divide C M, the semi-conjugate, into the same number, in the points A, B, P, and N. From C, draw C S perpendicular to V H, and parallel to it; from the points D, E, F, and G, draw D S, E S, &c., to meet the circumference in points S. Through A, draw a line parallel to C H, and make the ordinate, A I, equal to D S. Draw B J parallel to C H, and equal to E S. Draw also P K and N L parallel to C H, and respectively equal to F S and G S. The points M, L, K, J, I, H, are true points of the ellipse, and other points of it may be found by drawing the ordinates in the same manner for each quadrant; and means may be taken for drawing the curve as indicated in the previous problem.

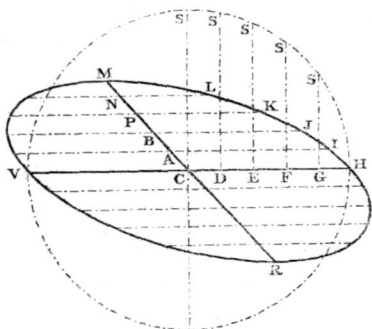

Second Method—By means of intersecting lines.—Let A B and D E be the given diameters, inter-

secting each other at C, the centre of the ellipse, and let A B be the greater. Through E and D, draw F P and H G parallel to A B, and through A and B, draw G P and H F parallel to D E. Divide A C and G A into the same number of equal parts, in

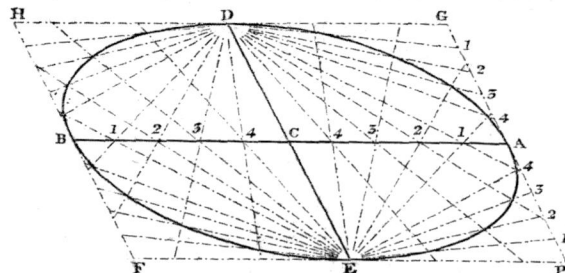

the points 1, 2, 3, and 4. From D, draw lines D 1, D 2, D 3, and D 4, to the divisions in G A; and from E, draw lines through the points of division in A C; these being produced, will intersect the former, and indicate true points of the curve, namely, the intersection of E 1 and D 4, of E 2 and D 3, of E 3 and D 2, and of E 4 and D 1. By proceeding in the same manner with the remaining quadrants, other points may be found, and the curve drawn as already indicated.

PROBLEM 153.—Two equal diameters of an ellipse being given, to describe the curve.

Let A B and C D be the given diameters, which intersect each other at their middle point, and at any angle. From A and B, draw lines A E and B F, intersecting C D at right angles; and from C and D, draw lines perpendicular to A B. These will intersect the first drawn perpendiculars at points G, F, and E, H. From G, with the radius G C, describe an arc, C A; and from H, with the same radius, the arc B D. From E, with the radius E A, describe the arc A D; and from F, with the same radius, the arc C B, which will complete the figure required. It is evident that if the equal diameters intersected each other at right angles, the construction would cease, and the figure would be a circle.

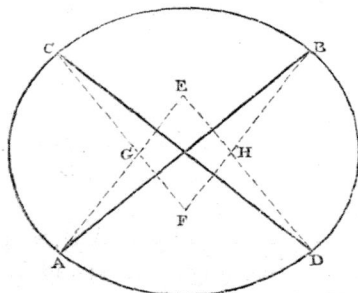

PROBLEM 154.—An ellipse being given, to find the centre, and to draw the transverse and conjugate diameters.

Let A B C D be the given ellipse. First, to find the centre: Draw two parallel lines, A B and E F, meeting the curve in E A B F. Bisect these lines, and through the points of bisection draw G H, to meet the figure in G and H.   Bisect G H in O; this point is the centre of the ellipse.   Next, to draw the axis: From O, with any sufficient radius, describe an arc of a circle, cutting the ellipse in points C and D; join C D by a straight line, and

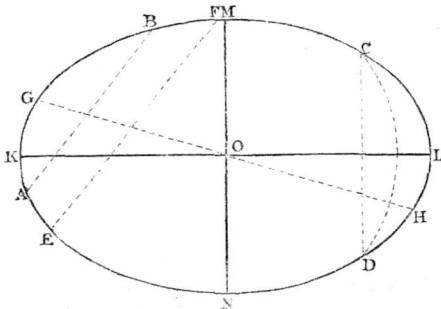

through O draw K L, perpendicular to it, meeting the curve both ways; this is the transverse axis; and a line, M N, drawn at right angles to K L, through the centre O, is the conjugate diameter as required.

PROBLEM 155.—To describe the curve called the ogee, or *cima recta* and *cima reversa*.

First, to construct the *cima recta*.   Let A B and C D be two parallel lines, in which the point A is the point of recess, and C the point of projection of the required curve.   Join A C by a straight line, and bisect it in E.   Bisect C E in F by a line perpendicular to it; and from C draw a line at right angles to C D, produc-

ing it to meet the perpendicular at F, in a point G. Bisect A E in H by a line perpendicular to it, and from A draw a line at right angles to A B, to meet the perpendicular to A E in a point I.   From G, with the radius C G, describe the arc C E; and from I, with the same radius, describe the arc A E. Then is A E C the required curve.

Next, to construct the *cima reversa*.   Let A be the point of recess, and C the point of projection, in the parallel lines A B and C D.   Draw A C, and bisect it in E.   Bisect C E in G, by a line perpendicular to it, producing it to meet C D in D.   Bisect A E in F, by a line perpendicular to it, and produce it to

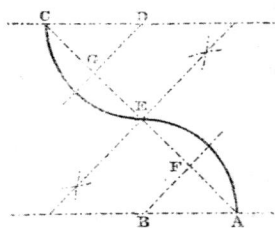

meet A B in B.   From D, with the radius D C, describe the arc C E; and from B, with the same

radius, the arc A E.   Then is A E C the *cima reversa* required.

It is evident that both the constructions are capable of infinite variation, both as to the quickness of the curve, as also to the position of the point of contrary flexure, E; both of which will very materially affect the character of the line.   The present construction is derived from standard Roman examples.   In Greek ornament, the ogee is usually quirked, and generally also in the Gothic.

PROBLEM 156.—To describe the contour of the *scotia*, or hollow moulding.

First Method.—Let A and C be the extremities of two parallel lines, A B and C D, of which A is the point of recess, and C the point of projection. From A, let fall a perpendicular A E, upon C D; and from C raise a perpendicular to C D, making C F upon it equal to the sum of the half of A E, and two-thirds of C E. From F, with the radius F C, describe a semicircle, G H C.   Through G and

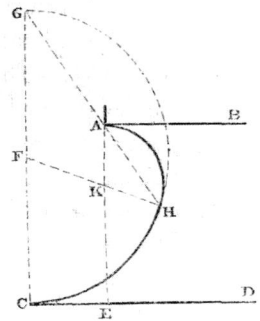

A draw a line, producing it to meet the semicircle in H, and join H F, intersecting A E in K.   From K, with the radius K A, describe the arc A H, which will complete the scotia A H C.

Second Method.—Let A and C be the extremities of two given parallel lines, A B and C D. Draw B D perpendicular to them, and make B N equal to the third part of B D. Draw A E parallel and equal to B N, and join E N by a straight line. From E, with the radius E A, describe the quadrant A F.   Produce N E to G, until E G is equal to the third part of E F.   From G, with the radius G F,

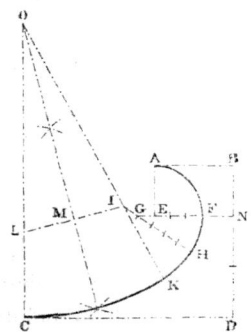

describe an arc F H, whose chord is equal to two-thirds of E F.   Join G H, and produce it to I, until G I is equal to one-fourth part of G H.   From C, raise a line C O, perpendicular to C D, and upon it make C L equal to I H.   Join I L, and bisect it in M, by a perpendicular line produced to meet C L in O.   Through O and I draw a line, and produce it towards K.   From I, with the radius I H, describe the arc H K; and from O, with the radius O K, describe the arc K C, which will complete the contour of the scotia.

Third Method—By an elliptical curve, drawn by means of ordinates.—Let A B and C D be the given parallel lines. Join A C by a straight line, and from the middle point, E, describe a semicircle upon it. Draw E F perpendicular to A C, and E G parallel to D C, and equal to E F. From any point, H in A C, draw H I parallel to E F, and H K parallel to E G, and equal to H I. Draw M N parallel to E F, and M L equal to it, and parallel to C D; proceed in the same manner for any number of points, and the curve may be drawn through the extremities A, K, G, L, C of the ordinates, as already indicated.

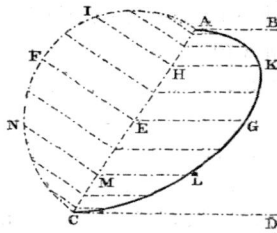

PROBLEM 157.—To describe the contour of an ovolo, the height and projection being given, and the tangent at the receding extremity.

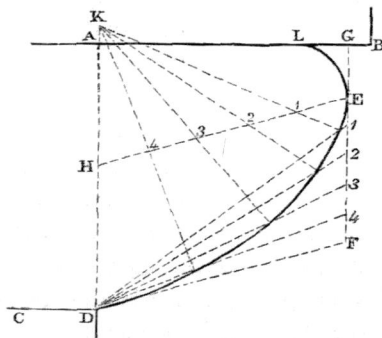

First Method.—Let A B and C D be the parallel lines, between which it is required to describe an ovolo. D A being the height or distance between them, E the projection of the curve, and D F the tangent at the receding extremity D. Through E draw a line, G E F, perpendicular to A B, producing it to meet the tangent D F in F. Make D H upon D A equal to E F, and produce D A to K, until H K is equal to E F. Join H E. Divide H E and E F, each into the same number of equal parts, at points 1, 2, 3, 4. From D, draw D 1, D 2, &c., to the divisions in E F, and from H, through the divisions in H E, draw lines, producing them to meet those drawn from D. The points of meeting of D 1 and K 1, of D 2 and K 2, &c., will indicate a number of points in the curve, corresponding to the number of pairs of lines. Points in the remaining part of the curve, E L, may be found in a similar manner, drawing lines from D, through points of division in H E, to meet lines drawn from K, to points of division in E G, or E G produced. When a sufficient number of points have been found in this manner, the curve may be drawn through them. By this construction, the extremity of the conjugate diameter is between D and E, and gives the moulding a full appearance. By the following method, the extremity of the conjugate diameter is made to coincide with the receding extremity D, and produces a very beautiful moulding.

Second Method.—Let A B and C D be the parallel lines, D the receding extremity of the curve, E its projection, and D F the tangent at D. Through E, draw a line G E F perpendicular to A B, meeting the tangent D F at F. Make D A perpendicular to D F. Join E D by a straight line, and bisect it in H. From F, draw a line through H, producing it to meet D A in a point K. From K, draw K L parallel to D F. From E, with the radius D K, describe an arc intersecting K L in M. From E, draw a line through M, and produce it to meet D A in N. Make K O upon K L equal to E N. Then, with the semi-transverse axis equal to K O, and a semi-conjugate axis equal to D K, construct an ellipse or a part of one; the portion of it contained between A B and C D, will be the curve required. In this manner, by altering the portion of the ellipse, as well as the part of it employed, a great variety may be introduced into the moulding; and the workman's task will show itself in the judicious selection and application of an appropriate part of an ellipse of suitable proportions.

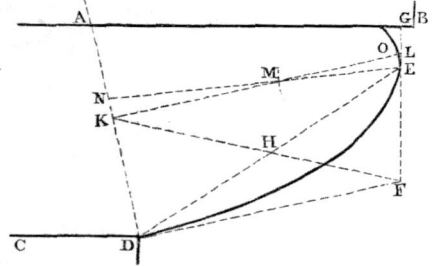

In the Roman examples, the ovolo is usually a quarter of a circle, which is easily described when the height is known; but when the projection is limited, and less than the height, it may be described as follows:—

Let A B and C D be the parallel lines, and let E D be the projection of the ovolo beyond the perpendicular B E. From B, with the radius B E, describe an arc of a circle, and intersect it at F by an arc described from D with the same radius. From F, with the radius F D, which is equal to B E, describe the arc D B, which will be the ovolo required.

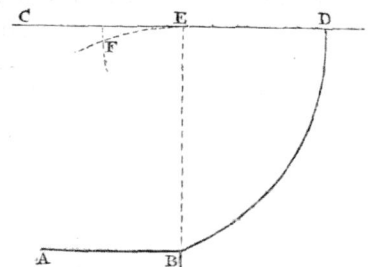

PROBLEM 158.—Two parallel straight lines being given, to describe a curve that shall be tangentical to them, at points that are not in the line which is perpendicular to both.

Case 1.—*First Method.*—Let it be required to describe a curve line touching two parallel lines, A B and C D, at their extremities A and C. Join A C by a straight line, and bisect it in E. Through E draw F G, parallel to A B or C D. Make E F upon F G equal to E A, and from F draw F H, intersecting A C at right angles. From A draw A K, perpendicular to A B, to meet F H in K; and from C draw C L, perpendicular to C D, meeting F H in L. From K, with the radius K A, describe an arc A F; and from L, with the radius L F, describe the arc F C. Then is A F C the curve required.

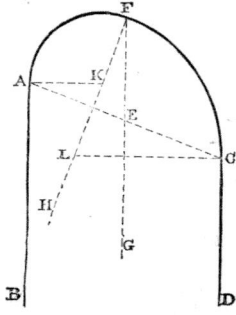

Second Method.—Let A and C be the extremities of two given parallel lines, A B and C D, of which A E is the distance from A to the point where the perpendicular C E, from C, falls upon A B. Upon A E construct the half of a regular polygon, as E *f g h k* A, the half of an octagon whose diameter is A E. Produce C E to L, until E L is equal to the sum of the sides of the half polygon. Bisect C L in *m*, and raise *m n* perpendicular to it, and equal to A E; upon it construct a half octagon, *m r o p q n* A, equal to that upon A E. From *q*, with the radius *q* A, describe an arc to meet the production of *p q* in R. From *p*, with the radius *p* R, describe the arc R S, to meet *o p* produced in S. From *o*, with the radius *o* S, describe an arc S T; and from *r*, with the radius *r* T, describe the arc T C, which will be tangential to C D at C, and the curve will be completed.

This latter construction, when well executed, produces a very uniform and beautiful curve. It will be understood that all these methods of connecting lines by means of curves, may be employed not only for hollow and projecting members of mouldings, and so forth—as for example, in the upper part of the side-board, Plate XIII., or in the work-table, Plate LVII., Fig. 5—but are also applicable for the determination of larger parts, as, for instance, the form of panelling, to fill irregular spaces, &c. When applied in the Gothic style, they give the contour of the rampant arch.

Case 2.—Let A B and C D be the given lines, and let the curve be also tangential to A C at the point E. From A, upon A B, make A F equal to A E; and from C, upon C D, make C G equal to C E. From E, raise E L perpendicular to A C. From F raise F H perpendicular to A B, to meet E L in H; and from G draw G L perpendicular to C D, to meet E L in K. From H, with the radius H F, describe the arc E F; and from K, with the radius K E, describe the arc E G. Then is F E G the curve required.

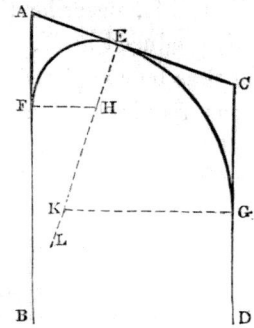

Case 3.—Let A and C be the extremities of two given parallel lines, A B and C D, and let it be required that the curve shall also touch a line which forms an angle with A B, equal to *a b c*. From any point E in the production of A B, let E F be drawn, making an angle B E F equal to *a b c*, and meeting C D produced in F. From E upon E F, make E G equal to E A; and from F, make F H upon E F equal to F C. Join A G and H C by straight lines, which will intersect each other at K. Through K draw L M parallel to E F, and describe the curve, as in the last case, to touch L M in the point K.

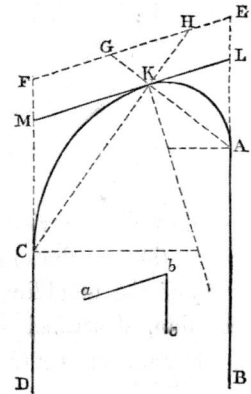

PROBLEM 159.—To construct a spiral curve, of which the radiant is given.

First Method.—Let A B be the given radiant. Divide A B into five equal parts, and from the extremity B draw B C perpendicular to it, and equal to one-fifth part of A B. Divide B C into five equal parts, and draw D C at right angles to it, making it equal to four-fifths of B C. Draw D E parallel to B C, and equal to four-fifths of C D. Join B D and C E by straight lines. From E draw E F parallel to D C, meeting B D in F; from F draw F G parallel to B C, meeting C E in G; from G draw G H parallel to C D, meeting D B in H, and proceed in the same manner for any number of centres required. Next, from B as a centre, with the radius B A, describe a quadrant B I, to meet B C produced in I. From C, with the radius C I, describe the quadrant

h

219

Another form of the T square is that called a *bevel*. In this, the stock is formed of two equal pieces of wood, b and c; the blade a, is fastened flush with one of them, b, while c is made so that it can turn upon a centre, and be fixed in any position with a thumb-screw. By this means the blade, and the piece c, being arranged at any angle, and fastened, parallel lines making that angle with the side of the board may be drawn, and also any number of other parallels may be drawn from an adjoining side which shall be at right angles to those first drawn.

The *set square* is another exceedingly useful instrument. It consists of a thin piece of wood, about the thickness of the blade of the T square, and in the form of a right-angled triangle, as Fig. 1. It is also sometimes made in the form of a trapezium, one of the angles of which is a right angle, the other angles being also of some determined and useful measure. Fig. 1 is a good form, having the angle at a a right angle, that at b equal to 30°, and that at c equal to 60°; these angles will be found serviceable in the construction of some triangles, hexagons, &c. In Fig. 2, a is a right angle, that at b is half a right angle, or 45°, and that at c is an angle of $67\frac{1}{2}°$; these are of great use in constructing squares, and octagonal figures. They may be of any size; but one of the most convenient is that in which the longest side may be about eight or ten inches.

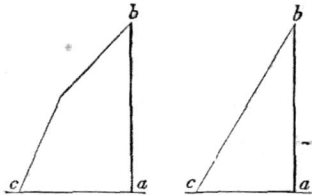

The set square will be found a great aid in drawing short perpendiculars, without the trouble of moving the T square from one side of the board to the other. For this purpose, one of the sides about the right angle must be laid against the edge of the T square, and the other adjusted so that the line drawn along it shall pass through any point. It may also be employed, with the straight edge, for drawing perpendiculars to any line whatever; **first bringing one of**

the sides a b about the right angle, to coincide with the line, then, placing the ruler against the hypothenuse a c, the square must be moved upon the edge until the third side b c is in such a situation that the line drawn along it will pass through any given point d. The set square affords a most convenient means of drawing parallel lines, not only from its easy application, but also that it is less liable to inaccuracy than most other methods. Let a side a b be made to coincide with the given line, and against a c let a ruler be placed. If the square is now moved upon the edge of the ruler, until any given point e coincide with a point in a b, the line drawn along this side will be parallel to the given line; and it is evident that any number of parallel lines may be drawn in the same manner. It need scarcely be remarked, that any inaccuracy in the edge of the ruler will produce corresponding errors in the lines drawn, because, if the side move in a curved direction, the different positions of either of the other sides will no longer be parallel to one another.

There are two or three different kinds of parallel rulers, which may be used sometimes with advantage. One of these consists of a single rule, in which is fitted an axis carrying two little rollers of equal diameters—one at each end, and the instrument moving upon these, its edges will maintain a position parallel to that to which it may have been adjusted. The edges of the rollers are toothed to prevent them from slipping instead of rolling on the paper, which would destroy the parallelism of the lines. Another kind is formed of two plain rulers, connected by two equal pieces of metal turning on centres, which must be equidistant in each;

they must also be placed so as to be always parallel to one another, that is, so that the four centres may form a parallelogram in whatever position they may be placed. To use this instrument, the edge of one of the rulers must be brought to coincide with the given line; the other ought then to be held firmly by one hand, while the first is moved until the edge is brought to the place of the required parallel; it is now, in its turn, to be held while the line is drawn. Care should be taken that the ruler does not slip during any part of the process, otherwise error is introduced. These rulers answer their purpose very well for short lines, or where great accuracy is not so much looked to as speedy work; but the T square and the drawing board are always to be preferred, and also the method by means of the set square and ruler.

We have already described the ordinary compasses used for making circles, but it sometimes happens that a circle, or its arc, is required of a larger radius than can be managed with such instruments. In this case, it is necessary to employ the *beam compasses* or *trainer*, as it is sometimes called, and which may easily be formed to describe circles of any size. It consists of a bar of wood C C, generally of well-seasoned mahogany, and of

any required length; upon one face of this a slip *a a* of brass, or of some kind of hard light-coloured wood, is inlaid, upon which is marked a scale of feet and inches, with fractional parts of the latter. Two brass boxes, A and B, are fitted on the beam, one of which, B, may be moved throughout its length, and retained firmly, at any required point, by a clamping screw F. The other box, A, has a limited motion, for nice adjustment, by the screw D, and may be fastened by the clamping screw E. Both boxes have points G and H attached, for one of which may be substituted a pencil-holder or a pen. In the sides of the boxes are two openings, *b* and *d*, through which the scale upon the beam may be seen, and the instrument set. The method of using this kind of compasses is easily understood from the description of the parts; for the box A being placed so that the divisions of its scale coincide with that upon the beam, the box B and its point may be placed at any required distance from it. If, again, it is required to transfer a distance with accuracy, the points being placed by hand as nearly as possible, the slow motion effected by the screw D affords the means of perfecting the setting of the instrument to any minute quantity.

Arcs of large circles may also be described by means of the principle pointed out in Prob. 48, and illustrated by Prob. 49. For example, the angle contained by a semicircle is a right angle; hence it may be described by means of a square, the sides of which, B D and B E, are a little longer than the diameter

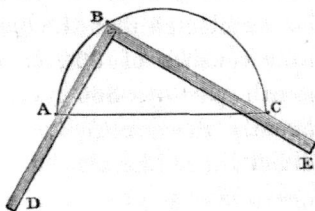

A C. Two pins are fixed at A and C; the square being moved between these, the point B will describe a semicircle which may be traced by a pencil, or marked in any way that is more convenient. In the same way any arc of a circle may be described if its angle is known; that is, if any three points in it are given, merely substituting such angle for the square in the diagram.

Besides the circular curve, the cabinet-maker generally requires others, which, with the exception of the ellipsis, it is necessary to draw by hand. These are of constant occurrence, and in order to facilitate the production of clean and finished drawings, a number of *sweeps* will be found exceedingly useful. These consist generally of thin pieces of pear-tree wood of different figures, the edges of which are cut into a variety of curves as in the figure. The use of this kind of rule is simple. The drawing having been sketched by hand, and the curves indicated as nearly as possible, some part of a sweep may be found which will nearly coincide, either wholly or in part, with the curve to be described, and it may then be drawn with a pen or pencil in the usual way; care must be taken in shifting the sweep that the ends of the lines nicely unite with one another so as to appear continuous, otherwise a very disagreeable effect is produced, not unfrequently spoiling the whole drawing. A few of these curves, of different forms, being procured, portions of them will generally be found to agree with any kind of line that may be required. This method, it must be observed, ought not to be employed in drawing complicated ornamental work, especially if on a small scale; such should always be drawn by hand, as greater ease and freedom may thus be attained, while stiffness and formality are avoided.

The construction and employment of scales of different kinds, is a matter of great importance to every draughtsman, being one of the chief means whereby drawing is made available in the mechanical arts; without their aid, the workman would scarcely be able to carry into effect any design, with that degree of certainty which is desirable in perfecting his productions. For this purpose, the design or working drawing is always constructed to a scale which ought in all cases to be given, in order that the workman may refer to it, and know the relative dimensions of the different parts. One of the scales most frequently in the hands of the cabinet-maker is that of feet and inches, with their subdivisions; his work is generally designed to this scale, though seldom to the full length of the foot, but a certain space is assumed to represent a foot, as in Fig. 1; and is subdivided into twelve

parts, which represent inches; if the scale is sufficiently large to require it, these may be again subdivided into tenth or eighth parts. In this way, Fig. 1 represents a scale of three feet altogether, but it may be extended to any number. Fig. 2 is a scale in which the space assumed is the same as in the former, but is made to represent ten feet, and this is divided into ten equal parts, each of which consequently represents one foot; the use is similar to the last. It ought to be observed that in making these scales, the numbers of the smaller divisions ought to be placed in an order from right to left, and the larger in the contrary direction; this is more convenient for taking off measures, as, for instance, in taking in the compasses a distance of one foot nine inches from Fig. 1, or fifteen feet from Fig. 2.

It is evident that in measuring distances on scales of the foregoing construction, the eye must be depended on when fractional parts of the smaller divisions are required—a method that may be sufficient for many purposes. In drawings on such a small scale as Fig. 2, the principal measures ought to be marked in figures, and the mouldings and other details on a larger scale, if they are to be understood at all. One of the most convenient modes of obtaining minute subdivisions of short lines, is by the construction of what is called a *diagonal scale*. For instance, a scale of feet and inches may be thus simply formed. Draw seven lines equidistant and parallel to one another, containing six spaces of equal breadth, Fig. 1. The length A B, to repre-

sent a foot, being determined, lines are drawn parallel to one another at right angles to those first drawn, and at a distance equal to A B, a scale of

feet is thus formed. From the middle point of A B, the last division on the left hand, draw the diagonal lines 6-0 and 6-12; these will intersect the parallel lines, and indicate the inch divisions or the twelfth parts of A B, which may be numbered as in the diagram. Another kind of diagonal scale, and one that is very useful for general purposes, particularly where measures are to be subjected to any process of arithmetic, is that called the decimal diagonal scale. This is represented in Fig. 2. Eleven equidistant parallel lines are drawn, containing ten spaces of equal breadth. These are intersected at right angles, as in the former case, by parallel lines A D, B E, C 1, &c., which are equidistant, and indicate the numbers of the assumed unit of measure of the scale. The lines A B and D E of the last division on the left hand, are next divided each into ten equal parts, and, lastly, lines are drawn from B to the first division, from E in D E, from the first division in A B to the second in D E, and so on. The unit of measure, A B, is thus divided into 100 equal parts, or its hundredth parts are known. Thus, if the distance from the perpendicular 3, 3, to the point 6 in A B is taken, it will be 3·6 or $3\frac{6}{10}$; if the distance from n in the same perpendicular, and on the sixth parallel, is taken to o, its intersection with the sixth diagonal, the distance will be 3·66 or $3\frac{66}{100}$. In a similar manner, if A B is 10, then the first measure will be 36, and the second 36·6; or if A B is 100, then the first will be 360, and the second 366, say feet, or any other measure. The ivory or boxwood scales, contained in cases of mathematical instruments, have, on one side, lines divided in this way, generally a half inch and a quarter inch, but the draughtsman frequently requires other scales; these he must construct for himself. On the other side of the same ruler the inch is divided into 15-20, &c., numbers of parts. There is, besides, a scale of chords marked C, which is of use in drawing lines at given angles to one another. The construction and use of this scale will be easily understood from the diagram. The straight lines B A and B C are drawn at right angles to one another, and a quadrant A C described between them with the radius B C. It will be recollected that the quadrant consists of 90°, or the fourth part of 360°, consequently the arc A C, being divided first into nine equal parts, and each of these again into ten, the whole will be divided into ninety parts or degrees. Let the chord A C be drawn, and from C, with a radius equal to the distance from each point of division in the arc, describe arcs of circles to meet the chord A C as shown. A C is thus converted into a scale of chords, from which angles may be measured in the following manner. Let it be required to draw a line at an angle of 50°, with B C a given line. From B, with the chord of 60° taken from the scale of chords, describe a sufficient arc of a circle, and intersect it by an arc described from C, with a radius equal to the chord of 50° taken from the same scale. Through B and this point draw a line, which will form the required angle with B C. Should the angle be greater than a right angle, the line must be produced, and the supplemental angle of that given, or its deficiency from two right angles employed. By reversing this operation, any given angle may be measured; that is, an arc is to be described, with the chord of 60°, from a scale, and the chord of the intercepted part of the arc measured upon the scale. It must be recollected that the chord of an angle of 60° is equal to the radius of the circle of which it is a part, and hence the reason of the construction.

Angles are also measured and set off by an instrument called a *protractor*. This is simply a semicircular piece of brass or horn, the centre of which is marked; the circular edge is converted into a double scale of 180°, which are marked, in contrary directions upon the instrument, for the purpose of avoiding some trouble in find-ing supplement-al angles. The

use of the protractor is very easy; for instance, let it be required to draw a line at an angle of 40°, with a given line B C. The centre of the instrument being placed at the point where the angle is required, and the straight side to coincide with the given line, the angle may be marked off with a fine pointed pencil or other sharp point; a line B D is then to be drawn through this and the point B, which will form the required angle with B C; or, if it is required to find the measure of a given angle D B C, the centre of the protractor must be made to coincide with the vertex of the angle, and the straight side with a side of the angle; its measure may then be read off by observing where the other side intersects the edge of the instrument. The protractor is sometimes made in the face of a parallelogram, the scale being marked by lines radiating from the central point to three of the edges, the fourth side coinciding with the diameter. In employing such an instrument, without great care error is apt

to arise, from the great obliquity of some of the lines with its edge, rendering it difficult to mark an angle with any degree of accuracy. The semicircular protractors are generally to be preferred.

The different divided lines that have been mentioned as occurring on ordinary rulers, will be found useful individually; but as they are unalterable, they can only be employed when they happen to suit the scale on which the construction is to be made. The *sector* is an instrument by which this is obviated. This consists of two flat rulers moving round an axis or joint, exactly as in the carpenter's common two-foot rule. The centre of this joint is marked, and from it several scales are drawn on the faces of the rulers, and also some close to the edge or on it. The whole of these scales are not of equal importance to the cabinet-maker, but such as he will find useful we shall proceed to explain. The sector is usually six inches in length when shut, but it is sometimes made of twelve inches, and when fully opened, may be employed as an ordinary measure by the scale of inches and parts at its edge. The other scales which proceed from its centre are double, or each scale is laid twice on the same face of the instrument, once on each leg. The principle of its con-struction is derived from the proportionality of the sides of similar tri-angles. Thus when the legs of the instrument are opened to form any angle A C I, a number of similar triangles are formed by connecting points in each, which are equidistant from C, as E, D, B, in the one, respectively with F, G, H, in the other; the sides and bases of each of these triangles have the same common proportion, or C F : E F :: C G : G D, and the same for the others.

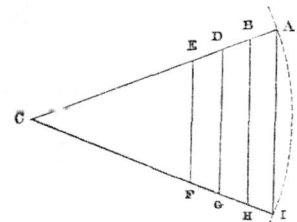

The instrument is used in connection with the compasses, not only for its adjustment, but also for taking the distances from it. Any distance measured on the scales of the sector, from the centre C towards A or I, is called a *lateral distance;* and any space, as from E to F, taken between the corresponding divisions of the scales of the same kind, is called a *transverse distance.*

The radiating scales on the rulers are, on one side, the line of lines, marked L; the line of secants, S; the line of chords, C; and the line of polygons, Pol.; on the other side, a line of sines, S; and two lines of tangents, T. There are also some logarithmic scales on this side. Of these scales, it will be sufficient to explain the use of the line of lines, the line of chords, the line of sines, and the line of polygons. It must be observed that each of the sectoral scales have three parallel lines, across which the divisions of the scale are marked; now, in taking transverse distances, the points of the compasses must be always set on the inside line, or that next the inner edge of the leg, for this line only, in each scale, runs to the centre.

The line of lines is simply a scale of equal parts adapted to the length of the sector. This is divided into ten primary divisions, and these again into ten secondary, which are sometimes subdivided into four equal parts. By this line a given line may be divided in any proportion; proportions may be found to given quantities; and right-angled triangles constructed, or their sides found.

To divide a given line in any required proportion, say that the parts shall be to each other as 2 and 3; these numbers, being added together, make 5. The length of the given line must now be taken in the compasses, and made a transverse distance between 5 and 5 on the scales. The transverse distance between 2-2, and between 3-3, are the lengths of the parts required, as may be seen by dividing the line 5-5 at *a*, making 5 *a* equal to 2-2, the remainder *a* 3 will be found equal to 3-3. In the same manner a line may be divided into any required number of equal parts, say 5. The length of the line being made a transverse distance between 5 and 5, and the sector retained in this position, the transverse distance between 1-1 will be the fifth part of the line, and, being measured upon it, will be divided as required. When a line is too long to be made a transverse distance, it must be bisected continually until it comes within the sector. Thus, if the given line is of such a length that the fourth part only can be made a transverse distance, then the distance between 4-4 will be the part required, and not 1-1. Scales may also be constructed, by this means, of any given length, and containing a given number of equal parts; thus, a scale of fifty feet, to be four inches in length, may be formed by making the transverse distance, from 5 to 5, equal to four inches; then the transverse distance between the corresponding decimal divisions, on the line of lines, will be the scale of feet required. These uses of the line of lines will be found very serviceable, particularly in altering scales in any required proportion.

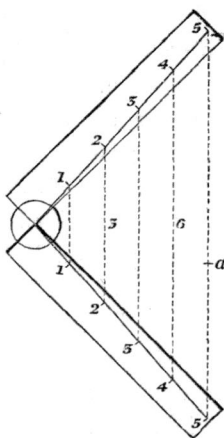

A fourth proportional may be found to three given lines or quantities by the following means. Let the lines given be 2, 3, and 4, say inches; in this case the scales of equal parts on the sector must be considered to represent inches. Make the transverse distance 2-2 of the first term equal to the lateral distance of the second, that is, 3 taken from the scale; the transverse distance of the third term 4-4, will give the fourth term, or the distance 4-4, measured upon the scale laterally, will show how many inches and parts make up the required quantity; here $2 : 3 :: 4 : 6$, as in the diagram. This rule is very usefully applied in increasing or diminishing a given line in any required proportion, say to diminish a line of 4 inches in the proportion of 8 to 7. Open the sector until the transverse distance 8-8 be equal to the lateral distance of 7. Next mark the point to where four inches will reach as a lateral distance taken from the centre, then the transverse distance taken at that point will be the line required. A third proportional to two given lines, as of three and four inches, is found, when in an increasing ratio, by making the transverse distance 3-3 equal to the lateral distance 4, the transverse distance of 4-4 measured laterally, will give the third proportional sought, or $5\frac{1}{3}$ inches; in a descending ratio, the transverse distance 4-4 must be made equal to the lateral distance 3, when the transverse distance 3-3, measured laterally, will give $2\frac{1}{4}$ inches, which is the proportional required.

The two scales of lines on the sector may be placed at right angles to one another, by a means employed in the construction of perpendiculars, namely, that any triangle, whose sides are respectively 3, 4, and 5, equal parts, is a right-angled triangle; therefore by taking 5 parts from the scale, and making it a transverse distance between the lateral distance 3 on one scale, and 4 on the other, the two scales will be placed at right angles to one another, and may be used for finding the sides of right-angled triangles; for instance, let the given base be 6, and the perpendicular 5, then the transverse distance between 6 on one scale and 5 on the other, measured on the scale laterally, will be about $7\frac{4}{5}$, which is the length of the hypothenuse or third side. Or, if the hypothenuse 8 is given, and another side 5, then take 8 in the compasses from the scale, and from 5 on one scale, observe where the transverse distance 8 reaches on the other; then from that point to the centre is the third side, which will be found to be about $6\frac{1}{4}$.

To find a mean proportional between two lines, as between 40 and 90, the scales of lines must be set at right angles to one another; find half the sum of the given quantities, which is 65, and half their difference, which is 25; then take the lateral distance 65 in the compasses, and placing one foot on 25 in one scale, extend the other to the opposite scale and observe where the transverse distance 65 falls; the lateral distance, in this case 60, is the mean proportional sought.

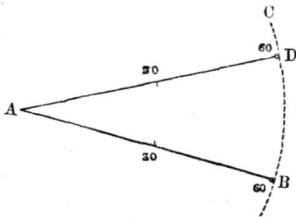

The sectoral lines of chords are more convenient than the single scale, since they apply to any radius contained within the transverse distance 60-60, at all openings of the sector. To protract an angle of less than 60°, say an angle of 30° at A, on a given line A B. Opening the sector at pleasure, take the transverse distance 60-60, from the line of chords, and with this radius describe an arc B C; set off from B to D, the transverse distance 30-30, and draw the line A D, then is D A B the required angle. When the angle is more than 60°, and less then 90°, set off the transverse distance 60-60 on the arc B C, and also a transverse distance equal to the difference between 60° and the required angle. If the angle exceed 90°, it is better to describe a semicircle, and set off either one or two transverse distances equal to the difference between 180° and the required angle. To protract a small angle, say of 6°, make an angle of 60° and measure off from the arc the transverse distance of the difference 54°.

The lines of polygons (marked *Pol*) are placed along the inner edges of the sector, and are used for the construction of regular-sided figures of from 4 to 12 sides inclusive. They are adapted to the divisions of the lines of chords, and the transverse distance 6-6 is equal to radius. To construct a polygon, say of eight sides, of which each side shall be equal to a given line, make the given line, a transverse distance between 8-8; then take the transverse of 6-6, and with this as radius describe a circle; take again the transverse of 8-8 and measure round the circumference, and complete the figure, by drawing lines from point to point. To describe a polygon within a given circle, make its radius a transverse to 6-6, then take the transverse of the required number of sides, and measure round the circumference as before.

The only other sectoral lines* that we shall describe, are the lines of sines marked S. Their

* In the use of the sectoral lines there is a perplexing discrepancy between the theory, which is perfect, and the practice, which is extremely liable to error. The various lines are never divided with absolute mathematical accuracy; and even if they were, the constant application of the points of the compasses must necessarily widen the divisions. It requires some dexterity of manipulation to compensate the minute errors of excess in deficiency.

principal use to the cabinet-maker is in the construction of ellipses. Let A B be the longer diameter of an ellipsis, and C D the shorter. These must be drawn at right angles to each other, bisecting at E, which is the centre of the ellipsis. Make A E the half of the longer diameter a transverse distance to 90-90, and take the transverse distances of 10°, 20°, 30°, 40°, 50°, 60°, 70°, 80° successively, and apply them upon A E, from E towards A, as at the points 1, 2, 3, 4, &c. Through these points draw lines parallel to E C, or perpendicular to A E. Next, make E C a transverse distance to 90-90, and take the transverse distances of 80°, 70°, 60°, &c., and apply them successively to the perpendicular A E, as 1 *a*, 2 *b*, &c., and so many points will be obtained through which the elliptical curve will pass. The operation must be repeated for each of the four quarters of the figure.

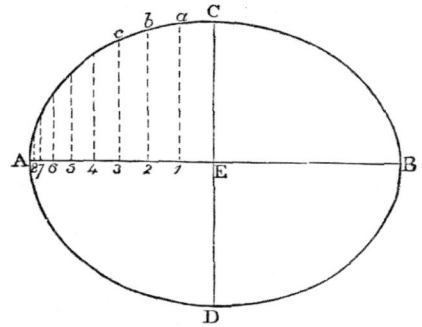

DRAWING.

Drawing is the art of delineating any object on a plane surface, by so representing its parts in their relation to one another, that a distinct idea may be conveyed of the form of that object, and of such of its properties as may be capable of being expressed by the means employed, as lines, shadows, &c.

Outline is the most important part of drawing; and as more is expressed by this means than any other, it demands so much the greater attention on the part of the designer. Drawing divides itself into two branches—the one executed by the eye and hand alone, without the aid of any instrument except the pen or pencil, this is called *free-hand drawing;* the other is the more exact and rigorous delineation of forms, by the help of scales, measures, and instruments of different kinds, named *geometric drawing.*

Drawing as employed by the cabinet-maker is of easy attainment, requiring only a little pains and perseverance to overcome the few difficulties that lie in the way. Free-hand drawing is not independent of taste, yet consists chiefly in the education of the eye, in judging of lines and distances—and in command of hand to express them. For this purpose,

i

in the absence of regular instructions, a few curves may be drawn, by means of a large sweep, of such a kind as described in page lxi. These may be imitated by hand as accurately as possible, of the same size first; and when sufficient facility and correctness have been attained, they may afterwards be drawn of any greater size, either upon large coarse paper, or upon a black board set upright. This will in time give freedom and boldness of hand, but care must be taken not to hurry, or to pass over inaccuracies. Another very useful exercise for the eye is the division of lines, and judging of distances, &c.; for instance, a line may be drawn and divided into two, three, or more equal parts by the eye, and the correctness of the divisions verified by using the compasses; a line may next be divided into unequal proportional parts, corresponding with those of another divided line, and the exercise verified by Prob. 28 of Practical Geometry. By proceeding in this manner, great precision of hand will be attained. The student may then copy forms more and more complicated, and lastly draw from natural objects, beginning with the simpler forms, and advancing to those that are more intricate. Proceeding thus, step by step, considerable power of execution may be arrived at, but it is always to be borne in mind, that in any progressive acquirement each step must be firmly secured before proceeding to the next; since hurrying, in a matter that depends almost entirely on practice, is a sure way to lose time, and it is far better and easier to bestow pains at first, than to have careless habits to correct afterwards. Figures drawn by free-hand are seldom accurate enough for working drawings; and for detailed proportions, or the formation of different parts intended to unite and concur in the formation of a regular whole, the geometric methods of drawing are absolutely necessary; and as these leave little or nothing to the discretion of the draughtsman, the work is performed with an exactness approaching to mathematical accuracy. The workman ought, however, constantly to exercise himself in judging of the relative measures of objects by his eye; he will thus acquire and retain correct ideas of their forms, which will present themselves as geometric pictures, of which all the parts are known, and be able to produce a representation of them from memory. The workman has frequently to exercise his powers in this way, and he ought to try to put upon paper at once what he has endeavoured to fix in his mind; for objects that are supposed to be indelibly impressed on the memory are sometimes from their very simplicity easily lost.

The repetition of a figure is exact and perfect only when each line of the copy is equal to, and corresponds with, a line in the model, and when the corresponding lines in each contain equal angles. The exact repetition of figures, and their enlargement or diminution, without the aid of instruments, offer no great difficulties to a practised eye. When great exactitude is required, the different methods of constructing rectilineal figures similar to one another, given in Prob. 100—105, may be had recourse to. The application is easy for all figures; since, however complicated a figure may be, by connecting the leading points by straight lines, a number of triangles, or other simple rectilineal figures, are developed, which may be easily repeated, and a corresponding number of points are thus necessarily placed in relation to one another that will regulate the whole reproduced figure. The same remark applies where the outline of the figure is composed of curved lines, since the general direction of these may be indicated by straight lines: for instance, the back of the hall-seat—Plate V., Fig. 4—may be readily copied by reducing the forms to a few straight lines, the direction of which is easily seen, and which will serve as guides for the position of the different curves which make up the outline of the whole. In some kinds of French work, where the forms are of a very indefinite nature, the lines of construction are not easily recognized, but imaginary lines, bounding and determining masses of form, can always be found to aid the draughtsman and designer. Take for example, the sideboard-back—Plate XVI., Fig. 6—in which the ornament presents very few lines that are not, in a great measure, at the will of the designer. The effective part of the ornament, resolves itself into a simple triangular mass, the summit of which is directly over the middle point of the length. The construction of a similar triangle in a like situation, when the design is to be repeated, will afford very efficient aid in making the drawing.

A figure may sometimes be easily copied by drawing a single line in any convenient direction through it, and observing the points where it intersects different parts of the outline. When the object is symmetric, as many of the forms are that the cabinet-maker has to treat, the proper line to employ is the axis of symmetry, or that line which divides the whole into two equal and identical figures. For instance, the pillar and block table—Plate XVII., Fig. 1—may be so divided by a line let fall perpendicularly from the middle of the top line; and the figure may be essentially repeated by the ruler alone, by simply setting off the relative lengths of the lines for the determination of the projecting parts. Sometimes panellings may be easily copied or constructed by dividing the space by a few lines; for instance, the fret at the lower part of the hat-stand—Plate VII., Fig. 3—can be easily repeated, if lines are drawn through the middle of it, parallel with the sides; the different points of contact of the curves may then be marked with the positions of the centres, and the space filled in very readily with the curves. The upper part of the same stand is more complicated, and will be most easily repeated by observing what points lie in the same straight lines, parallel and perpendicular with the sides. Diagonal lines may also be employed with advantage, when the form indicates them; as, for instance, in the end of the occasional table—Plate LIV., Fig. 5—where the little knob below the rosette will be seen to be a central point. The same remark applies to Fig. 6.

It has already been observed that any design intended as a guide to the workman is always drawn to a given scale. The reduction of such drawings, and more especially the enlargment, is frequently necessary. This is usually effected by adopting a second scale, either greater or less in the given proportion; the different parts of the drawing to be repeated are then measured upon the original scale in feet and inches, and the same number of feet and inches are taken from the second scale, and thus a similar figure must necessarily be produced. In full sized working drawings, the foot measure is adopted as the second scale.

One of the most convenient and exact methods of repeating a drawing, either on the same or of a different size, is by determining the relative position of a number of its points by horizontal and vertical lines: thus dividing the surface into a number of squares, and repeating the same, either of the same size or proportionally greater or less; the figure is then drawn upon this, taking care to mark within each square all that is contained in the corresponding square of the copy.

The annexed figures represent the drawing-room

Fig. 1.   Fig. 2.

chairs—Plate LXV., Fig. 5—ruled off for reduction in this manner.

It will be readily understood that when the parts of the subject to be copied are very minute or irregular, the size of the squares into which the parallelograms are divided, must be proportionally smaller; or where the intricate part of the drawing occurs, the squares over it fall to be subdivided, to assist the eye in making the outline.

If the design to be copied is too valuable to permit of the squares being actually drawn upon it, the same end may be attained by substituting fine silk threads for the lines. These must be stretched tightly across an open frame, on pins placed at equal intervals, so as to form a network of squares over the open space. By a modification of this method, proportions of length and breadth may be altered, at the same time preserving the design. This is effected simply by altering the proportions of one of the sides of the parallelogram on which the drawing is to be made, dividing it into the same number of parts with the corresponding side of the parallelogram containing the original figure.

When a drawing is not of much value, it may be copied by pricking through the leading points with a fine needle, and using these marks as guides. Tracing paper may also be used sometimes with advantage. This is simply paper that has been saturated with oil or varnish, and dried. It is laid over the drawing, and the outline is traced with a pencil; when finished, the lines may be seen distinctly by laying the transparent paper upon any white surface. Another mode of tracing is by rubbing a sheet of paper, of suitable size and thickness, with black lead or coloured chalk, going over it with a bit of crumpled paper until it ceases to colour the finger when touched lightly; by interposing this with the prepared side next a sheet of blank paper, and placing the drawing above, the forms may be readily traced by any small smooth point passed along the outline. Care must be taken not to press too heavily with the tracer, but a little experience will show the amount of pressure that is necessary. When it is not convenient to fasten the drawings together upon a board by means of pins, a few weights will be found very useful; these ought to be rather heavy—and covered with some kind of soft woollen cloth—to prevent the paper from slipping. The progress of the tracing may be occasionally inspected, to see if any parts have been omitted; but this must be done with great care, as in case of any disturbance of the papers, the re-adjustment is very troublesome.

Another means of enlarging and reducing drawings is by means of an angle, sometimes called the *angle of reduction*. The principle depends on the proportion of the sides of similar triangles. Suppose it to be required to reduce to a third, or to give

to the lines of the copy a third of the length of those of the subject:—Upon a line A B, mark with the compasses any three equal spaces from A to C. From C, with an opening equal to one of these spaces, describe an arc of a circle, and intersect it at D by another described from A, with the radius A C equal to all three parts; lastly, draw A D, then D A B is the angle required. If, now, E F be a line of the pattern, take this as radius, and from A describe an arc G H intersecting A B and A D at G and H; the chord of this arc is the length required, or the third part of E F. It is evident that the construction may be advantageously applied either for enlarging or diminishing proportional lengths, and that is a very correct method. It may be remarked, that, as a general rule, the correct enlargement of any drawing is rather more difficult than its reduction. This is easily accounted for, since any slight error in measuring the distances is multiplied proportionally to the increase of size; while, on the contrary, an error of the same extent on a diminishing scale may become inappreciable in the reduced copy.

An instrument called the *proportional compasses* is employed for facilitating the process of enlargement or diminution. This is a kind of double compasses, the four points of which may be arranged to any proportion. It consists of two shanks, crossing each other on a centre which is either fixed or moveable. The moveable centre is preferable, since it may be adjusted to give a great variety of proportionals. The construction of the instrument is very clearly shown in the annexed engraving. A B D E are the shanks, and C is the centre, which moves up and down in the slots or openings. On the faces of the shanks are marked divisions of lines and circles, the use of which are best illustrated by examples. By the scale of lines, a line may be divided in any proportion that falls within the range of the instrument. To divide a line into a proposed number of equal parts—say nine, or to find its ninth part; the in-

strument must be shut close, and the centre moved until the line across it coincides with the ninth division on the scale of lines, and then fastened by turning the screw; the compasses being opened until the line can be received between the points of the longer legs, the distance between those of the shorter will then be the ninth part sought. By the scale of circles, a regular polygon may be inscribed in a given circle. For example, to inscribe a regular polygon of twelve sides; the instrument being closed, the centre is to be moved until the line upon it coincides with the twelfth division on the scale of circles, and fastened there. The radius of the circle is then to be taken between the points of the longer legs, when the distance between those of the shorter will be the side of the polygon required. The proportional compasses are, on the whole, a very convenient instrument; the chief objection is, that the points are apt to get out of order, and it is plain that if any one of them gets a little worn, the scales are no longer of any use, as they must necessarily afford incorrect quantities.

There are a great variety of instruments by which drawings may be copied mechanically; these are generally called *pantographs*, but our space will not admit of entering on their details. The best instrument of the kind is the invention of the late Professor Wallace, of Edinburgh, called the *eidograph*. None of these contrivances are, however, of much use unless made with a mathematical accuracy that renders them very costly; but even if it were otherwise, the cabinet-maker will find it infinitely more to his advantage in every respect, to depend on himself and his own powers of execution, founded on a correct eye and a ready hand, both of which may be attained by practice.

The copying and repetition of curved lines is effected very much in the same way that other figures are made similar, that is, by determining a number of points which may serve as guides for drawing them. For this purpose, the lines of construction, or those lines that have been used for in-

dicating the general form of an object, may be frequently employed, and found sufficient. Thus, if A C is a curved line that it is desired to repeat, a straight line may be drawn in such a direction as to intersect it in the greatest number of points, as at A, B, C. Another line being drawn where the curve is required, and of suitable length, may be similarly divided, and the points of division will be a great assistance in placing the curve properly, and giving its true character. It is of course necessary to observe where the curve is at the greatest distance from the line, as at *d* and *e*, and to make them relatively in the copy. This may be done by measuring, if necessary. One of the best methods of drawing curved lines is that by projections, as indicated in Prob. 152. For instance, let A B be a

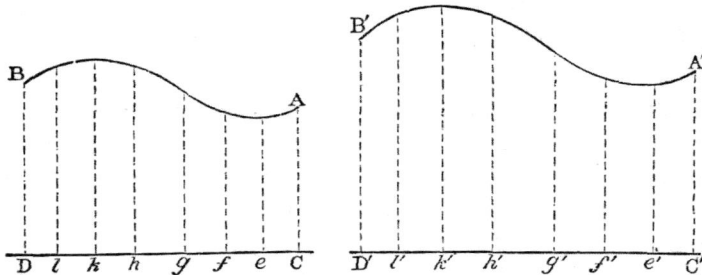

given curved line, a straight line C D being drawn in any convenient situation, any number of perpendiculars are let fall upon it from points in the curve, selecting the most important, which are generally those where the curve is at its greatest projection, and where it changes its direction. The curve line is now easily repeated, either on the same or a different scale, as in the diagram, where it is enlarged one-fourth; the process being simply the division of a line C′ D′, which is one-fourth longer than C D, into the same proportional parts at the points *e′*, *f′*, *g′*, &c.; from these perpendiculars are raised, each of which is made one-fourth longer than the corresponding lines at *e*, *f*, *g*, &c., in C D. A curve is then drawn through the extremities of these lines, precisely similar to that given.

The rendering of curved lines is one of the nicest operations that the cabinet-maker has to execute, whether in drawing or in his work. This is the case not only in the imitation of a line already drawn, but, in making a design, the selection of an appropriate curve to suit a given situation is one of those points in which taste may be advantageously displayed. For the actual drawing of the line upon the work, when the curve is not given or a pattern used, various methods are employed. One of the best is by an instrument constructed upon the principle in the last diagram. For the line C′ D′ a long rule is substituted (about five feet will be a convenient length), in this is made an open groove extending to within about half an inch of each end, and for greater strength, there may be a support in the middle. Upon the upper part is a second set of open rulers, which may be moved to any part of the first, and fastened there, by a thumb-screw passing through both. By means of their open grooves, they may be extended, shortened, or set at any angle, with respect to the long ruler. They

represent the perpendiculars D B, &c. At their extremities C A are holders, or notches, in which a long thin slip of steel may be inserted, that may easily be made to assume any given curve by arrangement of the rulers. When this is done, the whole may be moved about without danger of disturbance, and may be applied where required, and the curve drawn with as much facility as a straight line. With such an instrument, it will be found convenient to have more than one steel slip, because the curve is affected by its stiffness. The whole of the rulers ought to be divided to a scale of feet and inches, so that perfect accuracy may be attained in the enlargement of any given curved line, by taking the measures and distances from the drawing. The ingenious workman will have no difficulty in making such an instrument for himself, and in the end it will save him much trouble. There is another very convenient mode, applicable in a variety of cases, and which may be adopted when the curve is in a great measure left to the taste and discretion of the workman. This consists in the employment of a thin slip or rind of elastic wood, about a quarter of an inch square in substance, and seven or eight feet long. When the work is framed, as, for instance, the back of a sofa, the slip of wood is placed on it, and being bent to a curve, is prevented from moving, and may be further adjusted by fastening in small nails where required; when all is arranged to the satisfaction of the workman, a pencil line may be drawn along the edge of the rind upon the framing, which will serve as a guide in shaping. Whalebone may also be advantageously employed in this process, and will be found to possess advantages that wood has not, especially when the curve is quick.

There are some methods for the enlargement or reduction of mouldings, that are more directly applicable to this purpose than others. One of these is founded on the principle employed in Prob. 102, for the construction of figures similar to one another having their sides parallel. Thus, let A B be a moulding, of which A C is the projection, and B C the vertical height; suppose that it is required to alter its dimensions, say to make it one-half larger. Through B draw a straight line B E, parallel to A C, and produce C B from B indefinitely towards F. Next, from each of the points indicating the members of the moulding, or other desirable points, let fall perpendiculars upon B C, meeting it in *d*, *e*, *f*, and from the same points, perpendiculars to D E. From B, as a centre with radii equal to the distance between it and each of the last drawn perpendiculars, describe quadrants meeting B F in g, h, k, F. Next, from any convenient point B' in D E, draw B' C' perpendicular to it, or parallel to B C, making it in the required proportion, as in the present case, one-half longer than B C. This line represents the vertical height of the new moulding. Through C' and C draw a line, extending it to meet D E in E, and through E and F draw a line to meet the production of C' B' in F'. If lines are now drawn from E through each of the points d, e, f, g, h, k, in C F to meet C' F' in points d', e', f' g', h', k', the whole line C' F' will be divided similarly to C F. From C', d', e', f', draw lines perpendicular to B' C', or parallel to D E, of indefinite length. From B' as a centre with the radius B' F', describe a quadrant to meet D E, and from the point of meeting raise a perpendicular to intersect that drawn from C'; the point of intersection at A' will indicate the projection A' C' of the new moulding. Quadrants described in the same way from B', with radii

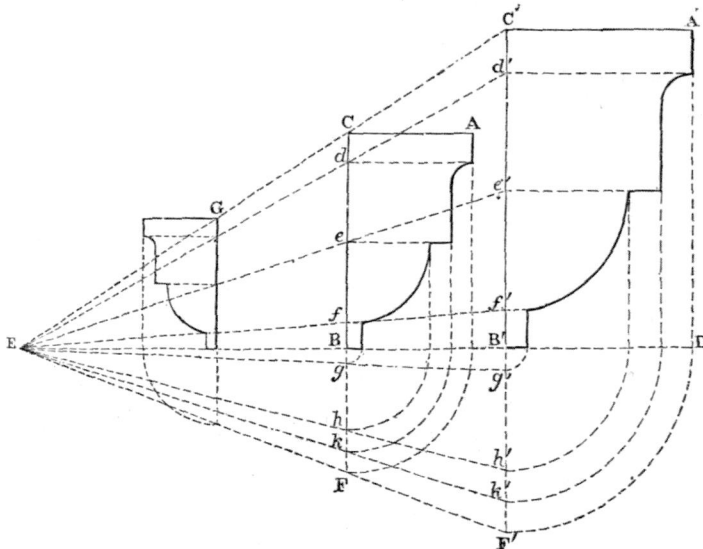

B' k', B' h', B' g', will meet D E, and perpendiculars drawn from these points, to intersect those drawn to C' B', will indicate successively the different points of the members sought, and the moulding may be drawn in the usual manner. If the moulding were required to be reduced, then the vertical line must be reduced in the given proportion, and it would be situated as at G, between C and E. By this method the moulding may be reversed, with the same ease that it is reproduced, by merely reversing the projections, as at G.

The following is another excellent method :—Let A B be the profile of a moulding, B C its vertical height, and A C the projection; let it be required to reduce the dimensions of the moulding one-third part. From B, one extremity of B C,

draw a line at any angle with it, as B' C', perpendicular to it, making it equal to two-thirds of B C. From each point of the members of the moulding, draw lines parallel to C A, or perpendicular to B C, to meet B C in points d, e, f. Draw C' C, and from d, e, and f, lines parallel to it, meeting B C' in points d', e', f'. From C', d', e', f', draw lines perpendicular to C' B, of indefinite length. Next from C with radius C A,

describe a quadrant to meet C B in g, and from g draw a line parallel to C C' to meet B C' in g'. From C', with the radius C' g', describe a quadrant, or make C' A' equal to C' g'; this will be the projection of the new moulding. From B and e, with radii equal respectively to their perpendicular distance from points in the profile, describe quadrants meeting B C in h and k, and from these points draw lines parallel to C C', meeting B C' in h' and k'. Make the projections from e' and B respectively equal to e' h' and B k', which will afford a sufficient number of points for the construction of the moulding, and it may be easily completed. It is plain that the projection may be made upon either side of C' B, as may be convenient.

The proportions of mouldings may be varied by similar means, that is, a given profile may be altered either in its horizontal projection, retaining the vertical height, or in its vertical height, retaining the horizontal projection, simply by increasing proportionally the lines in the above construction which determine these respective dimensions.

It frequently happens, that in a drawing or design, the only key to the true profile of a moulding is to be found in a mitre, where the members may present themselves under quite different aspects and proportions, the outline of the moulding being produced, in this case, by an oblique section. The true profile may, however, be easily derived from that of the mitre. Let A B be the profile of a moulding, at a mitre of which A C is the horizontal projection, and C B the vertical height. Through

B draw a line of indefinite length parallel to A C, and from A let fall a perpendicular to meet it in D. From B, as a centre with the radius B D, describe a quadrant to meet the production of C B at E. Draw the chord E D, and from its middle point F draw B F. This line B F is the true horizontal projection of the moulding. From any number of points, as *a*, *b*, *c*, *e*, in the profile, let fall perpendiculars upon B D, to meet it in points *f*, *g*, &c., and from the same points draw lines of indefinite length parallel to A C. From the points *f*, *g*, &c., draw lines parallel to F D, and meeting B F in *k*, *l*, &c. Next, from B with radii equal to B F, B*k*, B*l*, &c., describe arcs of circles meeting B D respectively in points *m*, *n*, &c. From *m* raise a perpendicular to intersect at *p* the parallel to A C, drawn from the point *a* in the profile; from *n*, a perpendicular to intersect at *q* the parallel from *b*; and proceed in the same manner with the remaining points. These will indicate the true projection of the moulding, and it may be easily completed.

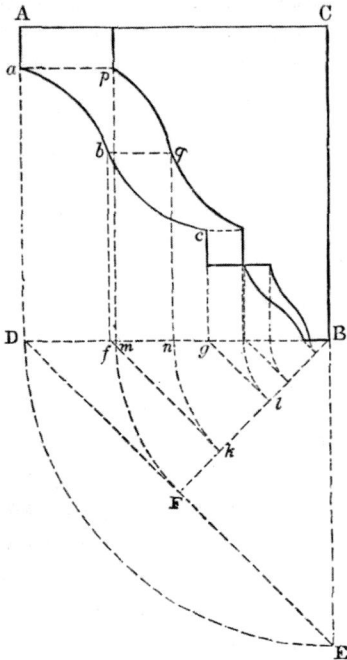

It is frequently of great importance to have exact drawings of actual mouldings. There are various modes by which this is effected with greater or less exactitude. One of those most commonly used in practice is to measure a number of perpendiculars to a given line, and to lay down the profile by finding a number of points in it. Thus, if A B is a moulding, a straight-edge C D is held firmly against it, and the perpendicular distance between it and any sufficient number of points is ascertained by actual measurement, at the same time observing the points upon C D, where the perpendiculars fall. The construction then becomes the same as Prob. 103. A good method is to apply a strip of lead, which being pressed against the moulding, will take its form very exactly; it may then be removed, and the line drawn upon

paper by its means. It is needless to observe that the lead must be of a sufficient substance to retain the form when removed, and not so thick as to present any difficulties in taking the impression: when the moulding is large, it may be thicker than when it is of small size. Clay and putty are also sometimes employed when the mouldings are small. The best method, when practicable, is to make a perpendicular saw cut through the moulding; into this a paper may be introduced, and the profile traced. Besides these methods, there is a very beautiful contrivance for taking tracings of mouldings by an instrument devised for the purpose, by Professor Wallis, of Cambridge. This consists of a board, upon which a point is made to trace any moulding by a parallel motion, composed of two parallelograms working together. A B is a board of 10½ inches by 11½ inches, D is a plate fixed to the board about the middle of the shorter side. E, E are two arms, each 7 inches long, turning upon centres at the extremities of D, which are about 3 inches apart, and also on F an arm of equal length with D. The first parallelogram is thus formed, the sides of which are movable, and will be parallel to each other in all positions. Two other arms G G, of the same length with E E, are jointed at one end to the arm F, and at the other to the carriage H. This forms the second parallelogram, the sides H and F of which being parallel to one another in all positions, H and D will be so also. By this arrangement, the carriage H may be moved over every part of the board, and all its positions will be parallel to one another and to D. The carriage with the tracer K L M is one of the principal parts of the instrument. The part of the tracer L M is placed in a frame having a pointed screw at M, and a collar at L, so that the whole may be made to revolve upon its axis. K L is nearly a semicircle, and the point K is exactly in the axis. At N there is a button upon the tracer, which serves to guide its motion along the surface of a moulding, as well as to turn it upon its axis. The carriage has a pencil holder O attached. It is plain that, as the carriage and tracer are parallel in every position upon the board, that any point in the carriage will travel in the same path as the tracing point, and consequently if K is made to pass over the profile of a moulding, or other object, the pencil O will mark a line exactly the same upon the board, and of the same size. K L is curved, in order that by its power of rotation it may enter the inflection of mouldings, where a straight tracer would be inefficient, as seen in the diagram. It is necessary that the instrument should be held firmly in one position during the whole process of tracing; to effect this two retaining pieces or supports are attached to the back of the board, which may be adjusted and fastened to any position by two thumbscrews. The paper can be attached to the board by any of the usual means; the best method is by a couple of flat spring-holders, as at P and Q, the latter being placed near the inner upper corner, to prevent the paper from being rubbed up. The instrument does not require very nice workmanship, the essential points being that the arms E E and G G should have exactly the same distance between the joint-holes, as also the holes in the pieces D, F, and H; and that the point K should be exactly in the axis of rotation of the tracer. The parallel motion may be made of thin slips of sheet or hoop iron.

PERSPECTIVE.

Linear perspective is the method of drawing the true representation of objects on a plane surface, through the application of geometrical rules, by which their outlines are determined, and such as they would present themselves to the eye when placed in a known position.

A perspective representation will be easily understood if it be supposed that the eye being placed in a fixed position, a transparent plane is interposed between it and an object in such a manner that the

object can be seen through the plane; if the form is then traced upon it, the outline thus produced will be a true perspective delineation of the object. By the rules of perspective the representation of things can be produced whether the objects themselves are actually present, or only their dimensions

and position known. The different planes and lines by which this is effected have received denominations that require some explanation. In every perspective operation three things are to be distinguished, namely, the object to be represented—the observer—and the plane upon which the representation is to be made.

An object is seen by rays which proceed from it in right lines, in every direction, from every point in it. Those which meet the eye of the observer are called *visual rays;* for instance, the rays C A and B A, proceeding from C B to the eye of the observer at

A, are visual rays. These form an angle C A B at the eye which is called the *visual angle*, and the apparent size of any object depends on the measure of this angle, and all objects of the same size appear greater or less according to their distance from the eye; that is, if a line is at double the distance of another from the eye, it will appear of only half the length.

The plane upon which the drawing is to be made is called the *picture*, and is always supposed to be placed between the observer and the object, and the points where it intersects the visual rays, as c and b, determine the perspective representation, as of C B. The picture is always supposed to be placed in a position perpendicular to another

plane, called the *ground plane*, as H G in the former figure, or A C; it is upon this that the objects for representation are placed, and on which the spectator stands. The line of intersection of the ground line and picture, as B B (in the *third* diagram), is called the *base* of the picture; and the point P′, the *centre*. The straight line D D′, drawn through P, parallel to B B, is the *horizontal line*, which is every-where level with the eye, and is the *vanishing line* of all the planes parallel to it or perpendicular to the picture. The line M N, drawn through P′, per-pendicular to D D′, is called the *vertical*, and is the vanishing line of all vertical planes that are perpen-dicular to the plane of the picture. The *points of distance*, D D′, are equally distant from P′; and D P′, P′ D, are each equal to the distance of the observer's eye from the picture. As an example of the way in which the lines operate, draw *a* P′ from the point *a* in the base B B, and *b* D from another point *b*; then will *a* P′ represent an infinite line perpendicular to the picture; P′ *a* B will be a right angle in perspective; and *b a c* a perspective representation of an isosceles triangle.

The preceding may be too severe in theory for a mechanical work, and we shall, therefore, confine our further notices of perspective to a few simple problems, in which points, lines, planes, and solids, are brought into true position and configuration on the plane of the drawing.

Before proceeding to the problems, it is neces-sary to define terms with reference to their method of construction. This we shall do with the assistance of the annexed dia-gram, which itself requires some little previous explana-tion. H L G X is supposed to be a transparent verti-cal plane, the side

H L being uppermost; the whole of this plane is also supposed to be occupied by so much of the pic-ture as lies between its base and the horizon, or, in other words, it takes in the whole ground view, but no part of the sky. This being understood, G X is the *ground line*, or base of the picture. H L the *horizontal line*, parallel to the former, is that ima-ginary line which forms the common boundary of earth and sky, and on which the perspective lines of all objects come to a point, or vanish. P is the *point of station*, or the position which the spectator occupies to look upon, or delineate, the view or object; the height of his eye reaches to the top of the transparent plane, and is directly opposite to the point, C, the *centre of the picture.* The *pro-spective angle*, *v* P *d*, contains sixty degrees, and

includes all that the eye can effectively take in of any prospect without moving the head or changing the position; every picture is therefore, according to strict perspective rule, contained under this angle, and the objects to be delineated must all be brought within it by assuming a proper point of station. The points *v d* are termed the *points of distance*, they being the extreme limits of the picture on the right and left. The point *v* is also a *vanishing point;* in the present diagram it is identical with the point of distance, but this coincidence arises from the mere accident of the line *a b* (of which *v* is the vanishing point) lying parallel to, or in the same angle with, the line P *v*. If the line *a b* be represented by *e f* on the transparent plane, it must be evident that if it were continued, it would pass across the plane, and vanish in the horizontal line at the point *v*. If these definitions be clearly com-prehended by the young draughtsman, the follow-ing problems will be divested of all difficulty and obscurity:—

PROBLEMS.

I. *To find the place of a given point in the per-spective plane.*

Let the given point be A; then as a preliminary operation, draw G X the ground line at a little dis-tance from it, and, parallel thereto, H L the horizon-tal line; assume the point of sta-tion P, and draw from it perpendi-cularly to the line H L, when C will be the centre of the picture. To avoid repetition, this preparatory operation is to be understood as applying to every problem.

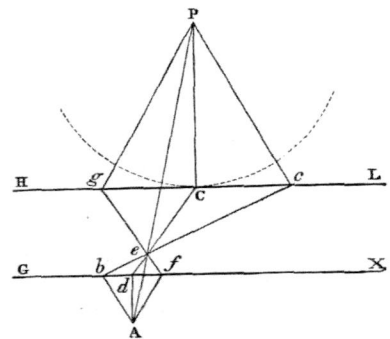

The apparent intricacy of the diagram arises from our having included in it three different methods of finding the place of the point.

1st Method. Draw from the point A in an oblique direction to G X, as A *b*, and from the point of station P draw P *c* parallel to A *b*, and join *b* and *c*; then draw A *d* perpendicular to G X, and draw from *d* to the centre C; the intersection of the lines *b c*, *d* C, at *e*, gives the place of the point A in the per-spective plane.

2d Method. Draw A *b*, P *c*, as before, and also *b c*; then draw from the point A to the point of sta-

k

tion P, and the intersection of A P by bc gives e, the place of A in the perspective plane.

3d Method. Draw A b, P c, as before; draw A f at pleasure, and g P parallel thereto; join b to c, and f to g, and the intersection of these lines bc, fg, gives e, the place of the point A.

II. *To place a line in the perspective plane.*

All original lines *perpendicular* to the ground and horizontal lines, vanish in the centre of the picture; and all lines *parallel* to the ground and horizontal lines, will likewise be parallel to them, when brought into the perspective plane. Thus, D E is represented in the perspective plane by fg, and would, if continued, vanish in the centre C; and A B is represented by bc, which is parallel to the ground line G X, and the horizontal line H L.

The complexity of the illustrative diagram arises from the line being placed in three positions; but there is a manifest advantage in bringing the several operations into juxtaposition, as we thus see at a glance how variously a line of the same length is represented in the perspective plane, according to the direction in which it lies with respect to that plane.

1st Case. When the line is parallel to the ground and horizontal lines, as A B. Draw P A, P B, from the point of station P, to the extremities of the line A B; join B to the ground line at pleasure, as B a,

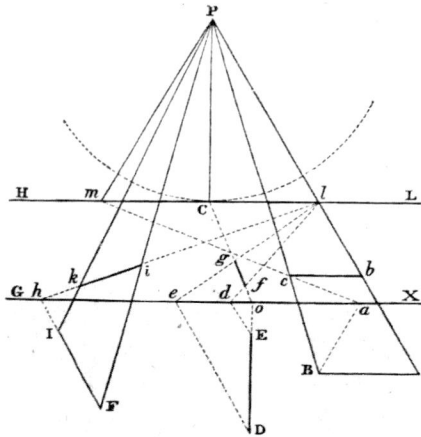

and draw P m parallel to B a, also draw $m a$; the line ma will intersect P B in c; draw through c parallel to G X, and bc will be the representation of A B in the perspective plane.

2d Case. When the line is perpendicular to the ground and horizontal lines, as D E. Continue D E to G X, as D E o; draw D e at pleasure, and parallel thereto E d, and P l parallel to both; draw from l to d and e, and from o to the centre C; then will fg represent the line D E in the perspective plane.

3d Case. When the line lies obliquely to the ground and horizontal lines, as F I. Continue F I to h on the ground line G X, and draw P l parallel to F I h; join lh, and draw P F, P I, from the point

of station P to the extremities of the line F I; then is ik a representation, on the perspective plane, of the line F I.

III. *To represent a triangle in perspective.*

Let the given triangle be B A D. Continue the oblique lines A B A D to the ground line G X, as A B a, A D b; draw P f parallel to A D b, and P g parallel to A B a, and connect f to b, and g to a. The intersection of fb, ga, gives the angle e, the perspective representation of the angle A. Draw from the point of station P, to B and D; and where the lines P B, P D intersect the lines fb, ga, draw the line cd; then will ced be the perspective delineation of the triangle B A D.

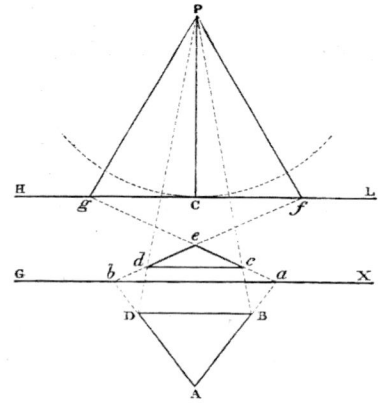

IV. *To represent a square in perspective, when placed obliquely to the perspective plane.*

Let the given square be $abcd$. Continue the sides ab, ac to G X, as abe, ach; likewise continue the sides bd, cd to G X, as bdg, cdf; draw P n parallel to ach and bdg, and P o parallel to abe and cdf; draw from n to the points g and h, and from o to the points e and f. The points of intersection $kilm$ define the perspective representation of the square $abcd$.

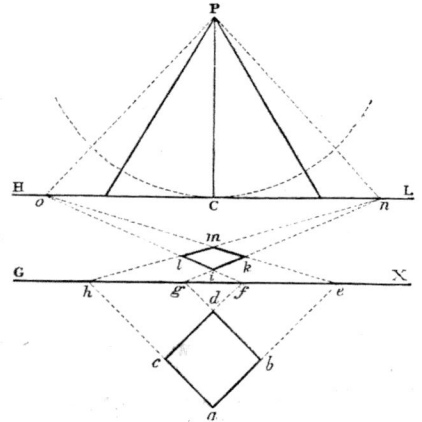

V. *To represent a square in due perspective, when placed parallel to the perspective plane.*

Let the given square be $abcd$. Continue the sides ac, bd, to the ground line G X, and draw the diagonal bc, continuing it to e; draw P f parallel

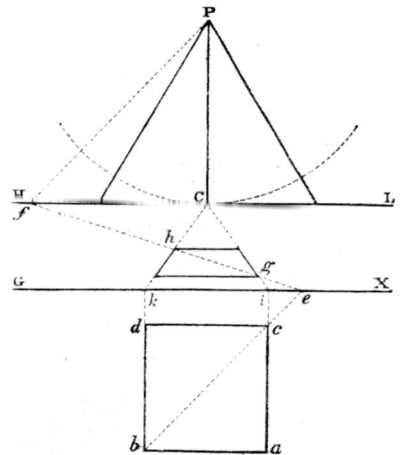

to *b c e*, and join *f* to *e*; also draw from the centre C to the points *i* and *k*; draw lines parallel to the ground line through the points *g* and *h*, where the line *e f* intersects the lines C *i*, C *k*. We have thus obtained the representation of *a b c d* in the perspective plane.

VI. *To represent a pentagon in perspective.*

Let the given pentagon be A B D E F. Continue the lines A D, B E to *a* and *e*, and draw P *f*, P *d*, parallel to B E *e*, A D *a*, and join *a* to *d*, and

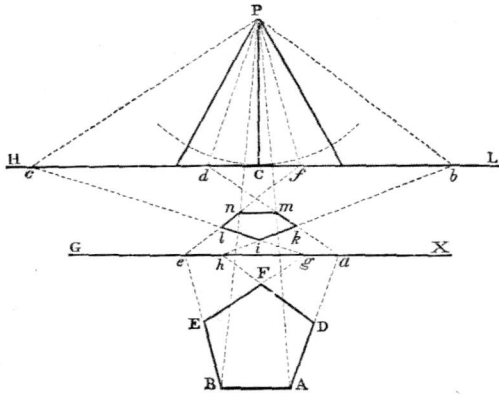

f to *e*; continue the lines D F, E F to *g* and *h*, draw P *b*, P *c* parallel to D F *h*, E F *g*, and join *c* to *g*, and *b* to *h*; and draw from P to the points A and B. The intersection of the lines *b h*, *c g*, gives the angle *i*, corresponding to A F; the lines *b h*, *c g*, are intersected by other lines *a d*, *f e*, in the points *k* and *l*, and *i k*, *i l*, are perspective sides of the polygon A B D E F, that answer to F D, F E; then *a d*, *f e*, are crossed nearer to C, by the lines P A, P B, in the points *m* and *n*, and *k m*, *l n*, are the perspective sides answering to A D and B E; and joining the points *m* and *n*, we obtain the side *m n* corresponding to A B. The given pentagon A B D E F is therefore represented in the perspective plane by *i k m n l*.

VII. *To represent a hexagon in perspective.*

Let the given hexagon be A B D E F I. Continue A D to *a*, E I to *d*, and draw through the points D and F to *b*; the lines A D *a*, B F *b*, E I *d* being parallel, draw P *h* parallel to any one of them; continue B E to *f*, D F to *c*, and draw through the points A and I to *e*; and the

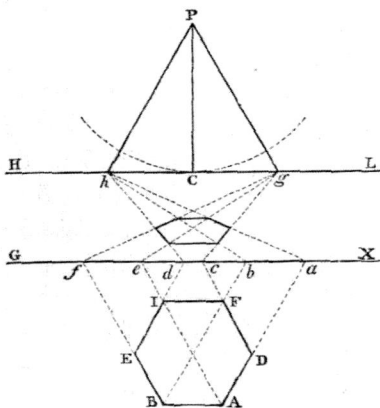

lines B E *f*, A I *e*, D F *c*, being parallel, draw P *g* parallel to any one of them; draw from *h* to the

points *a*, *b*, and *d*, and from *g* to the points *c*, *e*, and *f*, and the intersections of these lines from the points *g* and *h*, will give the perspective outline of the hexagon.

VIII. *To represent a circle in perspective.*

Let the given circle be *e a b f d c*. Draw the square A B D E without the circle, and let the sides A B D E be parallel to the ground line G X, and continue A D B E to the ground line. Draw the diagonals B D, A E, continuing them to *g* and *h*; also P *k*, P *i*, parallel to B D *g*

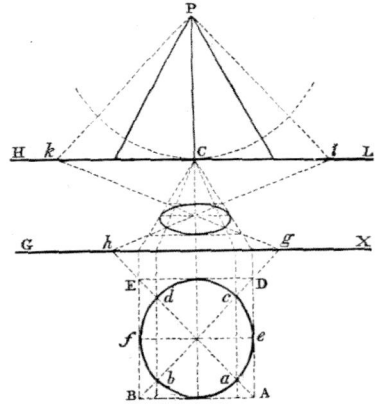

and A E *h*, and join *k* to *g*, and *i* to *h*. Through the points *a b c d*, where the diagonals A E B D intersect the circle, draw the lines *a c*, *b d*, parallel to A D and B E, and continue them to the ground line; draw likewise through the centre of the circle in like manner; and also the diameter *e f*, parallel to the ground line. All the perpendicular lines vanish in the centre of the picture; therefore draw from the point C to all their intersections with the ground line. These lines from C will intersect the lines *g k*, *h i*, in various points; and if from some of these we draw the perspective parallels answering to E D, *f e*, B A, as shown in the diagram, we obtain the points and bounds of a continuous curve which is the perspective delineation of the given circle.

IX. *To represent a cube in perspective, when the original lines lie obliquely to the perspective plane.*

Let A B D E be the base of the cube. This base, or ground plan, is first to be put into perspective by Problem IV. Then from the angular points of the perspective base raise perpendiculars; and on any one of the points *a*, *b*, *c*, *d*, (but more conveniently on *a* or *d*), erect a perpendicular equal to the height of the cube —let it be *a g*, on the point *a*. Draw from *g* to *f*, cutting

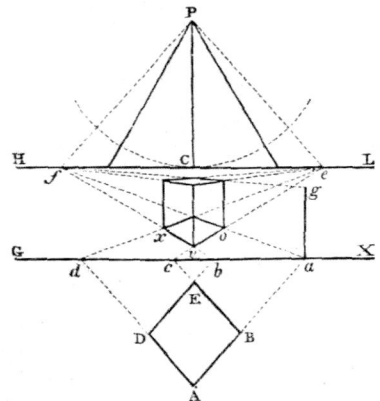

the perpendicular *o*; draw from *e*, through the intersection, cutting the perpendicular *v*; draw from *f*, through this last intersection, cutting the perpendicular *x*; and draw again from *e* to this intersection in x. Thus the top of the cube is determined and the whole figure defined, as shown in the diagram.

X. *To represent a cube in perspective, the original lines being parallel and perpendicular to the perspective plane.*

Let A B D E be the base of the cube, which is first to be put into perspective by Problem V. Then on the point a erect the perpendicular $a\,c$, equal to the height of the cube. Raise perpendiculars likewise from the angles of the perspective base. Then draw from c to the centre of the picture; and the line c C will cut two of these perpendiculars, and form one side of the top of the cube. Draw lines parallel to the ground line, or horizontal line, through the points where c C intersects the perpendiculars, and thus obtain the two sides of the top of the cube which lie parallel to the perspective plane. These parallel lines will cut the other two perpendiculars; and a line drawn from C through the intersecting points, will give the fourth side of the top of the cube. And thus the whole figure will be formed, and a cube of the given dimensions be transferred to the perspective plane, as required.

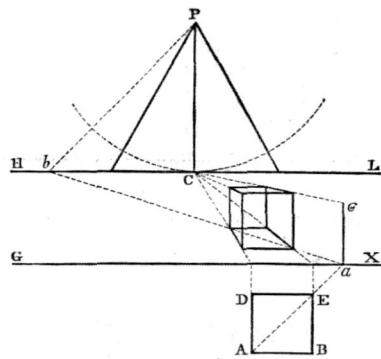

XI. *To represent a pyramid, or solid angle, in perspective.*

Let A B D E be the base of the pyramid, which is to be put into perspective by Problem IV. From c, the centre of the base A, B, D, E, draw the line $c\,a$, parallel to B D and A E; and on a erect the perpendicular $a\,f$, equal to the height of the pyramid. Draw lines from the opposite angles of the perspective base, and they will intersect in the centre of the pyramid, on which raise a perpendicular. Draw from f to g, and the line $f\,g$ will mark the height, h, of the pyramid in the perspective plane. Lastly, draw from the angles of the perspective base to the point h, and the figure will be completely formed, and delineated in the terms of the problem.

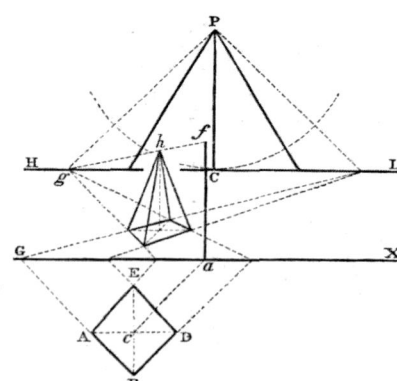

XII. *To represent a cylinder in perspective.*

Let the circle A B D E be one end of the cylinder.

This is first to be reduced to a perspective plane, by Problem VIII.: then erect on the points b, c, the perpendiculars $b\,d$, $c\,e$, equal to the height of

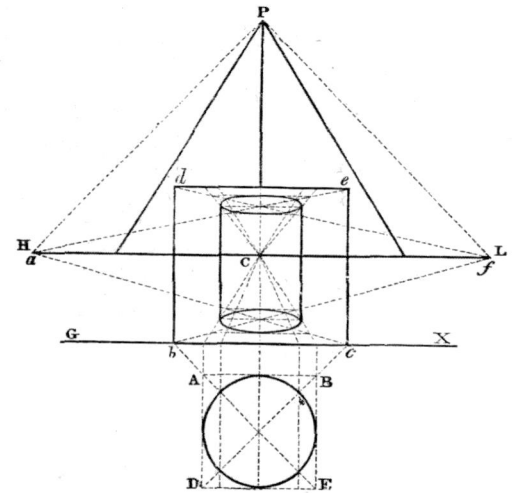

the cylinder, and join d and e. Draw from e to a, and from d to f; and having set off on $d\,e$, the several divisions or intersections in $b\,c$, draw from C to the points so obtained in $d\,e$, and also draw parallels to $d\,e$ to give the top of the cylinder, in the same way that parallels are drawn for the base, according to Problem VIII. The ends of the cylinder being determined, it remains only to draw the parallel lines connecting them, and the figure is completed.

The preceding problems are illustrated by diagrams on a small scale, and that, for the obvious reason, that larger illustrations would have spread over many pages the information which is here compressed within four pages. But, for practice and instruction, it is desirable that the young draughtsman construct his figures on a much larger scale, making each occupy a space not less than the size of our page. The advantages of such enlargement must be apparent; the lines of construction will not crowd together confusedly, and the points of intersection, by which the outlines of figures are determined, will be projected with much greater precision. And, moreover, this mode of practice will enable the draughtsman to introduce much variety of construction, and derive from these elementary problems a thorough knowledge of all the principles contained in them. It may be of advantage to notice in detail some of the variations which may be introduced into each problem.

In connection with the first problem, which determines the position of a point, we may introduce a variation in the height of the vertical plane, or plane of projection. Thus, whilst other portions of the figure are laid down proportional to the diagram, let the space between the ground line G X, and the horizontal line H L, be increased or diminished; or, in other words, suppose the height of the eye, which is measured by the space between the ground and horizontal lines, to be greater or less. It will thus be seen, how the point A takes a different position in the plane of delineation, according to the greater or less elevation of the spectator's eye.

The three cases of the second problem are to be constructed separately, to dispel any confusion that may result from their union in one diagram, and also to admit such variation on each case as may be desirable. Thus, in the first place, take the line D E, which is perpendicular to the ground line G X, and placing it at various distances from G or X, see how it comes into the vertical plane, under these several conditions; and then construct with different heights of the eye, or horizon, and so learn how the position and length of the line are affected by the height of the eye. Treat the lines B A and I F in a precisely similar manner. The young student must not suppose that he has exhausted a problem when he has constructed it precisely as it is shown in the printed diagram; but, on the contrary, he must analyze and vary its details until every elementary principle involved in it becomes clear and satisfactory to him. Indeed, unless this be done, the knowledge of perspective to be derived from the twelve problems is very limited; but if the plan recommended be followed, they will be found to contain all that is necessary in the way of general instruction, and quite sufficient to carry the draughtsman on in the application of the principles to any varieties of objects, under every mode of assemblage.

The third problem presents a triangular area for projection on the plane, and this offers a large field for practice. The triangle may have its base D B parallel to the ground line, yet be situated at any distance from G or X; it may have its base at any angle to the ground line, with the same variation as to distance; its figure may be varied at pleasure; it may be brought nearer to, or removed further from the ground line; and it may be projected with any height of eye, or horizon. And let it not be thought that these variations of construction are profitless repetitions; since from each one new ideas will be obtained, and the general principle more clearly demonstrated.

The fourth and fifth problems give two cases of the projection of a square: in the one, its diagonal is perpendicular to the ground line; and, in the other, its side is parallel to the same line. These problems admit all the variety of construction referred to under the third problem. The side may lie nearer to or more distant from the ground line; it may vary in position with regard to G or X; its side may lie at any angle to the ground line; and it may be projected with horizons of greater or less height.

The seventh and eighth problems project the pentagon and hexagon; and it is most important that all the varieties of construction be employed upon them, since polygonal figures, from the number of lines of which they are composed, come so differently into the plane, according to the point of sight.

The circle completes the series of plane figures, and the method of its perspective projection is shown in the eighth problem. The variations in this case are the removal of the circle nearer to or farther from the base line; placing it more or less obliquely to the point of sight; and viewing it from different heights of the eye, or horizon. With a low horizon, the circle projects very elliptically, as shown in the diagram; but if the point of sight be considerably elevated it loses less of its circular figure, and especially when it comes into foreground, or very near to the ground line.

It is supposed that thus far the young draughtsman will make a separate diagram, on a large scale, for every variation of the several problems that has been recommended, and not attempt to combine two or three projections in one drawing, which would confuse him and frustrate the purpose in view. Having now, however, become conversant with the projection of plane figures under every variety of aspect and position, it is desirable that he should retrace his ground, and familiarize himself with the projection of a number of similar plane figures placed contiguously. Thus, taking the equilateral triangle D A B in problem third, let him repeat it along the ground line, and then draw a line through the angular point A of each triangle, which will thus form a double series, the one filling up the intervals between the other. Let him connect with this line of alternating triangles, two other lines precisely similar. Here, then, he will have a tesselated pavement of triangular pieces closely fitting into each other; and the projection of the whole figure on the plane of delineation will only be a repetition of the operation for a single triangle. In his first trials at these more complicate constructions, it may be advisable that the draughtsman have beside him a number of tints of colour, so that the different steps of his projection may be apparent, and stand out separately from the rest. It must be observed that the projection of a tesselated pavement does not necessarily require a process so tedious as finding the figure and position of every triangle, but it is best to commence on this principle, and, after a little practice, equally certain, but shorter methods, will suggest themselves. Diamonds, squares, polygonal figures, and circles may be similarly combined; and if the young artizan will labour heartily and industriously through this class of projections, he will become a thorough master of perspective, so far as bases and ground surfaces are concerned.

The ninth and tenth problems give the projection of the cube. Its base is a square, and may, of course, be placed, with reference to the ground line, as variously as the square itself. This being a solid, and not a mere surface, the value and effect of a low or high horizon will be very apparent. If the eye be considerably elevated, and the cube lie in the foreground, little more than the top or upper face will be seen; but if the cube is five or six feet high, and the horizon low, the side or sides only will be visible. The student will soon learn, from a variety of projections, what height of horizon is most pleasant to give agreeable form to the object, and avoid those abrupt angles which are termed *violent* perspective.

Problem eleven shows the perspective representation of a pyramid on a square base. This admits all the different modes of projection referred to in the preceding paragraph. If the pyramid be five or six feet high, and the horizon low, only one or two of its triangular sides can be seen; whilst a high horizon, if the pyramid is in the foreground, will lose its altitude, and the area of the base only will be visible with the lines of its angular sides meeting in the centre. Pyramids are not uniformly on square bases; and it will be a useful practice to project them on triangular, pentangular, and polygonal bases. These operations involve no difficulty, since the student is presumed to be thoroughly conversant with the projection of every plane figure under all conditions of aspect and position.

The twelfth problem gives the perspective of the cylinder, and, in connection with this, a patient working out of all the varieties of projection is absolutely necessary, since the most important elementary principles will be demonstrated at every step.

The draughtsman having now grounded himself thoroughly in the *separate* projection of the solids, under all accidents and circumstances, he must proceed to combine them; and, to do this, he must lay down their bases, under all conditions, with reference to the ground line, and transfer them accurately to the plane of delineation, and then raise the solids upon them, according to the rule for the simple figure.

The purpose of the remarks we have offered is to show that the elements of perspective are few and simple, at least for all practical purposes, and that a very sufficient knowledge of the art may be attained, without spending half a life-time in the study of those awful treatises in which lines and angles mix in most admired confusion, and present ingenious labyrinths that few persons have skill or patience to thread. A severe mathematical theory undoubtedly lies at the root of perspective, but the ordinary requirements of mechanical art can safely take the elements it establishes, without all the cumbrous load of proof, however elegant in its demonstrations and captivating to an enthusiast in mathematical science.

LIGHT AND SHADE.

In this department of his art, the draughtsman requires the following materials: a selection of good sable and camel's hair pencils of various sizes; a piece of the best China ink; three cakes of fine water colours,—lake, gamboge, and Prussian blue; and a Wedgewood palette for grinding the ink and colours, with cells to contain the various tints required. Such pencils should be chosen as, when wetted, terminate in a fine point, free from all straggling hairs. India or China ink is tested by the metallic lustre of its fracture, and by a powerful scent of musk; the last criterion is not, however, always decisive of quality, as many of the inferior inks are scented in imitation of the genuine kinds; it is, therefore, safer to rely on the appearance of the fracture, and the smoothness of the ink when ground upon the palette. The lake should be a rich crimson; not the dull heavy colour which, under this name, is usually included in ordinary drawing-boxes. Gamboge can be had at a very cheap rate in the lump, but it is far better to have it in the cake; in the latter form it is purer, and therefore combines more freely with the other colours in the formation of a neutral tint. Prussian blue should be very rich in the tint: this and the preceding colours are also to be tested by grinding; none will work satisfactorily, or mix properly, if gritty particles exist in them. These colours are seldom required by the mechanical draughtsman separately; their principal use is for the preparation of a fine mellow neutral tint, which is much more pleasing in a drawing than the harsh blackness of Indian ink, particularly if it include large shadowed surfaces requiring considerable depth of tone. The method of mixing this tint is to grind down the three colours upon the palette separately; then combine with the Prussian blue as much lake as will compose a rich purple, and add gamboge till a fine pearly gray colour is formed. No drawing can be properly shaded with fewer than three gradating tints, some draughtsmen use so many as five, and hence obtain great richness and depth in their shadows. These are to be prepared in the cells of the palette, and their relative strength properly proportioned; then dip a clean pencil in each, and draw broad strokes side by side on a piece of waste paper; when these are dry, it will be seen whether they have the gradation and depth required for the drawing.

The cabinet-maker may sometimes need to colour his drawings, to see the true effect of the combined materials, and also to give a customer a perfect idea of the intended article. To do this effectively, he must familiarize himself with the colours of woods in their natural state, and also when overlaid with French varnish. He must likewise study the character of the veinings and markings of the woods, and be able to represent these with freedom and richness of effect. Some length of practice and careful observation will be necessary to make the eye and hand skilful in this department; but the workman who has trained himself to this point of art, may fairly claim some precedence in the workshop, as one who has raised himself beyond the mere mechanics of his profession. A box of colours, containing twelve cakes, as ordinarily assorted, will be abundant material for the draughtsman's purposes; and the preparation of the various tints can be thoroughly understood only by continual practice, and training the eye to distinguish the most delicate variations of colour. To become skilful in representing the veins and markings of woods, the young artisan must first learn to outline them with his pencil freely and correctly.

Whatever objects are represented by linear drawing, the appearance of substance, roundness, and distance, may be given to them by an artful distribution of light and shade. If a circle be drawn upon paper, and the interior filled up with any even colour, it will represent a circular plane. When, however, an object has different degrees of shade, the lightest parts appear to come prominently forward, whilst the darker parts apparently recede, in proportion to the variations and depth of shade. For example, draw a circle as before, and, in place of covering the entire surface with an even tint, leave it light in the centre, and deepen the shadows towards the circumference; it will then present the appearance of a ball or sphere. The roundness of a cylinder or column is produced in the same manner. When the draughtsman can give due light and shade to these two solids, he can have no difficulty in imparting apparent substance to all curvilinear forms.

The proximity or remoteness of flat surfaces is produced by even tints of different depths; and in them also the lightest parts approach the eye, and the darkest retire from it. In mechanical drawing the light is usually supposed to come from the top of the drawing, and at an angle of forty-five degrees.

Let us suppose a drawing finished in outline, and ready to receive the light and shade. If China ink is determined on as the medium, grind down a sufficient quantity on the palette, and prepare three tints in so many different cells. The first tint is very light, and is to be applied to plane surfaces which retire from the eye; and all circular forms are to be entirely filled in with it, excepting the central light, which in a globe is a small circle, and in a column or cylinder, a broad, white line; it will also form the projected shadows on the high lights. The second tint must have sufficient strength to separate plane surfaces that retire still farther from the eye, to form the projected shadows on the first tint, and to give roundness to circular bodies; in applying it to these last, care must be taken to leave a portion of the first tint uncovered towards the centre, as a secondary light; and a narrow strip of the first tint is likewise to be preserved at the circumference, as a reflected light. If an ivory ball be held in the hand and the light suffered to glance upon it obliquely, it will be seen that the darkest shadow does not fall upon the extreme circumference, but at a very sensible distance from it; and this fact requires especial attention, for the appearance of roundness can never be properly brought out, unless the faint reflected light be preserved on the shadowed side. The third tint must have considerable strength; it is used for projected shadows on the second tint, and for perfecting globular and circular forms; observing, in this case also, to preserve a portion of the second tint towards the centre, and a smaller portion towards the circumference. If there should be a number of parts in the drawing requiring different depths of shade to discriminate their recession from the eye, intermediate tints must be prepared before we commence, for the strength of the finishing tint will never justify its use as a flat tint of any great extent. If the neutral tint, which we have recommended in preference to India ink, be adopted as the medium of giving shadow, the process of mixing and applying the gradating tints is precisely the same.

Some dexterity is required in handling the pencil, both to produce an even flat tint, and to give a pleasing idea of circular form; and the young aspirant must not be discouraged if, in his first essays, he should fail to give the decisive touch and bold finish of an experienced artist. A conquest achieved without labour is worthless; and all things, that are not practically impossible, can be accomplished by persevering industry. A few hints may obviate first difficulties, and assiduous application will overcome others. Young artists are too apt to work their pencil dry, which always destroys the evenness of the tint, and produces disagreeable seams, and likewise gives a harsh and meagre appearance to the drawing. The true method is, to use as large a pencil as the nature of the drawing will permit, and to keep it well charged with colour, for the largest surface will never be disfigured by a sinking of the tint or by seams, so long as we keep the paper flooded with colour, and thereby prevent the formation of dry edges as we proceed. When laying on a flat tint, the surface should be covered as rapidly as possible, as a farther preventive of sinking; afterwards the drawing should be placed a little aslope, and all the superfluous colour gathered up from one corner of the surface with a pencil that has been moistened in clean water. This done, lay the drawing level again, and on no account touch the tint till it has dried. The shadows of circular bodies and all gradating shadows require skilful management; any sudden transition from light to shade produces a disagreeable effect. Lay on the tint with a large full pencil; then with another pencil moderately moistened with clean water soften off all the edges of the tint. If this be done adroitly, light and shade will blend with each other in such a way that it can scarcely be detected where light ends and shadow begins. It will be obvious that the tint must not at first be laid down to the full breadth of the shadow, as we necessarily extend it by the process of softening off. Every succeeding tint must be softened in the same manner; so that as the light blends with the first tint, so the first tint must blend with the second, and the second with the third. These are all the verbal instructions that can be given for producing judicious and pleasing light and shade; and if the young draughtsman conjoin with them a love of his art and close application, only one more requisite is wanting to insure his success, and that is—*time*.

THE

CABINET-MAKER'S ASSISTANT.

PRACTICAL OBSERVATIONS ON CABINET-MAKING.

INTRODUCTION.

IN attempting to furnish some practical observations on the Art of Cabinet-making, one of the greatest difficulties in the outset is to determine at what point to begin; so as, on the one hand, to avoid presuming too much on the previous knowledge of the reader, and on the other, of presuming on it too little. In the one case, the observations are apt to be to some extent unintelligible; and in the other, to be thought commonplace or trivial. Believing that in the greater number of elementary treatises the first of these errors has been the one fallen into, we shall endeavour so to frame our remarks as to render them useful to the inexperienced workman, though it should be at the risk of appearing, to the better instructed, to be descending to greater minuteness than is really necessary; while for him we trust to be able to bring forward some information on the materials, processes, and methods of construction—the result of our own study and experience—which even he may acknowledge to be both novel and advantageous. We therefore submit the remarks that follow to the favourable consideration of cabinet-makers in general, believing that those who have already made the greatest progress in acquiring knowledge, will be found the most willing to receive instruction, and the most ready to overlook any imperfections that may occur in our treatment of the subject.

We have for long been convinced that the vast majority of our artizans bestow far too little thought upon the articles which they manufacture, whether as respects the materials of which they are constructed, the method by which they are made, the purposes they are to serve, or the designs after which they are fashioned. The result of this is,

that modes of construction, useful forms, and elegant designs, which have originated with the thoughtful few, are copied and re-copied by the unthinking many, without any intelligent appreciation of why this particular method of construction has been chosen, why this form and proportion of parts is more suitable than another, or of what were the principles of taste and purposes of utility which led to their adoption. And, as a necessary consequence, the articles thus unintelligently copied, have a constant tendency to degenerate in character in the hands of the copyist.

One of the leading causes of this state of things is doubtless the imperfect training given to apprentices. It is too often the case, that while the young workman is instructed what to do, he is seldom told the reason for doing it in the way pointed out to him. Obedience is too much depended on, and thinking intelligence too little. The apprentice thus learns to perform certain pieces of work in a certain manner, and, by steady application, he becomes an active and efficient workman; but his reasoning faculties having been left dormant by his master, and he himself never having had the curiosity to inquire into *whys* and *wherefores*, he seldom attains any peculiar eminence in his trade, and rarely becomes an originator himself, or an intelligent copyist and improver of the plans and designs of others. We are glad to think, that though this is the rule, there are many exceptions; but few who have had much experience among workmen will be inclined to deny the general accuracy of these statements. Another cause of this state of affairs is the want, till lately, in this country, of Schools of Design. While in France, and other continental states, the young workman has long had the means within his reach of acquiring such a knowledge of art as would

A

243

destitute of that massive richness seen in other species of the pine. Specifically, it is distinguished by having the leaves fivefold, numerous and slender, of a bluish-green colour, and three and a half inches long. The cones are from four to six inches long, composed of smooth scales rounded at the base, and having the apex thinly covered with white resin. The trunk, which tapers considerably from the base to the summit, is free from branches for two-thirds of its height; the limbs, which are short and verticillate, are disposed in stages one above the other, and terminate in three or four upright branches at the top of the tree.

The felling and transporting of this description of timber from its native forests, affords employment to a large number of our British colonists in Canada and New Brunswick. The parties engaged in the work are called *lumberers,* and generally lead a life of extreme hardship and privation, alternated with seasons of riot and indulgence. Hired by a master lumberer, or associated in a party having a common interest in the proceeds of their labour, these men set out in the end of summer for the remote forests which are to be the scene of their winter's toil. Selecting a spot near the banks of a river, and in the midst of as much timber as possible, they divide themselves into three gangs; one of which cuts down the trees, another hews them, and the third is employed in hauling the timber to the banks of the nearest stream, or to the river itself. Rudely lodged in a log cabin, and coarsely fed, they spend the winter, which often lasts until the middle of May, in unremitting toil. The approach of summer, which swells the river with the melted snow, rather increases their hardships, as it then becomes necessary for them to get the timber afloat and rafted; an operation which cannot be effected without the lumberer being day after day, and that for weeks together, wet up to the middle, and often immersed from head to foot. When the timber has been floated down to the seaport, the rafts are taken to pieces and disposed of; which puts the poor lumberers in possession of a whole year's earnings at once. It will readily be conceived, that they often deepen the effects of their lengthened privations, by the brief indulgence in dissipation which follows.

The amount of pine timber annually imported to Britain from our North American colonies, on an average of eighteen years, ending 1841, is 9,634,776 cubic feet, employing upwards of three hundred vessels, the aggregate tonnage of which exceeds one hundred and sixty thousand tons.

Introduced into this country as an article of commerce about thirty-five years ago, yellow pine has almost entirely superseded the red and white pines,

or Baltic Timber, which, up to that period, were the only kinds available for the purposes of the cabinet-maker. From its larger growth, its comparative freedom from turpentine and resinous matter, and from its being much softer, it is much better fitted than either of the others for being veneered on, or for interior finishing. The modern cabinet-maker, accustomed to this material, so easily wrought and so free from bias, can scarcely conceive of the difficulties experienced by his less fortunate predecessors; who, for their interior fittings and beds for veneering on, had nothing better than white or red pine, with their innumerable joinings, their flint-like knots, and almost endless shrinkings.

Of the various ports from which yellow pine has been shipped, the popularity has waxed and waned in no common degree. At one time, to advertise a cargo as from Mirimachi, was sufficient to insure its immediate sale; but, whether from the extensive exportation, or from a great fire, which a few years ago destroyed a vast quantity of timber there, recent importations have not obtained nearly the same popularity. The exports from Chaleur Bay for a time successfully disputed the precedency; but these, in turn, have given place to the timber from St. John, New Brunswick, which at present is, on the whole, the best fitted for cabinet-work. The earlier importations of it, we are aware, obtained, and perhaps deserved, a bad name. But more recent cargoes have done much to wipe away the reproach. While the first specimens which met our observation were distinguished by remarkable harshness and strength, accompanied by innumerable black soft knots, what we have met with latterly has been much milder in its character, and entirely free from the kind of knots mentioned. It is, however, by no means safe to purchase, without selection from the importations from any port; for every cargo contains wood of various qualities.

In the case of the house carpenter, there is less need of careful selection; for, from the nature of his demands, a profitable use can be found for timber of any character. If fine, it may be husbanded for interior finishing; but if coarse, can readily be got rid of in large masses for beams, and other covered work. The cabinet-maker, from having no such opportunities of disposing of coarse wood, requires to be more particular in his choice.

The faults in fir, to be chiefly guarded against, are *shakes,* twisted growth, and coarseness. We place the chief evil first, for while wood of twisted growth, or very coarse, may be made something of, when full of shakes it is almost good for nothing. We need scarcely say that the *shakes* to be dreaded are not those visible on the sides of the log, presenting cracks at a right angle to the surface, which are merely the effects of exposure; nor are those in the end of the log, which are seen to radiate from the heart; those most to be feared are *ring shakes*, that is, cracks in the end of the log which follow the grain, or annual rings. These, accompanied by an appearance of damp, show that the log is of a kind that, when cut up and dried, will scarce hold together. But many logs, otherwise fine, are unfit for the cabinet-maker, on account of their twisted growth; that is, from the grain, or fibres, not running parallel to the sides of the log, but being twisted round in the manner of a rope. Boards cut from such a log are sure to twist in drying, and prove troublesome after being wrought. Coarseness, that is, gnarled growth, and numerous knots, which ordinarily render their presence obvious to the most unpractised eye, is also to be guarded against by the careful buyer. In general, a good fir log is to be known by its having the ends dry and firm, and free from the appearance of softness and resinous streaks.

Cutting up.—From the way in which wood is assorted in lots, when exposed for sale, it is not to be expected that all the logs in a lot will be of one quality. On the contrary, as is natural, the indifferent and the bad ones are mixed with the good, and sold along with them. Hence the necessity of attention to the cutting up of the various qualities into thicknesses suited for the purposes for which they are best fitted. If the log be very coarse, it should be cut into boards for packing cases, or the like. If the appearances indicate harshness or strength, it is evidently best adapted for framing, of various sorts. But when a mild and clean log presents itself, it should naturally be cut into thinner boards, for panels, or gables and tops, to be veneered on. The recent introduction of fine fir varnished with copal, as a material for the manufacture of furniture for second or inferior bedrooms, which now obtains rather extensively in large mansions, lends an additional value to timber of this quality. But as every log, however fine, contains more or less of coarse wood near the heart, it is of importance to dispose of this to the best advantage in cutting it up. Many are in the habit of cutting planks of 3 inches, or $3\frac{1}{2}$ inches thick, from the heart, with the view of working up the coarser wood in veneered pillars, or the like; but we regard it as the better plan to take off a few $\frac{1}{2}$ inch, or $\frac{3}{4}$ inch boards, which, however coarse, can be got rid of in drawer shelving, or tops and bottoms of carcases, where quality is of little importance. But in this, as in other matters, experience is the best guide; and, from the varieties of demand, will

conduct different parties to results which, although opposed to each other, are nevertheless best suited to their respective cases. There is one consideration, however, which should not be overlooked in any instance, namely, which way the draughts are to be run through the log. In determining this, regard should be had to two things—the direction of the heart shakes, and the fact that every log has one side finer than the others. It is desirable that the cuts should not cross the heart shakes, and that they should run parallel to the fine side of the wood. When both of these can be attained, it is most profitable; but where they cannot, it is perhaps the least evil to run the draughts in the direction of the shakes.

RED AND WHITE PINES.—We deem it unnecessary to say much regarding red and white pines; but with the view of affording all the information which is likely to prove interesting or useful to the cabinet-maker, shall briefly notice them, in order. The red pine of commerce is denominated, by botanists, *Pinus Sylvestris*, the wild or Scotch fir. It is very extensively distributed over the surface of the globe, being found in almost every country of Europe, and in the more temperate and colder parts of Asia. Although indigenous to this country, and attaining to considerable perfection in various districts, the colder climate of Russia, Denmark, Norway, Lapland, and Sweden, seems most favourable to its full development; and in these countries it is to be found of fine quality, and in prodigious numbers. In favourable situations this species of pine attains a height of from 80 to 90 feet, and is from 4 to 5 feet in diameter at the base. The bark is thick and furrowed, the leaves are *in pairs*, of a pale green colour, and from $1\frac{1}{2}$ to fully 2 inches long; the cones thick, short, and not much pointed.

The white pine, or deal, of commerce, is the *Pinus abies*, or spruce fir of botanists. Of this there are three species known in trade, the Norway spruce, and the white and black spruces, or *Abies alba*, and *Abies nigra*, of America. This is a tall and stately tree, reaching sometimes the height of from 150 to 200 feet. The leaves are solitary, scattered upon the branches, and of a dark green colour; the cones from 5 to 7 inches long, and about 2 inches in diameter.

The red pine, although of the highest value in ship building, house carpentry, and all kinds of work exposed to the action of the atmosphere or of water, is, as we have already said, ill adapted to, and almost never used, in the manufacture of cabinet furniture. The white variety, possessing more strength than the yellow, and less charged with turpentine and resinous matter than the red, is better fitted for a number of purposes than either of them. This wood, although grown in Britain, and extensively imported from America, is found in the greatest perfection in the northern parts of Europe, from whence large supplies are annually shipped, for consumpt in this country. Instead of being sent in logs, it is cut up into planks of 11 inches broad by 3 inches thick, and from 18 to 22 feet long, which are called *deals*, and when shorter, *deal ends*; or into pieces of $6\frac{1}{2}$ inches broad by $2\frac{1}{2}$ inches thick, and 20 or 21 feet long, known as *battens*.

There are several sizes to which this variety of fir may be applied, which renders it desirable that the cabinet-maker should have it in stock. Cut into boards of $\frac{1}{2}$ inch thick, it is suitable for plain deal backs; in $\frac{3}{4}$ inch boards, it will be found useful for bed bottoms; or if cut $1\frac{1}{4}$ inches thick, it will make excellent tenter frames, or the like, where strength is required. It is very unsuitable for veneering on, as, in the course of shrinking, which it will continue to do after being pretty carefully dried, it will leave the harder veins projecting above the softer, to the great detriment of the appearance of the article for which it has been used.

From its being offered for sale in planks, there is little need for directions as to the purchase of it. We may notice, however, that there is ordinarily the option of buying the planks as they lie, or of picking them. The cabinet-maker will generally find it profitable to pay the small additional charge for having his choice, and so secure the finer timber. This is distinguished by having small annual rings, or being close in the grain. In selecting, care also should be taken to avoid deals or battens which contain the heart of the tree, or which are of twisted growth.

Seasoning.—Every one knows that it is of the greatest importance that wood should be well seasoned, previous to its being manufactured; and that, in attention to this, the quality of the article, and the character of the maker, are alike involved. Let the design be faultless, and the execution perfect, if the material be unseasoned, disappointment to the purchaser, and disgrace to the manufacturer, must inevitably be the result. All, therefore, who seek to attain the reputation of being good cabinet-makers, ought to make certain of the thorough seasoning of their wood. The process of drying may be said to commence from the time that the timber is felled and squared, as either immersion in water, while being rafted down the rivers to the sea, or subsequent exposure to the action of the air, has the tendency to abstract from it the natural sap. This may be

continued, to some extent, while it remains in logs, by taking care to give the air admission on all sides, raising them from the ground on *clean* blocks, and keeping free spaces between; at the same time, noticing that any top covering of slabs is separated from the logs, which it shields from the sun, by fillets of wood. The mention of *clean* blocks may appear trivial, but experience shows, that if these be in a decayed state, they taint the timber which rests on them. If logs are suffered to lie on the soft damp soil of a woodyard, and especially if there are weeds or fungous matter around them, the effect is to impregnate the wood with the seeds of decay, before it is brought into use.

It is, however, not desirable that fir should remain long in the log, as the tendency of the air acting on the surfaces alone, while the body of the wood is unaffected by it, is to produce shakes or cracks, which earlier cutting up would have prevented. When sawn into planks and boards, these should be laid in horizontal piles, with fillets placed at intervals between them, or set upright in racks, divided by fixed fillets. The timber placed upright, will dry sooner than that laid horizontally, but will not generally be found so flat and straight; as the pile, if carefully raised, forms a press to keep the whole in order.

One unacquainted with the subject, would be ready to think that timber would dry but slowly, if allowed to remain exposed in all kinds of weather; but experience proves, that the natural sap is extracted more thoroughly by the action of the external atmosphere, even although accompanied with moisture, than by any artificial means. Wood so seasoned, is much less likely to be the subject of change afterwards, than that which has been dried by artificial heat. All wood used in the manufacture of furniture, should, previously to and in the course its being wrought, be placed in a temperature several degrees higher than that to which the finished article will probably be exposed; this, however, should be preceded by a course of seasoning in the open air. Where heat alone is relied on, it will be found that the outer surface is hardened to a degree that prevents the evaporation of the moisture from the internal part, and that the imprisoned sap will betray its presence, by its subsequent efforts to escape. It is scarcely possible, by any course of treatment, to prevent wood from shrinking and warping under atmospheric influence. We have seen pine that had formed part of a church steeple for between two and three centuries, when taken down and sawn into small pieces, shrink and expand considerably, both in length and width, when exposed to changes of temperature and to the action of the air. So satisfied, by repeated experiment, of the impossibility of rendering any kind of wood impassible by seasoning, was an ingenious watchmaker, who wished to form pendulum rods of it, that he at length found it necessary to char the rods, and in their heated state plunge them into copal varnish, which, by excluding the air, attained the desired result.

The shortness of the time which circumstances allow for the seasoning of material, by the ordinary method which we have recommended, often renders it necessary to expedite the process by having recourse to more artificial means. When a drying room, heated by means of stoves, steam, or hot water, is made use of, it is of great importance that a free circulation of air should be had. Entering at the lower part in a hot and dry state, it escapes at the upper, charged with the moisture which it absorbs in the heated state. When, on the contrary, such rooms are made as air-tight as possible, the wood is then surrounded by a warm but stagnant atmosphere, which retains whatever moisture it may have acquired from the evaporation of the sap in the wood.

As to the time necessary to the proper seasoning of wood, a cabinet-maker of any experience will have little difficulty in determining. The presence of moisture is indicated by a peculiar smell, by the readiness to shrink and warp, and mainly by the weight; for no piece of wood can be said to be thoroughly seasoned, until it cease to become lighter from evaporation. Difference of thickness will of course render it necessary to employ a longer or shorter time in the process; and the purposes to which the wood is to be applied must also be taken into consideration, for it is possible that wood may be rendered too dry.* The fear of this, however, need disturb the cabinet-maker but rarely indeed. If it be objected, that beds for veneering on require to be damp in proportion to the state of the veneer to be laid on them, we will afterwards show that it is very easy to make them so, without having recourse to unseasoned wood, from which the natural sap has for the purpose not been thoroughly withdrawn.

BIRCH.

It has been common for writers on woods to speak in a very slighting tone of the birch, and to treat of

* We recently saw an instance of this, in an otherwise very well finished public building. In the upper flat, of which on one side the windows were designed to stand open, the floor had been so completely stove-dried, that when exposed to the external air it had expanded, so that it presented a series of curves equal in number to the boards of which it was composed.

it rather as a tree of graceful form and beautiful foliage, than as yielding wood of great utility, and most inviting appearance. While the white birch, or *Betula alba,* and the weeping birch, or *Betula pendula* of Europe, may deserve no higher consideration, it is widely different with the birch of American growth. This, in regard to the cabinet-maker, occupies a place of no mean importance. For a long period it has furnished the staple commodity in use, for almost all the purposes for which hardwood is required: and more recently, the finer specimens of it have been employed in the manufacture of bed-room, hall, and even drawing-room furniture.

Of American birch, there are seven varieties; but of these we shall mention only the three which are commonly imported to Britain, namely, the *Betula lenta,* or mahogany birch, the *Betula excelsa,* or yellow birch, and the *Betula nigra,* or black birch. The *Betula lenta,* or mountain mahogany of America, called also mahogany birch, and sweet birch, is, on account of the excellence of its wood, the most valued. We have seen many specimens, which, in a finished state, rivalled in beauty the finest mahogany. These were of the kind familiarly called *curled:* a descriptive designation warranted by its resemblance to curled mahogany, in having the plane surface variegated by a series of semicircular shades of colour, alternately light and dark, occasioned by the different angles at which the light falls upon the grain of the wood. A figure will most simply illustrate the manner in which this effect is produced. Let the serpentine line represent the undulating growth of the grain lengthways, and the straight line, the saw draught which runs through the log; it is plain, that at each undulation traversed by the straight line the grain is presented at opposite angles to the surface, and hence the variety of colour is produced. The semicircular form of these shades is occasioned by the sawdraught crossing the annular rings of the tree. It is difficult to convey by mere description an idea of the rare beauty of such specimens as we have mentioned: for when finished in French polish, they possess a transparent appearance, suggestive of coloured crystals or precious stones, having the light reflected from a surface polished at different angles, rather than a plane surface of wood. Birch of this quality is well suited for the manufacture of hall furniture, when the design of it is rather plain than enriched with carving: also, for bed-room furniture, when the apartments in which it is to be placed are not large. In a room indifferently lighted, or contracted in its dimensions, the use of birch, from its light colour and transparent surface, has an excellent effect, as the articles seem rather to retire than obtrude themselves, as those in a darker coloured wood appear to do. These remarks will render it evident, that we do not approve of the practice of colouring birch, with the view of making it resemble mahogany. To use colouring matter, whether in the form of vegetable juice, or gum in solution with the polish, is, we apprehend, only to spoil good birch when applied to it; inasmuch as the stain or gum has the effect of destroying that transparent lustre which we regard as its principal beauty.

It may be objected to our strong recommendation of finely figured birch, that it is very liable to shrink and warp. The truth of this will be readily admitted by all who have any experience of its use; but these defects may be counteracted by careful seasoning in the first place, and, further, by avoiding the use of it in the solid, wherever it is practicable to apply veneer. In wardrobe doors, or in the footboards of beds, let both panels and framing be of suitable fir; which will be found, if properly prepared, quite able to resist the natural tendencies of the birch veneer.

Birch logs of the quality of which we have been speaking, bear but a small proportion to the whole amount imported from Quebec, the port from which this variety is shipped for Britain. It is to be found growing not only in Canada, but also in the middle states of Pennsylvania, New York, and the Jerseys; but from these localities the cost of transmission forbids its being sent to this country.

This tree is found to prefer a deep rich soil, is of rapid growth, and when it attains its greatest dimensions, reaches a height of 70 or 80 feet, and a girth of from 9 to 12 feet. It is exceedingly handsome in appearance, budding remarkably early in the spring, when its leaves are covered with a thick coat of down; this disappears later in the season, and leaves them of a bright and lively green. The trunk is straight, and is often clear of branches for a height of from 30 to 40 feet from the ground; the branches are quite smooth, the leaves thin, oblong, tapering to a point, and beautifully serrated. They possess a peculiar fragrance, which they retain after being dried in a stove, affording by infusion an agreeable diluent, superior to some of the common teas of commerce.

YELLOW BIRCH.—The *Betula excelsa* of botanists yields wood much like the last mentioned, but paler in the colour. The trees attain an equal height, but are of smaller girth than the former; rarely exceeding 7 or 8 feet.

BLACK BIRCH.—*Betula nigra* is smaller in size, duller in the colour, and less variegated in the figure of the wood, than either of the species already mentioned, still it is imported into this country in such quantity as to have led to its name being applied to American birch in general. This is, perhaps, to be accounted for by the fact of this variety having been much earlier introduced to Britain than the others. Large quantities are annually exported from St. John, New Brunswick; Pictou, Nova Scotia; and from Cape Breton island. In 1839, the imports of American birch amounted to 336,151 cubic feet, while the consumpt (307,450 feet) nearly equalled them.

Purchase of Birch.—Most of the remarks which we made regarding the purchase of fir, will be found of equal value in reference to birch; we shall, therefore, only make a few additional remarks, which are specially applicable to it. And first, we would recommend the young buyer to select logs in which there is as little sap wood as he can find in the parcel exposed for sale. In birch, the sap wood, even when fresh, is much inferior to the perfect wood, and is peculiarly liable to decay in the course of seasoning in the open air. As in different trees, the sap wood bears very different proportions to the whole, an opportunity for selection is afforded, which it would be unwise to overlook. A glance at the ends of the log will at once enable an observer to judge of the amount of sapwood in it, as there is in colour a marked distinction between it and the matured wood. We would advise further, the purchase of large sized logs, in preference to smaller ones. In birch, the heart, and knots which radiate from it, often form a considerable part of the whole log; and, in a small tree, there is the additional evil, that in squaring and straightening it the best portion of the wood has been hewn away; and hence large timber, though bearing a higher price, will be found the most economical. In obtaining finely figured wood, the difficulty arises not so much from the trouble of selecting it, as from its absolute scarcity. The presence of fine figure is more evident in birch than in almost any other wood, the rough hewn sides of the log showing the transverse semicircular shades almost as plainly as the dressed surface. It is true, that there may be present these external signs, while the figure does not go far into the body of the wood; but the interior never can be fine, without betraying itself externally. Whole cargoes, however, are to be found, in which there are few or no logs of the desired quality.

Cutting up.—In cutting up birch into the various thicknesses in common use, the first thing to be attended to is the character of the log. Should it be of a plain description, it is evidently fitted only for chair rails, sofa stocks and scrolls, and bed stuff. In this case, perhaps the best way of cleaning the heart is to take a 2½ inch plank off each side of the opening draught, then 3 inch or 3½ inch planks for bed-posts; the remainder outwards, to be thrown into thicknesses for rails of common chairs, or for stocks. The heart planks if foul, that is, knotty or shaken, will cut up profitably into rails for easy chairs, or into rails of common chairs with sweeped seats. The rinding of birch, after it has been planked, into the breadths commonly required, for bed stocks and posts, or rails for telescope tables, &c., greatly facilitates the seasoning of it; but this should never be done until the planks are partially dried. When this is not attended to, it will be found much more liable to bend and warp, than it would be after having had a little time to season. It may excite surprise in some, to see sliding rails for telescope dining tables mentioned as one of the uses to which birch may be applied: but we have seen it used for this purpose with great advantage. The dressed surface of birch presents a smoothness, of which oak or Honduras mahogany is destitute; and hence it is much less liable than either of them to become rough from the friction which sliding rails are exposed to. When used for sliding rails, care must be taken to select birch of straight, close growth, free from figure and from tendency to warp, and above all, wood that is thoroughly seasoned. Where these qualities meet in birch, we are persuaded that it will be found nearly equal to Cuba mahogany, in suitableness for the purposes mentioned.

When a log that appears to be curled is to be cut up, it is of importance to examine it carefully, with the view of ascertaining in which way the finest figure is to be obtained. A mistake in this matter may considerably affect the value of wood obtained from a log of the finest quality, and should therefore be avoided if possible. As almost every log has one side of better quality than the others, so every figured log has most of the figure on one side. Various causes have been assigned for this, by different writers, but the fact is unquestionable. Some have supposed, that exposure to the sun of one side more than the other, accounts for its being finer than they; but we are disposed to agree with Duhamel, in regarding the difference as being caused by the tree having had freedom to sway or bend to the side on which the fine wood is found. It is certain that the largest deposit of wood has always been found in the hollow side of a bent log. Our present business, however, is rather to make use of the fact than to ascertain its cause. In cutting a figured log of birch, then, we would recommend that the saw draughts should run parallel to the side which has the greatest appearance of being curled,

and would not regard the crossing of the heart shake transversely, as furnishing a good reason against it. When the wood is so finely figured as to be principally cut into veneers, those planks which are shaken can be rinded into narrow breadths, and sawn into veneers suitable for framing, bases, cornices, or the like. From such a log it would plainly be wasteful to cut thick planks. If used in the solid, it should only be in ⅝ inch, or ¾ inch boards, for clamps or mouldings, to go into work along with fine veneers; or into ½ inch and 1⅛ inch boards, for the seats and backs of hall chairs, or for panels, where these need to be solid, as in the case of French beds.

Seasoning.—We have already remarked, that in birch, the sap wood is peculiarly liable to decay in the course of seasoning in the open air. This indicates the desirableness of using all suitable means to preserve it from those influences which are the causes of decay; and, first, we would recall attention to what is said, in former observations, on the best mode of treating wood while in the log. If true in respect of fir, the hints there given have tenfold force when applied to birch, which deteriorates far more readily when exposed to the soft damp soil of a woodyard, to contact with weeds, or fungus matter. We would further notice the propriety of having the wood piled, or placed in " the horse," *immediately* after being sawn into planks or boards. If allowed to lie close together, as laid off from the saw, especially if the weather is wet, the sap-wood will, in the course of a very short time, discolour and spread the seeds of decay. When piled, care should be taken that the covering is sufficient to prevent the rain from getting in between the boards and lying on the surfaces. It may perhaps occur to some readers, that we are forgetting the cost of the labour which we recommend to be bestowed on the stock in the woodyard. But the experience of the best regulated establishments has shown this expenditure to be the truest economy; while, on the other hand it would, if desirable, not be difficult to adduce numerous instances in proof of the serious loss entailed by a contrary course of treatment.

We would recommend one exception to the rule of carefully covering up birch, namely, when it is to be applied to the purpose of making sliding rails for telescope tables. Here we would suggest the propriety of rinding the planks, which should be cut ¼ inch thicker, and rinded ¼ inch broader than the finished size, and laying out the rinds to the action of the weather. The effect will be, to extract thoroughly the natural sap, to warp the pieces to the full extent of their tendency, and so to secure that no change shall take place upon them after

B

sions. The quality of the wood is greatly affected by the nature of the soil on which it is grown; that produced on poor land being stunted and brittle, while that grown in a free loam mixed with gravel, possesses, in the highest degree, that toughness and elasticity which constitute the principal value of the timber. The wood of the ash, though not so durable as the matured or heart wood of the oak, surpasses it and all our indigenous trees in elasticity and adhesiveness of fibre; and is, on account of these properties, universally used in the manufacture of articles where these qualities are particularly required, such as implements of husbandry, wheel carriages, ship-blocks, oars, and various portions of machine work. It possesses the additional recommendation of becoming useful when quite young, the wood being as durable and perfect then, as it is when it has attained its greatest dimensions. Those who have had the most experience, consider it most valuable at the age of from thirty to sixty years.

The ash tree is so remarkable for elegance of form and beauty of foliage, as to have been called the Venus of the forest. The principal stem rises to a great height in an easy flowing line, while the branches, as they lengthen, take generally a graceful sweep; and the looseness of the leaves corresponding with the lightness of the spray, the whole forms an elegant depending foliage. The colour, also, which is of a light and agreeable green, harmonizes and contrasts well with trees of a more sombre hue. It is very late of coming into leaf, rarely before the beginning of June, and its foliage falls suddenly with the first frosts of autumn, however early in the season these may happen. There are three or four varieties of the common ash grown in Britain, which we need not enumerate, as they are cultivated rather on account of their ornamental appearance, than with the view of yielding profitable timber. Guided by the principle of making those trees only which are of importance to the cabinet-maker the subject of special notice, we turn to the ashes of American growth. Of these, botanists enumerate more than thirty distinct species, the most important of which is the *Fraxinus Americana*, generally called the white ash. This species is a native of the United States, and also of Canada; from which it is annually exported to this country in large quantities, varying in amount from 7000 to 25,000 feet. The circumstances most favourable to the growth of this species, are a cold climate, and a moist soil, such as is furnished by the edges of a swamp, or the banks of a river. In such situations, it is found to attain a height of eighty feet, and a diameter of three or four feet, and having the trunk perfectly

straight and undivided often to the height of more than forty feet. On large trees, the bark is deeply furrowed, divided into small squares, and so light in colour, as to have given rise to the name of *white* ash, by which it is known throughout America. The leaves are twelve or fourteen inches long, composed of three or four pair of leaflets, surmounted by an odd one, and present a remarkable contrast of colour, the upper surface being of a light green, while the under side is nearly white. While the timber of this species bears a considerable resemblance to that of the common ash of Britain, it is neither so hard nor so tough; and hence is better fitted for the use of the cabinet-maker. From the time of its being extensively imported, it has gradually and to a considerable extent superseded the other woods used for the interior fittings of chests of drawers, wardrobes, and similar articles of furniture. For the preference, two reasons may be assigned; namely, the entire absence of smell which distinguishes ash, and the ease with which it is wrought as compared with the cedars, &c., formerly in use for the purposes to which ash is now applied.

Purchase.—The principal use to which ash is meant to be put, indicates the desirableness of selecting such logs as are distinguished for the mildness and cleanness of their timber; and the appearances which mark these qualities are obvious to any careful observer. As in the case of most other woods, so in ash, the thinness and closeness of the annual rings, or, in other words, the fineness of the grain, marks the degree in which it is characterized by mildness. An examination of the end of the log will at once furnish evidence on this head.

On turning to the sides, take notice whether the grain is straight and close, and whether there is little appearance of gnarled growth or marked figure. Where these are present, the wood may be expected to be strong and coarse, difficult to work, and liable to warp. Attention should also be paid to the appearances of soundness near the heart of the timber, as it is not by any means unfrequent to find a large portion of it the subject of the dry rot. The existence of this is ordinarily indicated by the soft, spongy, and discoloured appearance of the ends of the tree, especially near the heart.

Cutting up.—As it can scarcely be expected that all the logs in a lot of ash should possess the mildness and cleanness which are desirable in wood to be used for interior fittings, it is of importance to take care that any which are of an opposite character should be cut up for a different purpose. Instead of sawing them into thicknesses for drawer stuff, let them be cut into planks suitable for chair rails, sofa stocks or scrolls, or bed-stocks. For

sions. The quality of the wood is greatly affected by the nature of the soil on which it is grown; that produced on poor land being stunted and brittle, while that grown in a free loam mixed with gravel, possesses, in the highest degree, that toughness and elasticity which constitute the principal value of the timber. The wood of the ash, though not so durable as the matured or heart wood of the oak, surpasses it and all our indigenous trees in elasticity and adhesiveness of fibre; and is, on account of these properties, universally used in the manufacture of articles where these qualities are particularly required, such as implements of husbandry, wheel carriages, ship-blocks, oars, and various portions of machine work. It possesses the additional recommendation of becoming useful when quite young, the wood being as durable and perfect then, as it is when it has attained its greatest dimensions. Those who have had the most experience, consider it most valuable at the age of from thirty to sixty years.

The ash tree is so remarkable for elegance of form and beauty of foliage, as to have been called the Venus of the forest. The principal stem rises to a great height in an easy flowing line, while the branches, as they lengthen, take generally a graceful sweep; and the looseness of the leaves corresponding with the lightness of the spray, the whole forms an elegant depending foliage. The colour, also, which is of a light and agreeable green, harmonizes and contrasts well with trees of a more sombre hue. It is very late of coming into leaf, rarely before the beginning of June, and its foliage falls suddenly with the first frosts of autumn, however early in the season these may happen. There are three or four varieties of the common ash grown in Britain, which we need not enumerate, as they are cultivated rather on account of their ornamental appearance, than with the view of yielding profitable timber. Guided by the principle of making those trees only which are of importance to the cabinet-maker the subject of special notice, we turn to the ashes of American growth. Of these, botanists enumerate more than thirty distinct species, the most important of which is the *Fraxinus Americana*, generally called the white ash. This species is a native of the United States, and also of Canada; from which it is annually exported to this country in large quantities, varying in amount from 7000 to 25,000 feet. The circumstances most favourable to the growth of this species, are a cold climate, and a moist soil, such as is furnished by the edges of a swamp, or the banks of a river. In such situations, it is found to attain a height of eighty feet, and a diameter of three or four feet, and having the trunk perfectly

straight and undivided often to the height of more than forty feet. On large trees, the bark is deeply furrowed, divided into small squares, and so light in colour, as to have given rise to the name of *white* ash, by which it is known throughout America. The leaves are twelve or fourteen inches long, composed of three or four pair of leaflets, surmounted by an odd one, and present a remarkable contrast of colour, the upper surface being of a light green, while the under side is nearly white. While the timber of this species bears a considerable resemblance to that of the common ash of Britain, it is neither so hard nor so tough; and hence is better fitted for the use of the cabinet-maker. From the time of its being extensively imported, it has gradually and to a considerable extent superseded the other woods used for the interior fittings of chests of drawers, wardrobes, and similar articles of furniture. For the preference, two reasons may be assigned; namely, the entire absence of smell which distinguishes ash, and the ease with which it is wrought as compared with the cedars, &c., formerly in use for the purposes to which ash is now applied.

Purchase.—The principal use to which ash is meant to be put, indicates the desirableness of selecting such logs as are distinguished for the mildness and cleanness of their timber; and the appearances which mark these qualities are obvious to any careful observer. As in the case of most other woods, so in ash, the thinness and closeness of the annual rings, or, in other words, the fineness of the grain, marks the degree in which it is characterized by mildness. An examination of the end of the log will at once furnish evidence on this head.

On turning to the sides, take notice whether the grain is straight and close, and whether there is little appearance of gnarled growth or marked figure. Where these are present, the wood may be expected to be strong and coarse, difficult to work, and liable to warp. Attention should also be paid to the appearances of soundness near the heart of the timber, as it is not by any means unfrequent to find a large portion of it the subject of the dry rot. The existence of this is ordinarily indicated by the soft, spongy, and discoloured appearance of the ends of the tree, especially near the heart.

Cutting up.—As it can scarcely be expected that all the logs in a lot of ash should possess the mildness and cleanness which are desirable in wood to be used for interior fittings, it is of importance to take care that any which are of an opposite character should be cut up for a different purpose. Instead of sawing them into thicknesses for drawer stuff, let them be cut into planks suitable for chair rails, sofa stocks or scrolls, or bed-stocks. For such uses, too, it may be prudent to take a board off each side of the heart draught in a log which, rather coarse at the heart, is on the whole fitted for being cut into thin wood. The main use of ash, however, is to furnish material for drawer sides, bottoms, and *mounters*. By mounters, we will be understood by tradesmen to mean the cross bar of $3\frac{1}{2}$ inches broad by $\frac{3}{4}$ inch thick, which is used to divide into two parts the bottom of a long drawer, for the sake of strengthening it to bear the weight of the contents. The usual thickness for the sides of large drawers is $\frac{9}{16}$ inch, and for the bottoms of such, $\frac{3}{8}$ inch. Where the drawers are of small size, the $\frac{3}{8}$ inch usually employed for bottoms will be found thick enough for the sides, while the bottoms need not be more than $\frac{1}{4}$ inch thick. In determining the order in which these various thicknesses should be cut, we have found it advantageous to take the thickest clefts nearest the heart. This throws the cleanest wood into the bottoms; and should the boards cut for sides prove coarse, they can either be jointed for the purpose, or cut up into the grooved fillets which are extensively used by good tradesmen.

It is of importance that ash logs should be sawn into the various thicknesses for which it is suitable, as soon after it is got into the wood-yard as possible; as we know of no wood which is more liable to crack and shake when exposed in the mass. Nor is it sufficient to avoid this, that it be cut into half logs; for even in this state, the efforts of the natural sap to escape from the centre, will have the effect of producing deep rents on all the sides. In order to prevent this, recourse is sometimes had to the sinking of the logs in ponds of water, where these are available. We regard this as a practice of very questionable utility; for while it is true that immersion will prevent splitting, it is certain to have the effect of inducing discolouration and decay.

Seasoning.—As in the case of beech, so in regard to ash, where it is very strong and hard, it may be of advantage to allow the boards to lie close together for a few weeks after being sawn, with the view of rendering them more tender and easily wrought. But in the case of wood of ordinary mildness, this is not advisable. Generally, it will be found the wisest course to *pile* the boards immediately after they are cut. In doing so, regard should be had to the fact, that, from the nature of the wood and the thinness of the clefts, they are extremely liable to warp and bend in the drying. In order to overcome this tendency, it is of importance that they be laid on a straight and level bed of blocks, closer than is ordinarily required, and that the fillets which separate them should be of equal thickness, and placed

exactly above each other, so as to secure the perfect straightness of all the boards in the pile. After being exposed for two or three months, let the whole be turned over, and the boards be laid upside down, with the same care; thus will be secured the fairest chance for the material, when seasoned, being found in a workable condition. Should it be objected that the course recommended is laborious, we can only reply, that the first labour is the least, and that pains taken in the seasoning will prove gain in the working.

ELM.

Although the wood of the elm is now much seldomer used in the manufacture of furniture than it was formerly, we regard it as having a natural claim to be noticed in any account of the woods suitable for cabinet work. The elm, called by botanists *Ulmus*, has been the subject of much diversity of opinion in regard to the number of its species and varieties; some authorities enumerating as many as twelve distinct species, while other writers refer all of these to one species, *Ulmus campestris*, or common elm, and regard the others as varieties merely. This difference of opinion is easily accounted for, by the fact, that the seed of the elm does not all prove true to the tree from which it is gathered, but is apt to produce varieties differing more or less from the parent plant, and from each other. Among the cultivated elms of this country, individuals are found differing as much from each other as if they belonged to distinct genera; and yet there are such a number of kinds intermediate, that classification is found a matter of extreme difficulty, even to those who have paid the greatest attention to the subject. Most botanists, however, are agreed in classifying the elms of British growth under two species, namely, the *Ulmus campestris*, the common, or English elm, and the *Ulmus montana*, the mountain, Wych, or Scotch elm. The first of these is seen in its greatest perfection in the southern and midland parts of England, where it not only forms the avenues of the finest public walks and drives in the vicinity of towns, but forms a large proportion of the timber chosen to adorn the parks and surround the residences of our nobility and gentry. It is of rapid growth, and often attains a height of from seventy to ninety feet, and a diameter of four or five feet. The trunk is tall and straight, and the branches are subordinate to it, throughout its entire length. The leaves are small, doubly serrated or toothed, and are, when matured, of a dark green colour, and rough surface. The flowers, which are of a purple colour, sometimes appear very early in the season, and cover the branches as fully as the subsequent leafy foliage, presenting a singular and beautiful appearance. The common, or English elm, if not indigenous to Britain, must have been introduced at a very remote period; as we find various localities in England to which its name seems to have been attached in the times of the Anglo-Saxons.

The *Ulmus montana*—the Wych, or Scotch elm, is distinguished from the common, or English elm, in having a much more picturesque appearance, attaining a larger size, and yielding timber of a better quality. Instead of a straight continuous trunk of upright and formal growth, it forms a large spreading tree, in which the stem, frequently covered with gnarled excrescences, generally divides itself, at no great height from the ground, into large diverging limbs, which, of free and graceful growth, are rendered pendulous by the weight of foliage they bear. In point of size, too, it considerably exceeds the common elm; for while the largest specimen of that, of which we have any notice, namely, Piffe's elm, in the vale of Gloucester, measured, at five feet from the ground, about sixteen feet in circumference, we find mention made of one wych elm grown in Suffolk, which, at the same height from the ground, was twenty-seven feet in circumference; and of another in the parish of Roxburgh, called the Trysting elm, which, at a height of four feet from the ground, measured not less than thirty feet in circumference. But the principal difference in favour of this species, is in the quality of the timber which it yields; which, by all practical men, is admitted to be superior both in durability and value. This superiority would seem to have been well known in ancient times, for we find the use of the wych elm, in the manufacture of bows, enjoined by statute. The timber of both species, however, possesses in common the quality of resisting the action of water; and hence has long been extensively used for the keels of vessels, for wet foundations, water-works, piles, pumps, and the like. It is also, from its toughness, preferred for the naves of wheels, for the shells of tackle blocks, the gunwales of ships, and all purposes which require a wood that will bear rough usage without splitting.

But the circumstance that principally calls for the present notice of the elm, is its extensive use in the manufacture of furniture up to a very recent date. Although, at present, it is rarely used except for the commoner sort of Windsor chairs and similar articles, not more than twenty years have elapsed since it formed a principal material for drawing-room furniture of the best description. When employed in the manufacture of fine furni-

ture, the large trees of twisted growth, which, when cut, present a fine laced appearance, or waved unevenness, were selected for the plainer parts of the work; and veneers cut from the gnarled excrescences, or curls, for the principal parts, such as table tops, or the surface of cabinets. These excrescences are caused by the stoppage or peculiar diversion of the sap, occasioned by the lopping off large branches or constitutional defect; and annually increasing in size, deposit a curiously veined and marbled wood, which, when cut off and carefully seasoned, are found to yield veneers of rare beauty. Perhaps the main cause of furniture made of this material going out of fashion, is to be found in the fact that, in order to finish it well, an amount of labour was required that the majority of purchasers were unwilling to pay for. This great amount of additional labour was rendered necessary, by the small size, irregular form, and faulty texture, of the pieces of veneer which could be obtained. In order to cover a large surface with small pieces of veneer of an irregularly circular or oval shape, very much more work was needed to join them to each other, than is required in the case of mahogany or rosewood. But even when this was effected, a greater amount of time was employed in filling up the smaller or larger holes usually found in the veneers, arising from openness of texture, and the admixture of loose bark or gum; all of which required to be carefully filled, in order to produce a solid surface to receive the polish. In the manufacture of such articles, taste, skill, and time, were productive of a result which leads us to regret that work of this description is rarely called for, except for the purpose of matching suits of furniture.

While we think it unnecessary to speak particularly of the purchase and cutting up of elm, it may be useful to call the attention of those who occasionally require it, to the necessity of very carefully seasoning the curls, or wart-looking pieces, usually cut into veneers. If this be neglected, the veneers will not hold together, but, in consequence of their varied texture causing unequal progress in drying, will split in all directions. Even where the greatest care is taken beforehand, the veneers may present, after being cut, a very uneven surface. As in the case of the curled birch veneer, this may be overcome by the sudden application of heat and pressure, which will have the additional effect of shrinking the veneer to its least dimensions before it is laid, and prevent subsequent opening of the joints and pores in the surface. It is scarcely possible to carry too far the drying of the veneer before it is laid, whether as regards the larger pieces, or the smaller bits which are filled into the holes. From the irregular shape of these, it is difficult to join them with sufficient nicety. Any imperfection in this respect, will be greatly remedied by the application of the glue, which will expand the previously dried wood, till it completely fill the space into which it is inserted. In connection with this subject, it may be useful to the young workman for us to notice the propriety of making all his joinings in irregular and waving lines, similar to those which are described by the figure of the wood. It is plain that this will cause more work than making them in straight lines, but the additional labour will be far more than repaid, in their being rendered almost invisible. We would mention further, that the small holes of which we have spoken, should, as far as possible, be fitted with pieces of wood rather than with sawdust and glue, or gum shell-lac; neither of which make such a solid surface for the reception of polish.

Before leaving the subject, we may also notice, that many persons of experience deem it of great advantage to the beauty of the wood, that pieces which are to be cut into veneers, should be buried for some months previously in a heap of horse dung. This is said to have a wonderful effect in improving the show or figure, which we are inclined to credit, from knowing that the same course is followed on the Continent with great benefit, in the case of pieces of the walnut tree intended to be cut into veneers.

From Canada, there is annually imported into Britain, from 40,000 to 50,000 cubic feet of red elm, the *Ulmus rubra* of botany, similar in appearance, but inferior in quality, to the elms of British growth.

OAK.

Of the oak, or *Quercus*, botanists enumerate not fewer than one hundred and fifty distinct species, and it is doubtful whether all are included, even in this large number. Distributed over a large portion of the earth's surface, in almost every variety of soil and climate; and possessing a wonderful power of adaption to these, it presents a wide field for description. But we shall confine our attention to those species which are indigenous to Britain, or which are imported into this country for the use of the cabinet-maker. The *Quercus robur*, or common oak, which is indigenous to Britain, has, by some naturalists of eminence, been divided into two distinct species, namely, the *Quercus pedunculata*, peduncled or common oak; and the *Quercus sessiliflora*, or sessile fruited oak. Externally, the difference between these is marked, by the first

having the acorns supported on short stems, or as it is termed, pedunculated; while the second has the acorns sessile, or without the supporting stems; the leaves, also, of the first are larger, and the bark darker in the colour, than the second. But a more important difference has been asserted to exist, in the qualities of the timber yielded by them respectively; that of the pedunculated, or common oak, being regarded as superior, both in strength, toughness, and durability, to that of the sessile fruited oak. While some naturalists of eminence draw this distinction, others, of not inferior note, contend that the difference is only one of variety, not of species; and that each variety furnishes timber inferior or superior to the other, according to the quality of soil on which they have respectively been raised. By practical men, the difference, if it exists, has been entirely overlooked; for the timber of both kinds has always been used, indiscriminately, for the most important purposes in which oak is employed.

Without presuming to decide which of the two opinions is the more correct, we shall proceed to such observations as apply equally to all oaks of British growth. These would appear to have been held in high estimation in the remoter periods of the history of the island; though, for a very different reason than any of those which now obtain for the oak such an important place amongst our forest trees. During the Saxon rule, and even after the time of the Norman conquest, the oak was valued chiefly for the acorns which it yielded, and which were used, not only in general, for the fattening of the herds of swine, which constituted a great part of the wealth of our Saxon ancestors, but also, in seasons of scarcity, were rendered available for human food. Strange as this statement may appear to modern readers, it is rendered less wonderful on referring to the experience of our British troops, who, in the absence of a well-supplied commissariat during the Peninsular war, were sometimes glad to satisfy the cravings of nature with this humble fare. Of such importance, in respect to the food which they yielded, were the oak forests considered, that we find some of the Saxon kings passing laws for their preservation; and others rewarding their powerful military retainers, or dowering their daughters, by settling on them the produce of a certain portion of oak forest. But an advancing civilization soon elevated the oak to a higher place in the national estimation, and connected it intimately at once with the maritime superiority, and the religious sentiment of the British people. We find indications of the estimate which, at a very early period, had been formed of its fitness to supply material for sea-going vessels; in the remains of large and rudely-fashioned canoes scooped from the oak, which have been at different times disinterred in various parts of the country. The construction of these vessels, which are common only to the earliest stages of society, would seem to prove the use of the oak, for such a purpose, to have commenced at a date, perhaps, earlier than the Roman invasion. What was thus early begun, has been continued down to the present day; and whether, in the oared galleys of the Saxons, the three-masted vessels of the times of the Tudors, or in the first-rate Indiaman, or British ship of war of our times—the oak has formed the staple material. So identified, indeed, is the oak with naval architecture, that the British government has long deemed it necessary to commit to the care of the same department in the public service, the rearing of the timber, and the superintendence of the dock yards. There are three qualities possessed by the oak, which procure for it the distinction of being regarded as the fittest material for shipbuilding; namely, strength, toughness, and durability. Any one of these qualities, taken singly, may be found, in an equal degree, in some other species of timber: but in no other species are all three found combined in the same degree. Another recommendation to the ship-builder is the crooked growth in oak, which, forming short turns and elbows, furnishes pieces suitable for what is called *knee-timber*. But the extensive use of oak timber, in early times, was not confined to the ship-carpenter; for we find that, in all the older ecclesiastical edifices, it furnished material not only for the heavier timbers, but also for the beautiful interior decorations, many of which have excited the admiration of all succeeding ages. So invariably has it been employed in the religious buildings reared by the piety or superstition of ancient times, that it has, from the association of ideas, come to be regarded as the only material congruous with the nature of any of the more expensive structures erected for religious purposes. The matchless screen of the minster at York, the stalls of the cathedral at Gloucester, and the shrine of the chapel of Edward the confessor, in Westminster Abbey; all were of oak. The practice of modern times would seem to sanction the canon of taste here implied; for we have invariably, in the circumstances, if not the same material employed, at least an imitation of it given by the painter. In the interior fittings of our ancient baronial halls and castles, and in the furniture with which they were provided, the exclusive use of oak prevailed to an equal extent. Although the successive introduction of walnut, mahogany, rosewood, and other fancy woods, may, for a time,

have rendered oak less popular in the private mansions of the great, recent years have shown a revival of the taste which prefers it as the most suitable material for the furniture of the hall, and the library, if not of the spacious dining-room. For these purposes, the wainscot, imported from Dantzig, Memel, and Riga, has, in modern times, been employed almost to the exclusion of British oak. The grounds of preference are, that the wainscot is milder in its character, and more easily wrought than the British oak; but, chiefly, that in it the grain is finer, and more interspersed with the ornamental markings or flower, from the septa or medullary rays in the wood. In common phrase, "*the champ*" is better. We have often heard these qualities, in wainscot, attributed to a particular process of steeping which it is said to undergo after being cut; but, after careful inquiry, are persuaded, that the difference between it and common oak does not arise from any peculiar mode of treatment, but from an original difference in the species, and, in part, from the nature of the soil on which it is raised. The name wainscot, is derived from the purpose for which it was extensively employed, before the introduction of plaster as a finishing for interior walls, in Germany, Holland, and on the Continent generally. It is composed of two words, "*wandt*," a wall, and "*schot*," a defence; which, at first descriptive of the use to which oak was extensively put, came, at length, to be applied to the wood itself. The common name given in England to the panelled lining of an apartment, was "the wainscot" or "wainscotting," which generally consisted of oak. The name thus acquired, has been retained to the present day; and, although not correctly descriptive, is serviceable in distinguishing the article referred to, from the oaks of British growth, and those which are imported from America.

In external appearance, there is a considerable difference between the common or British oak, and the *Quercus cerris*, the Turkey or mossy-cupped oak, which is imported into this country under the name of wainscot. While the common oak has ordinarily a short trunk of from six to twelve feet high, which divides itself into large crooked limbs, but little inferior to the main stem, the Turkey oak is of a pyramidal growth, having a tall straight trunk, which often reaches a height of forty or fifty feet, and to which the branches are subordinate, rarely assuming the large size, or tortuous form, of the limbs of the common oak. In illustration of the remarkably straight growth of the oak which is imported under the name of wainscot, we may mention, that it is a common practice to split the trees into two halves, simply by boring a hole in the top, at the beginning of winter, and filling it with water, which, expanded by the action of frost, forms a wedge sufficiently powerful to split the tree in two throughout its entire length. The occasion for thus dividing the trees, seems to be the necessity of reducing them in bulk to fit them for being floated or rafted down the rivers Dwina, Niemen, and Vistula, from the mountain sides where they are grown, to Riga, Memel, and Dantzig, the ports from which they are shipped to Britain. Of the importations from these three ports, the wainscot of Riga is the most valuable for the purposes of the cabinet-maker, and brings by far the highest price. They, however, are not of uniform value, but distinguished by the names "crown," and "common," into a fine, and an inferior quality. Although in respect of strength, toughness, and durability, wainscot is decidedly inferior to the common oak, it possesses all these qualities in sufficient degree to warrant the employment of it in furniture and interior finishings, for which its ornamental appearance renders it much more suitable. We accordingly find that, for such purposes, it has almost entirely superseded the oak of native growth. Nor is it the sole rival with which our indigenous timber has had to contend; for there is annually imported, from Quebec, from 200,000 to 300,000 cubic feet of oak of American growth. Upwards of seventy distinct species of oaks have been enumerated by naturalists, as indigenous to America; varying in importance from a lowly shrub, to the loftiest forest tree. Of these, we shall mention only the two which, in value, approximate to those of European growth. The *Quercus virens*, or live oak, is that which, in the quality of its timber, bears the closest resemblance to our common British oak, and is, in the United States, regarded as the most valuable for shipbuilding. The general Government has at different times laid out large sums in the preservation and establishment of plantations of live oak, with the view of supplying the naval dockyards with suitable materials. This species being confined to the southern States, has not, we believe, been imported into Britain as timber, nor has the attempt to cultivate it in this country been successful, the climate being too cold to permit its growth, except in very warm and sheltered situations. The *Quercus alba*, or white oak, which is abundant in the northern States of the Union, is that which is imported from Quebec, to supply the British market. Inferior to the common or British oak in strength and durability, and to wainscot in fineness of grain and beauty of figure, it is nevertheless extensively used both in carpentry and cabinet-making. Costing not more than one-half of the price of wainscot, it is often employed in the manufacture of hall furniture of an inferior description, for plate chests, gun cases, and similar articles. When it is of fine quality, even good tradesmen employ it for the inferior or subordinate parts of furniture, of which the principal surfaces are in wainscot; but in all cases, a practised eye can readily detect the difference. It is also extensively used for the rails and slides of telescope dining-tables, and other purposes which requires toughness and strength in comparatively small bulk of wood. Like all the other species of oak, it holds a large amount of natural sap, with which it parts very slowly, and the evaporation of which shrinks the wood to the extent of about one thirty-second part less than its original size. It is also very liable to warp and twist in the course of drying, which points out the great necessity of carefully selecting for purchase such logs as are straight grown, and avoiding such as have the grain twisted after the manner of a rope. Where this is the original tendency, scarcely any amount of seasoning is sufficient to counteract it; on the contrary, it will show itself not only in the course of working, but even after being manufactured, when exposed to a variation of temperature. This is peculiarly mischievous when it is used for the purpose of making sliding-rails; which, requiring to be wrought at intervals, are found to be out of order just when they are wanted, and when there is not time to adjust them.

In purchasing a lot of American oak, it may not be possible to avoid including one or more logs of the twisted growth which we have described. But care should be taken, that pieces of this nature are cut up into thicknesses suited for purposes where the tendency to warp will be productive of the least harm. Indeed, we are persuaded that less loss will result from using it as common hardwood, than from applying it to uses which its cost would render desirable, but which it is unfitted to serve. Where, from the necessity of economy of production, it is found requisite to employ American oak for finishing purposes, attention should be given to the selection of such pieces as have least of the oaky appearance; or, in other words, which are closest in the grain, and have the best figure, or *champ*, and, in consequence, most closely resemble wainscot. In the selection of wainscot for purchase, it is also needful to have respect to the same rule; for entire lots of it are to be found which are of strong oaky growth, and possess but little of the mildness, closeness of texture, and beauty of figure, which render it valuable in preference to British or American oak. It is also of importance to choose lots in which the logs are straight, and of considerable size. When

c

they are small, and much bent, they are necessarily less economical in the cutting out, and require, for most purposes, an additional number of joints. As we have already said, wainscot is, to a considerable extent, imported only in half logs; and hence, few boards cut from it are found to be straight at a greater breadth than eleven inches. The half logs are of a greater breadth than this, it is true, but they can only be cut in one way, to secure the beauty of the wood; that is, the draughts must run from the split side to the round side. This takes them either perpendicularly or obliquely through the silver grain, or medullary rays, which yield the ornamental marking, or *champ*. This will be found in the greatest perfection in those planks, the surfaces of which are at a *small* angle with the lines of the silver grain; these should be selected for cutting into veneers, or for fine $\frac{1}{2}$ inch or $\frac{5}{8}$ inch thick boards, for panels or the like. A cut will most simply illustrate our meaning.

We have, in the figure, a section of a half log of wainscot, in which the annular rings are represented by the semicircular lines, and the silver grain, or medullary rays, are seen radiating from the heart to the circumference. A draught run from *a* to *a*, as in the dotted line, would present a more showy surface than a draught from *b* to *b*, in which the silver grain is presented more obliquely. A glance at the figure will furnish another reason for running the draughts from the split side to the round side of the half log, namely, that it avoids the waste which would be occasioned at the round side, were they cut in the direction of the dotted line from *c* to *c*. But before leaving the subject of the silver grain, or medullary rays, we would earnestly invite the attention of young workmen to a careful study of the laws which regulate the show or figure of the timber which they are engaged in working. Many, from not having had their thoughts directed to the results which can be produced by an intelligent acquaintance with these laws, are guided in their mode of treating a piece of wood, by a simple regard to ease or convenience. In consequence of this, it is regarded as a matter over which they have no control, whether, when finished, it shall be showy or plain. Whereas, on the contrary, the result, in all cases where a piece of wood can be worked in two ways, is entirely in the hands of the workman. Suppose he is called on to run a moulding in oak; if he run the plane parallel to, or at a small angle with, the silver grain, he is sure to bring out all the show which the wood possesses; but should he run the plane on the edge of the silver grain, he will render the moulding as plain as the wood is capable of making it. The knowledge of this alternative resting with him, ought to be sufficient to induce any young man, desirous of rising in his business, to make the subject a matter of careful study. It is, perhaps, not going out of our way to remark, that the union of mental effort with physical toil, of which we have specified an instance, is the natural way to render bodily labour less irksome while it lasts, and, eventually, to raise the workman above the necessity of engaging in it. But to return to the cutting of wainscot from the log, it may be observed, that as it is impossible to get all the logs in a lot, or even all the planks in the same log, equally showy, the plainer wood should be cut into the thick planks required for bed-posts, truss-legs, table-pillars, the feet of hall chairs, and the like. In articles of such bulk, although generally plain, it will ordinarily be found practicable to turn the showy side to the front, or prominent part of the job

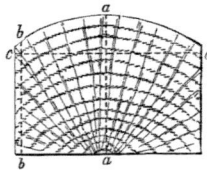

But the main thing to be attended to, in the treatment of oak or wainscot, is the seasoning; for, if manufactured before it is dry, it will split and open in every direction. This tendency will only be increased, and the evil aggravated, by attempting to hurry the process by any application of artificial heat, with which we are acquainted. From the extent of the shrinking which takes place in drying, when the outer part is dried, while the damp heart remains undiminished in bulk, the outer rind must necessarily crack. Should an attempt be made to fill these cracks with thin slips, however neatly inserted, they are sure to show themselves in course of time. The inner part, when reduced to its least bulk by drying, will carry the previously seasoned outer part with it, and eject, as intruders, the slips which have been inserted before the seasoning was complete. To prevent this, there is nothing for it but to subject the material to a course of thorough seasoning in the open air; the tediousness of which will be amply compensated by the result.

It would be improper to close our notice of oak, without adverting to what is called *black oak;* that is, timber which, from long-continued immersion in water, or from being imbedded in a moist mossy deposit, has changed from its natural colour to black, or an intermediate hue. Salt water has the effect of changing the colour of oak, which has been submerged in it for a sufficient length of time, to a deep black, but the process would appear to be very tedious; for the timber of the " Royal George," which sunk with Admiral Kempenfelt, and a numerous crew, in 1782, when fished up about seven years ago, was found to be but very partially affected, the heart of it being but little changed, although at each end, and on the outsides of the various pieces, the discoloration had reached to a bluish green. We had an opportunity of examining the wreck of part of the Spanish Armada, which, after lying nearly two and a half centuries under water, was recovered on the north-east coast of the island about twenty-five years ago; and in this, as in the former case, the natural colour of the wood had changed to a jet black. In both cases, the timber was unchanged in quality, remaining as firm and sound as ever it had been. Most, although not all of the specimens of black oak disinterred from bogs and mosses which we have seen, have been less firm and sound in quality, and not so deep in the colour as the last mentioned of those recovered from the sea. Indeed, there is perhaps no material presented to the cabinet-maker, which is the occasion of so much trouble and annoyance in the manufacture, as the moss or bog oak. Proprietors on whose land it is found, are naturally fond of having it made into articles of furniture, but are little aware of the difficulty of the task. Although, on being dug up, it may seem perfectly firm and compact, yet on being exposed to the action of the air, in the great majority of instances it shakes and cracks to an extent that is scarcely conceivable by those who have not witnessed it. And in pieces which are more compact, the tendency to warp is so great, as to render it almost impossible to work it in bulk, with the hope of its remaining *fair*. The only chance of making creditable articles of furniture from it, is first to dry it very slowly under cover of a cellar or outhouse, and then to cut it into veneers; which, if dried with equal care, may stand pretty well when laid on a proper bed. Of course, this rule must be taken with the exception of retaining as much of the wood solid, as may be required for mouldings or other portions, such as chair feet, and turned or carved work, which cannot be veneered. It will be found of advantage in lending cohesion to the naturally open texture of the wood, to rub in *size*, or weak glue, into such parts of the surface as can be conveniently cleaned afresh after the glue has dried. This, by shutting out the air, will lessen the chances of the article cracking after it is manufactured. To attain the same end, it is of importance that the French polisher should, immediately after the surface is cleaned, fill up the pores with blackened plaster of Paris.

Maple.

Of Maple, called in botany *Acer*, there are about thirty-six distinct species, of which two are indigenous to Britain. The first of these, *Acer pseudo-platanus*, the great maple, sycamore, or mock plane tree, is a robust hardy tree, which grows to a size equal to that of the oak, ash, and other trees of the first rank; and is little affected by exposure, whether from the sea breeze, or the highest winds in inland situations. It has an erect stem, which, diverging into large angular limbs, with a strong spray supporting a large unbroken mass of foliage, affords an impenetrable shade from the rays of the sun, and a shelter from the blast. This recommends it as an excellent break-wind for mansions in exposed situations, and as a companion to other trees of a less hardy nature. From early spring till late in autumn it is covered with leaves, which at first of a yellowish tint, deepen into positive green, giving place, at the close of the season, to a bright reddish brown hue, not less beautiful than either. The bark is of a fine ash gray colour, broken into patches of different hues by the casting off old flakes, which tend to increase the picturesque appearance of the tree. The second species of maple indigenous to Britain is *Acer campestris*, the common or field maple. Ordinarily placed in hedge-rows or copse-woods, and cut over as a bush or shrub of inferior growth, it is in many districts of the country very rarely planted and treated as a tree; and hence, few specimens of it are found which have attained the magnitude that, in an appropriate soil, it is capable of reaching. In favourable circumstances, and under proper treatment, it arrives at dimensions but little inferior to that of trees of the first rank, and presents a very handsome outline, and picturesque appearance. Of the foreign species which have been introduced and extensively cultivated, the most important is the *Acer platanoides,* or Norway maple. As its name implies, it is a native of Norway; but is also found growing extensively in Russia, Germany, Switzerland, and France. Like the great maple, it is hardy and robust, withstanding the effects of the sea breeze as well on the coast of Britain, as it does on its native shores of the Baltic and western coast of Norway. In size and general appearance it is very similar to the great maple, although its foliage is not so heavy; and its leaves are, when fully expanded, larger in size, and lighter in the colour. The timber of these three species is similar in appearance and quality; being of a whitish colour, close and compact in the grain, easily wrought, and little liable to warp. These qualities have recommended them as a suitable material for turnery, patterns for foundries, the soles of mangles, cutting boards, and for various pieces of machinery. Except in rural districts, European maple has been used to a very small extent in the manufacture of furniture, and would scarcely have called for notice here but for its affinity to the American species, which yield the wood known as *Bird's-eye maple,* one of the most beautiful materials employed in the manufacture of cabinet furniture.

Bird's-eye Maple is the wood of *Acer saccharinum*, the sugar maple, rock maple, or hard maple; it is indigenous to America, and is found in greatest abundance between the forty-third and forty-eighth degrees of latitude. In the northern parts of the States of New York and Pennsylvania, it is said that there are not fewer than ten millions of acres which produce these trees, at the rate of about thirty to an acre. It is also abundant in Canada, New Brunswick, Prince Edward's Island, and Nova Scotia; and is thence imported in considerable quantities into Great Britain. In America, it is less valued on account of its timber than for the saccharine juice, which it yields in such quantity as to furnish a large proportion of the sugar used by the inhabitants of the rural districts and back settlements of the country. The process of collecting this sap, and manufacturing it into sugar, is worthy of passing notice. In the end of February, or beginning of March, while the ground is still covered with snow, on a site conveniently near to the trees from which the sap is to be collected, a shed is raised to shelter the sugar boilers from the weather. Their implements and utensils are few and simple, consisting of a few augers, tubes, troughs, buckets, and boilers. Operations are commenced by boring holes of $\frac{3}{4}$ inch diameter, and $\frac{1}{2}$ inch deep, obliquely, ascending into the trunks of the trees, at about 18 or 20 inches from the ground. Into these holes are fitted tubes of elder, or sumac, which convey the sap, to the extent of from one to three gallons per day, into the troughs placed to receive it. These are, once every day, emptied of their contents, which are placed in barrels near to the boilers. The evaporation is effected by means of a brisk fire, during the application of which to the boilers the contents are carefully skimmed; and when the liquid has been reduced to a syrup, after being strained, it is poured into moulds, and the molasses drained from it. The result is the production of a sugar, which, when refined, may even compare with the finest used in Europe. The quantity produced must be very large, for single trees are often found to yield as much as 30 lbs. weight in a season.

But it is as an ornamental wood that the maple calls for our attention; and in this respect its claims are considerable. The figure in maple of highest repute is that known under the name of 'bird's-eye' —a designation which it has acquired from the small dots, or little conical projections, with a small hollow in the centre, which, in the finished work, bear a strong resemblance to the eye of a bird. The cause of these appears, on examination, to be the existence of internal spines or points in the bark, on which the successive layers of wood are moulded in a series of abrupt curves, corresponding to the spine or point which causes them. A simple figure will illustrate our meaning. Let *a b* be the saw-draught,

which runs in a straight line through the fibres of the wood, curved by the projection of the spines from the bark *c d*; this renders apparent the cause of the seeming projections. But in order to account for their beauty, it must be noticed that at each intersection of a curve the fibres are presented at a different angle to the light which falls on the surface, and hence the variety of light and shade, transparent and opaque. Another beautiful figure in maple is that known familiarly as *fiddle-back figure*, from pieces of that kind being usually chosen to form the back part of violins. It may be described as consisting of a series of small undulations in the grain, which, as in the case of the *bird's-eye* figure, are transformed into varied beauty when traversed by the straight line of the saw-draught. In the plane finished surface it resembles closely the undulations on the sands of the sea shore, caused by the ripple of the waters. There is a marked difference between this and the *bird's-eye* figure, in this respect, that while the one is peculiar to maple, the other is found in mahogany, and various other woods.

The maple would appear to have attained celebrity, as an ornamental wood, even amongst the Romans; for Pliny dilates at length on the beauty of the specimens furnished by that which grew in Istria and Rhætia, and says that it exceeded in loveliness even the *citrus*—a tree which was regarded as of such value, that instances are on record of single tables formed of it being sold for sums varying from £8000 to £11,000 sterling. While in modern times, which have rendered us familiar with the products of the western hemisphere, this estimate may justly be deemed extravagant, still it will readily be admitted, that for a variety of purposes, this material is eminently suitable. In mirror and picture frames, or other articles, in which it is associated with gilding, there is, from its pale colour and transparent lustre, a congruity and suitableness which is not possessed in the same degree by any other wood with which we are acquainted. The qualities specified render it also a very appropriate material for the manufacture of furniture for a drawing room, which happens to be imperfectly lighted, or which is from any cause sombre-looking and dull. In such an apartment, with an exposure to the north, and a paper and carpet of rather dingy hue, we have seen it employed with the happiest effect. Nor is it less appropriate to the requirements of a well-furnished bedroom. It will be found of the greatest service as furnishing a variety to the " mahogany room," the " oak room," or the " birch room," in a large mansion. Let the chamber be rather small or dark, if maple is used for the entire suit of furniture, its size and cheerful aspect will apparently be greatly increased. But irrespective of dimensions and light, there is in maple a peculiar adaptation to the adornment of an appropriately-furnished sleeping apartment. Suggestive to the fancy of purity and happiness, it seems to combine in furnishing, to as great an extent as mere accessories can do, the subordinate elements of an agreeable bed chamber.

Maple veneer is also well adapted for the interior fittings of Davenport writing-desks, or similar articles of drawing-room furniture, which require to be nicely finished internally; as it not only presents an agreeable contrast in colour to the rosewood, walnut, or mahogany, used for the external surface; but also, from its pale hue, gives the appearance of cleanness, and serves to reveal more perfectly than a darker material would, the contents of the article when it is placed in the shade.

Unlike most other woods, maple is very liable to shrink *lengthways.* Inattention to this peculiarity may be productive of considerable inconvenience in the subsequent widening of mitres, or butt joints, which were perfectly close at the time they were made. The cause of the evil is easily explained. By a reference to our figure, it will be seen that the grain of the wood, from its frequent undulations lengthways, partakes nearly as much of the character of side wood as of end wood. The bed on which the maple veneer is laid, say mahogany, on the contrary, from the straightness of its grain, is not liable to any sensible decrease in length in the process of drying, after being subjected to the action of moisture in the application of the glue with which the veneer is laid. In order to prevent such a result, it is needful that the veneer should in every case be shrunk to its least dimensions before it is laid down.

The pale colour of maple has led to its being frequently used for the bordering of surfaces, of which the main body is veneered with walnut or rosewood; and also to its being employed to furnish the alternate squares in draught boards, where they are introduced into the tops of tables made of the same material as the darker squares. The effect of this is very good, but is frequently greatly marred in the polishing; by the use of French polish made of dark gums, or which contains colouring matter. This polish, which, in so far as the dark veneer is concerned, is beneficial, or at least harmless, has a very bad effect on the maple; as it not only dulls the lustre of its bright spots or undulations, but substitutes a dirty reddish tint for the naturally pure colour of the whole. In the lighter-coloured woods generally, but particularly in maple, it is of importance that the polish used should be as transparent and colourless as possible. Even where they are combined with a darker material, we would recommend that this rule should be adhered to; for it will be found that the purity of the lighter parts of the article, will more than compensate for any loss which the darker sustain from the absence of colouring.

The quantity of maple imported into Britain is so very limited, as to leave the purchaser but little choice of different growths; the finest we have had an opportunity of examining was brought from St. John, New Brunswick. It is of importance that the buyer be on his guard against trees which are of impure colour, or disfigured by stains; as it is not uncommon that such as have the finest figure are rendered valueless by the presence of dull greenish streaks, the result of the tree having died before being cut down, or of improper exposure afterwards.

SATIN WOOD.

Although much less popular now than formerly, as a material for furniture, satin wood is so pretty in itself, and is still so extensively used, as to render it needful to notice it in a work like the present. The finest kind of this wood was found, growing in great abundance, in Hispaniola; an island so named and first discovered by Columbus, and subsequently known as St. Domingo and Hayti. A thirst for gold seems to have been the master passion of the early navigators, and appears to have left the majority of them little leisure and less inclination to observe the wonders of the vegetable kingdom, which the New World presented before them. The Spanish colonists who succeeded them, and the French bucaneers who, a century later, effected a settlement on the island, were equally regardless of the immense forests of mahogany, satin wood and other timber, which have since proved a source of wealth to the exporters, and furnished a supply of new and beautiful materials to the manufactories of Europe.

The selecting and cutting of timber for the purposes of exportation, was induced by a series of occurrences, in themselves of a calamitous nature. Previously to the Revolution in the mother country, towards the end of last century, the French colonists had confined their attention to the production of sugar, coffee, cotton, and indigo, and exported these in large quantities. Encouraged by the liberal policy pursued by the French Government, the colony rapidly attained a degree of prosperity altogether unprecedented. Though occupying little more than one third of the island, it far surpassed in opulence not only the Spanish part, but the whole Spanish West Indies. This thriving state of commercial affairs experienced a severe check in consequence of the revolutionary struggle in France. The promulgation of republican doctrines in St. Domingo, containing a numerous coloured population, many of whom were in a state of slavery, led to a war of races, marked during its continuance by extreme ferocity, and leading eventually to the massacre or expulsion of the white population, the cessation of industrial pursuits, and the ruin of commerce. But this change in the state of society, had one effect of more importance to our present subject than any of the social or political changes at which we have felt it necessary to glance, in so far as it led to the more extensive cutting and exportation of the fine woods with which the island abounded. The black population, disinclined to the continuous labour of the plantations, allowed these to go to waste, and had recourse to the spontaneous supply of commodities for export furnished by their almost interminable forests. Amongst the other woods thus brought into notice, satin wood was exported in large quantities into Britain, and rapidly rose into general favour. Close in the grain, of a pale yellow colour, and elegantly veined, it presented an agreeable variety to the more sombre coloured woods, of which drawing-room furniture had been commonly manufactured, and for a number of years it was extensively used in preference. That it did not retain this eminence is to be accounted for partly from the caprice of fashionable taste, and partly from the fact that when polished with bees' wax, the mode then in use, it speedily gave off its colour and presented a pale blanched appearance. This defect has been remedied by the introduction of French polish, which preserves the colour; but the wood had fallen into disfavour before the remedy had been discovered, or rather, before it had found its way to Britain. Another cause of the comparative neglect into which satin wood has fallen, is its greasy nature, which renders it liable to part from the bed on which it is glued in veneer, or at joints where it is framed or wrought solid. This oily matter, held in the cellular tissue of the wood, gives it a highly aromatic odour, and renders it very inflammable. Although fallen into disrepute as a material for entire suites of drawing-room furniture, it is still employed for articles of ornament, interior finishings, picture and mirror frames, and such purposes as maple is used for. The reasons which recommend maple for these uses, apply with nearly equal force to satin wood. Lightness of colour, beautiful figure, and a silken lustre, which has given rise to its name, all indicate its fitness for being *associated* with gilding and mirror plates; or for being *contrasted* with the darker woods, where variety is desired. In addition to what is used for furniture, a considerable quantity of satin wood is employed in the manufacture of brushes and fancy turnery. The supply is drawn not only from St. Domingo, but also from Porto Rico and Nassau in the West Indies, and from Singapore and Bombay in the East Indies. The relative values of the different growths will appear from a statement of their present prices. St. Domingo wood costs in London £14 per ton; Porto Rico wood, £10; Nassau wood, and those of East India growth, about £8. The wood of India and Ceylon is paler in the colour and less handsomely figured than that grown in the West Indies, but is of the same species. The name given by botanists to this wood is *Chloroxylon swietenia*. It is a variety of the same family to which the mahogany tree belongs; is *leguminous*, or bean-bearing, and yields an oleaginous matter known as *the oil of India*.

A fuller account of the natural appearance and habits of this wood would have been desirable, but hitherto there has not appeared any full account of the botany of the West Indies from which such information could be drawn.

Walnut.

The common walnut, or royal walnut, named by botanists *Juglans regia*, is a native of Persia, whence it was brought by the Greeks. It appears to have been early introduced into Italy, and was known amongst the Romans as the Nut of Jove. We have no authentic information as to the time of its introduction into Britain, but mention is made of it in the earliest botanical records. Its fruits furnished the first inducement for its cultivation, and afterwards the useful and ornamental character of its timber secured for it permanent attention. In ancient Italy, it was highly valued for its beauty, and, according to Strabo, great prices were paid for tables and other furniture manufactured from it. In France and other continental states, from an early date, every encouragement has been given to its increase and cultivation. Evelyn, whose *Sylva* was written in the seventeenth century, says that it was abundant in Burgundy, and that 'in several places betwixt Hanau and Frankfort in Germany, no young farmer is permitted to marry a wife till he bring proof that he is a father of such a stated number of trees; and the law is inviolably observed to this day, for the extraordinary benefit the tree affords to the inhabitants.' In Britain, walnut appears to have been the first wood which superseded oak as the material for furniture of an expensive description; and it is not difficult to account for the preference. Closer in the texture and susceptible of a higher polish, softer, and hence more easily wrought, differing in colour, and often curiously veined, it naturally came to be regarded as the appropriate material for the furniture of apartments of which the interior finishings were in oak. The introduction of mahogany and other exotic woods, it is true, effected a great change in the general taste, and caused walnut for a long period to be regarded only as a material for gunstocks; for which its specific lightness and strong lateral adhesion rendered it eminently serviceable. The quantity required in Britain for this purpose, during the late war, greatly enhanced the price, and led to the cutting down of a large proportion of the trees growing throughout the country; and in France, it is said, that about the year 1806 not fewer than 12,000 trees were annually required for this purpose alone.

Within the last few years another change has taken place, and walnut furniture has again become popular. Fine old specimens of chairs, cabinets, tables, &c. that had been quietly resting in the lumber rooms of our large mansions, have been brought to light, repaired, and polished, and either reinstated in their former places, or sold at prices that would have astonished their long-departed makers. The great demand for these antique specimens of furniture has naturally led to the resuming of the manufacture of similar articles; and hence we find that in drawing-room furniture especially, walnut is now very extensively employed. One circumstance that has contributed to the renewed popularity of walnut, is the revival of a taste for marquetry or inlaid work, for the lively and variegated colours of which this wood forms a very appropriate ground. Of an olive brown colour, interspersed with darker and lighter veins, it acts as a foil to the light and parti-coloured ornaments, which, in the form of centre-parts, corner ornaments, or borders, are inserted in it. Of the common walnut grown in Europe, the qualities are various, some yielding much finer veneers than others. The importations from Italy are most valued, and at present are sold in London at prices varying from 9d. to 1s. per superficial foot. The growths of France are next in value, particularly those of Auvergne, in which the black and red veins are almost invariably found distinctly marked. We had recently an opportunity of examining a parcel of planks brought from Smyrna, which were very pale in the ground, and inferior in the marking; they were sold at 7d. per foot. There are some very fine trees, of large size, to be found in the parks of our nobility and gentry, but they are not numerous, and are seldom exposed for sale. In order to increase the limited supply from these various sources, recourse has been had to the black Virginia walnut, or *Juglans nigra*, a considerable quantity of which is now imported into Britain from America. It is denominated *black*, to distinguish it from the white walnut, or *Juglans alba*, of which there are several varieties, known under the general name of hickory, the wood of which is much lighter in the colour, and less valuable than the black walnut. The importations of black walnut, since the increased demand for it in this country, have been considerable. In quality, it is decidedly inferior to that of European growth, as is indicated by the price, which is only about $4\frac{1}{2}d.$ per superficial foot. What we have seen is of a dull uniform brown, having little of the figure which is necessary in ornamental furniture. It is, however, serviceable when wrought in the solid, for the inferior parts of articles of which the principal parts are veneered with finer wood, and for chairs, couches, pillars, brackets, balls, or the like. Finely-figured veneers of this wood are considered so valuable as often to be sold at from 2s. to 3s. per foot. These are the produce of trees that have grown upon rather dry and poor soils, and which are, in consequence of their slower growth, closer and firmer in the grain, than those which have been more quickly raised on rich and deep soils. The most beautifully marked specimens are yielded by cutting the large roots of such trees into veneers, after placing them in heaps of dung for a considerable time, which has a wonderful effect in deepening the markings and enriching the ground. At a recent public exposition of furniture, &c., in Paris, a *secretaire*, veneered with this material, excited universal admiration.

Although walnut is at present a fashionable material for furniture, we are disposed to think that there is little probability of its continuing to be so for any great length of time. We arrive at this conclusion on the ground that it is destitute of one of the three elements of beauty in wood, namely, *lustre* or *transparency*. It possesses the other two, *colour* and *figure;* but these enter more largely into the character of other woods, as mahogany, maple, satin wood, &c., which possess the additional recommendation of being lustrous and transparent in a high degree. It is inferior also, we think, in colour and figure to rosewood, which has not the advantage of being lustrous or transparent. For these reasons, we expect that it will speedily decline in public estimation, but in the meantime it is necessary for every tradesman who would keep up with the times, to direct his attention to the manufacture of it.

ROSEWOOD.

Rosewood is the produce of the Jacaranda, of which there are several varieties. It is indigenous to the East Indies and the Canary Islands, to Africa, and Central America; but the principal importations into Britain are from Brazil, where it is grown of the finest qualities, and in great abundance. Of the quantity imported into this country, on an average of the five years from 1840 to 1844 inclusive, we find nearly 2000 tons per annum entered for home consumption. The importations from Rio de Janeiro furnish the largest-sized and best-figured wood, and bring a considerably higher price than those from Bahia, the other principal seaport, situated about 800 miles to the north of Rio de Janeiro. Amidst the profusion of beauty and grandeur which distinguish the vast virgin forests of Brazil, the Jacaranda is too striking to be overlooked by the traveller. Von Spix, a German naturalist, who visited them, says, 'Among these sovereigns of the forest, the rosewood tree attracts the eye by the lightness of its double feathered leaves; the large gold-coloured flowers dazzle by their splendour, contrasted with the dark green of the foliage.' The name commonly given to this wood, *rosewood*, is descriptive of the fragrant smell of the wood itself, and not of any odoriferous properties possessed by its foliage or flowers. It has furnished occasion for frequent remark, that it is almost always exported in *half logs*, and not in whole trees. The reasons for thus *splitting* or *sawing* up the trees (for the division of them is commonly so rudely effected, as to partake of the characters of both) seem to be, that in the absence of navigable rivers, or roads of easy passage, it is necessary to reduce the weight of the pieces, for the purpose of facilitating their transport from the interior of the country to the sea coast; and further, that the trees are generally so faulty in the heart, that little, if any, loss arises from dividing them. The trees, unlike most other woods, are never squared, and for this reason, that the best wood is always found at the outside. The rudely-halved, unsquared, and crooked appearance of the planks,

forbid the idea of the wood being sold by measurement, and accordingly it is purchased by the weight, as ascertained and stamped on the ends at the custom house. The prices at present current are, for good *Rio* wood, in lots, about £20 per ton; and for *Bahia* wood, about £12 per ton. Single planks are to be found worth double the highest price we have quoted, and inferior lots are to be had at a lower figure than the lowest mentioned; but in order to get good lots of large-sized wood, with a mixture of veneer planks included in them, it is necessary to give the prices stated. An inferior kind is occasionally imported from Honduras, and sold at about £7 per ton; but it is so soft, porous, and ill coloured, as to be fit only for the manufacture of ordinary furniture.

In selecting rosewood for purchase, it is of importance to attend to the size, soundness, colour, and figure, of the planks, of which the various lots are composed. Planks of a small size, although bought at a lower price than larger wood, will be found less profitable to the cabinet-maker. For the manufacturer of picture frames, or of brushes, the narrow breadth is less objectionable; but in purchasing it as a material for furniture, the full-sized wood, although it cost more money, will be found the most economical. It is a matter of greater difficulty, in general, to secure *sound* wood, than to get it of a proper size; since, in importations of a fine quality, it is not uncommon to find the greater proportion of the planks, or half logs, scooped out on the heart side as if designed for pumps or canoes; and this may be the case to a considerable extent, even although it does not appear at the ends of the wood. Pieces that are marked by sudden bends lengthways, are to be avoided as suspicious, where there is no opportunity to turn over and examine them. But the *colour* is of more importance than either size or soundness in rosewood. Much of it is to be found of a dull light brown colour, resembling nothing more than a dried peat; whereas in wood of good quality, the ground is of a clear sharp colour, varying in depth of shade from orange to dark red, having the graining or figure distinctly marked in black. In seeking to ascertain the colour, it is desirable to learn what it is near the heart; for often a thin rind of good coloured wood is found on the outside, enclosing a very inferior heart. The value, of course, is greatly increased when the wood is well coloured throughout. In seeking for wood of a fine figure, special attention is to be paid to the appearance of the annular rings, as seen in the ends of the planks. When the concentric circles of red and black are found regular, or only slightly irregular, much show or figure is not to be expected. But when, on the contrary, they are found in waving and tortuous lines, a good figure is certain to be found. Another indication of fine figure is the plank being marked by knobby protuberances, which, when pierced, are found of a light colour. These, when intersected by the straight line of the veneer saw, produce an abrupt dash of light, which contrasts very agreeably with the sober aspect of the general surface; and, therefore, planks having these knobs, and other indications of figure, should be carefully selected for veneers, while the plainer pieces are reserved for chair wood, couch-feet and scrolls, table-pillars and claws, and solid work generally. In cutting up veneer planks, regard must be had to the form of the concentric circles, in order to bring out the best figure which the plank is capable of exhibiting; and this object will be best secured by making the saw-draughts run as nearly as possible parallel to the circles. The annexed figure exhibits a transverse section of a plank, in which the concentric rings present the irregular form necessary to produce a fine show or figure. If this plank were sawn in the direction of a line drawn from e to f, the surface would show the smallest amount of figure of which it was capable, and would consist of a series of nearly straight lines of red and black alternately. But if a draught were run from a to b, and then another from c to d, the surfaces would present a beautifully variegated figure, the richness of which would be greatly increased were the knobby protuberances found elevating the grain lengthways. Rosewood, in this respect, presents a remarkable contrast to mahogany; for in it the finest figure is secured by causing the saw-draught to go right across the concentric rings, instead of parallel to them. The cause of this difference is, that in rosewood the medullary rays, or transverse septæ, are hardly distinguishable; and hence, there is almost none of that lustre or transparency which lends the chief beauty to mahogany, maple, birch, and other woods, in which the medullary rays are large. Rosewood is remarkable for the large quantity of gum and oleaginous matter which it contains; is, consequently, difficult to dry or shrink to its least dimensions; and is less easily held by glue than most other woods. Hence it is desirable to cut up such planks as are to be used in the solid, into thicknesses suitable for the various purposes to which they are to be applied, as long before using them as possible. If intended for chairs, a plank next the heart will be most profitably cut into front-leg thickness; a thickness for two or three back-legs in depth, say 4½

inches or 6¼ inches, may be taken next, and the remainder, which will be narrow, may be thrown into clefts for clamps or mouldings. It may be found profitable to take up another plank of nearly the same quality and colour, and cut a thickness for claws off the heart, and then one to serve for chair-top rails, couch-feet, and scrolls; the remainder, if any, to be cut into ⅜-inch stuff for fret work, beads, and the like. In order to secure the quicker and more thorough drying of the material, we consider it profitable, in establishments where the uniformity of the demand justifies it, to cut up the planks not only into thicknesses, but also depthways, into the various pieces of work which retain pretty nearly the same outline edgeways, although the facial lines may require to be varied, as patterns change. This mode of cutting will be found conducive to the more speedy and complete seasoning of the material, and will also, by careful lining, effect a considerable saving. Any difficulties to which this mode of breaking out wood may give rise, in settling for work done by the piece, may, we apprehend, be readily overcome by a judicious foreman in dealing with reasonable workmen.

In drying rosewood, it is of importance to take care that it is neither exposed unsheltered to the rays of the sun, nor suddenly to artificial heat; for either will have the effect of producing cracks, which, even although they close, cannot be concealed in the finished work. To make good furniture of this wood it is especially necessary that it be gradually and thoroughly seasoned; otherwise it is sure to betray the neglect afterwards.

Another peculiarity of rosewood is, that much of it is very porous, and that the pores are elongated on the surface, in a way that renders it difficult to produce a good solid body of polish on it. To remedy this, various plans have been tried. Size of various kinds has been employed to fill in the pores; but although well papered off, it furnishes a very harsh and ungenial surface to polish upon, and shrinks below the surface afterwards. Blackened bees'-wax has been rubbed in, and then cleaned off; but this has the effect of preventing the polish from getting properly riveted in the wood, and causes it, when the article is in use, to peel off on the least friction. The best remedy yet discovered, is, after the surface has been finished by the cabinet-maker, to rub it carefully in with plaster of Paris, coloured with rose-pink, which, after being set, is to be carefully papered off. This does not shrink like the size; and has the effect of preventing the oil used with the French polish from finding a hiding-place in the pores, whence it afterwards exudes on exposure to the air, and eats off

D

which are commonly imported into Britain. These, however dissimilar, are not distinct species, but varieties of one species, whose qualities are determined by the soil on which they have respectively grown. The harder, more compact, and beautiful varieties, are the produce of dry and rocky soils; while the larger and softer wood is grown on low and marshy grounds. The mahogany tree of Honduras is a most magnificent and splendid object, compared with which the largest oak, the king of our forests, dwindles into insignificance. The enormous size and height of the trunk, the vast spread of its branches, and the space of ground covered by its roots, are alike remarkable. Some idea of the magnitude of the growing tree may be formed from the measurement and weight of the logs which are occasionally cut from it. The largest of which we have any account was seventeen feet long, five feet four inches broad, and four feet nine inches thick; it weighed fifteen tons, and contained 5136 superficial feet of one inch thick. The tree is often found 100 feet in height, rising nearly sixty feet in column from the spur to the limbs, which diverge into numerous branches that form a large and handsome head, covered with shining green leaves, and spotted with tufts of flowers, of a reddish or saffron hue. The leaves are about eight inches long, divided into leaflets about two and a half inches long, which are in pairs from three to five in number. The fruit is of an oval form, about the size of a turkey's egg. The tree is easily raised from the seeds, and it thrives in most soils, varying in grain and texture with the characters of each. It is almost impossible to give more minute circumstances attending the growth of this valuable tree, as its progress to maturity is scarcely perceptible within the life of man; we may state, however, that not less than 200 years is regarded as the average period which it requires to reach its full maturity.

In Honduras, the season for cutting mahogany usually commences about the month of August. The labourers employed consist of gangs of from twenty to fifty men, having a conductor, who is styled captain, and an intelligent observer, named the huntsman, whose duty it is to search the woods to find labour for the whole. Cutting his way through the woods to some elevation he ascends one of the highest trees, and minutely examines the country. At this season, the leaves of the mahogany tree are invariably of a yellow reddish hue; and a practised eye can readily discern, at a great distance, the spots where the wood is most abundant. These ascertained, the huntsman descends, and, unaided by compass, or any other guide than the recollection of his observations,

proceeds, with almost unfailing accuracy, to the scene of promise. Should the nearer view confirm his expectations, his next care is to retire without leaving any traces of his discovery behind him, that might enable competitors in the same pursuit to profit by his labours. Despite of his care, however, it not unfrequently happens that his track is perceived, and others take the promised spoils out of his hands. When the treasure is found and secured, the operation of felling commences, and as many trees are cut as will occupy the gang during the season. These are commonly felled at about 10 or 12 feet from the ground, the axe-man being elevated on a stage of convenient height. The man thus employed appears to be in a situation of some danger, but an accident is of rare occurrence. A sufficient number of trees being cut, the gang rear habitations for themselves on the banks of the nearest river, down which the timber is to be floated to the port of shipment, and in the construction and arrangement of these dwellings, much taste is frequently displayed, whilst the rapidity with which they are raised is equally remarkable. The next operation—and that one of great toil—is to form roads from the mahogany village to the spot where the wood is cut, the main road being directed as nearly as possible to the centre of the cuttings. Each man clears about 100 yards of road per day, clearing away the under-wood with his cutlass, and employing his axe or fire to level the larger trees; and these last he employs in the construction of bridges, for transit across the streams that intersect his road. If the trees lie much dispersed, miles of road and many bridges have to be made, branching out in various directions from the main road. The road-making is usually completed by the month of December; and then commences the cross-cutting of the trees into logs, and the squaring of the logs, with a view to lessen their weight, and render them more manageable in their transit from the forest to the river. By the month of April all is ready, and the ground in proper condition for carrying the logs to the river. This operation must be completed during the months of April and May, the earth being softened at all other periods of the year by heavy rains, and made impassable by trucks heavily laden. To this task, therefore, the whole force of the gang is directed, some being employed in loading, others in driving the oxen, and the remainder in cutting food for them. There are usually seven pairs of oxen, with two drivers to each truck, and six trucks to a gang. The labour of loading and driving, on account of the intense heat of the sun during the day, must be performed in the night-time, and by torch light; which renders the scene extremely picturesque and interesting to a stranger. The six trucks, extending to a length of nearly a quarter of a mile on the road—the great number of oxen—the half naked drivers, each bearing a torch—the wildness of the forest scenery—the rattling of chains, and cracking of the whips—and all this at the hour of midnight, present more the appearance of some theatrical exhibition, than of the sober industrial pursuit which has fallen to the lot of the wood-cutters of Honduras. On arriving at the river side, the logs, marked with the initials of the owner, are thrown in, to await the rising of the flood in sufficient strength to float them down to the sea. Nor is long delay necessary; two or three weeks of the heavy rains which now prevail, being sufficient to swell the rivers to a height more than sufficient to float the logs. The gangs follow in a kind of flat-bottomed canoes, called *pitpans,* to guide and facilitate their progress, until they are intercepted by a boom, placed at the mouth of the river. Here each gang claims its own logs, and, forming them into large rafts, floats them to the wharf of the owner; where they are taken out of the water, and subjected to a more particular trimming, to fit them for shipment. A large proportion of the entire exportation from Honduras is sent to Britain, which, on an average, amounts to nearly 4000 logs per annum. This variety of mahogany is commonly called *Bay-wood,* and is now used by cabinet-makers chiefly for veneering upon, for inferior parts, or for articles of solid furniture. The earlier importations were distinguished from the present, by containing a much larger proportion of hard showy wood, much of which was cut into veneers, and was well worthy of being used for finishing purposes. Thirty or forty years ago, bay veneers were nearly as much used as those cut from Spanish wood, but they have since been almost entirely superseded by the latter. Two causes have contributed to the change, one being the inferior quality of the wood now imported; and the other, that while Spanish wood improves in appearance after being manufactured, bay-wood loses its colour and force of expression from lengthened exposure. But not only has it almost entirely ceased to be cut into veneers, it is also much less used for solid work, such as chair frames, dining-table tops, and the like. This may be in part accounted for, by a considerably increased demand for it by machine-makers, coach-makers, carpenters, and ship-builders, which has had the effect of raising the price of large-sized and good firm wood: and further, the increased importations of small-sized Spanish logs, sold at a moderate price, have furnished the cabinet-maker with a harder material, equally suitable

for many of the purposes for which bay-wood had been employed, and not more expensive. Still, for panels, door-framing, and table-tops, which are to be veneered upon; and also for all pieces of work that are required to be specially free from warping or change, we have no material equal to good bay mahogany. Whether in instruments that are to be submerged in water, or those which are to be exposed to atmospheric change, we have no wood equally impassible: and hence, for levelling-rods, tide-gauges, and similar articles, it is the material almost exclusively employed. Mahogany, of all kinds, possesses another valuable property, namely, durability; and in this respect it is equal, if not superior to, any other wood with which we are acquainted. Although, while in the tree, it is subject to the attacks and ravages of various insects, we have never seen nor heard of any instance, in which, after being manufactured, it has suffered from this cause. It cannot be reckoned an exception to this statement, that when planted in thin clamps or veneers on any of our home-grown hardwoods which fall speedily to decay, it should be perforated by the insects which destroy them; for we never find it attacked when detached from other woods. A remarkable proof of the durability of mahogany was furnished in June 1846, when several competent judges met to inspect various specimens of timber, which, six years before, had been placed in a fungus pit, for the purpose of testing their powers of resistance to dry rot. Of the various woods which had been subjected to this test, comprising English and American oak, African and East Indian teak, elm, ash, mahogany, and other woods, every description of timber, except the mahogany, was in a greater or less state of decay; but it was found to be in a perfectly sound state. While experience has shown that mahogany possesses, in a high degree, the qualities which we have mentioned, the main cause of its becoming and continuing so extensively popular as a material for furniture, is its beautiful appearance. The general colour of even the plainest kind is agreeable, and the finer sorts are distinguished by a variety of beautiful configuration and transparent lustre, that claim for this the first place among our furniture woods. Of the earlier importations, those from the island of Jamaica furnished a great proportion of the largest and most beautiful wood, of which we have seen several specimens in old furniture, marked by a wild irregular figuring and deep colouring, more resembling tortoise-shell than the mahogany in use at present. The trees nearest the sea were cut first, those near streams capable of floating them to the sea followed, until all the mahogany which would repay the cost of its transmission had been removed. We learn from missionary intelligence and books of travel, that many noble trees are yet standing in different parts of the island, which the difficulty of removal alone has preserved. It is surprising that no attempt has been made to continue the supply of accessible wood, by planting the waste lands, of which every proprietor has some within his range, and which, although unfit for almost any other purpose, would nevertheless be quite suitable for nurseries or plantations of mahogany.

Mahogany is imported in large quantities from the island of Cuba into Britain. On an average of five years we find nearly 1200 tons per annum entered for home consumption. It is sold under the name of Cuba mahogany, to distinguish it from Honduras and St. Domingo mahogany. It is much closer in the texture and harder than Honduras wood, and, in these respects, is nearly equal to Spanish or St. Domingo wood, to which it bears a considerable resemblance. It is generally paler in colour, and even when well marked with figure, wants the force of expression which distinguishes good Spanish wood. Unlike the latter, Cuba wood does not improve in the working, nor does it acquire the same rich mellow appearance from lengthened exposure after being manufactured. But the main defect of Cuba wood lies in the dark brown spots and streaks with which a great part of it is disfigured, to an extent that forbids its use for finishing purposes. The cause of these peculiar markings we cannot explain, but we have heard them attributed to the attacks of insects, whose perforations of the earlier and more tender layers of the tree, had, either from some colouring properties in themselves, or from the introduction of external air and moisture, produced the blemishes described. We are inclined to favour this idea, from having found many logs thickly marked near the heart, while the outer layers, to the thickness of five or six inches, was wholly free. But however caused, the liability of Cuba wood to this defect, renders the purchase of it uniformly troublesome and hazardous. Where the blemishes are distinctly marked externally, the purchaser will of course offer only such a price for the wood as the purposes it is fit to be used for will afford. But it is no uncommon occurrence to find a log giving strong indications of show or figure, and having no appearance of the dark spots or streaks, which yet, when opened, proves to be worth a far less price than has been paid for it. This uncertainty of value involves, on the other hand, the possibility of procuring really good logs at a price far below their value. When

this wood is found free from the fault described, it is very useful. If plain, it may be advantageously cut into bed pillars, chair wood, table legs, sofa feet, &c. For these purposes it is not necessary that the logs be of a large size, as wood of 18 inches deep, or less, will cut out quite as well, and cost less than logs of a larger size. When 19 inches deep and upwards, and of fair quality, the logs are called *table-wood*, and are cut into thicknesses suitable for dining-table boards, dressing-table tops, and ledgings. For dining-tables made on the old principle, whether on legs or on pillar and claws, it was deemed necessary to have the boards about 24 inches deep, or even broader. But since telescope dining-tables have come into general use, boards of a less breadth are found to suit quite well. Indeed, we are disposed to think boards of 20 inches or 22 inches deep are preferable to those of a larger size. They are lighter, and, consequently, more easily added to or taken from the table, and therefore less liable to injury; besides, the most convenient enlargement of a table is by boards, each of which are fully the breadth of a chair, for in this way the size of the table can be exactly suited to the number of the company. In selecting a table log, it is important to observe the length of it, whether it is long enough to yield two boards, or is not much longer than one board. Either of these is preferable to a log of an intermediate size, which would necessarily leave a considerable portion of the wood to be used for inferior purposes, and thus enhance the price of the table-boards. But good table-wood is often so scarce, that the purchaser must frequently buy logs, which otherwise suitable for his purpose, are yet of an inconvenient length. In cutting up such logs, it becomes a question of importance whether they should be cut the whole length into thickness for table-boards, leaving a number of short lengths after cross-cutting the boards. This question will be answered differently by different persons, according to the varying nature of their demands; some finding in the manufacture of small articles, ample use for all their cuttings of seven-eighths or one inch wood, while others find it more profitable to cross-cut the boards at the proper length, and to leave what wood is beyond in thick plank, which can afterwards be cut into chair-tops, rails, &c. Where this latter plan is resorted to, it is necessary, in cross-cutting the boards, to be very careful to prevent their splitting, which they are very apt to do. To effect this, a cramp should be put on each side of the saw-draught, only one board taken off at a time, and that carefully covered on the newly-cut end with canvas, glued, to exclude the air, before the cramp is removed. Each board in succession should be treated in the same way until the whole are cut off, when the thick cutting which remains should also be glued and covered with canvas. It will be noticed that we have spoken of the thickness of table-boards as seven-eighths of an inch or one inch. These different thicknesses are made use of in different localities, and while we would not presume to decide authoritatively on the matter, we may be allowed to express our opinion, that in tops which *are not* clamped, seven-eighths of an inch wood is thin and meagre in appearance, while in tops that *are* clamped, it may suit very well. For the tops of dressing-tables of a plain description, the usual thickness is five-eighths of an inch; while for those of a better kind, three-fourths of an inch, or even seven-eighths of an inch thick tops are used. The ledgings are usually half an inch thick; but the ledgings of washing-tables, in consequence of their greater depth, require to be of five-eighths of an inch wood. When practicable, it is important that the ledgings should be of the same log with the tops; and this can ordinarily be attained without loss, by using for them the faulty or shaken boards, which are unfit for tops. When a log is cut into boards of the thicknesses specified, there can be no difficulty in working it up into mouldings or clamps of one kind or another, if it should prove unsuitable for the purposes designed. But Cuba wood may be of a quality fit for cutting into veneers; and occasionally considerable prices are paid for it with this view. As in treating of Spanish or St. Domingo mahogany we shall have occasion to mention the different kinds of figure, and their external appearances, the hints we propose to give regarding the purchase of veneer logs will be found equally applicable to Cuba wood, and need not be anticipated.

When, instead of being fit for veneers or good solid work, a Cuba log is found much spotted or streaked with brown, perhaps the best use that can be made of it is to cut it into thicknesses suitable for the sliding rails of telescope tables. For these, we know of no material equally free from liability to warp; and in them the discolouration is of no consequence whatever. We have also seen it cut with advantage into five-eighths of an inch and three-fourths of an inch thicknesses, to be used as beds for veneering. Where the veneer employed has a strong tendency to warp and draw, Cuba wood will be found to offer a greater resistance, and to stand better than even Bay mahogany.

Before referring to Spanish mahogany, we may briefly notice, that, about twenty years ago, there was a considerable importation into this country of what was called African mahogany. It was a native of Western Africa, shipped from Gambia, and designated by botanists, *Khaya Senegalensis*, of a genus very closely allied to the *Swietenia*, or true mahogany, to which its wood, when cut, bore a strong resemblance. When first introduced, and before its true character was known, a considerable quantity of it was bought and manufactured into furniture. A very short experience of its qualities, however, served to drive it out of the market; and it has now fallen into entire disuse. Brief, however, as was its term, it did serious damage to several makers, who had used it largely, in ignorance of its qualities. When new and fresh, it had a fleshy colour, which, on continued exposure, deepened into a dirty purple, of a most disagreeable appearance. Nor was it only in colour inferior to genuine mahogany; it altered much more in drying, did not hold glue so well, and, consequently, the furniture made from it gave general dissatisfaction.

Spanish or St. Domingo mahogany is grown in the island of St. Domingo or Hayti; from which the annual exportations have greatly increased since the beginning of this century. In the year 1801, the whole amount exported was only 5217 feet; in 1821, the export amounted to 55,005 feet; while in 1841 it had increased to 7,525,461 feet. Since that date, the exportations have undergone but little variation. Of the whole amount exported from Hayti, about one-sixth part is imported into Great Britain, where the consumption seems to have kept pace with the supply; for on comparing the consumption of 1831 with that of 1837, we find it increased nearly fourfold, the amount in 1831 being 280,000 feet, and in 1837, no less than 818,900 feet. Of the whole amount imported into Britain, nearly a half is brought to Liverpool; which is resorted to not only by the chief buyers and consumers of the United Kingdom, but is also visited by purchasers from the Continent. From the Liverpool market, France, Germany, Russia, and even India, have of late been drawing supplies of Spanish mahogany. The large supply in this market naturally attracts purchasers; and an additional reason for preferring it is the liberal mode of measurement. Mahogany is not sold by weight, like the finer fancy woods, the irregular shapes of which forbid measurement; nor is it measured by the cubic foot, like the more common woods, but by the superficial foot. In other words, the contents of the log are stated in the number of square feet of boards, each one inch thick, which it will yield. To do this fairly, an allowance of fully one-eighth of an inch ought to be made for each saw-draught that would be necessary to cut the log into one-inch boards. A further allowance should be made for the loss in taking the slabs off the sides of the log, to straighten and clean it; and further, should there be unsound and faulty wood at the ends of the log, such as *shakes* or *rots*, an allowance should be made for these also; the result of the whole being to make the purchaser pay for the number of superficial feet of one-inch wood which the log will yield, and no more. These allowances on the measure are generally believed to be more liberally given in Liverpool than elsewhere, and hence its popularity amongst buyers; of whom those who come from the greatest distance are often heard to say, that the extra allowance on the measurement of their wood is more than sufficient to cover the expense of their journey to purchase it. We have made these remarks on measurement with the view of furnishing a useful hint to our less experienced readers, many of whom may not have a demand great enough to warrant their going to purchase at Liverpool. When it is expedient to resort to a nearer market, the buyer should either purchase by the Liverpool measure, giving a profit to the middleman who has brought it within his reach, and whose trouble must be repaid; or examine carefully for himself, by the directions we have given, whether the log or logs will yield the number of superficial feet which they are said to contain.

It is worthy of remark, that the mahogany imported under the name of St. Domingo wood is of varied quality, and is the produce of widely-distant localities. From the celebrity attained by the exports from St. Domingo city, it has become customary to carry the growths of other localities coastwise thither, and ship them for foreign markets under the common name. The cargoes thus collected are ordinarily of less value than those which consist of wood grown in districts more adjacent to the city; the latter is therefore usually distinguished by the name of city wood. Good quality consists in the wood being close in the grain, and of firm texture; or fine, in opposition to coarse; and of a kind nature, in contradistinction to the harsh and brittle hardness which is frequently found in mahogany. Bad quality is marked by the grain being porous, and of a gray and smutty appearance; and also by the specific lightness of the wood. The *colour* of mahogany is a principal element in determining its value, and varies in shade from a pale yellow, resembling pine timber, to a deep red. The colour most esteemed is a medium between the extremes, rather nearer the pale than the dark shade mentioned. Wood from the city is chiefly of a rich generous hue, varying from gold colour to ruby; but its superiority over other importations, consists principally in the transparency and beauty

of figure by which it is distinguished. *Figure*, in mahogany, may be divided into two kinds, namely, *roe* and *mottle*. Roe is that alternate streak, or flake, of light and shade running with the grain, or from end to end of the log. If the streak be regular in size and unbroken, it is little thought of; but if the flakes be broad, and if the light and dark parts have a tendency to blend, yet strongly contrast with each other, and are variedly broken in their progress, then it is considered fine. Mottle is that mark in the wood which, in a polished board, at first view appears like something raised upon the surface, and leads an observer to feel if it be a plane or not. This figure is much varied in form, and has had distinctive names given to the various kinds, of which we may mention the following:—*Stop-mottle* mostly arises from angular grains, and is in broad flashes, frequently diverging from a centre, like the foot of a bird; *fiddle-mottle*, so called from its resemblance to the figure often seen in the wood used for the backs of violins, and the cause of which we have endeavoured to explain in treating of Maple. *Rain-mottle* is another variety of this figure which is greatly valued; it is somewhat similar to fiddle-mottle, but is in larger and longer marks. These last are rarely found to penetrate into the heart of the log, and hence in cutting it is usual to take a plank for veneers off each of the four sides. Another well-known figure is the *plum-mottle*, so called from its resemblance to a section of a plum-pudding. It is rather hazardous buying logs giving indications of this figure, as the spots, which arise from indentations of the grain, often turn out disagreeably dark in colour. But this is by no means invariably the case, many specimens being found quite free from this blemish, and variegated in a most agreeable manner. Another variety is the *peacock-mottle*, so called from the eyes in it, resembling the spots in the tail of the bird after which it is named. A log, strongly marked with this figure, was sold in Liverpool for nearly £1000. Of all the varieties of figure, however, stop-mottle is the most esteemed; and, when united with broad roe of good quality and fine colour, constitutes the highest perfection in mahogany. It is not uncommon to find a price as high as 12s. per superficial foot paid for a log which possesses these recommendations; and on rare occasions, 15s. and even 20s. per foot has been given. Another variety of figure, but now much less popular than formerly, is the *curb*, or that peculiar feathery marking, which is caused by the log being cut above where it has diverged into two separate hearts, each forming the centre of a limb of the tree. The wood deposited between these two, before they finally separate into the forked shape, is often found very beautiful, and was, till lately, highly prized for veneering panels, sideboard backs, and moulded fronts, for drawer fronts, and round table tops, on which the curls radiated from the centre. Plainness or variety in the appearance of mahogany depends essentially, and chiefly, on the position of the fibres as presented to the light. When they lie parallel to the axis of the tree, the wood has a uniform and plain character; and the more contorted, interwoven, and, at the same time, regular in their distribution the fibrous masses are, the greater the beauty and richness of expression. The comparative abruptness of these transitions in the fibre, constitutes the chief distinction between roe, mottle, and curl.

The longitudinal and transverse sections of the fibre, or the *rip* and *cross cut* in plain wood, present the extremes of condition and of distinction of shade. Between the right angle which these sections form with each other, there is a varying range in degree of dip and direction of fibre, which develops the characteristic appearance of fine mahogany. The weather-seasoning and sunlight, and also the polish on finished surfaces, beautifies the wood, by intensifying the difference of shades produced by this variety in the fibrous arrangement. Good wood, besides its permanent expression of figure, when seen from a single point of view, exhibits a varying beauty as the observer alters his position, the lights and shades dissolving into, and alternating with each other. This illusion of change defies the imitation of the painter, and is unconsciously one of the chief attractions which mahogany furniture presents.

A practical knowledge of cabinet-making is indispensable in the selection of woods, particularly those of the more expensive sorts. In addition to the quality of logs, the consideration of their length, in connection with their breadth, determines their fitness for the various uses of the trade. Attention to this circumstance is of especial importance in buying mahogany.

Table wood is amongst the most useful, and considering the quantity with its required quality, it is the most expensive. Telescope table tops are made from 4 feet 6 inches to 5 feet 6 inches long; and the breadth of the leaves or slip tops from 21 inches to 30 inches. These dimensions determine the selection of a log not less than 5 feet long by 22 inches in depth. If the tops are mounted on pillar and claw, they are usually wrought in three breadths, and consequently a log of less depth, say from 19 to 22 inches, will suit. If the log exceeds what is above stated, by 6 or more inches, the over length will clear away faults, or may be wrought up into clamps for the moulded edges of the tops. If the log be an

expensive one, and more than one length of tops, it is obviously more economical that it should be one or more exact additional measures of the length required, so that the wood may be wrought up without loss. Under such circumstances, the greater the length of a log it is the more valuable, as it can be cut up more advantageously; besides, if faults do occur in a long length, there is room for selection, and avoidance of blemishes; whereas, a log 5 feet long, which appears adapted for tables when opened, is frequently found to be a little shaken at one or both ends, however sound it may have appeared externally, and probably not one table board can be got out of it. In selecting wood for Pembroke tables, the same considerations have to be kept in view; their usual size is from 3 feet 6 inches to 3 feet 9 inches. The bed portion of the top is from 22 to 24 inches wide, and each of the wings about half this breadth. Quality, colour, and figure are here requisite also, but this being a less expensive kind of table than the telescope, it is customary to make them of wood inferior in these respects. Defective tops of longer length may be wrought up in these tables, and this is the more conveniently done, as in them only one and the same side of the wood is at any time exposed. These tables are not now so common in good houses as formerly, a smaller size of turn-over table, on pillar and claw, having taken their place. As the quality and figure of wood varies considerably in different parts of a log, in cutting up table wood the boards should be marked in the order in which they lie to each other in the log, by numbering them on the edge, beginning at the one side, and proceeding to the other. This is of less importance if the wood be intended for telescope tables, as in them the loose tops are so adjusted as to fit whichever sides are brought together; but in turn-over tables where the boards are permanently joined in forming the tops, it adds much to their appearance that the grain, colour, and figure of the parts be well matched; and as there is always greater likeness in these respects between the nearer than the more remote boards of the log, the marking guides in making such adjustments more perfectly and rapidly.

The apparent direction of the heart or centre should be carefully attended to in the selection of a table log. If the tree, when growing, has been crooked, the heart of course retains its original divergence from the direct line, when the timber is cut straight in forming the log.* The bend, in such case, may have been so great as that the heart in its

* The necessity of compact stowage is one of the chief reasons for squaring the logs.

E

course will crop out on the side of the log, and again dip into and traverse it diagonally. As the wood surrounding the heart is usually plainer, and is easily distinguished, this oblique direction of it through the breadth of the log, invariably deteriorates the quality of the timber.

This condition of the heart renders the wood unfit for tables, from its unequal shrinking, and consequent liability to warp and split in seasoning. It is, besides, less fit for telescope tables, where the tops are loose, than for tables on pillar and claw, where the fixed joints and the bars below keep the boards under constraint.

There is a further objection to the use of wood of this character for the sort of tables last referred to, that as the boards in the top should match together in their general figure and quality, this, from their irregularity of expression, is done with difficulty, or very imperfectly. In laying open such a log, the saw-cut should be made as nearly as possible in the same plane as the wandering heart, and not at right angles to it. By this means the plainer wood, with any defects or blemishes at the heart, may be planked off by the saw, whereas, if it be cut the opposite way, these defects will be dispersed through all the boards.

Chair-wood logs require less attention to size in their selection than to colour, straightness of grain, and firmness of texture. This is especially true in regard to wood intended for front legs, and in this less when they are turned than when sweep-moulded. Till lately the profile of the most common pattern of back-leg required it to be cut out the flank-way, and the broader the wood there was the less waste of material; but this style of chair, in mahogany, is now falling into disuse. The profile in the most prevalent pattern of back-leg is a segment of a circle, the wood being cut the deep way, and the style of the chair presented in front. The log selected for this purpose is first laid open, to ascertain its quality, and, if found suitable, it is then cross-cut into blocks the proper length of back-legs, and sent to the saw-mill. There is, by this means, no waste, as formerly, in intermediate cuttings, the saw-draught at once separating the wood into sweeps, the required thickness. Chair logs should not square less than 16 inches, so that if laid open through the centre, the sweeps may present such a breadth as to admit at least three legs being moulded on their face. This should be regarded as a minimum size of chair log. In the event of its turning out faulty in the centre, it may come in for bed-pillars; it will also pretty evenly divide for turned legs of the ordinary size. This eventual use of a log, supposed to be suitable for chairs, will determine the safest lengths to be selected in purchasing. Lengths of 8 feet, 8 feet 6 inches, or 9 feet, or multiples of these, are the most suitable.

Veneer logs require more skill and greater knowledge of cabinet-making for their selection than those for any other purpose in the trade. The expected quality of the veneers will determine the use they are likely to serve, and will consequently regulate the considerations of price, and the choice of dimensions. It is a good general maxim to be kept in view, in the selection of woods, that the lengths chosen should be determined by the diameters; for this the practical skill of the buyer must find application; but, generally, this relation of the dimensions is not so important in a veneer as in a table log, and less in chair wood than in either. The cross section, or the end of logs, is the best criterion of their general character; by the inspection of the wood in mass it can be judged pretty accurately whether the quality indicated on the side is continuous throughout. This is especially true in judging of veneer logs from the arrangement of the fibres of the wood, which fits it for veneers, and the indications of its quality from this reason are the more decided, the richer the wood. The reason of this may be briefly explained. In cross-cutting a *veneer* log, the general mass of the wood is cut at right angles to its length, but the fibres of the wood, whose contortions and overlappings give richness to its expression, are not cut at the same, but at very varying degrees of angularity. From this reason, the end of the log presents the characteristic appearance of the wood pretty faithfully, the various shades being shown on the end, from the same cause as those on the side, if not with equal distinctness. The different kinds of figure are not discovered with equal facility on the end view, and in most cases it requires a practised eye to distinguish them. Roe or shade is always easily observable; mottle frequently, but with greater difficulty; the roe by a strong deep colour, and the mottle by faint flakes running from near the centre to the outside. It is further important to observe whether the indications of figure are uniform throughout the log, or otherwise; if they become indistinct, or fall off towards the heart or centre, the rich or veneer wood will be confined chiefly to the outer side; and, on the contrary, when greater depth and variety of shade are apparent toward the centre, the outside may be expected to be the plainer wood. Such irregularity in quality depreciates the value of the timber, and limits its use to fewer and inferior purposes.

Curls.—In selecting a log for curls, particular attention should be paid to the width between the two centres or hearts, with the view of ascertaining the probable length of the figure. When the centres are unusually wide, a long length of curl may be expected suitable for the panels of wardrobes; and, on the contrary, when the centres are near, the curl is likely to be fit for short panels only, or for the star tops of tables. A defect in the quality of the curl is frequently caused by the ordinary circumstances in the growth of the tree, which go to form it. This is due to partial detachments of the branches, at short intervals, before their complete divergence from each other at the top of the stem. The formation of *in-bark* at these points is destructive of the value of the curl. The external indications of this fault are generally not very decided. The most certain and conspicuous mark is when there is the appearance of bark, imbedded or interposed between the concentric rings of the exposed sections of the several branches. This defect may exist in the absence of this symptom, as the log may have been cross-cut at a point where the branches are solidly united. Upon this supposition, it is important to observe whether the concentric rings of the wood at the contiguous parts of the branches are regularly formed, or whether they are distorted, as if by mutual pressure, in their growth. There is a greater probability of the existence of this blemish in the curl in the former case, than in the latter. Their dimensions and soundness are the chief considerations to be kept in view in examining the more common kinds of wood. In the ornamental sorts, in addition to these, other qualities claim attention, and, accordingly, greater discrimination is necessary, as those are increased in number and varied in character. Required excellencies are met by their corresponding defects, and the distinct perception of the indications of both is necessary to a correct and well-balanced judgment. An excellent preparative to the study of wood, is a general knowledge of structural and physiological botany. An acquaintance with the character of woody fibre, and with the chief circumstances that attend its growth, will impart greater acuteness and accuracy to observation, while a knowledge of the distinguishing names of the different parts of the stem of trees, and of the uses which these serve or express in their structure, will furnish the language of distinction and description.

A correct opinion of the quality of timber might be readily formed, if the general appearance of the outside of the log correctly indicated its entire character; but when even an approximation to a correct judgment depends so frequently on a variety of obscure hints, carefully collected, which blend their influence in forming a general impression of its

nature, it is the more necessary to sharpen the powers of observation by careful and attentive study.

It is well known that good judges of timber are rare, and that it is always a great recommendation to a workman to possess a thorough knowledge of these materials of his trade, while to an employer or foreman, who conducts or superintends an extensive business, an acquaintance with woods, their several varieties, particular qualities, and usual prices, is all but indispensable. None of the woods deserve or require such particular attention as mahogany. In it great loss may be incurred through ignorance, while it is well known that a successful purchase has often given a decisive turn to the fortunes of a business. The risk of loss on the one hand, and the uncertainty of a profitable purchase on the other, are reasons sufficient to induce an attentive study of this the most important wood used in the trade. Competent skill removes this uncertainty; and while it imparts greater security, it also alleviates much of that anxiety of mind which arises from a hazardous investment. From the number of different woods used by the cabinet-maker, and the variety in dimension and quality of the several specimens of each which present themselves, no precise rules can be given for their selection. Suggestions of a general sort are all that can be offered; the practical knowledge and peculiar skill which qualifies for purchasing safely, can only be attained by personal observation and attentive study. This valuable acquirement has hitherto terminated with the individual possessor, and no attempt has been made to preserve and disseminate the results of mature experience. Much that is dependent on personal sagacity and acumen is of course incommunicable, but many useful hints and existing maxims for the selection of woods thrown together after some system, would assist the inexperienced, and add to the general stock of intelligence in the trade. A methodic inspection of woods has the recommendation of directing the attention to a series of particulars in succession, so that the observer, instead of resting in an indefinite general impression of any specimen under examination, may come to form a distinct and positive judgment of its qualities. No wood extensively used in cabinet-making is better suited thus to exercise the judgment of the workman than mahogany. This wood embraces three great varieties, possessing different properties, which adapt them for various general uses in the trade; in addition to this, there is the further diversity of the several specimens of each in quality and dimension, which points out their respective fitness to particular kinds of work. The inspection of the wood in log should go far to predetermine these conclusions, and, accordingly, the requisite skill required for this purpose. The circumstances which give this wood the appearance of fineness, have been already referred to. Observation may be further assisted, by pointing out and classifying the defects incidental to mahogany. The consideration of unsuitable form or dimension in the log is here purposely avoided; both faults being obvious, and their importance easily determined; attention is chiefly directed to those less apparent blemishes in the timber, which arise either from peculiarities in the growth of the tree, or from external causes affecting it.

These defects may be severally designated General, Local, and Accidental.

GENERAL.—When the blemish is not partial and limited, but extends to the whole or the greater part of the log, such as—

Colour—when this is of a pale unvaried character, approaching that of American birch, or Havannah cedar, or of a deep red.

Coarseness of Grain—the appearance of which is often such as no quality of finish can ameliorate; it is, besides, frequently accompanied with defective colour and harshness in the figure.

Dotted—when the wood wears a fungoid appearance, or that of extreme age, as if the tree had been fast decaying, or perhaps was quite dead when cut down.

Brittleness and Softness in the Fibre—the usual accompaniments of that appearance of the wood previously referred to.

Wandering Heart.—The character and external symptoms of this blemish have been already referred to. Although the quality, colour, and figure of the wood be in general good, its use is limited, and its value lessened by this defect. It is not uncommon to find the heart so crooked in its course in an otherwise fine log, as to prevent it yielding one sound board.

LOCAL—when the defects are confined to a portion of the wood, or distributed at considerable intervals through its mass, leaving the greater part sound, such as in the occurrence of

Knots.—These, when large, are often accompanied with much plain wood. They are more injurious when they occur in the depth than in the thickness of the log. If in the depth, the log must be cut on the side, so as to clear off the knots on one or more of the boards. This causes loss, as the thickness of the log thus determines the breadth of the boards. When this fault occurs on the edge of the log, it is of less consequence, as the breadth is then preserved.

Spots occasionally accompany some peculiarity

of figure in the wood, as in plum mottle, already referred to. These blemishes, in this figure, are sometimes offensively dark; and frequently they break out into numerous small fissures, with *inbark*, which are widely diffused over the sides of the wood, and so render it valueless.

List.—This, in figure and distribution, is like straight roe, running with the general direction of the grain, and is of a dark cloudy colour. It appears to be caused by the irregular deposition of the secretions in the wood. This also frequently occurs, but in minute degree, and of the same colour with its other defects, in wood with plum mottle figure.

Stains are of various hues, and are often irregularly dispersed throughout the log; frequently, from their dingy colour, they appear to be the incipient symptoms of decay in the wood.

Cork centre, with its almost constant accompaniment, *worm-holes,* the soft, spongy character of the wood rendering it easily penetrable by worms. This defect frequently extends considerably round the centre, and is of a pale colour. The logs in which it occurs are generally raw in grain, and specifically light—the usual indications of rapid growth in the tree.

Curls, when of useful dimensions, and of suitable quality, rank next in value after table and veneer wood; but when formed on the stems of trees, in the growth of branches, they are a serious blemish in the timber. The indications of their presence in the log are quite decided, and easily observed. If at the top of the trunk the tree has spread out into many branches, curl may be expected in connection with each, and on the end of the log the medullary centres, with their concentric layers, are the symptoms of its presence. These indications are still more decided from the oblique section of the branch made on the side of the log, exposing, with greater certainty, the character of the surrounding timber.

ACCIDENTAL DEFECTS are those which arise from external circumstances, affecting the timber in the tree when growing, or after it is cut down, such as

Shakes.—This defect presents two varieties, one of which runs with the grain of the wood, and the other directly or obliquely across it; each is commonly accompanied by a distinct and characteristic difference in the appearance of the wood. In the straight shake, the wood, for most part, is otherwise sound in colour and fibre; but in the cross shake it is usually defective in both these particulars, being brittle, and of a dull, dark colour. In the former case, the defect is confined to the heart or its vicinity; in the latter, it extends irregularly through the mass of the wood. Local disease in the tree, and a consequent arrestment of its growth in the parts affected, may account for the lengthwise rending of its timber, but the cross and irregular fractures, apparently destructive of its vitality, are most probably caused by the disruptive action of electricity, and the defective quality of the wood may be a consequence of the subsequent decay of the tree.

Rot.—The occurrence of this on the outside of a log, either on the end or side, is a conspicuous fault, and liberal allowance in the measure is usually given for clearing it off. It sometimes lurks in the timber without any distinct external indication either of its existence or extent. Large cavities and decayed masses are frequently found in the heart of logs, while very faint and indistinct symptoms of these appeared on their outside. This defect, in most cases, may be considered the consequence of soft centre, and its decay. Interior rots are frequently caused by decayed branches, exposing the inside of the tree to atmospheric influence and the attack of insects; knots are frequently accompanied with decayed wood, and their soundness on the outside, taken together with apparent firmness of heart in the log, are the only certain indications of the absence of rot internally. This defect occurs in St. Domingo wood more than in Honduras, and less in Cuba wood than in either.

Worm-holes are common to all kinds of mahogany, but they occur less frequently in Cuba wood than in the others. This defect is easily seen when it appears in the sap, or on the edge of the log, but the indications of its existence in the heart are much less decided, and its occurrence much more injurious; wood partially affected with this blemish, may be wrought up as a bed for veneering on, when only the veneered side is exposed, as in the tops of loo-tables; probably, also, in the veneered gables and ground-framing and panelling of the doors in rosewood cabinets, the insides of which are imitation grained.

Adzing of logs, beyond what is necessary in forming them, is a deception practised for the purpose of concealing plainness, or of exaggerating the appearance of figure in the wood. This has the character of a defect in logs having a hollow side, as there is greater waste than might otherwise be in clearing the timber of the adze marks. It is also a proper reason for sharp inspection, and of claim for more liberal measure on the part of the buyer, to cover the loss from this intentional irregularity in the surface.

A good practical method of prosecuting the study of mahogany, or of the woods in general, may consist in first carefully attending to the several external indications of the quality of the timber in the log, and from these predicating a distinct judgment of its character; and when the log is laid open, a comparison between this original opinion, and the now disclosed character of the wood, should be made. Such exercise sharpens the power of observation, and tests the judgment.

A STATEMENT of the IMPORTATION into BRITAIN, with the CONSUMPTION and STOCK of the different sorts of MAHOGANY, for the last Seven Years, ending Feb. 1.

	IMPORT.			CONSUMPTION.			STOCK.		
	Average from 1845-1849.	1850.	1851.	Average from 1845-1849.	1850.	1851.	Average from 1845-1849.	1850.	1851.
Honduras Logs.....	3,651	3,379	4,030	3,619	2,351	4,561	1091	1400	869
St. Domingo Logs..	12,408	18,815	21,152	11,615	20,095	21,029	3220	2959	3082
Cuba Logs..........	4,329	1,567	2,296	4,402	1,459	2,257	939	127	166

TABLE of IMPORTS of MAHOGANY of every description, into the UNITED KINGDOM, for the Years 1838 to 1849 inclusive; and of MAHOGANY from ST. DOMINGO, CUBA, and HONDURAS respectively, into the PORT OF LIVERPOOL for the same period.

	IMPORT INTO LIVERPOOL, FROM				Total Imports into the United Kingdom.
	St. Domingo.	Cuba.	Honduras.	Total.	
Year.	Tons.	Tons.	Tons.	Tons.	Tons.
1838	2360	270	3666	6,296	23,336
1839	2540	972	4121	7,633	25,859
1840	1630	373	2716	4,719	23,115
1841	1865	200	2479	4,544	19,502
1842	2080	180	1128	3,388	16,938
1843	1510	765	2726	5,001	20,284
1844	3215	1766	4473	9,454	25,622
1845	5127	4458	4891	14,476	38,351
1846	3480	2819	7503	13,808	40,238
1847	3836	888	4045	7,769	34,009
1848	1603	2139	1757	5,499	31,668
1849	5121	1025	4911	11,057	29,012

Relative Number of Feet to Weight.—Returns are made to the custom-house, for statistical purposes, upon the estimated ton. The ton weight, if from the city of St. Domingo, in logs, usually yields *for sale* from 290 to 310 feet, and from 270 to 290 feet in curls; from other parts of Hayti, from 300 to 320 feet in logs, and from 290 to 300 feet in curls. From Cuba, the average is 290 to 300 feet to the ton; and from Honduras 330 to 350 feet to the ton.

CEDAR.

This name is given to several trees which differ much from each other in their botanical characters and relations, and in their properties and value in the arts.

The *Cedar of Lebanon* (*Pinus cedrus*), by the sanction of ages, and from many interesting associations, is unquestionably the most celebrated tree which bears the name. It is equally distinguished for its vast size, and for the irregular grandeur of its form. It is superior in picturesque effect to all other evergreen coniferous trees, and when arrived at maturity, or approaching those gigantic dimensions which it acquires in its native climes, may be justly considered as one of the most magnificent of the vegetable creation. The growth of the cedar is tained from Para, one its Northern provinces; it is found also in the other adjoining regions of South America. In the several places of its growth, it is variously named; at Darien it is called *Amarilla*. Nothing is known of its botanical character. It is sometimes imported as squared timber, but most frequently in round logs, ranging from 9 to 14 inches in diameter. The wood is straight and close in the grain, about the texture of American birch, but much heavier; its general colour is a golden yellow, or light orange; on end section, the annular ranges are waved and of slightly varying shades; this circumstance imparts a minutely veined expression to the wood in plank, which much enriches and beautifies it. The characteristic and finer colour, is frequently intermixed with dingy streaks of a yellowish brown, and fissures and cracks often occur, extending considerably round the heart. Were this wood uniformly coloured, and free from defects, it would be a very valuable cabinet-wood.

Canary wood although suitable from colour and texture, as an ornamental cabinet-wood, yet its small dimensions, faults in colour, and heart blemishes, confine its use within narrow limits; it is little employed except in marquetry and turning.

A wood called *Vigniatico* which resembles canary wood closely, and by some supposed to be identical with it, is also imported from Brazil. This name appears to be a corruption of a general term, *Vinhatico*, given by the Portuguese to several yellow woods, besides the variety in question under that name, imported from Brazil.

CAMPHOR WOOD.

Camphor Wood is the timber of the *Laurus Camphora*, and is found in Japan, China, India, and Brazil. It grows to a considerable height, dividing into many branches, and covered with smooth greenish bark; the leaves are ovate and lance shaped.

The root, wood and leaves, have a strong odour of camphor; this substance is found to lodge everywhere in the interstices of the wood, also in the pith, but most abundantly in the knots and crevices. It is obtained by dry distillation and sublimation. The camphor is often found concrete in cavities and fissures in the heart of the tree. This secretion is obtained from several others of the *Lauraceae*. Camphor wood is imported in logs and planks of large size. It is a light soft wood, frequently spongy, coarse in grain, of a dirty greyish yellow colour, irregularly interspersed with streaks of iron grey. Its dimensions, but chiefly its fragrance, are its sole recommendations for cabinet-work, and that only for internal finishings. It is used also in turnery.

JAPAN WOOD.

Japan Wood or *Bukkum Wood, Caesalpinia Japan*, is a product of China, Siam, Pegu, the Coromandel coast, and the Islands of the Eastern tropical seas. It is found also in Brazil, and is obtained from a tree of the same genus as Brazil wood.

It is imported in sticks 1 to 4 inches in diameter, and 3 to 8 feet long; it is close in grain and heavy, and abounds in defects, chiefly from the growth of the wood, being crooked, and deeply indented.

The colour is a beautiful orange, which deepens on exposure to a rich reddish brown; it is used in turnery, but its faults limit it to small articles; it is exported abundantly by the Chinese for treenails in ship building. It also yields a beautiful red dye.

TULIP WOOD.

Tulip Wood is imported from S. America, chiefly from the Brazils, in round sticks, trimmed and cut like King wood, which it resembles in figure and in general dimensions, being usually from 2 to 7 inches in diameter. The prevailing colour is a flesh-red, varied by streaks of a deeper tint of the same. These blended colours are very beautiful, but not permanent; the wood besides, from its frequent unsoundness at heart, and other blemishes, is very wasteful. It is used in the smaller articles of cabinet work, and in turnery.

It is often scarce, and sells at about £25 per ton.

A wood, bearing the name of the French tulip wood, which comes from the East Indies, chiefly from Madras, appears to be an excellent cabinet and turnery wood, and is held in great esteem by French cabinet-makers. It is much straighter in the grain, and softer, than the Brazilian wood of that name; the darker streaks present a more decided contrast to the ground colour, which is an orange-red. This wood is resinous, but has no odour.

HOLLY.

Holly (*Ilex æquifolium*), is found in most parts of the northern hemisphere, being dispersed throughout Europe, North America, Japan, Cochin-China, &c. In Britain it is one of the most beautiful native shrubs or low trees.

Although ordinarily seen as shrubbery, and as forming hedge-rows, yet there are many examples in England and Scotland of hollies 40, 45, and 50 feet high, with trunks varying from 2 to 4 feet in diameter. Holly is an evergreen, having beautiful deep green glittering spinulose foliage; this prevailing colour is prettily contrasted with the coral hues of its berries, and in some of its varieties by a white and gold border on its contorted leaves. The wood of the holly is white, very hard, uniform and close in grain, and susceptible of a fine polish. It admits of being dyed of various colours with great facility. It was formerly much used, chiefly in the white state, or when dyed black, for lines or *stringing* in cabinet work. It is used also in cross-veneering portions of the case work inside of pianofortes, in the construction of harps, and extensively in the manufacture of painted Tunbridge ware. Holly is exceedingly apt to split when newly cut, and when exposed in seasoning; it is, at the same time, liable also to become spotted and stained from the mutual chemical action between its sap and the constituents of the atmosphere. To prevent the occurrence of these blemishes, the wood, when felled, is cut into the form and dimensions required for its several uses, as veneer or other planks, or as round blocks for turning. With a view to extract the sap, and to preserve and improve the whiteness of the wood, these pieces are then boiled in water for many hours. Immediately after boiling they are placed into a compact heap, and closely covered up, to prevent the wood from splitting from the too rapid action of the air in cooling and drying. A species of fermentation now takes place, and a fungoidal growth of a greenish hue, and to some depth forms on the wood. As the heap dries, after the lapse of several weeks, the covering may be gradually removed, and the mildewed appearance brushed off. As the boiling necessarily operates superficially on the wood, from surface to centre, it will always vary in its efficiency and completeness, and that the more decidedly according to the duration of the process, and as the masses acted on are large or small; the larger pieces requiring longer time, that the effect may penetrate to a greater depth. Under all circumstances the heart is but partially affected, and is still liable to stain if the wood, when newly cut up, is again immediately laid together. For this reason veneers, when newly cut, should be kept asunder for a day or more, and thicker wood for a much longer period; for resting in contact for a few hours will cause stains to appear. By suitable care, holly will be fit for use in five or six months.

LIME TREE.

Lime Tree or Linden Tree. Most of the species of the order *Tiliacea*, to which this tree belongs, are found generally distributed within the tropics, forming diminutive plants, shrubs, or trees, with elegant flowers, usually white or pink. A few species are peculiar to the northern parts of either hemisphere, where they form timber trees of stately growth. Of the lime tree there are two great varieties, the European and American, severally known to botanists as the *Tilia Europea*, and the *Tilia Americana*. The former has been long naturalized, and by some affirmed to be indigenous to Britain; its geographical distribution embraces a great portion of the middle and north of Europe. From its graceful form, rapidity of growth, and highly odoriferous flowers, it is a favourite avenue tree in Holland and Germany, and also in England. Honey procured from the flowers of the lime tree is esteemed the finest in the world.

Among native trees, the lime ranks in the first class in point of magnitude, frequently attaining a height of 80 or 90 feet, with a trunk of corresponding dimensions. In Switzerland and Germany there are lime trees of an enormous size, and one in the county of Norfolk is mentioned by Sir Thomas Brown as being 90 feet high, with a trunk 48 feet in circumference at $1\frac{1}{2}$ feet from the ground.

The smooth bark of this tree furnishes the materials from which bast mats are made. After being macerated in water, the bark separates into layers. These mats are mostly fabricated in Russia and Sweden, where the fibre is also sometimes manufactured into nets; and in Carniola it is even woven into a coarse cloth for ordinary clothing. The American variety of lime present few points of distinction from the European. In foliage and dimensions they are very similar: in the character and uses of the timber they are identical. It is found in Canada and the northern parts of the United States, but in Virginia, Georgia, and the Carolinas, is only met with in the Alleghany mountains. The wood of the lime tree is very light in colour, approaching to white, or yellowish-white; it is close and straight in grain, of a fine texture, and nearly as soft and light as deal. It stands well after being properly seasoned, but is not suited to any use wherein it might be exposed to frequent alternations of moisture and dryness.

From its inert character it makes an excellent ground for japanned and inlaid work, and is used for the frames of the best japanned chairs, inlaid with mother of pearl. This wood, from its even texture, capacity of sharp outline, freedom from knots, and general facility of working, is well suited for carving. The works of Gibbons at Windsor Castle, and St. Paul's, London, are of lime tree.

It is employed in general turnery, and also used in the sounding boards of harps and pianofortes, and the key levers of the latter, and in various parts of other musical instruments; it is also used in panelling carriages, and in the manufacture of toys.

It is sold at an average price of from 1s. 6d. to 2s. per cubic foot.

ALDER.

Alder (*Alnus glutinosa*), possesses very wide geographical distribution, being found throughout the whole of Europe, by the margins of streams, or in marshy grounds. It is widely dispersed in similar localities throughout Asia and Northern Africa, and a species, said to be identical with it, grows in Canada and other parts of North America. It is indigenous to Britain, and is one of the most common trees. In dry soil it frequently does not grow beyond the dimensions of a large bush, and, even under more favourable circumstances, seldom rises above 30 or 40 feet in height. The wood of the alder is soft, and of a homogeneous texture, and not capable of enduring much lateral strain. When growing, the timber is of a white colour, but upon being cut down and exposed, it changes to a deep red; this afterwards fades into a flesh-colour of different shades, which it retains. The timber of old knotty trees, and that of the root of others, is often beautifully veined, and chairs and tables made of it possess all the beauty of the curled maple, with the addition of a deep rich reddish tint.

In Scotland and the north of England, this wood is frequently used in furniture; suitable specimens are, however, comparatively rare, and they are usually sought after and employed by those who have a partiality for articles made of native grown timber.

From its durability under water, the alder is sometimes used for piles, pipes, and the barrels of pumps, and in inferior turning, such as toys, powder boxes, brushes, bobbins, &c., and also in making patterns for founding.

CHERRY TREE.

Cherry Tree (*Cerasus Sylvestris*). This tree has various other popular and also local names, such as Gean tree, Merry tree, Wild Black Cherry, Merries, &c. Pliny relates that Lucullus, the conqueror of Mithridates, introduced it into Europe from Asia, now nearly 2000 years ago. From Italy it was speedily propagated to most European countries, so that "other lands had cherries, even as far as Britain beyond the ocean." The cherry is, however, considered by some to be indigenous to many parts of Europe, and to be also a native of England, where it is cultivated chiefly as an ornamental tree, and for its fruit.

In average and moist soil the cherry, or gean tree, in little more than half a century, attains a height of from 60 to 70 feet, with a diameter from 20 to 24 inches. The wood of the mature tree is thus large enough for general purposes. It is, besides, in texture and colour suitable for ornamental work, being close grained and firm in fibre, in colour approaching a plain and pale mahogany; and in durability second only to the oak. The cherry tree is another of several instances wherein the culture and use of a valuable native timber has been superseded by foreign imports. In Britain, cherry wood is little used by cabinet-makers, and specimens of furniture made of it are rare; but in France, and other parts of the Continent where this tree abounds, it is extensively used by the cabinet-maker, turner, and musical-instrument maker.

LOCUST WOOD.

Locust Wood. This name is common to three great varieties of timber of considerably dissimilar qualities, the products of trees of widely different botanical characters. They are known to botanists as the *Robinia pseudacacia, Hymenea courbaril*, and *Gleditschia triacanthos*.

The *Robinia pseudacacia* is a native of North America, growing most abundantly in the Southern States, and generally diffused throughout the whole country. Of this tree three varieties are common, popularly distinguished as the red, green, and white locust wood. They are so called from the prevailing colour of the duramen or heart-wood. These variations in the appearance of the timber, are probably due to difference of soil, situation, and climate. The locust tree grows rapidly; and under favourable circumstances sometimes reaches a height of 70 feet, and 4 feet in diameter. As it is very branchy, the bole is usually short, and seldom straight for any considerable height. The branches often contain as many cubic feet of timber as the main trunk, and are armed with strong hooked spines. It is remarkable for the smoothness of its leaves, which close themselves at night, and for the more enduring freshness of its verdure as compared with many trees. In its most attractive period, bunches of white and yellow flowers hang gracefully from the branches, and contrast beautifully with the deep shining green of its luxuriant foliage.

Locust tree has been extensively propagated in Europe, especially in France and England. In the latter country, specimens of considerable size were growing in the year 1640. Its growth in a good sandy soil is so rapid, that it has been known to attain a height of sixteen and even nineteen feet in four years. In ten years it gains a height of 20, 30, and even of 40 feet. When at mature growth, which it reaches in about forty years, it is not of more than the average dimensions of timber trees, yielding then between 40 and 50 cubic feet of available timber.

The wood is close grained, very hard, of a greenish-yellow, with a slight tinge of red in the pores, and finely veined. It is exceedingly tough and durable, having been known to remain quite unimpaired, although entirely exposed to extremely varying atmospheric influence for nearly a century. As the result of numerous and carefully conducted experiments made in the Government dockyards and elsewhere, locust wood was found to be " heavier, harder, stronger, more rigid, more elastic, and tougher, than the best English oak."

In shipbuilding, tree-nails made of locust wood are esteemed superior to bolts of iron, in consequence of which it is imported for the Government and other building-yards. In North America it is more highly valued by the cabinet-maker and turner, than any other native timber. The locust is one of the very few trees planted by the Americans.

Hymenea Courbaril, the second tree enumerated, whose timber bears the name of locust wood, is found in the West Indies, Guiana, and Brazil. The usual dimension of this tree is from 60 to 80 feet in height, and 5 or 6 feet in diameter; it sometimes attains to a vast size, several varieties of it, when at mature growth, being the giants of the South American forests. Martin describes some specimens seen by him in Brazil, of such enormous dimensions, that fifteen Indians with outstretched arms could only barely enclose one of them. Close at the root, they were 84 feet in circumference, and 60 feet where the boles became cylindrical.

In good and characteristic specimens, this wood has a veined and variegated appearance. The prevailing colour is a rich reddish brown, diversified by streaks of a lighter and darker hue. These last frequently expand into irregular flakes, which deepen to nearly black, and by presenting a varying contrast with the lighter tints, enhance and beautify the general expression.

This wood possesses all the important qualities of a valuable cabinet-wood. In dimension of timber, in colour, figure, and texture, it is well suited to the manufacture of the larger and more expensive articles of furniture. It has hitherto been comparatively little known to British cabinet-makers, but from the elegant and ornamental character of the articles of furniture, manufactured of this wood and shown by the Austrians in the Great Exhibition, it is probable that it will soon be introduced into general use in this country.

Gleditschia triacanthos, the last of the three trees, whose timber has been called locust wood, is better known as the honey locust. It is a native of North America, and is found chiefly in the Carolinas and Virginia. It attains a height of 50 to 80 feet, and when young, its trunk and branches are covered with prickles, which, hardening as the tree becomes older, form a formidable defence. Its foliage which is of a light green colour, is very elegant, and its seeds which are covered with a sweet pulp, yield, when infused and fermented, an intoxicating liquor, much prized by the American Indians. The wood is coarse grained; it splits with great ease, and is little used.

SAUL, or SAL TREE,

Shorea robusta, is one of the largest timber trees of India, common over the eastern and western peninsulas, and the adjacent islands, and extending northwards to the foot of the Himalayas. Saul is esteemed the best, as it is the most extensively used timber in India, for beams, rafters, and various other building purposes; and in the north-western provinces, it is employed in all government works. It is stronger and tougher than Sissoo or Teak, yet not so passively durable as the latter, but for heavy strain or active wear, it surpasses any other Indian timber. The wood is close grained, heavy and of a uniform light brown colour, and in India is extensively used for furniture. The tree yields a balsamic resin, used in the temples of India, under the name of ral or dhoona, as an incense; by Europeans, under the name of dammer, for the same purposes as many other resins, and in the dockyards in Bengal as a substitute for pitch.

SISSOO.

Dalbergia sissoo is a tree well known throughout the Bengal Presidency, and highly valued on account of its timber, which furnishes the Bengal shipbuilders with their crooked timbers and knees. The trunk which is generally crooked, is lofty and frequently 3 or 4 feet in diameter. The sissoo has numerous spreading branches, pinnate leaves, with small drooping leaflets, imparting with their foliage, and the tree generally, a light elegant appearance. It is universally employed both by Europeans, and natives of the north-west provinces, where strength is required. In structure, it resembles the finer kind of teak, the Godaverian variety, but is tougher and more elastic. *Dalbergia latifolia* another and superior sort of sissoo, is a product of the Malabar coast. It is much darker than the former, being of a greenish black, with lighter coloured veins running in various directions, and takes a fine polish. This variety, called by the English Indian rosewood, and black-wood tree, and by the natives, *sit sal*, is one of the largest trees in India, attaining a circumference of 15 feet. Both sorts possess the qualities of good cabinet-wood, in dimension of timber, firmness of texture, and average appearance.

Sissoo with Saul is, for general purposes, more extensively used in Bombay and the north-west of India than any other timber.

JACK WOOD.

Jack Wood is the timber of *Artocarpus integrifolia*, and is a variety of the bread fruit tree. This tree is a native of India, and belongs to a class of trees that are extensively distributed over East India, both continental and insular, and also over the islands in the South seas. It is likewise extensively cultivated in the West Indies; its fruit being a favourite food with the negro population.

The specific character of the tree, as its scientific name imports, is founded on the entireness of its leaves, which are undivided, not lobed, or sinuated. The fruit, the production of which gives such importance to this class of trees, is pear shaped, of varying size, and grows on the trunk and larger branches. That on the branches, and farthest up the tree, is about the dimensions of the human head; but it gradually becomes larger the farther down it grows, till, on the stem near the root, it attains to the bulk of the body of a full grown man. The fruit is luscious, and has a powerful smell, of the flavour of strawberries. Its edible quality appears to be owing to the presence of starch, in its succulent heads. These at first contain a very tenacious milky juice, which subsequently hardens into the consistency of newly-made bread, and is as white as snow. The taste is insipid, with a slight sweetness, somewhat resembling wheaten bread. The natives prepare it by boiling or frying in palm oil. Europeans use it at dessert, with salt and water, like olives.

Jack wood, in colour and grain, resembles a rather coarse and inferior variety of mahogany. In cross section, the concentric rings are seen to be variously and alternately coloured in different shades of brown, the wood in plank presents a minutely streaked appearance, which, at near view, imparts to it considerable richness and elegance.

The general colour of the wood, when first cut, is yellowish brown, which deepens on exposure into a reddish brown. It is harder and heavier than mahogany, and abounds in white, gritty, silicious particles in its pores.

In India, jack wood is extensively employed for all purposes in house carpentry and furniture; and in England for cabinet work, marquetry, and turnery.

BEEF WOOD.

Beef Wood.—This name, obviously depending on the colour of timber, ceases to be distinctive among red woods of otherwise uncertain character, and of near or uniform shades. Accordingly, many woods have this name, but that sort which is most commonly designated beef wood, is known also as Botany Bay oak, and is imported from New South Wales, in round logs about 9 feet long, and from 9 to 14 inches diameter. In general colour, it is more intensely red than mahogany, with occasionally dark veins, small, slightly curled, and minutely dispersed throughout the entire surface. Some specimens are pretty. It is used in turnery, in veneers for bordering and for small cabinets and brush backs, and in the manufacture of Tunbridge ware.

The descriptions given in the foregoing pages by no means exhaust the woods that might have been brought under notice; but, intentionally, the list has been restricted to those best known, and most extensively used, as little advantage could accrue to the practical man from vague notices of timbers whose nature and qualities are imperfectly known. The endeavour has been to assist the cabinet-maker in estimating the qualities, and recognizing the kinds of timbers by their appearance and properties, and, at the same time, to indicate the most suitable purposes for which they may be used, the method of treating them, and their commercial value. A few additional particulars have been added concerning the growth of the trees, and where they flourish; but it is to be regretted that, especially respecting many tropical woods, so little precise information exists; a desideratum which might soon be supplied, were importers to procure from the producing countries accurate intelligence of the growth and habits of the trees, with portions of their inflorescence, fruit, and foliage. By inspecting these, scientific men would be enabled to tell to what class of plants the trees belong, and thus a flood of light would be thrown on a subject which, at present, is admittedly very obscure.

VENEERING.

VENEERING is the process of overlaying a prepared surface or ground with thin wood. This art was known to the ancients; Pliny speaks of it as a recent invention, in his time, and descants on thus converting the cheaper into the most valued woods, by plating the former with the latter. He praises the ingenuity evinced in cutting a tree into thin slices, and thus selling it several times over. The citrus, the terebinth, various kinds of maple, box, palm, holly, and the root of elder and poplar were the woods then employed for this purpose. As at present, glue was used in fixing the veneers. At this period, furniture so embellished, was esteemed as a luxury; and, from its great expense, was confined entirely to the mansions of the most affluent persons. The skill possessed did not apparently extend to veneering continuously a large surface, but was chiefly confined to patch-work and inlaying; the desideratum felt then, and for a long time afterwards, being the means of properly cutting and laying veneers of large dimension. It is only in modern times that veneering has had that extension which makes it a matter of public interest. Its general use dates from a period considerably later than that of the introduction of tropical woods into Europe, for the manufacture of furniture. The comparative scarcity and consequent expense of the finest furniture woods, their unfitness, in general, for being wrought in the solid state, from their fibrous structure, usual dimensions of timber, and difficulty in working, together with the inconvenient weight given to many articles of furniture, made of them, seem to have suggested the notion of employing the finer woods in overlaying others which were cheaper, lighter, less liable to warp or fracture, and of greater facility in working. Improvements in veneer-cutting, and veneering have powerfully contributed to beautify, extend, and economize cabinet-making, and thus to disperse the products of this manufacture through all ranks and conditions of society.

In veneering, the chief particulars demanding attention are, the suitable character of the ground, its preparation, with that of the veneer, the general process of working, with the attendant circumstances proper or incidental to the operation. These will be considered in their natural order, along with various practical examples of important cases of frequent occurrence in the experience of the workman.

The proper quality and condition of the timber forming the ground for the veneer must, in all cases, be carefully attended to. The choice of the cabinet-maker is here confined within narrow limits, as comparatively few woods are suitable for this purpose; particularly if, under the condition of fitness, we include also the comparative expense of material and of facility in working. The American yellow pine and Honduras mahogany are highly esteemed, and most extensively used; the latter wood is well adapted, from its firm texture, for undulating surfaces and shaped-work; both are straight in grain, large in size, and usually sound; they do not readily warp or split, are free from offensive juices, and are easily wrought. Woods possessing great strength of fibre, and closeness of grain, such as white pine, birch, beech, or elm, do not suit well for veneering on, especially for large purposes; being comparatively difficult to work, and more resisting and intractable under the application of remedies to any defects in the wood or faults in the workmanship that occur. Woods which abound in unctuous or resinous juices, such as red pine or rosewood, are also unsuitable; their exudations interfering with the action of the glue. American oak, and Havannah or swamp cedar, are frequently used as a ground for veneering on; the former suits well, the latter, indifferently, being too soft, brittle, and raw in grain. Black Virginia walnut, extensively used by American cabinet-makers, is well adapted, from its size and other qualities, for the veneered gables, door frames, and panels of cabinets, or for massive shaped-work. But no original quality in the timber will relieve from the necessity of its suitable preparation for veneering purposes; it must be properly weather-seasoned (for a year at least, the time required depending much on the thickness of the timber), and afterwards, for a short period, fire-dried. The latter process tones the wood to the temperature of a dwelling-house, and ensures that residuary shrinkage consequent on the escape of the aqueous vapour always present in the out-of-door atmosphere, with which the wood continues to be saturated after it has been seasoned. The glue employed in veneering on such timber dries properly, the water in it being readily absorbed by the pores of the wood, and the thin gelatinous layer interposed between the surfaces speedily hardens, giving them the due adhesion to each other. Otherwise, if the

G

ground be wet, the wood being already saturated, the water of the glue is not taken up, while the continued exudation of moisture from the ground maintains the glue in a liquid state, till it decomposes or putrefies, when it loses its adhesive power, and the veneer in consequence peels off. This occurs only in extreme cases, when the wood yet retains its natural juices, or has been wrought too soon after being cut up. Partial, but imperfect seasoning, is attended with consequences of a like kind, although less mischievous; in this case the glue may dry, and the joined surfaces apparently adhere sufficiently, but the ground in a dry apartment soon shrinks to its minimum dimensions, when the veneer becomes either blistered, by starting from the ground at intervals, or becomes shrivelled and uneven on the surface. This defect becomes particularly conspicuous when the shrinkage is unequal, from any irregularity in the form of the ground, or from some imperfection in its timber. In the selection of wood for veneering, especially if the surface be large, choice should be made of a piece free from knots, shakes, and strong figure.

When the surface to be veneered is broad, such as in the case of tables, sideboard tops, or of door panels, the veneer should be laid on the side of the ground which is next the heart of the tree; this side in any case may be easily observed, by inspecting the end of the board, and noticing the direction of the growth rings of the wood. The annexed cut will serve to explain the propriety of this preference of the heart side for veneering on. *Fig.* 1 represents a cross section of an exogenous tree,

Fig. 1.

with its concentric rings. A plank *a, b, c, d,* cut diametrically, presents the rings equally disposed on opposite sides of the line *e f* drawn through the pith centre; the fibres forming the ring segments being thus similarly circumstanced in respect of shrinkage; the board, if equally exposed in seasoning, remains flat across. A plank *g h i k* cut out of any other portion of the tree, will be found, as an effect simply of drying, to curve outwards, presenting the heart side of it convex. This arises

from the contracting force being greatest in the longest continuous lines of fibres, as will be explained on referring to the diagram. The number of fibres, and consequently their contracting power in the line *l, m, n,* proportionally exceeds the number and force of the fibres in the line *l, o, n,* the same amount which the curve of the segment exceeds its chord in length. The plank accordingly tends to take the form indicated by the dotted lines *p q r s.*

A veneer, therefore, when laid on the heart side of the board is resisted in contracting, while drying, by this natural convexity of the ground; whereas, when it is laid on the outer side, the energies of both ground and veneer unite in drawing the veneer surface hollow. Where a perfectly flat surface is required, or where the ground has to be veneered on both sides, as in the folding tops of card tables, it is customary to cut up the board into narrow breadths, and alternately reverse the pieces, and join them together so as to equalize and distribute their different tendencies to curvature.

Fig. 2.

The ground, of whatever form or extent, must be uniform and smooth, free from sudden irregularities or fibrous roughness. Where the planes of direction are meant to be straight, they should be strictly so; when curved, they should be regular. The veneer is thus more easily laid, and from its extreme thinness it does not admit of the reduction of any inequalities of the surface afterwards. In preparing a flat ground, it is first planed; any remaining irregularities are then wrought off with the toothing plane; the blade or iron of which is grooved, lengthway on the face, so as always to present a serrated edge, whose projections or teeth dig into the wood, and work off its minute inequalities of surface.

Fig. 3 presents a form of toothing plane, better adapted for working large surfaces than that ordinarily in use. The plane

Fig. 3.

should be provided with two irons, one having finer teeth than the other; the coarser being required for the ground, and the other for the veneer. The cannel, or grinding bevel of the irons, should not be longer than that of other planes, as otherwise the irons are apt to vibrate in their action, and tear or dig out portions of the surface. The toothing action takes place first in the direction of the grain, then obliquely across it, cutting off any irregularities, and thus flattening the surface. Besides the general use of smoothing the ground, the toothing process increases the extent of glued surface by the indentations of the teeth in the ground and veneer, and ensures the retention of a sufficiency of glue between them, when they are acted on by the caul or the hammer, in extruding the excess of glue. A round soled plane, similar to the ordinary hand-plane of that form, is used in toothing the hollow segments of circles, such as the veneered sweeps of table blocks, &c. Quick and varied curves, on being wrought to outline, are toothed with a rasp, or with the toothing plane iron detached. On the ground being toothed, it is sized over with thin glue, wrought into it with a sponge or the hand. The size, on drying, stiffens those fibres of the wood raised by the previous operations, so that they are easily shaved off by a steel scraper, or by the toothing plane short-set for the purpose.

When the surfaces are large, such as in the tops of loo tables orside boards, and the wood, dry previous to the operation of sizing, the side of the ground next the veneer requires to be soaked with water to expand it. As the moisture must penetrate the wood some distance, the board may be laid for a few hours on a bed of wet sawdust, *Fig.* 4. This expansion of the ground serves to counteract the

Fig. 4.

shrinkage of the veneer, and is especially necessary when the ground happens to be very dry, and the veneers are hammer laid. It is usual to swell and veneer loo table-tops in halves, and panels in pairs. When the wood is deemed sufficiently swelled, it is then sized, and allowed to harden just enough to fix the fibres raised by the toothing and damping. This method is practicable only when the ground is finished plain on the edge, no mouldings at this stage of the work being planted on it; otherwise the mitres and joints are apt to be forced open. To avoid this the ground and veneers are treated differently; the former is allowed to remain straight, and the veneers are dried and pressed between heated boards, to preserve them straight, and then cauled. The ground may be secured by bars screwed on below; these are slightly rounded on the edge, and are left on until the veneer is completely dry; the bars may also be used as a security when any of the methods referred to are adopted.

The perfection to which the cutting of veneers has now been carried, leaves little to be said on their preparation or treatment before they are laid. Veneers should not be kept in a very dry atmo-

sphere, more particularly the richer varieties of them; an out-house or ground floor, where they are under the ordinary moisture and temperature of the seasons, is most suitable. Before they are laid, the traces of the veneer saw should be toothed off; this gives greater pliancy to the veneer, and ensures its closer approximation to the ground. When the veneers are stout and resisting, and are to be hammer-laid, or cauled on a curved or convex ground, they may be reduced thinner by the toothing process.

Two methods are ordinarily resorted to in veneering such curved surfaces as occur on the pillars and blocks of tables, fronts of sideboards, or on mouldings in general; the one is to strengthen or support the natural tenacity of the veneer on its being bent; the other, to increase its flexibility. The former is effected by glueing on the outside of the veneer canvas or calico, to preserve it from fracturing under the unequal pressure of the caul, while the veneer is being pressed down; the latter, by subjecting the veneer to the action of moist steam, a process similar in principle to that employed by shipwrights, in bending their planks to the required curvature. Veneers having a strong roe or curl, from the extreme irregularity of their grain, suffer by being subjected to a sharp heat, or to extreme moisture, their contractions and expansions being so very unequal that they speedily fracture; accordingly, they require to be carefully covered with canvas whenever they are laid on a curved surface, and in all circumstances must be cauled down. When the veneer for any surface consists of several pieces, and these marked by a waved or extremely irregular figure in the wood, as frequently occurs in rosewood, or without any decisive indications of grain or direction of fibre, as in Amboyna-wood, yew-tree, oak root, or birds'-eye maple, it is customary, in forming the joints, to follow the prevailing direction of the figure in the wood, or to join the pieces together, in lines which are least likely to be detected by the eye in the finished work. To effect this, the edges of the veneers are lapped on, and glued to each other; after the glue is dried, a fret saw is made to pass through both thicknesses together, tracing by the cut the intended line of the joints, which, on the superfluous wood on both pieces being chipped off, are quickly and perfectly formed. These waved joints in the veneers, when the required conveniences are at command, are better, and as expeditiously made, by this method, as those that are straight and wrought by the plane; they are, besides, often more economical than the others in the saving of veneer, and, under the circumstances supposed, always more elegant. The joints after being prepared in the above manner, are put together in the dry state, and connected by slips of cloth glued over them. On these being dried the veneers are then cauled down.

Veneers are laid by two methods—by the hammer or by caul. Hammering is a process of easy application when the veneer is of a mild and pliant nature. For some work this method is more convenient and expeditious than cauling—such as for border finishing, for slipping, for cross or feather banding, the laying of sweeps, and generally for small work. Some extensive surfaces, not otherwise easily accessible, are best to be done by the hammer; such as the tops of sideboards, or commodes, when these are clamped to thickness from under. Hammered surfaces are not generally so secure in standing as those that are cauled, in consequence of the veneer requiring to be moistened on its upper side with water or thin glue, to counteract its tendency to curve up from the ground, and also to admit of the hammer gliding easily over the surface. The form of the hammer is given in *Fig*. 5. The handle is fixed into the head, low down, so as to give the operator greater leverage power over it. A blade of steel, $\frac{1}{8}$-inch thick, is inserted into the head below, having its under edge rounded

Fig. 5.

along its length, so as to concentrate the pressure exerted on the hammer, and assist the smoothness of its action. The form given to the head above, furnishes at once a good hold, and an easy rest for the hand. In laying a large veneer with the hammer the assistance of several hands is required; the ground and veneer are gently heated previous to glueing; the glue is then spread on both, and the veneer, on being laid on the ground, is coated over with thin glue, and rubbed down with the outstretched hands of several persons. The hammers are then applied, at first, in sweeping over the whole surface, to reduce any undue swellings of the veneer, and to exclude the air. The more close and effective action then commences of two persons or more, on opposite sides, proceeding from the middle towards the sides and ends; the head of the hammer is urged against the veneer with one hand, while the handle receives a rapid horizontal motion to right and left, being made to travel from centre to side with a wriggling step, carrying a wave of the superfluous glue under the veneer before it. The veneer is, from time to time, coated at

the parts requiring it with hot size, to maintain the warmth, and relieve the friction of the hammers. Greater flexibility is given to the veneer by keeping up the wet and heat; it is thereby prevented from cracking and curling up at the sides. The glue becomes stiff on being chilled, and the pressure of the hammer behind the wave is apt to break the veneer, from the abrupt bend to which it is subjected. If, by slowness in the operation, arising from the extent of surface, fewness of hands, or the temperature of the workshop, the glue under the veneer becomes cold and stiff, its warmth and fluidity may be quickly restored by passing a hot smoothing-iron swiftly over it. The use of the iron should not be prolonged after the glue has been forced out, otherwise the continued heat is apt to raise the veneer. The quality of the process gone through is now tested by smartly tapping the veneer surface all over with the extremity of the hammer handle; if the sound is hard, the contact is complete; if dull and hollow, the application of the hammer must be renewed. Occasionally veneers are met with which in certain parts of them, from heart wood, or peculiar conformation of grain, are extremely difficult to lay perfectly; such parts, after some hours, may be easily reduced by the partial application of the caul, when the surrounding portions are cooled and contracted. In very dry workshops it is often advantageous, at the conclusion, to lay the veneered board face-down on the floor, and covering it with shavings or sawdust, to prevent too rapid drying.

The process of cauling veneers is distinguished from that of hammering them by the pressure, which is necessary to urge the veneer into close contact with the ground, being applied at once over its whole extent, and maintained until the parts united cool and consolidate. Cauls may be described as a means of conveying heat, and of transmitting pressure to the whole surface of a veneer at once, in laying it; they must vary in form and dimension, corresponding with the ground to which they are applied, requiring to be perfectly parallel to it, and the force exerted on them must be uniform in its distribution over its entire extent. They are generally made of pine-wood, sometimes of wood with canvas continuations for abrupt curves. Cauls, formed of bags of suitable size, partially filled with hot sand, are frequently employed in veneering hollow and irregular surfaces; canvas or girth web is commonly used in cauling cylindrical grounds, such as table pillars, round pedestals, or potstands. The pressure exerted on the caul is ordinarily by screw action, variously applied; for general purposes the common hand-screws are suitable; but in the treatment of broad surfaces these are inefficient or tedious. *Fig.* 6 presents an apparatus which is found very effective; it consists of a rect-angular frame of hard-wood, 3½-inch thick, formed of two pillars, with two cross rails framed into them. The upper rail is tapped by a series of screw holes, through

Fig. 6.

each of which a wooden screw is made to pass, the ends of the screws act together on bars, which cross the caul, and transmit the combined force of the screws to it, and thence to the veneer. The screws have a square tapering head, which fits into a hollow iron key, the upper end of which is wrought into a bar, to give it sufficient leverage, for turning the screws. Several such frames are required; their breadth between the pillars and their number depend on the dimensions of the sur-face to which they may be applied. When at use they are sufficiently effective if set apart from each other nine or ten inches. The caul, *Fig.* 7, con-sists of a number of separate planks, four or six inches broad, and two inches thick, which are slotted to-

Fig. 7.

gether, by cross bars morticed at exactly equal distances through the whole series; by this arrange-ment the breadth of the caul may be varied at pleasure, according to the character of the work. Two such cauls are necessary when the ground is to be veneered on both sides at once, or when the ground is thin wood, such as in door pannels; but, when the ground is stout, one may be sufficient, in which case the veneer is laid face-down, as shown in *Fig.* 6, with the bars crossing the back of the ground. In proceeding to lay veneers on both sides of a board with this apparatus, the caul screw frames are mounted on a suitable trestle or stool, and set apart from each other at equal intervals; one at each end of the board to be veneered, and the intermediate space equally divided between the others. A slip of deal is then run edgeway along the top of the upper rail, and fixed by hand-screws to the projecting top of the pillars; this keeps the screws in their places, and maintains the whole steady. The cauls being prepared flat and smooth in the surface, are rubbed over with linseed oil or grease, and then heated; the oil prevents the caul from adhering to the veneer, by means of any glue which may ooze through its joints or elsewhere.

The under caul is then, keeping the heated side up, slid quickly through the frames along the top of the under rails. On this under caul the ground with the veneers are laid, and upon them the upper caul is now placed. The bars are then adjusted under the screws, and the centre course of screws, taken lengthway along the several frames, is now rapidly urged home with a moderate force, so as to express the superfluous glue from the centre of the veneer, towards the sides and ends. The course of screws next in order on each side of the centre one are now wrought, and so with the others on to the two outsides. All the screws are now strongly tightened up, and the pressure is maintained for about four hours; by the end of which time the veneer and ground will have cooled, and adhered securely to each other. The screws should not be left on with full tension over night, as they and the frames are likely to be impaired by such continued action; besides, in cases where it is not desirable, a permanent flatness is thus apt to be given to the veneered ground. It may be more convenient that the cross bars be screwed to the upper caul per-manently, more particularly if the usual dimensions of the grounds veneered are large, and generally uniform. The upper caul alone is necessary when the ground is thin, and veneered on one side only; the under caul, in such case, serving to resist the pressure merely. In absence of an apparatus of the above sort, broad flat surfaces are laid by means of cross bars, and the ordinary hand-screws aided by cramps, as may be. Deficiency and inequality of pressure, and comparative slowness of manipulation, by which heat is lost, are the chief objections to this method. Flat surfaces are generally easily laid, the pressure required being simple in direction, and acting parallel to the plane of the surface. In curved grounds, circular or various, there is greater difficulty, the pressure necessary being often com-pounded of several directions of force, requiring, from the peculiar shape or condition of the piece of work under operation, some exercise of skill in the workman to resolve these into two or more single forces of available direction, whose joint action will be effective. On these uneven surfaces it is fre-quently found convenient to employ several cauls in succession, or those having canvas continuations of them to carry the veneer over abrupt changes of outline or return curves. Mr. John Meadows, of London, has recently patented an apparatus, by which the same veneer may be carried continuously without break or joint, over all forms of curved surfaces, or of angles. This is effected by a series of cauls hinged to each other, and acted on by direct screw pressure, and by lever power, supported through the centre of the rich wood in each veneer, as in *Fig.* 12; along this line, from the tapering end of the veneers, other pencil lines are swept across, with a compass, at equal distances on each veneer, passing through the parts that are alike

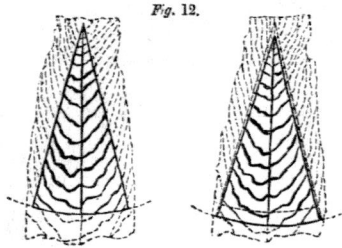

Fig. 12.

and most striking and characteristic in the figure of the wood. These cross lines serve to identify the parts so marked with certainty, and assist much in matching the veneers on the ground. The divisions of the top being now drawn on the ground, a tapering mould of thin wood, half of the determinate size of the veneer, is then made. The shape of this half-mould is drawn on the veneers, the mould being applied, in succession, to both sides of the centre line on each veneer, having its tapered end adjusted to the centre point from which the cross sweeps were struck. The two outside veneers of the quantity selected always differ most from each other in their figure; this difference is often so great as to render it necessary, for the proper effect, to distribute the veneers on the top after a particular order. Ordinarily, the top one of each pair of veneers is simply turned over, and brought side to side with its fellow; and all are laid according to their numerical succession, the last and first being thus finally brought together. The other method referred to is shown in *Fig.* 13, where the first and last pair of veneers in the series are laid opposite to each other; the next two most remote pairs are placed on the alternate sides of these first, being the continuous numbers. Following the same order,

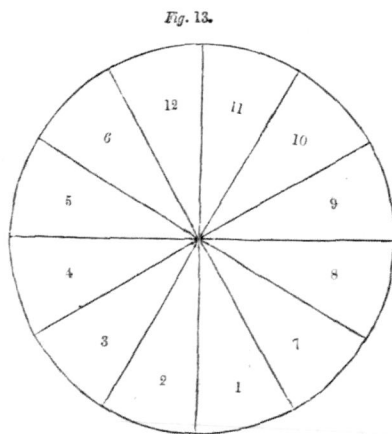

Fig. 13.

the others that remain are put into their proper place, and thus the circuit is completed, any diversity in the figure is thus more equally distributed. If the veneers are cauled, and laid in close succession to one another, each must be left to dry completely before the succeeding one is put down. That first laid, after it has dried, is carefully stripped on both sides, and the adjoining veneer is fitted to it. To support this veneer to the joint, a thin slip of deal is temporarily sprigged

to the ground, along the outer edge of the veneer, between which slip and the veneer first laid the one now in process is inserted, and urged home like a wedge; and so on with all the others. It is obvious that as little moisture as possible should be applied to curl-veneers in laying them.

The glue used by the cabinet-maker is a jelly made of the refuse portions that are pared off the hides of animals, before they are subjected to the tan-pit for conversion into leather. Good glue is translucent in the cake, of a clear amber colour, and, when dry, hard and brittle. Inferior varieties are more or less opaque or muddy in appearance, arising from their mixture with impurities incidental to their preparation, such as lime or other mineral ingredients, or from errors in the process of manufacture. Glue made from animal matters in a state of partial putrefaction is inferior in strength, and, when moistened, emits the odour, while it retains the peculiar qualities of such a condition. On this glue being boiled, gases are disengaged from it which become entangled with the glue, and give it a frothy consistency. An apparently similar effect may also arise from the mixture of the glue with other gelatinous substances, with which, on boiling, it does not coalesce, such having a less specific gravity than the other materials, and consequently boil at a different temperature. Glue very recently made, although of good quality, exhibits, in some degree, this frothiness of appearance when boiled; it is, for this reason, better that the glue be some months old before it is used.

In extensive workshops, glue is prepared in large quantity at once, for general use. The cakes are broken into small pieces and put into a large boiler, and soaked for some hours with as much water as will cover them. On the application of heat, the glue dissolves and boils; the boiling is continued for an hour or more. Water is added from time to time, to replace that evaporated in the process, and the glue is finally diluted to a degree rather greater than is suitable for general work. During subsequent heating by the workman, the excess of water is soon dissipated, and the glue thickens to the proper consistency. The boiler may now be removed from the fire, and its contents left in it to cool; or the glue may be poured into an iron trough, or one of wood, tin lined, from which source the workmen can replenish their glue-kettles as needed. To prevent dust or other impurities mixing with the glue, the kettle should be provided with a metal lid, notched in the edge to admit the brush handle. Frequently the glue is boiled in the workman's kettle, and that over an open fire. This circumstance causes the frequent preparation of the glue in small quantities, involving a loss of time, and, besides, the fuel usually at command in a workshop, chips of wood and shavings, flames up and soils and chars the glue, while the temperature necessary within a limited time to dissolve the glue, requires that energetic boiling of the water which is constantly attended with the inconvenience of its effervescence and overflow.

Glued surfaces are considered to cohere from the joint action of several forces, and these are, the pressure of the atmosphere, the adhesion of the glue to the wood, and its own proper tenacity. None of these forces, taken singly, will explain the strength of a well-made glue joint, which greatly exceeds the known energy of the first of these, the strength of a joint being often greater than that of solid wood; for when it is fractured, the separation does not at all times occur through its complete length, and even when this does take place, some of the fibres of the wood are almost invariably torn out. For the full efficacy of the second of these forces, certain qualities in the wood itself are necessary, seeing that to some woods the glue adheres better than to others; of these mahogany and deal are examples. The tenacity of the glue, or that force with which its particles adhere to each other, is the proper measure of its quality; if deficient in this,

either from original inferiority in the substance itself, or from its being diluted too much with water, the joint will be deficient in strength, however good the workmanship.

The *rationale* of the action of glue in joining wood appears to be, that the fluid gelatinous matter interposed between the surfaces, in adhering to the wood, penetrates also its pores for some distance, where it hardens, and thus articulates the parts together. This saturation of the pores forms over each surface in contact an air-tight layer, by means of which the supplementary force of the atmospheric pressure is obtained, while the incremental tenacity of the glue, or the mutual adhesion of its particles, consolidates and secures the whole. This view explains the necessity of having the glue of a certain consistency, and of keeping the surfaces warm for the operation. If the glue is too thick, its adhesion to the wood is lessened, as it does not penetrate the pores sufficiently; if too thin, the capillary action of the pores solicits the glue into the wood of both surfaces, and partially ruptures the connection between them. That the surfaces should be hot is more necessary in the former case than in the latter, in order to maintain the liquidity of the glue, and to expedite its drying. These considerations apply equally to veneer surfaces as to those of solid wood.

WOOD-CARVING.

In the following observations on wood-carving, no description will be given of the tools and benches used, as the learner will acquire a knowledge of these more readily and efficiently under a master, than from the most lengthened treatise. It will be taken for granted that the young carver is already skilled in the ordinary mechanism of his art; and an attempt will be made merely to lay before him certain principles, attention to which will enable him to detect the errors of the ordinary routine, and assist him to elevate himself from being a mere workman, to the higher position of a thinking artist.

Sculpture falls into two great divisions—

1. THE ROUND, OR FIGURE COMPLETE ON EVERY SIDE;—

2. SCULPTURE IN RELIEF, that is, wrought on a ground and rising from it. Of this there are three degrees—high relief (*alto-rilievo*), in which the ob-

jects are highly raised, and often almost detached from the ground, having a prominence of one-half or more of the natural projection; low relief (*basso-rilievo*), where the objects merely swell out on the ground, and project but little; and sunk relief, or countersunk, where the outlines are sunk below the surface, and the objects do not project above the level.

Carving in the round is applicable to the human figure and the whole animal creation, and such inanimate objects as may be introduced as accessories. In copying complete forms, there is no perfection short of the realization of living nature; no bar but that of the artist's power, which he may extend day by day: the gallant hound, with pricked ear and eager eye, and every straining muscle quivering with intense energy, and the bird's ruffled plumage, will tax to the utmost the cleverest hand. These, however noble a field for the wood-carver,

H

can scarcely be considered ornament, and are generally introduced but sparingly. As the earth is specially adorned with verdure, so the more fitting materials for ornament are to be found in the vegetable kingdom; and as here we see, in fact, each plant rising from and supported on its mother earth, so in ornamental carving, plants require to be employed on a ground, and should never stand alone; they must, therefore, be referred to carving in relief.

Carving in relief is not an entire truth, like carving in the round, which actually produces the form as it exists in nature; there we see that the foliage is distinguished from the ground by colour; here both are the same in colour and material. Hence it becomes a conventional or partial view of nature; and consequently, the perfectly free study of nature as we see it, is checked, until we can determine the limits of the sphere still open to our endeavours.

We must make no arbitrary rules, but seek only for those natural principles which are calculated to guard the learner from error. Such laws and traditions of the workshop are as numerous as the prejudices and mistakes of their masters; but true laws are few, and their only object is to save the student from being misled.

The most essential thing in every art is to consider what means we have at our command, what it is possible to produce with those means, and what the inherent properties of the material forbid. We thus place a definite goal before our view, and do not lose time in attempting what is beautiful and appropriate in one art, but impossible in our own.

The material is solid wood, which it is impracticable to carve into forms almost as slight and delicate as the flowers of the field. Against such an attempt its extreme fragility would almost be argument sufficient. But carry patient care to the utmost, and you produce a form still clumsy when compared with its original; where now are the varied colours which distinguish flower from leaf, and both from the ground, or the climber from the tree round which it twines? You have done your utmost to sever its connection with the ground from which it has been hewn, but the strength and elasticity of the real plant are wanting, and a touch will break it into a thousand pieces. The aim of art is not deception, for the common scene-painter or wax-flower modeller will easily imitate a curtain or a bunch of grapes, so that birds and men shall be deceived for a short space. True art is an adaptation of natural beauties to the material employed. Thus, carved foliage must not pretend, by any quality, to be other than a part of the wood from which it has emerged; it must possess the necessary strength of material to

fit it for the daily use to which it is to be subjected, nor must any part be made, to appear even, as if detached from its support. The true idea would seem to be, that the material from which it springs is so pregnant and teeming with beauty that it bursts spontaneously from its ground, like the rich vegetation heaving and swelling up from its moist bed of the primeval earth; and accordingly it is always most beautiful to see the leafage swelling up in one part softly from the ground, while another is thrown boldly up, as if caught by the breeze.

To copy nature too closely, leads thus to a neglect of other and more essential qualities; and a modified treatment is necessary; for even if we go as far as the strength of wood will allow us, it will still look frail to the eye. A good practical rule seems to be, to leave the wood as thick as you would be obliged to model it in clay, that is, in good working order. You will find that no great portion will stand alone without extraneous support. In applying this rule, the nature of the work must guide us as to the greater or less strictness with which it is to be enforced. It must be closely attended to in large and important pieces of furniture or decoration, but in more capricious and lighter objects we may relax in our severity, and allow more or less play of tendril or spray; but in all cases there should be a sufficient portion massed upon the ground, to show that these lighter parts are playful stragglers from the general design. Again, if the carving is to be gilt, the apparent change into a solid metal will allow greater license.

The power of representing space is also denied to sculpture; drawing is an abstraction; and, by linear perspective, objects can be shown gradually receding into the distance; but it only professes to be a partial delineation, and no actual form is there present to show the deceit. Painting, indeed, simulates the real form, but colour and aerial perspective, by making the diminished objects and their shadows appear dimmer and grayer, as in nature, complete the illusion. Sculpture is impotent to produce this effect; for, however the forms may be diminished in true linear perspective, the colour is as positive on the smaller as on the larger foreground figures; no atmosphere can intervene in the few inches of extra depth, and thus to the educated eye every attempt to reproduce pictorial effect is a failure, however palliated by skilful execution. No figure or portion of the sculpture can be represented as apparently farther removed than the actual plane of the ground on which it rests, and one part cannot be represented nearer to the eye than its real projection. This is a rule constantly violated since the *renaissance* of the art. Ghiberti introduced this false element into the reliefs of his celebrated gates of the Baptistery at Florence, and the example has spread till we have seen architectural compositions and pictures—such as Da Vinci's Last Supper, and Raphael's cartoons—copied in wood and in metal. This is a false road for sculpture, from which the works of Flaxman have done much to rescue it.

There is one general rule which applies principally to designing; but should here be mentioned, as a skilful carver is often called upon to design, or at least arrange details. No decorative adjunct should be allowed to become an essential constructive part, or assume the place of a real support in any work. Every good design should be constructed in the simplest and most natural manner, the lines good, the parts well-proportioned, and the general form graceful; so that, were no ornament added, it would still remain simple and elegant. Hence all figures and animals used as supports are bad; and though, by altering the lower part, you ensure that the caryatid shall not run away, you only produce an unnatural monster, as unfitted as ever for the purpose. The easy remedy is to introduce a bracket column or pilaster as obviously the real support, and then the figure becomes an ornament to the design. So again, all imitations of trees or reeds, used as columns, chair-backs formed of actual stems, curtain-rods with ends like flowers, are bad; they are lies. If real, they would be absurd, and, being put to do real duties, they are shams; whereas, let the column, chair, or pole-end exist with the foliage and flowers overlaying, twining around or gushing out of the solid wood, and you recognize them at once for what they are—ornaments. The worst and vilest instances of this bad taste, though bepraised by guide-books, and stared at in faith by sight-seers, are the huge pulpits in the Flemish churches, where the priest discourses from a leafy arbour, inhabited by parrots and monkeys, his head over-canopied by a carved tree, as large as life, loaded with fruit, flowers, and cherubs.

As a branch, severed from its parent stem, is an imperfect and now useless object, so a literal copy of a plucked sprig does not form a legitimate ornament. Before it can be ranked as ornamental art, it must show evidence that man's intellect has acted on it, and reduced it into harmony and fitness with the purpose to which it is applied. This harmony manifests itself in the two qualities of symmetry and proportion; whose presence, indeed, is essentially necessary, before an imitation of nature becomes transmuted into art.

Symmetry is an equal harmony, or balancing of the parts which form the whole; and proportion, the relative differences between all the parts. In a well-grown tree each branch varies in size and shape from every other, gradually decreasing in regular proportion from the base to the top; while the mass of branches on the one side counterbalances the mass of those on the other, and the tree is equipoised, or symmetrical. Symmetry, without proportion, produces monotony; and proportion, without symmetry, confusion. The whole of composition lies in the harmony of these two qualities. Proportion requires that there should be variety in the parts, and symmetry, that one side, or division, should be equivalent to the corresponding one. Every leaf and group may be different, and a large mass may be balanced by several small ones; but there should be the same general contour and weight of masses. Artistic expression depends on the adjustment of these two principles; as, on the predominance of one or other, the severe or playful character of the ornament depends.

Ornamental carving depends, for its principal effect, on light and shade, and here she reigns supreme; for, however inferior the form may be, light and shade are nature's own, and lend themselves to a thousand expressions. The general rule should be to produce soft and rounded masses, swelling up in one part like the hills and mountains in nature; in another spreading out like the plains at their feet, and contrasted here and there by a sharp, cutting edge or bold projecting-line; while, in parts, the points may be thrown up to catch bright sparkles of light. Of course, the changes are infinite, according to the effect to be produced; but generally, hard, sharp, cutting lines should be used with discretion, as contrasts to the prevailing ornament, otherwise the carving will become poor and hard. The modern plan of cutting the ornaments for panels and small pieces of carving separately, and fixing them on the ground when polished, is one great source of hardness and tameness; for the junction of the ornament with the ground must everywhere show a hard angular line, detaching the carving from the ground. Indeed, it is impossible to produce the effect of good Gothic carving, without cutting it out of the solid wood, a point which has been closely attended to in the new Houses of Parliament.

A very beautiful instance of the contrast of successful treatment is the architrave of Ghiberti's gates, at Florence, of which a portion is found in every drawing-school; where the leaves of the egg gourd are thrown up as if caught by the wind, and contrast with the smooth oval fruit and broad-winged birds.

If garlands are introduced, let them be such as could be formed of twined flowers, and not solid masses of flowers and fruit, stuck as closely as possible together, without stalks, or of leaves stuck in a solid lump, which could never exist without needle and thread.

In ornamenting mouldings, the lines must always cross the moulding, in order to exhibit the profile, and never run in the same direction. The forms used should not be too positive or deeply cut. The Greek mouldings are a good study of well-adapted ornamentation: they are never so deeply cut as to interfere with the profile, nor to allow the shadow of the ornament to prevail over that produced by the general form. In Roman mouldings, on the contrary, the ornament usurps too much importance; the leafage is coarse and deeply cut, and the indentations so many that the outline is apt to be lost; and, in place of long and well-defined lines of light and shade, a confused richness is the only effect produced.

All woods that are tolerably close-grained, and of uniform colour, are suited to carving; but handsomely-figured woods, such as finely-mottled rosewood, zebra-wood, mahogany, or bird's-eye maple, on the contrary, lose their own beauty, and destroy the effect of the workmanship. Pear, lime-tree, and chestnut, being tough, moderately soft, and close-grained, are the best suited of all woods to the carver's tools; but, unless stained, they want colour to fit them for general use in ornamental furniture. Those best qualified, by their colour, for decorative purposes, and for exhibiting, at the same time, beauty of modelling, are holly, oak, walnut, and similar woods, which retain a moderate polish, and have no strongly-marked figure to interfere with the most delicate light and shade: they are also the woods best adapted to the Gothic style, where the parts are generally small, and rectangular forms and angles prevail, and where the carving is often delicate and in low relief.

Mahogany has a smooth grain, well suited to the carver; but the style of ornament should be broad, and the forms round and smooth, to display fully its rich colour and smooth grain, which is susceptible of a very brilliant, and yet soft polish. Finely-figured wood is entirely thrown away on elaborate work, and accordingly, for such, colour is the great quality we must select. Maple, satin-wood, and figured birch, are not desirable, for the same reason; besides which, the alternate layers of hard and soft wood render them difficult to cut. Rose-wood is the least fitted for carving of all the woods used in furniture; its long open grain requires filling up with so much polish, that every curve shows a sharp dash of light like polished metal; while its dark and rather dull colour, when cut across the grain, absorbs the light, and entirely obliterates the distinction between half-tints and shadows; so that all we should aim at, in ornamenting rose-wood, is to produce sharp sparkles of light, glittering like dew-drops on a dark ground. Elaborate modelling is entirely lost; a bold free ornament, opposing strongly the black deep shadow against bright sparkling lights, is best suited to it; when the wood is very orange in colour, then these objections are lessened.

Ebony, in spite of its dark colour, takes such a soft smooth surface, free from metallic glitter, that it is well adapted to objects of moderate dimensions; its great hardness and the labour of working it, together with constant flaws and defects in colour, cause it to be generally replaced by pear-tree, which, if well stained, is of a richer black than ebony itself.

Having now mentioned those great principles which distinguish the functions of an artist-carver from that of a mere workman, let us impress on the young student the importance of an attentive study of drawing and modelling in clay, as the only means by which he can rise to eminence. Drawing is the first training of the hand, and the means by which he can take memorandums of the beauties he may fall in with, and of the ideas that arise in his mind; but modelling, above all, must be his daily study and guide. It is the only means of acquiring freedom of hand and bold sweeping curves, before his fingers have been cramped by long years of toil, and of preserving that power when once gained.

The great reason why the French have hitherto excelled us in wood-carving is, that they always model their ornament completely before beginning it in the wood, by which means they judge of the effect, and easily make any alterations. It is much more economical; there is no uncertain trying, or fear of boldly cutting away the waste; the carver saves half his time, and the work is better done; nothing has to be done twice over. In England, how much carving, too costly to be abandoned as destroyed, has already, when half done, lost all beauty of proportion, from the wood having been cut away during a few hours' absence of the directing head; the workman is dispirited, and the work is turned out, at last, deformed with clumsy gluing on, in the attempt to restore its original character.

CABINET-MAKER'S ASSISTANT.

DESCRIPTION OF THE PLATES.

PRELIMINARY REMARKS.

IN commencing the description of the Plates a few words may be offered on their arrangement, and the manner in which the descriptions will be treated. The designs for the furniture of each apartment, or series of apartments of a similar character, are numbered consecutively, so as to form a distinct group, and be of easy reference. These groups are arranged in the order in which the apartments to which they refer usually present themselves in houses of the larger size. Thus, as being the entrance apartment, *Hall furniture* naturally comes first; this will be followed in order by *Dining-room and Parlour furniture*, as being the rooms next approached; after these *Library furniture* will be taken up, to be followed in succession by *Drawing-room furniture*, *Bed-room furniture*, and a short section on general details and *miscellanies* which do not properly classify under the heads into which the subject has been divided.

The descriptions will mainly relate to the practical construction of the several designs in the plates, and be so treated as to explain and obviate any difficulties that may occur to the tradesman in carrying the designs into execution. While, to avoid tediousness, many things must either be stated as to be done *in the ordinary way*, or else passed over in silence, it will be our endeavour fully to explain the parts of construction, regarding which any doubt or difficulty is likely to arise. Sometimes several methods of construction will be given, with remarks on the advantages and disadvantages of each, leaving the tradesman to adopt the one best suited for the quality desired, and the price to be obtained, for the article in hand. To avoid repetition throughout the descriptions of a series of designs, parts similarly constructed, after having been once described, will not be noticed in the succeeding figures, or else merely by reference to the description of the figure under which a notice of the part in question is to be found. Sections and diagrams of construction will be introduced wherever they are deemed necessary for the elucidation of the text.

HALL FURNITURE.

The furniture, painting, and decorations of the hall, lobby, or entrance room of any mansion, whether large or small, or by whatsoever name it may be called, should be rather of a quiet and sober description, than have the least tendency to gaudiness; for it is obvious that much show, particularly of positive colouring and gilding in the hall, staircase, or approaches to the more important rooms, tends to destroy the richness and brilliancy of these apartments, and to lessen the effect they would otherwise have by contrast, were due relation preserved between the furniture and decoration of the approaches and that of the more important rooms. In large and well arranged mansions, this principle is steadily kept in view; and though the rooms throughout be decorated with bright colours, gilding, and pictures, these are either entirely excluded from the approaches to the apartments, or else used very sparingly. Sculpture, and articles of taste and *vertu*, of quiet and unobtrusive colouring, are employed as hall decorations, which, while they impart a feeling of comfort and a certain richness of effect, do not detract from the splendour of the public rooms of the mansion.

Armorial bearings, so frequently displayed on hall furniture, may, with advantage, be blazoned in their true colours, and gilding introduced where gold forms part of the blazon. Such an introduction of gold and colours supplies an agreeable point of relief, and tends to give sprightliness to the piece of furniture to which they are applied; but the employment of positive colour throughout, or the hatching of the ornaments with gold, should rather

*a**

diameter; the arms towards their extremities are tapered slightly in their thickness. This is effected by grounding them down in the face, so as to relieve a band which is gradually formed on their outer edge, and terminates its greatest depth at the scroll. The two lowest arms, at their under edge, are united with the ornament overlying the cross rail; the parts are wrought separately, and then joined.

Fig. 2, in its under part, resembles several of the preceding. The large circle in the upper part supplies the place of the centre and side standards, and cross arms in the others. The rim should be wrought of four segments, and made up of three thicknesses, forming together $1\frac{1}{8}$ inch thick. The joints of the segments are made to pass each other, for strength, and the middle thickness is made of cross wood. The face of the rim is cross banded. A hollow moulding is carried round the inner and outer edges of the rim. The diagonal bars, $\frac{3}{4}$ inch thick, are half checked into each other, and fitted into the circle, and fixed by dowels passing through the rim into their ends. The rim is fitted and dowelled to the top of the centre standard, and fixed to the side standards, by screws passing through the hollow at their top into the rim; the outer edge of the rim is slipped with veneer. The centre ornaments are planted on at the crossing of the bars. The top ornament is formed of three pieces, carved separately, and screwed on.

Fig. 3, in configuration and ornament, combines the elements of several of the preceding, with some varieties and additions. The frets are grooved in; the standards are first framed together by the cross bar, and the frets are slid into the grooves from the upper and lower ends. The arched top, formed of a single piece, is then fitted down, and the standards are let into and fixed to the box; the vases on the top of the side standards are let in with a pin; the tie in the centre of the arch is scribed into the moulding; the coronet with foliage is then planted on.

CLOCK CASES.—PLATE VIII.

These examples are designated wall clocks, as they are supported on a bracket, or hang on the wall, instead of resting on the floor. Besides being an article of hall furniture, they are of frequent use in public offices, places of resort, &c. They are usually made of oak, frequently of mahogany, and sometimes of satinwood, or deal painted in flat tints, and the carving hatched with gilding. The style of the design and character of the apartment for which the clock is intended, determine the material and manner in which it should be executed.

In fig. 1 the head is of one piece, and extends to the bottom of the truss-shaped ornaments on each side, where it joins with the framing of the door opening: it is wrought of $2\frac{3}{4}$ or 3-inch wood. The bissel surrounding the dial is turned on and gilt; a brass ring, glazed, is hinged to the bissel and secured by a lock. The door moulding is checked to receive the fret from behind. A thin panel, with coloured silk, is put in behind the fret, and a plate of glass in front preserves the silk from dust. The drops at the bottom of the case are let in with a pin, and the torus moulding is broken round them and carried back. The ornament below is formed of three pieces, which are joined behind the drops, and fixed to the sides and bottom of the case. The front of the clock is attached to the casing behind, which encloses the works.

Fig. 2 has the front of the head formed of $\frac{3}{4}$-inch wood, and fretted with coloured cloth shown behind the openings. A hollow moulding is carried round the front margins of the frets on both edges, and gilt. Within the fret a circular ground is formed for planting the bissel moulding. The head stands out from the body of the case $1\frac{1}{2}$ inches; the door is glazed; the side ornaments below are kept back $\frac{1}{4}$ inch from the line of the case front; the large moulding and bracket at the bottom go back to the wall.

Fig. 3 has a plain ground, with the ornamental parts of the head and lower end planted on the face. The side mouldings, with their overlying foliage, are attached to the side of the door opening. The icicles, under the sweeped moulding on the top, should be gilt. The bissel is brass, and gilt. This pattern might be executed in rosewood, and would be much enriched by the mouldings and carved portions being hatched with gilding.

Fig. 4 may be wrought out of fir wood, and either painted in flat tints relieved by gilding, or entirely gilt; the head requires 3-inch wood. The side mouldings and bottom ornament are attached to the door frame. The door is glazed, with a silk covered panel behind the fret.

CLOCK CASES.—PLATE IX.

These examples have the front of the head formed of one entire piece. The clock work is enclosed within a circular casing behind, which is built of fir wood, and veneered round; this casing follows the general outline of the front, and is attached to it; it is perforated on both sides, for emitting the sound when the hours are struck. The head, so formed, is fixed to a frame, on which, in figs. 2 and 3, the upper part of the cornice mouldings are planted. The inside of this frame is grooved, and made to correspond with the outside dimensions of the body of the case, so as to receive its top within it; hardwood fillets, which work into the grooves, are screwed to the sides of the case, and on these the frame, with the attached head, slides off or on as required. The entire back is enclosed by a board, which is shaped at the upper end to the interior of the case containing the mechanism. The interior of the case must be clear for the descent of the weights. The usual depth of the case inside, from back to front, is 6 inches, but some bulky compensation pendulums, such as the mercurial, require 8 or 9 inches, to allow sufficient room for the weights to pass.

In Fig. 1, the case is entire, extending from below the head to the base. The front, containing the door opening, is framed up the whole length. The sides are feathered into the front with a plough, and checked behind to receive the back; the whole is then wrought flush and veneered. The ornaments on the front and sides are planted on. The door is glazed, and opens at the second band above the shield. The interior of the back, opposite the door, should be veneered or covered with cloth. The feet are wrought in three pieces, the front and the two sides: they are mitred at the corners in front, and afterwards carved; the back connecting them is lap-dovetailed in, the moulding above is wrought separately, and planted on.

In Fig. 2, the head is made of wood 1¾-inch thick, and has the bissel turned on the solid. The frame which connects the head with the body overlies the egg moulding at the top of the case, forming the block of the cornice. The pedestal and body are wrought separately, and afterwards joined. The pedestal is hollowed in the front and sides with the fore-corners canted. The method of constructing

Fig. 14.

the pedestal and the adjoining parts is shown in *fig.* 14. The front, *a*, and the side, *b*, collectively

expressed by the dotted lines, are clamped up of deal, upon a ground of the same, ⅞ inch thick, dovetailed together, and afterwards hollowed to a radius of 16½ inches; the clamps are 2 inches thick, where they mitre at the front-corners. The top moulding, *c*, rests on the top of the pedestal, and projects beyond it 1¾ inches; the hollow member below stands beyond the flush ¼ inch; the space behind the moulding is pieced out so as to finish flush with the inside of the pedestal ground, and join with the body of the case, *d*, where it is fixed within the pedestal. The canted corners, *f*, are clamped with solid wood, ⅜-inch thick, to form the sunk panels. The front, *g*, forming the door opening, is framed up of solid wood; the stiles are 2¼ inches thick, and taper in breadth from 1⅝ inch at top, to 3¾ inches at bottom; the cross-rails are ⅞ inch thick. As the body of the case requires, for secure attachment, to pass about 2 inches within the pedestal, the sides must be made so much longer, and the under cross-rail broader. The frame is wrought flush behind, where it applies to the case, the difference of thickness in the stiles being thrown to the front. The upper ends of the stiles are reduced to the thickness of the cross-rail, and wrought flat across; and their inner edges, all down, are brought to the same thickness, as a ground for the door to act on; the side pieces are then gradually scooped hollow, from above downwards. The sides of the case must be of solid wood, 1¼ inch thick, so as to work in with the sweep of the mouldings on the top of the pedestal. The door, *h*, is glazed. The base block is formed of one solid piece, 2 inches thick, and the scrolls are glued on to the required depth; the back scrolls, *d* (*fig.* 15), must be wrought so as not to project behind, that the case may

Fig. 15.

stand close to the wall. The shell in front of the block is set in between the carved scrolls.

Fig. 3, in the chief points of construction, is identical with the preceding. The body of the case at the top is rounded over to where the head is attached, and then veneered. The foliage on the upper corners is planted on. The moulding on the top of the pedestal is mitred round after the pedestal and body are joined. The panel, with its mouldings, is formed of one piece, and fitted to the hollowed front of the pedestal, then carved and planted on. The base includes the carved moulding, the square block, and feet. The feet are each separately wrought of one piece, and screwed on.

Fig. 4 requires 3½ or 4-inch wood for the head. The bissel is turned on the solid. The position

*b**

and character of the pilasters, on the body of the case, gives it greater breadth across than any of the others. The case, with its pedestal, is shaped, as shown in the plan sketch (*fig.* 16), so as to present a ground for planting the trusses and pilasters. The door acts on pivot hinges, and sweeps under the cornice and over the pedestal mouldings.

Fig. 16.

DINING-ROOM AND PARLOUR FURNITURE.

Dining-room furniture should be characterized by three qualities—convenience, solidity of construction, and absence of gaudiness. In the furniture of a family apartment in daily use, strength and solidity of construction are absolutely necessary for tear and wear; and any structural form, ornament, or decoration that interferes with comfort is to be discarded. Richness of effect, rather than showiness, is to be aimed at, and that by the use of good materials, and by masses of colour judiciously harmonized, without being monotonous; decided contrasts should be but sparingly used. The sideboard being the chief article of furniture in the room, the other articles of plenishing ought to be kept in subordination to it, and consistent with it in style and decoration. Having to contrast with plate, the sideboard should have a species of richness that looks well alone, and, at the same time, sets off the service of plate to the best advantage. Positive contrasts of various-coloured woods, gilding, decorations in brass work or ormolu, tend to interfere with unity of design, and disturb the effect of plate; such modes of ornament should be therefore avoided. Sufficient effect may be obtained by the use of beautiful woods, carefully wrought, and enriched occasionally by carving, inlaying, or fret-cutting. For variety, woods of different shades, but not of different colours, may with advantage be used together, and ornaments of bronze employed instead of carving.

PEDESTAL SIDEBOARD.—PLATE X.

The dimensions of the pedestals, with the proportional length of the drawer between them, are the principal determining measures of the sideboard. The usual height of the top is 39 inches, the width from 26 to 30 inches, and the length from 7 to 9 feet, according to the size of the room. The example here presented is plain in style, and simple in construction. The doors are flush panelled and veneered over, the mouldings and shields being clamped on. The back, between the pedestals, is closed in by a panelled frame, with the projection of base carried round it; this is screwed to the back edge of the inner gables, which, in consequence, are kept the thickness of the frame narrower than the outside gables. The pedestals are adjusted to their position by two pins glued into their upper ends, which pass into the top. They are then screwed firmly to their places, so as to support and regulate the action of the drawer fitted between them. This drawer has the sides grooved, and is made to act upon fillets screwed to the inner gables. A piece, forming a field for the centre ornament, is planted on the middle of the frieze drawer; it is fitted exactly between the listels of the upper and under mouldings, and wrought flush with them. The moulding, which is carried round the gables, is attached to the top; it is formed on a fillet of wood, clamped on the edge of a strap of deal 3 inches broad. The top is veneered and finished square, and slipped with veneer on the edge. The ground of the top is made of $\frac{7}{8}$-inch deal, clear of knots, and sound; the required thickness being made up by clamping below, lengthwise, and across at the ends and middle. If the top, in drying after being veneered, remains convex on the upper side, this can be easily rectified by cutting at intervals through the cross clamps, under the most convex portions of the top, small pieces of a wedge form, and chipping these parts out, and increasing their breadth by inserting at their edges thin slips of wood, then glueing and driving the wedges home, and so forcing the top straight. Should the top happen to become concave on the upper side, from the contraction of the veneer in drying, this may be remedied by running grooves, an inch apart, into the cross clamps, and fitting freely into them fillets of wood with strong glue. The top is then forcibly bent, and maintained slightly convex on the upper side till the glue in the grooves is thoroughly dry. The back is let into the top the thickness of the ground, and screwed; the bevelled moulding of the back rests on the top. The end view shows the top moulding in profile, the required projection of the top behind, and the centre drawer, indicated by dotted lines.

PEDESTAL SIDEBOARD.—PLATE XI.

Fig. 1 is of a simple character, and in construction resembles the example given in Plate X. The top may be formed of $\frac{5}{8}$-inch solid wood, clamped with deal to the required thickness: the ovolo moulding on its edge is planted on, and placed so as to present the listel above of the proper depth. The part of the moulding on the ends of the top, and also the returns of the brakes, should be formed of cross wood, so that the grain of the wood may be continuous with that of the top itself. The pieces for this purpose must be carefully seasoned, and should be grooved and feathered on the top. They are not mitred, at the fore-corners, into the front mouldings, but are put on before them, and planed flush with the square edge of the top, and then butt-joined with the mouldings in front. The hollow below the top is separately prepared and planted on. A block $\frac{1}{2}$-inch thick is planted on the drawer front, and the mouldings on its upper and lower edge are carried round it; small side trusses, $\frac{1}{4}$-inch thick, are joined to the edge of the block, and in front they are made to finish flush with the lip of the upper and lower mouldings. The drop below is let in with a pin. The brackets under the ends of the drawer are fixed by screws passing through the inner gables. The doors are wrought flush as a ground for the shaped panels, $\frac{5}{16}$-inch thick, which are planted on them; on these again the small fielded centre panels are glued down, and the mouldings carried round their edges. The general appearance of the design may be improved by increasing the breadth of the straight portion of the back to six inches. The ground of the pediment, above this part, may be formed of deal, pieced on the edges to show solid wood, when it is profiled with the top moulding, which is planted on the face. The ground and fret are both completely finished before they are glued together. The semicircular ends are formed of deal, veneered on the face, and the mouldings, which are turned, planted on: their upper edges are then slipped with veneer.

Fig. 2.—From the enriched character of this design, no great extent of plane surface is presented; it is consequently not so well adapted for wood possessing large or striking figure, as for that of a minutely variegated and plainer character, such as oak. The stage is framed and fitted with drawers. The exact measures of the stage being determined, those of the ground frame are so much less by the greatest depth of the mouldings planted on it. The position of the cross rails are regulated by the same condition, which again determines the spaces from the frieze drawers. The stage frame in plan and vertical section is shown in *figs.* 17 and 18; the dotted line, *a a*, marks the outside of the mouldings, which are carried round the front and ends of the ground frame; the lines *b b* the ground, with the thickness of the wood employed—the front portion of the ground being the three drawer fronts. Four blocks, *c c c c*, $1\frac{1}{4}$-inch thick, are

planted on the extreme ends of the two outer drawers, and around these the frieze mouldings are

Fig. 17.

Fig. 18.

carried, forming the brakes shown in the drawing. The six cross rails of the frame are cross headed with solid wood. These headings are tenoned into the long rails, *d d, fig.* 18, and they show solid wood on the drawers being drawn out. By this means, also, the action of the drawers is rendered more smooth, and the cross rails are kept from warping. The drawers are made to abut against the frame in the line *c f*. The back rail of the frame, *g*, should not be finally glued till the drawers are fitted, as any irregularity in breadth, dimension, or workmanship, may thus be more easily remedied. The large moulding on the drawer fronts must be of solid wood, as the panelling shown on it is formed by grounding down. The doors, which are sunk panelled, have their stiles, the united breadth of the pilaster grounds, and door framing. The circular head of the door is formed by piecing up the inner corners (*fig.* 19). The pieces are mitred together, and glued to the adjoining parts of the stile and rail—the grain of the wood being made to run with these parts: the whole is then flushed off and veneered. The mouldings

Fig. 19.

stand out beyond the flush, are glued to the inner edge of the frame, and form a check for the panel. The pilasters are $\frac{5}{8}$-inch thick, and solid; the drops at their top and bottom are planted on $\frac{5}{16}$-inch thick. The back is formed of two thicknesses—the one in front of $\frac{3}{8}$-inch solid wood, the other of $\frac{5}{8}$-inch deal. The front board is wrought to pattern, and perforated in the centre. This figured opening is traced on the board behind, and the space marked is veneered and polished; the two thicknesses are then glued together. The top moulding, which forms the profile of the back, is planted on the face, and has a hollow moulding wrought on its inner edge. The prism-shaped panels, with the ground on which they rest, are made of two pieces separately wrought, glued together, and planted on. The fret pediments are of $\frac{5}{8}$-inch wood, and dowelled on.

Fig. 3 has the top resting immediately on the pedestals, as in Fig. 1. The corners of the pedestals are canted, and recede from the line of the doors at an angle of 45°, or $\frac{1}{2}$ a square mitre; consequently the cant is thrown equally on the doors and the gables. The pilasters, of solid wood, are $3\frac{1}{8}$-inch broad, and $\frac{5}{8}$-inch thick. From their position, the doors require to stand beyond the front edge of the gables $2\frac{1}{8}$ inches. The inner pilasters are attached to the doors, and the outer ones to the gables; to these last the doors are hung. The propriety of fixing to the gables the outside pilaster of each door is obvious, as otherwise the trusses on them would prevent the doors from opening to the square. The ground for the moveable pilaster is glued to the side of the door frame before the latter is veneered. On veneering the door, the edge of the veneer on the stile is made to join with the pilaster. The frets on the pilasters are wrought $\frac{1}{16}$-inch thick, and planted on a ground $\frac{5}{16}$-inch deep. The doors are in all respects similar to those of Fig. 2, excepting the upper rail; the greater breadth of which serves as a ground for planting the bordered fret. The moulding on the ring is similar to that on the door stile, but smaller. The length of the drawer is determined by the distance between the trusses on the inner pilasters; that being the space within which it must act. The drawer opens at the outer ends of the fretted panels, in the manner shown in *fig*. 20. The breadth of the moulding on the base determines the projection of the frame around the front and sides of the pedestal. The canted corners are

Fig. 20.

wrought flush with the face of the shaft of the pilaster, and dovetailed into the front, D, and side of the frame, E, *fig*. 21. On this ground a block, C, is glued down—being made the proper thickness and breadth for carrying round the base moulding. The upper edge of the base is bevelled, and slipped with veneer, before the moulding is planted on. The back is pieced

Fig. 21.

on the upper edges and ends with solid wood, and veneered on the face. The ornament at the centre and top of the back is separately wrought, and the scrolls terminating the top moulding are fitted into it. After the front of the back is finished, the fret is planted on. This last consists of five pieces—two, forming the top, which are butt-joined in the centre,

the two ends, and the straight portion at the bottom. These several parts are profiled and adjusted at the points of contact previous to fret cutting.

Fig. 4 has the pedestals tapered on the sides. They are two inches narrower at the top than at the bottom. The doors are sunk panelled, and the moulding (*fig*. 22) is made

Fig. 22.

to lap on the stile. The pilasters are $\frac{1}{2}$-inch thick, and the small panels on their front are $\frac{3}{8}$-inch thick, and fielded on the edge. The trusses are formed of two pieces—the scrolled portion and the foliage below it being separately wrought. Between the pedestals behind, the space is filled by a frame flush panelled and veneered over; a base is formed on its under edge corresponding with that of the pedestals, and mitred in with it.

The back has a mirror in the centre, surrounded by a rim, with a moulding planted on its edge. The lip of the moulding projects within the rim, forming a check in which the plate rests. The rim is made up of segments of two $\frac{7}{8}$ thicknesses of deal $2\frac{1}{4}$-inch broad. These are cut of various lengths, so as to strengthen the rim by

Fig. 23.

making the pieces lap over the butt-joinings on the sides alternately. The ends of the rim are connected by a bar, *a* (*fig*. 23), which is $\frac{7}{8}$-inch thick, and in breadth $\frac{3}{8}$-inch less than the depth of the check which the thickness of the sideboard top forms behind. The bar is checked flush with the fore-edge of the rim, and glued and screwed. The semicircular moulding, *b*, which is turned, is then planted on, and the outer edge of the rim is afterwards veneered. After the rim is polished, the plate, *f* (*fig*. 24), is laid

Fig. 24.

into the checks, and maintained in its place by blocks, *c*, three inches long, that are glued at short intervals around the inner edge of the rim. The mirror has a framed back, made of $\frac{3}{4}$-inch deal, and panelled. It is fitted within the rim, as indicated by the dotted lines, and made to rest on the blocks, and is fixed by screws passing through it obliquely into the rim. The entablatures, which adjoin the mirror at each end, have their ground formed of 2-inch deal. They are made to stand in advance of the rim $\frac{3}{8}$-inch. For this purpose they are in front checked on the sideboard top, and at their inner ends behind, the rim is checked into them, leaving a lap of $\frac{3}{8}$-inch thick in front of the mirror. The rim moulding abuts on the top of the entablature at *e e, fig.* 23. The moulding at its base may, for the protection of the plate, be carried along the front of the mirror. The bar, *a*, would, in consequence, require to be made of sufficient breadth, as a ground for the moulding, which should lap over like that on the rim, forming a check for the plate.

PEDESTAL SIDEBOARD.—PLATE XII.

This design, in construction and embellishment, differs considerably from any of the preceding. The ground of the back is of deal, 1-inch thick, and of one piece, checked and screwed at the ends into the adjoining sides of two pedestals. The centre of the back is increased in breadth, and projected $1\frac{1}{4}$-inch in front by clamping. On this part a ground panel, with an ornamental scrolled border, is planted. The panel and border may be wrought together of one piece, $1\frac{1}{2}$-inch thick. The panel being grounded down, and the small raised panels planted on its field; or, otherwise, the larger panel may be separately wrought, and of sufficient thickness to project, as shown in section Fig. D, and the scrolled border formed of four separate pieces, fitted round it. The scrolled head of the clock is made of wood 4-inch thick. The bissel is separately wrought, and let into the upper moulding of the back, then applied to a ground formed for it on the head, and fixed by screws from behind. The dial and clock-work is let in from the front, and behind a space is cut out to admit the work. The bracket and shelf shown in the profile, Fig. C, are fixed by screws passing through the back. The fret pediments on the ends of the back are made of 1-inch wood, and the band on their edges is formed in relief. Before veneering the top, the ovolo moulding on its edge is planted on. The projecting centre part of it, having the rounded ends, is first planted. It is formed of a piece whose finished breadth is $3\frac{1}{2}$ inches. The end pieces are then mitred with or scribed to this. In the drawing, the frieze drawer is shown as straight in front, but, from the projection over it of the brake on the top, it would be more elegant to project the drawer also,

so as to correspond in outline with the parts overlying it: in this case, the drawer front would require to be built at the ends. Two designs for the decoration of the pedestals are given. The pedestal door, to the right, shown in section Fig. F, is flush panelled, and veneered over with the shield and mouldings planted on. Ornamental pieces of rich wood, $\frac{1}{4}$-inch thick, are fitted within the brakes of the mouldings, and glued down on the door. On the left-hand door a raised panel is planted: it is made to lap on the framing all round, as shown in section Fig. K. The coved and torus mouldings are mitred round the panel in succession, after which the field is veneered. The carving round the panel is formed of four pieces $1\frac{1}{2}$-inch thick, which are fitted to the edge of the mouldings and glued down, or they may be screwed on from behind. Any slight inequalities in the joinings may be remedied after the parts are fixed. The grain of the wood, in all the parts, should run lengthwise with the door. The coved moulding of the raised panel on the gables, is pieced out on the corners to form the brakes. The cabinet between the pedestals, including the base on which it stands, is separately made. The doors are flush panelled and veneered over. An elliptical bead attached to the right-hand door laps over the left at their joining. The distance between the trusses on the inside gables, determines the united breadth of the doors that being the space available for their opening. Two stiles—whose breadth slightly exceeds, say $\frac{1}{8}$-inch, the greatest depth of the trusses, are fixed—one at each end of the cabinet; and to these the doors are hinged. The ring moulding on the doors is shown in section Fig. L. The hollow side of the triangular corners is made to sweep from the same centre with the ring. These corners are formed of mouldings on the door to the right; and on the left by small bevelled panels, with rebated margins.

PEDESTAL SIDEBOARD.—PLATE XIII.

This design is well adapted for oak; and, from its rich and massive character, it should be executed of a large size, that sufficient space may be given for combining boldness with delicacy in the details of its decoration. The pedestal doors require wood $1\frac{3}{8}$-inch thick: they are sunk panelled, and the mouldings are checked, to recess the door $\frac{3}{8}$-inch, and are made to lap on the stile. The trusses are dowelled to the sides of the frame; and, together with it, form the true breadth of the door. There are two panels in each door, that in front is $\frac{5}{16}$-inch thick, and fretted; the large figured spaces in the corners being cut through, and their edges bevelled; the interior smaller spaces may either be grounded down ¼-inch into the panel behind, and the scrolled frets planted close: or inlaid with darker wood, and the ornament produced upon it by inlaying with wood of a lighter colour. *Fig.* 25

Fig. 25.

presents a cross section of the pedestal door, half-width, in a line passing through, and including the nodule above the ring in the centre. The ring is turned and cut into four equal pieces, between the ends of which the ties, which are solid, are interposed and fitted. The head is fixed by screws passing through the panel from behind. The four trusses should be profiled together out of a single piece, and the tie on the shaft of each afterwards planted on. The stage frame is made similar to that of Fig. 2, Plate XI.; the exact measures being determined by the dimensions of the sideboard, and the greatest depth of the front mouldings. The large ovolo moulding may be variously made, according as the panelling and foliage on its front are wrought in relief, or planted on. If in the former manner, it may be wrought in the solid, or clamped with 1¼-inch wood, and then veneered over; in the latter, it may be made of fir, and veneered, and pieces forming the ornamental parts may be glued up of three thicknesses, and cauled together to the curve of the moulding as a ground, and afterwards cut to figure and planted on. The rosettes on the end drawers, and the husk and leaves on the centre one, are separately wrought and let into the front. The top is veneered after the moulding on its edge is planted on. The back is formed of deal 1¼-inch thick, pieced with solid wood on the ends and centre, and veneered, as represented in the drawing, with wood of a lighter and darker shade; the former being the margins of the panels, the latter their fields. The mouldings are made to lap over the sides of both veneers. The mouldings on the top of the back, extending from the semicircle towards the ends, may be each formed of a single piece; and also the upper mouldings of the panels, which are parallel to them; all these mouldings are planted on the face. The semicircular moulding, and its overlaying ornament, are together wrought out of the solid; they are formed of three separate pieces; the centre or top part, which is fitted between the scrolls and checked, so as to be flush behind, and lap down in front; and the two segmental side pieces which are scribed edge-on to the ground, and from above down, for about ⅓ of

their length, are made to lap 1½-inch on the front, to form the scrolls and foliage, and below to mitre in with the adjoining ends of the top moulding. The thickness of wood required for these parts is about 2¾ inches.

The two similar carved ornaments on the top of the back, on the opposite sides, and at the base of the semicircle, are each formed of two pieces; the head portions, with their scrolled extremities, rising obliquely from behind, and resting on the outer end of the flat parts of the top mouldings, which mitre in with the semicircle; and the scroll shown in front as connectedly passing from under the mouldings, and recurved from before backwards. Small ornamental cylinders, laid horizontally, are made to fill the space between the semicircle, and the insides of the scrolls, where they are butt-joined, and the parts fixed by dowels. The other extremity of the ornament is fixed by screws passing through from behind; wood 3 inches thick is required for these parts. The shield is wrought of wood 2¾-inch thick; the ring is turned on, and its inside flattened as a ground for the head, previous to which the carving on the shield is blocked out. The head is carved separately, and screwed on from behind.

The cabinet between the pedestals is recessed 5 inches, measuring from the fore-edge of the inner gables. This space on the outside of these gables is clamped with wood, solid or veneered, 1⅛-inch thick. In the front, and towards the centre of the clamp, a hollow is wrought to a radius of 3½ inches; the line of which sweeps from the outer edge to within 1½-inch of the back of the clamp, where a flat border of that breadth is left. If the clamp is veneered, a panel is formed on the bottom of the hollow, by planting a small moulding on the face; if solid, a groove ¼-inch deep may be carried round to mark off the panel. Pendant foliage is shown above the panel, which may be wrought in high relief by inserting a piece into the ground of the hollow. The clamp forms a check behind, which determines the position of, and forms an attachment to, the cabinet between the pedestals. The base, with its moulding, must correspond with the outline of the clamp. The doors are flush panelled, and the ornamentation of them may either be produced by fret cutting—a piece of cloth being introduced behind the fret—or by inlaying the ground of the pattern with wood of a darker colour.

SLAB SIDEBOARDS.—PLATE XIV.

Slab sideboards differ from pedestal sideboards in being more fitted for the display of plate or articles of *vertu*, and less for a place of deposit.

Fig. 26 shows the manner in which the stage frame, and that of the base, should be wrought;

Fig. 26.

the rounds and hollows of the outline of the ground are formed by clamping with deal, *c, c, c,* upon a frame so constructed. The operation is guided by moulds of the ends and front, previously formed, and must be accurately done. The clamps for the frieze moulding are wrought by the same mould, and must be $1\frac{1}{4}$-inch thick; the centre clamp may be cut out of two lengths, and butt-joined in the middle; the carved ornament in the centre of the rail will cover the joining. The scrolls, shown on the end mouldings, are wrought on the solid. The foliage under the rail, and between the front trusses, consists of three pieces, the centre and two sides; these last are cut out to the sweep of the front rail, and made to work in with the top of the trusses; corresponding pieces are cut out, but of shorter length, and fitted to the outsides of the front trusses. The carving shown on the frame, over the front trusses, is wrought on the solid and apart; the advancing hollow sweeps of the front and end mouldings are flushed with the ground frame, and the carved parts are planted on. The top is clamped to thickness the usual way; and, when wrought to shape, the mouldings, which are hand-wrought, are dowelled on; care being taken that the dowells are bored parallel to each other, and, as nearly as possible, at right angles to the surface into which they are driven; few dowells, judiciously inserted, are quite sufficient to adjust and secure the mouldings firmly to their place. As consider-able difficulty may be experienced in bedding the mouldings properly, after being nearly fitted, they may be temporarily glued to their place; and, when dry, a smooth and broad bow-saw blade may be care-fully passed between the moulding and the ground, so as to cut off any little inequalities on either, and thus bring them more expeditiously to a joint; the same method might be resorted to with the frieze moulding. The front and end top mouldings should be fitted, mitred, and glued down first; and the short pieces, for the brakes, after. The listel above the moulding should be afterwards slipped with veneer, and any slight defect in the joints of the mouldings with the top, may be concealed by bringing the veneer to join edgewise with the moulding above. The front trusses are fixed by dowells passing

through the blocks, T, T, on the frame. The back trusses are placed so as to stand clear of the framed back; they are dowelled to blocks, D, D, fixed within the frame. In both, the high projections may be brought out by clamp-ing. The top of the base is in all respects treated as the stage top in framing, and boarded above; the edges of the board being previously slipped, and the mouldings planted on them, it is then glued and strongly blocked to the cross-rails, and afterwards veneered. The frame enclosing the back is flush panelled, and checked and screwed into the back of the base and stage frame; the mouldings, with their carved corners, are planted on the veneer.

The back is formed of two thicknesses of solid wood, that in front requires $\frac{3}{8}$-inch, that behind may be $\frac{5}{8}$-inch thick; the front portion is veneered over, and then cut through to the figure of the panels; the ground behind is polished at the ex-posed parts, and the pieces cut out are reduced to size, moulded on the edge, and clamped down; the carving on the corners, excepting the small scrolls, is separately wrought and fitted on. The scroll work and foliage, around the edges and in the centre, are planted on the face. The heart-shaped carved work surrounding the initials, is shown as hooked on the descending sweep of the top scrolls; the parts in contact alternately under and overlaying each other. This arrangement is produced by keeping the scroll rather full in thickness, and thinning off the part below, so as to make it appear to dip under, emerge, and overlay the other. The whole centre carving is formed of one piece, and is first planted down; the top mouldings, the ends of which terminate in a calyx from which the foliage seems to issue, are afterwards fitted on.

Fig. 2 resembles Fig. 4, Plate XI., in the stage, which may be fitted with drawers. The hollow curve of the frieze moulding, on the return of the brakes, is formed of two solid pieces, mitred in the angle; the pieces are slip-dowelled together, and, when profiled, are afterwards taken asunder, and the large moulding is formed on them separately; they are then, finally, glued together, and their surface is wrought off. The centre drawer opens, and the end drawers abut, at the spring of the curve. It may be most convenient to form the top of $\frac{1}{2}$-inch board, clamped to thickness; the ovolo moulding, in such case, being kept down, so as to leave the listel to project. The trusses are wrought of $3\frac{1}{2}$-inch wood, and are fixed by dowells to the stage and base. The frame enclosing the back is sunk-panelled; the mouldings on it are checked on the framing, and the panels are let in from behind.

The ground of the back may be of solid wood, or of deal, and in either case veneered; labour is saved by making it solid, in consequence of the shaped ends and perforated centre requiring the exposed edges to show solid wood; if made of deal, the ends of the ground, and also the centre, must be pieced with solid wood; that on the centre must be inserted into the ground, with the edges feathered and grooved into it; the surface, after being flattened and prepared, is veneered over. The centre ornament is wrought of $1\frac{1}{4}$-inch wood, and, when completely finished, is clamped down; the back is then perforated, and wrought to profile of ornament. The top moulding is wrought of a piece with the upper part of the carving on the ends, and is clamped on the face. The panels on the back are formed by planting the shaped mouldings on the face of the veneer.

SLAB SIDEBOARD.—PLATE XV.

This design is well suited for oak; and, to give it proper effect, should be executed of a large size. The pillars are blocked out square, and are profiled, as stated under Plate I. They are then framed up with the ground of the stage, and the drawers are made to act between them. The brakes on the front and ends are formed on the square heads of the pillars, which stand out beyond the line of the frame $1\frac{1}{2}$ inches. The large moulding is solid, so as to admit of the panelled foliage, and other ornaments, on its surface, being wrought in relief. The moulding is carried round the entire front and ends; in the order of work, it should be first planted on the heads of the pillars, between which the parts forming the fronts of the drawers are afterwards scribed in. The ends of the drawer fronts so shaped, are made to lap beyond the drawer, the body of which is, as usual, square wrought, and made to act between cross rails morticed in from back to front, as shown in the diagram given under Plate XI., Fig. 2. The top is formed of $\frac{7}{8}$-inch deal, and clamped to thickness. After the top is wrought to size, pieces forming the ground, for the projection of the brakes, are glued on its edge. The moulding is then mitred round, and the whole surface is flushed off and prepared. A board of solid wood $\frac{3}{8}$-inch thick, after being wrought to the proper shape, is clamped on the top, and forming, by its thickness, the upper member of the top moulding. The frame of the base, if made of solid wood, requires to be $1\frac{1}{8}$ inch thick, and must be lap or mitre dovetailed in the fore-corners; if made of deal and veneered wood, $1\frac{1}{4}$ inch thick is necessary. The top of the base is boarded over with wood of the same thickness as that of the frame;

this part must be recessed from the front and ends, to form a check for the moulding, which is carried round its edge; it is also kept within the line of the back rail, the thickness of the upright framing behind. The base must be strongly made, and the top firmly blocked down, so as to form a secure and unyielding attachment to the pillars in front, and to the back framing. This last consists of three distinct frames, flush panelled and veneered, which are severally checked into the adjoining sides of the four pilasters at the back, and made flush behind with the stage and base. The pilasters are morticed into blocks that are glued within the back rails of the stage and base frames; small fielded panels are planted on their fronts. The ground of the back is prepared of two thicknesses, similar to that of Plate XI., Fig. 2. The front board should finish $\frac{3}{8}$-inch thick, and solid; that behind, $\frac{7}{8}$-inch, and of deal. The mouldings bordering the frets are fitted into the prepared openings, and should stand out beyond the ground $\frac{3}{16}$-inch. The pieces for forming the frets are fitted to their place before being cut; after which, and when completely finished, they are planted. The small ornamental pedestals are first planed up square, and the vases on their top turned on the solid, and carved. Previous to planting the mouldings on them, the pedestals are fixed to their place on the back; the two at the ends are dowelled on, the others are half checked, and planted on the face, and the top mouldings are abutted on them. Small panels, $\frac{5}{16}$-inch thick, with bevelled edges, are planted on the body of the pedestals. The wood forming the foliage which surmounts the semicircle, requires to be $1\frac{1}{2}$ inch thick; it is fitted to outline, and maintained 2 inches broad for carving; when completely finished, it is fixed by screws. The frets require $\frac{3}{4}$-inch wood, and are dowelled down. The ring is turned separately, and the shield is planted within it.

SIDEBOARD BACKS.—PLATE XVI.

From the examples here given, backs may be selected suitable for several of the designs of sideboards contained in the preceding plates, or the elements of their configuration and ornament may be variously blended together, or partially modified and adapted to other designs; care being taken, in such adaptation, to preserve unity of style and harmony of proportion.

Fig. 1 is formed of a board of deal, veneered, with the mouldings planted on the face, and slipped with veneer on the ends and upper edge. The block resting on the scrolls is a solid piece, with the mouldings returned on the ends. The tie is let into the block. The shield, which is veneered, has the grain of the veneer laid in the direction of its length.

Fig. 2 has the ground pieced on the upper edge, at the centre, before it is veneered. The centre ornament, including the scrolls on the top moulding, is wrought of one piece. The ornaments on the ends are checked, and made to lap on the front, so as to butt against and work in with the top moulding, the straight part of which is separately wrought.

Fig. 3, like the preceding, has the ground formed of deal, and veneered, with the top mouldings and centre ornaments planted on the face. The small pedestals at the ends are dowelled on, and in horizontal section appear as in (*Fig.* 27).

(*Fig.* 27.)

Fig. 4 has its centre projected by clamping with a piece $\frac{3}{4}$-inch thick, around which the mouldings above and below are mitred. A panel $\frac{3}{8}$-inch thick, having a small hollow wrought around its edge, is planted on the face of this raised portion; overlying this is an ornamental border, inclosing a panel separately wrought, and of a single piece—the panel within being grounded by cutting through the border, which is thinned off inside. This construction is shown by a vertical section through the centre of the back (*Fig.* 28). The panels on each end are $\frac{1}{2}$-inch thick, and veneered with rich wood on a ground of solid wood, with their edges fielded down. The ornamental pediment is dowelled on, and requires wood $1\frac{1}{2}$-inch thick.

(*Fig.* 28.)

Fig. 5 has the ground solid, and may be veneered or not, according as the wood is plain or figured. The carving is planted on the face; the centre part with the scrolls may be formed of one piece; the stem from which the latter appear to issue, and the end scrolls are entire, and wrought together. The shield is planted on.

Fig. 6 has the ground solid and veneered; it is pieced, on the upper edge, so as to profile with the carving on the ends and centre, which is planted on it. The panels on the ground are $\frac{5}{16}$-inch thick, and veneered with rich wood. The shell carving, on the centre, requires 2-inch wood; it is of one piece, and distinct from the flowers on each side; the latter, with the flowers at the ends and the top moulding between them, are wrought of one piece, $1\frac{3}{4}$-inch thick. The scrolls which form the ends are planted on the face, and butt-joined below the flowers.

PILLAR AND BLOCK TABLES.—PLATE XVII.

In pillar and block tables the dimensions of the block are variable; the breadth across its centre, and the expansion of its limbs, severally, depend on the diameter of the base of the pillar, and the size of the table top; $\frac{2}{3}$ of the breadth of the latter is usually taken as the measure of spread for the block. The form and construction of block, suited for five of the examples here given, is shown in (*Fig.* 29.) Fig. 4 differs from the others. The block is framed up of three pieces of deal A B B, $4\frac{1}{2}$ inches broad, by $2\frac{1}{2}$ inches thick; batten wood at half breadth is frequently used for this purpose. Diagonal pieces C C for forming the sweeps are let into the limbs of the frame, and the inner corners D D are blocked up with short wood; the top surface is then flushed off, and, afterwards, if the block is to be finished plain, as in Fig. 1, it is clamped

(*Fig.* 29.)

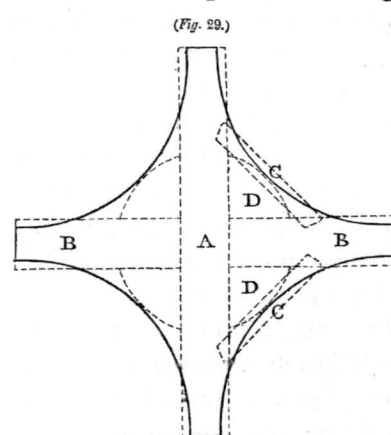

with deal $\frac{5}{8}$-inch thick, before the sweeps are cut out; but if, as in Figs. 2, 3, 5, and 6, the mouldings on the blocks are formed on the clamps, which are solid, the blocks are sweeped out and veneered on the edge before the clamps are glued down. Besides the above method, the blocks are frequently formed from three thicknesses of wood glued together, the grain of the centre one being, for sake of strength, made to cross that of the others. The wood, in this case, must be well seasoned, as, from the irregular mixture of end and side wood, the shrinkage will be unequal, and apt to show through the veneer. When the sweeps are to be carved, solid wood has to be planted on, and in such cases any defect in seasoning is not so readily apparent. A mould for making the block in this way is of especial advantage in piecing up and economising the wood.

Fig. 1 has the pillar four-sided, and paned on the corners; the panes are of equal breadth throughout, the taper being altogether formed on the sides. The body of the pillar is made up of four pieces of deal, $1\frac{1}{4}$-inch thick, and of the entire length shown, with about 5 inches additional for forming the tenons on each end, by which it is attached to the upper and lower blocks; two of the pieces are cut out full to the diameter and taper of the pillar, the

c *

hinges of the flap door; hardwood fillets are screwed to the sides within, forming, by their interspaces, grooves into which the loose leaves are slid; the sides and bottom are then wholly cloth covered. The flap door is made of solid wood, 1½-inch thick, and cross headed; tenons or dowels are inserted into the exposed ends of the sides of the holder, and corresponding mortices, or bores, *m, m*, into the inside of the flap; these assist in supporting the sides of the leaf-holder under the action of the slides. The top of the leaf-holder has the same projection all round as the rounded ends of the table-top; it is moulded on the ends and returns of the brake, and clamped below, so as to mitre-in with the other mouldings. The rounded ends are built up of sweeps of deal 1½-inch broad, and veneered. The mouldings on the edges may be formed of cross wood planted on, or, if the grain is to be lengthwise, the mouldings, after being wrought, may be rendered flexible by immersion in moist steam, and then bent to the round of the table. The fixed portions of the top are screwed to the rounded ends and leaf-holder; the former recede from the inner ends of the rim exactly the amount of projection given to the sides of the latter. The ends, *l, l*, are boarded below with hardwood, 1¼-inch thick, so as to form a secure attachment for the supporting pillars; these bottom boards are kept back from the flush of the ends of the built frames the united breadths of the three bars *f, g, h;* they abut against these bars when the table is at its least size. Continuous with the hardwood bottom, the outer part of the round is boarded with deal ¾-inch thick; both boards are finished flush below, the difference of thickness being thrown to the inside. The supporting pillars have hardwood blocks dowelled on their upper ends, and are finally fixed on by screws passing through the blocks into the bottom boards.

The joints of the tops are slip dowelled; the pins and bores are formed on alternate sides, and are made exactly to correspond to each other in number and position. The number is usually five— one in the centre of length, from which the others are set off equidistant, two towards each end; those nearest the ends are placed over the catch. By this arrangement it is indifferent what boards are made to join, the dowels and boards being made to fit each other in any arrangement.

In working the tops, they are first planed up, brought to the requisite thickness and breadths, and squared in the ends; they are then surface-finished

below, and clamped for the moulding; they are afterwards carefully jointed and dowelled, and the catches put on. The fixed portions of the tops are first brought together, wrought off, and trimmed flush in ends; the slides are then drawn out, and the leaves are individually in succession put in, wrought flush with the previous parts, reversed and adjusted in the surface and ends; the slides are then drawn out the entire length, and all the leaves are placed in and braced together. The moulding on the edge of the top is then wrought, and finally the surface of the table is glass-papered and finished.

Small-Sized Telescope Dining Tables.

The frame and slide construction of an elliptical telescope table are shown in (*Fig.* 33). This table, at least size, is 5 feet 2 inches, by 4 feet 10 inches, and is capable of being extended to 14 feet: it

(Fig. 33.)

stands on six turned legs, for which two pillars with claws or blocks might be easily substituted. In this, as in the preceding example, the outer slides are shortened, on account of the ends being rounded; consequently both designs are better suited for tables of small size than those having square ends, wherein all the slides may be of equal length. The figure presents the under side of the table, showing the position and attachment of the legs and slides, the form of the rim, and projection of the table top, drawn to a scale of ¼ of an inch to the foot. The two outside and the two inside slides, A A and B B, are fixed by screws, which pass through them into the top; they are also dovetailed into the rim; the outer pair is so at both extremities, and cut in the middle at the opening joint of the top, where transverse bars C C are dovetailed into the adjoining ends of the slide and rim; this supports the rim, and strengthens the parts so connected against the traction of the *screw expander*. Between the fixed slides five other pairs D D′ E E′ F are made to act; two of these D D′ move in connection with the outer fixed pair, and two, E E′, with the inner; the middle slide F is, relatively to these, stationary, and maintains the connection between them. The several pairs of moveable slides have a stretching rail dovetailed into their inner ends; these rails, as shown in the cut, come together when the slides are pushed entirely

(*Fig. 34.*)

in; they are bored in the centre, so as to allow the screw to pass freely through them. A bar G is screwed to the under edges of the middle pair of slides F, into which the two centre legs are morticed; the other legs are let into the rim by regulated dovetails, and screwed from the inside, as shown in plan, (*Fig. 34.*) The mutual attachment of the slides is shown in (*Fig. 35*); those marked D and D′ are T grooved, as when drawn out they are not so well supported at their extremities as the others, which are feathered and grooved only. The slides are conveniently moved by an apparatus

(*Fig. 35.*)

(*Fig. 36.*)

(Fig. 37.)

(*Fig. 38.*)

(*Fig. 39.*)

called a *screw expander*, examples of which are shown in (*Figs.* 36 and 37); these severally, are suitable for tables which extend 12 and 15 feet. This arrangement consists, essentially, of a screw and tube-nut, which are fixed centrally within the ends of the table frame, and parallel to the slides, so as to make the line of traction in the screw to be exactly at right angles to the joints of the top. The tube is fixed in position, but is free to revolve by the action of a crank handle. The screw is supported lengthwise on the top of the table pillar, or on bars crossing the table, and, in either way, secured to its place by holdfasts, which brace it down. To suit large tables, one or more additional screwed tubes are introduced; these act alternately, as nut and screw, penetrating each other like the parts of a common telescope.

Large-Sized Telescope Dining Tables.

The plan of a telescope table with square ends is shown in (*Fig.* 38), drawn to a scale of ½-inch to the

foot. The slide action of this table, when extended, is shown in (*Fig.* 39), on a scale of ¼-inch to the foot, and a cross section of the slides in (*Fig.* 40), on a scale of 1½-inch to the foot. With an equal number of slides, square-ended tables are capable of greater extension than when the ends are rounded as the curves encroach upon the length of the slides. This table is supported on four legs, A A A A, which are framed in with the ends of the rim; the sides of the rim B B form the two outside fixed slides, and are at one end morticed into the legs; at the other they abut against the legs opposite, and are free to pass out or in as the table is being extended or contracted. The two inside fixed slides, C C, are dovetailed into the end rail. Two cross bars G G are dovetailed into and screwed to the centre pair of slides F F; to these last the *screw expander* is attached, and greater breadth is given to F F (*Fig.* 40), to admit of the cross bars being partially sunk into their edges. When the slides are drawn out,

(*Fig.* 40.)

they are apt to droop in the centre of their united length; to counteract this tendency they should each be wrought slightly convex on the upper edge about ⅛-inch. The sum of this convexity is considerable on the whole length; and by thus giving an arched form to the slides, they are maintained at their proper level.

TELESCOPE TABLES.—PLATE XIX.

Fig. 1 is a design for a telescope table, in the Gothic style. The stand is so made that, on extending the table, the columns, which appear an integral part of it, are drawn away in connection with the ends, leaving the middle portion alone as the central support. The transverse block, to the ends of which the columns are adjusted, is formed of three pieces framed together; one of these is the entire length between the columns, the two others are half lengths, and morticed into opposite sides of the first, in the same line, and at right angles to each other. All the corners of the block are plain stop-chamfered. From the extremities of the block spring four curvilinear buttresses, the upper ends of which abut against, and are dowelled to the top of a small octagonal pillar, which is introduced between them rather to form a point of attachment than as a means of support—a separate support being unnecessary. The buttresses and pillar are fixed to the table by a cross bar of hardwood, which is first dowelled down on their ends, and afterwards screwed below to the middle pair of slides, and to the rim of the table. The buttresses below must be wrought flush and square up with the ends of the base block, so that when the columns are withdrawn, the parts may present a finished appearance, as in (*Fig.* 41), a tudor rose, or other flush ornament, being carved on the extremities of the block to relieve the plainness.

Each column is in one piece throughout its length, and is clamped at the lower end to form the moulded base, the profile of which is afterwards

(*Fig.* 41.)

formed at once on all the columns placed together: they are left square at the upper end, where the mouldings forming the capitals are mitred round them. Before paning the shafts of the columns, the corners are chipped in the lathe, and the beads at both ends are at the same time formed. The vandyking, which overlaps like tiles on a roof, is drawn on the panes, and cut; each lap, as shown Fig. 2, is formed by bevelling the part below it upwards and inwards. The elongated drops at the bottom of the rounded laps, formed on the alternate panes, are planted on; they are turned from a cylinder of wood, temporarily glued together in halves, and afterwards split asunder. At their lower end the pillars present the appearance of being strongly united with the base block, by the ends of the latter passing through and projecting beyond them. This expression is given to these parts by pieces dowelled endwise on the front of the pillars, which continue the direction of the lines of dimension in the arms of the base block: before they are finally fixed, the pieces are ogeed on the ends, and separately carved. This illusion is rendered more perfect by the apparent insertion of wedges, with ornamental ends, at each side, into the neck of the projecting parts. Fig. 3 shows the moulding on the top, the square block below it is formed by clamping. On extending the table, the rim parts in three, opposite the lines of junction of the tops—the middle piece of the top being fixed and stationary. The rim is shown enlarged in Fig. 4, and has the fore angle of its lower edge stop-chamfered and wrought into a double ogee, and at the ends a leaf sunk carved. The cross rails, which form the ends of the rim, are finished below like the sides; they are morticed between the latter, leaving the carved ends of the sides to project beyond them. As the Gothic style is rather stern and angular, depending much for its effect on bold light and shadow, oak, walnut, and our home-grown furniture woods in general, are better suited to it than mahogany, or most foreign woods, whose brilliant colour and high polish are better shown in smooth curved surfaces.

As a general rule in carving Gothic leaf ornaments, the carver should procure leaves of the tree he intends to adopt, and observing not the form of any single leaf, which may be defective, but the general form common to all, carefully follow it, exaggerating the size and relief of the large ribs and projections, and suppressing the smaller and less marked features. The sycamore or plane-tree leaf, with its pendulous fruit introduced between the interstices, is that which has been selected for this design.

Fig. 5 is a table on the same plan as the foregoing, and is shown extended. The ornamental work is a modification of the Italian style, and is carved out of the solid wood. The pillar of the stand is the chief central support, and is larger in proportion to the others than those of Fig. 1. At the bottom, it is let into and shouldered on the large ring-moulding, as marked by the dotted lines, (*a, a, Fig.* 42). This construction is necessary to strengthen the projecting lip of the hollow and bead below. The body of the pillar passes

(Fig. 42.)

through the ring, in the line *b*, and is morticed into the circular block, *d*, on which the ring rests. Four flat stretchers are fitted and dowelled, *e, e*, to the edge of the circular block, and wrought flush with it above and below, before it is finally fixed to the pillar. The wood forming the stretchers must be sufficiently thick to allow for the relief carving on their upper side, and for the greatest diameter of the turned ends which join with the scrolled supports. A projecting moulding is formed on each end of the turned part of the stretchers, that on the extremities of the latter forms the shoulder against which the scroll joins. At their upper end, the scrolled supports are fitted and screwed into the angles of a four-sided cap, which is turned, paned, and fitted on the pillar.

When the table is closed, the bottom curve of the scrolled supports is made to abut against the hollow of the base of the columns, as in (*Fig.* 43). The stand rests on eight castors, four of which are fixed in the extremities of the scrolled supports, which, in consequence, spread suddenly out, as in (*Fig.* 44); and four are screwed to blocks, fixed under the stretchers at the line of their greatest breadth. The columns are turned, leaving sufficient wood for the carving, which, both on these and on the centre scrolls, should be in moderate relief, and carefully rounded, so as to present no hard outlines, and with scarcely any undercutting, as that would prevent the foliage from forming one harmonious mass with the curves, on which it is wrought. The upper moulding of the top is wrought on the boards; the others are

(Fig. 43.)

Fig. 44.)

formed on the rim, and extend the entire length of the table, the loose tops having portions of the rim continued on them.

TELESCOPE DINING TABLES—PLATE XX.

Fig. 1 is a side elevation, and Fig. 2 an end elevation, of a telescope table in the Italian style, enriched by natural foliage. A sketch plan, corresponding with Fig. 1, and showing the position and arrangement of the supports, is given in Fig. 3. The scroll supports are each of an entire piece, and require wood 5 or 6 inches thick; but for economical working, a piece to form the small scroll at bottom, with its appendage, may be dowelled on. The lower ends of the supports rest in capsules, turned and carved separately, and screwed on with the castors sunk into them. The centre part of the rail is stuffed, to serve as a foot-cushion, the ground of it being a box without bottom, the sides of which are of deal, 1 inch thick, and the ends formed of stout blocks, fixed by dowels passing through the sides. This construction admits of the rail being either spring or cushion stuffed. A small moulding which borders the stuffing is carried round the box. From the inside of the end of the box, screws are sent through into the dependent scroll of the supports, by which the latter are strongly braced to their places. Additional strength may be given to these dependent scrolls, and to their attachment to the stuffed rail, by connecting these parts by a strap of iron beneath. The scrolled supports are slightly tapered upwards, and their upper ends are dowelled to a rail, which is screwed to the under edge of the table frame. The leafage in front is carved, and lies on a double ogeed moulding; and the back is gently rounded to the band—see section, (*Fig.* 45). The centre pillar may be introduced or not, according to the length of the table. The large ring-moulding on the pillar is turned and fitted on; and the lower extremity of the pillar is paned square as a shoulder for the claws, which are dowelled on it.

(Fig. 45.)

Fig. 4 is a side elevation, and Fig. 5 an end elevation, of a table in the Gothic style. The legs are wrought in with the table-frame, and should not be of less than 3-inch stuff. Their edges are chamfered, either with a double ogee or plainer chamfer, according to the degree of richness required. In the centre of the rail, the chamfer is carried up, and a leaf is carved in the hollow. The end rail is carried through the top of the legs, and projects sufficiently to receive the cap of a columet, which descends the leg and pins the end of the stretcher, the drop below appearing as the end of the column. The stretcher is a solid piece, the centre being sunk down to receive an inch or so of the stuffing.

SIDE TABLES.—PLATE XXI.

Fig. 1 has the top framed of deal with a large veneered moulding carried round the front and ends; the brakes are formed on blocks planted on the ground; the scrolled ornaments are first fitted to ground and profiled, then indented into the front, and afterwards separately carved, finished, and fixed in. The shaped pillars are made of wood 2 inches thick; a band or border, $\frac{5}{8}$-in. broad and $\frac{3}{8}$-in. thick, is planted on both sides of each pillar. This border is projected beyond the flush of the pillars edgewise $\frac{5}{16}$-in., so as to present a border on both edges, the space inclosed by the borders on all sides, may be fretted or inlaid. The pillars are framed together side to side by three cross rails, the two lower bear the shelves, and the upper rail is dovetailed into the heads of the pillars, and screwed to cross bars fixed in the under side of the frame. The middle cross rail is morticed in; two fillets are shown on its edge, the upper one being formed by the projecting end of the shelf which rests on the rail. The front of the shelf is similarly finished by clamping below. The lower cross rail is dowelled in, and is moulded, with a check formed below, into which the shelf is screwed.

Fig. 2. The top frame is similar to Fig. 1; the moulding on it must be solid if the frets are wrought in relief, and if they are planted, the wood forming them must be glued up of three thicknesses, and cauled to the profile of the ground previous to being cut; or, better than either, the figure of the ornament may be formed by inlaying. The shaped supports may be made of two pieces, each forming one of the arched feet and pillars; the former being of solid wood 1½-inches thick, laid horizontally, the latter of fir wood of the same thickness, slipped on the edges and morticed into the feet; both are afterwards flushed off and veneered on the sides. Or otherwise the supports may be made entirely solid, and the feet dowelled to the side of the upright, in this case the scroll brackets above are wrought out of the solid. In either method, the trusses below are separately wrought and planted on. A groove is wrought on the inside of the supports to receive the ends of the arched fret; the shelf below is dowelled in between the ends. Two cross rails are dovetailed within the top frame from back to front, between which the pillars are tenoned and screwed.

Figs. 3 and 4 are similarly made. The legs are shaped out of square blocks, and wrought flush with the rails of the top frame; the large moulding is

then carried round the front and ends of the frame. The cabled panels and small trusses on the squares of the legs, Fig. 3, are planted on. The spandrels on both figures are fixed to the legs and rails by screws.

RISING SIDE TABLES.—PLATE XXII.

These tables present the convenience of varying the number of shelves, by means of a telescope slide action formed in the supporting pillars. The first three examples have four shelves when drawn out, which number may with facility be reduced to three or two. Each of the supporting pillars consists of three distinct parts, and the shelves are attached to the corresponding divisions in these pillars. The lowest and middle portions are chambered, and receive within them the parts they support, so that when the table is depressed to its least height, the two upper portions of the pillar disappear, the highest part passing into that below it, and both together into-the lowest part. The two upper shelves A B, (*Fig.* 46), move with the slides E F, the two lower C D, are permanently fixed; the lowest shelf is wrought into a groove and dowelled between the pillars; all the other shelves are dowelled on the ends of their supports. Openings are cut through the shelves B C, to allow the slides to pass. The slides must be fitted accurately, and made to move freely within the receiving chambers; their motion is regulated, so as to assist their easy ascent, and prevent their too rapid descent, by counterpoising weights of lead $g\ g\ g\ g$, cast to a convenient shape; of these there are four to each pair of slides, the sum of whose weight is equal to that of the shelf and slides together. The weights are attached to the edge of the slides, and are shaped to suit the space within which they are to act. To obtain the proper weight for each counterpoise, weigh each shelf and its two slides together, and take a quarter of this amount for the weight of a single counterpoise, there being four of them.

(*Fig.* 46.)

The weights are suspended by cords attached to the bottom of the slide, and are carried over pulleys $h\ h$, fixed in the upper end of the chamber in which the slide acts. The pulleys are of brass ½-inch diameter. Besides facility of motion, the slides must be kept from passing out, and also maintained at their proper height; the former is effected by glueing thin blocks of wood to the edge of the slides within the chamber; the latter, by springs formed of wood or steel, *i, i*, sunk in the slide behind, which, when the slide passes down is depressed, and when drawn up, starts out and rests on the top of the shelf.

Figs. 4 and 5 are a convenient combination of the dining table leaf-holder, with the rising side table. The leaf-holders here designed are cases consisting of two panelled frames, forming the front and back, bound together by a top and bottom of deal dovetailed into their edges. The front frame of Fig. 4 is wrought flush, with a raised panel planted on; the corresponding part of Fig. 5 is sunk panelled, with a moulding carried round the frame. The receiving or chambered slides of the side table are dowelled on the edge of the front, and wrought off with it. Fillets, cloth covered, are screwed on the top and bottom of the case, leaving intervals between them into which the loose table tops are slid; in Fig. 5 these interspaces are divided the whole height, by dovetailing pieces edgeways into the top and bottom. This method has the convenience of suiting any difference of breadth in the leaves. The leaf-holder is rendered more accessible by having a door at each end. The bracket and moulded pilaster on Fig. 4 are wrought together, and the lying trusses are both joined to the pilasters. The corresponding parts of Fig. 5 are wrought out of one piece. The movable shelf, in both examples, has a moulding planted on its fore edge and ends, which is of a breadth to lap down and receive the top of the leaf-holder within it, when the shelf is depressed. In Fig. 4 this is done completely; but, in Fig. 5, the upper member only of the top moulding is concealed.

DINING-ROOM CHAIRS.—PLATE XXIII.

All the designs here given have their seats fixed. Figs. 1 to 4 inclusive, have the back legs framed up parallel to each other; these, along with Fig. 8, are straight across the back; the others in the plate, as ordinarily, have the back hollowed, with the back legs diverging at their upper end.

In Fig. 1 the semicircular top is dowelled down on the legs and scroll rounded from before backwards. The panels are formed by grounding, and are rounded on the face, their field being sunk carved. The cushion behind is separately stuffed on a frame which is made to fit within the back; it is let in from behind, and fixed by screws passing through the frame into the legs. The back of the frame is then covered and gimped round the edges. The shaft of the front leg is parted by grooves, ¼-inch broad, terminating in a bore at both ends. The moulding on the seat frame is cross wrought on the squares of the legs.

In Fig. 2, the back legs at the seat rail are 2½-inches broad. The top, which is dowelled down on them, forms the greatest breadth of the back. In framing these parts together, the proper position and exact depth of the dowel holes must be carefully attended to, so as to prevent their appearance when the looped openings on the sides are cut out. The front legs are shaped so as to spread out below, in front and on the sides; they are framed in, flush with the seat rails, the latter being clamped on their lower half, and with the legs form a ground for planting the moulding on the seat frame.

Fig. 3 has the stay in the centre of the back tenoned into the seat rail; the top is dowelled down on it, and on the legs, and afterwards cut out to figure. A small hollow moulding is carried round all the inner front margins of the chair back. The seat frame and front legs are wrought similarly to Fig. 2.

Fig. 4 has the back executed similarly to Fig. 1. The front legs are framed in with the seat rails, and the moulding on both is sunk carved or inlaid, and planted on.

Fig. 5 is framed up in the usual manner of vase-backed chairs. The seat rails are 3½-inches broad; of this breadth 2½-inches are of hardwood, slipped on the lower edge, with 1¼-inches of solid wood, to show as such on forming the sweeps below the seat. On their lower half the rails are cross-clamped on the face with ⅜-inch solid wood, thus making the grain of the rails to run with that of the front and back legs, and affording depth of wood for grounding the triangular spaces on the adjoining parts of both; and also for forming in relief the leaf ornament on the centre of the front rail. A small hollow moulding may be formed on the inside corners of the legs, and continued around the under edge of the seat rails on the sides and front.

Fig. 6, the back is framed up similarly to Fig. 5. Its projecting sides, formed by pieces dowelled on the legs, are curved forward so as to sweep with the stay and top rails: the latter is dowelled on the legs after the side pieces are put on. A raised bead or fillet is carried round the inner margin of the back. The seat frame is made separately from the fore legs; the latter are checked and shouldered in front, under the edge of the frame, and pass up within it behind, and are there glued and screwed.

Fig. 7 is in all respects wrought like Fig. 5. The top is dowelled to the legs at the point of their greatest width, so as to give sufficient strength to the frame. The stay, from its deep curvature, requires to be fitted and framed up without resistance or strain, as it would otherwise be easily fractured.

Fig. 8 has the back wrought separately of a single piece, similar to a hall chair. The interior of the back is grounded down around the margin of the cushion, which is highly stuffed on the solid wood. The seat rails require to be 3½-inches broad, for sweeping out below. They *(Fig. 47.)* are cross clamped with ⅜-inch wood on the under half, similar to Figs. 5 and 7. The bead on the front rail is wrought on the solid. The manner in which the front leg must be framed in is shown in *(Fig. 47)*.

DINING-ROOM CHAIRS.—PLATE XXIV.

The designs in this Plate are, in their outline and general construction, similar to vase-backed chairs; and, excepting Fig. 3, are all loose seated.

Fig. 1.—A projecting moulding, carried round the seat frame, is planted on the rails, and cross wrought on the squares of

d *

the legs, which, before being framed up, are pieced out by ⅜-inch clamps on the front and sides, to form the projection.

Fig. 2 has the panel in the back made of solid wood ⅝-inch thick, with a raised border in front ⅜-inch deep, planted around its sides and bottom; the top portion of the band, along with the carving, requires 1-inch wood. The panel is let in from behind, and made to join with the apparent stay, the ends of which are formed on the legs; it is fixed by screws or dowels passing through the apparent stay, and through the seat and top rails. The back cushion is stuffed on a loose panel ½-inch thick, previously fitted within the band on the ground panel, and fixed by screws sent through the latter from behind.

Fig. 3.—In this example the top rail is not cut through but grounded at the ends, where the marginal moulding inside is carved and scrolled. The back stay is shown as in advance of the legs, its scrolled ends being carved on them, and its middle portion shouldered between; or otherwise, the stay may be of one piece, separately carved, and grounded on the legs, and on another stay framed between them. The seat rails are shaped out, and clamps ½-inch thick, of a corresponding form, are planted on them. The truss legs are carved after being morticed and adjusted to the seat rails.

Fig. 4 has the frame of the back cushion let in from behind, and fitted between the seat and top rails, to which and to the legs it is screwed from behind.

Fig. 5 has the back panel fitted, finished, fixed, and stuffed, similarly to Fig. 2. The carved ornament on the front rail is profiled, then indented; separately carved, and lastly glued down.

Fig. 6.—The top rail joins down on the legs at the greatest breadth of the back, forming with them the carved shoulders of the side scrolls. The looped openings are afterwards cut out, and the border of the cushion is formed in relief on the legs. The triangular space between the seat, scroll, and band below, is not perforated. Fillets are screwed on the inside of the legs to carry the stuffing. The back is cloth covered.

Fig. 7 has the back stay framed in, leaving a space between it and the seat rail for the stuffing of the seat to pass. The frame for the back cushion (*Fig.* 48), is fitted between the legs; at the top it is shaped so as to support the general outline of the stuffing, and is fixed by dowels *a, a,* to the scrolled ends of the legs, below; it is dowelled to the stay at *b,* and on the sides screwed to the legs at *c, c, c, c.*

(*Fig.* 48.)

The truss legs are dowelled to the corner of the seat frame.

Fig. 8, in the back, is made similarly to fig. 7. The cushion frame extends down to, and is dowelled on, the back rail of the seat. The seat moulding is wrought similar to that of fig. 1.

CHAIRS.—PLATE XXV.

The designs on this Plate are well suited for either the dining-room or the library. The contour of the first three examples approaches that of the hall chair, to which, with minor modifications, they might be easily adapted. Fig. 4, besides its fitness for the dining-room, presents the chief elements of the devotional chair. They are all loose seated.

Figs. 1, 2, and 4, have the back cushion stuffed on a panel ½-inch thick, previously fitted within a raised border, ⅜-inch deep, formed on a ground panel, which last, in Figs. 1 and 2, is framed in between the pillars. The corresponding part of Fig. 4 is dowelled from under the seat rail, and from above fixed by screws passing through the semicircle. The loose panels are fixed to the others by screws passing through from behind.

Fig. 1.—The semicircular top is turned and chamfered on the outer and inner edges; a moulding is mitred round its ends, where it joins down on the columns. When the semicircle is in its place and before it is fixed, the pieces forming the frets are accurately fitted in, then lined out and fretted. The frets are finished and fixed on before the semicircle is finally dowelled on the pillars. A screw passing through the top of the semicircle, connects the cushion frame with it.

Fig. 2.—The semicircle is turned and planted on the face of the ground panel of the back. The back legs may be made the entire length, or the part surmounting the capitals of the columns may be dowelled on.

Fig. 3 has the back rail of the seat pieced with solid wood, and made of sufficient breadth to admit of its upper edge being wrought in with the band, around the inside of the back legs. The back cushion is stuffed on a frame previously fitted in; it is fixed by screws. The truss legs are dowelled to blocks fitted within the corners of the seat frame.

Fig. 4.—The capitals of the spiral columns are separately turned and carved; they are fixed by pins, turned on the ends of the spiral columns, which pass through them into the semicircle. The front feet at the top are projected so as to recess the seat rails 1/16-inch.

EASY CHAIRS.—PLATE XXVI.

Easy chairs, as their name imports, are especially adapted to those sedentary and reclining attitudes of person which are most favourable to repose or relaxation. They are usually large, low-seated, and spring-stuffed, with a sloping back. In executing Figs. 1 to 4 inclusive, thin profile moulds of the front and back legs and haunch rails are at first made, and according to these, the wood for the chair is lined out full, on the board. When sawn out and faced up, the wood is again more accurately lined, and the framing-shoulders, with the position and length of all the mortices, previously marked on the moulds, are set off on it. A little over wood is left on the profile of the legs, above and below the several side mortices, which is wrought off after the sides are framed together. When the legs are shaped out, they should be carefully adjusted, parallel to each other, across the haunch mortices. This is necessary to preserve the seat frame parallel, and, besides, from the great length of the back legs, a slight inaccuracy at the seat rails becomes, when the chair is framed up, increased, and quite apparent at the top of the back.

Fig. 1.—The frets are dowelled down on the haunch rails, and are fixed above, by screws passing through the elbow rails, after the latter have been framed into the back legs. The seat cushion may be either fixed or loose; if the former, fillets must be screwed to the inside of the haunch rails to carry the stuffing; for a similar purpose, fillets are fitted between the cross rails of the back; they are screwed along the side of the back legs, following their general outline, but narrower, so as to form a uniform check for the stuffing; if the seat cushion be loose, a separate frame resting on the back and front rails of the seats, as in ordinary cases, is required to support the stuffing.

Fig. 2.—The front legs and elbow stumps are of one piece, and, so also, the back legs; the latter, however, may be formed of two pieces, butt-joined in the line of the seat, and dowelled together. The elbow rails are framed in with the sides of the chair. A panel, cloth covered, is let into the space between the seat and elbow rails; it is supported behind by fillets, screwed on the rails, forming a check for its sides. The circular ends of the panel lap on the elbow stumps and back leg, which are grounded down. A moulding, which laps on the panel, is planted around the space between the rails. The fret, after being completely finished, is screwed on the face of the panel.

Fig. 3.—The scrolled elbow stumps are dowelled down on the seat rail; on the top of these the elbow rails, on being framed into the back legs, are screwed down. The space between the side rails is filled by a cloth-covered panel, around which, and lapping on it, a moulding, planted on the rails, is carried.

Fig. 4.—In tapering the front feet, downwards, the scrolls on both sides of the toe, are wrought in relief below, and on the turn at the hinder part of the leg, upwards, terminating in a leaf ornament under the seat rail; the extremity of the leaf is formed by piecing it out below the rail. The elbow rail is formed of two thicknesses, the lower of which is solid and made to project, forming with that above it, a check for the stuffing; the projection is rounded into a bead, which, at the inner end, joins in, with a similar moulding planted round the opening between the seat and elbow rails.

Fig. 5 is circular in the back, with the fore feet set obliquely to the front. The general method of construction is shown in (*Fig.* 49.) The front rail is fitted and clamped with solid wood, on a hardwood ground; it shoulders with the feet in the lines *a, a*. The back feet *b, b*, are framed up between the ends of the circular seat rails, being dowelled in. Two hardwood standards, *c, c,* forming a part of the back frame, are strongly tenoned into the back feet, before the latter are framed up. The standards are made to incline back at the top, an amount depending on the profile form given to the back. A hollowed cross rail, *d*, is dowelled down on the standards; on this the top rail of the chair is glued down. The moulded band, which borders the stuffing, extending from the leafage on the top to the front feet, is formed of three pieces; the part forming the elbow stump, joins down on the foot, at the line *e*, and unites with that on the elbow rail, at the joint *f*; this part, in the order of work, is first dowelled on; it is clamped behind with deal, and receives into it below, at the back, the stuffing rail *g*; and above, the elbow rail is checked into it and into the standard *c*; on this rail the part *f, i*, is clamped, and at the line *i* it unites with the ascending side piece *i, k*, which last is clamped with deal and dowelled to the standard *c*, and receives down on it the ornamental top rail. The top rail and the band, down to the line, *f*, require 2½-in.

(*Fig.* 49.)

solid wood; the elbow stumps, from *f* to *e*, require 3-in. wood. All the carving is executed after the chair is framed together.

Fig. 6.—The front is framed up, and all the parts of it are carved at the same time. The elbow, scroll, and leg are of one piece, requiring 3¼-in. wood. Standards are inserted into the hind feet, to form the back framing, as in Fig. 5; on the sides and top of these the pieces forming the carving are dowelled.

TABLE AND CHAIR LEGS.—PLATE XXVII.

In this Plate are shown, Figs. 1 to 5, designs of turned and truss legs for hall and other tables, with the depth of framing and form of top and rail moulding proper to each; and Figs. 7 to 12, designs of chair legs, the larger and more massive suitable for oak or mahogany; the smaller and lighter, for rosewood or satinwood.

Fig. 1 has the ball of the leg formed of a separate piece, which is indented, turned, and then paned; the small panels on the panes may be formed in relief, or they may be face moulded in one piece together, then profiled separately and indented. The buttons on the band on the top of the shaft are let in with a bore, and the dart shaped ornaments below are indented.

Fig. 2 has the profile of the carving on the ball, formed in the lathe. The shield on the square of the leg, and the panels on its lower extremity are planted on.

Fig. 3 has the ball of the leg square wrought. The leg is first wrought out in the lathe immediately above the ball, and below it, from the drop downwards, leaving a square block from which the ball with its appended decorations is profiled.

Fig. 4 requires not less than 3½ in. wood. On being profiled, it should be adjusted and fitted to the frame before being carved; it is attached to the frame in the ordinary manner.

Fig. 5 has a check cut out of the top of the truss, on the bottom of which the table frame rests; this part extends backwards, and is carved and wrought in with a moulding under the rail. The frame abuts against the side of the check, which part is wrought into the carved foliage, that curves out under the top moulding. The ear-shaped opening on the side is not perforated, but grounded down.

Fig. 6, from its form and plainness, is suitable for satinwood (which, from its light colour, does not shade well in small mouldings, or surface carving), but may also be made of mahogany, if the diameter measures of the design are enlarged.

Figs. 7, 9, 11, and 12, are best adapted for oak, but the first three may also be made of mahogany. Fig. 12 is for a hall chair, and is alternately square wrought, and turned along its length, from the bead under the rail to the top of the shaft; the leg is turned, and the ball paned. The shaft, with the drapery on it, is profiled square, and the latter afterwards carved on the face; the drops below are indented. Fig. 8 and 10 are for drawing-room chairs, and should be of rosewood, walnut, or satinwood.

SOFAS.—PLATE XXVIII.

All the figures here have the seats square framed, with the hind feet turned, and the backs separately wrought and screwed on. Figs. 2 and 3 have the hind feet shaped and framed in, with the rounded corners. The backs are fixed, being wrought on the frame.

Fig. 1.—The elbow stumps are dowelled down on the feet, with an incline back of 4 inches at the top; below they are square with the feet, and recede ⅛-in. from the flush, on the front and sides; towards the top they gradually wind outwards to give the top scroll an overlay at the ends of the sofa. The stumps require solid wood, 3½-in. thick, and are clamped behind with deal. Two pieces of hardwood, 1¾-in. thick, a, (Fig. 50), corresponding in facial outline, and breadth, with the stumps, are dowelled on the back feet, with an incline backwards of 2½ inches at the top. The back, on being screwed to these pieces, receives a corresponding slope with them. Three cross bars, b, c, d, are fitted between the front and back stumps; the upper bar, b, is checked in, and nailed down on the stumps, forming the elbow; the others are let into grooves; the lowest bar, d, is kept 1½-in. above the seat rail; to this the cloth in stuffing the end of the sofa is nailed. The frame for the back is made of deal 1 in. thick, and consists of two long rails e, f, and four cross ones, of

(Fig. 50.)

which g, h, are two. The end bar, g, is made flush with the outer edge of the stumps a, to which it is screwed. The moulding on the back is planted on the face, and the upper edge of the back is veneered. The hind feet are made to stand out beyond the back rail ¾-in.; on this projection the back is made to rest.

Fig. 2.—The ends of the frame towards the back are carved of a parabolic form, which in outline sweeps with the position given to the elbow scrolls. The mould for working the ends may be easily traced by the hand, but if greater accuracy is required, a parabola may be drawn, by the method of ordinates, whose diameter and altitude are severally 24 and 18 inches, the vertical half of which curve is the form given to the ends of the sofa (see Practical Geometry, page 51). The elbow scrolls are dowelled down on the feet with an incline backwards of 5 inches at the top. They have a face breadth of 3½-inches, with a depth of 14 inches. The hind legs a (Fig. 51), are dowelled between the adjoining ends of the back and end rails b, c. A standard d, which forms a part of the back frame, is strongly tenoned into each leg, having an incline backwards of 2½-inches at the top. The top rail of the back, e, is morticed down on these standards, and also on two others that are framed into the back rail of the seat. The elbow is built on a curved rail g, the ends of which are checked into the back of the elbow scroll, and standard d. The pieces h, after being butt-joined to the standard, and glued down on the rail g, are fixed at the ends by dowels sent obliquely through them into the standard. The whole is then wrought off, and the joinings are overlaid with pieces of canvas, saturated with glue. Stuffing rails i, i, i, are carried round, parallel to, and 1½-inch

(Fig. 51.)

above, the back and ends of the seat frame; these have their ends inserted into the back of the elbow scroll, into the top of the back leg a, and into the framing of the back f.

Fig. 3 has the ends wrought similarly to Fig. 2. Two upright pieces, terminating the curve of the ends, are morticed between the seat and elbow rails: the latter are dowelled down on the top of the balusters.

Fig. 4 has each of the front feet, with the elbow stumps, of one piece. On the feet being turned, the front half of the parts forming the stumps are sawn down, and cross-cut above the square of the foot; the exposed surfaces are cleaned, and the detached pieces are temporarily glued together, turned, carved, and polished; then split asunder, and planted on the parts from which they were originally cut. In other respects this example is finished similarly to Fig. 1.

SOFAS.—PLATE XXIX.

The upper design is framed in the usual manner. The moulding on the seat rails and back is similar in character, being rounded, (as shown in the section figure), and planted on the face. The elbow stump has an incline back of 2¼-inches at the top; its appearance from above, along with its connections, is shown in a separate figure, on an enlarged scale. The decorations on all these parts are intended to be formed by inlaying, but a somewhat similar effect may be produced by grounding and sunk carving.

The lower figure has the spiral pillar and front foot of one piece. The fore-edge of the end stuffing is attached to a plane pilaster, behind the pillar, and tenoned into, and between the seat and elbow rails, as shown in section. The scrolled cap of the pillar is separately carved and dowelled on.

SOFAS.—PLATE XXX.

In the upper design, the seat being first framed up, the ends are then formed, and the back is afterwards separately made,

(Fig. 52.)

and fixed by screws. The elbow scrolls are 1½-inch thick, and clamped on a hardwood ground; after being carved they are dowelled down on the feet. An ogee presented obliquely to the front, as shown in section A, is formed on the face of the scroll: (Fig. 52) shows the latter in section, where they join down on the feet. The centre ornament of the back, with the moulding on which it rests, is formed of one piece, 2¼-inch thick, which extends to, and mitres with the hollowed sweep of the end portions of the moulding.

(Fig. 53.)

These last are ⅞-in. thick, and planted on the face, or otherwise, as shown in section C, the centre ornament may be dowelled on; the recurved ends of the leafage being separately made, carved, and indented.

The lower design has the framing of the back, and of the seat behind, made as described under Plate XXVIII. A method of framing up the scrolls and front feet is shown in (Fig. 53).

The end rail, *a*, is joined on behind, and dowelled to the front rail *b*. The corner so formed, is cut off in the line *c, d*. The hardwood ground, *e, e*, of the scroll is dowelled down parallel to the line *c, d*, and flush with the centre corners, thus forming, with the depth of the seat rails, a ground on which the elbow scrolls are clamped and dowelled. The scrolls require 3-inch wood, and the moulding on them is shown in section G. The bottom of the elbow scroll is wrought off flush with the under edge of the seat rails, and the feet are dowelled to them; the position of the feet is indicated by the lines on the wood-cut, and the form and depth of the carving on them in section F. The clamp forming the moulding on the front rail is fitted, glued down, and wrought before the elbow scrolls are fixed on; it is made in two lengths, which are butt-joined in the middle behind the centre ornament. The elbow scrolls abut on the ends of the rail moulding, and the small scrolls terminating the latter are wrought on the former. The carved ornament on the centre of the front rail is formed of two pieces, joined vertically in the centre, and indented; it is shown in section E.

SOFAS.—PLATE XXXI.

The upper design has the seat frame dovetailed together in the fore corners, and the feet glued and screwed on after: or, otherwise, the front rail may be framed in between the extremities of the end rails, and the latter then tenoned into the front feet. The hind feet are framed up with the seat rails. The elbow scrolls, and the ends of the sofa, are wrought like those of Fig. 1, Plate XXVIII. The flowers which hang from the scrolls are, after being carved, partially indented into their place and dowelled on. The front and end rails are similarly finished, but the latter are not recessed; they are ground, veneered, or clamped, with thin wood, and, when polished, the fret, which is $\frac{6}{16}$-inch thick, is then glued down; the ornamental lentils and dots are afterwards planted on. A projecting square fillet is planted on the upper edge of the rail, and a torus, or other moulding, on the lower. The centre of the back, extending, on both sides, to the curve of the moulding beyond the leafage, is wrought from one piece of solid wood, 3 inches thick; the further portions of the moulding mitre in with the centre, and are planted on the face, and veneered on the top. The ring surrounding the head may be turned and planted on; the ornaments on its edge may be shaped facially, in the lathe, and then profiled. The head is separately carved, and, when finished, is screwed on from behind.

The lower design has the upper end of the front feet checked down to the ground of the carving; they are then framed in flush with the ground of the seat rail. The front and end rails are similarly finished; the enriched round moulding on them is separately wrought of $\frac{1}{8}$-inch solid wood; it extends the whole length and breadth of the frame, and is planted on; the border, on both edges of the round, being mitred and glued down after. The scrolls adjoining the feet, and below the rail, are separately carved and screwed on. The elbow scrolls are made of 1-inch wood, clamped on a ground of hardwood, the flowers suspended by an apparent ring, from the scrolls, are fitted to the latter, and fixed by dowels. The carving on the back is of one entire piece, 3½-inches thick, extending on each side to the mitre angle, at the extremity of the leafage; the further parts are mitred in and planted on. This design may be executed either in mahogany or in rosewood; if, in the latter, the thickness of the material employed may be less than that above indicated, and the recessed and delicate parts of the carving may be hatched in gold, or gilt.

DETAILS OF SOFAS.—PLATE XXXII.

Figs. 1 to 5, have the front of the sofa first formed. The hardwood grounds for the elbow scrolls are checked in flush with the face, and also shouldered on the upper edge, of the end of the seat rail, where they are glued and screwed. The feet, which are solid, are dowelled on the under edge of the rail, and also flush with it in front. These parts serve as a flat and a uniform ground for the clamps of solid wood which form the carving.

In Fig 1, the elbow and foot are clamped with one piece, which unites to the adjoining part on the seat rail previously glued down; from the cant given to the scroll above, and the form of the foot at the bottom, the thickness of wood required is 1¾-inch; that on the rail being ⅞-inch.

Fig. 2 is wrought similarly to Fig. 1, and of wood 1¼-inch thick. In this example the foot need not be clamped, but made of the entire thickness, and projected in the framing, beyond the ground of the adjoining parts, an amount equal to the thickness of the clamps on them. The clamps of the rail and scroll abut together, and join down on the foot.

Fig. 3. The clamp, on the elbow and foot, consists of two pieces; that, on the former, joins to the rail at the lower extremity of the wing; that on the foot has its upper end, on which the leafage is formed, scribed into the clamps on the rail. The trefoil figure in the centre of the foot, from the neck upwards, is a separate piece, which is first profiled and indented into the rail, and the line of depth, for the carving, accurately marked on its edges; it is then detached, carved, and finally fixed in its place. Wood, 4-inch thick, is required for the elbow, and 1½-inch thick for the clamp on the foot.

Fig. 4 is clamped similarly to Figs. 1 and 2, and requires 2-inch wood. The flower festoon, which overlies and hangs from the neck of the scroll, and the eagle's beak, may either be carved on the solid, or procured, in embossed leather or gutta percha, from the manufacturers of these articles.

Fig. 5 is wrought in the same manner as the foregoing, requiring also wood 2 inches thick. The column is half thickness, and is planted on the recessed ground of the scroll, the lower members on it mitre in with the moulding on the front rail.

Fig. 6 has the feet framed in flush with the ground of the rails, and the moulding on the latter is carried round the front and the ends. The scrolls are dowelled down on the rails.

Figs. 7, 8, and 9 are the free ends of rosewood couch backs, the solid wood is feathered, or dowelled end on, to the deal framing of the back, and extends below the bottom line of the carving about 3 inches, so as to present the latter above the seat cushion. The thicknesses of wood required for these severally are 2-inch, 1¾-inch, and 2¼-inches. Corresponding to each of these, and immediately below them, on the Plate, are three examples of couch feet; they are framed up with the seat rails, the mouldings on which are wrought in with the carving on the feet.

Figs. 10 to 14, inclusive, are examples of the fore feet and elbow scrolls of rosewood couches, with the front rails shown in cross section. The foot and scroll in all these, excepting Fig. 11, are together formed of one piece. The projecting leafage, overlieing the rail, or under it, as in Figs 10, 13, and 14, is indented or fitted on, after the parts are framed up. The thickness of wood for these varies from 3½ to 4 inches.

LIBRARY FURNITURE.

The library, the name of which sufficiently indicates its distinctive use, may be described as the gentlemen's drawing-room; for, as the ladies receive their friends in the drawing-room, the gentlemen, in like manner, generally receive those visitors having business with themselves individually, in the library. As a matter of convenience, also, on occasions when the formalities of fashion may with propriety be merged in the free and easy intercourse of friendship, that apartment is not unfrequently converted for the time being into a drawing-room, and still oftener it is used also as a parlour. Consequently, it should be alike free from the heavy stateliness of the dining-room, or the gaudy and formal, because studied, disorder or negligence of the drawing-room; but nevertheless allied somewhat to the one in its sober hues, and to the other in the richness rather than the lightness of its furniture. By this means its protean character will be well maintained; and by keeping the decorative always in subjection to the useful, it will be rendered, what it ought to be, the most comfortable room in the dwelling. Oak is a favourite wood for the furniture of the library, and suits admirably for carrying out the character of the room above indicated; but mahogany, rosewood, &c., may likewise be used, according to taste; that employed in making the book-case determining the general character of all the other pieces of furniture.

It may be observed, however, that in some houses the library forms one of the drawing-room suite of apartments; opening into it, when occasion demands, by folding doors. In such cases the woods employed in making the book-cases and the general decorations of the room, though they ought not to be the same as those of the drawing-room, should, in every respect, harmonize with the furnishings of that apartment. By following such a course, not only is a great scope allowed for the exercise of taste, but a unity of design and feeling is maintained throughout the series of apartments, contributing, in a high degree, to produce that pleasing elegance which ought to be the aim of all concerned in the furnishing and embellishing of a house.

BOOK-CASES.—PLATE XXXIII.

Figs. 1 and 2, are designs of book-cases, similar in plan, but differing in the details of ornament. The body, or carcass of each, is formed in two heights, connected together by a framed surbase, interposed between them, to which they are severally screwed. Each of these main divisions, again, consists of three distinct parts, which are separately made and screwed together. The outside gables, with the exposed parts of the others, are of solid wood; all the rest being of deal. Previous

to framing the carcasses, and after the wood for them is surface wrought, it assists accuracy and expedition in working to set off the full and exact profile of the whole job, with that of the mouldings and other parts, on a slip of deal; and, at the same time, the cross measures over the gables, doors, and pilasters, on a single rod; this serves as a sure reference for measurements, and as a constant check on the accuracy of the work. The doors of the upper centre carcass are hinged to the gables; the left hand door is shut by slip bolts, sunk in the ends and edge of the inner stile, which pass into perforated brass plates sunk into the cornice and surbase. The right hand door locks on the left; the line of junction in Fig. 1 is concealed by an ornamental bead, planted on the right door, which projects ¾-inch, and is checked to lap on the adjoining stile of the left. The doors on the wings lock on the gables of the centre which projects beyond the former 3-inches. All the pilasters, on the upper part, are attached to the doors; the stiles of the latter being made of sufficient breadth as a ground for them. Before being glued to the doors the pilasters are veneered and polished on the face; and the bordered frets, when finished, are planted on them, to conceal the joints; the inner edges are then slipped with veneer. After the pilasters are planted on, they, along with the doors, are flushed and veneered on the outer edges. In Fig. 2, the pilasters are ornamented with small panels and rosettes, the former being veneered with rich wood, and inlaid. The doors are glazed, either with a single plate in each, or as represented in the drawing with several; in which last case, the astragals are mitred into the stile mouldings, and grooved and feathered behind, to form the checks for the glass. With a view to strength, the slips or feathers are glued into the grooves, with their ends inserted into the back of the stile moulding, and also fitted tightly between the stiles. The doors on the under part of both designs are sunk panelled. The panels of Fig. 2 are inlaid, those of Fig. 1 have a raised, sunk carved, or inlaid panel planted on them. A raised border is formed on the body of the pilasters, within which the carving, after being finished, is, in both cases, planted; that of Fig. 1 is fixed by screws passing through the pilaster from behind. The two outside pilasters, on each design, are fixed to the doors; the two inside are fixed to the centre carcass; the ground, for the latter, is formed by the frame, to which the curtain and fringe are attached. This

(Fig. 54).

frame is made of deal, 1-inch thick, and consists of two upright stiles, and one cross rail at top; the stiles are sunk flush into the fore edges of the top and bottom of the carcass, within which the frame, after being shaped out and slipped with veneer on its inner edge, is fitted and blocked behind: the frame is then veneered on the face. The fringe is attached to the inside of the frame, and the curtain is suspended from rings which move on an iron rod, the ends of which are bent, and made to hook into staples or eyes, screwed on the frame within. The enclosed space is designed for depositing maps, globes, specimens, &c. The inside of the book-case is provided with movable shelves, resting on serrated racks or on pins, attached to, or inserted loose, into the gables. Two varieties of the former, along with one of the latter, method of support are shown in (Fig. 54). The first consists of pairs of toothed slips, a, a, 1¼-inch broad by

⅜-inch thick, exactly similar to, and equidistant from, each other, that are glued on along the insides of each pair of gables, and flush with their fore and back edges. Cross bars b, b, of the same thickness, bearing the shelves c, c, are fitted between the slips, and made to rest on the projecting teeth. The slips are prepared from a single piece by a plane for the purpose. The other method is by serrating the gable the entire breadth, by means of the plane referred to, and bevelling the ends of the shelves c, c, to fit; here the wood of the gables should be not less than 1-inch thick, and of Bay mahogany. The same sort of wood is most suitable for the gables when the shelves are supported on pins, as the bores for them are more smooth and resisting. The pin holes should be equidistant, and similar in height on both gables, and to stand out ½-inch, with their exposed ends slightly rounded.

The books in the shelves are arranged in a decreasing scale from below up; the largest books occupying the bottom shelves, and the next less those in succession upwards; the propriety of this arrangement is obvious. From the particulars of the length and breadth of the largest books, along with the required number of ranges, the absolute dimensions of the book-case are deduced; these being conditions which must be fulfilled whatever modifications the views of stability in the structure or elegance in the design may require. The usual dimensions and sorts of books are the following :—

Large folio, 18 × 14 in.	Large 8vo, 10 × 7 in.	Large 18mo, 7 × 5 in.
Small do., 16 × 11½ ,,	Small do., 9 × 6 ,,	Small do., 5½ × 4½ ,,
Large 4to, 14 × 10 ,,	Twelves, 8 × 5 ,,	Large 32mo, 5 × 3½ ,,
Small do., 11½ × 9 ,,	Small do., 7½ × 4½ ,,	Small do., 4½ × 3 ,,

The base, surbase, and cornice, are each, in both examples, framed up the entire length. The base proper is that part which is the ground support in the direct line of descending pressure; from the cornice downwards, solid below solid is the true principle of construction. The ornamental parts are mechanically non-essential, but are superadded for the purposes of beauty and effect.

BOOK-CASES.—PLATE XXXIV.

Fig. 1 has the body or centre of the book-case recessed 3 inches; the doors, on this part, are, in consequence, pivot hinged. In (*Fig.* 55), this method of hinging is shown, as it appears on removing the cornice. A and B are the carcasses of the centre part and wing, which are screwed together; C, C′, are, respectively, the door when shut and open; e, is the pivot, or pin on which it turns, which is tightly driven into the door stile, in the centre of its thickness: it passes through,

(*Fig.* 55).

and is supported by a small brass plate sunk into the wood. The position of the pin is exactly determined by the half thickness of the door stile, and by the length of the side of a right angled isosceles triangle, d, e, f, whose perpendicular height, g, e, is equal to that half thickness. A gauge set to these measures in succession, and run on the end of the stile, from its face and edge, will give, where the lines intersect, the proper point for inserting the pivot. The stile on its outer edge, d, h, is rounded to the radius e, d; it describes the curve, d, h, i, on the door being opened or shut. This curve is wrought out of the adjoining gables of the centre A, and of the wing B, on the edge and side of these severally. It may be

convenient to screw the gables first together, and draw the curve on the parts at once by a mould. The curve may be freely wrought out, but as exactly as is compatible with the smooth action of the door; for by giving too much space in the curve, the door stile in the centre being unsupported, is apt to yield backwards, and expose the joint in front. On the book-case being temporarily screwed together, the base, surbase, and cornice, are centred for the door pivots by means of a veneer mould of the door top applied to the parts. The pins pass through, and are secured to their place, by brass plates sunk into the wood.

The upper doors have their mouldings checked and lapped on the frame: the rounded corners of the moulding are turned, and butt-joined with the other parts. As these doors are glazed, each with a single plate of glass, they must act smoothly; their framing must be perfectly parallel, and made of wood not liable to warp. A bead, screwed on, is carried round within the door frame behind the plates, keeping them in their place; it should first be temporarily screwed on, and a slip of wood, the exact thickness of the plate, made to pass round the frame, gauging the space between the door moulding and the bead, wherever the screws are inserted. On the screws being withdrawn, and the bead removed, the plate is put in, and the bead is then replaced, and finally screwed on. The under doors, on the wings, are flush panelled, and the mouldings on these, and on the centre doors, are planted on the face. Panels, cloth covered, are shown behind the frets. The cornices on the wings are separately made; that on the centre being a detached piece, fixed to its place by screws passing through a block glued on it behind; or otherwise, the several cornices may be framed together, the centre one being tenoned between those on the wings, and the under moulding carried round the whole. The carved ornament requires 2½-inch wood in the centre, and is dowelled on. The circular pediment on the wings are dowelled on; they, along with the vases at their ends, should recede from the front to the line of the cornice frieze; if, in this position, from the projection of the cornice mouldings, the pediments appear too low, they may be raised by blocks, or by increasing their breadth on the under edge. The mouldings which border the pediments are turned, and with the other ornaments in front, are planted on the face.

Fig. 2.—All the pilasters on this design are inlaid with a raised border; those on the wings are attached to the door frames. The centre is without doors; the pilasters on it, after being finished, are dowelled on the edge of the middle divisions; similar half pilasters are fixed on the gables of the upper part; the rounded corner and cross mouldings being planted on after the pilasters are glued down. The exposed shelving in the centre may be draped with cloth. The curtains below, with the rods from which they hang, are treated as those of Fig. 2, Plate XXXIII.

BOOK-CASE.—PLATE XXXV.

In the execution of this design, the body, or carcass work, is similar to that of the foregoing. The middle portion of the book-case is projected beyond the wings 3 inches; the pilasters on it are fixed to the gables; those above are grounded on haffits to which the doors are hinged, and on their outer edge finished flush with the latter, and with the gables. Corresponding haffits are fixed on the adjoining gables of the wings; these, from oversight have been omitted in the drawing. The paneling, and other decorations on the shaft of the pilaster, are $\frac{5}{16}$-inch thick. The under middle doors are hinged to the pilasters, those on the wings, above and below, to the gables. The under doors are sunk panelled: the frets on those in the middle part are ⅜-inch thick; the ornamental panels on the others are ¼-inch thick, and have a border formed on them by bevelling the edges. Sections of the cornice and base mouldings are presented in figs. 56, and 57: the panels, on the frieze of the cornice, are ⅝-inch thick. The vases, on the top, are fixed in the perpendicular line of the frieze; their under part must be of sufficient height

(*Fig.* 56.)

(*Fig.* 57.)

to bring them full into view, as seen from the front. The top ornament is clamped on the face, for the centre scroll work, on a ground ⅞-inch thick.

BOOK-CASES.—PLATES XXXVI. AND XXXVII.

These two Plates, with others in the series about to be referred to, furnish designs whereby a library may be fitted up in a neat and uniform manner, the several portions of its furniture agreeing with each other in their style of design. Plate XXXVI. shows the book-cases for one side of the room, with a design for the chimney-piece, surmounted by an appropriate mirror; the cases for the second side of the room are shown in Plate XXXVII., with a suitable design for the door of the apartment; the cases for the third side of the room would be a simple adaptation of those shown in the drawings to the proper length; in the fourth side of the room the windows would occur, and if a case is desired on the pier between them, it would be merely a repetition of two compartments of one of those shown in the drawings. The table, Plate XL. (*Fig.* 1); the chairs, Plate XLII. (*Figs.* 1, 2, 3), and the window cornices, Plate LXXI. (*Fig.* 1), are well suited to accompany these book-cases in the same apartment, being all designed in a similar taste.

PLATE XXXVI.—Both book-cases here given are formed in two heights, of a single carcass in each. They are divided inside by two upright divisions into three nearly equal compartments. The two outside doors are hinged to the gables, and lock on the middle door, which again is hinged to the division on its right, and is stopped on that on its left, where it is slip bolted into the cornice and surbase: consequently the middle door can be opened only after the others have been opened. Or, otherwise, the middle door may be feathered in the ends, and made to move freely to right and left, in grooves formed in the cornice and surbase: the parts grooved must be clamped with solid wood. A bead, or slender half column, with a capital and base, is planted on each of the outside doors,

(*Fig.* 58.)

and made to lap on that between them. The base and cornice mouldings are shown in section (*Fig.* 58), along with the method of glueing them up. The decorations on the pilasters are ⅜-in. thick, those on the upper doors ¼-in. The vases surmounting the cornice are turned and carved, and the wings are afterwards fixed on them.

The ground of the mirror frame on which the mouldings and other ornamental parts are planted, is two inches thick; it consists of a cross rail at top, tenoned into two upright stiles. The inner edge of the ground all round, is checked for the plate; leaving a fore lap, ⅜-inch thick, to which it is applied. The belt that borders the frame inside may with advantage be gilded; consists of four pieces, two on the sides on which the scrolls are formed, and two across above and below, which are checked into the others. The supporting ties along the sides and top of the belt are half checked into it, and into the fore lap of the frame, the rounded ends being wrought off.

The glass plate below rests on a rail, ⅞-inch thick, which connects the pilasters, being dovetailed into them from the under side. A moulding similar to, and mitreing in with that forming the base of the pilaster, is planted on the edge of the rail, lapping on the plate. This arrangement is not shown in the drawing. The fillet which crosses the plate below might be supported by ties checked into the upper member of the moulding on the bottom rail. The trusses on the ends of the frame below are 1¼-inch thick. A panelled frame, ¾-inch thick, fitted and screwed within the checks, protects the glass plate behind.

PLATE XXXVII.—This book-case has its upper part made in four carcasses; of which the centre or body constitutes two, and the wings one each; and the under in three, the centre being in one piece. Both heights are divided inside into six compartments. The pilasters on both divisions are similarly fixed; those at the ends are attached to, and move with the doors; those in the middle are dowelled on the gables of the centre part; being made flush with them outside. All the end doors are hinged to the gables, the others on the lower part to the fixed pilasters; the upper doors may be similarly hinged if the decorations on their corners are dispensed with, otherwise they must be pivot hinged. The corner ornaments of the latter are ¼-inch thick; the pivots, in consequence, must be inserted that amount, fully, farther in on the end of the door stiles, so as to permit the door to open. A hollow corresponding to this increased radius of the door must be wrought out of the parts which adjoin it.

The figure to the left is the work of the joiner, being a door for the apartment, having its architraves and other decorations designed in keeping with the book-cases.

SECRETAIRE BOOK-CASES.—PLATE XXXVIII.

This piece of furniture is adapted either for a library, a parlour, or a bedroom, according to the use to which it is put. It consists of two heights; that above is suited for containing either a small library, or a particular selection of books. The under portion is filled with drawers; the upper one of which is provided with a hinged front which folds down, forming a writing board; the interior of this drawer is fitted up with small drawers and pigeonholes. The under drawers, according to the room in which the secretaire is placed, may furnish a convenient deposit for maps, philosophical instruments, or mineralogical or botanical specimens; or they may be devoted to general use, as a repository for body-clothes or napery.

Fig. 1 is in the Moorish or Alhambra style. It has the upper part divided inside into two compartments. The doors require 1½-inch wood; they are first framed up with a small hollow wrought on the stiles and bottom rails; the upper corners inside are then bosomed, to form the round. The face of the door frame, from the top down to the spring of the curve below the circle, is next checked down ¼-inch, and this part is then veneered. The triangular corner spaces are further grounded down ¼-inch, and veneered in the bottom with wood darker than that of the door frame, or otherwise, according to taste. The spaces and frets are entirely finished before the latter are glued down. The circle is turned, and made to lap on the door frame; below, it mitres-in with a curved piece, which is butt-joined to, and laps on the stile. The pilasters consist each of a half column, surmounted by a vertical panel, with a raised border; the panels are grounded on the recessed part of the door frame. The middle pilaster is attached to the door on the right, and laps on that on the left. In the under carcass, there are below three true drawers; those above them project 1½-inch, and are only apparent, being *shammed* on the hinged fold, forming the front of the secretaire drawer. The body of the drawer is strongly made, the ends requiring ⅞-inch Bay mahogany; into these the bottom is checked and screwed, and the top and back dove-tailed. The fold acts between the pilasters, being of the same length as the drawers below. The method of hinging it is shown in (*Fig.* 59). The fold *a,*

(*Fig.* 59.)

and the bottom of the secretaire *b,* require to be of the same thickness; at the hinge, they are half-checked into each other, the breadth of the check being equal to the thickness of the wood; by this means the point *c* is kept in the same plane, whether the fold is open or shut. The fold is supported by a strong iron hinge *d,* the two limbs of which *e, f,* are respectively sunk flush into the ends of the fold *a,* and secretaire *g,* and abut against each other in the mitre line *k c.* In addition to the hinges on its ends, the fold is supported towards the middle of its length by two small edge hinges. When the fold is closed, as shown by the dotted lines, it is caught and fixed by a spring-catch *i,* sunk within the ends of the secretaire. The small drawer casing and the pigeon-hole divisions may be fixed in the surrounding parts of the secretaire drawer, or they may be formed in a separate case, and fitted in from behind. The

(*Fig.* 60.)

small drawers and pigeon-holes may be variously arranged; the example given in (*Fig.* 60) is generally approved of. Here the

pigeon-holes are ranged above the drawers, the space in the centre is closed by a small door opened and shut by a secret contrivance, and is fitted up with drawers and pigeon-holes for depositing cash or important documents. The door is hung on pivots inserted into its sides, at about ⅜-inch from the top. The divisions forming the pigeon-holes are barely ⅛-inch thick; those between the drawers are ¼-inch full; both are slipped with solid wood on the edge, and moulded with a bead plane. The upright divisions adjoining the sides of the small door, present the same fore-edge thickness as the others; these require ½-inch wood, checks being formed on them within, by which the door is stopped in locking it. As shown in (*Fig.* 61),

(*Fig.* 61.)

the checks, *a a,* for the door are continued of the same depth across the upper ends of the divisions; grooves *c,* in which the pivots move, are formed in these cross checks. The corners, *b,* formed by the two checks, are rounded off. The door, in consequence, on being pressed inwards at the top, yields back, and tilts out below— affording a hold by which it is raised parallel to the cross checks, and thrust into them.

The decorations on the frieze and pilasters may be carved or inlaid. Figs. A and B show, on an enlarged scale, the details of the ornamental capitals; figs. E E′ the drawer nob in front and profile.

Fig. 2 is in the Elizabethan style, and very similar in construction to the preceding. The doors have raised mouldings; the frets on their upper corners are fitted and fixed to the moulding, and also flush with it inside, so as to apply properly to the glass; the front of the secretaire includes the two upper apparent drawers. Figs. C and D present two designs for the profile of the pilaster brackets; Figs. F F′ show the drawer nobs in front and profile.

Each of these examples may be provided with a secret drawer in the frieze, forming a convenient place for drawings or private papers. The front of the drawer forms the frieze, and may be made to extend over, and finish flush with the gables; in such case, the mouldings immediately under the top are planted on the drawer front, and the sides of the drawer act on the gables. The drawer is locked by means of a catch or spring, formed of an elastic slip of wood, fixed on the under side of the bottom, at right angles to it; the slip at the inner end is obliquely indented into, and screwed on the bottom, leaving the other end free, and standing out; it is so placed, that the drawer, on being pushed in, is locked by the spring starting out and abutting against the inner edge of the fore-edge below. To raise the spring, the secretaire has to be opened, and the spring pressed up from below.

PANELS IN FRET-WORK.—PLATE XXXIX.

Frets, for decorating panels, usually consist of duplicated halves, whose figured parts are symmetrically arranged along a central line or axis; the effect produced being made to depend on the connection, equipoise, and harmonious distribution of similar elegant forms and profiles. Frets should agree in style, and in other general characters, with the piece of furniture in which they are employed— being sober or playful in delineation, bold or slender in details, according as the latter is formal or fanciful, massive or delicate, in its treatment. The proper thickness of frets varies with the character of the wood employed; and should be greater when the wood is soft and brittle, as in mahogany or oak, and less when it is hard and tough, as in rosewood, zebra wood, or satin wood. When a fret is very tender and delicate in its parts, it may, to preserve it from risk of fracture, be planted upon a polished ground prepared to receive it; and, to give greater richness and relief, the ground may advantageously be made of a darker or contrast colour.

Fret-panels are ordinarily wrought of three thicknesses, the middle one being made to cross the grain of the others; in frets of rosewood, stout veneers are considered sufficiently thick, in those of mahogany, the centre thickness is most frequently $\frac{1}{4}$-inch beadwood. In glueing up the pieces, the surfaces should first be well toothed, and the glue employed should be rather thin; the cauls require to be well heated and powerfully screwed down, and left on for about four hours, till the glued surfaces are cooled and consolidated.

Figs. 1 and 2 are in the Moorish or Alhambra style, and are suited only for a piece of furniture designed in the Moorish taste. They may be finished by gilding and painting in positive colours in the manner peculiar to that style; and, in such a case, the other parts of the work in which they are employed should be carried out in a similar manner, that unity of purpose may pervade the whole. They require a tough and hard wood, owing to the delicacy and tenderness of many of the parts.

Figs. 3 and 6 are in the Louis XV. style, and are well suited for rosewood. They require to be made of stoutish wood, owing to the veining of the leaves, which may be done partly by the fret-saw, but chiefly by surface-working.

Figs. 4 and 5 are in the Elizabethan style, and, from their massive character, are well suited for oak or other light-coloured wood. Towards the upper part of Fig. 5 several small horizontal bands are planted on after the fret is cut.

LIBRARY TABLES.—PLATE XL.

Fig. 1. The supporting pedestal in this design requires to be strongly made. It is provided with a door in front; the sides and back are sunk-panelled, and made so as to appear framed; the method of construction is shown partly in Fig. 2 on the plate, but more completely in the annexed cut (*Fig.* 62). The gables of the pedestal are two upright boards of deal, $\frac{7}{8}$-inch thick, into the ends of which a top and bottom are dovetailed; one similar board forms the back. The boards, at the same time, form the fields of the panels, and are, in consequence, veneered in the centre; they are also the ground on which the frames d, d, d, which surround the panels, are planted. The frames are $\frac{5}{8}$-inch thick, have a moulding carried round their inner edge, and are veneered on the face; they are joined to the boards, forming the carcase of the pedestal, before the latter is framed together. The interior of the pedestal may be left a free space for maps or portfolios, or it may be shelved for general purposes. The back may, at first, be temporarily sprigged to the gables, as at g, and then blocked inside, k k; the corners are afterwards planed off in the line h i, making equal angles with the sides and back. Blocks, also, are glued on along the fore-edge of the gables, inside, with which they form the canted corners in front; they require to

be of solid wood, as the door acts between them. On the corners being formed, the pilasters, b, b, b, b, are planted on. The ornamental brackets are screwed on from the inside of the canted corners.

(*Fig.* 62.)

The door is framed, sunk-panelled, and pivot-hinged. The door-stile, m, is bevel-checked on the block k; n, n' present the appearance of the other stile and hinge when the door is shut and open. The projecting decorations of the door-stile determine the position of the pivot on which the door revolves. This point, for practical purposes, cannot be accurately marked on a figure of so small a scale; suffice it to say, that it lies in the line of the block k, parallel to the gable—its exact position being where that line, if produced, intersects the front line of the decoration. The panelled fret is let in from behind, and applied to the door-moulding; the rhombus on its centre is veneered and inlaid.

The tops of library-tables are usually made of deal, being framed and flush-panelled; they are moulded around the edges with solid wood, and bordered on the face with veneer; the interior of the top is leather-covered and embossed. In this case, from the character of the moulding on the top, it may be more convenient, that instead of flush-panelling the frame, it be overlaid at one breadth with deal, $\frac{1}{2}$-inch thick, having the upper member, a, (*Fig.* 63), previously planted around its

(*Fig.* 63.)

edge. Before glueing down the board, the moulding on the frame is planted and wrought. The rim, c, under the top, is separately wrought and fixed by screws. The top is connected with the pedestal by means of a frame which crosses both diagonally; this frame is first screwed to the top, and is so placed as to maintain the latter parallel to the pedestal; the extremities of the frame rest on, and are screwed to, the corner brackets; additional strength may be given to the connection of the parts by screws sent through the top of the pedestal into the frame.

The base is formed of two pieces, crossed at right angles, and half-checked into each other; the angles are bosomed by diagonal pieces dovetailed in. On the ends of the base being rounded, its edge all round is cross-bordered with veneer; the moulding on its top is separately wrought on a clamp $\frac{5}{8}$-inch thick, which may be of solid wood, or of deal, and veneered on the top.

The second design on the Plate, like the ordinary consulting-room table, consists of two pedestals supporting a connecting frieze-frame and top, and having two fronts, with drawers, entering from each. The drawer in the frame over the knee-hole is provided with a writing-board, hinged within its front. The frieze-frame is entire, extending the whole length; the four corners of it are morticed into blocks, 4-inch square, which extend down to, and rest on, the capitals of the rounded pilasters; it projects beyond the body of the pedestal ¾-inch all round.

The method of forming the outer corner of the frieze-frame, with that of the pedestal under it, is shown in (*Fig.* 64). The true lines in the cut represent the frame, the dotted ones the under-lying part of the pedestal. The front and end rails, *a, a'*, are tenoned into the corner block, B; on the latter, a quarter round is formed in front. The gable of the pedestal, *c*, recedes from the fore-edge of the carcass top *d*, 2½ inches; the projecting part of the latter is cut-in an equal amount, from the line of the gable—thus forming a rectangular corner. An upright fore-edge, *f*, is dovetailed into these cornered ends of the top and bottom, into which, and into the opposite gable, the horizontal fore-edges between the drawers are dovetailed. A diagonal piece, *g*, connects the edge of the upright with that of its adjoining gable, forming a ground for planting the rounded pilaster. The block, forming the corner of the frieze-frame, is made to lap down in front of the pilaster-ground; for this purpose the block is cut out behind in the line *i, k, l*. The frame is made to pass down similarly on the pilasters adjoining the knee-hole—the pieces forming the lap being dowelled on its under edge. The inner pilasters are planted on a ground of deal, ⅞-inch thick, which is slipped with solid wood on its inner edge, and is half-checked on the fore-edges, and sunk flush with them, and with the edge of the adjoining gable. The pilasters are returned on the corners of the pedestal; they are sunk-panelled by means of a raised border planted on; the carving in front is separately wrought and glued on. The decorations on the rounded pilasters, and on the frieze-frame, are carved in relief.

All the drawers are recessed with a moulding planted round their fronts. The upper drawer of the pedestal has its front broader than its sides, an amount equal to the depth of the arch on the former. An ornamental key and drawer handle, in keeping with the design, are shown in Figs. 3 and 4; these should be executed in bronze or else bronzed with the veining gilt.

WRITING TABLES.—PLATE XLI.

Figs. 1 and 2 are Davenports—the desk parts of which are made in the ordinary manner—requiring wood ¾-inch thick for the body and hinged fold; the latter may be made of deal, or of Bay mahogany, cross-headed—the solid wood forming the mouldings being planted around its front and ends; it is afterwards veneered below, and bordered above with veneer, and leather-covered. Fig. 1 is either mitre or lap dovetailed, according as it is made of solid wood or veneered. A small drawer, *a*, (*Fig.* 65), for holding pens, ink, &c., is fitted into the right end of the desk towards the back; it is usually about 10 inches long, and hinged to a block, *b*, which moves with the drawer in the space *c*. On the drawer being pulled out, it is stopped by the attached block, and folds in conveniently to hand, along

the end of the desk. The fretted ledges, which are formed of three thicknesses, are dowelled down on the desk-top. In Fig. 1, the base is a flat frame of hardwood, 1¼-inch thick, which is bordered on the edge with veneer, and overlaid by a ⅝-inch clamp of solid wood, having mouldings wrought on its edge all round. The pillars are turned and then carved; they are fixed in position by pins formed on their ends. The general effect of this design may be considerably enhanced by hatching the carving on the pillars in gold, by substituting gilt-tooling for blind-tooling on the leather covering, and by bordering the ornaments of the fretted ledge with a narrow gilt outline.

In Fig. 2 the sides are framed up, and panelled similarly to those of Fig. 1, Plate XL. The pedestal drawers are recessed and moulded around their fronts. The left end of the pedestal is distinguished from the right, by being closed with a single panel having a moulding carried round it, and a small carved ornament planted on its centre. The ends of the desk are panelled by a planted, raised border; the leaf ornament and the panel on which it is planted are both finished before they are glued together. The base is footholed in front like that of Fig. 1, it is lap-dovetailed together, and clamped on the top, its projecting ends form a rest for the supporting scrolls. The scrolls require 3½-inch wood, and are fixed by screws sent through the top of the base and the bottom of the desk. The effect of them may be much heightened by partial gilding.

Fig. 3. In this writing-table the plinth is made of deal, dovetailed together, and veneered; the brakes in front are glued on, and the mouldings mitred round. Cross-rails or corner blocks of hardwood must be sunk into the base below to receive the castors. The outside gables are framed—the inside ones are plain and dovetailed together, with divisions for drawers; the latter are dovetailed into the gables, and the grounds for the columns are half-checked on them, and made flush with their edges. The pilaster-grounds must be lined up of a sufficient breadth to receive the columns in front, and to admit the drawers to pass quite clear. The top should be of Honduras, and veneered, with the mouldings planted round, and made to project sufficiently to rest on the caps of the columns. The columns are flattened a little behind on their greatest projections, so as to apply to the grounds to which they are screwed from within. The cases for the top are made separately, and screwed on—one may be with pigeon-holes, and one with shelves for books; the desk must also be made separately and screwed on, a small ledge should be fixed on it behind. The centre shelf should be hinged at the back, and either let down with a rack or with small spring bolts at each end. The gallery may either be of fret-work or of bronze. This design is well adapted for mahogany, with the mouldings and portions of the columns ebony or ebonized—the ornaments containing the handles ebonized—and the handles either of bronze or silvered.

LIBRARY CHAIRS.—PLATE XLII.

The first three figures have their top rails dovetailed on; this, considering the depth of sweep cut out of the rails below, is the strongest and most secure mode of fixing them. All the decorations on the back legs are wrought on the solid, except-ing the small bevelled panels, which are planted. The ornamental work on the front rail of all the designs, from the moulding on the seat frame downwards, is formed by pieces varying in the several cases, from ¾ to 1½-inch thick, which are fitted and dowelled under the seat rail, and shouldered and tongued between the legs; the pieces are first fitted, then detached, profiled, carved to pattern, and finally fixed on.

Fig. 1 has the mouldings on the seat-rail planted on, after the chair is framed up; the mitred corners of the mouldings are blunted by slightly rounding them; the small knob in the centre of the back is placed in a sunk channel, and does not project beyond the flush of the back.

Fig. 2 has the upright stay in the back scribed under the top rail, and dowelled between the latter and the cross stay: the apparent bottom-end of this part is wrought on the cross stay. The moulding on the seat is cross wrought on the front legs; the square heads of the latter are reduced, to give the moulding greater prominence.

Fig. 3.—The under edge of the cross-stay joins on the back rail of the seat: the stay is perforated after the back is framed up. The front legs are framed in flush with the seat-rails; and the moulding around the seat, and the decorations of the legs, are planted on.

Fig. 4 is flat across the back. The frame surrounding the cushion is formed of two stiles and a bottom rail; it is below dowelled between, and framed up with the back legs. The top rail requires 2-inch wood; it is first joined down on the spiral columns, and on the free ends of the cushion frame; it is then detached, shaped out below, and carved on the face. The shell is carved out of the solid. The bordered fret surrounding the cushion is planted on: it is formed of five pieces, the curved and the straight piece on each side, and the bottom piece, which mitres in with the others. A frame carrying the stuffing of the cushion is fitted in from behind, and fixed by screws.

Fig. 5.—The top rail joins down on the legs, through the centre of the brake on the back; at this part, the curve on the back leg may be pieced out by clamping. The back legs and top rails are bordered, on both edges, by a bead wrought on the solid; the interspace being carved on the face. The stuffing of the back may be effected on checks formed on the legs and top rail; or, on a separate frame, fitted in, and screwed on from behind. The two borders surrounding the front legs and rail, with the enclosed carving, are severally wrought apart, and planted on.

Fig. 6 has the back made similarly to that of Fig. 4. The top rail, from a line across the top of the columns, being of one piece, and dowelled down; it requires 3-inch wood. The cushion frame may be supported, in the centre, by screws sent through the pillars; the screw heads being covered by pateras. The carving on the front-rail is separately wrought, being first mitred on the seat frame; it is bordered on both edges by a square fillet carried round the seat.

DRAWING-ROOM FURNITURE.

THE drawing-room being the principal apartment of a house, and appropriated to the elegancies, refinements, and amusements of modern society, its furniture and decorations afford full scope for the display of taste in the owner, and of ingenuity in the artists or tradesmen he may call to his assistance. The uses of the drawing-room naturally suggest that its furniture and decorations should wear a light and cheerful aspect, and that its general colouring should be gay rather than grave. Beauty and elegance of expression being the main features to be studied in this apartment, there is not the same

necessity for subordinating the ornamental to the useful, as in furniture intended for the dining-room or library; ornament may, consequently, be more freely introduced, richer materials employed, and greater license taken, both in the forms and in the colours adopted. Variety of form is very desirable, and playfulness of design may be freely introduced in such articles as are more for show or amusement than for actual use, and of these a drawing-room usually contains a fair share; but while aiming at variety of form, consistency of style should be maintained, and no piece of furniture introduced obviously at variance with the prevailing character of the furnishing of the room. This would be a gratuitous remark, were not such improprieties so frequently committed, often resulting in giving an expensively furnished apartment very much the appearance of a curiosity shop. Variety and brilliancy of colouring, but without theatrical display, is very appropriate to the drawing-room, and, when properly managed, is productive of the best effect. Through fear of offending good taste, or of producing an effect verging upon tawdriness, neutral tints and colours, slightly removed from white, relieved by gilding, have been extensively adopted for the walls; and the various draperies have been made to match one another in colour so nearly as to give but little relief and variety. While such treatment seldom produces jarring and incongruity, it is generally wanting in liveliness of expression, and frequently marred by insipid uniformity. In many instances, a bit of decided contrast colour, introduced in small quantity into a room treated in this manner, is of great value in giving clearness and decision to the general effect. Were the principles of harmonious colouring more generally understood, the selection and arrangement of colours for the drawing-room would soon assume a more decided and artistic character. It is therefore evident that to this result the cabinet-maker ought to work in co-operation with the upholsterer and decorative painter; and that all, in due relation to the architect and to each other, should combine to produce a whole, in which the harmonious arrangement of the parts, as to form, position and colour, is as carefully observed as in a skilfully painted picture; the rules applicable to the one being equally suited to the other.

It is the more necessary to insist upon this intimate connection of the various branches of the decorative art, from its having, of late, become so extensively subdivided—an arrangement, in some respects, advantageous, from the superiority of execution obtained by it, combined, in many cases, with diminished cost of production; but liable, from the want of co-operation, to produce the grossest violations of propriety and taste. Among the more glaring instances of such violations, we need only refer to many of the carpets, and other decorations now in use, attractive to the uneducated eye by their extreme elaboration of design and brilliancy of colour, but which, when placed in their proper position, only serve to destroy the purity and tone of every other colour associated with them, and effectually disturb the repose and harmony so essential in a well-furnished drawing-room. The same want of propriety is as frequently seen in the work of the cabinet-maker, where hard and persistent forms are made to obtrude themselves on the eye with most unpleasing effect, instead of quietly blending with the other decorations, and forming part of a pleasing and well-compacted whole.

Straight lines, with their necessary sharp and angular convergencies, should, as much as possible, be avoided; substituting, in their stead, graceful and flowing curves, gently varied in their character, so as to avoid abrupt transitions, or monotonous uniformity. If this holds good in relation to the more massive and stationary portion of the furniture, it is still more applicable to those articles that are immediately intended for luxurious repose, where any sense of hardness and angularity should never be tolerated, but lines expressive of the softest and most pliant curves, aided by the skill of the upholsterer, should here be made suggestive of all the comfort and ease that such combinations can convey.

The woods most in favour at present for the ornamental purposes of the drawing-room, are rose-wood and walnut-wood. The former is so well known as to require little or no comment, except that its usual dark and heavy character is frequently felt to be incapable of harmonizing with some styles of decoration in which lightness is essential; on this account, therefore, and also from the peculiar beauty of grain it frequently exhibits, walnut-wood has of late been very extensively used: it associates well with almost any style of decoration and colour of material, without either detracting from them, or intruding upon the eye. For the purposes of carving, it has many advantages; it is more easily worked, and the lights and shadows are more clear and effective than in rosewood; while, in flat surfaces, some of the finer specimens of veneer, from their great variety of figure, admit of most elegant combinations. In large and important work, in this wood, where relief and effect are required, gilding, judiciously introduced, is productive of the best results.

CHIFFONNIERS.—PLATE XLIII.

The chiffonniers represented on this Plate are, in point of construction, very similar to each other; and much that has been said on the construction of sideboards, is applicable to them. The plinths and friezes should, for the sake of convenience, be made separate from the carcasses. The breaks may be formed on the plinths, by gluing on the grounds blocks of from 1½ inch to 2 inches in thickness, according to the projection of the pilasters; they are then veneered and finished off, when the top moulding, previously worked in a length, is mitred round, and, for security, blocked from beneath. The friezes may be provided with a drawer the whole length, on the front of which, the moulding, after being worked to its character, is mitred round, and then finished by the carver. The carcasses, from their simplicity, require no explanation. The tops, or slabs, are, in these designs, intended to be of marble; but, if made of wood, deal may be used, with the mouldings first planted round, and flushed off, and the surface veneered.

Fig. 1 has the doors flush-panelled and veneered; the circles, enclosing the carved heads, may be turned, and the rest of the moulding mitred into and around them to the design. The two smaller panels, enclosed in the angles of the doors, may be defined by mitring a ¼-inch bead, or other suitable small moulding, to the shape required. The field of the inner panel is grounded down ¼-inch; and a piece of fret-work, ⅛-inch in thickness, is inserted. The carved heads in the centre require wood of 2 inches to 2½ inches in thickness, to produce the necessary relief and effect. They are secured from behind by screws. Heads moulded in plaster, similar to those in the design, may readily be procured, and if either bronzed, or tinted to the colour of the wood in which the chiffonnier is wrought, would form a cheap and effective substitute for carving; or electrotypes in copper might be taken from those in plaster, and employed in their stead. The pilasters, which are affixed to, and open with the doors, should be about 4½ inches broad (Fig. 66.) in their widest part; they are shaped at the sides, and also in front, as shown in the profile, (Fig. 66). The top and bottom ornaments of the astragal dividing the doors, may be turned in one piece, and afterwards cut in half. The best construction for the back is to frame its lower division of deal, and veneer it; the moulding should then be mitred round the inside of the frame, forming a check for the veneered panel, which is put in from behind; on this, a smaller raised panel of solid wood, ⅜-inch thick, having a moulding wrought round its edge, is veneered and planted. The shelf, if not solid, should have the moulding planted round before veneering; and, when finished, can be fixed to the lower back by screws from above. The upper part of the back, having to be shaped to the carving, should be veneered on solid wood, otherwise the edges, after being shaped, will require to be veneered. The brackets which support the shelf should not be less than 1-inch in thickness, rebated behind to admit the back, thus avoiding unseemly joints; they are fixed by screws from behind, and by dowels at top and bottom.

Fig. 2 differs from the above in having plate-glass introduced into the back, the rebate for which is formed by the moulding, that is, planted on the stile, being allowed to project ½-inch beyond the inner edge of the frame. In all other respects the construction is similar to that of Fig. 1.

Fig. 3.—In this design the doors are sunk-panelled, the panel being let in from behind; on the fields of these, raised panels, ⅜-inch thick, are planted. The carved pilasters having, in some parts, a bold projection, require to be about 3½ inches thick, to

produce the necessary effect. The brackets supporting the shelf
are carved in the solid, and have their ornamental terminations
dowelled on. The decorations of the frieze are wrought separately, and planted.

Fig. 4.—The doors are flush-panelled, and veneered over;
the mouldings on them are mitred to the shape, and planted on
the face. The columns, after being turned and carved, require to
be flattened at the back, removing nearly one-fourth of their
diameter, so as to bring them under the caps, and close to the
grounds on which they are planted.

CHIFFONNIER.—PLATE XLIV.

This design is similar in construction to those on Plate XLIII.,
but has more importance given to the back, which here forms
a very conspicuous feature. In order to insure the requisite
firmness and stability, the back should be framed in one piece,
extending the whole height; the top part, behind the shelves,
being flush-panelled, and the mouldings planted on the face. The
shelves have the mouldings on them returned on the ends, to
preserve uniformity; the middle shelf is screwed on from behind.
The shelves are ¾-inch thick, and the brackets require 1½-inch
wood; they may be treated as described under Plate XLIII.
Fig. 1. The members of the fret-work pediment have their edges
bevelled throughout, thus giving additional force and richness,
by forming a double outline to the figures; the brackets may,
with advantage, be treated in a similar manner. The pediment
requires ¾-inch wood; the spear-heads on it may be wrought
separately, and dowelled on. The details of mouldings, &c.,
given on the Plate, render those portions sufficiently intelligible without farther description. The fret-panels of the
doors are of different designs, that selection may be made,
according to taste, not that two designs so different are intended to be introduced in the same chiffonnier; an additional
design for the fret-panel is also given in Fig. 3. In the end
view, for the same reason, a design for the brackets is given
different from that in the elevation, and it is in some respects
the better of the two. The design of this chiffonnier would
not be marred were it made with one shelf instead of two; in
that case, it is the upper bracket and upper shelf that should
be left out; the fret-work pediment would then be placed on
the lower shelf.

CHIFFONNIERS.—PLATE XLV.

This Plate contains two examples of winged chiffonniers, which,
in some parts of their construction, differ from those already
described. They are each formed in one carcass, the top and
bottom of which extend the whole length, are recessed in
the centre part, and receive, at the proper distances, the two
inner gables, which are morticed in. (*Fig.* 67.)

(*Fig.* 67.)

Fig. 1.—The several parts of the friezes and inner gables,
forming both angles A of the recessed centre, are clamped so
as to sweep together in the curve which is formed on them.
The construction of the plinth is shown by (*Fig.* 68), being
simply dovetailed together in deal; blocks are fitted into the
inner angles at A A, and shaped out; after which the whole is

veneered, and the moulding, of solid wood, formed on the edge
of a slip of deal, is planted on its upper edge. The frieze frame
is similarly constructed, solid wood being planted round to

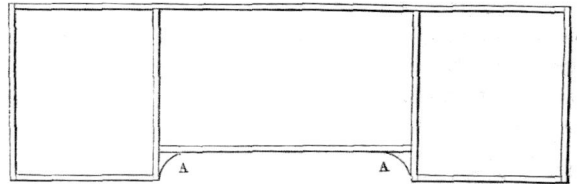
(*Fig.* 68.)

form the moulding. The carved ornaments at the angles are
formed by working a single piece of solid wood, sufficient for
the whole of them, to the exact curve of the moulding, then
mitring portions together to fit the angles, after which they are
carved upon a saddle of soft wood. As the carved back is
intended for the reception of plate-glass, and being, at the same
time, light in character and delicate in decorations, it should,
for sake of strength and sharpness of outline, be made of
Bay mahogany, or some other hard and straight-grained wood.
There being no brackets in front to steady and support the
mirror with its frame, this is effected by continuing the ends
of the ground frame, 4 or 5 inches, below the bottom rail, to
allow of their being screwed to the back of the frieze, as shown
in (*Fig.* 69). This frame should be made ⅝ths or ¾ths of an inch

(*Fig.* 69.)

narrower than the carving; so that, when the latter is screwed
on from behind, it will project over the inner edge of the frame,
forming a rebate for the glass.

Fig. 2 is so similar in construction to the above, that any
additional remarks are unnecessary.

CHIFFONNIERS WITH HIGH MIRRORS.—PLATE XLVI.

Fig. 1.—This design is well adapted for being executed in
dark oak or walnut, with the ornamental parts throughout
relieved and heightened in effect by partial gilding. The ornament is in the Byzantine manner, a style of decoration that has
rarely, if at all, been applied to the purposes of modern cabinet-
work. Though possessing considerable resources, and great
variety and beauty of expression, its distinctive merits, and
susceptibility of adaptation, have been too long overlooked or
neglected by decorative artists. The ornamental details of the
remains of Byzantine architecture in Italy, especially in the
oldest edifices of distinction in Venice, and the illuminated
manuscripts of the Byzantine period preserved in our museums,
supply the designer with suitable materials for decorations in this
style. The chiffonnier is simple in construction; the base and
frieze are separately made; the ornament on the latter is first
shaped to the ground, then profiled, carved, and planted. The
gables are sunk-panelled, and finished ornamentally like the
door. The ground of the panel forms the true gable on which
the bordering frame, ⅜-inch thick, and the other decorations,
are planted. The doors require 1½-inch wood; and are also
sunk-panelled, and bordered around the frame by a fillet,
which, along with the moulding, are planted on the face; a
hollow, or other small moulding, is carved round the inner

edge. The carved panels of the doors require 1-inch wood; these, after being profiled and perforated, are carved to pattern, and fixed by screws from behind; coloured silk or velvet, covering the panel, is introduced behind, to give richness and effect to the ornament. The outer pilasters are attached to the doors; that in the middle is dowelled on the centre division of the carcass. The moulding on the glass frame is separately wrought, and planted on a ground frame, 1½-inch thick; the carving is wrought in pieces, and dowelled or screwed on, at the most convenient points; the portions of the foliage which overlie the moulding, are separately made and fitted on.

Fig. 2 is decorated in the Moorish style, the ornamental details being based on those of the palace of the Alhambra. This style has, as yet, been but little employed in this country for cabinet-work, though the French have produced some very excellent adaptations from it. It is admirably suited for gilding and polychromatic embellishment; and, if the style of the Alhambra be fully carried out, such enrichments are really necessary. Moorish ornament may, however, be adapted to our domestic requirements, and very rich and agreeable effects produced in it without the application of colour. Those who wish to study this style, and satisfy themselves of its capabilities, will find valuable assistance by consulting Murphy's *Arabian Antiquities of Spain*, and the works on the Alhambra, by Owen Jones and by Girault de Prangey.

The design Fig. 2, may be entirely executed in deal, and painted in the polychromatic style, using the primary colours on the ornamental parts, and relieving them by gilding. Were the painted surfaces enamelled, it would give greater permanence and value to the colours, and impart to the whole a lustrous and highly-finished appearance. Such treatment, however, would require a special or complementary arrangement of colour for the room in which this piece of furniture is placed; and also, that similarity of design and treatment, though in a modified form, be carried out in the rest of the furniture of the apartment, to preserve consistency. This design may also be effectively wrought out in woods of various colours; in which case the chiffonnier would have a more subdued effect, than if treated in the manner we have just described, and would also approach more nearly to the character of drawing-room furniture commonly in use. For example, the plinth, the frieze, and the carved pilasters, may be made of walnut wood; the doors veneered in satin wood, with their mouldings also wrought in wood of light colour, with exception of the inner member, which should be dark; the ornaments on the panels inlaid in lime-tree, dyed in bright colours, the ground for the ornaments being a dark neutral colour, produced in the same manner, making the general effect of the panel be, to tell dark on a light ground, the dark mass being relieved by the radiant form and colours of the inlaying; the ornaments on the frieze inlaid in various colours, like the panels, but made to tell light on a dark ground. The effect may be further heightened by bordering the leaves of the inlaid parts by a fine gilded outline, and by hatching the carved pilasters in gold. The mirror-frame may be wrought in deal; but better in lime-tree, and gilded; the gilding being relieved by a good deal of burnished work, and by the partial introduction of colour. Several variations of this method of treatment will readily suggest themselves.

CABINET.—PLATE XLVII.

This cabinet is decorated in the French style, and, if executed in rosewood, would form a very useful and elegant article for the ante-drawing room. The character of the design would be maintained with equal effect if worked out in walnut or mahogany, where these woods are employed in the furniture of the

apartment. In construction it is similar to a chiffonnier, having a secretaire drawer in the frieze, with the upper carcass shelved for books, &c.; the latter part is made and finished separately, and, as usual, is fixed in its place by dowels and screws. The doors require wood not more than ¾-inch thick. The rebate to receive the plate-glass is formed by planting the carved mouldings on the face of the door, as shown in the section B, which presents also the character of the moulding on the front of the brackets. A break, corresponding with the projection of the bracket, is formed on the cornice, as shown at section A. The pedimented ledge on the top is of solid wood ½-inch thick, on which, as a ground, the carved ornaments are planted. The space enclosed by the carving in the centre of the ground is perforated, and so also the figured spaces or panels on each side of it; the two end portions of the ledge, shown in side view, are, at their points of contact with the back and top, dovetailed into the one and dowelled on the other. The secretaire drawer opens between the end panels, and is similar in construction to that described under Plate XXXVIII., but different and simpler in its interior arrangements; one plan is given (*Fig. 70*) which, in a cabinet of this kind, will in most

(Fig. 70.)

cases be found suitable; but the arrangement may of course be varied as circumstances and convenience dictate. The drawer front is veneered flush, and the panels and carved work surrounding them planted on the face;—of the character of these mouldings, as well as those forming the frieze, section D will be found sufficiently explanatory. The lower part is so similar to the chiffonniers already described, that little explanation is needed beyond what is furnished by the design itself and the sections accompanying it. The gables or ends are panelled to correspond with the front, simply by planting on in the usual manner. Both carcasses are closed in behind by panelled frames of deal; that on the book-case may be cloth covered, inside, or flush-panelled, veneered, and polished. An agreeable variation of this design may be made by omitting the doors on the lower part, enclosing it instead by silk curtains, enriched with ornamental needlework, suspended from a brass rod, the ends of which would be inserted in the upper part of the pilasters.

CABINET.—PLATE XLVIII.

This is another cabinet on the same plan as the one just described, and differing only in the style of its decorations, which is Elizabethan. The fret-work pediment on the top is ½-inch thick; that on the doors not more than ¼-inch. The frets are prepared, in the usual manner, of several thicknesses; each of them, along with the portion of the band connected with it on the top and sides of the door, is formed of a single piece; the sides mitre in with a corresponding piece at the bottom. The frets and bands attached to them are fitted into the rebate formed by the door-frame and moulding, and glued to the projecting lip of the latter. Another good method of fixing the frets is to rebate the inner edge of the doors, on the front, for the thickness of the fret-work, which, when the doors are veneered, then is fixed in its place, and the mouldings,

(Fig. 71.)

being planted so as to lap over, effectually secure it, and also cover the joints—as the section of the door style (*Fig. 71*) will suitable either for a Drawing-room or Bed-room; and, with a little variation, would make effective Work-Tables.

LOO TABLES.—PLATE LV.

This Plate contains four designs for Loo Tables, in styles differing greatly from those previously described, and exhibiting a marked originality in the combination of parts and general treatment.

Fig. 1. The moulding on the top, being free from carving, it may be treated by the second of the processes given in the introductory part of the description of Plate LIII. The lower part should be made in three portions, namely, the pillar, the collar, and the claws. The pillar is turned and afterwards finished by the carver, and the upper portion of the collar is also turned, and the lower part afterwards shaped in the manner shown in (*Fig.* 88) elongated over the claws. The

(*Fig.* 88.)

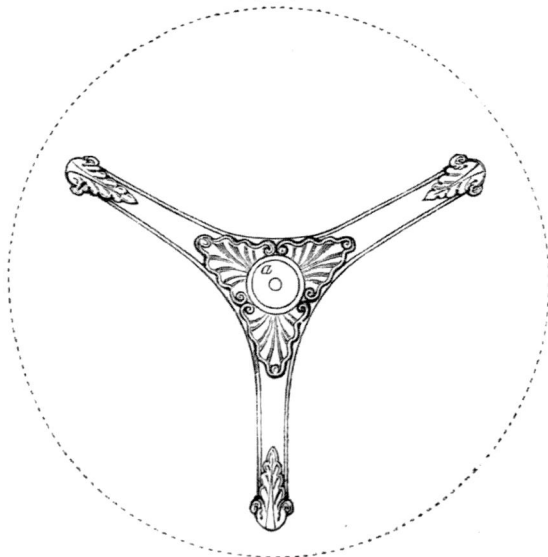

claws may be dovetailed into a centre-piece, in the manner shown at (*Fig.* 79).

Fig. 2. The arrangement of the lower part of this table requires that the upper block be made somewhat different from those of the tables previously described, in order to provide a sufficient bearing for the three smaller pillars; this may be accomplished by framing the block of 2-inch Honduras or birch, 3 or $3\frac{1}{2}$ inches in width, as shown at (*Fig.* 89).

(*Fig.* 89.)

Fig. 3 presents a simple and effective mode of enriching the rim, which in this instance is first veneered and finished off as if intended to be left plain; the shaped work previously prepared and shaped is then laid on, and may be either solid or veneered, but in either case should not exceed $\frac{1}{4}$ or $\frac{5}{16}$-inch in thickness; the carved ornaments are finished separately, and then glued in their places. The standards of the lower part require to be about $2\frac{3}{4}$-inch thickness when finished, they are tenoned or dowelled to a centre-piece, as shown at (*Fig.* 90). This figure is a section of (*Fig.* 91) on the line *b, b, d* represents the centre-block, *c* the standards, and *a, a, a*, the position of the joints; or, the joints may be formed at *e, e* (*Fig.* 91), in which case the piece of wood required for the centre-block

would be of much smaller dimensions. Oak, or walnut, are the woods for which this design is most suited.

(*Fig.* 90.)

(*Fig.* 91.)

Fig. 4 presents a table in which gilding may be introduced with good effect, associated with any of the more choice woods. From the arrangement of the lower part, this table does not admit of the top being turned up in the ordinary manner. The top block being connected with the scrolls rising from each limb of the base-block, it, in consequence, exceeds considerably the usual dimensions of this part in other tables. It should be secured to the clamps by four thumb-screws, as shown at (*Fig.* 92). In constructing the lower block, the

(*Fig.* 92.)

ground should be framed or halved together of $1\frac{1}{2}$-inch pine, as shown at (*Fig.* 93), a process which has been before de-

(*Fig.* 93.)

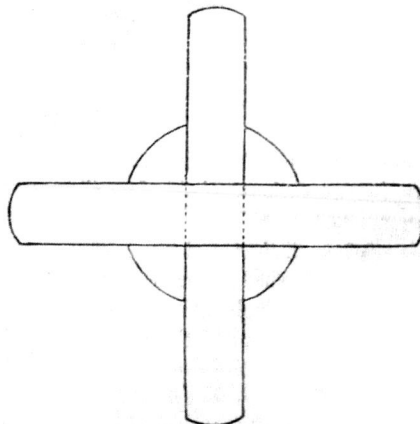

scribed under Plate XVII. This ground should be accurately shaped to the proportions required and veneered; the moulding has to be placed on it, the simplest method of doing which is to turn the centre part *b* (*Fig.* 94) out of solid wood, the moulding being accurately described on its edge; four other

(*Fig. 94.*)

pieces of solid wood should then be carefully shaped to the limbs of the block, and the moulding accurately worked on their edges—they may then be mitred into the circle in the manner shown at *a, a, a, a.* These mitres are in a great measure concealed by the base of the table-pillar. If the nature of the wood renders this plan inexpedient, a counterpart of the block *b* (*Fig.* 95), may be made, smaller in size, an amount, equal to the projection of the moulding, all around. This piece *c* should be firmly glued on to the other, and in the rebate so formed the solid wood for the moulding should be planted, the joints being concealed by the upper square of the moulding *a*, formed by a clamp of ⅜-inch solid wood covering the whole. The swan-necked scrolls may be of bronze, with the leafage tipped with gold; they may be fixed by screws sent through the upper and lower blocks.

(*Fig. 95.*)

OCCASIONAL TABLES.—PLATE LVI.

Fig. 1.—As this small table depends for its effect on sharp and well-defined shadow, it is not suitable to work it in woods of varied colour, or in those whose lustre is only shown to advantage in smooth rounded contours. We shall therefore assume that it is made of solid wood, having the top made of inch stuff, with a thickness glued on beneath the outer edge, and the moulding worked out of the solid. In forming the ornament depending from the under surface of the top, four square blocks, with their lower ends turned or canted, should be prepared, into which the intermediate ornaments are doweled at the ends; these are finally cut on the curve out of solid wood, then shaped and carved, and the whole is doweled into the under side of the rim; small blocks may be glued at the back of the pendant squares to stiffen them, if thought necessary. The four standards are then shaped out of 1¾-inch stuff; the foliated ornament at their foot is relieved by the carver on each side. The circle in the centre is turned out of 2¼ wood; the moulding carved or not. It should then be carefully notched out to receive the standards, the notch being ⅜ less than the width of the standard, which must be grooved in so that the circle goes slightly into the standard, to conceal the joint. The standards must then be screwed to a bearing-piece at the top, and

doweled below to the top of the plinth. The plinth is made of ⅝ stuff, on the edge of which the moulding is worked, with a thickness glued on below, and shaped. The feet are shaped out of solid wood, carved, and a sinking made, if requisite, to receive the castors.

Fig. 2.—This table is suited, from its greater richness, for an inlaid, marble, or marqueterie top. The ground of the top should be got out of mahogany, thicknessed up beneath, and the wood for the moulding planted on all round; the square edges being banded with veneer, and the top veneered. The rail is shaped as in the design, and carved leaves placed on it as brackets where they are shown. The centre column must be got out right to the bottom, the upper part turned, and pieces doweled on for the three scrolls. The standards and claws must then be shaped, as shown in the section (*Fig.* 96), and doweled together without gluing first. It is now ready for carving, after which it must be glued up fast, and the joints are afterwards trimmed by the carver. The scroll supports may be of from 2½ to 3-inch stuff, and the claws 3-inch towards the foot, of course, widening towards the centre.

(*Fig. 96.*)

Fig. 3.—The top is made of Honduras, and veneered, with a moulding planted on it. Below, and at each end of the top, is a wide rail, forming a rim, to receive the columns, and the side-rails are dovetailed into them. If the wood be expensive, the rail may be veneered with a bead planted round the lower edge, or clamped with a thickness of ½-in. to 1-in. stuff, on which a moulding may be worked. The columns must be fitted and turned, leaving wood for the wreaths; gluings may be put on the caps to form the projections, but the better way is to shape the whole top ornament with the two caps out of one solid piece, and then put long dowels through it into the columns. The stretcher is turned, and the claws shaped out of 3-inch solid wood, tapered on each side towards the feet, with a piece of ¾ stuff, which is shaped and moulded on the edge, and laid on their tops; it is then doweled and glued together, the stretcher being tenoned into the claws. The castors are, as usual, sunk in the feet.

Fig. 4 is made exactly like Fig. 3, excepting that the end standards join down on the arched feet in the straight line drawn between the angles which their profile makes with the feet. The carving which completes the bottom of the standard, is wrought on the feet. The standards require 2½ to 3-inch stuff, and are doweled on; the feet are shaped out of solid 3-inch wood.

LADIES' WORK TABLES.—PLATE LVII.

Fig. 1 is a design intended to be executed in mahogany; the bag to draw out from the end, being in this way much more convenient for a lady's use when sitting before the table. The part shown in the design above the bag is the front of a drawer, the interior of which is fitted up in the usual manner, and provided with the proper requisites for needle-work. (*Fig.* 97) presents a convenient method of dividing off the interior of a rectangular work-table drawer. The divisions are made of pencil-cedar, and may be silk covered; their edges are frequently embellished by silver lines. The drawer is pulled out by means of the scrolls at each end, which serve the purpose of handles. The

(Fig. 97.)

top, being made to lift up, should be furnished inside with a small mirror, inclosed within a tastefully ornamented border. The four scrolls which support the top should be finished before they are fixed, except at that part where they join the pillar, to which they are secured by means of screws. The pillar is turned the whole length, the claws being dovetailed or doweled into it.

Fig. 2 is a design to be executed in ebony, relieved by silver lines, &c. The top is well suited for mounting in a mosaic work of fine spars or marbles, inclosed within a Buhl border, executed in ebony, silver, and tortoiseshell. The body of the table is hexagonal or six-sided; the top is made on a ground of ⅝-in. Honduras; it is hinged, with a moulding planted around it. The inside of the frame under the top is provided with a movable tray, furnished with the requisite fittings, or these may be fixed as shown in (*Fig.* 98), where the usual manner of setting off the interior of a hexagonal work-table is presented. The part corresponding to the drawer, in Fig. 1, being fixed in this example, access to the bag is obtained through the centre space *a*, which is covered by an ornamental

(Fig. 98.)

lid; the upper end of the bag, as shown by the dotted lines, passes up within the top frame, and forms a check on which this lid rests. The bag is formed by working a piece of sufficient thickness and length to form the six sides to the sweep required, and then mitring these together, and afterwards panelling them. Or the wood forming the bag may be made up of three thicknesses, of stout veneer, glued together, and cauled down on a mould, having the required outline of the bag; when the gluing is completely dry, the gores are cut out, and mitred together. Two pieces of deal, shaped to the inside size and figure of the bag, above and below, may be temporarily employed, to form a ground on which the mitring is effected; the bottom piece may, however, be permanently fixed, as a means of attaching the bag to the pillar. The mitres are strengthened by keying the angles outside; this is done by inserting slips of veneer with glue into slant cuts of the saw; on these being properly dry, the surface of the bag is smoothed off, and the panelled openings are then cut, and moulded around the edges; the mitre cuts are concealed, by afterwards veneering the borders which surround the panels. The upper portion of the table is shouldered to the pillar within the calyx, the interior of which is outlined and bottomed by the turner; the parts are fixed together by a strong screw from the inside of the bag. Down the stem of the pillar a silver line should be inserted. The tips of the flowers and ends of the fruit should be relieved in the same manner.

Fig. 3 furnishes another design for hexagonal tables, to be

executed in rosewood. The top part of this table is supported by three scrolls springing from the pillar, much in the same way as Fig. 1. The bag is made in the same manner as in the table just described. There are six leaves on the upper portion of the pillar, one running up each scroll, and one intermediate. The divisions of these leaves may be so managed, as in a great measure to conceal the joints.

Fig. 4 is designed for rosewood, with the upper part made in the same manner as the others. The scrolls, in this instance, require to be made each in one piece, from the top to the insertion of the claws; they are joined in the centre, and doweled together, and the claws fitted under each; the scrolls are secured by screws, as in (*Fig.* 99), *a*. The upper part of the table is secured to the lower by a screw bolt, *b*, *b*, which, passing from the inside of the bag through the pillar, is tightened underneath by means of a nut. The leaves, at the bottom of the bag, touch the scrolls, which arrangement affords an additional means of strength, by admitting of a screw being passed from the inside of the bag into the scrolls.

(Fig. 99.)

Fig. 5 is a design suitable for maple-wood, relieved by ebony mouldings and inlaying, and, in construction, is similar to those already described. The inside should be fitted up with coloured silk, and the fret work on the panels relieved by the same material.

Fig. 6—a design suited for rosewood and satin-wood, relieved by gilding. The top to be inlaid with various coloured woods, inclosed within a circle, the angles being filled up with Buhl-work, executed in tortoiseshell, &c.; the first and third moulding on the top, the mouldings around the panels of both frame and bag, portions of the scrolls and foliage, and the mouldings on the block, are the parts to be gilt. The panels of frame and bag being of satin-wood, these parts are, in consequence, separately made, and the upper part is screwed to the lower by means of a bolt, as described under Fig. 4.

DRAWING-ROOM SOFAS.—PLATE LVIII.

The details of construction given in the description of Plate XXVIII., and several following Plates, are equally applicable to the sofas figured here. It will be only necessary to notice the peculiarities in the ornamental details, in which alone the difference consists. The frames are made, the solid wood planted on the fronts, and the feet doweled underneath, precisely in the manner formerly described.

Fig. 1.—In this design the lines of the foliages, with a little care, may be so arranged as effectually to break or conceal the joining of the feet to the frame. The peculiarity of execution consists in a portion of the foliage which springs from the end of the front rail being made to clasp, as it were, the base of the elbow; it will only be necessary, when planting the solid wood on the front rail, to make provision for the additional thickness required, when the whole can then be carved and finished together.

Fig. 2 differs simply from sofas already described, in the styles of the ornament, the mode of execution being precisely similar.

Fig. 3 presents a marked contrast to most of the preceding designs, both in arrangement of lines, and details of ornament. It is, however, doubtful, whether the broad and decided angularity observed in the treatment of some of its parts, may not be objectionable. In such case the difficulty

(Fig. 100.)

may be surmounted by softening the lines, and modifying the angular features of the design, in the manner shown in the accompanying figure.

Fig. 4.—This design is so similar to those figured in Plate XXVIII., as only to require an explanation of the ornament in the centre of the back; the solid wood for which is doweled firmly to the deal framing, and afterwards carved, care being taken to preserve an easy graceful line for the edge of the stuffing.

DRAWING-ROOM SOFAS.—PLATE LIX.

Fig. 1 is a sofa designed in the French style, in which the various members are doweled, and skilfully relieved, as to render it admirably suited for satin-wood and gold, or for gilding entirely. The same design, carefully wrought in rosewood, will also prove very effective and pleasing. In constructive details it is similar to the designs on Plate XXXI. The centre of the back is in one piece, as far as the dip in the moulding, where the end pieces are mitred up to it. The solid wood on the front rail is also in three pieces, arranged in a similar manner.

Fig. 2 bears so close a resemblance to Fig. 2, Plate XXXI., that a reference to the description given for that design will furnish all the information required.

DRAWING-ROOM SOFAS.—PLATE LX.

Fig. 1 is another very graceful design, in the French style, eminently suited for gilding, or finishing in white and gold. In this design the seat frame is first made of birch, to the shape of the design; upon it the back is built up of birch and pine, in the manner shown and described under Plate XXVIII., Fig. 2. Around the ground framing of the back, the solid wood required for the carved work is carefully and securely planted: great attention being paid to the security and soundness of the joints. It will be found in practice, that, after the various pieces are fitted in these places, much of the heavier parts of the carving may be more readily roughed out before being finally fixed, which is also desirable for this further reason, that the risk of jarring and disturbing the joints will be thereby considerably lessened.

Fig. 2 requires to be built up in the same manner, observing,

of course, the same precautions in fixing and working the mouldings, &c. The clusters of leaves and fruit may be separately wrought and indented.

COUCHES.—PLATE LXI.

The couches on this Plate will be readily constructed from the descriptions already given.

COUCHES.—PLATE LXII.

The general construction of these couches will be readily understood.

Fig. 1 is best suited for execution in the lighter coloured woods, such as maple, or satin-wood, or birch, and the character of the ornament is such as to admit of its being considerably improved and illuminated by a judicious introduction of gilding.

Fig. 2 is a design better adapted for rosewood or mahogany, in either of which woods it would prove a very effective and elegant couch.

DRAWING-ROOM CHAIRS.—PLATE LXIII.

It is presumed the general construction of vase-backed, or drawing-room chairs, is sufficiently understood, as to render any particular explanation in this place unnecessary, especially as many of the remarks in page 25, relating to the dining-room chairs on Plates XXIII. and XXIV., are equally applicable to those now under notice—as a rule, however, drawing-room chairs should be smaller and decidedly lighter in character, than chairs intended for dining-room purposes—grace and elegance being requisite in the one case, solidity and strength essential in the other.

Fig. 1 exhibits a simple design framed together in the usual manner of vase-backed chairs, but from the quick sweep of the under part of the stay, it is necessary that the joint should be formed in the manner shown in (Fig. 101) a, a. The moulding on the face of the back is simply three beads, as shown in (Fig. 102):

(Fig. 101.)

(Fig. 102.)

(Fig. 103.)

that on the legs being made to correspond. This back may be either stuffed into a rebate, sufficient wood for this purpose being left on the inside, which serves also to give additional strength to the back; or the space may be fitted with a loose panel, which, when stuffed, is put in from behind, and secured by screws.

Fig. 2 is another vase-backed chair, framed upon a light coloured wood, inlaid with a darker one. In other respects it is similar to the one just described.

Fig. 3 differs only in ornamental details, the construction being similar.

Fig. 4 has the back moulded, the character of the moulding is shown at (Fig. 103).

ments. Their style is intermediate between French and tester bedstead, being less expensive than the latter, and esteemed more elegant than the former.

Fig. 1.—The head-posts are square, measuring on the side about 4 in.; they are made up of birch, 3-in. thick, clamped on their exposed sides, namely, the front and its adjoining inside, with solid wood, 1-in. thick. At their upper end, the posts terminate at the cap below; they extend to the under edge of the side rails, where the turned feet are doweled on them; they are chamfered on three corners, and their decorations are planted on. The short foot-posts are of solid wood, 6-in. square; the ball of the turned feet may be brought out by clamping. The side and end rails are made of birch 2¼-in. thick, and are veneered on the face. On the surface of the veneer being finished, the bordered frets are glued on the veneer; these require to be $\frac{5}{16}$-in. thick, the outside layer being thicker than the others, as the frets are relieved on the front by the carver. Around the frets a raised border, ⅜-in. thick, is then planted; the upper edges of the side rails are afterwards veneered.

The frame of the footboard requires solid wood, 3-in. thick. The side rails of the frame are doweled between the top and bottom; the lines of the joints being the upper edge of the bottom rail, and the diameter line of the circle along the brakes. The border, surrounding the outer edge of the frame, is ⅝-in. thick, and is planted on the face; the straight portion of this border below extends down, on both sides, to the bed rail, forming a ground on which the bottom moulding of the footboard is planted. The panel of the footboard is made of ⅞-in. deal, and laid with a choice veneer; it is let in, from the outside, into a check formed for it on the frame: in this process the panel is first profiled, and its outline drawn on the face of the frame, the thickness of the panel is then gauged on the inner edge of the frame, and the space, to form the check, is cut out true to these lines. The panel being thus kept exactly flush in front, a small moulding, planted on the frame, is made to lap on it, covering the joint. The front and sides of the frame for the canopy are of solid wood, ⅞-in. thick, and dovetailed together; these parts are panelled by means of a raised border, ⅜-in. thick, which is planted on; the frets, as in the case of the rails, being previously glued down. The apparent blocks, forming the corner ornaments of the cornice, are each made up of two pieces, clamped on the face, and mitred on the angle. The canopy behind is connected with a vertical frame of deal, 1½-in. thick, which, in length, extends across, and rests on, both posts; while its breadth corresponds with the depth of the arch of the canopy. This frame is fitted, and doweled between, and is, behind, wrought off flush with, the sides of the canopy. A block of solid wood is glued within each angle, formed by the two frames where they join; by this means the canopy is slip doweled on the posts.

The canopy is maintained in position by a strong straight bar of iron, which is screwed to the head-posts and vertical frame behind. A flat frame, or lathe, is fitted within the cornice, leaving a space between of ⅜-in. broad, for the valance, which is nailed to the edge of the lathe. Two right-angled iron brackets, screwed to the posts, serve to support the lathe, which again is connected to the cornice by tongued catches screwed on from above.

Fig. 2 is made like the preceding; the head-posts and canopy are similarly treated; the apparent prolongation of the former, above the cap, is a thin piece planted on the frame. The ground, for the canopy frame, is dovetailed together; in front, it may be pieced out on the upper edge with deal to receive on it the cornice moulding. The thin pieces, forming the margin of the panels, are mitred together on the fore corners of the frame; and so conceal the dovetails. The framing of this bed may be connected by screws in the ordinary manner; the heads of which may be concealed by the oval pateras.

HALF TESTER BEDSTEADS.—PLATE LXXIX.

The principal difference in construction, between the designs here given and those on the preceding Plate, consists in the character of the footboard; in both the present examples it is let into the foot-posts; a groove being mortised out of each. This is effected before the posts are turned; the grooves being temporarily filled tightly with a piece of wood, to prevent their lips from chipping in the lathe. The footboards are framed, and flush panelled, with a moulding planted on the face. The panels may be inlaid, or covered, with figured cloth; they are let in from the outside, and applied to a cheek cut out of the framing; with a view to greater strength, they may be strongly blocked from the inside, and are stuffed over. The head-posts extend the whole height, and may be of hardwood, veneered or clamped, on the exposed sides, while the decorations are all planted on. The bed rails are sunk panelled by means of a raised border which is planted on them. The decorations, under the rails of Fig 2, are slip doweled, and are brought near to the outside, so as to admit the curtain pawn to pass behind them. Both these beds should be framed together by the screw, Fig. 7, Plate LXXXV. The cornices of both designs are similarly constructed; the supporting brackets may be slip doweled, or secured to their place by screws sent through the cornice from the top, and also through the posts from behind.

HALF TESTER BEDSTEAD.—PLATE LXXX.

In all essential particulars of construction, this design resembles either of the preceding. The head and foot posts are wrought square, and the panels are grounded down and veneered. Their mouldings and frets are, after being wholly finished, planted on. The triangular ornaments on the top of the foot-posts are carved on the solid. The small panels below are made to cover the screw heads, and are movable. For other methods of bracing the posts, and framing together, the reader is referred to the description of bed-pillars, under Plate LXXXV. The mouldings in the four posts are carried around the rails; the top edge of the latter is veneered. The footboard is sunk panelled, and doweled, between the posts; the ornament in its centre is inlaid. The cornice is mitred into the capitals of the pilasters, into which the head-posts are formed. The back of the cornice is screwed to a cross rail, which is dovetailed edgeways into the top of the posts. The fret brackets, supporting the cornice, are fixed as described under Plate LXXIX.: these may be of bronze, or of wood, made up in three thicknesses. The frets, on the angles of the posts and rails, are slip doweled on these parts.

BEDSTEAD (MEDIEVAL).—PLATE LXXXI.

The woods most suited for this style of design are oak, birch, and walnut; or any light-coloured wood may be used, but not mahogany, which, to show the full beauty of its grain, requires broad and rounded surfaces. The corresponding ends of the bed and canopy are framed permanently together; they at once join on to the side rails, and the ridge rail of the bed, and are secured by ordinary bed screws. Each of the two centre standards is mortised flush into the end rail of the bed, which again is tenoned into the posts. The latter are 3½-in. thick, and project, on each side, ¼-in. beyond the rails; the standards, rails, and shaped arms, are wrought flush, and are 3-in. thick; to this thickness, also, the foot-posts are made to taper at the tops, where the arms, which have been previously shouldered into, and doweled on to, the standard, are adjusted and doweled on; the line of the joints on the side may be partially concealed by a sunk patera and leafage. The arms on the corresponding part at the head of the bed are made to join down on a straight cross rail, which is tenoned into the posts. The standards sensibly taper, both on the thickness and breadth, from where the lower arms join to them up to the top. This expression of taper is shared by the upper supporting arms and the arch of the canopy, giving to these parts greater lightness of appearance. The upper arms are tenoned into the standard, and shouldered on it obliquely, as shown in (*Fig.* 108). From the upper part, *a*, the standard is further reduced to a breadth which it maintains to the top. The arch may be formed of two pieces doweled together, and then joined down on the standard; or the latter may pass up and receive on its sides the two segments forming the arch; the latter is the better method. To assist the action of the cramps, in framing the parts together, a notch of wood should be left on the upper edge of each segment; these may be wrought off after.

(*Fig.* 108.)

In addition to the ends, the wood-work of the roof consists simply of three rails, one on each side below, tenoned into the segments of the arch, and also the ridge rail; all of which are secured by screws passing through the ends. The ridge rail may be continued to any depth that may be deemed necessary for stiffness to the bed, as this will depend much on the close and secure abutment of the rails, and on the strength of the screws. The contour of the roof may be completely maintained through its entire length by ribs spanning the distance between the side and ridge rails; two such ribs will require to be screwed to the inside of each of the ends, to distend the cloth.

The poles for the curtains must be fixed outside, being supported by passing through the ends of the curved arms at the head and foot. The ornament is extremely simple, the carving being merely sunk in the solid wood. It may vary in richness from simple outlining, leaving the figure almost flat, to the most careful modelling, in which, however, under-cutting must be avoided, or any such depth as shall interfere with its presenting a surface in harmony with the predominant idea of flatness. Most of the wood-work is also chamfered lengthwise, either with plain chamfering or ogeed, still preserving the square profile in section, as in the cross rail at the head and foot. The panels of the head-board are represented as stuffed; those of the foot-board as covered with tapestry, stained light. The draperies, whether rich or not, should have a pattern treated in flat unshaded colours; all chintzes, or silks, with flowers shaded and drawn in close imitation of nature, are inadmissible, as they violate the principle which guides the ornament of the wood-work throughout. The valances may be embroidered if there be any difficulty in finding a pattern suited to their form; but with a pattern merely powdered with fleur de lis, crosses, or diapers, this is likely to be unnecessary. Gymps should be sparingly introduced on the edges and principal lines; they may, however, be run with good effect on the circular canopy from the divisions of the valances to the ridge, as in the design. In summer, the effect of this bed would be lightened by substituting white muslin for coloured curtains around the foot.

POSTED BEDSTEADS.—PLATE LXXXII.

The designs on this Plate are similar to each other in all the chief particulars of construction. The head and foot posts are of equal length; those at the head, when exposed, are of a square form, and of solid wood, or of hardwood laid with stout veneers, and are finished ornamentally; they are usually of birch, 3½-in. thick, tapering to 2½ in. at the top, and cloth covered, the head piece of the curtains being carried round and tacked on them behind. The foot-posts of the figure to the left are square wrought; and clamped at the parts of greatest diameter. The capitals, including the square blocks on which the cornice rests, may each be formed of a separate piece from the posts and doweled down. The panels on the square of the posts are removable, being fixed to the post by catches, so as to cover or expose the framing screws as needed. The foot-posts of the other design on the Plate are turned above and below the square, and afterwards carved. The foot-board is framed and panelled; the top and bottom rails being tenoned into the ends. The wood of the frame requires to be of a breadth to admit of the figure of the panels being cut out of it. When the panel openings are profiled, checks are wrought around their edges inside to receive the panels, the forelap of the check has a hollow moulding wrought in its edge. The panels are cloth covered. After the top edge of the frame is profiled, the top mouldings at the ends are fitted on. The scrolls at the centre of the top are separately prepared, then planted and wrought off. The foot-board of the figure to the right may be joined up in one breadth of solid wood, and cross-headed at the ends; or it may be made of 1¼-in. deal, and veneered over; the top moulding is planted on the face on both sides, and veneered on the top. The shaped panels, ⅜-in. thick, with the other decorations, are planted on the face. The foot-boards are doweled into the posts.

The head board is framed, fitted between the head-posts, grooved in the end, stuffed inside, and slid into its place on tongues mortised into the posts.

The cornices are supported by a frame lathe of 1-in. wood, which rests on the top of the posts. This lathe, when the curtains are suspended from iron rods attached to it below, is distinct from the cornice, with a space of ⅜-in. between them around the sides and foot end, to admit the valance, which is tacked to its edge; in such case the cornice is attached to the lathe by tongued catches.

In the present examples, the lathe *a*, as shown in (*Fig.* 109,)

(*Fig.* 109.)

is glued permanently to the cornice *b*, and, with the cornice, is veneered below. The sides of the lathe, at the foot end of the bed, are tenoned, and joined to the corresponding part of the cornice; they receive on them the end which is fitted, and glued to the cornice within the returns; this arrangement is necessary when the curtains are suspended from poles fixed into the head of the posts, as in these examples, wherein those parts are wholly exposed to view. The poles are let full into the posts for two or more inches.

The cornice consists of three separable parts—the end with its returns of about 8 in. long attached, and the two sides, which abut against the returns. When the cornice is framed together, these ends approach, but not so closely or firmly as is necessary for the strength or elegance of appearance. A simple device is commonly resorted to for bracing home the joints. The abutting ends are tongued and slip-doweled together, so as to maintain the various parts and members of the mouldings flush and uniform with each other. As shown in (*Fig.* 110), a slip of hardwood, 1½-in. broad, and ¾-in. thick, is glued and screwed on within half-an-inch of the joints, across each of the four adjoining ends of the returns and sides of the cornice; each pair of slips taken together when screwed on is slightly wedge-shaped and tapered from below up. Another piece, ¾-in. thick and 3-in. broad, is checked out to the form and depth of the pieces screwed on, and made to pass on them tightly from above down, so as to force home the joint and maintain it secure. Brass catches, of a suitable construction, are frequently employed for this purpose; the method referred to, however, is cheap and efficient.

(*Fig.* 110.)

The decorations surmounting the cornice are put on in the usual manner. Posted beds should be mounted on French castors; these are completely concealed from view when the bed is fully mounted, and their action is easy and smooth.

STATE BEDSTEAD.—PLATE LXXXIII.

This design, in its lower parts, does not differ materially in construction from the ordinary four-posted bedstead: it is square-framed, having four short posts or pedestals in the angles. The pedestals in the body are not less than 6 in. square, the panels on them are grounded down, the mouldings of the base and capital are mitred around them, and the carving at their upper end is planted on the face, the pieces being mitred together on the several angles. The four columns on each pedestal are centred, as shown in (*Fig.* 110); they are fixed by a pin and bore, having their bases, which are 4 in. in diameter, just touching each other. The caps of the columns are separately made, each being fixed by a pin turned on the column; their diameter is such that they require to be flattened where they come into contact with each other; they are connected together by small iron plates, which are sunk and screwed into them from above. A solid piece, wrought ornamentally, is doweled on the top of each group of columns, forming a support for the cornice. These pieces at the foot of the bedstead are turned, and each is decorated with four small inverted trusses, which rest on the several columns, and are fixed to the turned piece. The corresponding pieces on the head posts are shaped, carved, and perforated from the front in the form of a Gothic arch. The bed rails are recessed from the front, on the sides, and foot end, thus making the pedestals to appear in relief. The foot-board laps down in front of the end rail, covering it completely, and presenting on its under edge the same finish which is given to the lower edge of the side rails. The head-board is framed up strongly of 2½-in. deal, having its upper edge pieced with solid wood to form the figures. The piecing may be variously effected; two methods are shown in (*Fig.* 111). According to one of those methods, four principal pieces are required—two on each side *a, a,* (6-in. thick), forming the lower half, and the attire of the reclining figures; the moulding connected with this part may be wrought on the solid, or, if esteemed as more convenient, it may be separately wrought and planted on a prepared ground. Another piece, *b,* 8-in. thick, joins down on the head-board and side pieces in the line *c, d,* passing under the arms of the figures; the joint and the opposition of the grain of the wood in the parts should be hidden as much as possible by the folds given to the dress in

(*Fig.* 111.)

carving. A fourth piece, *e,* 10-in. thick, is joined on the last in the line, *f, g,* to form the middle-winged figure, as the head

(*Fig.* 112.)

is in advance of the wings, and both parts project inwards, overshadowing the sleepers; additional pieces may be clamped on the face, to give the due projection to the parts. The dotted lines on the cut suggest another method of gluing up the wood; for the carving in this case, the line *h, i,* is that of a butt joint of two pieces, which is formed in the medial line of the centre figure. It may be desirable to execute the centre figure separately, and to adjust and fix it on from behind. The cornice consists of four principal parts, which are separable, the two ends and two sides; those parts at the angles being slip dovetailed together, and secured by angle plates. The ground on which the cornice mouldings are planted is formed of deal 1-in. thick; the semicircular parts of it are made in two thicknesses; the ends of the semicircles are half checked on the short horizontal pieces, which again being dovetailed into the sides, with them form the angles of the cornice. At the head, square blocks are glued on the ground to form the brakes; the turned blocks on the corresponding parts at the foot may be scribed on. The depth of these brakes and blocks is about 3½-in. measuring on the top moulding of the cornice. Attention to this is necessary, as the valance, which is nailed to the roof, passes between the two inner columns, on its being carried round to the ends. After the mouldings on the cornice are planted, the turned blocks may be notched on the angles of the ground, and then mitred in with the adjoining part of the moulding, and finally screwed to the end of the cornice; this latter particular is important, as in dovetailing the ground the pins of the dovetails are formed on both ends of the sides, which parts in consequence are first put on the bed, the ends being driven home after. The ornamental brackets on the angles of the cornice below are doweled on, and are let in by the end into the ornamental pieces which are fixed on the pillars. The vases are turned, separately carved, and slip doweled on the top. The leaves on the cornice should be profiled from one or more long pieces shaped to the ground, and then separately carved. The roof of the bed is made with straight horizontal sides, and arched ends dovetailed at right angles into them. These ends are not apparent in the drawing, from being cloth-covered on their upper edge; they follow the general outline of the tops of the arches, and are at both ends kept apart from them about ⅜-in., so as to admit of the valance being interposed between. The ornamental ridge pole of the roof is tenoned between the ends of the cornice; a block is carried along its under edge on each side for attaching the cloth of the roof; the apparent convexity of which is formed by straining the cloth stiffly between its points of attachment, the centre of the curve being supported on each side, by a stretching rod mortised between the circular ends.

BED PILLARS.—PLATE LXXXIV.

Fig. 1.—This design is for mahogany pillars; being suitable for the common thickness of wood for posts of this description, namely, five inches. The can is turned by itself, and joined round the pillar. Excepting the can and buttons, and the clamps of the base, this pillar is solid throughout. The panels covering the bed-screws are fastened by ball and plate catches, as shown in (*Fig.* 112), or by two screw nails, which fasten like dove-tails upon the post.

(*Fig.* 113.)

Fig. 2.—The pillar shown in this figure should be made of oak. This wood being less costly than mahogany, it is better to have it the whole thickness, since the labour of clamping and mitring will not be compensated by any saving thereby effected in the wood. The drops under the can, and the decorations above the base-moulding, are planted on. The pillar is turned the whole length of the twisting, and a third of the capital: the remainder of the capital being wrought square. If no twisting lathe is at command, the spirals may be hand-wrought, and, as preparatory to this, take a piece of girth-web, and tack it to the front and centre of the pillar, just above the can; then wind the girth round it spirally, making eight turns between the can and the capital; taking care to terminate the spiral on the front side, as otherwise the capital will appear to *throw*, for want of support. When the girth is fixed, draw the spiral lines along its edges with a pencil, after which it may be removed and the work begun. A flat twist is made, in the first place, which the carver afterwards deepens and finishes. This design does not admit of panels on the surbase to cover the bed-screws.

Fig. 3.—This pillar is for mahogany, and is turned its whole length. The can is put on in the same manner as Fig. 1.; and the buttons and drops are sunk in. The slide panels on the surbase are also fixed as in Fig. 1.

Fig. 4.—The design exhibited in this figure is adapted either for oak or mahogany. If made of oak, whole wood is to be used, for the reason given under Fig. 2; and the pillar is to be turned its whole length, leaving *wants* for the octagonal sides. If mahogany is used, the mouldings above the surbase, and also the base mouldings may be planted and mitred. As this pillar tapers to the top, as much wood may be taken off the thickness, at that part, as will make all the small mouldings. These last are wrought the cross way of the wood; and the best method is to cross-cut them at their breadths, and plant them continuously on the edge of a board, and work them all in one length. This pillar must be fastened by the patent screw, Fig. 7, Plate LXXXIII., as the design is not suitable for panelling.

Fig. 5.—This is intended for mahogany, and is turned from the upper mouldings of the surbase, all below which is square. The large bead or can is planted as in former cases; and the base and upper mouldings are mitred on. The slide panels are the same as in Fig. 3, and other examples.

BED PILLARS.—PLATE LXXXV.

Fig. 1.—This pillar is intended to be made of Bay mahogany, veneered with Spanish wood. It is turned the whole length of the shaft and surbase. The base moulding is made separately, and fixed on with dowels; and the mouldings constituting the can above the surbase are formed from a ring of wood, separately made, and let into a groove turned on the pillar; as shown in Plate I., Fig. 1; the inserted piece being afterwards turned and carved on the pillar. The capital is also of Spanish wood, carved separately, and is fixed upon the shaft by a tenon. This pillar must be covered with a strong mottle veneer, which, when polished, gives it a clear, plain, light effect, being its principal beauty. The portions of the pillar above and below the can are separately veneered, and each with one piece. In proceeding to lay the veneer it is first brought to its proper breadth at each end, allowing, besides the absolute measure, $\frac{3}{16}$-in. more for one of the sides to overlap the other; it is then stripped straight on the edges, and laid by means of girth web rolled tightly around it on the pillar. As the process is a little tedious, and during it the glue is apt to cool, after the web is wound round the pillar the glue is heated, and, at the same time, the web is tightened strongly up, by moistening the whole surface with hot water before a blazing fire; turning the pillar, and exposing all parts of it in succession to the heat. The whole is allowed to dry for a day, after which, the girth web is unwound, and the veneer is washed clean; the overlapping side is now carefully stripped back by a rebate plane, until the edge of the underlying side begins to appear; a hot iron is then coursed along the veneer at this part, to dissolve the glue retained under the projecting side, and so to reduce the inequality of surface: the two edges of the veneer being thus brought to abut together, and the joint accordingly formed. Sliding panels, usually placed on the surbase to cover the screws, are not applicable to this pillar; and their use is obviated by adopting the patent screw, Fig. 7, the construction of which is so simple as to require little explanation. It consists of a strong iron screw, which deeply penetrates the posts from the inside of the framing, at an angle of 45 degrees. The body of the screw passes through the centre of an arch of iron, which, while its extremities act on both rails, urging them home, re-acts equally, and at the same instant, against the screw, the action of which solicits the post powerfully inwards. The ends of the arch are resisted by their partial insertion into the wood of the rails, where, also, for the same purpose, iron plates crossing the rails are screwed on. The head of the bracing-screw is formed into an eye, through which a lever is made to act in turning it.

Fig. 2.—This pillar is also to be made of mahogany, and turned the whole length from the square, or top of the surbase. The can is octagonal; the moulding on it is separately made, being worked in one length and mitred round. The ground for the moulding is formed on the original thickness of the wood for the pillar; which, at this part, is not entirely turned, but has merely the corners chipped off. The screw heads are covered with sliding panels. The base mouldings are mitred and clamped; as much wood as will serve this purpose may be cut down from the several sides of the post at the top before it is turned.

Fig. 3.—In this design the turning commences at the top of the surbase. The can is formed, fixed, turned, and carved, as in Fig. 1; and the ornamental part above the can is gorged out, the pillar being left so much thicker for the purpose. The base mouldings are mitred and clamped as in Fig. 2. As the effect of the surbase would be injured by the sliding panel, this pillar must be fixed like Fig. 1, by the patent screw, Fig. 7.

Fig. 4.—This is adapted either for oak or mahogany, and is wrought in the same way as Fig. 3. The buttons on the can, and the small detached ornaments in the cavetto, above it, are sunk in.

Fig. 5.—This pillar is to be made of mahogany, and to be wrought in the same manner as Fig. 2, all above the surbase being turned, and all under it square. The shaft is octagonal,

h ✻

and starts from the round above the can. The method of starting and finishing the panes, shown in this example, has a very good effect. The surbase has sliding panels for the screws, the button above each panel being sunk in.

Fig. 6.—The design here given is intended for oak, and the whole pillar is solid except the can, which is split and put on as in Fig. 1, and the base moulding which is blocked from one piece and fixed with dowels. The pillar is turned the whole length from the base moulding to near the scrolls of the capital, and to preserve the octagonal form as large as the wood will admit, the turner must leave, on the greatest diameters, *wants* or flat spaces nearly the size of the panes. To enable him to do this, suitable wood must be given to him, and, for guidance, a full-sized draught of the design. After the wood is turned, draw on the lines for the octagon in the usual way. This is done by fixing the pillar in what is termed a *reeding* box (*Fig.* 114), which is a long box without top or bottom, about

(Fig. 114.)

nine inches square inside, and about nine feet long, and made of inch and quarter deal. It is provided with movable ends, through which pivot-centres a, b, are driven for suspending the post when under operation. Grooves b, c, d, &c., are wrought in the sides of the box, into which the end a, may be slid, to fit different lengths of posts. The ends may be varied in height to suit the requirements of work, and, in such case, the sides are braced together by a wooden screw, f, which, passing through one side, acts in the other opposite. On the pillar being laid in the box, divide its circumference into eight equal parts with the compasses; then with a reeding gauge draw pencil lines through the points of division along the entire length of the pillar; this being done, the octagonal sides on it are formed by flattening the surface between these lines.

This pillar is screwed to the stock in the same way as Fig. 1. In place of the patent screw, Fig. 7, however, the contrivance shown at Fig. 8 may be used, which is quite as simple and efficient. The exact breadth of the stock B is drawn on the side of the post at the proper height, and a second breadth, D, with about an inch additional, immediately below the first. Then work out of this lower measure a groove 1½-in. broad, and of a depth equal to the intended length of the tenon, continuous with this mortise, and of the same depth a receiving dove-tail is wrought out of the upper breadth, which widens inwards and narrows towards the top; with this a dove-tail, formed on the end of the stock, is made to correspond. This construction is shown by A, Fig. 8, and by section A B, Fig. 9. The framing is effected by inserting the dove-tail of the stock into the groove, and raising it into the receiving part, where it is maintained by the block d, which fills the groove, and is urged home, either by cramp or hammer, after the wedge c is driven in. When the bed is to be taken down, on driving out the wedge c the whole framing will come asunder readily.

COTS AND CRADLES.—PLATE LXXXVI.

Fig. 1 is, in the body and head, framed and sunk panelled. The side framing is wrought to shape; it is 2½-in. broad, by ⅞-in. thick, with the end rails mortised into the sides; the latter only are veneered before the frames are put together, the end rails being cross-veneered after. The two end frames are each formed into quadrant curves, which are half checked on each other below, and above are tenoned or checked into a cross

rail. The end frames abut on, and are glued and screwed to, the ends of the side frames. They are made to project so as to form a ⅜-in. raised border on the side, which is cross-veneered. The panels are cloth covered and set in from the outside; they may be supported behind by fillets, sprigged on the framing, or by a check wrought out of it before it is put together; the panel mouldings and frets are afterwards planted on. The sides are connected at the bottom by a keel-piece, which is screwed on them and on the ends. The head is formed of three pieces, the two sides and top; these are made up as frets in three thicknesses, making together about ½-in. The proper curve is given to the pieces by cauling them on suitable moulds. The back of the head is similarly prepared, and, after being shaped and panelled, is doweled down on the body. The sides of the head are then fitted to the back and body, and doweled on the latter. The circular top is then joined down on the sides, and keyed to them from the inside, and canvassed over at the joints. After all these fittings are made, and before they are finally fixed, the panelled openings on the head are cut out, and the mouldings around them mitred in. The pieces cut out form the panels, which, after being trimmed and cloth covered, are restored to their original position. After the head of the cot is attached to the body, the moulding around the upper edge of the latter is planted on. A square fillet is formed around the head in front, by planting on the face a cross band ¼-in. thick, which works in with the upper member of the moulding on the body. The upper edge of the moulding and of the fillet, is cross-banded. The cot is suspended by looped brass rods screwed to it at each end, and carried over strong studs fixed into the supporting pillars. It may be necessary that the stretching rail below be made more massive and stronger in its attachment to the pillars than is shown in the Plate. The length of this rail is obviously determined by that of the cot, including the greatest projections on the pillar. The cot is stuffed inside.

Fig. 2, in the body, is built of ⅞-in. deal. The segments should generally go completely round the end, their joinings being effected chiefly on the sides; each layer might be independently formed, and the pieces for strength made to half lap on each other at their abutments. On the whole being glued up, it is then wrought to shape on the outside, and smoothed off within. The body may be cross-veneered or done up in colours, with the mouldings and other decorations gilt. The panels on the sides are cloth covered. They may be either formed flush, the cloth being nailed on the body, or the pieces may be cut out, covered, and, after the mouldings are planted, replaced from the inside and blocked. The mouldings may be wrought to shape out of the solid in quarter lengths, and butt joined; or they may be wrought in half lengths, and steam bent around the ends, and butted in mid length. The fret ornament around the bottom is 1/16-in. thick; it is by the upper edge checked into the body, and then lapped over by the moulding. The bottom is checked in from below. The head in front view is semicircular, and is formed of seven ribs to the two in front, which together form the semicircle; a piece of solid wood, for the carving, similarly shaped, is glued on to the ribs and edge of the body. The carving is executed and the parts fitted before they are finally fixed; after which the other ribs are adjusted, the whole being brought together at the top, and secured by screws, and by cloth glued on. The head is cloth covered outside, and stuffed within. The crown, which surmounts the head, is gilt, and rests on a crimson tasselated cushion.

Fig. 3.—The body of this cradle is a large moulding, of solid wood, thin wrought and adjusted to the overly, and mitred in the four corners. The mitres, on their upper and under edges, are secured by small iron plates, which are sunk flush into them, diagonally, and screwed on. The carving on each corner is formed of two pieces, which are grounded and mitred together. The bottom is formed by a board screwed on, upon the edges of which the mouldings, shown in the design, are planted; to this bottom the rocking feet are doweled or attached by screws sent through from within. The head is built of staves of solid wood, on which the carving in front is wrought. The ends of the staves are made to project, so as to form together a fillet round the back of the head.

Fig. 4 is, in all important particulars, similar in construction to Fig. 3.

WARDROBES.—PLATE LXXXVII.

The sort of wardrobe, of which the designs on this Plate are examples, is usually made in a single carcass, with a loose cornice and base; frequently they are made in two carcasses, the interior adjoining gables of which are screwed together; in such case, the moulding shown between the doors, which in the single carcass is glued on the door stile, is of a breadth corresponding to the thickness of both inner gables, and is planted on one of them, flush with the inside, and projecting beyond the outside so as to lap on the edge of the other gable, which is brought close up behind the moulding, before both gables are screwed together. Whatever method is adopted, the wardrobe, interiorly, is divided into half, if not, by the construction of two distinct and separate divisions; then by one centre division, mortised between the carcass, top and bottom; most frequently this centre division is stopped short below, being mortised into a horizontal division, dove-tailed into the gables at about 10-in. from their lower end; by this means, a drawer space, the entire length of the wardrobe, is cut off, which forms a convenient deposit for small clothes or napery. Of the two upper spaces, that to the right is fitted with drawers and trays; there are usually three drawers and four trays, the drawers being under; the latter are separated from each other and from the trays, by fore-edges and shelves. The trays are made to run on fillets screwed to the gables. The space to the left and also the carcass back, which is framed and panelled, are cloth lined, and provided with hooks at the top for hanging dresses.

Fig. 1.—The four corners are wrought into a quarter round on the gables of about 2½-in. radius. The rounded corners stand in advance of the top and bottom edges of the carcass about ½-in., and the doors which fit between them are, in consequence, sunk this amount, and stand out, their remaining thickness forming a long brake in front; the base and cornice are made to correspond with the outline thus given to the carcass.

Fig. 2 is made like the preceding, but is square in front, and embellished by two ornamental columns, ¾ of the round, which are doweled on the doors or screwed on from the inside.

Fig. 3.—The pilasters on the doors are sunk panelled by means of a raised border planted on, within which a small moulding is afterwards mitred and fitted. A block and vase, continuous of the pilaster, are planted on and above the cornice. The doors are sunk panelled. An ornamental panel, with a moulded border, is planted on the field of the door panel. The ornaments on the angles of the doors are together wrought out of one piece, then cut asunder, and planted on.

Fig. 4.—The fret on the door, enclosing the moulding on the top, is formed of two pieces, mitred together in the centre; each pair may be glued and fretted together, then separated, fitted, and planted. The top ornament is formed of ½-in. wood; it is slip doweled on the top, and afterwards cut.

WARDROBES.—PLATE LXXXVIII.

These designs are of a plain character, and require, for effect, that they be executed in rich wood; each should be constructed in three carcasses, the two outer of which, or wings, should be entirely a free space within, for hanging dresses, and cloth lined, or furnished below with one drawer, each about 12-in. deep; the centre part is provided with drawers and trays. The cornice and base of each design are entire.

Fig. 1 has a projecting centre, on the gables of which the doors on the wings are made to lock. The panel of the centre door is a mirror plate; the door frame, in consequence, must be of 1½-in. wood; the plate is protected from behind by a panelled frame ¾-in. thick. The two inner pilasters move with the centre door; the outer pilasters are attached to the doors of the wings. The block in the centre above the cornice, along with the frets at each end of it, are set back parallel to the front of the cornice frieze, and fixed by screws.

Fig. 2 has the doors all in one plane, with the centre one pivot-hinged; they are flush panelled, with a raised panel planted on each. The two centre pilasters are fixed, and those at the ends are, as in Fig. 1, attached to the doors of the wings. They are stop chamfered on the corners to within 3/16-in. of the door stile, and the other decorations on them are inlaid.

WARDROBES.—PLATE LXXXIX.

The general construction of this wardrobe is sufficiently apparent from the design; the wings are made and adapted similarly to those of the preceding. The doors are flush panelled and veneered over; two styles of decoration are shown on them. The mouldings and relievo figures on both are planted on the face. The pilaster on the door to the left is wrought from one piece of solid wood, the truss and base are made to abut to and lap on it; the tie ornament in the centre of the shaft is planted on. The carving around the circular moulding on the door to the right, is formed of two pieces of 2-in. wood, joined together in the centre. The drawers and cabinet between the wings are separately made, and in the ordinary manner. The cabinet doors are pivot-hinged; a slip of wood ⅝-in. thick, moulded on the fore edge, is interposed all around, between the cabinet and the top of the drawers, so as to make the doors sweep clear of the drawers' top; this, although not apparent in the design, requires to be introduced. The two interior gables of the wings may be of solid wood, or veneered only as far as they are exposed, the continuation backward being of deal. The mouldings on the cabinet doors are planted on the face of the door framing, and made to lap inwards, forming a check for the frets, which again are closed in from behind with a panel, cloth covered; the heads on the centre of the frets are screwed on from behind. The several parts of the large moulding on the cornice are first mitred, then carved and planted; the angles are trimmed after the whole is glued down.

WARDROBES.—PLATE XC.

The designs on this Plate are formed in two heights, which are united together in the bottom line of the columns and pilasters. The upper portion is divided interiorly, as described under Plate LXXXVII.; the under part is a case containing a large drawer, which acts between the base and surbase, and extends the whole length, between the gables, with its front lapping over their edge. Sometimes, and more ingeniously, the drawer front is made to pass within the gables, being stopped flush with them; and the pilasters are hinged to the edge of the gables, and made to lock on the drawer.

The doors on the figure to the right are flush panelled; on the panel of each, as a ground, an ornamental panel of solid wood, 1¼-in. thick, is laid; the ground panel might be dispensed with by increasing the breadth of the doors' framing, and making the ornamental panel to lap on it. A hollow moulding is wrought on the solid around this panel, and its edges are pieced out to form the brakes on its sides. After this raised panel is shaped and glued down, the mouldings of the door frame are mitred and planted around its edge; the field of the panel is veneered with rich wood; the panel on the drawer front is similarly treated. The pilasters are separately made, and, on being wholly finished, are planted on the door frame. The cornice ground, in the centre of its front, is pieced out and veneered, forming a ground on which the top mouldings are planted.

The other design, on the Plate, has the doors also flush panelled, with an ornamental panel planted on. The columns are slightly flattened behind, and applied to, and screwed on, the door stile. The shaft of the columns is veneered. The capital and base of the column are doweled on; the moulding surmounting the former is paned. The carved top of the door moulding is of one piece, 2-in. thick, of cross wood, and includes the curves which join on to the ends of the stile moulding, the grain of both pieces being made to run alike. This part, in the order of work, is first planted, and the adjoining parts are abutted to it. A raised panel, ⅜-in. thick, is planted on the drawer front, and the moulding is carried round it; on this ground the other decorations are successively glued down. (*Fig.* 115) presents the cornice in cross section. The ornament, on its top, requires 2-in. wood, with the chief projections of the carving brought out by clamping.

(*Fig.* 115.)

PILASTERS AND BRACKETS.—PLATE XCI.

The pilasters and brackets, designs of which are shown on this Plate, are principally intended for wardrobes; they might also be employed on bookcases, or adapted to decorate the front of other carcass work. Each example is surmounted by an appropriate entablature, which may be considered either as forming part of the pilaster, or as separate from it, and suggestive of a style of cornicing becoming the piece of furniture on which the pilaster or bracket might be displayed. In executing the profile of any of these designs, when several pieces are required, it is more expeditious to cross work them all at once out of a single piece, or to glue the pieces temporarily together for this purpose; those for the top and bottom together, and severally apart, any projections on the sides being afterwards brought out by clamping.

Fig. 1 is adapted for oak or mahogany; it is relieved behind and also around the scrolls by various perforations; the turned drops on the under part are doweled or screwed on.

Fig. 2 is suitable for mahogany or rosewood; it is also well adapted for gilding, if this should accord with the character of the piece of furniture on which it is introduced.

Figs. 3 and 4 should be executed in oak; the latter may be partially gilt.

Figs. 5, 6, 7, 8.—These brackets may be detached from connection with any more extended design, and employed as an

independent means of support. In such case they should be treated freely, according to taste or fancy, and may be executed in solid wood, and partially gilt, or in deal, and done up in gold and colours. They may also be employed on a pilaster ground, with a base or bottom piece to correspond, as in the other designs on the Plate.

WASH-STANDS AND DRESSING-TABLES.—PLATE XCII.

Fig. 1.—This design, with its decorations, is founded on the Moorish style of the Alhambra. The top and ledges should be of marble, resting on a moulded frieze, the ground of which is framed into the top of the legs, as shown, (*Fig.* 116). The legs, after being turned, are reduced in the square at the top, so as to work off flush with the rails; the turned corner-caps, and the mouldings which mitre with them, are then fitted and planted on. The order of operation being thus, the caps are first notched on the corners; they are then mitred, and the mouldings on the front and ends are afterwards adjusted to them. The ledges are, as usual, pinned down on the marble top; the back and returns are united at the angles by means of small pillars of wood or marble, surmounted by carved vases; if the pillars are of wood, the back is checked into them behind, and secured by screws sent through the marble into the wood; the returns being let into grooves, wrought into the front. The bracket for supporting the water bottle is fixed on from behind. The stretcher is of solid wood, and is doweled from under to the bottom of the legs, the stump feet being afterwards doweled on.

(*Fig.* 116.)

Fig. 2 is a Gothic wash-stand, well adapted for oak of a light or dark variety, the top and the ledges to be of marble; the latter may be of wood. The frame under the top is separately made, and the moulding is planted on around it; at the ends it is doweled down on the shaped cross-bar, which again is similarly fixed to the pillar. The stretcher below is mortised between the bottom blocks.

Fig. 3.—The top is of marble, and forms about two-thirds of a circle: the rim under it is of solid wood turned and doweled down on the supports; and, as the back is straight, a cross rail, the thickness of the moulding, unites the ends of the rim behind, being half checked into them. The two shaped supports behind are doweled together, edge to edge, in the same plane, the one in front being fixed to these at right angles. The back may be of solid wood and attached to the rim by screws, or it may be of marble, and made to rest on a check, formed by the projecting back rail, being also attached to the top in the usual manner.

Fig. 4.—The top, with its ledge, and also the mirror sole, may be of marble; the moulding under the top is formed on a flat frame, consisting of a front and two ends of solid wood; the back rail may be of deal. The pedestals are separate; and on the table being fitted up, they are united together by the bracket which crosses the knee-hole and supports the drawer; and by the fore-edge that borders the drawer above, which is dovetailed into the gables, but chiefly by the moulded frame which crosses, and is screwed to, the top of both pedestals.

The mirror supports, on being profiled, are fitted to the sole; they are attached by screws, wrought into the standards, which are made to pass through the marble, and secured by nuts from under. They are afterwards separately carved, finished, and finally fixed; if the sole is made of wood, the supports are simply doweled on. The mirror frame is built up of two ½-in. thicknesses of mahogany; the fret on it is made up in the usual manner, and checked in flush from the fore-edge of the frame; the moulding is then planted on, and made to lap on the glass; the outer edge of the frame is slipped with veneer.

Fig. 5.—As in this design the moulding under the top is planted on the body of the pedestals; the top itself, in consequence, rests immediately on both. The pilasters intersect the moulding, and pass up to the top; they are planted on a ground formed for them on the pedestals, and are chamfered on the angles, the other decorations on them are carved out of the solid. The frame supporting the glass is made entire, and formed of two equal thicknesses, that behind, for sake of strength, being made to cross the front thickness obliquely. At the top, the pieces do not mitre, but lap on each other, and, during the process, the frame is stiffened below by a cross rail temporarily screwed on the bottom. The standards, on their outer edge, are chamfered from both sides to the joint line in the middle. They are made to lean backwards, and are supported from behind by a piece shaped like the other feet, so that the standards have a tripod support. The position of the mirror may be made secure and permanent by pinning the standards into the top. The glass frame is made similarly to that of Fig. 4, the moulding being planted on and made to lap within a ground frame, forming a check for the plate, the outer edge being slipped with veneer.

MOULDINGS.—PLATE XCIII.

The mouldings, the designs for which are here given, are all of full size. The assemblage, arrangement, and relative dimension of the parts, forming each of the examples in the series for cornices, may be considered as judicious and elegant, but arbitrary; other and equally suitable combinations may be made of the various members or elements, dispersed throughout the several designs; requiring the exercise of judgment and taste in the cabinet-maker for their selection and adjustment. The various entablatures may be wrought in such parts, separately, as are most suitable either for the economy of materials, or for convenience of working. Lines are drawn behind several of the mouldings, suggestive of the thickness and breadth of solid wood required for their execution. If the mouldings are to be veneered, the reader is referred to p. 56 of this work, where that process is considered in detail.

The other mouldings on the Plate are adapted to the stiles of doors that are sunk-panelled, or for bordering the edges of raised panels; the particular character and dimension of each of the mouldings will readily suggest its adaptation for one or other of these purposes.

MOULDINGS.—PLATE XCIV.

The various combinations of mouldings shown on this Plate, are presented in full or available size, along with their profile and perspective expression; the absolute dimensions given may, however, be easily modified and adapted, while the same form and proportion is preserved among the *parts*, or, as previously stated, other groupings of the forms may be effected, according to taste, or the character of the work on which the mouldings are to be displayed. Besides the uses of the mouldings for table tops, with their rims, and for chiffoniers, &c., as suggested in the title, the profiles are generally well adapted for turnery, where the mass is considerable, and the members are bold and expansive.

PORTABLE BED CHAIR AND OTTOMAN SEAT.— PLATE XCV.

The piece of furniture variously shown, in the design here given, is admirably adapted for the military man or traveller,

when subject to circumstances wherein the conveniences which it furnishes are not otherwise easily attainable. It is so contrived as to admit of three distinct uses, with a corresponding change in the arrangement and appearance of its parts suitable to each; it may, with facility be converted, on occasion, either into a chair, bed, or open seat; and in this last, which is its most compacted shape, it may be stowed into a stout trunk, of moderate dimensions, and easily carried.

The seat is square framed; its front is made in the ordinary manner. The haunch rails, being exposed on both sides, should be of solid wood 1¼-in. thick; they require to be about 3¼-in. broad, as they have to receive within them the bed-frames when folded; they are in front mortised into the prolonged upper end of the legs, flush inside, and are, at the back, lap-dovetailed into a cross rail of the same dimensions; the under edge of this quadrangular frame being made to correspond in height with the upper edge of the front rail; the dimensions of the interior space requires to be about 28 inches, measuring between the sides; and, from back to front, 25 inches.

A drawer case, made of ⅞-in. wood, corresponding exactly in form and dimension with the outside of the chair seat, is glued and screwed to the rails from under, and wrought off flush with them; the case extends forward, close to the inside of the front rail, to which it is fixed by screws sent through it from within. The sides and closed ends of the case, and the edges of the drawer opening, are of solid wood; its top and bottom are of deal. The moulding around the case below is partly scribed on to the back of the front legs, and a screw is sent through each corner into its adjoining leg. The turned back feet are doweled on. The bed frames are of solid wood and cane woven in the centre. The frame, within the seat, is permanently fixed, and made to rest on the top of the drawer case. The second in order is hinged to that first named, having the knuckle of the hinge to the upper side, and half pin up, so that these two frames may fold directly down on each other; the third frame has the knuckle of the hinge down, requiring this frame to fold to the under side of the second, on that being raised to fold on the first; when so arranged, they come to be adjusted as they should be shown in Fig. 1—there being an inadvertency in the drawing at this point, three pairs of hinges being apparent, whereas only one, and that the under pair, can be shown. The supporting legs are secured to their position by iron screws, wrought into their upper end, which are made to act in plate-nuts that are sunk under the outer sides of the second and third frames, as shown in Fig. 2. These legs, when the piece of furniture is altered from being a bed to being a chair or seat, are stowed away into the drawer. The mattress for the bed consists of three separate pieces, corresponding to the three folds; these also are united edge to edge, and by ties or buttons, so as to fold on each other and conveniently stow into the drawer; when the article takes the form of a chair, one portion of the mattress is used as the seat cushion. The elbows are framed in the ordinary manner; they are hinged to the side rails, and when folded down, as in Fig. 3, the scrolls require to pass in behind the front feet; and, in consequence, they must recede from the front the full thickness of the feet. The top is hinged to the upper edge of the back rail of the seat; it is stuffed inside and also without, where it is covered with a sewed piece, as shown in Fig. 3. When the top and elbows are erect, they are locked together by spring catches or hooks.

Fig. 4 is a trunk for containing the chair, and opens on the side; it may be of oak, with japanned corner clasps, or of deal, and leather covered.

STEAM-BOAT RAILINGS AND CLOCK.—PLATE XCVI.

The fretted rails, designs of which are here shown, are intended to surmount the first tier of berths in a steam-vessel, and to enclose and form the front of the second tier, being made to pass along the sides and around the stern. The rails consist of parts, whose lengths correspond to those of the several berths, and whose adjoining ends are united, by means of small pillars, into which the rails mitre above and below; the pillars rest on, and are doweled to, the elbows of the sofas of the lower berths.

Fig. 1.—This railing is in the Flemish style, and should be made of rosewood; the fret is, as usual, made up in three thicknesses, and relieved on the face by carving; it is put in and secured by a stout panel from behind; sometimes there is a groove made in the upper and under moulding to receive the fret, as shown in section at A.

Fig. 2 is in the Elizabethan style, and for oak; this rail is made similarly to the last, being different only in detail; it is presented in section at B.

Fig. 3 is in the same style as the preceding, but to be executed in rosewood; here there are two portions of the rail presented, the smaller of which is at the stern, and over it the ornamental clock is placed; it being fixed on a veneered ground formed on the rudder case. The pendant flowers and fruit on the rail are gilt; and so also the small moulding in contact with the fret; the vases are hatched with gold. In all other respects this rail resembles the preceding. The clock case requires wood 6½-in. thick; it is made of deal, and entirely gilt; the dial may be white or silvered. This rail is shown in section at C.

DETAILS, &C.—PLATE XCVII.

The sketches on this and the two following Plates, although detached from the connections in which they were originally presented, will readily suggest to the experienced cabinet-maker their particular use or easy adaptation.

Figs. 1 and 2 are well suited for the corner ornaments of the doors of such cabinets, as are shown in Plates XXXVIII. and XLVIII.; or the carved part may be wrought in relief and fretted, or the figure alone may be inlaid.

Figs. 3 and 5 are truss brackets, suitable for the top and bottom of pilasters; the foliage on both is similar to that on Fig. 1; the moulding which borders the latter is similar to that which caps the upper trusses; this uniformity of style would adapt these parts for being displayed on one common ground.

Figs. 4 and 6 are brackets which might be employed for supporting the upper and under shelves of a chiffonier respectively.

Figs. 7, 8, and 9, are key-hole ornaments; the first two of which may be inlaid, or the whole may be separately carved and planted.

Figs. 10 and 11 are panelled ornaments, and may be employed of greater dimension, according to surface.

DETAILS, &C.—PLATE XCVIII.

On this Plate are shown the front and side views of four details of a massive character; the designs are wrought out by the fantastic combinations of animal and vegetable forms, and are highly novel and ornamental.

Figs. 1 and 2 represent a truss support suitable for a hall or bagatelle table, slab side-board, or under part of a book-case or other cabinet. It may be done up in oak or in colours, and partially gilt.

Figs. 3 and 4 are two views of a design intended for being attached to fixed pilasters on an open cabinet, and generally also can be made to serve purposes similar to the preceding.

Figs. 5 and 6 exhibit a bold and effective design for the front of a sofa, couch, or easy chair; it might also be introduced with good effect on the bottom ends of a half tester bedstead. A form, approaching to this, is sometimes given to the ends of sofas for the saloons of steam-vessels; such require to be very massive, and the grain of the wood in the head must run so as to preserve the greatest possible strength in the parts having least support.

Figs. 7 and 8 display a striking and highly original treatment of the pilaster of a cabinet below, and the subjacent portion of the base by the introduction of a griffin figure, the body and appended carving of which unites the pilaster and base, and passes down to near the bottom of the latter.

DETAILS, &C.—PLATE XCIX.

All the details on this Plate are so approximately related in general style, that they might be displayed together on one piece of furniture.

Fig. 1 is a top ornament suitable for a bookcase, wardrobe, sideboard, or chiffonier; it is also well adapted for a mirror, in which case it should be gilt.

Fig. 2 might be employed as a decoration for door panels.

Figs. 3 and 4.—A pair of either of these might be displayed on the top of the wings of a wardrobe or bookcase, one at each end of Fig. 1.

Figs. 5 and 6 are appropriate devices for ornamenting the grounds of pilasters.

ORNAMENTS ADAPTED FROM NATURE.—PLATE C.

Fig. 1 is a study of leaves and berry of the hawthorn (*Crataegus oxyacantha*).

Fig. 1, *a*.—In an adaptation for a circular compartment, the centre group of berries must rise semicircularly, the stalks and leafage to lie flat upon the ground, with the large leaves swelling gently up in rounded forms towards the middle of their broader parts. The outer group of berries must have the lower layer in half relief only, with those above lying on them, fully rounded, so as to induce, from their numerous convexities, a sparkling reflection of light.

Fig. 2 is the common pea (*Pisum sativum*), of which Fig. 2, *a*, is an arrangement, for the spandril of an elliptical arch; the lower pods must lie in high relief on the ground, the large leaves immediately above them rising in rounded masses, where they are not repressed by the stalks. Each pair of leaflets must be arranged so that the lower one is in very low relief, while the upper swells up considerably.

Fig. 3 is a study from the *Sonchus oleraceus*, being a variety of the sow thistle, of which Fig. 3, *a*, is an adaptation for a capital, having the stems carrying buds between the leaves; smaller leaflets are arranged symmetrically around the ovolo.

Fig. 4 is a study of rye-grass (*Secale cereale*), of which Fig. 4, *a*, is an application to a frieze, along with the common ground ivy (*Glechoma hederacea*), festooned between it. Here the leaves of the latter must rise in full rounded masses, contrasting with the more angular forms of the grass; one side of many of the leaves should nearly disappear into the ground, and the back leaves and leaflets near the grass should be but faintly detached from it.

Fig. 5.—Studies of *Penicillaria spicata*, the bulrush, and the leaves of a water plant; the latter is very common in ponds and ditches.

Fig. 5, *a*, is an ogee moulding, ornamented with both the above; the cylindrical head of the bulrush is shown as shrouded by the folding leaves of the water plant.

ORNAMENTS ADAPTED FROM NATURE.—PLATE CI.

Fig. 1.—A study from nature; it is a small plant found commonly in hedges.

Fig. 1, A.—Adaptation of the above as a perforated gallery, the application of natural forms to this purpose represented merely by outline on a flat surface, requires a more rigidly geometric treatment than where the surface is relieved by carving; it is also necessary that the points should be protected by being made to touch; otherwise it would be too liable to be broken. The rounded form of the mushroom is introduced below to support the leaflets, and by its semicircular curve, to contrast with the rigid, straight lines. The novel and agreeable effect produced by the introduction of this humble plant, serves to prove that no objects in nature, however simple or insignificant, should be considered as beneath the attention of the ornamental designer.

Fig. 2.—Study from the sow thistle.

Fig. 2, A.—Part of a support for a small table. The capital composed of the sow thistle, with leaflets arranged around the necking. The shaft is worked out of a circular turned piece, with a panel sunk on three faces, each containing a grass or some other simple upright plant. At the base, tendrils of the convolvulus bend over, like scrolls, with a leaf between them. The rib, carried up the angle, connects them as a stem with the leaves which bend over at the top. The bulb is ornamented with ivy leaves and berries, which must be kept in low relief, so as not to destroy the contour.

Fig. 3.—A screw mount; the outer part is perforated; the forms are adapted from a very beautiful plant, which is seen climbing in the hedges, with dark green shining leaves, and red berries. The centre part has an inlaid ornament, composed of ivy leaves and berries twined round a geometrical arrangement of lines. The peculiarities of the ivy are all indicated, even to the small roots which support it.

HALL TABLES.

Fig 2.

Fig 4.

Fig 1.

Fig 3.

366

Fig 1

Fig 2

Fig 3

9 6 3 0   1   2   3 Feet

P. Thomson Del.

J. H. Le Keux Sculp.

BLACKIE & SON, GLASGOW, EDINBURGH & LONDON.

HALL CHAIRS.

Fig. 1.

Fig. 3.

Fig. 7.

Fig. 2.

Fig. 6.

Fig. 1.

Inches 12   9   6   3   0   1   2   3 Feet.

368

PLATE II.

HALL CHAIRS.

Fig 4.

Fig 3.

Fig 2.

Fig 1.

Fig 8.

Fig 7.

Fig 6.

Fig 5.

Inches 12   6   3   0   1   2   3 Feet

Fig 2

Fig 4

Fig 1

Fig 3

Inches 12   9   6   3   0   1   2   3   4   5 Feet

HAT and UMBRELLA STANDS.

Fig.1

Fig.2

Fig.3

Fig.4

Fig.5

Fig.6

Inches.0 9 6 3 0   1   2   3   4   5   6   7   8   9 Feet.

PLATE VII.

HAT AND UMBRELLA STANDS.

Fig.3.

Fig.2.

Fig.1.

J.H. Le Keux.

P. Thomson Del.

Inches 12   9   6   3   0   1   2   3   4   5   6   7 Feet.

PLATE VIII

CLOCK CASES.

Fig. 4.

Fig. 3.

Fig. 2.

Fig. 1.

PLATE IX

CLOCK CASES.

Fig 4.

Fig 3.

Fig 2.

Fig 1.

Inches 12 9 6 3 0 1 2 3 4 5 6 7 Feet.

PLATE XI

PEDESTAL SIDEBOARDS.

Fig 2

Fig 4

Fig 1

Fig 3

Inches 12 9 6 3 0   4   5   6   7 Feet

PLATE XII

PEDESTAL SIDEBOARD.

Scale for the Details.

377

PLATE XIII

PEDESTAL SIDEBOARD.

Inches 12 9 6 3 0   1   2   3   4   5   6 Feet.

F.Thomson. Del.

J.H.Le Keux Sc.

PLATE XVIII.

PILLAR AND BLOCK TABLES.

Fig.4.

Fig.1.

Fig.3.

Fig.6.

Fig.2.

Fig.5.

CONSTRUCTION OF TELESCOPE TABLES.

Fig. 1.

Fig. 6.

Fig. 3.

Fig. 5.

Fig. 2.

Fig. 4.

TELESCOPE TABLES.

Fig. 1

Fig. 2

Fig. 3

Fig. 4

Fig. 5

PLATE XX

TELESCOPE TABLES.

Fig. 1.

Fig. 2.

Fig. 3.

Fig. 5.

Fig. 4.

G. Inglis Sc.

Inches 12 9 6 3 0   1   2   3   4   5   6   7 Feet

PLATE XXI

SIDE TABLES.

Fig 2.

Fig 1.

Fig 4.

Fig 3.

5 Feet.

4

3

2

1

0

Inches 12 9 6 3 0

PLATE XXII

RISING SIDE TABLES.

Fig 3

Fig 2

Fig 1

Fig 5

Fig 4

Inches 12   9   6   3   0   3 Feet.

Inches 12   9   6   3   0   5 Feet.

PLATE XXIII

DINING ROOM CHAIRS.

Fig 4.

Fig 3.

Fig 2.

Fig 1.

Fig 8.

Fig 7.

Fig 6.

Fig 5.

Inches 12 9 6 3 0   1   2   3 Feet.

F. Thomson and Carl Bornbach, Del.

J. H. Le Keux Sc.

PLATE XXV

DINING ROOM CHAIRS.

Fig 4

Fig 3

Fig 2

Fig 1

Fig 8

Fig 7

Fig 6

Fig 5

Inches. 12 9 6 3 1 2 3 4 Feet.

PLATE XXV.

CHAIRS.

Fig 4

Fig 3

Fig 2

Fig 1

Inches 12 9 6 3 0 1 2 3 Feet.

PLATE XXVI.

EASY CHAIRS.

Fig 2.

Fig 4.

Fig 3.

Fig 6.

Fig 1.

Fig 5.

Inches 12   9   6   3   0   1   2   3   4   5 feet.

T.H. Le Keux. Sc.

P. Thomson, Del.

PLATE XVII.

TABLE AND CHAIR LEGS.

Fig.5.

Fig.4.

Fig.3.

Fig.2.

Fig.1.

Fig.12.

Fig.11.

Fig.10.

Fig.9.

Fig.8.

Fig.7.

Fig.6.

Inches 12   9   6   3   0   1   2   3 Feet.

PLATE XXVIII.

S O F A S .

Fig. 2.

Fig. 1.

Fig. 4.

Fig. 3.

Inches 12 9 6 3 0   1   2   3   4   5   6   7 Feet.

Inches. 12   9   6   3   0   1   2   3   4   5 Feet

Inches 12   9   6   3   0   1   2 Feet

Scale for the details

Inches 12   9   6   3   0   1   2   3   4   5 Feet.

Inches 12   9   6   3   0   1   2 Feet

P. Thomson Del.

J.H. Le Keux Sc.

BLACKIE & SON. GLASGOW, EDINBURGH & LONDON

DETAILS of SOFAS.

Fig 6.
Fig 5.
Fig 4.
Fig 3.
Fig 2.
Fig 1.

Fig 14.
Fig 13.
Fig 12.
Fig 11.
Fig 10.
Fig 9.
Fig 8.
Fig 7.

3 Feet
2
1
0
3
6
9
Inches 12

397

Fig 1

Fig 2.

Inches 12 9 6 3 0   1   2   3   4   5   6   7   8   9   10   11 Feet

P. Thomson Del.   J. H. Le Keux Sc.

BLACKIE & SON GLASGOW EDINBURGH & LONDON

PLATE XLIV.

BOOK-CASE.

400

PLATE XXXV.

BOOKCASES WITH CHIMNEY PIECE AND MIRROR.

Inches 12 9 6 3 0

10 Feet

401

RANGE OF BOOKCASES.

Fig 1

Fig 2

Inches. 12 9 6 3 0   1   2   3   4   5 Feet.

F. Thomson Del.

J.H. Le Keux Sc.

BLACKIE & SON. GLASGOW, EDINBURGH & LONDON.

Fig.1.

Fig.3.

Fig.2.

Fig.4.

Fig.5.

Fig.6.

Inches 12   9   6   3   0   1   2   3   4 Feet.

P. Thomson Del.

J. B. Le Keux Sc.

BLACKIE & SON, GLASGOW, EDINBURGH & LONDON.

PLATE XL.

Fig. 1.

Fig. 4.

Fig. 3.

Fig. 2.

Fig. 5.

Inches 12   9   6   3   0   1   2   3   4   5 Feet

Fig. 1.

Fig. 2.

Fig. 3.

Inches. 12   9   6   3   0   1   2   3   4   5

PLATE XLII

LIBRARY CHAIRS.

Fig 3.

Fig 6.

Fig 2.

Fig 5.

Fig 1.

Fig 4.

Inches 12   9   6   3   0   2   3 Feet

PLATE XIII

CHIFFONNIÈRES.

Fig. 2.

Fig. 4.

Fig. 1.

Fig. 3.

CHIFFONNIER

Fig. 5

Fig. 4

Scale for the details

6 Feet

Inches 12

409

PLATE XIV

Fig 1.

Inches 12   9   6   3   0   1   2   3   4   5 Feet.

Fig 2.

P. Thomson Del.

J.H. Le Keux Sc.

BLACKIE & SON, GLASGOW, EDINBURGH & LONDON.

410

PLATE XLVI.

CHIFFONNIÈRES with HIGH MIRRORS.

Fig. 1.

Fig. 2.

Sketch plan of Jambs.

414

Fig. 2.

Fig. 3.

Fig. 4.

Fig. 1.

PLATE LIII.

LOO TABLES.

Fig 2

Fig 1

Fig 4

Fig 3

PLATE LIV.

OCCASIONAL TABLES.

Fig. 3.

Fig. 6.

Fig. 1.

Fig. 4.

Fig. 2.

Fig. 5.

Inches 12   6   0   1   2   3   5 Feet.

BLACKIE & SON. GLASGOW EDINBURGH & LONDON.

417

Fig 2

Fig 4

Fig 1

Fig 3

Fig 3.

Fig 4.

Fig 1.

Fig 2.

PLATE LVII.

WORK TABLES.

Fig. 3.

Fig. 2.

Fig. 1.

Fig. 6.

Fig. 5.

Fig. 4.

Fig. 2.

Fig. 1.

Fig. 4.

Fig. 3.

Fig 1.

Fig 2.

Inches 12 9 6 3 0   1   2   3   4   5   6   7 Feet.

BLACKIE & SON. GLASGOW, EDINBURGH & LONDON.

Fig.1

Fig.2.

Inches 12   9   6   3   0   1   2   3   4   5 Feet.

P.Thomson Del.

J.H.Le Keux Sc.

BLACKIE & SON. GLASGOW EDINBURGH & LONDON

COUCHES.

Fig 1.

Fig 2.

Fig 3.

Fig 4.

Inches 18   6   3   0   1   2   3   4   5 Feet.

Fig 1

Fig 2

Inches 12   1   2   3   4   5 Feet.

DRAWING ROOM CHAIRS.

Fig. 3

Fig. 2

Fig. 1

Fig. 6

Fig. 5

Fig. 4

OTTOMAN SEATS.

Fig.3

Fig.6

Fig.2

Fig.5

Fig.1

Fig.4

427

PLATE LXV

DRAWING-ROOM CHAIRS.

Fig 3

Fig 6

Fig 2

Fig 5

Fig 1

Fig 4

Inches

3 Feet

428

PLATE LXII.

NATIONAL EMBLEM CHAIRS.

Fig. 3.

Fig. 6.

Fig. 2.

Fig. 5.

Inches 12   9   6   3   0   1   2   3 Feet

Fig. 1.

Fig. 4.

Carl Hambuch Del.

J. H. Le Keux Sc.

Fig. 1.

Fig. 2.

Fig. 3.

Fig. 4.

Inches 12 9 6 3   1   2   3 Feet.

J.H.Le Keux Sc.

BLACKIE & SON, GLASGOW, EDINBURGH & LONDON.

430

Fig. 2.

Fig. 4.

Fig. 1.

Fig. 3.

Fig 1

Fig 2

Inches 12   9   6   3   0   1   2   3   4   5   6   7 Feet.

BLACKIE & SON, GLASGOW, EDINBURGH & LONDON.

432

Fig. 1

Fig. 2

Inches 12   9   6   3   0   1   2   3   4   5 Feet.

P. Thomson Del.

J.H. Le Keux Sc.

BLACKIE & SON. GLASGOW EDINBURGH & LONDON

433

Fig. 1

Fig. 2

Fig. 3

Fig. 4

Inches 12   6   6   3   0   1   2   4   Feet.

Fig 1

Fig 2

Inches 12   9   6   3   0   1   2   3   4   5 Feet.

DRAWING ROOM CHAIRS.

Fig 3.

Fig 6.

Fig 2.

Fig 5.

Fig 1.

Fig 4.

OTTOMAN SEATS.

Fig.3

Fig.6

Fig.2

Fig.5

Fig.1

Fig.4

PLATE LXV

DRAWING ROOM CHAIRS.

Fig 3.

Fig 2

Fig 6

Fig 5

Fig 1

Fig 4

Inches

PLATE LXVI

J.H. Le Keux Sc.

NATIONAL EMBLEM CHAIRS.

Fig. 3.

Fig. 6.

Fig. 2.

Fig. 5.

Fig. 1.

Fig. 4.

Carl Hambuch Del.

439

Fig. 1.

Fig. 2.

Fig. 3.

Fig. 4.

Inches 12 9 6 3   1   2   3 Feet.

J.H. Le Keux Sc.

BLACKIE & SON. GLASGOW, EDINBURGH & LONDON.

PLATE LXVIII.

HIGH BACKED CHAIRS.

Fig 1

Fig 2

Fig 3

Fig 4

Inches 12   9   6   3   0   1   2   3   4 Feet.

PLATE LXXX.

ANTIQUE STATE CHAIRS.

Fig. 3.

Fig. 2.

Fig. 1.

Inches 12   6   0   3   6   5 Feet

442

PLATE LXX.

ANTIQUE HIGH-BACKED CHAIRS.

Fig 3

Fig 2

Fig 1

Inches 12

Feet

Fig. 1.

Fig. 2.

Fig. 3.

Fig. 4.

Fig. 5.

Inches 12 9 6 3 0   1   2   3   4 Feet.

Fig. 1.

Fig. 2.

Fig. 3.

Fig. 4.

Fig. 5.

Inches 12   9   6   3   0   1   2   3   4   5 Feet.

T. Thomson Del.

445

PLATE LXVIII.

WHAT - NOTS.

Fig 2.

Fig 1.

Fig 3.

446

Fig. 4.

Fig. 8.

Fig. 3.

Fig. 7.

Fig. 2.

Fig. 6.

Fig. 1.

Fig. 5.

3 Feet

Inches 12

Fig 5.

Fig 2.

Fig 4.

Fig 1.

Fig 3.

FIRE SCREENS.

Fig. 2.

Fig. 4.

Fig. 3.

Fig. 1.

449

PLATE LXXVII

FRENCH BEDSTEADS.

Fig 2

Fig 3

Fig 4

Fig 5

Inches 12 9 6 3 0   1   2   3   4   5   6   7   8 Feet

PLATE LXVIII

HALF TESTER BEDSTEADS.

Fig 2

Fig 1

Inches 12 9 6 3 0

10 Feet

451

HALF TESTER BEDSTEADS.

Fig. 2.

Fig. 1.

Inches 12 9 6 3 0   1   2   3   4   5   6   7   8   9   10 Feet.

HALF TESTER BEDSTEAD.

PLATE LXXXI.

BEDSTEAD.—MEDIEVAL STYLE.

454

PLATE LXXVII.

POSTED BEDSTEADS.

P. Thomson Del.

J. H. Le Keux Sc.

455

Fig. 1.   Fig. 2.   Fig. 3.   Fig. 4.   Fig. 5.

Inches 12   9   6   3   0   1   2   3   4   5 Feet

456

PLATE LXXXV.

BED PILLARS.

Fig. 1.

Fig. 2.

Fig. 3.

Fig. 7.

Fig. 8.

Fig. 9.

Fig. 4.

Fig. 5.

Fig. 6.

Inches 12 9 6 3 0 1 2 3 4 Feet

PLATE LXXXVI

COTS and CRADLES.

Fig. 2.

Fig. 4.

Fig. 1.

Fig. 3.

P. Thomson Del.

J. H. Le Keux Sc.

inches 12   9   6   3   0   1   2   3   4 Feet.

Fig. 1.

Fig. 2.

Fig. 3.

Fig. 4.

Inches 12 9 6 3 0   1   2   3   4   5   6   Feet.

Fig 2.

PLATE LXXXI.

WARDROBE.

Inches 9 6 3 0 1 2 3 4 5 6 7 Feet

461

PLATE XC.

WARDROBES.

PLATE XCI.

PILASTERS AND BRACKETS.

Fig 4.

Fig 3.

Fig 6.

Fig 8.

Fig 5.

Fig 7.

Fig 2.

Fig 1.

PLATE XCII.

WASH STANDS and DRESSING TABLES.

Fig. 2.

Fig. 5.

Fig. 3.

Fig. 1.

Fig. 4.

CORNICE MOULDINGS AND MOULDINGS FOR PANELS.

FRET-RAILS & CLOCK FOR STEAM-BOAT CABINS.

Fig 1.

Fig 2.

Fig 3.

Inches 12   9   6   3   0   1   2   3   4   5 Feet

Fig. 1.

Fig. 3.

Fig. 2.

Fig. 4.

Fig. 5.

Fig. 6.

Fig. 8.

Fig. 7.

Fig. 9.

Fig. 10.

Fig. 11.

Fig. 1

Fig. 4

Fig. 7

Fig. 8

Fig. 5

Fig. 6

Fig 1.

Fig 5

Fig 2.

Fig 6

Fig. 3.

Fig 4

PLATE C.

ORNAMENTS ADAPTED FROM NATURE.

Fig. 2 a.

Fig. 3.

Fig. 3 a.

Fig. 2.

Fig. 5.

Fig. 1 a.

Fig. 4 a.

Fig. 1.

Fig. 4.

Fig. 5 a.

472

ORNAMENTS ADAPTED FROM NATURE.

Fig. 3.

Fig. 1.

Fig. 2.

THE PRACTICAL CABINET MAKERS DESIGN BOOK

BY H. THOMSON

PUBLISHED BY J. CAMPBELL & Co. GLASGOW.

INDEX.

PLATE 1.

HALL.

PLATE 3

HAT STANDS

PLATE 4

HALL TABLE

THE PRACTICAL CABINETMAKER'S DESIGN BOOK.

HALL FURNITURE.

PLATE 1.—HAT STAND.

Example in Byzantine style. Appears to best advantage when made of yew-tree root. Plinth, plain and veneered ; turned column ebonized. Capitals effectively cut, with ebony mouldings springing from back, and along outside member of back on top. Square columns and entablatures inlaid with ebony. Ebony mitred round inside of arch. Top, black marble, with under moulding. Back, three panels, centre one mirror-plate ; outside ones, walnut, encased with ebony bede. Dark oak, with light-coloured mouldings, would be applicable to this design.

PLATE 2.—HAT AND UMBRELLA STAND.

This design differs from preceding one, being of greater dimensions, and suitable only for houses of larger size. It is an Umbrella as well as a Hat Stand, the one portion serving as a support for the other. This design is suitable for dark oak. Bars and panels chamfered. Rods supported by brackets, and chamfered and screwed on from behind. The drip boxes are strongly made, and fitted with zinc cases.

PLATE 3.

Fig. 1.—The difference between this and the preceding design is, that the table is supported on turned pillars. A brass rod is fixed at each end to receive umbrella which rests in drip pan. See Plate 2. Bars and scroll work on back chamfered. Mirror should be sufficiently high and proportioned, so that easy access may be obtained.

Fig. 2, similar to Fig 1.—Proportions same. Suited for medium-sized houses. Pan stretches whole length. Brass rod fixed in front. Bars and pilasters chamfered.

PLATE 4.—HALL TABLE.

Design Italian. Suited for oak. Must be strong and massive. Ornament $\frac{1}{8}$ in. wood, planted, not of a lighter colour, and stained for contrast. Top, $\frac{1}{2}$ in. wood, clamped, of fir. This is an advantage, as indentations may be more easily removed from the solid, than if it had been veneered, as is usual.

PLATE 5.

Example in Pompeian style. Best adapted for black and gold. Top, black marble. Rails framed in the ordinary way. Ornamental parts and lines hatched with gold. Pateras planted.

Fig. 2.—Design in Gothic style. Top may be veneered, but it is most useful, and appears to best advantage, when of $\frac{3}{8}$ or $\frac{5}{8}$ in. wood, clamped with fir. Legs chamfered and turned at bottom. Oak most suitable.

Fig. 3.—Table leaf example. Style, Gothic, suited for dark oak. Ornaments planted, same wood, lighter colour. Arches chamfered inside. Caterfoil may be planted or sunk. End brackets pierced and chamfered. Dimensions usual, and if properly executed, forms a handsome table

PLATE 6.

Example in Gothic style. Ordinary dimensions, construction massive and substantial. Oak wood most suitable for this design. Chair, back upholstered, chamfered all round stuffing; pateras light wood, planted. Elbows or arm rests chamfered and opened up. Bench same as back, stiles chamfered with sunk pateras. Ends kept secure by octagonal stretcher. Breadth of seat, 23 inches. Chair and seat should have a recline of about 1½ inches. Table plain; pateras lighter wood, and planted. Droop turned and incised. Ends cut through with a chamfer taken from the corners. Plinth veneered.

INSTRUCTIONS IN THE ART OF DESIGNING OR DRAWING.

The theory of design is a knowledge which only can be acquired by studying the best works of art, and reading authors' criticisms on the accomplishments of great artists. Once a knowledge of the theory of design is attained, although the student may be unable to portray on paper any object, he still may be able to judge works of art, and by frequently examining these, and coming in contact with experienced and esteemed critics, his knowledge will be greatly increased and good taste acquired. The mechanical portion consists in the application of the hand, which is guided by the understanding in producing the various forms which may be desired. When the object has been removed from before the eye, the mind only retains a confused idea of the detail; therefore, theory and practice are inseparable in art. By continued practice, the hand will acquire freedom, and will

delineate on paper the impression made on the eye, every object taking its proper order. The student should thus be careful not to vitiate the eye, as it is the organ which is employed in collecting thoughts for the mind to work on. Many objects daily presented may, if properly used, considerably develop both eye and hand in the appreciation and display of art. Invention is thus merely a proper organization by the hand of ideas collected by the power of vision. If, therefore, the designer has a store of material laid up, and his hand trained to work with his eye, he will never be in want of new ideas, and will more easily and speedily produce a more original subject than the dreamer in art who is ever waiting till his mind is imbued with some magnificent idea, which, of course, he never realizes, as these ideas in art are only attained by continuative and unwearying application. The student, therefore, who is determined to be master of his study, will carefully use his eye, and diligently use his hand, as these and constant application are the only producers of success in art.

DRAWING.

The manual portion of drawing consists of Outline and Relief. Of these, the first mentioned is the more important, and comprehends form and proportion. It is therefore necessary that the designer gives close attention to it. Free-hand drawing is executed by the hand, directed by the eye—no instrument, save the pen or pencil, being used. Geometrical drawing being a more exact delineation of forms, requires the application of the scale and other instruments of various kinds. Drawing, as required by the Cabinetmaker, may be obtained by application, and a small amount of perseverance will soon overcome that which may appear a serious obstacle. The student should first give his attention to the free-hand section of the Art. This consists chiefly in the judging of proportions and lines. Too much should not be attempted at the outset of the study, as thereby

PLATE 6.

A.J.Thomson.

HALL.

PLATE 7.

SIDEBOARD.

A Thomson.

PLATE 8.

SIDEBOARD.

the student, not succeeding so well as he anticipated, may become disheartened, and the consequence of this would be a deterioration of taste—a matter which should always be guarded against. To avoid this it might be well that a selection of the more simple curves of these plates be practised on at first, commencing by copying these lines exactly as to size, and then to increase the size in direct proportion. If this be practised, the student will soon acquire freedom of hand. The student must be careful not to hurry, but be very accurate, and gradually more complicated forms may be executed with precision, subsequently advancing to those of more intricacy and detail. Freehand is essential for working all kinds of drawing; and judgment ought to be exercised in the relative dimensions of different objects, the eye in all cases being the guide. In drawing Cabinet Furniture it is necessary that geometrical methods may be resorted to, in order to give accuracy to the detail. An easy method of copying any figure is by dissecting it with convenient lines, intersecting the main portions. Another easy way is by studying the vertical and horizontal divisions of the piece. This may be used in an exact or enlarged or diminished drawing. These must always be of correct ratio, and the squares capable of being produced in the copy. If the design does not admit of squares being drawn on it, silk threads may be substituted for the lines, or these may be drawn on tracing paper—which, when fixed, will not produce any disadvantgeous result to the draughtsman.

Plate 6a.—HALL CHAIRS.

Fig. 1.—Has semicircular back, with moulding planted on top, terminated with droops. It is pierced to relieve the shield, under which a bede is planted. The corners of the seat are round. Legs turned and opened up.

Fig. 2.—Has moulding planted on back, resting on turned pillars. The shield is also planted. Legs turned. The pillars and legs are opened up with a coiled vein.

Fig. 3.—Back pierced and chamfered. It is upholstered, having turned pillars at each side. Legs turned and opened up, as in Fig. 2.

Fig. 4.—The back of this chair has wrought moulding planted on the front, and chamfered inside. It is pierced to relieve the shield. A narrow fielding runs from it, diminishing as it falls. Seat square, with moulding carried round the edge, and deep-shaped rail in front. The ends are pierced and the corners chamfered.

Plate 7.—PEDESTAL SIDEBOARD.

Design for dark oak. Style nearly Pompeian. Dimensions ordinary. Pilasters and all ornamental portions relieved with gilt lines. These lines are inserted with small gouge. Gold leaf should be used, as it is more brilliant than powder or liquid. (Pateras, ebony, hatched with gold.) Those on pedestals show one inch projection. Chamfered pateras, and sunk. Base should have sufficient projection to receive pilasters. These open with doors. Sunk panels, with raised portions. These portions should be of rich wood. Back pilasters same as others, only thicker, to receive mirror-plate. Ornaments glued. Centre one screwed.

Plate 8.—SIDEBOARD.

Example here represented is well adapted for mahogany. The length is 7 feet 9 inches over stage; height, 36 inches to top of stage. As no extent of plain surface is here exhibited, on account of the enriched character of the design, the wood should not possess a very striking appearance, except that which is used for top of stage, end panels, and plinth, for which the veneer should be carefully selected. The doors are flush panelled. The end raised panels are clamped on, the stiles being built and veneered over. The pillars should be almost entire. The pateras and bars are planted on stage. The back is mirror-plate, with small pedestals at each side, which are usually surmounted with bronzes. The centre ornament is wrought on, except the festoon, which may be cut separately. The other ornamental parts are grooved. It is chamfered inside all round, also outside of frame, commencing where the top moulding terminates, and decreasing as it approaches the vase, which should be eccentrically shaped to admit being close to the wall.

PLATE 9.—SIDEBOARD.

This design is adapted for oak, walnut, or mahogany. The construction is of a rich and massive nature, and specially adapted for a large-sized Sideboard; so that there may be sufficient space for the boldness of the design and delicacy of the detail. The trusses on the pedestals are dowelled to the sides of the frame. Doors are sunk-panelled. The stage is framed and fitted with drawers, the exact measures being determined by the dimensions of the Sideboard and the greatest depth of the front mouldings. The large oval may be made in various ways, according to the decorations on its front, which may be wrought in relief or planted on. The back is mirror-plate. The pillars are turned, having octagonal plinth and carved capitals. The centre ornament may be wrought separately, and fixed on.

PLATE 10.—SIDEBOARD.

This design is in the Gothic style, and suitable for oak only, which should be of a dark shade. The ornaments are kept in their natural colour. The plinth is bevelled and veneered over. The doors are sunk-panelled. The ornaments are $\frac{1}{8}$ in. wood, planed. The arch, springing from husks, is chamfered, and may be wrought solid, with sunk pateras and incised ornaments, or veneered over, with pateras and ornaments planted. The carved frets should not be stained, but treated the same as the other ornaments. The stage frame is fitted with drawers, as usual. Back, mirror-plate. The frame is wrought solid, bevelled and incised sunk pateras. The centre ornament is wrought in relief.

PLATE 11.—BUFFET SIDEBOARD.

This design is adapted for oak or mahogany, and, to give good effect, should be executed in large size. The style differs from the Pedestal Sideboard. The construction is more massive and the dimensions larger, and thus adapted for spacious dwelling-houses. It is more useful for the display of plate or articles of *vertu* than as a place of deposit. The pillars are blocked out square and wrought in relief. They are then framed up with the ground of the stage, and drawers, when required, made to act between them. Brakes on front stage should have a projection of about $1\frac{3}{4}$ inches, those at end about three inches. Stage veneered. Moulding carried round the centre, front, and ends. Top formed of fir, clamped with wood about $\frac{3}{8}$ in. thick, which, when wrought to the proper shape, forms by its thickness the upper member of top moulding. Base must be strongly made, and pillars firmly attached. Back framing is flush-panelled and veneered. Back is mirror-plate, with shelves at each side, veneered and planted. Shafts of pillars are turned. Plinth paned, of five sides. Carved capitals. Top of frame is veneered. Outside moulding and all other ornamental parts are planted on face.

PLATE 12.—SIDEBOARDS.

Fig. 1.—This design is adapted for mahogany. The length is 5 feet 3 inches over stage moulding. Height, 33 inches. The end doors are sunk-panelled, the centre being flush. They are all on one plane, the stage and base being entire. One drawer in centre. The back is mirror-plate. The carved ornament is planted. The tie is fitted on top of moulding.

Fig. 2.—Dimensions same as Fig. 1. The base is chamfered and veneered over. The centre door hinged so as to clear the brackets. The stage can be made with one or three drawers. The back is panelled with mirror-plate The ornament should be effectively cut.

PLATE 9

SIDEBOARD

PLATE 10.

SIDEBOARD.

PLATE II

BUFFET SIDEBOARD

PLATE 12.

SIDEBOARDS.

Fig 2.

Fig 1.

SIDEBOARDS

FIG.1.

FIG.2.

FIG. 2.

SIDEBOARD.

SIDEBOARD

TABLE LEAF CASES.

FIG.1.

FIG.2.

FIG. 3.

PLATE 13.--SIDEBOARD.

Fig. 1.—This design is only suitable for mahogany. Sideboards after this plan are usually made 7 feet long over stage moulding, and 36 inches in height. The pedestals are round-cornered and sunk-panelled; these are veneered over, with mouldings clamped on. The stage is framed and fitted with drawers. The top is veneered over. The back is formed of a deal board, veneered. The moulding and bede are planted on the face. The edge is slipped with veneer.

Fig. 2.—This is of the same dimensions as Fig. 1, and is best adapted for being wrought out in mahogany. The pedestals are raised-panelled. The centre doors sunk-panelled. The stage is fitted with drawers. The back is veneered over. The mouldings and shield are clamped on. The top moulding terminates with a turned piece split, and having enough projection to receive it. The edge is slipped with veneer.

PLATE 14.—CHIFFONIERS.

The examples here given are of a plain character. The length over top moulding is 5 feet, the height is 2 feet 6 inches.

Fig. 1.—This example is suited for mahogany only. The base is plain, with no moulding on top. The pedestals are round-cornered and flush-panelled. The moulding is curved at the top, and clamped on. The centre door is raised panelled. The drawer between pedestals has bede planted on the face. The back is veneered over. A small part of the ground may be solid where the centre ornament is planted. The remainder of the upper edge is slipped with veneer. The scroll and husk are clamped on the face. The shelf and brackets are screwed. The shelf has moulding carried round it and veneered on top. The brackets are perforated.

Fig. 2.—This design is adapted for light wood, such as American Ash, Pitch Pine, &c. It is wrought solid. The base is bevelled. The pedestals are sunk-panelled. The stiles and the centre door are chamfered. The drawer between pedestals has bede planted on the face. The mouldings and shield are clamped on. The shelf has chamfer taken off the corner. The brackets are incised.

PLATE 15.—SIDEBOARD.

This design is best suited for mahogany. It would also look well in oak. The pedestal corners are broken and veneered over. The styles are treated in a similar manner, and sunk-panelled, with clamped mouldings. The back between pedestals is flush-panelled and veneered over. The base is carried round. The arch between pedestals is veneered over, and has moulding and ornaments clamped on the face. The stage is fitted with drawers. The top may be veneered or clamped with solid wood about $\frac{3}{8}$ in. in thickness. The back is mirror-plate, surrounded by a wrought moulding about $2\frac{3}{4}$ in. broad, resting on entablatures at each end. The centre ornament is wrought separately.

PLATE 16.—SIDEBOARD.

This example is well suited for oakwood. The pedestals are sunk-panelled, veneered over, and the mouldings clamped on. The canted corners are relieved with carved trusses. The back, between the pedestals, is closed in by a flush-panelled frame, with the projection of the base carried round it. The stage is framed and fitted with drawers. The top is veneered over. The back is mirror-plate, surrounded by a veneered frame, with mouldings planted on the face and top. The centre ornament is wrought on the frame. The radius of the sweep may be determined by referring to the scale. The mirror has a framed back made of deal, and panelled and fixed to the frame by screws.

PLATE 17.—TABLE LEAF-CASES.

Fig. 1.—This example is adapted for oak. The base is bevelled and veneered over, surmounted by turned pillars supporting bracket, which is pierced and carved. The corners are chamfered. It is flush-panelled and veneered, with moulding clamped on. The back is formed of deal, veneered, with moulding planted on the face. The top edges and sides are slipped with veneer.

Fig. 2 is best suited for mahogany. The pillars are complete, having been turned and cut. The panels are raised. The back is executed similar to Fig. 1.

Fig. 3 is also adapted for mahogany. The turned pillars are entire. The base is bevelled and veneered over. It is flush-panelled. The back is solid. The top has no frieze, but consists only of a wrought moulding, and, with Figs. 1 and 2, may be veneered, or of solid wood, clamped, of fir to the required thickness.

DRAWING—*Continued.*

There is a variety of methods for the enlargement or reduction of drawings, and many instruments may be used for that purpose. One of these, the proportional compass, is a useful and convenient instrument. It is like the ordinary compass, but pointed at both ends. If you wish to divide a space into any number of equal parts, close the instrument and shift the centre until the line across it coincides with the division required, and indicated on the scale of lines, and made tight by turning the screw. The compass is then opened until the space can be received between the points of the longer legs; the space between the shorter will be the part sought. The points of this instrument are very apt to get out of order, one becoming more worn than the other; consequently the scales become useless, as they must necessarily be incorrect. Our space will not admit of our entering on the details of the various methods and instruments which may be used for copying drawings mechanically; but if the cabinetmaker can confidently rely on his own powers of execution, on the foundation of a correct eye and trained hand (both of which may be acquired by application), he will find these to his advantage in every respect. It will be understood that any drawing

intended as a guide to workmen ought in all cases to be drawn to a scale. Tracing paper can always be advantageously used. It may be made by saturating clean white paper with good drying oil, and allowed to dry. It may be also had ready for use at an artists' furnisher's. The way to use it is to place it on the drawing, and trace the outline with a fine-pointed lead pencil. The lines may be distinctly seen when finished, by placing a sheet of white paper under the tracing. Another method of tracing that may be adopted is by using a sheet of paper previously rubbed in with black lead or coloured chalk, and afterwards come over with soft paper until the colouring ceases to come off when touched lightly. The clean sheet of paper is placed on the drawing board, after which the prepared side of the tracing paper is placed next to it; the drawing is then placed on the top, and the forms may be traced down by passing a smooth-pointed instrument over the lines, taking care not to cut the paper. The instrument used is properly called a stile. Some draughtsmen prefer using lead weights to hold down the tracing paper instead of pins; also a small piece of mirror glass, having one edge perfectly straight. This being placed uprightly in the centre of any design, the equal-sided reflection gives the general appearance of the design with accuracy and less labour. A large mirror will be found a very good critic. Hold the drawing before it; the design is thus in the reverse way, and defects may be remedied. The exact execution of figures, and their reduction or enlargement without mechanical aid, offers no difficulty to the experienced eye. In drawing an equal-sided object, such as you see in Plate 71, the centre line is laid down first; the extreme height and breadth is then blocked in—the square block at the top—and the other members are measured off, these being at right angles with the centre line. You next proceed to put in the shaft and main features, and lastly, the detail. The sofa-foot (No. 1 in this Plate) may be easily and accurately

502

FIG. 1.

FIG. 2.

FIG. 3.

FIG. 4.

PLATE 20

SOFAS.

copied in this way. The ornament in the square block can be executed by putting down straight lines from corner to corner, and through the centre. These will serve as guides for the position of the curves. A good example for this may be had—the dining-room chair (Plate 22, fig. 3). Lay down the centre line, then proceed to put in the height and breadth of the back, and the side rails. Having fixed their centre, draw another line between the centres of the side rail and stay, place the point of the circular to this line, extend to outside of rail, and this gives the radius for the sweep. Other imaginary lines, determining or bounding the various forms, will be a considerable aid to the student in the execution of the design. The nature and number of these lines vary according to the figure which is to be copied. In this branch of the art of drawing it will be often necessary to resort to mechanical appliances and geometrical principles. As the limits of this work will not admit our entering on an explanation of the science of geometry, the student will find it to his advantage to acquaint himself with a few of its elementary principles.

PLATE 18.—TELESCOPE DINING TABLES.

Telescope Tables are so called from their slide action, by which they may be extended with facility to various lengths as required. Their qualities in this respect are their chief recommendations.

Fig. 1.—This design is for a table in mahogany, and shown closed. The dining-room side tables are used for the disposal of the loose tops. In working the fixed top, they are brought together and trimmed flush. It is then extended. The leaves are put in and wrought flush with the previous parts, being reversed and adjusted. The table is then extended the whole length, and the moulding wrought on the edge of the top, the upper members of which are wrought on the boards. The others are formed on the rim, and extend the whole length of the table. The columns

are turned and carved. The design is a double one.

Fig. 2.—This is an example in the Gothic style. It is best adapted for oak wood, and is on the same plan as the preceding. The pillars show two designs; they are both hexagonal. The carving of the ornament should be sharp and bold in relief.

PLATE 19.—TELESCOPE TABLES.

These examples show the end elevations of this class of table. Fig. 1 is a design for mahogany. The outside edges are rounded off with a wrought moulding. The inside ones are chamfered. The base is turned and carved. The patera is sunk and wrought on the solid. Fig. 2 is an example in the Gothic style, and is adapted for oak wood. The corners are chamfered. The ivy-leaf ornaments forming the decorations are sunk. The patera is sunk and wrought on the solid. The pillars and droop are turned. A more pleasing effect will be produced by planting the ornament, which should be stained and of lighter wood from the same tree. The patera also should be planted and stained, and raised or sunk flush with the grounding.

PLATE 20.—SOFAS.

The upper design is framed in the usual manner. The centre ornament of the back, with the moulding, is formed of one piece. The end portions extending from the centre ornament are planted on the face. The elbow stumps are dowelled down on the feet, having an incline of four or five inches at the top. They wind outwards, thus giving an overlay at the ends of the sofa. The hind legs are dowelled between the adjoining ends of the back and end rails. The standard forming part of the back frame should have an incline of about $2\frac{1}{2}$ inches back at the top. The top rail is morticed down on these standards, with two others that are framed into the back rail of the seat. The carving should be bold and round, the feet deep plated. The lower design has the elbow stumps clamped behind with fir. Two pieces of birch are dowelled on the hind feet, having an incline backwards of 2½ inches at the top. The frame for the back is made out of ⅞-inch fir wood. The centre ornament of the back is about 2¼ inches thick. The moulding and scroll running from it is ¼ inch thick, planted on the face and slipped with veneer on the upper edge. The decorations on the elbow, &c., are incised. Both these designs are adapted for mahogany.

PLATE 21.—DINING-ROOM CHAIRS.

The designs given in this plate are similar in construction to vase-backed chairs. Figs. 1 to 4 inclusive have their seats fixed. The back is hollowed.

Fig. 1.—Back rounded off. Bead carried round the inside. It is framed up in the usual manner of four pieces dowelled, including back legs and stay. The moulding on the seat rail is planted on before it is framed up. Best suited for mahogany.

Fig. 2.—The back of this chair is wrought similar to Fig. 1, excepting the stay, which is carved after it is framed up. It has the addition of a bend on the outside, terminating with a husk. A narrow bead runs round the inside, forming part of the stay, which must be deeply cut, to give relief to the scroll and rosette. The hollowed moulding on seat rail is planted on before it is framed up. This design is best adapted for mahogany.

Fig. 3.—In this design the back is chamfered all round. It is flat on the face. The stem and husk are sunk. The patera has no projection. It is relieved from the grounding. The fluted legs should be deeply cut to give relief. This design is most suitable for oak.

Fig. 4.—This example is in the Gothic style. The back is chamfered and cut through at top, which part is also chamfered. The stay is carved. The patera is cut on the solid, in the same manner as in Fig. 3. The seat rail is chamfered. The legs opened up with a simple ornament. This design is also best adapted for oak.

PLATE 22.—DINING-ROOM CHAIRS.

Fig. 1.—Is framed up in the usual manner of vase-backed chairs. The back legs are framed up parallel to each other, converging at their lower end. The back is hollowed. A bead is carried round the inside and on the top, which terminates with a flower. The back is cut through, where it falls into the stay. The projecting moulding, carried round the seat frame, is planted on the rails, and wrought on the squares of the legs. This design is best adapted for mahogany.

Fig. 2.—The back of this chair is hollowed. The outer and inner edges are chamfered. The decorations are sunk. (This back must be fitted and framed up without resistance or strain, owing to the curvature of the design.) The seat rail is framed up flush with the squares of the front legs, across which the projection is planted, mitred at corners, and butting against the back legs, where they diverge from the lower part. This design is most suitable for dark oak.

Fig. 3.—The back of this chair is straight, with turned pillars. The upright stay is dowelled down on the seat rail. The decorations are sunk. The pateras are wrought on the solid, and do not project beyond the flush of the back, which is chamfered on the outer and inner edges. The moulding on the seat frame is carried across the squares of the front legs. The pateras are wrought in the same way as on the back. The shaft, scribed coil. Oak wood is most suitable for this design.

Fig. 4.—This design is of a more elaborate character than any of the preceding. It is wrought similar to Fig. 3, but has the back stuffed. The seat frame has moulding cross-wrought on the square of the front legs. The decorations are wrought as described in the preceding design. Oak wood is best suited for this kind of chair. If it be dark, the patera should not be stained; if light wood is used, it may be preferable to have them darkened.

FIG. 1

FIG 2

FIG. 3

FIG. 4

DRAWING—*Continued.*

The value of ornament consists in its being used to relieve blankness, and to add beauty wherever it is applied. It may be divided into several branches of design, and in each case it is governed by different principles. We will look at it here in its two great divisions—the *flat* and the *round.* The flat is to be regarded as a vehicle of colour, giving contrast in light and dark; the round as a contrast of light and shade. In ornamental design the floral detail should not be merely copied from nature, but should be aided by art. The treatment of plants in this way is termed conventional, as it departs from their natural development. If they were imitated exactly, both in detail and order of development, it would be termed natural. This treatment is seldom found in the various styles of ornament, such as Egyptian, Grecian, Roman, and Italian, and to this day, in many instances, we use the same detail as were adopted by the ancients.

If we go back about 2000 years we find ornament at its greatest height. Although at that time the useful arts were in their infancy, we are convinced that then ornament had reached maturity, for man passed the most of his time in the regions of fancy, and has left to us an inexhaustible flow of talent. It is good for us that it has been so with ornamental art, for, living as we are in an age of bustle and anxiety for our daily wants, we have not that time to bestow on the beautiful which is expedient for the refinement of taste, and thus we are compelled to go and draw from the ancient wells.

DRAWING INSTRUMENTS.

Previous to entering on the description and use of drawing instruments it may be necessary to some of our readers who are not acquainted with miniature drawings of cabinet furniture to call their attention to those designs which are executed in perspective. It is understood that every cabinetmaker is familiar with the general proportions relating to cabinet furniture; and if the student is not a cabinetmaker, he is in all likelihood connected in some way or other with the craft, thereby affording him the opportunity of consultation should he meet with any difficulty. It will be observed that some of the accompanying designs are shown in elevation, which enables the workman to take the sizes speedily, and it also serves as a working drawing. The most of these designs are shown in parallel perspective, the system of drawing commonly used by draughtsmen (although not correct as to the rules laid down in perspective), being an expeditious way of delineating geometrical objects, and more convenient to the workman, especially when no working drawings are given; also, showing the general appearance of the job, which is not always the case in elevation drawing.

The accompanying designs are all drawn to scale, which should prudently be resorted to when taking the sizes from the perspective designs, as certain parts of these appear to diminish as they recede, also the gables, where, in many instances, no profile is given, it not being thought necessary, as they are all made about the same size. In taking the measurements of a sideboard, for instance, the breadth and height over stage may be taken, also the base and pedestals. The back is taken separately. The surface of the top of stage is not included. The breadth of the back is determined by the breadth of the stage. It is narrower in the drawing, so it is lower proportionately. Suppose the plate has been determined at six feet broad, and it measures six inches less in the drawing, if the top is half the length in height, it will be three feet high by six broad. The same rule is applicable to many of the examples given in the accompanying plates; and, as there is little or no perceptible diminution in the detail, there should be no difficulty whatever in working out he design.

PLATE 23.—EASY CHAIRS.

Fig. 1.—This chair is adapted for mahogany. The front legs and elbow stumps may be of one piece, or they may be of two pieces, dowelled and butt-jointed. The projecting moulding is planted on the rails, and cross-wrought on the squares of the legs, and carried round the seat frame. The back frame is made to incline back at the top, the amount of incline depending altogether on the design of the chair. The cross rails are hollowed. The band which surrounds the stuffing is formed of several pieces, and carved after the chair is framed up.

Fig. 2.—This chair is adapted for oak. The front legs and elbow stumps are of one piece. The rosettes and other decorations are wrought on the solid. The back is straight. The stuffing is bordered with a wrought moulding. The ornament must be very simple.

Fig. 3.—This chair is suitable for either mahogany or oak, or any of the various other woods used in chairmaking. The moulding on the seat and frame is planted on the rails and finished before they are framed up. The elbow stumps may be dowelled down, or they may be of the same piece as the front legs. The back is framed up straight, having an incline back at the top. The decorations are simple, with the exception of the griffin's head.

PLATE 24.—BOOKCASES.

PLATE 25.—BOOKCASE.

The design given in this plate is of a plain character and of the usual dimensions. The chiffonier, or lower portion, is fitted with one or more drawers. The doors may be flush-panelled if preferred, and the end shields clamped on. The pilasters have about one inch projection. The plinth is bevelled and veneered over. The cornice consists of a wrought moulding and coping. The pilasters terminate with pointed ornamented finals. These are of solid wood.

PLATE 26.—BOOKCASE.

The proportions of this bookcase are similar to those of Plate 25. It is best suited for oak wood. The plinth is bevelled. The pilasters have about $\frac{3}{4}$-inch projection. They are chamfered and incised. The ornaments on upper pilasters are wrought on the solid. The doors are sunk-panelled. The stiles are chamfered. The doors of upper carcass are also chamfered. The cornice consists of a wrought moulding, surmounted with ornamental coping, which is about $\frac{3}{8}$-inch thick. The turned vases terminate the pillasters.

PLATE 27.—BOOKCASE.

This design is well suited for mahogany. As usual, the carcass, or body, is framed in two heights. The centre division of the under portion is fitted with a drawer, which may be used as a writing desk. The doors have chamfered shield panels. The pillars are fixed. The arch between the pillars is solid wood perforated. The pillars in the upper carcass are fixed to the doors, which are hinged to the gables. The centre and right-hand doors lock to the left, and the left to the right. The doors are glazed with a single plate each. The bookcase is provided inside with movable shelves. The books should be arranged in a decreasing scale from the bottom shelves. The centre ornament or cornice may be fixed on. The full size may be taken from the profile given on this plate. It is judicious to lay down the exact profile of the job for reference to measurements.

PLATE 28.—BOOKCASE.

This design is suited for oak. It may be of dark wood, with the mouldings and other ornamental parts of lighter wood. The pillaretts are turned and planted on the door stile, and appear resting on the base, which has projection to receive it. The decorations on door stiles may be sunk and stained, or cut out of $\frac{1}{8}$-inch wood and planted. If planted this way, the wood should be of a

PLATE 23

EASY CHAIRS

PLATE 24.

Fig. 2.

BOOKCASES.

Fig. 1.

PLATE 23

BOOKCASE

PLATE 26.

BOOKCASE.

PLATE 27

BOOKCASE

PLATE 28

BOOKCASE

PLATE 29

BOOKCASE

PLATE 31

CONSULTING TABLES

lighter or darker colour than the grounding. The rosettes are relieved from the solid. The droops on side doors are turned and planted. In the upper portion the doors are chamfered, and have the turned pillars fixed. The entablatures are relieved in front. The decorations on doors are wrought in relief; the cornices formed of wrought moulding, with turned vases and ornamental coping, cut out of solid wood about ⅜-inch thick. The shield is relieved; the circle planted in the moulding. The droops are turned.

PLATE 29.—BOOKCASE.

This example is in the Italian style, and best suited for dark oak. The doors on outer wings are hinged on the gables. The decorations on pilasters are relieved from the solid. The arched doors in the centre are pivot-hinged. The left-hand door locks to the right, the right-hand to the left. The centre panel remains fixed. The semi-circular mouldings are clamped on the face. The carved fluted pillars open with the doors. The doors are framed up and veneered over. The centre wing in upper portion is open. The shelves are draped with ornamented leather. The pateras on frieze are planted. The ornament in cornice is planted. The shield is boldly carved.

PLATE 30.—BOOKCASES.

Both these are adapted for oak wood. In this instance half-designs only are given, so as to economise space and admit them being drawn to the inch scale. In the upper design the pillars are checked to receive the shelves. These are draped with ornamented leather. The pillars are turned ; the capitals slightly cut ; the Gothic arch chamfered and perforated. The under design is similar in construction. The hanging ornament is perforated. The small droops are turned separately and glued. The top must have sufficient projection for the caps, and the base prepared to receive the pillars.

PLATE 31.—LIBRARY TABLES.

The upper design of this plate is a plain one, and got up after the manner of ordinary consulting-room tables. It consists of two pedestals supporting a connecting frieze frame and top. It has two fronts ; each one is fitted with drawers. The centre drawer in the frame may be fitted with a writing board, as shown in plate 32, fig. 2. The frieze frame is entire, and extends the whole length. The semi-circular arch over knee-hole is of solid wood. This design is suitable for mahogany or oak.

The second design is of a more elaborate description. The style, old English. The construction is similar to the above. The pedestals are enclosed with doors, flush-panelled. The frame is fitted with drawers, and projects at the corners beyond the pedestals, and thus appears resting on the ornamental brackets. The pedestals are made with drawers entering from each side. The outside gables are panelled. The knee-hole arch is of solid wood, and perforated. The plinth is bevelled and veneered over. The tops of these tables are made of fir, and framed and moulded round the edge with solid wood, and bordered on the face all round with veneer. The top within the veneer is covered with leather, which is decorated with embossing and gilding.

PLATE 32.—LIBRARY TABLES.

The top of the octagonal consulting table is formed of fir, with mouldings mitred round it, and bordered on the face with veneer. Within this border it is covered with leather. The frieze may be draped with leather, or ¼-inch wood may be adopted. The decorations are surface-wrought. The droop is turned.

The second design on the plate is entirely different from any of the preceding. The pillars are turned and carved. The drawers are veneered over, with carved moulding planted on the face, and should have ornamental escutcheons in keeping with the design. The outside ends have planted moulding. The brackets supporting the centre drawer are solid, cut through. The writing board is leather covered, also top of table. Oak is best adapted for this design.

PLATE 33.—SOFAS.

The upper design in this plate has the seat framed in the usual manner, with the moulding clamped on the face. The decorations on the square blocks are planted. The feet are carved. The back is stuffed over. No wood is shown beyond the seat frame. This sofa is adapted for oak, and upholstered in leather.

The second figure has a wrought moulding carried round the back, which is planted and veneered on the upper edge. The centre part is formed of a solid piece framed up with the back. It is planted where the ornament terminates. The foot (turned) and elbow may be of one piece. The latter has rosette glued on. The seat frame moulding is cross-wrought, and mitred round the elbow stump. This design is also adapted for oak and leather.

PLATE 34.—LIBRARY CHAIRS.

Fig. 1.—This chair is intended for oak and leather, relieved with gilt studs. It is plain in design. The seat is framed up with the legs and a torus carried round it. The legs are square and chamfered. The ornaments are glued on. The back is stuffed over. The frame terminates with a scroll.

Fig. 2.—The seat rails have moulding clamped on the face and dowelled into the square blocks. The corner ornaments are glued down. The back is stuffed over, and appears resting on turned pillarettes.

Fig. 3.—This chair is similar in construction to the former. The legs are turned and framed up with the seat rails. The decorations are wrought solid. The back is shaped. The top ornament is wrought on. The pillarettes are turned.

Fig. 4.—This design is in the Italian style. The legs are blocked out on the square. The seat rails

are recessed a little from the square blocks. The decorations on these parts are incised. The back is straight. The pillarettes are turned. The diminutive arches are formed of one piece of solid wood about ⅜-inch thick.

PLATE 35.—LIBRARY CHAIRS.

Fig. 1.—This has the seat frame dovetailed into the legs. These are turned. The decorations are wrought in relief. The back is shaped. The edges are chamfered. It is cut through near the top.

Fig. 2.—This chair has moulding clamped on the seat rails, cross wrought on the squares of the legs. The latter are turned and carved. The back is shaped. The decorations are wrought in relief. The edges are chamfered.

Fig. 3.—This is framed up in the usual way. The decorations are all wrought in relief. The back is shaped and stuffed over. This chair is adapted for mahogany.

Fig. 4.—The seat rails are framed up with the legs, along with the stretchers. Seat rail chamfered. The back is shaped. The edges are chamfered. The decorations are sunk. This chair is adapted for oak, upholstered in leather or velvet, and relieved with gilt studs.

DRAWING INSTRUMENTS—*Continued.*

DRAWING BOARDS.—The draughtsman ought to be provided with several drawing boards of different dimensions. These should be made of well-seasoned wood; mahogany will be found very suitable for this purpose. Deal may be used, especially where the drawing board is of large size, and admits of the use of drawing pins, which cannot be used conveniently with a mahogany board. The mahogany board keeps its shape longer, and the material being harder, it is less liable to accidental injury. The drawing board must of necessity be perfectly flat and smooth on the surface, and the sides ought to be at right angles to each other, as these are of great service as guides in the drawing

PLATE 33

SOFAS

PLATE 34

CHAIRS

PLATE 36

EASY CHAIRS

of lines. It is also advantageous to have the board jointed to prevent its twisting, and clamped at the ends. It may also be framed up as a panel, with the stiles mitre-jointed around it, thus showing no end wood, which is very desirable, as it is liable to spring if the wood is not thoroughly seasoned. Drawing boards of large size should be of several pieces, closely jointed, with the ends clamped with a strip one inch broad, and the corners rounded.

SQUARES.—The most useful of these instruments is the **T** square. It is so well known that any description of it is almost unnecessary. It consists of a long, thin piece of wood, called the blade. This is fixed at right angles into another piece of wood, called the stock. In the *bevel* **T** square the stock is made of two equal pieces, the blade being fastened to one of them, while the other is made to turn upon a centre, and may be fixed in any position by means of a screw; and thus the blade and the stock may be set at any angle of the side of the board, and any number of parallels drawn.

Walnut is a very suitable wood for making the **T** square of. The blade should not be less than 1-12 inch in thickness, and rounded or bevelled on the edge. Mahogany, with an ebony edge, is also a good blade. The size of the square should correspond to the size of the drawing board. In using the instrument, the stock is held in the left hand, slightly pressing it to the edge of the board —the fore-finger and thumb resting on the upper and under edges of the blade, the right hand being thus free for the use of pen or pencil. The pen or pencil ought to be pressed slightly against the blade, as too much pressure is apt to shift its position.

The *set square* is another simple but very useful instrument. In some cases it consists of three pieces, mitre-jointed, thereby showing no end wood. It ought to be less than 1-12 inch in thickness. Ebony, satin-wood, rosewood, or other close-grained hard wood is most suitable for these. The right, obtuse, and acute angles should be made, and these

are of use in the construction of cornered figures. They may be of any length of from 4 to 12 inches. Both these and **T** squares should be highly French-polished, being thus less liable to catch dust. The set square is very useful in drawing short perpendiculars and angle lines without the moving of the **T** square to the under side of the board. In using it the right-angled side is placed against the edge of the **T** square, and adjusted to the point through which the line shall pass.

Parallel rulers will be found useful sometimes, but they are of no great use to the cabinetmaker. The **T** square ought always to be preferred. There are several kinds of rulers of different construction. One kind consists of a single rule, with two metal rollers, teethed, to prevent slipping, and placed in similar situation at each end. Another, also of a simple construction, is made of two plain rulers, connected by two pieces of metal of equal length turning on centres.

CURVES.—These are generally made out of pear-tree wood, and of the thickness of the ordinary small set squares, and of different figures. Curves are used for putting in the finishing line with the pen or pencil. The drawing having been sketched by the hand, some portions of the curves may be found nearly to coincide with the sweep or curve to be described. In some instances, in putting in the lines in parts, care should be taken not to have them broken, or to show any perceptible joining of the parts. The elementary student ought to be judicious in the use of these curves, using them as seldom as possible, especially on ornamental work—as such, if sketched by the hand, will possess that freedom from stiffness which shows the expert draughtsman.

TRAMMELS.—These are sometimes termed beam-compasses, and are used for making large sweeps where it is necessary for a circle or its arc to be of an unusual radius. This instrument consists of a square wooden rod, and may be made to any required length. A slip of hard wood or brass is sometimes inlaid, having a scale or scales marked on its face. Two brass boxes are fitted on the beam or rod, and are capable of being retained in any fixed position by means of a screw. One of these must be fixed at one end; the other can be adjusted according to the radius required. Both of the boxes have points attached to them, which may be substituted by the pen or pencil as occasion requires. We have given this full description in order that there may be no difficulty in the use of this instrument.

THE COMPASS.—This instrument is so familiar to every one in the trade that a description of it is hardly necessary. In selecting a compass, particular care should be directed to the nature of its joint, as of these there are various kinds. The joint ought in all cases to be formed of two different metals. We are of opinion that brass and steel make the best joint. The axis ought to be on the nut and bolt principle, and should consist of a steel pin, with a broad head, slit, so as to admit the turn-screw. A flat nut is screwed into the other end, and has two holes pierced in it, so as to allow a slackening or a tightening at pleasure. This is the most superior kind of compass, although the simple screw joint might be found serviceable for ordinary uses, but the rivet joint ought always to be avoided—as, after it is several times used, it becomes a nuisance. The steel at the points is another consideration. It ought always to be of the best tempered material, and so sharp as not to tear or in any way injure the design. These points will require to be occasionally set with the oil-stone, and every draughtsman ought to know how to do this. In using the compass, it must be wrought with one hand, so as to allow the other free for any contingency. The thumb and the first and second fingers are only required in its management.

The SPRING DIVIDER is another very useful kind of compass, and may be always used with a due regard to accuracy. It is formed entirely of well-tempered steel. A fine screw is attached to one of the legs by means of a small pin, the other end passing through the other leg. By means of a nut running on the screw, any radii can easily be adjusted. The student ought always to unscrew this instrument when finished with it, as the contraction is very injurious to the elasticity.

CIRCULAR OR BOW COMPASS.—This compass is of various sizes and different kinds. The Bow Pencil consists of a small compass with a short handle—one leg is fitted with a pencil-holder, the other has a steel point, and sometimes made so as to introduce a needle point. Superior small circulars for accurate drawing are fitted with joints, the advantage of which will at once be seen, as these always keep the points on the perpendicular. These joints ought to be fitted with screws for their regulation, and the main joint on the nut and bolt-screw system. The Bow Pen is similar to the pencil, only constructed with a drawing pen.

The SPRING CIRCULAR may be used for particularly fine work. It is similar in construction to the spring divider. For larger circles the big compass may be used, substituting a pen or pencil for one of the steel points.

DRAWING PEN.—The drawing pen consists of two fine steel blades fitted with a screw for regulating what is to be the thickness of the line. One of these blades, instead of being fixed into the handle, is sometimes attached to it by means of a hinge, with a steel spring to act in opposition to the screw. This kind is by far the superior, as it enables the blades to be cleaned and sharpened when necessary. The tips of the blades, when close, must be exactly the same—as, if not, the instrument is useless. The oil-stone will be found useful in regulating the blades of the pen. In using the pen, the ink or colour with which it is charged ought always to be supplied by a fine camel's-hair pencil, and carefully cleaned after use by a piece of blotting paper or a linen rag. In its use it is to be wrought the same as the compass, by the thumb and first and second fingers, and it must be kept perpendicular, only carrying its own weight, and guided by the ruler.

PLATE 37

PLATE 38

CHIFFONIER

PLATE 39

GHIFFONIERS

PLATE 40

STEP MIRROR

PLATE 42.

LIBRARY EASY CHAIRS.—PLATE 36.

Fig. 1.—This design is in the mediæval style, and adapted for oak wood. The pillars on the back are turned and clamped on the edge. The balustrade under elbow is cut out of solid wood about ⅞ inch in thickness. The elbow stump and turned leg is formed of one piece, the decorations of which are wrought in relief. The seat frame is framed into square blocks. This chair should be upholstered in velvet.

Fig. 2.—This chair is suitable for oak or mahogany. The elbow stumps and turned legs may be of one piece. The decorations are wrought in the solid. The seat frame is butt-jointed into the square blocks. The back is straight across. The semicircle may be turned, and has the centre ornament planted on. The brakes at each side are mitred. The trusses are clamped on the sides. This chair should be upholstered in leather.

DRAWING-ROOM FURNITURE.
PLATE 37.—CHIFFONNIER.

The example given in this plate is in the Renaissance style. The frame is intended for gilding, and is made of wood, while the festoons and other ornamental parts are of composition, the whole so constructed as to encase a mirror-plate. The top is white marble. The design may be executed in walnut, rosewood, or other rich wood. The end doors have glass panels, thus exposing the plate that may be disposed on the shelves. The pilasters are inlaid. The ornament is planted separately.

PLATE 38.—CHIFFONNIER.

This is a design in the Italian style. The decorations on the turned pillars, and other portions of the back, may be of composition. The vase is of a flat shape. The pateras are planted. The top is marble. The pillars are turned and carved, and remain fixed. The centre doors are glass panelled, and the styles chamfered inside. The outside semi-circular and quarter-pillars are

planted, and move with the doors. The pilaster in the centre is a fixture, and, with the upper portions of the doors, is relieved with inlaying. The end panels are raised, and show two designs.

PLATE 39.—CHIFFONNIERS.

These designs are plain and of small dimensions, and are different from any of the preceding.

Fig. 1 has the frieze and plinth separately made from the carcass. The top is intended to be of marble. The panels are of mirror-plate. The pillars remain fixed. The back is mirror-plate.

Fig. 2, although entirely different in design, is similar in construction. The top should also be of marble. The pillars remain fixed. Mirror-plate panels. The pilasters on the back may be wrought solid, and have the frieze veneered. The rosettes, mouldings, and other decorations planted.

PLATE 40.—MIRROR FRAME, WITH STEP.

The design given in this plate is in the Renaissance style. It is intended for gilding. The frame is formed of wood and composition, and relieved, and some parts with burnishing. In some cases pigment may be added, but must be used prudently. It may be applied in this case to the grounding of the head, which is in alto-relief. The colour should be light blue, pale pink, or white. The step is of white marble, and hatched with gilding.

PLATE 41.—MIRROR FRAME, WITH STEP.

This is an example in the Italian style. It is similar in construction to the preceding one. The columns are turned. The step is marble. The pillars on pedestals are turned.

PLATE 42.—CABINETS.

Fig. 1.—The design in this plate is intended for ebony and inlaying. The rosettes on centre door are planted. The end doors have bent glass panels.

Fig. 2.—This is of large dimensions and adapted for dark, rich wood, relieved with inlaying and gilt hatching. The flutes on pillars and pilasters may be gilded, and the other lines inlaid. The centre door panel should project beyond the stiles. The pillars are turned, and move with the door. The outside doors have glass panels. The shelves are covered with cloth. These are for the display of plate or articles of vertu. The pilasters may be fixed, or made to open with the doors.

PLATE 43.—CABINETS.

Fig. 1.—This design is in the Renaissance style, and plain in idea. The pilasters are intended for inlaying. They may also be incised. The doors have glass panels. The back is inlaid, and has panel of mirror-plate.

Fig. 2.—This is a larger and more elaborate design. The style is Italian, and the wood most suitable is walnut. The pilasters and decorations on door-stile and frieze are inlaid with light wood. The fluted pilasters may be relieved with gilding. The doors have all glass panels as in Fig. 1.

DRAWING MATERIALS.

PENCILS.—These ought always to be of the best quality, and we consider the pure Cumberland lead as best adapted for drawing purposes. There are various grades as to hardness or softness of these, but all ought to be so hard that they can be cut to the finest point without breaking. Those of hard quality should be used for working lines, circles, and straight lines, as they keep the point longer, and make a much clearer line than a softer pencil. The line can also be more easily cleaned or erased by India-rubber. It is often requisite to use one or more kinds of pencil for the same drawing. When drawing straight lines the pencil should be cut with a flat or chisel point. The flat side ought to be placed next the ruler. The line is thus drawn with more accuracy than with a round-pointed pencil, and retains its sharpness a greater length of time. The chisel point is also particularly suitable for the pencil circulars. Pencils to fit the circular may be had ready for use, but we always find it more advantageous to cut the ordinary drawing pencil to the size required. The reason for this is evident, namely, that you have thus the same quality of lead for all the lines, which gives a finish and appearance to the drawing that could not be otherwise obtained.

CRAYONS.—These may be had of any colour, but the department of drawing (Cabinet designing) which this treats on, requires principally three colours, viz., white, black, and red. These crayons cannot be cut in the same way as pencils. From the exceeding brittleness of their composition they must be sharpened backwards from the point. These, like the ordinary pencil, may be had of various degrees of hardness or softness. One way of using them is for tracing down the outline, drawing or sketch (which may be on cartridge paper), on the crayon paper, which should be previously stretched on a drawing-board. It is then outlined and finished by stumping and hatching. The unnecessary removal of lines should be avoided, so as to preserve the surface of the paper, and also to allow the chalk to work freely. Bread free from grease, neither too new nor stale, may be used for removing lines or reducing tints. Coloured paper should be used so as to form the medium tint of the drawing. The white chalk producing the high lights, it is not necessary to work it with a sharp point. This should rather be avoided. The drawing ought to be protected from the hand by a sheet of paper. The port-crayon should not be heavy. The stumps should be hard and soft, tapering to a point. A piece of chamois-leather will also be found useful. Willow charcoal may be used to sketch out the forms, and may be dusted off with a feather or silk handkerchief. It will also be found exceedingly useful in large drawings.

CHINA INK.—This very useful article may be had either in a liquid or solid state. The former is generally inferior to the latter. It ought always to be of the best quality, and its permanency genuine. It should be pure black, and free from

PLATE 44

LOO TABLES

any sediment. To make the ink ready for use, rub it up in a saucer with a little clean water. Any depth of colour may thus be produced—a solid black if required. The ink ought always to flow free from the pen, and the addition of a little ox-gall ought to be added, as it gives the ink a better catch on the paper. It may also be had in a liquid or solid state.

PAPER.—As there is a great variety of kinds of paper adapted for different purposes, the draughts-man must acquaint himself with the different qualities of this extremely useful article. Paper for drawing purposes should be hard in texture, and should stand the India-rubber without ruffling or breaking the surface, and should absorb water or colour slowly. The qualities of paper may always be tested by moistening with the lips. If it absorbs like blotting-paper it ought not to be used. It is always advantageous to strain the paper well on the board, more especially if a fine drawing is to be desired, and if it is to be coloured. If the paper has to stand many washes it is essential that it should be strained. Although this method is simple to some, at the same time great care and skill is required in the straining of large sheets. The paper is laid flat on the board, with the side to be used down. It is then sponged all over with clean water, and allowed to stand a few minutes more or less, according to the density of texture. It is then turned over and placed square with the board. A straight-edge is placed on the surface of the edge, and held down firmly with the left hand, allowing about half an inch margin. The forefinger is passed under this, and a little thin glue applied with a brush. It is then replaced by passing one finger over it. When the paper has two different sides, the right side may be proved by holding it up to the light, and reading the maker's name on the side to be used.

CARTRIDGE PAPER.—In selecting this paper, care should be taken to see that it can stand the India-rubber without ruffling the surface. Paper of this kind is adapted for preliminary sketches and work-ing drawings. Drawing paper should be selected of a hard texture and smooth surface. Fine card-board may also be used. Whatman's hand-made paper is extremely serviceable, also his antiquarian paper. The last-mentioned is peculiarly adapted for water-colour and mechanical drawings of all kinds, as it is not easily affected by continual washes of colour, and may be subjected to rough usage without injury.

CRAYON PAPER.—This paper is entirely different from the above. It is of a soft texture, and con-sequently not able to stand erasures with the India-rubber. It is used for chalk drawings, sepia sketches, and soft pencil drawings. It is not at all adapted for colouring. A variety of colours may be had in this paper. Grey or brown will be found most suitable in working up a chalk drawing. The colour of the paper serves for the middle tint. The white may be used for lights, but it must not mingle with the black chalk. Chinese white may also be used with good effect. It is applied in the same way as water-colour. India-rubber should not be applied to this paper. The design may be sketched in charcoal, and then dusted off, leaving a faint impression; or it may be drawn on cartridge paper and afterwards traced down.

TRACING PAPER should be strong and trans-parent, but not thick. It should be protected from exposure to the light and the atmosphere, as these are apt to give it a brown colour and destroy its transparency.

PLATE 44.—LOO TABLES.

In the manufacture of drawing-room loo tables, much care and experience is required, especially with the top. Fig. 1 in this plate has the top supported by three turned pillars, dowelled into the claws. The vase in centre is turned and carved. In Fig. 2 the top of the table is supported by dolphins (which may be made looking either three or four ways) resting on a plinth. This table would be well adapted for gilding.

PLATE 45.—COUCHES.

Fig. 1.—This couch has the seat framed into the square blocks of the legs. These are turned and carved. The small brackets are glued on afterwards. All the other parts of the couch are stuffed over, and it is thus well adapted for fancy needlework.

Fig. 2.—This design is simple and similar in construction to Fig. 1. The legs are square, carved on the face, and framed up with the seat-frame. The back is stuffed over. The cord carried along the front forms the scroll on the elbow, from the terminus of which the tassel is suspended. For the exposed parts of these couches, the most suitable woods are walnut, rosewood, or ebony. The frames can be made of birch, and constructed in the ordinary way.

PLATE 46.—CHAIRS.

Fig. 1 has the seat rails dowelled into legs and the mouldings cross-wrought. Fig. 2.—This chair is wrought in a similar way, but has a break in the seat. The back is carved. The top rail is dowelled into the entablatures of the pillars. These are turned and opened up. Fig. 3.—The back is shaped, carved and champfered at the corners. The stay is dowelled into the back. The legs are turned and framed up with the seat. Fig. 4.—The back of this chair is shaped and carved. The top rail and stays are dowelled. The front legs are turned and carved, and dowelled into the seat rails.

PLATE 47.—CHAIRS.

Fig. 1.—The seat rails are dowelled into the square blocks. The back is shaped. The decorations are incised and carved. If preferred, pebbles may be substituted for the rosettes. The chair should be made in very dark wood or ebonized. Fig. 2.—This design has the top rail dowelled down on the turned pillars. The stay is flat, resting on and supporting semi-circles. The legs are turned and carved. The moulding on seat-frame is cross-wrought on the squares of the legs.

Fig. 3.—The seat-rails are dowelled into the squares of the legs. Those are fluted and carved. The squares and the rosette in the centre are cut on the solid. The other decorations are incised. The pillars on back are turned, fluted, and carved. The circular moulding may be turned and dowelled into the entablatures of the pillars. The small tie on the top is planted. Fig. 4.—The back is dowelled into the entablatures of the pillars and down into the seat-frame. The decorations are all wrought on the solid. The seat-rails are dowelled into the square blocks. The legs are turned. The decorations are wrought solid.

PLATE 48.—EASY CHAIRS.

Fig. 1.—The back is shaped. The decorations are wrought in relief. The elbows are shaped with the seat. A wrought-moulding is carried round the seat-frame. The front legs are turned and carved. Fig. 2.—The top rail of back consists of a wrought-moulding. The ornament on top may be planted. The pillars are turned with the blocks, cut or planted. The elbow is shaped with the seat. The elbow stumps and front legs may be of one piece. Fig. 3.—The back of this chair is wrought in relief. The elbow stumps and front legs may be of one piece, and the seat-rails dowelled into the blocks, the moulding on the edge having been previously planted.

PLATE 49.—SUNDRIES.

Fig. 1.—COMMODE. This design can be well executed in ebony and gold hatching, rosewood, or walnut. The pillars are turned, and remain fixed. The door has glass panel or mirror-plate, as may be desired. The panels above semi-circle are planted.

Fig. 2.—FIRE SCREEN. This design may be wrought out in walnut or ebonized oak. The panel can be of glass, clear or embossed. The claws are dowelled into the pillars. The arches are of one piece, and fixed into the pillarettes, which again are fixed down on the squares of the stretcher. The small drops are turned, and fixed

PLATE 45

COUCHES

2

3

4

FIG. 1

FIG 2

FIG. 3

FIG. 4

PLATE 48

EASY CHAIRS

FIG 3

FIG. 2

FIG. 1

PLATE 49

SUNDRIES

PLATE 51

CHAIRS

PLATE 52.

Fig 1.

Fig 2.

Fig 3.

W.Thomson.

VALLANCES.

PLATE 53.

Fig 1.

Fig 2.

Fig 3.

VALLANCES.

AThomson

separately. The pateras are wrought solid. The vases above pillars may be turned. The ornament on top is wrought separately and fixed.

PLATE 50.—FENDER STOOLS.

Fig. 1.—This design is plain, and adapted for walnut. The feet are turned. The upper members are the same as the moulding carried round the bottom of the rails. Fig. 2.—The design here given is best adapted for gilding. The ornament is clamped on the rail, and the feet are screwed on. Fig. 3 is also suitable for gilding, and may be made of walnut or rosewood. The rails may be dowelled or dovetailed into the corner blocks. If it is not to be gilded, the rails may be of fir or birch, and clamped on their under edge with solid wood, and afterwards carved. The feet may be turned with the corner blocks, or turned and fixed separately. The above articles afford ample scope for the display of taste; but harmony, contrast, and keeping, must be strictly observed. Different arrangements of colours might be here suggested for the covering of the stools. When gilding is adopted, light blue next the gold will harmonize as well, or if not better, than any other colour. Purple and maroon would also be suitable. Light blue, deep pink, salmon colour, or amber, might be used with walnut or other similar woods. Green may be used, but only when no flowers of another colour are sewed on the covering. Crimson may also be suitable, but these colours will not give contrast when used as a ground for embroidery. Gimp, or cording of yellow silk, blue, and red, should never come together, neither should yellow and green, nor bright yellow and bright red. Scarlet and yellow do not harmonize well. When a fender stool or other article is covered with sewed work of leaves or flowers, the effect is completely destroyed by surrounding these with gay colours. The intense brilliancy of colour in flowers cannot be reproduced in any fabric, or even in painting. In order that the flower may stand out, they should be relieved with a dark background, and very deep shadows. This will help considerably, and appear not like wool, but flowers.

PLATE 51.—DEVOTIONAL CHAIRS.

Fig. 1 has the legs framed up with the seat-rails. These are fluted and carved. The back appears supported by two pillars, turned and opened up. The ornament on top is wrought solid. Fig. 2 has front legs turned, fluted, and carved, and are framed up with the seat-rails. These have a bead carried all round. The ornament or front is fixed under the rail. These chairs may be upholstered to taste, but the same rules ought to be observed as those laid down for fender-stools.

PLATE 52.—WINDOW VALLANCES.

Fig. 1.—This pole is intended for gilding. The flutes may be burnished. The pediment is screwed down. The grounding of the centre may be coloured with pale blue, pink, or white. Fig. 2 can be made of mahogany, and may be gilded, and have gilt rings. The vases are turned, and glued down on the brackets. These are wrought in relief. Fig. 3.—This pole is suitable for mahogany with gilt rings. The ends are turned separately, and with the pole are fixed into the brackets. These poles appear supported by the brackets, but may be fixed in the ordinary manner.

PLATE 53.—WINDOW VALLANCES.

Fig. 1.—This is a design for cornice, and intended for gilding. The monogram and other ornaments on frieze are planted. The ornamental vases may be of a flat shape. The other decorations are cut on the solid. The brakes should project about 1½ inches. Fig. 2.—This example is plain and may be produced in light wood. It consists of a wrought moulding, opened up with a moulding planted on the surface of top, and ornamented with small pieces of solid wood glued down on the edge. Fig. 3.—This cornice is more massive. It may be wrought in light wood, or black and gold. The decorations on the frieze are merely incised lines. The Vallances of these poles and cornices must harmonize with the furniture and decorations of the rooms.

PLATE 54.—HALF-TESTER BEDSTEAD.

The design on the plate is adapted for light oak. The cornice consists of a wrought moulding opened up. The ornamental terminals at corners are cut solid, and glued down with the coping. The bed-end has turned pillars, incised and carved; also sunk panel. The ornaments are cut out of $\frac{1}{8}$ inch wood, and planted. The trefoils are treated in the same way. Above these are planted panellings and mouldings. The mouldings and planted portions should be of a lighter or darker colour to give contrast. The bed may be draped according to taste, but care must be taken to produce the proper effect with its arrangement and the wood.

PLATE 55.—PARISIAN BEDSTEAD.

The example on this plate will appear to best advantage if constructed of walnut. The ornaments on head may be glued down on the wrought moulding which appears resting on the pillars. These are rounded off above the capitals, not to allow much projection beyond the moulding. The pillars are turned and carved, with square base chamfered with decorations cut on the solid. The bed-end has turned pillars carved and fluted, and octagonal base panelled, and has a bead mitred around it, carried along the stocks. The ornaments above the pillars are planted. The panel is raised and has a semi-circle taken out to receive the rosette which is planted. The carving on moulding is wrought in relief. The stock is ornamented with a narrow bead planted on the face.

PLATE 56.—PARISIAN BEDSTEAD.

This example is best suited for light wood, such as Hungarian ash, pitch pine, light-coloured oak, or American ash. The pediment may be incised, and have its lines coloured. The moulding planted

on the edge forms one of the members of the cornice. The squares on frieze are planted of $\frac{3}{8}$-inch wood, and have the quarterfoils cut out. The pilasters are chamfered and incised. The pillars are chamfered and panelled. The mouldings may be mitred round. The ornaments at top may be planted or wrought solid. The turned piece on top may be glued down. The small arches are cut out of solid wood, which forms the grounding on which the mouldings above are planted. The cross-bar panels are framed up in thick stiles, chamfered.

PLATE 57.—PARISIAN BEDSTEAD.

This bedstead may be made of the same kind of woods as those of plate 56. The semicircular moulding is planted and opened up, also the inside moulding. A bead is planted all round next to the stuffing. The other decorations are planted. The character of the design is carried out in the stuffing. The end is flush-panelled. The wrought-moulding is planted on the edge of the stiles, and the panel fitted in behind. The trefoils on frieze may be planted or relieved from the solid. The moulding above is opened up. The pillars are turned, and have carved capitals. The base is panelled, and has a moulding mitred round it. The small brackets may be glued to the stocks.

PLATE 58.—HALF-TESTER BEDSTEAD.

The design of this plate is well adapted for walnut. The pilasters are planted and relieved with incised work. It may be flush-panelled. The ornament and rosette are planted. The cornice consists of a wrought-moulding, carved, with carved pediment. The drapery may be according to taste. The cornice is hung with a heavy woollen fringe, over this is hung the vallance. It is bound with gimp, and the other ornaments formed of silk cord.

PLATE 59.—PARISIAN BEDSTEAD.

This example is best suited for light wood. The

PLATE 54.

HALF TESTER BEDSTEAD.

Thomson

PLATE 55.

PARISIAN BEDSTEAD.

PLATE 56

BEDSTEAD

PLATE 57.

PARISIAN BEDSTEAD

555

PLATE 59

PARISIAN BEDSTEAD

557

PLATE 55.

WARDROBE.

PLATE 60

WARDROBE

PLATE 61

WARDROBE

WARDROBE.

A Thomson

PLATE 63

WARDROBE

PLATE 64

WARDROBE

head pillars are turned, and have their upper portions carved. The turrets are semi-octagonal, and with the cornice are opened up. A wrought moulding is planted all round the stuffing. The end has cornice moulding opened up. The octagonal turrets appear resting on the pillars. These are turned, and have carved capitals and plain shafts. The base is chamfered and panelled, and has a moulding mitred round at the bottom. The panels may be flush. The mouldings chamfered and pierced. The stock is bevelled on top, and veneered over. It should have a solid piece of wood clamped at the bottom about 2½ inches deep. It may be cut out with the bow-saw and chamfered. The small droops may be turned and glued on.

Plate 55A.—WARDROBE.

This design may be wrought out in oak, with incised lines stained, or ebonized and relieved with gold lines. The pillars are turned and remain fixed. The base has a semi-octagonal projection to receive them. The centre panel is mirror-plate. The panels on stiles are planted. The outside wings are flush panelled. The corners have bevelled panels planted on. The cornice moulding is relieved with incised lines. The trefoils can be planted on the frieze.

Plate 60.—WARDROBE.

This design is intended to be wrought out in light oak, pitch pine, Hungarian or American ash, or other light coloured woods. The centre panel is mirror-plate. The columns are turned and fixed to the stiles, and move with the door. The stiles are bevelled. Two designs of panels are shown here. The left wing has bevelled moulding wrought on the solid. The decorations at corners are also wrought in relief. The right wing has the panel fitted behind a chamfered moulding planted on the edge of the stiles. The base is bevelled. The cornice has wrought moulding opened up. The two brakes have projections to receive the capitals.

Plate 61.—WARDROBE.

This is another design also suitable for light coloured woods. Two different examples are given. The centre panel is mirror-plate. The stiles are chamfered. The other decorations are planted. The pediment has a border chamfered on the edge. The surface is relieved with incised lines. The left wing has chamfered stiles, and sunk panels, plain. The right wing has cross and upright bar panels. The stiles are chamfered. The decorations are planted or wrought solid. The base is bevelled.

Plate 62.—WARDROBE.

This design is adapted for walnut. The centre door has mirror-plate panel. The columns are turned and carved, and may remain fixed. The base and cornice are broken to receive them. The vases may be turned and fixed down. The pediment is wrought in relief. The cornice is carved. The decorations on frieze are planted. The outside doors have carved laurel planted above the panels.

Plate 63.—WARDROBE.

The design on this plate is best suited for light wood. It is of the usual dimensions of a two-doored Wardrobe. Two designs of panels are shown. The doors are hinged on the gables behind the columns. These are turned, and fixed on the corners, and move with the doors. The cornice has octagonal projection at the corners. The base is bevelled, and veneered over, and has projection at corners to receive columns.

Plate 64.—WARDROBE.

This wardrobe is similar to the preceding in construction and dimensions. If the shafts of the columns are plain, as shown on one half of the design, the doors may be hinged in front, the column remaining a fixture. Otherwise they may be hinged on the gables. The cornice is formed of wrought mouldings, and opened up. The base is bevelled and veneered over. The decorations on column are incised. Two different panels are given, but they are similarly wrought. The mouldings are bevelled.

PLATE 65.—WARDROBE.

FIG. 1.—This wardrobe is adapted for pitch pine. The door stiles are chamfered. The panels are sunk, and consist of jointed bars, bevelled at the joints. The cornice consists of wrought mouldings, with antifixes, glued on top. Fig. 2.—The design may be wrought out in birch, American ash, bird's-eye maple, or similar woods. The cornice is relieved with pediment in centre. In part it is a continuation of the cornice mould-ing. The outside member is clamped on the edge. The centre ornament may be planted or relieved. The brackets are incised and clamped on. The doors may be flush panelled, and have chamfered mouldings. The base is bevelled, and open under-neath. The wardrobe is fitted with drawers and trays, and space left for hanging, which is lined and fitted with hooks.

PLATE 66.—TOILET TABLE AND WASHSTAND.

The designs given in this plate are intended to be wrought in walnut. The toilet table is fitted with jewel drawers. The standards may be incised or relieved with pinching. The pillars are turned and carved. The pilasters behind are chamfered, with moulding mitred round the bottom. The washstand is the same, with the exception of the marble top.

PLATE 67.—TOILET TABLE AND WASHSTAND.

These examples are intended to be wrought in Hungarian ash, pitch pine, or other light coloured woods. The style is mediæval. The standards are wrought in relief. The table standards are chamfered and wrought in relief. The plinth and sole stretcher are bevelled. The squares on frieze

may be wrought in relief. The washstand is the same in construction. The standards are different, but wrought in the same way.

PLATE 68.—DRESSING TABLE.

This design may be carried out in various woods. Mahogany, walnut, or yew tree, may be adopted. If the latter, it must be relieved with dark mouldings. The standards may be incised and carved where they terminate. A ground plan is given of the pedestals and top. Underneath a suggestive design is given for a marble slab and shelf for washstand to match.

PLATE 69.—DRESSING TABLE AND WASHSTAND.

The examples given on this plate will appear to best advantage if wrought out in light oak, or similar light coloured woods. The dressing-glass frame is pierced and chamfered. The jewel drawers are sunk about $\frac{1}{4}$-inch, and relieved at each end with trefoil. These may be wrought in the fol-lowing way :—Glue eight pieces of wood together, not less than $\frac{1}{4}$-inch in thickness, draw the trefoil on each side, and cut out with the bow-saw, and finish the edges. They will separate when put into water. They are clamped on the face and finished with the drawers, and should be flush with the outside and sub-division when the drawers are closed. The standards are chamfered and pierced. The pedestals have chamfered corners. The panel mouldings are pierced and chamfered. The base is bevelled and veneered over. The ornament between pedestals is cham-fered, and has the droops turned and glued on. Washstand.—Another design for door panels is given here, but the same panel must be carried out in suit, whichever may be adopted. The pedestals on this plate are the same. This door may be flush panelled. A wrought moulding is clamped on the edge of the door-stile, butting against the corner ornaments, also clamped. The ornament inside may be formed of $\frac{3}{4}$-inch wood,

PLATE 65

WARDROBES.

Thomson.

PLATE 69

TOILET

PLATE 70

TOILET

DETAILS.

CHAIR LEGS.

SOFA FEET.

PLATE 72

SUNDRIES

pierced and chamfered, clamped on the face. The top is white marble, the back of which may be relieved from the solid. The frame may be fitted with drawers.

PLATE 70.—DRESSING TABLE AND WASHSTAND.

These designs, like the preceding, are adapted for light coloured wood. The dressing-glass frame is chamfered. The ornament inside is relieved from the frame. The standards may be cut out of one piece. The jewel drawers may be flush, and have the ornament clamped on the centre. The pedestals are chamfered. The top may be fitted with drawers. The base is bevelled and veneered over. The doors may be sunk panelled, with wrought moulding clamped on the edge of the stiles. The ornaments on these may be planted, but would be better wrought in relief, and have the stile solid wood. The arch between the pedestals is pierced and chamfered, and has small droops turned and glued on. A bead forming a semi-circle is planted on the face. Washstand.—The pedestals are square. The doors may be sunk panelled. The base is bevelled. The top may be of white marble, or inlaid with encaustic tiles; or it may be made with the tiles framed in a margin of ebony.

PLATE 71.—DETAILS OF CHAIR LEGS AND SOFA FEET.

Chair legs (figs. 1 and 3) may be wrought in oak or mahogany. The others are best suited for mahogany. Fig. 1 is curved and fluted. Fig. 2 has the ball relieved. Fig. 3 has the shaft fluted. Figs. 4, 5, and 6 are plain, but will admit of being relieved, if preferred that way. Sofa feet (figs. 1, 2, and 3) may be wrought in oak or mahogany. Figs. 4, 5, and 6 are suited for mahogany. Fig. 1 has the square block relieved. The shaft is fluted. The ball has leaves relieved in a simple way. Fig. 2.—The square is wrought in relief, and the shaft is fluted. Fig. 3 has the principal member opened up. Fig. 4 has the bead opened up with twist.

Figs. 5 and 6 are plain, but may be opened up if required.

PLATE 72.—SUNDRIES, CHAIRS.

Fig. 1.—In this design the back may be straight, with chamfered corners. The legs are chamfered and relieved, and framed flush with the seat rails. Fig. 2.—The back may be straight across, chamfered and counter checked. The trefoil is cut through. The front legs are squared and chamfered, and framed up flush with the seat rails, and has the small brackets glued on. Both these chairs will look best in light coloured wood, and both have fixed seats. Towel rails.—Fig. 1 is suitable for light wood. It is of one piece cut through, and may have five or six rods. Fig. 2 is adapted for light wood, is of one piece cut through, and has five rods. Fig. 3 is adapted for light wood, but may be made in mahogany or walnut. It is of two pieces, dowelled at the base. It is cut through and bevelled at ornamental parts, and fitted with four rods and stretcher at bottom. Fig. 4 may be wrought in oak or other wood. The semi-circle is dowelled down on the pillars, and these have their shafts turned, leaving the blocks square and dowelled down on the base. The rods are fixed into the square blocks, also the circle with quatrefoil pierced and bevelled. The stretcher may be fixed at the bottom. Fig. 5 is suitable for light wood only. The pieces are counter-checked, and may be fitted with five rods and stretcher.

PLATE 73.—PERMANENT WASHSTANDS.

The upper design on this plate is adapted for oak wood. The style is Mediœval. The mouldings are clamped on the face, and the ornamental portions are wrought and planted separately. The droops are turned and carved. The standard in centre may be formed of one piece. It projects at top and bottom, and has corners chamfered. The front panels may be flush or sunk. The moulding is clamped on the face. The ornamental part is cut out of ¼-inch wood, and clamped on inside the moulding. The ends are veneered over, and have the mouldings clamped on the face. The base is bevelled. The under design is adapted for mahogany and white marble. The pillars are turned and relieved from the solid. The wrought mouldings above are clamped on the veneer. The pilasters may have planted panel or bead. The panel may be sunk or flush. The ends are veneered over, and have a moulding clamped on the face. The base is veneered over, and wrought moulding carried round.

Plate 74.—DETAILS OF SIDEBOARD PILLARS.

These pillars may be wrought out in various woods. Figs. 1, 2, and 3 are specially adapted for wood such as oak; fig. 4 for mahogany; figs. 5 and 6, oak or mahogany. Fig. 1 has capital carved and other parts plain. Fig. 2 has capital carved and shaft incised. Fig. 3 has capital boldly relieved. The shaft takes the form of the quatrefoil. This pillar may be formed of three pieces, and dowelled together. Fig. 4 is of one piece, turned, carved, and fluted. Fig. 5 has boldly carved capital. The decorations on shaft are incised. This pillar may be adapted for different purposes. It may be formed of walnut, and have the capital and moulding under it gilded, also the incised lines on shaft. Fig. 6 is turned and wrought in relief entire. The capital is relieved, and the shaft incised and relieved. It may be wrought out in walnut, and after the same manner as described in fig. 5.

Plate 75.—TABLE LEAF CASES.

The two examples given in this case are specially adapted for oak wood. They are fitted behind with enclosed space for the reception of the telescopic table leaves. Fig. 1. The base is bevelled and veneered over. The doors are flush-panelled. The wrought-mouldings and other ornaments are clamped on the stile. A bead or moulding is planted on the edge of the right-hand door, and projects half-way over the stile,

thus securing the other door when locked. The pedestal top is formed of a piece of fir, clamped on the edge with solid wood, which forms the moulding, and is veneered over the top. The brackets are formed of one piece, relieved and pierced. The top has moulding and bead planted round it, in which the back and sides, of solid wood, are fixed down. Fig. 2 is more elaborate in design. The base is bevelled, and has brakes at ends to receive pillars. These are turned, and remain fixed. There is but one door, and it is hinged in front. It may be formed of several pieces of wood, jointed and veneered over. The mouldings and other decorations are clamped on the face. The four trefoil arches may be cut in one piece, and under these a small turned portion is planted. The butt of the arches and mouldings is jointed against it. The hanging trefoils may be wrought in relief. The small drops are turned. The brackets are cut through and chamfered. They are of the usual dimensions of what-nots, or upright table-leaf holders.

Plate 76.

Details of Plates 9 and 10 described in page 4.

Plates 77 and 78.—SHIP'S CABIN OR SALOON.

STERN.—The settee has turned legs, plated. The frame and seat-rails are chamfered. The centre ornament is carved and fixed. The rudder hop is panelled and inlaid. The frieze is also relieved with inlaying. The settee may be made of walnut, and upholstered in crimson velvet. The other parts should be of light-coloured wood, and relieved with walnut moulding and inlaying. TRANSVERSE SECTION—The grounding may be of birds-eye maple, or other light-coloured wood, and relieved with walnut moulding and inlaying. The sideboard has mirror back, encased in gilt frame, relieved with hatching. The pilasters are walnut, and have gilt capitals, and are inlaid. They are clamped on the stiles, and move with the

PLATE 74

SIDEBOARD PILLARS

PLATE 75

TABLE LEAF CASES

PLATE 76.

PLATE 77

SHIP CABIN

THWARTSHIPS, FORWARD

SIDEBOARD

DOOR

BRAKE, AFT

STERN

DOOR

LONGITUDINAL SECTION

SHIP CABIN

LONGITUDINAL SECTION

DOOR

582

PLATE 80

SHIP CABIN

TRANSVERSE SECTION

PLATE 81

DETAILS of PLATE 80

doors. The panels are relieved with inlaying. The mouldings are walnut. The moulding and bead on stage, and the moulding on the base, are also walnut. The doors are hinged at gables. The doors on each side of sideboard have embossed or enamelled glass panel. The lower panel is of cast-iron, perforated, and is decorated with colour and gilding. The mouldings are walnut, likewise the moulding round the door. The space between panels is relieved with inlaying. The pilasters have gilded capitals, and walnut shafts, relieved with inlaying of light wood, or gold lines. The mirror has gilt frame, the pilasters of which are incised. The top moulding is relieved with small pieces glued on. The small book-case is fitted with two glass doors. LONGITUDINAL SECTION—The pilasters and door are the same as already described. The frieze (along the passage) between beams, is of cast-iron, perforated, and relieved with colour and gilding. Elsewhere the frieze is relieved with inlaying. The panel and other mouldings are walnut. The under panels are cast-iron, perforated, and decorated. The large panels contain pictures, such as flowers, landscapes, and other high-class sketches of pleasing and interesting subjects. The picture is painted on paper prepared for oil painting. The panels, of plate glass, are embossed and gilded. The picture is laid down on the plate, with dial varnish between, and pressed out at the sides, the same way as laying veneer. The small pilasters are walnut, inlaid or hatched, and gilt capitals. The panel under window is inlaid. The decorations on each side are inlaying. The frieze is also inlaid. The settee is continuous, and is already described.

Plate 79.—SHIP'S CABIN.

LONGITUDINAL SECTION —The pilasters have gilt capitals and walnut shafts, fluted and gilded. The lower parts are inlaid. The intersecting mouldings are gilded. The frieze along passage has cast-iron panels, perforated and

decorated, elsewhere it is relieved with inlaying. The small hanging pilasters have gilt capitals, and walnut shaft, fluted and gilded. The base is of the same wood as the grounding. The intersecting mouldings and ornament under are gilded. The frieze moulding under beams may be gilded. The other mouldings are walnut. The panels above settee may be decorated with painted flowers or trophies. The mouldings surrounding these are walnut. The turned parts at top and bottom are gilded. The decorations around window are inlaid. The settee frame is walnut. The legs are turned. The door has glass panel, embossed with flowers or ornament. The mouldings are walnut. The under panel is perforated cast-iron, decorated. The decorations between panels are walnut and inlaying. The semi-circular arch above door has a walnut moulding planted on the face, the grounding being of light-coloured wood. The large panels between pilasters contain oil paintings, and embossed and gilded plate-glass, surrounded with gilt mouldings. The under panels are perforated cast-iron, painted.

Plate 80.—SHIP'S CABIN—TRANSVERSE SECTION.

This design is a continuation of the previous one. The doors and pilasters are the same. The side-board has mirror-plate back and gilt frame. The stage and base may be relieved with walnut mouldings. The doors are sunk, panelled, and inlaid. The pilasters have gilt capitals. The remaining parts are walnut. The flutes are gilded. The centre door opens between pilasters. The others open in the same way, or are hinged to gables, and the pilasters planted on the door stiles.

Plate 81.—DETAILS OF PLATE 80.

The Sideboard back is formed of semi-circular mouldings, opened up. The centre ornament is carved separately. The eagle is also cut separately and glued on. The pillar is turned, and the top dowelled into it. Three examples of capitals are given for pilasters, but the one adopted must be carried out in the whole suit. They are carved in fir and gilded. The cast-iron panels on this plate are described with Plate 80. In drawing these for the pattern-maker, or carver, they must necessarily be drawn larger than required, to allow for the shrinking of the metal in casting, as in every casting the metal shrinks proportionably about one-eighth inch to every foot. When a wood pattern is made, the iron pattern is cast from it, from which the working castings are taken. The pattern has thus undergone two castings, and consequently two shrinkings. Sometimes the patterns are modelled in clay, stucco, or wax, and afterwards cast in lead, and then in iron, thereby retaining all the delicacy of detail in a hard substance, which may be handled with freedom, whereas a wood or lead pattern is liable to being easily broken or injured. In making the pattern, allowance must be made for the draw from the sand or loam; for this purpose the edges are slightly bevelled (not squared, as in other cases), and the ornament cut, so that it may be lifted clean from the mould. Thus, then, in a wood pattern, a quarter of an inch to the foot more than the cast size is allowed for the two shrinkings. If in stucco or lead, or if the wood pattern is to be cast in lead and the iron taken from it, three-eighths inch to the foot must be allowed for the three shrinkings.

PLATE 82.—SHIP'S CABIN—TRANSVERSE SECTION.

The grounding is of light wood, relieved with dark mouldings, inlaying, and gildings. The shafts of pillars may be walnut, incised and gilded. The capitals are gilt. The decorations above may be planted. The hanging pillar has gilt capital. The shaft is of dark wood, incised and gilded. The rosettes are planted. The door has glass panel, walnut or rosewood moulding, and inlaying. The sideboard has mirror-plate back, in gilt frame. The stage and base have projections to receive the

pillars. These are fixed to the stiles, and move with the door. They are relieved with incised lines and curved capitals. If the pillars are dark, the capitals and lines may be gilded. The doors are flush panelled. The mouldings and decorations are clamped on the face.

PLATE 83.—SHIP'S CABIN—LONGITUDINAL SECTION.

Same wood as described in Plate 82. Pillars also similar in decoration. The windows are draped with vallance and curtains. The continuous settee is stuffed over, and embroidered, and hung with heavy fringe. The frieze has planted decorations and carved mouldings, relieved with gold hatching. The ventilation panels are of cast-iron, and decorated. The oval panel is plate glass, with painted flowers, or other subjects, as previously described. The carving around it should be gilt. The other mouldings may be of dark wood, also the moulding planted on each side. The other panels are relieved with inlaying. The rosettes are planted. The passage is draped with vallance and hangings, which must be in keeping with the other upholstered work.

PLATE 84.—BED ENDS.

The upper design on this Plate is intended for inlaying. A wrought moulding is clamped on the face of the frieze of the top stile. The pateras are planted. The fluted pilasters may be rounded at the corners, and clamped on the face of the stiles. The latter, along with the panel and stock, are inlaid. The under design may be wrought in light wood, solid and incised, or dark wood (such as walnut) and inlaid. The panels may be raised, or relieved with inlaying. The stiles have small circles taken out of the corners, and chamfered all round. They are framed up with the pilasters. These have the inside corners bevelled. The pateras on frieze are planted. The wrought moulding above is opened up.

PLATE 82

SHIP CABIN

587

PLATE 83

SHIP CABIN

PLATE 84

BED ENDS

PLATE 85.—TOILET TABLE ENDS.

Fig. 1 has turned pillars, opened up. The stretcher is bevelled on top. The upper portion is pierced, chamfered, and relieved. The droops are turned. Fig. 2 may be of one piece. It is bevelled at corners, and pierced and incised. The patera can be wrought solid. Fig. 3 is pierced and chamfered, and relieved with incised lines. The droops are turned out of the square piece. The square block is butt-jointed to the stand. Fig. 4 is pierced and chamfered. The plinth is bevelled on top. In Fig. 5 the pillars are turned and incised. The other portions are chamfered and incised. The pateras may be relieved or planted. Fig. 6 has the pillars turned and incised. The upper portion has bevelled corners and turned droops. The pillars are fixed down on the plinth. The stretcher is also fixed into the plinth, and is relieved with incised lines.

PLATE 86.—TABLE LEGS.

These designs are adapted for telescope-table legs, and may be wrought out in various woods. They are all turned, with the exception of Fig. 8, which is hexagonal. Fig. 1 has main feature carved and shaft fluted. Fig. 2 ought to be more boldly carved. The upper half alone of the shaft is fluted. In Fig. 3 there is little decoration. It must thus be wrought out clean and sharp. In Fig. 4. the decorations are nearly all incised. The little balls may be turned and fixed. The upper portion of the shaft is fluted. These incised lines may be ebonized, or coloured if preferred. In Fig. 5 the decorations are incised and wrought in relief. Fig. 6 is a bold design. The pateras on centre of shaft may be wrought solid or in relief. The upper portion of the shaft is incised. In Fig. 7 the decorations are all incised, with the exception of the pateras, which may be planted. The small rings at the bottom and middle of the shaft may be done by pinching. Fig 8 is the most elaborate in design. The decorations on the middle of the shaft may be planted. The other portions are

relieved with incised lines. The small arches on the upper portion are boldly relieved. The small turned droops are fixed on.

PLATE 87.—CAPITALS.

These designs are chiefly adapted for Wardrobe pillars, but may be applied in various other ways. Fig 1 is plain, and would require to be boldly cut. Fig. 2 is much more elaborate, and would be suitable either for pillar or pilaster. Fig. 3 has shaped overhanging scroll meeting in the centre, the leaves of which almost cover the other portions. In Fig. 4 the flowers may be cut separately and glued on. The pillar shaft is relieved with incised lines. The little falls are turned and fixed on separately. Fig. 5 has pateras cut round the upper portion. The remainder is nearly covered with the leaves. This might also be applied to a pilaster. Fig. 6 has three shells at the lower part. From behind these the foliage springs. This capital may also be applied to a pilaster.

PLATE 88.—BRACKETS.

The design of Fig. 1 is in the form of a truss. It may be applied to a Sideboard to support the stage, or by placing two together, and having a pillar between them fixed at the wings and scrolls, and down on a plinth. This would form a telescope table-end. In this case the cross bar at top should have a piece of wood clamped on above the griffins' heads, else they will be hidden from view. Fig 2 may be used as a shelf bracket, or may be applied in various other ways. Fig. 3—This bracket may be formed of wood of about $1\frac{1}{2}$ inches in thickness, except the head and terminus of the scroll, which should be thicker, especially the former, as it is bold in relief. This bracket may be applied to various pieces of cabinet furniture, and may be carved on one or both sides as required. Fig. 4 may be used as a shelf-bracket. It terminates at both ends with a turned piece. The thickness of the wood should not be less than half-an-inch, but may be guided by the size of the bracket.

PLATE 85

TOILET TABLE ENDS

H.Thomson

PLATE 87

CAPITALS

1

2

3

4

5

6

INS

2